Peter O. Müller, Susan Olsen and Franz Rainer (eds.)
Word-Formation – Language Contact and Diachrony

This volume is part of a larger set of handbooks to Word-Formation

1 **Word-Formation: History, Theories, Units and Processes**
Peter O. Müller, Susan Olsen and Franz Rainer (eds.)

2 **Word-Formation: Special Patterns and Restrictions**
Peter O. Müller, Susan Olsen and Franz Rainer (eds.)

3 **Word-Formation: Semantics and Pragmatics**
Peter O. Müller, Susan Olsen and Franz Rainer (eds.)

4 **Word-Formation: Language Contact and Diachrony**
Peter O. Müller, Susan Olsen and Franz Rainer (eds.)

5 **Word-Formation: European Languages**
Peter O. Müller, Susan Olsen and Franz Rainer (eds.)

Word-Formation
Language Contact and Diachrony

Edited by
Peter O. Müller, Susan Olsen and Franz Rainer

DE GRUYTER
MOUTON

ISBN 978-3-11-141408-9
e-ISBN (PDF) 978-3-11-142053-0
e-ISBN (EPUB) 978-3-11-142087-5

Library of Congress Control Number: 2025934171

Bibliographic information published by the Deutsche Nationalbibliothek
The Deutsche Nationalbibliothek lists this publication in the Deutsche Nationalbibliografie; detailed bibliographic data are available on the Internet at http://dnb.dnb.de.

Cover image: 1933bkk / iStock / Getty Images Plus
Typesetting: Meta Systems Publishing & Printservices GmbH, Wustermark
Printing and binding: CPI books GmbH, Leck

www.degruyterbrill.com
Questions about General Product Safety Regulation:
productsafety@degruyterbrill.com

MIX
Papier | Fördert gute Waldnutzung
FSC® C083411

Contents

Wieland Eins

1 Types of foreign word-formation

Abstract: This article aims to investigate linguistic reflexes of non-nativeness in word-formations. It will be argued that foreign word-formation subsumes processes that vary considerably in how much they differ from indigenous types of word-formation. Divergences between indigenous and foreign derivations and indigenous and foreign compounds may turn out to be marginal; yet there are non-native combinations that deviate significantly. As the term foreign word-formation subsumes both word-formation and borrowing, this article starts out by trying to disentangle how these processes are intertwined. It ends with some remarks on how specific donor languages predetermine secondary usage.

1 Constituting new sources of lexical innovation

Lexical enrichment of languages follows a wide variety of patterns. Coining novel words by simply inventing new lexical labels (*jeep*, etc.) is one of these but not a prominent one. Most new lexical items are products of word-formation. New words are generated by recombining existing elements of a language; elements that carry lexical meanings or morphological functions: a machine that computes is a computer.

Another large chunk of new lexemes is borrowed. Computers are as well-established around the world as its lexical label is; an English product of word-formation has turned into a borrowed lexical item in other languages. Borrowing as well as word-formation extends the repertoire of words; nevertheless, the us-

Wieland Eins, Tokyo, Japan

https://doi.org/10.1515/9783111420530-001

age of non-native words and structures is subject to controversial discussions in many language communities (cf. article 2 on foreign word-formation, language planning and purism).

It seems easy to distinguish between these two sources of lexical innovation. With regard to *computer* there is little doubt that English word-formation simply preceded the use of its product elsewhere. German *Computer*, for instance, retains linguistic features of English such as the word-initial <c> or the phoneme cluster /pju/. Still, the clear-cut distinction doesn't hold if Latin constituents like the verbal stem of Latin *computare* are used in English word-formations. In English, this is a combination of both word-formation and borrowing; foreign word-formation is the third major source of lexical enrichment of European languages (cf. article 4 on foreign word-formation in German, article 5 on foreign word-formation in English, article 6 on foreign word-formation in Italian and article 7 on foreign word-formation in Polish).

Foreign word-formation eventually sets in as soon as there is enough information available to decode the morphological structure of a foreign word. As far as a form like *computer* is concerned, there is nothing peculiar about a construction that refers to some sort of appliance carrying out whatever action is specified by the verbal stem. In more remote cases, it might be necessary to derive meanings or functions of non-native constituents by analysis of equally structured lexical items; we do not borrow morphemes, as Paul (1995 [1880]: 399) noted, we borrow words and begin to use their constituents as soon as we have figured out how they work and what they mean. Assuming that we are capable of decoding the concepts behind non-native elements by analogy despite scepticism here among cognitive linguists (e.g., St. Clair 2002: 17), foreign word-formation is more than the borrowing of non-native means to create new words. It requires a fair amount of linguistic analysis on the speaker's part to assign a secondary function to morphemes as well as to the constructions they form.

In some cases we fail, at least if usage standards of the donor language are what speakers of the recipient language are aiming for. Formations like German *Prinzessin* were obviously not analysed correctly if a feminine personal marker *-in* is added, not to French *prince*, but to a derived form that already includes that marker (*princesse*). The Italian pseudo-loanword *footing* 'jogging' is by no means ill-formed but nevertheless odd because none of the numerous meanings of this word in English even comes close to the way it is used in Italian, and Japanese *arubaito* is not German *Arbeit* but restricted to a very specific type of *Arbeit* that speakers of German also refer to by using a loanword: *Job*. It is a difficult task to integrate foreign words into a target language and just as intricate to master all aspects of foreign word-formation. That might be one reason why foreign word-formation trails borrowing at times by 100 to 150 years (Munske 1988: 63) or more.

Nevertheless, foreign word-formation gets easier with every new element added. The estimated 10,000 Greek and Latin loanwords in English adopted during the Renaissance (Baugh and Cable 1993: 227) established a stock of non-native words that was solid enough to render substantial foreign word-formation possible. Since the majority of loanwords in English appeared around 1800, thus, long after borrowing from classical Greek or Latin reached its peak (Scheler 1977: 48–52), it seems likely that foreign word-formation replaced borrowing as the dominant source of new words around that point of time – even though Neo-Latin as a potential source for borrowing may be underestimated (Rainer 2009: 47–50). According to the *Deutsches Fremdwörterbuch*, most foreign words in German are also word-formations rather than borrowed lexical items (Kirkness 1988: 234), and Schmitt (1996: 128) states that foreign word-formation in French not only outnumbers borrowings but also word-formation with genuine elements of French. Still, it is hard to tell in many cases whether words are borrowed or not. Even dictionaries might sometimes be misled by their specific perspective on foreign words (Barz 2008: 40–41), and the shift from borrowing to foreign word-formation might not apply to elements from all sources to the same extent (Kirkness 2001: 106–117). It is the means that vary, but the tendency of broadening the non-native part of lexica remains the same. Some European languages use foreign types of word-formation widely while others compensate for their hesitant use of those processes by borrowing to a greater degree.

It has been argued that German, as compared to English or French, has lexical deficits in either case because of its tradition of purism (e.g., Kirkness 1996: 13; see also article 8 on word-formation and purism in German), but the latter languages have also had their period of profound aversion to foreign influence. There was strong opposition to *inkhorn terms* in English as well as to non-native ways of producing them (e.g., Adams 1987: 129; Baugh and Cable 1993: 212–219), and even in French foreign elements have not remained undisputed (cf. article 9 on word-formation and purism in French). The Latin terminology of jurisprudence, for example, was by law replaced by indigenous French terms as early as 1539 (Settekorn 1988: 38–40). Nevertheless, the number of Latin lexical items in French is vast; there were no major typological gaps to be bridged. It is not surprising that Germanic languages predominantly accessed the Latin lexical reservoir through French until English became the primary source of these elements for the other modern European languages (Kirkness 1996: 12) which, again, makes sense because more than half of all English words are of Latin or Greek origin (Scheler 1977: 52). Obviously, there is nothing unusual about constituents crossing language borders numerous times.

The odds are that many such elements alter features on their way: German *Diathek*, for instance, refers to a 'slide collection', whereas the similar compound in classical Greek means 'testament' (Holzberg 1996: 1–2), and even elements without lexical meaning (affixes) may simply change their functions: English *-ic* as well as its German or French equivalents (*-ik*/*-ique*) forms nouns while its Greek predecessor *-ikós* derived nouns into adjectives (*aisthētikós* 'perceivable'). Secondary usage is not a matter of heritage alone; borrowed elements are used in the way they are needed, not necessarily in the way they were used in the donor language.

The stems involved here may be called "affixes" because they are bound (e.g., Schmitt 1996: 119–132). Since there is more to these elements than affix-like morphological behaviour, more specific ways to address them describe their features: Iacobini (2004: 69–95), for instance, refer to "elementi formativi neoclassici" in Italian. Yet there are numerous terminological suggestions for these neoclassical elements of word-formation. "Confixe" is one of them, a French term for bound roots used by Martinet (1979: 20) and Kocourek (1982: 108) which was introduced as "Konfix" to German linguistics by Schmidt (1987b: 50). Italian "confisso" is not very frequent, perhaps because "confix" has also been used to refer to elements of word-formation that are not stems (Mel'čuk 1982: 80–84). Other terms such as "quasi-morphème" (Tournier 1985: 87–88), "Intermorphem" (Volmert 1996: 227–230) or "Ponem" (also Schmidt 1987b: 49) essentially refer to the same type of constituent, just as "affixoid" does – if we disregard that affixoids are not associated with non-nativeness. Despite the criticism the concept faces (e.g., Fleischer and Barz 1995: 27–28), "affixoid" is used in Germanic linguistics (e.g., ten Hacken 2000: 353) and is also one of the more frequent ways to address these elements in Slavic literature on morphology (Scheller-Boltz 2010: 49–69). However, none of the ways of referring to these stems is as well-established as the English term "combining form", introduced by the *Oxford English Dictionary* (OED) in 1884 (Kirkness 2005: 451). Today this term is used in practically all works on word-formation published in English (e.g., Adams 1987: 128–138; Bauer 1998: 403–422; Lehrer 1998: 3–28; Warren 1990: 111–132 on English word-formation or Fradin 1999: 11–55 and Szymanek 1998: 467 on Romance and Slavic languages).

However, these elements are referred to, there does not seem to be a consensus as to what criteria the morphological classification of these stems should be based upon. Not even non-nativeness is a criterion all linguists agree on (e.g., Fleischer and Barz 1995: 122), and recourse to elements solely from classical languages as suggested by earlier approaches (Martinet 1970: 134–135; Marchand 1969: 5–6) has given way to broader categories not defined by the classical descent of its members (e.g., Schmidt 1987a: 27–35; Eisenberg 2006: 244–246). There seems to be a need for an additional morphological category; one question is where to draw the line between its members and other word-formation elements if combining forms share features with affixes (i.e. both are bound) and lexemes (i.e. both carry lexical information). The other one is how to define them if we take into account that the morphological features of these elements vary considerably. Some modify bases like affixes do, others function as bases for derivations, while the members of a third subset of these constituents are restricted to forming compounds. Either heterogeneous classifications or categories without distinctive features seem inevitable.

There are prototypical elements that meet all demands stated above (e.g., the constituents of *morphology*). Many others do not, such as those elements frequently used in international medical terminologies (*hyper-*, *-itis*, etc.). It is the fuzzy edges that are hardest to describe within this foreign subset of word-formation elements. Basically, the same counts for the processes of word-formation involved here.

2 Constituting new processes of word-formation

Linguists have been struggling to describe how Greek or Latin elements behave within modern languages. Obviously, foreign word-formation processes using Greek or Latin elements may lead to the same constructions in most European languages; it is a difficult task to label foreign word-formations by origin. Speakers of German do not necessarily know that *Musik* was formed in Latin, *Keramik* in French and *Pneumatik* in English (Munske 1988: 65), they don't have to because it does not really matter which language contributed a word to this international stock of words. Terms like "euromorphology" (Schmitt 1996: 119–146) or "learned word-formation" (Fradin 1999: 22–27) reflect this state of affairs; Bergmann (2000: 109) even refers to polygenesis here – to foreign word-formation that is European rather than word-formation specific to any one language. The common ground among these formations is their science-specific, rather than language-specific purpose and the recourse to a classical prototype constructed by the reanalysis of classical model-words that modern European languages share.

However, even if there is some process productive in all modern European languages, the first impulse should, of course, be to describe its products within the linguistic systems of any of these languages. Sections 3 through 6 will discuss how foreign the processes leading to foreign word-formations really are. If there is no systematically significant deviation from compounding or derivation with indigenous constituents, it makes sense to describe non-native word-formations within native models (e.g., Eisenberg 2006: 242–246). But on the other hand, word-formation subsequent to the borrowing of words not only facilitated the use of non-native morphemes in derivations and compounds; it also introduced linguistic structures unknown to modern European languages up to that point of time. Patterns such as those generally referred to as "neoclassical compounds" as in *morphology* differ considerably from the way regular compounds of these languages are formed. It is tempting to refer to different sets of processes in recipient languages – native ones (see sections 3 and 4) that allow foreign constituents and foreign ones (sections 5 and 6) that require them.

Within the neoclassical subset there is heterogeneous morphological behaviour. The "medical" elements *-itis* or *hyper-* mentioned previously may form compound-like words despite being affix-like in that they are bound, but compared to the elements of which *morphology* is composed, there are additional restrictions. *Morpho-* as well as *-logy* can be used as either initial or as final constituent of neoclassical compounds, and they form bases for derivations ([[*morph*]eme]/[[*log*]ic]) as well as neoclassical compounds. *Hyper-* and *-itis* do not; they require stems as co-constituents, and they are restricted in their use as either initial or final constituents in European foreign word-formations. Obviously, some foreign stems resemble affixes more than others. Given that we cannot even pinpoint word-formations with elements of this kind as being either cases of compounding or derivation, it is tempting to avoid this distinction altogether and subsume all these combinational patterns under one common label. Martinet's (1970: 134–135) and – more recently – Schmidt's (1987a: 28–33) approaches may be described in this way. In their models (*recomposition* and *recombination*), the origin of the constituents in the former and their non-nativeness in the latter case seem to be more significant than similarities between foreign and native compounds or foreign and native derivations.

Marchand (1969: 5–6), on the other hand, distinguishes between native and non-native processes that do not necessarily correlate with the origin of the constituents involved here. *Word-formation on a native* [English] *basis of coining* combines words (as compounds do) or words and non-words (found in derivations). Foreign formations, on the other hand, are combinations of non-words; thus, the only criterion for nativeness, as far as types of word-formation are concerned, is the presence of a word. English *hypersensitive* (containing a non-word and a word) as well as its equivalent in other European languages is a native word-formation within his framework despite its non-native constituents, whereas *hypertrophy* (consisting of two non-words) is not.

Other models expand native concepts somewhat in order to describe non-native combinations of non-words. Müller (2005a: 208), for instance, refers to *affix-combination* if bound elements lack the ability to function as both initial and final constituents, whether they are stems or not. These stems resemble native affixes in this sense, no matter how much lexical content may be assigned to them. Even most productive and semantically transparent stems turn into affixes because topological properties suggest such a classification (e.g., German *Biblio-*$_{[\mathrm{Aff}]}$*-thek*$_{[\mathrm{Aff}]}$ 'library').

In sum, there seems to be a tendency to infer hyperonymic models that include modern and neoclassical combinations (Schmidt, Eisenberg) or derivation- and compound-like processes (Martinet), and a tendency to define foreign processes of word-formation by exclusion. Whatever is not possible within indigenous models of word-formation is foreign (Marchand, Müller) – combining affixes, for instance.

There have been many more attempts to disentangle foreign word-formation processes as well as criteria its constituents can be defined by – some of these reflections lead to contradictory results: Bauer (1993: 214–215), for instance, uses potential participation in neoclassical compounding to define combining forms, whereas Donalies (2000: 154–157) takes derivability as the sole criterion for such a classification. The one thing all theorists agree on is that some distinct subtype of word-formation exists that is foreign. Since all of these approaches – with, perhaps, the exception of Müller's affix-combination – require the presence of foreign stems, the differences do not seem to be all that significant. The foreign process of word-formation might be termed "recombination", "recomposition" or simply "word-formation on a non-native basis of coining". But even if there is some foreign model of word-formation, we still do not know how to capture the behaviour of non-native constituents in native-like constructions. The following sections aim to investigate how foreign the different types of word-formation are.

3 Foreign derivation

There is nothing foreign about affixing some sort of functional marker to a stem. Many of these markers gradually emerge within a language as lexemes become opaque and eventually grammaticalize. German *-heit* or *-schaft* (Fleischer and Barz 1995: 158–163, 168–170), for instance, used to be stems but turned into bound morphemes with morphological functions rather than lexical meanings; they became affixes just like the predecessors of their English counterparts *-dom* or *-hood* did (Marchand 1969: 262, 293). In all Romance languages, *-ment(e)* is such a result of grammaticalization, and even foreign words may share that destiny: the English suffix *-ify* derives from Latin *facere* 'to make' (Hall 2000: 537). Given that grammatical units do not tend to change their features easily (compare inflectional markers), it is worth noting that the inventory of word-formation morphemes is not as closed a system as other modules of grammar seem to be. Still, grammaticalization is a minor source for secondary affixes, and so is coining in the sense of simply inventing new affixes: Fradin briefly discusses elements that came along with attempts to establish an appropriate nomenclature for chemistry in 18th century French – very few of them (*-ate* 'chlorate'/*-on* 'xénon') being "pure creations" (Fradin 1999: 25).

The overwhelming majority of secondary affixes result from the analysis of complex loanwords. As far as Romance languages are concerned, the model derivations were obviously Latin (Rainer 2004: 1705–1708); English drew on the same source to make up for its native affixes that were lost after the Norman Conquest (Baugh and Cable 1993: 177–179). Within the German inventory of prefixes, non-native elements also constitute the most productive and the largest class (Polenz 1994: 88); for a language widely relying on compounding to extend its native lexicon, this does not come as a surprise. Within verbal word-formation, some languages compensate for morphemic deficits by "prefixing" words as bound elements to a certain extent. Verbal particles, derived from prepositions or adverbs, have relational meanings, and denominal particles have lexical meanings rather than the synsemantic functions associated with prefixes. Within the non-verbal domain of word-formation, not even particles take over functions the limited number of indigenous prefixes do not cover. As far as the semantic function of, e.g., German nominal prefixes is concerned, it is basically restricted to negation, augmentation, and diminution (Fleischer and Barz 1995: 320–346), but there are plenty of borrowed elements available that either fit into one of these categories (see Klosa 1996: 373–395 and Ruf 1996: 335–344 on foreign means of negation and augmentation) or constitute new ones. A series of studies – *Studien zur deutschen Sprache* – conducted and published by the *Institut für Deutsche Sprache* (IDS) reveal contemporary and past usage of elements like *inter-*, *trans-* or *ex-* in German. Articles on other morphemes have been published in these volumes that have shaped discussions on foreign word-formation in German linguistics in recent years (Hoppe et al. 1987; Munske and Kirkness 1996; Stickel 2001; Müller 2005b and 2009), and there is Eisenberg's book on foreign words, which discusses foreign elements in German most comprehensively (Eisenberg 2011).

The inventory of indigenous suffixes is much more elaborate in all languages described here; nevertheless, the foreign subset of suffixes is large and extremely productive. The suffix in *computer* (from Latin *-arius*), for instance, is one of the most frequent nominal markers; all Germanic languages have it (Bloomfield 1933: 455). Impressive productivity also counts for German *-ieren*; given that German lacks the verbal alternatives English has (regul-*ate*/class-*ify*/random-*ize*), the high frequency of *-ieren* and its variants does not come unexpectedly (Eisenberg 2011: 259–261). Yet suffixes differ from one another in their degree of integration. Intonation patterns in German show that there are (older) Latin elements almost indistinguishable from indigenous morphemes and also (younger) constituents that retain non-native linguistic features: derivations with *-er* are native-like in that they are stem-stressed, whereas formations with *-ieren* are not. Not even elements of the same origin necessarily behave in the same manner.

The stems in foreign derivations are bound just as Latin or Greek roots are. There is no word *comput-* in English or in the languages that adopted the concept and the lexemes associated with it – only a bound root ([[*comput*]er]/ing]/able]/ ...). Native roots, on the other hand, are generally free. They do not need a word-formation element to become a free form; not even verbal stems do since they may require only an inflectional marker to form words (e.g., Dutch [[*reken*]en$_{\text{INFL}}$] 'to compute'). Even the bases of parasynthetic derivations that might be described as bound bases as a result of prefixation (e.g., French *enrichir* 'to enrich'; Rainer 2004: 1706) need only inflection and not word-formation ([*en*[*rich*]]ir$_{\text{INFL}}$]). Verbal stems and parasynthetic bases are word-like in this sense; the non-native bound roots are not. Stems like *comput-* fill lexical gaps without being lexemes themselves.

On the other hand, bound segments may be obsolete linguistic constructs altogether because the notion of forming new words from scratch by first analyzing and then recombining bound roots with derivational elements seems a little far-fetched. We might simply adapt borrowed words to our own purposes by substituting constituents of one word with elements taken from others ([[comput]*er*]/*ing*]/*able*]/...). It might be a specific type of word-formation process rather than a specific type of constituent which frequently occurs in foreign word-formations. Munske (1988: 64–65) terms this specific type of foreign derivation *affix-substitution* in opposition to *addition* – which is what we find in indigenous derivation.

Still, secondary verbs like English *sculpt* remind us that analysis actually happens; Beard (1998: 56) refers to backformation here, as the borrowed word *sculptor* lost its derivational suffix, leaving a base that could easily be integrated as a secondary verb of English. Backformation is not limited to foreign derivation (English *sightseeing* → *sightsee* / German *Staubsauger* 'vacuum cleaner' → *staubsaugen* 'to vacuum'), but it is a convenient way to form secondary word-formation paradigms based on complex loanwords.

4 Foreign compounding

Joining words to form another word is, of course, not limited by origin. As long as the constituents themselves are integrated into the language in that they carry all relevant grammatical and lexical information, there is no reason to look for another subset. Not even hybrid compounds appear to be restricted in any way; only the tendency that non-native elements are preferably used in a non-head position has been observed for German and English (Mackensen 1972: 98; Adams 1987: 129). The degree of morphological integration of loanwords in Germanic languages is remarkable in both hybrid and foreign compounds; non-native non-heads select native linking elements as the examples taken from Kürschner (2010: 847) indicate:

Danish	*station-s-hal*	*universitet-s-teater*
Dutch	*station-s-hal*	*universiteit-s-theater*
German	*Station-s-halle*	*Universität-s-theater*
Swedish	*station-s-hall*	*universitet-s-teater*

Nonetheless, there are differences in how compounds are formed. In Romance languages synthetic (verbal) compounds as in Italian *battimani* clap-hands 'applause' (Catalani 2004: 38–41) or Spanish *sacacorchos* pull-corks 'corkscrew' (Olsen 2000: 912) are quite frequent (see also Booij 2000: 858–859), whereas the corresponding exocentric model is rather insignificant in Germanic languages, though all of them seem to have isolated formations of that kind; Don (1998: 379), for instance, names Dutch *stampvoet* 'stamp foot'. It has been argued that these formations are lexicalized phrases (e.g., Rainer 2004: 1705), thus, products of syntax rather than word-formations, which eventually leads to the conclusion that Romance languages do not use compounding as much as Germanic languages do (cf. Olsen 2000: 911–913). Still, all European languages have compounds although there may be differences in how they are realized: German *Haustür* has its equivalent in English *front door*; German tends to form units on the morphological level, whereas English preferably makes use of word clusters, of *semi words* as Wurzel (2000: 39–41) termed units somewhere in between words and phrases. French, on the other hand, generally composes lexical items in opposite order of constituents (*porte de la maison*) just as Spanish (*puerta de la casa*) and Italian (*porta di casa*) do – even though there is more to compounding in French, Spanish and Italian, of course (e.g., Benveniste 1974: 171–176; Kornfeld 1998: 436–452; Bisetto 2004: 33–69). In any case, the concept of joining words to form another one allows for very different realizations (overview on subtypes of compounds in Dressler 2006: 23–44).

Still, none of the languages described here seems to retain foreign characteristics if foreign constituents are used. According to Cypionka (1994: 224), the sequence of constituents in hybrid formations in French corresponds to the French default in most cases (*scooter des neiges* 'snow scooter'; *prix standard* 'standard price'), and even the few German loan-compounds in contemporary English occasionally take on morphosyntactic shapes we would not expect: any google search suggests that English *kindergarten/kindergarden* has its "phrasal" variant in *kinder garden*. Needless to say, German forms compounds even if the model-word itself might best be described as one of Wurzel's semi words referred to above (English *top manager* > German *Topmanager*), and foreign compounding with French, Spanish or Italian constituents does not trigger inversion.

In compounds, foreignness is limited to the origin of its constituents. Still, there is one explicitly foreign type of compounding with rather limited disposition to interact with native modules of word-formation: neoclassical compounding.

5 Neoclassical compounding

From a lexical point of view, the type of word-formation discussed here is as foreign as it gets. It is not only that the constituents are non-native (*morphology*, etc.). The results of this type of word-formation do not seem to fit into the core lexicon of modern languages either. They are "éléments savants" (Martinet 1970: 134) – lexical units predominantly used in international scientific discourse. Even more recent works on foreign word-formation seem to imply that word-formation in general and combinations of this kind should be kept separate: Scholz (2002: 69), for instance, refers to "terminological combination" in Spanish, and the English term for the constituents of these complex units avoids the expression usually used to refer to constituents of word-formations: it is "combining form" and not "morpheme".

A closer look at the structure of these foreign word-formations reveals that there are morphological reasons for keeping them out of the core system. These combinations seem to violate the rules of word grammar. Compounds as well as derivations have heads. The major difference is that heads in compounds are not just heads in a morphological sense; they are "lexical heads" as well, while suffixes are not because this role is reserved for autosemantic morphemes – i.e. for stems. The final constituents of neoclassical compounds are stems in both senses but they are not words, which is disturbing in a way. If *morphology*, for instance, were a compound, the syntactic category should be determined by upward perlocation (Booij 2000: 860); *morphology* would not be a word because *-logy* is not. Yet we know that any such formation is not only a word, but in fact a noun with a word-final lexical head: the right-hand constituents of neoclassical compounds resemble heads of both compounds and derivations.

According to Selkirk (1982: 16, 119–124), this neoclassical type constitutes some discrete system of compounding. It may be a system in which we need to accept abnormal phenomena such as "bound words" (e.g., Fabb 1998: 69) or elements of word-formation that are underspecified in terms of categorical affiliation (Eisenberg 2011: 251–256, 283). But perhaps it is closer to the truth if we take into consideration that neoclassical formations like *morphology* might not be compounds at all. They could be regular derivations of multisegmental bases much like those described in section 3.

The notion of morphologically complex bases leaves us with non-words as lexical heads (*morpholog-*), which is not exceptional: non-native stems usually are non-words ([[*morph*]eme]). Still, compounding is involved here, because stems are joined together to form new lexical entities with new compositional meanings assigned to them. Selkirk (1982: 99) refers to "compound roots", whereas Donalies (2000: 155) argues that these complex units are simply combining forms themselves. If this is compounding, it is compounding that does not form words. Ten Hacken (2000: 354) suggests that bound compounds ([[*morpho*][*logo*]]) are derived to form words like *morphology* by some kind of suffix-substitution, the same process we have seen in foreign derivation (see section 3). But since the final vowels in these constituents (*morpho-*, *logo-*) do not seem to be anything but linking vowels, it might be easier to consider neoclassical compounding derivation of bound compounds containing minimal forms only ([[[*morph*]o[*log*] $_{\text{(COMP)}}$] *y* $_{\text{(DER)}}$]).

At first sight, the neoclassical linking vowels – in most cases Greek-based *-o-*, rarely Latin-based *-i-* (Höfler 1972: 125–136) – behave much like native linking elements do. They developed from inflectional markers into word-formation elements (Bauer 1998: 406), signalling compounding rather than some concept associated with the inflection marker that was reanalysed (for a discussion on linking elements in Swedish, German, Dutch and Danish see Kürschner 2010: 827–862). Dutch *boek-handel* 'bookshop', for example, is no less plural-marked than *boek-en-kast* 'bookcase' is (as far as the number of books referred to is concerned); *-en* does not imply "plurality" (Don 1998: 380–381). Still, it is not quite clear whether these elements are attached to the stems on their left (like inflection markers are) or simply inserted in between stems. As far as native linking elements are concerned, the preceding stem determines which one is used if there is a choice: Dutch *boek-en-kast* is grammatical but **boek-s-kast* is not. The linking elements in compounds with neoclassical stems, however, differ from those in regular compounds in this respect; formations like English *weatherology* show that it is not necessarily the compound-initial stem that determines the nature of the linking element. Neoclassical linking vowels do not seem to be linked to a stem (as suggested by ten Hacken's bound compound *morphologo*); they may only indicate neoclassical compounding. This specific type of foreign word-formation would provide a way of combining stems by insertion of a neoclassical segment, which does not mean that these formations are words. Neoclassical compounding is as foreign as it gets.

No matter how we try to capture the nature of these neoclassical combinations, there are good reasons for associating this type of foreign word-formation with some European prototype rather than with language-specific morphological systems. The prototype itself is stable, allowing only marginal adaptations to language-specific rules. The adaptations do not persist once the formations turn into internationalisms. German remodels the compounds originating in French or English according to the German realization of this prototype; it does not integrate English or French neoclassical compounds in an orthographically and phonologically unchanged form as it integrates other borrowed items from these languages – *Computer*, for instance. French neoclassical compounding shows how present this prototype still is as it disregards the morpho-topological default of French altogether once neoclassical stems are involved. There is no *gare d'aéro*, but there is an *aérogare* 'airport'.

6 Hybrid formation

Combinations such as French *aérogare* are both hybrid and compound, but they still differ from the hybrid compounds mentioned in section 4. They follow a neoclassical model due to the origin of one of its constituents; they form neoclassical compounds, not compounds. Nevertheless, there are formations in which it seems hard to draw the line: compounds with non-words in non-head position, for instance.

Bound elements as non-heads do not conflict with the morphological systems of modern European languages since prefixes do not behave differently. Still, there is no prefixation involved in cases like Italian *ecodisastro* (Iacobini 2004: 73), Spanish *ecosistema* (Scholz 2002: 105), German *Ökofreak* (Donalies 2000: 149) or Polish *ekobomba* (Scheller-Boltz 2010: 68) since the initial elements in these hybrids carry lexical meanings – which rules out prefixation –, but moreover they seem to mean something other than what we would expect. According to Reis (1983: 117), the initial elements in these formations generally refer to the concepts conveyed by neoclassical model-compounds; a German *Ökofreak* is some kind of 'ecological freak', Spanish *ecosistema* refers to an 'ecological system' and Italian *ecodisastro* or Polish *ekobomba* to a 'disaster' or a 'bomb' with regard to 'ecology'. Donalies (2000: 148–150) objects to this analysis. Nonetheless, any dictionary that indexes formations of this kind reveals countless constituents that seem to imply more than they overtly express, but only in rare cases is more than linguistic intuition available to show that some kind of neoclassical clipping is involved: Weinrich (2003: 930) has observed that these constructions neither denote a concept associated with *eco-* nor with the neoclassical compound *economy*. Obviously, German *öko-* as well as its cognates in other languages signals the presence of the neoclassical compound *ecology* which rules out the usage of *eco-* in other contexts: Italian *ecodisastro*, for instance, can not refer to an economic disaster.

Again we witness compounds with very unique features, and once again foreign word-formation might entail a combination of processes rather than a single compositional step merging a stem and a word. There is evidence that neoclassical compounds might be clipped to form constituents (e.g., Italian *ecologia* > *eco-*); constituents that are used in regular compounds (e.g., Italian *ecodisastro*). Given that neoclassical compounds themselves may be more complex than they seem (section 5), hybrid compounding may not be adequately described by the notion of minimal bound forms being attached to words.

The other hybrid pattern involving neoclassical constituents – non-words in head position – is somewhat awkward. It seems to belong to the domain of ad-hoc formations because they are easy to decode but apparently not useful enough to make it into the lexicon on a larger scale. Nevertheless, this process has existed for quite some time now; according to the *Oxford English Dictionary*, *weatherology*, for instance, can be traced back to the year 1823. Since we fail to identify some kind of model compound in *-ology*, etc., there is no use in assuming some kind of clipping either. The final constituents could be savant suffixes indicating a scientific approach to the entity specified by the element to which it is attached. If this is the case, there are multisegmental elements within the inventory of affixes (-[*o*[*logy*]]), elements with lexical meaning despite being affixes. With regard to French *-omanie*, Höfler (1972: 114–124) refers to a transition from (Neo-Latin) compounding to (French) derivation with these elements. But maybe these secondary suffixes are linguistic constructs given that morphemes share one common feature in any synchronic approach: morphemes are defined by their capacity to form regular words. Non-native stems as heads of hybrid word-formations are only capable of producing ad-hoc formations as it seems.

On the other hand, reanalysis of foreign stems as affixes is likely to happen because the transfer from one language into another one is often accompanied by the loss of lexical or morphological information as we have seen in the first section of this article. In fact, reanalysis of foreign elements unveils morphological characteristics that seem to be associated with foreign elements of word-formation only. Rainer (2004: 1705) points out that there are Latin prefixes that turned into synsemantic words of French (Latin *trans-* > French *très*), and occasionally affixes even develop into words with lexical meaning: *ex*, *macro*, even *isms* and many more are, in addition to their affixal use, secondary lexemes by now – in English as well as in other European languages. There are explanations for this behaviour, of course, ranging from clipping of model-words to usage-borne considerations. If elements are associated with more lexical content than plain affixes are, why shouldn't we use them accordingly? Hybridization is only one step on the way – an early one, according to Hoppe's (1999: 57) chronological register of *ex*-formations in German (*Exfrau* 'ex-wife' [1792]). But however these forms have evolved, it is a remarkable change in terms of categorical affiliation whenever bound forms turn into free ones.

The elements that remain plain affixes do not tend to leave the exogenic context they stem from; they derive predominantly non-native stems. Conflicting stress assignment rules might be a reason here. German words, for instance, are stem-stressed by default; thus, conflicts are inevitable whenever stem-shifting affixes are used. It makes sense to avoid conflicting rules within a linguistic system, and one way to do that is to refrain from hybridization. Formations like German *hausieren* 'soliciting' (lit. [['house']-ieren$_{(V)}$]) – not being stem-stressed – are rare. Nevertheless, most affixes are no longer restricted as to what kind of stem they can be attached to. The English suffix *-ness*, for instance, takes non-native stems (*nativeness*) and non-native *-able* forms hybrid words like *drinkable* (Bloomfield 1933: 454–455). Indigenous prefixes like *un-* can be attached to non-native words (1.a.) even though non-native words allow non-native prefixation, of course (1.b.). The only remaining genetic restrictions seem to affect the co-occurrence of non-native bound roots and native prefixes (2.a.) as well as non-native prefixation of native words (3.b.):

	English		German	
1.	a. *un-typical*	b. *a-typical*	a. *un-typisch*	b. *a-typisch*
2.	a. **un-morph*	b. *a-morph(ous)*	a. **un-morph*	b. *a-morph*
3.	a. *un-pleasant*	b. **a-pleasant*	a. *un-schön*	b. **a-schön*

We might expect hybrid derivation to be blocked by synonymous elements in the target languages (**apleasant*), but we have seen alternative ways of expressing the same thing (*atypical* – *untypical*). Redundancy is also not an issue here because alternate forms tend to develop specific qualities attributed to them. English *hypersensitive*, for instance, is as augmentative as English *supersensitive* is, but only *hypersensitive* carries an additional negative connotation. Conflicts in stress assignment cannot be responsible either because German *unschön* violates the (stem-stressed) default of German just as **aschön* would. In fact, there does not seem to be a systematic reason to avoid hybridization here; the tendency to stick to one language remains intact nonetheless. If this is the case, then the morphological behaviour is specific to the languages from which the borrowed elements of word-formation stem, at least to a certain extent. We will see that hybridization, even within the non-native subset, explains heterogeneous behaviour in some cases.

7 Language-specific reflexes in foreign word-formation

Given that integration into another linguistic system leads to all kinds of functional changes, we should not expect much of an impact from the languages in which borrowed elements originate; the term "neoclassical" reflects this underspecification as far as etymology is concerned. The generalization implied here is due to the path that lies behind the foreign elements but is also synchronically appropriate because of the similar functions both Latin and Greek elements have as tools for scientific discourse. On the other hand, younger anglicisms have similar (scientific) functions (Busse 2001: 143); not all of them are of Latin or Greek descent. Thus, the correlation between specific domains and specific languages does not seem to be a firm one, and it seems to be changing: Burmassova found that the figures for German anglicisms in contributions on science and technology in DIE WELT have declined in recent years; they have increased, however, in other sections of that journal (Burmassova 2010: 220–227). Time will tell whether the capacity to integrate anglicisms is about to be exhausted in some domains. In either case, if anglicisms develop one way or another within a specific domain, there is not a single foreign subset within the lexicon but a subset subdivided into groups defined by their origin.

There are additional domains with preferences of this kind. When it comes to food, languages like Italian come into play, despite the minor role it plays as a donor language these days (Schmöe 1998: 239–266). It is interesting that connotations seem to translate into word-formation elements in cases like *Mildessa* (Wegener 2010: 99), a German brand name for *sauerkraut* that gets an Italian touch by adding *-essa* to the adjective *mild*. It is even more interesting that Italian segments tend to be reinterpreted to a much greater extent than anglicisms are. According to Harnisch (2010: 113), the suffix in Italian loanwords like *Bambini* 'children' ceased to plural-mark their bases when used in German. Forms like *Bambinis* (pl.) or *Paparazzis* (pl.) indicate that the inflected Italian forms are mistaken for *i*-derivations denoting a person (compare German *Studi* 'student'). If, on the other hand, even bizarre elements of English like *-gate* or *-oholic* are used in much the same way in donor and recipient languages like German (Barz 2008: 52), French (Fradin 1999: 35–47) or Italian (Iacobini 2004: 76), there is little doubt that the source makes a difference here. Still, the most significant language-specific reflex seems to be the sheer amount of anglicisms compared to the limited number of elements from other modern languages.

A frequency effect of a different kind affects processes rather than words. The increasing productivity of patterns that are marginal in most languages has traditionally been ascribed to English influence; it still is (Burmassova 2010: 46–47). According to Carstensen (1965: 45–62), English clippings (e.g., *ad* 'advertisement') and blends (*smog* 'smoke and fog') in particular may have facilitated the use of these models elsewhere; Fradin (1999: 27–35) discusses both blends (e.g., *optimistique* 'optimistic and mystical') and amputated forms in French (e.g., *bibliothèque* → *bibli* 'library'); Barz (2008: 52–55) adds German backformation (e.g., verbal *nordicwalken* based on *Nordicwalking*$_{(N)}$) to the list of processes that might be more frequent due to the productivity of corresponding English models of word-formation. Even the suffix that this article started out with (*-er* in German *Computer*) has acquired an additional function in analogy to its use elsewhere: Eisenberg (2011: 264) points out that this suffix is not restricted anymore to exclusively derive verbal stems (compare German *Dampfer* 'steamer' having a noun as base).

One tentative conclusion would therefore be that English supplies terminology and alters patterns or frequency, whereas structures from other modern languages tend to be reanalyzed – they take on functions they did not originally have if they are adopted at all. We will see that there are language-specific aspects even within the one subset that has been described as a distinct and homogeneous morphological system so far – neoclassical formations.

Recalling what has been said about the Latinization of European derivation, it is tempting to associate neoclassical compounding with Greek; all constituents of neoclassical compounds mentioned here are of Greek origin. Perhaps this is more than coincidence. If we compare Greek- and Latin-based equivalents in today's terminologies, there is reason to correlate the origin and linguistic behaviour in foreign word-formation: *Microscope* is Greek, whereas *minimal* is Latin; *micro-* is initial element in neoclassical compounds only, while its Latin synonym is a base for derivations. Countless word-pairs show the same alternation in terms of how the elements are being used. The initial elements in *homo-geneous – similar* or *hetero-genic – vari-ant* refer to the same concepts (*homós – similis* 'alike'/ *héteros – varius* 'different'), but they are used in a way that is apparently specific to the language of origin. Modern European languages owe a great deal of their affixes and bases for derivation to Latin, and at the same time, the inventory of constituents of neoclassical compounds seems to be based almost exclusively on

Greek stems. Keeping this language-specific distribution in mind, there is a reason for stems to be restricted to either neoclassical compounding or derivation after all.

As far as analogous elements that behave much like affixes are concerned (e.g., [*super*[sensitive]] – [*hyper*[sensitive]]; Bauer 1993: 215), origin also makes a difference. There are no doublets like *hypertrophy* – **supertrophy* either in English or in other European languages, because the initial element in *hypertrophy* is Greek and therefore appropriate for neoclassical compounding, whereas *super-* is Latin and, thus, predestined to be a secondary affix. Since bound stems are not prefixed (see section 6), **supertrophy* does not work.

There are more conclusions to draw from the observation that the label "neoclassical" itself does not refer to one homogeneous class of word-formation elements and processes (Eins 2008: 248–260). The most important aspect remains that there are reflexes of origin still visible in terms of how elements are used – within the neoclassical context, but also outside of it. In modern foreign word-formation, it is complicated to pinpoint how foreign complex words exactly are because their constituents blend in, rather than initiate systematic changes. Nevertheless, this subset is not homogeneous, as some elements are more likely to be reanalyzed rather than used as suggested by the language of origin. Typological distance might be one factor, but extralinguistic reasons are probably more crucial here. In related languages, systematic deviation might be marginal but still be significant in terms of how many linguistic units are affected.

8 Concluding remarks

Foreign word-formation subsumes a rather heterogeneous group of processes, some being more deviant than others, depending on the language-specific point of view. Nevertheless, there seems to be only one type of foreign word-formation that deviates from indigenous patterns more than it resembles them. In modern European languages, neoclassical compounding constitutes its own, its European type of foreign word-formation. Perhaps additional functions of neoclassical constituents in hybrid formations such as lexeme-like usages of affixes or affix-like usages of stems simply show that reanalysis is an attempt to adjust foreign formations to indigenous patterns. Nevertheless, the neoclassical type of foreign word-formation remains intact.

9 References

Adams, Valerie (1987): *An Introduction to Modern English Word-Formation*. London: Longman.

Barz, Irmhild (2008): Englisches in der deutschen Wortbildung. In: Ludwig M. Eichinger, Meike Meliss and María J. Domínguez Vázquez (eds.), *Wortbildung heute. Tendenzen und Kontraste in der deutschen Gegenwartssprache*, 39–60. Tübingen: Narr.

Bauer, Laurie (1993): *English Word-Formation*. Cambridge: Cambridge University Press.

Bauer, Laurie (1998): Is there a class of neoclassical compounds, and if so is it productive? *Linguistics* 36(3): 403–422.

Baugh, Albert C. and Thomas Cable (1993): *A History of the English Language*. 4th ed. London/New York: Routledge.

Beard, Robert (1998): Derivation. In: Arnold M. Zwicky and Andrew Spencer (eds.), *The Handbook of Morphology*, 44–65. Oxford: Blackwell.

Benveniste, Émile (1974): *Problèmes de linguistique générale*. Vol. 2. Paris: Gallimard.

Bergmann, Rolf (2000): Zum Problem der Produktivität europäischer Wortbildung im Deutschen. In: Mechthild Habermann, Peter O. Müller and Bernd Naumann (eds.), *Wortschatz und Orthographie in Geschichte und Gegenwart. Festschrift für Horst Haider Munske zum 65. Geburtstag*, 103–114. Tübingen: Niemeyer.

Bisetto, Antonietta (2004): Composizione con elementi italiani. In: Maria Grossmann and Franz Rainer (eds.), *La formazione delle parole in italiano*, 33–69. Tübingen: Niemeyer.

Bloomfield, Leonard (1933): *Language*. New York: Holt, Rinehart and Winston.

Booij, Geert (2000): Inheritance. In: Geert Booij, Christian Lehmann and Joachim Mugdan (eds.), *Morphology. An International Handbook on Inflection and Word-Formation*. Vol. 1, 857–865. Berlin/New York: de Gruyter.

Burmassova, Svetlana (2010): *Empirische Untersuchung der Anglizismen im Deutschen. Am Material der Zeitung* Die Welt *(Jahrgänge 1994 und 2004)*. Bamberg: University of Bamberg Press.

Busse, Ulrich (2001): Typen von Anglizismen: Von *der heiligo geist* bis *Extremsparing* – aufgezeigt anhand ausgewählter lexikographischer Kategorisierungen. In: Gerhard Stickel (ed.), *Neues und Fremdes im deutschen Wortschatz. Aktueller lexikalischer Wandel*, 131–155. Berlin/New York: de Gruyter.

Carstensen, Broder (1965): *Englische Einflüsse auf die deutsche Sprache nach 1945*. Heidelberg: Winter.

Catalani, Luigi (2004): *Deutsch, Französisch und Spanisch im Kontrast mit dem Italienischen. Vier Beiträge zum Sprachvergleich*. Frankfurt/M.: Lang.

Cypionka, Marion (1994): *Französische "Pseudoanglizismen". Lehnformationen zwischen Entlehnung, Wortbildung, Form- und Bedeutungswandel*. Tübingen: Narr.

Díaz-Negrillo, Ana (2014): Neoclassical compounds and final combining forms in English. *Linguistik Online* 68(6): 4–20.

Don, Jan (1998): IE, Germanic: Dutch. In: Rochelle Lieber and Pavol Štekauer (eds.), *The Oxford Handbook of Compounding*, 370–385. Oxford: Oxford University Press.

Donalies, Elke (2000): Das Konfix. Zur Definition einer zentralen Einheit der deutschen Wortbildung. *Deutsche Sprache* 28: 144–159.

Dressler, Wolfgang Ulrich (2006): Compound types. In: Garry Libben and Gonia Jarema (eds.), *The Representation and Processing of Compound Words*, 23–44. Oxford: Oxford University Press.

Eins, Wieland (2008): *Muster und Konstituenten der Lehnwortbildung. Das Konfix-Konzept und seine Grenzen*. Hildesheim: Olms.

Eisenberg, Peter (2006): *Grundriss der deutschen Grammatik. Das Wort*. 3rd ed. Stuttgart: Metzler.

Eisenberg, Peter (2011): *Das Fremdwort im Deutschen*. Berlin/New York: de Gruyter.
Fabb, Nigel (1998): Compounding. In: Arnold M. Zwicky and Andrew Spencer (eds.), *The Handbook of Morphology*, 66–83. Oxford: Blackwell.
Fleischer, Wolfgang and Irmhild Barz (1995): *Wortbildung der deutschen Gegenwartssprache*. 2nd ed. Tübingen: Niemeyer.
Fradin, Bernard (1999): Combining forms, blends and related phenomena. In: Ursula Doleschal and Anna M. Thornton (eds.), *Extragrammatical and Marginal Morphology*, 11–55. München: LINCOM Europa.
Ganslmayer, Christine and Peter O. Müller (2021): Historische Fremdwortbildung. Forschungsstand und Perspektiven. In: Christine Ganslmayer and Christian Schwarz (eds.), *Historische Wortbildung. Theorien – Methoden – Perspektiven*, 105–144. Hildesheim: Olms (= Germanistische Linguistik 252–254).
Hall, Christopher J. (2000): Prefixation, suffixation and circumfixation. In: Geert Booij, Christian Lehmann and Joachim Mugdan (eds.), *Morphology. An International Handbook on Inflection and Word-Formation*. Vol. 1, 535–545. Berlin/New York: de Gruyter.
Harnisch, Rüdiger (2010): Integration und Isolation von suffixverdächtigen Fremdwörtern – das Deutsche in typologischer Perspektive. In: Carmen Scherer and Anke Holler (eds.), *Strategien der Integration und Isolation nicht-nativer Einheiten und Strukturen*, 105–122. Berlin/New York: de Gruyter.
Höfler, Manfred (1972): *Zur Integration der neulateinischen Kompositionsweise im Französischen dargestellt an den Bildungen auf* -(o)manie, -(o)mane. Tübingen: Niemeyer.
Holzberg, Niklas (1996): Neugriechisch und Eurolatein. In: Horst Haider Munske and Alan Kirkness (eds.), *Eurolatein. Das griechische und lateinische Erbe in den europäischen Sprachen*, 1–11. Tübingen: Niemeyer.
Hoppe, Gabriele (1999): *Das Präfix* ex-. *Beiträge zur Lehnwortbildung*. Tübingen: Narr.
Hoppe, Gabriele, Alan Kirkness, Elisabeth Link, Isolde Nortmeyer, Wolfgang Rettig and Günter Dietrich Schmidt (eds.) (1987): *Deutsche Lehnwortbildung. Beiträge zur Erforschung der Wortbildung mit entlehnten WB-Einheiten im Deutschen*. Tübingen: Narr.
Iacobini, Claudio (2004): Composizione con elementi neoclassici. In: Maria Grossmann and Franz Rainer (eds.), *La formazione delle parole in italiano*, 69–95. Tübingen: Niemeyer.
Kirkness, Alan (1988): Einleitung. In: *Deutsches Fremdwörterbuch*. Begonnen von Hans Schulz, fortgeführt von Otto Basler, weitergeführt im Institut für Deutsche Sprache. Vol. 7, 227–235. Berlin/New York: de Gruyter.
Kirkness, Alan (1996): Eurolatein. Überlegungen zu einem lexikalischen Phänomen und dessen Erforschung aus der Sicht eines Sprachgermanisten. *Sprachreport* 1(96): 11–14.
Kirkness, Alan (2001): Europäismen/Internationalismen im heutigen deutschen Wortschatz: Eine lexikographische Pilotstudie. In: Gerhard Stickel (ed.), *Neues und Fremdes im deutschen Wortschatz. Aktueller lexikalischer Wandel*, 106–130. Berlin/New York: de Gruyter.
Kirkness, Alan (2005): Zur lexikographischen Dokumentation eurolateinischer Wortbildungseinheiten: Vergleichende Beobachtungen am Beispiel *aero-*. In: Peter O. Müller (ed.), *Fremdwortbildung. Theorie und Praxis in Geschichte und Gegenwart*, 447–483. Frankfurt/M.: Lang.
Klosa, Annette (1996): *Negierende Lehnpräfixe des Gegenwartsdeutschen*. Heidelberg: Winter.
Kocourek, Rostislav (1982): *La langue française de la technique et de la science*. Wiesbaden: Brandstetter.
Kornfeld, Laura Malena (1998): IE, Romance: Spanish. In: Rochelle Lieber and Pavol Štekauer (eds.), *The Oxford Handbook of Compounding*, 436–463. Oxford: Oxford University Press.

Kürschner, Sebastian (2010): *Fuge-n-kitt, voeg-en-mes, fuge-masse* und *fog-e-ord*: Fugenelemente im Deutschen, Niederländischen, Schwedischen und Dänischen. In: Antje Dammel, Sebastian Kürschner and Damaris Nübling (eds.), *Kontrastive Germanistische Linguistik*. Vol. 2, 827–862. Hildesheim: Olms.

Lehrer, Adrienne (1998): Scapes, holics, and thons: The semantics of English combining forms. *American Speech* 73: 3–28.

Mackensen, Lutz (1972): *Traktat über Fremdwörter.* Heidelberg: Quelle & Meyer.

Marchand, Hans (1969): *The Categories and Types of Present-Day English Word-Formation. A Synchronic-Diachronic Approach.* 2nd ed. München: Beck.

Martinet, André (1970): *Éléments de linguistique générale.* Paris: Armand Colin.

Martinet, André (1979): *Grammaire fonctionnelle du français*. Paris: Didier.

Mattiello, Elisa (2018): Paradigmatic Morphology: Splinters, combining forms and secreted affixes. *SKASE Journal of Theoretical Linguistics* 15(1): 2–22.

Mattiello, Elisa (2022): *Transitional Morphology. Combining Forms in Modern English*. Cambridge: Cambridge University Press.

Mel'čuk, Igor A. (1982): *Towards a Language of Linguistics. A system of formal notions for theoretical morphology.* München: Fink.

Melloni, Chiara (2023): Neoclassical Word Formation. In: Peter Ackema, Sabrina Bendjaballah, Eulàlia Bonet and Antonio Fábregas (eds.), *The Wiley Blackwell Companion to Morphology*. Hoboken, NJ: Wiley-Blackwell [Online available at: https://onlinelibrary.wiley.com/doi/10.1002/9781119693604.morphcom053]

Müller, Peter O. (2005a): Deutsche Fremdwortbildung: Probleme der Analyse und der Kategorisierung. In: Peter O. Müller (ed.), *Fremdwortbildung. Theorie und Praxis in Geschichte und Gegenwart*, 199–218. Frankfurt/M.: Lang.

Müller, Peter O. (ed.) (2005b): *Fremdwortbildung. Theorie und Praxis in Geschichte und Gegenwart.* Frankfurt/M.: Lang.

Müller, Peter O. (ed.) (2009): *Studien zur Fremdwortbildung*. Hildesheim: Olms.

Munske, Horst Haider (1988): Ist das Deutsche eine Mischsprache? Zur Stellung der Fremdwörter im deutschen Sprachsystem. In: Horst Haider Munske, Reiner Hildebrandt, Peter von Polenz and Oskar Reichmann (eds.), *Deutscher Wortschatz. Lexikologische Studien*, 46–74. Berlin/New York: de Gruyter.

Munske, Horst Haider (2009): Was sind eigentlich ‚hybride' Wortbildungen? In: Peter O. Müller (ed.), *Studien zur Fremdwortbildung*, 223–260. Hildesheim: Olms (= Germanistische Linguistik 197–198/2009).

Munske, Horst Haider and Alan Kirkness (eds.) (1996): *Eurolatein. Das griechische und lateinische Erbe in den europäischen Sprachen*. Tübingen: Niemeyer.

OED (1989): *The Oxford English Dictionary.* Vol. 10 (Moul-Ovum) prepared by J. A. Simpson and E. S. C. Weiner. 2nd ed. Oxford: Clarendon Press.

Olsen, Susan (2000): Composition. In: Geert Booij, Christian Lehmann and Joachim Mugdan (eds.), *Morphology. An International Handbook on Inflection and Word-Formation*. Vol. 1, 897–916. Berlin/New York: de Gruyter.

Paul, Hermann (1995 [1880]): *Prinzipien der Sprachgeschichte*. 10th ed. Tübingen: Niemeyer.

Polenz, Peter von (1994): *Deutsche Sprachgeschichte vom Spätmittelalter bis zur Gegenwart*. Vol. 2: *17. und 18. Jahrhundert*. Berlin/New York: de Gruyter.

Rainer, Franz (2004): From Latin to French. In: Geert Booij, Christian Lehmann, Joachim Mugdan and Stavros Skopeteas (eds.), *Morphology. An International Handbook on Inflection and Word-Formation*. Vol. 2, 1698–1712. Berlin/New York: de Gruyter.

Rainer, Franz (2009): Die Integration des lateinischen Kompositionstyps *tauriformis* im Französischen und Italienischen. *Zeitschrift für romanische Philologie* 125: 45–84.
Reis, Marga (1983): Gegen die Kompositionstheorie der Affigierung. *Zeitschrift für Sprachwissenschaft* 2: 110–131.
Ruf, Birgit (1996): *Augmentativbildungen mit Lehnpräfixen. Eine Untersuchung zur Wortbildung der deutschen Gegenwartssprache*. Heidelberg: Winter.
Scheler, Manfred (1977): *Der englische Wortschatz*. Berlin: Schmidt.
Scheller-Boltz, Dennis (2010): *Präponeme und Präponemkonstrukte im Russischen, Polnischen und Deutschen. Zur Terminologie, Morphologie und Semantik einer Wortbildungseinheit und eines produktiven Kompositionstyps*. Frankfurt/M.: Lang.
Schmidt, Günter Dietrich (1987a): Vorschlag einer Modellierung der Kombinationen mit entlehnten Konstituenten. In: Gabriele Hoppe, Alan Kirkness, Elisabeth Link, Isolde Nortmeyer, Wolfgang Rettig and Günter Dietrich Schmidt (eds.), *Deutsche Lehnwortbildung. Beiträge zur Erforschung der Wortbildung mit entlehnten WB-Einheiten im Deutschen*, 25–35. Tübingen: Narr.
Schmidt, Günter Dietrich (1987b): Das Kombinem: Vorschlag zur Erweiterung des Begriffsfeldes und der Terminologie für den Bereich der Lehnwortbildung. In: Gabriele Hoppe, Alan Kirkness, Elisabeth Link, Isolde Nortmeyer, Wolfgang Rettig and Günter Dietrich Schmidt (eds.), *Deutsche Lehnwortbildung. Beiträge zur Erforschung der Wortbildung mit entlehnten WB-Einheiten im Deutschen*, 37–52. Tübingen: Narr.
Schmitt, Christian (1996): Euromorphologie: Perspektiven einer neuen romanistischen Teildisziplin. In: Wolfgang Dahmen (ed.), *Konvergenz und Divergenz in den romanischen Sprachen. Romanistisches Kolloquium VIII*, 119–146. Tübingen: Narr.
Schmöe, Friederike (1998): *Italianismen im Gegenwartsdeutschen. Unter besonderer Berücksichtigung der Entlehnungen nach 1950*. Bamberg: Collibri.
Scholz, Ulrike (2002): *Fachsprachliche Wortbildung des Spanischen, dargestellt am Beispiel des ökologischen Fachwortschatzes*. Berlin: Rhombos.
Selkirk, Elisabeth (1982): *The Syntax of Words*. Cambridge, MA: MIT Press.
Settekorn, Wolfgang (1988): *Sprachnorm und Sprachnormierung in Frankreich. Einführung in die begrifflichen, historischen und materiellen Grundlagen*. Tübingen: Niemeyer.
St. Clair, Robert N. (2002): Metaphorical blends, recruited frames and metaphors across cultures. *Intercultural Communication Studies* 11(3): 1–24.
Stickel, Gerhard (ed.) (2001): *Neues und Fremdes im deutschen Wortschatz. Aktueller lexikalischer Wandel*. Berlin/New York: de Gruyter.
Szymanek, Bogdan 1998 IE, Slavonic: Polish. In: Rochelle Lieber and Pavol Štekauer (eds.), *The Oxford Handbook of Compounding*, 464–477. Oxford: Oxford University Press.
ten Hacken, Pius (2000): Derivation and compounding. In: Geert Booij, Christian Lehmann and Joachim Mugdan (eds.), *Morphology. An International Handbook on Inflection and Word-Formation*. Vol. 1, 349–360. Berlin/New York: de Gruyter.
ten Hacken, Pius and Renáta Pancová (eds.) (2020): *The Interaction of Borrowing and Word Formation*. Edinburgh: Edinburgh University Press.
Tournier, Jean (1985): *Introduction descriptive à la lexicogénétique de l'anglais contemporain*. Paris/Genf: Champion Slatkine.
Volmert, Johannes (1996): Die Rolle griechischer und lateinischer Morpheme bei der Entstehung von Internationalismen. In: Horst Haider Munske and Alan Kirkness (eds.), *Eurolatein. Das griechische und lateinische Erbe in den europäischen Sprachen*, 219–235. Tübingen: Niemeyer.
Warren, Beatrice (1990): The importance of combining forms. In: Wolfgang U. Dressler (ed.), *Contemporary Morphology*, 111–132. Berlin/New York: de Gruyter.

Wegener, Heide (2010): Fremde Wörter – fremde Strukturen: Durch Fremdwörter bedingte strukturelle Veränderungen im Deutschen. In: Carmen Scherer and Anke Holler (eds.), *Strategien der Integration und Isolation nicht-nativer Einheiten und Strukturen*, 87–104. Berlin/ New York: de Gruyter.
Weinrich, Harald (2003): *Textgrammatik der deutschen Sprache.* 2nd ed. Hildesheim: Olms.
Wurzel, Wolfgang U. (2000): Was ist ein Wort? In: Rolf Thieroff and Peter Eisenberg (eds.), *Deutsche Grammatik in Theorie und Praxis*, 29–42. Tübingen: Niemeyer.

Wolfgang Pöckl

2 Foreign word-formation, language planning and purism

Abstract: Although word-formation by means of non-native linguistic elements is a widespread technique to enrich the vocabulary of languages, it has scarcely been taken into consideration by grammarians and linguists in a systematic way. Thus, many methodological problems have to be discussed in this field, and terminological confusion has to be clarified. The present article sketches differences among national attitudes towards foreign word-formation in the areas of linguistic research, language planning (and engineering), terminology planning, and purism. It is pointed out that foreign word-formation plays an increasingly important role in all types of texts and linguistic varieties.

1 Terminological inconsistencies

In the field of word-formation, linguistic terminology is generally rather unclear. Even the boundaries between well-established terms, such as *derivation* and *composition*, are disputed. Nowadays, with more and more attention being paid to what have hitherto been fringe areas of word-formation, such as blending, clipping or foreign word-formation, new terms have to be defined. Some advocate efficient use of a small number of terms that have a long tradition, while others prefer a more detailed terminology and differentiate, for instance, between *affixes* and *semi-affixes* (*suffixes* and *semi-suffixes*, etc.). German linguists are particularly prolific in creating new terms (*Affix*, *Halb-Affix*, *Eurofix*, etc.); to Schmidt

Wolfgang Pöckl, Innsbruck, Austria

https://doi.org/10.1515/9783111420530-002

(1987) we owe terms like *Kombinem, Komponem, Basem, Basokomponem, Präponem, Postponem*, etc. In French grammatical theory we find a multitude of different descriptive terms for bound morphemes such as *géo-* or *-thèque*, which are by no means being used in a consistent way. The *Trésor de la langue française* (1971–94), the most prestigious French lexicographic undertaking, uses different terms for elements that perform the exact same function: *anglo-*: élément préfixal, *germano-*: élément formant, *hispano-*: élément de composition.

Today, some European linguists would call these elements *confixes*. The new term *confix* is an excellent example of the terminological confusion that reigns in the area of word-formation theory, especially when we take into account various national traditions. Scholars of Romance languages and of German philology would see André Martinet (1979: 20) as the inventor of the term, which he used for elements of "composés [...] comme *thermostat* ou *philosophe*". It was taken up by Kocourek (1982) and from there adopted by Schmidt (1987). But while the term *confixe* has not been very fortunate in French linguistics, the correspondent German term *Konfix* enjoys a huge popularity (cf., for instance, various articles in Müller 2009). In the English-speaking world and in Slavic philology, however, the term is used to denote a (native) discontinuous morpheme or sort of circumfix (cf. Baiandina 2010, who describes the results of confixation in Russian as "formations préfixo-suffixales"). In German publications and dictionaries of linguistics we sometimes find *Konfix* translated by *combining form*, but Elsen (2013) has convincingly demonstrated that the two terms are not to be considered as synonyms. To resolve the issue of false friends at least for the present contribution, the decision has been taken to use the term *confix* in its English form, but with the meaning the term has in French and German linguistics.

2 Research traditions

The linguistic approach to scientific research into the processes and products of foreign word-formation in different languages can be linked to the practice of using foreign elements in the common language and integrating them into the vocabulary of the language in question. The English-speaking world has a tradition of treating this practice differently from speakers of German, French or Spanish.

It is widely known that the English language started to enrich its vocabulary in the Middle-English period by integrating loan words from Latin, often through French as an intermediary. This high number of loan words leads to a certain habituation, which would have long-term consequences for English word-formation, an observation made by Henry Bradley as early as the beginning of the 20th century.

> The custom of adopting Latin words at second-hand – through French – paved the way to the extensive introduction of words directly from Latin. This is the reason why the Latin element is so very much larger in the English vocabulary than in that of any other Germanic language [...]. Germany and Holland have certainly not been less, but probably much more, devoted to classical scholarship than England has; but their languages were not, in their middle stages, saturated with French loan-words, and consequently they were led to find expression for new ideas by development of their native sources, instead of drawing on the stores of the Latin vocabulary. (Bradley 1904: 93)

When the late Middle-Ages turned into an Early Modern era and English established itself as a language of science and the courts, English-speaking authors started to create more and more new words from Latin roots.

> The greater part of modern English literature has been written by men who were classically educated, and for readers who were presumed to have more or less knowledge of Latin. Probably there are very few of our scholarly writers who are not responsible for the introduction of some new word of Latin derivation. It has come to be felt that the whole Latin vocabulary [...] is potentially English, and when a new word is wanted it is often easier, and more in accordance with our literary habits, to anglicise a Latin word, or to form a compound from Latin elements, than to invent a native English compound or derivative which will answer the purpose. So much is this the case, that probably the authors of many of these coinages would be greatly surprised to learn that the words had never been used before, or even that they were not to be found in the ordinary dictionaries. (Bradley 1904: 94–95)

Taking this historical development into account, it is not surprising that those who work in the field of English linguistics have always described elements imported from other languages in rather matter-of-fact terms. They are not called *foreign words* or *elements*, but *borrowings* or *loanwords* (or *-suffixes*, etc.) and are seen as having enriched and enlarged the English vocabulary.

In contrast, the German-speaking world pays a great deal of attention to foreign words. This can be seen above all in the specialist dictionaries that are produced to record this section of the vocabulary and that do more to isolate these terms than to integrate them. So it has taken longer for the topic to reach specialised literature and for foreign morphemes to become the object of extensive and systematic analyses (cf. Müller 2005 and article 4 on foreign word-formation in German).

One reason for this could be that in German philology the vocabulary has been traditionally defined as being composed of a) native words, b) loan words and c) words formed from already existing elements. It is tempting to automatically group those three categories as a) and c) (= native) and b) (= foreign).

As can be seen by analysing the structure of a number of word families, word-formation based on foreign elements plays an important role in Romance languages. Frequently, a noun from the basic vocabulary coexists with an adjective of Latin or Greek origin and further derivations are based on the adjective (this is also common for English); just compare the German words *Stadt* / *städtisch* / *Städtebau* (→ *städtebaulich*), etc. with the French *ville* / *urbain* → *urbanisme, urbaniste, urbanité*; *urbaniser* → *urbanisation*, etc.) and the English word pair *town* / *urban*, etc.

The best publications in the field of Romance lexicography take this dissociation of word families into account by listing references to corresponding foreign elements under the headword from the basic vocabulary (for example under *ville* a reference to *-pole*; cf. *métropole*). The *Grand* (Rey 2001) as well as the *Petit Robert* (Rey-Debove and Rey 1993a), which define themselves as *dictionnaires analogiques*, highlight these elements by printing them in bold letters. In the Spanish *Diccionario de uso* by María Moliner (1998) we find similar entries (e.g., under *bosque* 'wood' the explanation: "otras raíces: 'daso-', 'forest-', 'nemo-', 'selv-'").

3 Methodical problems

When words formed from non-native lexical elements are to be analysed, there is often a difference between the judgment of speakers without linguistic knowledge, who can only go by their intuition, and the analysis of linguists basing their opinion on a linguistic theory. The main reason for these differences seems to be that theories of word-formation are generally based on the assumption that all processes and mechanisms of a language have to be explained rationally, while "naïve" users of a language simply activate their knowledge about other languages to get to (what they believe is) the meaning of a foreign word. This is why, for methodological reasons, the scholar of word-formation will often classify a loan word as a simplex, while ordinary native speakers who lack any theoretical knowledge will see it as a complex formation, which they will try to analyse.

Furthermore, even within the academic circles, there are controversies about how foreign words are to be analysed. Müller (2005: 23–24) uses three groups of German nouns that seem very similar at first glance to show three different opinions on what should be covered by word-formation theory (either only a), or a) and b), or a), b) and c)).

a) *Aktivität, Relativität, Rigorosität*
b) *Laszivität, Naivität, Neutralität*
c) *Gravität, Kapazität, Pietät*

The first group has been formed regularly, based on adjectives (*aktiv* → *Aktivität*); the examples of the second group, although the nouns are loan words, correspond to existing adjectives and can be analysed using regular word-formation rules (*naiv* → *Naivität*) while the third group must be considered to constitute opaque words without linguistic motivation, because no adjectives with the same root exist in German.

It is lucky that we are able to exactly reconstruct the etymological origin of the examples above, but this is not normally the case. Almost every single one of the rare case studies that have been conducted show that when neoclassical elements are involved, the hypotheses about the word-formation processes (especially in the field of "internationalisms" or "Europeanisms") stand on rather shaky ground – even those about terms from languages with a well-documented history. It is often impossible to research the history of a term without an exact and extensive knowledge about the history of the culture and the subject the term pertains to, but even with that basis there are many details that need a lot of work or luck to be convincingly proven.

Word-formation theories adopting the perspective of "ordinary speakers" (whose knowledge of foreign languages is supposed to be non-existent) and thus working strictly synchronically within one single language may lead to segmentations that possibly differ from the analyses that might be made by speakers with a background in humanities. To give an example: In the very extensive work on Spanish word-formation by Rainer (1993) we find the prefix *filo-* (*filoespañol, filocomunista*) next to the suffix *-ófilo* (*hispanófilo, bibliófilo*) (pp. 335–336, 624–625).

There is another problem of word segmentation that relates to both the form of the derivational morpheme and the form of the base, and has been mentioned in several publications, the latest of which is Elsen (2012). The following German verbs and their corresponding nouns – *informieren* / *Information, investieren* / *Investition, intervenieren* / *Intervention, exekutieren* / *Exekution* – show that the analysis of the verbs is easy to perform and is always identical (root + suffix *-ieren*), while we have to decide for the nouns if we want to accept an allomorphy for the suffixes (*-ation, -ition, -tion, -ion*) or opt for inconsistent roots. This shows that the boundary between base morphemes and derivational morphemes is not as clearly defined as could be expected.

4 Language structure and foreign word-formation

The way a language is structured naturally has a key influence on the potential for foreign word-formation. Starting from Bloomfield's universal principle that "[n]ormal roots combine with normal affixes, learned roots with learned affixes" (Bloomfield 1970: 252), Plank (1981: 132) introduced a refined scheme of compatibilities, that has become accepted as a guideline, at least for Indo-European languages (of course there are exceptions, even if they are not intended as a violation of the rules). According to this classification, the following morphemes can be combined:

- native base + native affix
- foreign base + native affix
- foreign base + foreign affix

but it is not possible to combine

- native base + foreign affix

This classification cannot be used, however, for derivations of proper names. An Italian dictionary of neologisms (Adamo and Della Valle 2003) contains terms like *pinocchiomania, benignimania* as well as *pottermania, tolkienmaniaco* found in newspaper articles published around the turn of the millennium.

Another area where Plank's classification is less and less applicable are formations with initial confixes. For example, many languages nowadays allow a combination of *bio-* with native words (German *Bioabfall* 'biological waste', *Bioladen* 'health food shop', *Bioreiniger* 'biological detergent'; Polish *biomasło* 'organic butter', *biopiwo* 'organic beer', *biosok* 'organic juice'; cf. Scheller-Boltz 2010: 343–344, 354–357).

Especially in languages that do not easily form compounds, derivation is used prolifically and in a variety of ways when forming words. The Romance languages are widely believed to be part of this category, with the explanation given that the Latin language itself was not very flexible when it came to forming compounds (this opinion was contradicted by Lindner 2002).

When looking into derivations occurring in Romance languages, we can observe an interesting phenomenon that has been interpreted by scholars of word-formation in different ways, namely the question of the extent to which point morphemes can be considered as base allomorphs. This is because in many cases an adjective is not derived from the noun, but made its own way into the language from the Latin (*cœur* 'heart' – *cordial* < Latin *cordialis*) or from the corresponding Greek adjective (*cœur* – *cardiaque* < *καρδιακός*), or it was even based on a reconstructed form (this happens frequently with anthroponyms: *Giraudoux* – *giralducien* < **Giralducus*).

Languages do not always choose the same derivational suffixes when integrating foreign words into their vocabulary. This can lead to false friends on the morphological level, as in the following examples: French *catastrophique* (like in the other Romance languages) – German *katastrophal* – English *catastrophic(al)*; French *pédagogie* – German *Pädagogik*, English *pedagogics*; French *despotisme* – German *Despotie*; French *conservateur* – German *konservativ* / English *conservative* etc.

At times, the suffixes themselves turn into false friends semantically: In Italian and Spanish, words with the suffix *-esco* have long been used primarily as relational adjectives (It. *lo stile dantesco* – 'Dante's style'; Sp. *la novela cervantesca* – 'Cervantes' novel'), while most other languages use the suffix only in a qualifying way; e.g., English *-esque*: "forms adjectives with the meaning, having the (artistic, bizarre, picturesque) style of –" (Marchand 1969: 286).

Pseudoanglicisms are a similar phenomenon – they seem to be loan words but actually do not correspond to any existing word of the English language. The German words *Beamer* 'overhead projector', *Layouter* 'layout man', *Looping* 'aerobatic loop', etc. would probably not be understood by English native speakers. Compound forms occur particularly frequently and are sometimes shared across a number of European languages. *Longseller* 'product sold successfully over a long period', *Oldtimer* 'veteran car' and *Autostopp* 'hitchhiking' are used in German, Italian, French and Russian (Pöllmann 2011). The word *wellness*, which is probably a German creation, has achieved such a high level of acceptance that authors of English texts are starting to use it. From a strictly synchronic point of view, this is the point at which it stops being a pseudoanglicism.

Languages with a rich tradition of forming compounds can normally integrate foreign words without changing native patterns. In German, foreign elements can be used as the initial or final part of the compound (*Chefkoch* 'chef, head cook', *Börsencrash* 'crash, collapse of the stock market'). In the English language, we find a pattern of word-formation that dates from the time of French rule but is not productive any longer and has the order determinatum – determinant: *brother/sister german, heir presumptive, court martial, postmaster general* (Marchand 1969: 81).

All modern Indo-European languages used in the area of technical communication have developed a form of composition which follows the Neo-Latin model and accounts for very interesting cross-language similarities. As technical terminology is generally regarded as highly prestigious in the modern world and has a high tendency to enter everyday language, it cannot be dismissed any more (as frequently occurred in linguistics until at least the 1970s) as epiphenomenon.

The models for this kind of word-formation were integrated into modern languages as loan words in the late middle ages and the early modern age, as for example Greek/Latin *bibliotheca* 'library' > French *bibliothèque*, Italian *biblioteca*, German *Bibliothek* (note that there is no corresponding loan word in the English language). One can observe an increased tendency to take apart compounds consisting of confixes and to use them to create new words. A modern example would be the French *biblio-* and *-métrie* (coined by Paul Otlet in 1934), which soon spread all over the Western World (English *bibliometrics* was introduced by Alan Pritchard in 1969).

This type of word-formation was so productive that many languages almost systematically increased their basic vocabulary by creating one new term from the Latin and one from the Greek.

Tab. 2.1: Etymological dissociation of the vocabulary in modern languages.

English	*sun*	*solar*	*helio*centric
German	*Sonne*	*solar*	*helio*zentrisch
French	*soleil*	*solaire*	*hélio*centrique
Spanish	*sol*	*solar*	*helio*céntrico

English	*eye*	*ocular*	*ophthalmic*
German	*Auge*	*okular*	*ophthalmisch*
French	*œil*	*oculaire*	*ophtalmique*
Spanish	*ojo*	*ocular*	*oftálmico*

Numerical terms also show this kind of feature: *half* = *semi-*/*hemi-*, *one* = *uni-*/*mono-*, *two* = *bi-*/*di-*, etc. Other examples are the term ‘twelve-tone music’, which is *dodécaphonie* in French, and the fear of Friday the 13th, which is called *paraskevidekatriaphobia* in English.

In some fields of knowledge (as, for instance, medicine) most European languages have integrated the learned technical terms into common language. In German, however, there is usually – due to purist tendencies in the late 18th and the 19th century – a native alternative to the international term. This solution makes it easier to address different audiences in the proper way: Depending on whether they are addressing colleagues or patients, a doctor can, for example, say or write *Apoplexie* or *Schlaganfall*, *Diabetes* or *Zuckerkrankheit*, *Gastritis* or *Magenschleimhautentzündung*, *Gynäkologe* or *Frauenarzt*, *Dermatologe* or *Hautarzt*, *Neurologe* or *Nervenarzt*. This kind of word-formation on two levels is also used in many kinds of texts for stylistic reasons because it helps to avoid repetition.

In recent times, techniques of foreign word-formation have increasingly been used for humorous constructions, the comical effect often being based on the hybrid form of the resulting words. To this end, neoclassical elements are combined with a colloquial word, or a word from specialist terminology or a modern foreign language (Pöckl 2009).

This kind of word-formation was found in the language of the students of 18th century Germany. One has to notice, however, that examples like the German lexicalised adjective *burschikos* 'pert' (from the German *Bursch* 'young man' and the Greek suffix *-ικός*) have lost their humorous touch over time (this might in time also happen to more recent formations of a similar type, as, for example, *Chefitäten* 'superiors', 'bosses').

Derivations based on patterns that are familiar from technical terminology are especially prolific. One example is medical terminology. Nowadays, most people know that the German medical suffix *-itis* means 'inflammation' and *-ose* means 'chronical or degenerative disease'. The base is made up from the name of the affected body part (e.g., *Hepatitis, Phlebitis*). In the word-formation process described above, the medical suffix *-itis* is used to indicate a pathological degree of the "content" indicated in the base: German *Telefonitis* (*Duden* 2009 entry), French *espionite* 'exaggerated fear of spies', *réunionite* 'excess of meetings' (both with entries in the *Petit Robert*, also found with *-nn-*) or Spanish *mieditis* 'excess of anxiety', *cuentitis* 'habit of making lame excuses' (both with entries in María Moliner's *Diccionario* 1998).

5 Language planning and foreign word-formation

The term *language planning* was introduced at the end of the 1950s by the Norwegian Einar Haugen, who today is mainly known for his *matrix of language planning processes* (Haugen 1987: 627). In this matrix, he looks at language planning from two perspectives: *status planning* and *corpus planning*. Today, we usually add a third factor: *prestige planning* (Haarmann 1990).

Status planning means that the authorities need to decide on the functions that the language should carry out in the present and/or the future (language of education, of administration, of the church, etc.).

Corpus planning is needed to ensure that the language can live up to all those functions in practice. For example: When in 1988 the Ladin language (*ladin dolomitan*) was declared an official language of the administration in the area of South Tyrol where it was spoken, there was no administrative terminology in this language and the local authorities did not possess any forms in Ladin (Lardschneider McLean 1994). In this case, corpus planning had not kept up with status planning and so the long hoped for presidential decree could not be put into practice right away.

The term *prestige planning* describes all measures designed to improve the acceptance of a certain language in its diverse functions – with members of other language communities spoken in the same area, but also with its own speakers. It is often noted that members of smaller language communities see an increased status of their own language as a burden, because they are now faced with the need to study the rules of their mother tongue, which they had mainly used orally before, in addition to those of the high status language they use at school or in their professional lives. Many speakers of the creole language Papiamentu, spoken on the Lesser Antilles, have huge reservations about its introduction as a language of instruction, as a large part of the population already has to master two or three major languages, namely Dutch, Spanish and English (Eckkrammer 2007). Another issue that is not always seen in a positive light is the use of a language in new domains, which, in theory, means an important increase in prestige. So, while Maltese translators and interpreters are doing their best to import EU-terminology into their language, many inhabitants of the island think that this is changing the nature of the Maltese language and that it would therefore have been better to use English as the official language for the EU (Pace 2011).

Linguists with specialisations other than the languages of the Western world see the language planning problems in Europe and the USA mainly as a cosmetic matter, and refer to the process as *language cultivation*. In contrast, language planning in countries where extensive changes have to be accomplished in a short period of time has been referred to as *language engineering* (Alisyahbana 1976). It is of course true that there are languages of the Far East and Africa for which fundamental decisions have to be made and carried out, but this also applies to a number of small European languages (cf. Tošović 2015 on word-formation and purism in Croatian and Raag 2015 on word-formation and language planning in Estonian).

The sociolinguist Heinz Kloss (1978) looked at this discussion from an alternative point of view and coined two important terms which were to become central to the linguistic debate on the topic. Sometimes, speakers (or language planners) are mainly concerned with distancing their language from genetically related (and usually geographically neighboured) languages. The term Kloss uses for this goal is *Abstand* 'distance'. Most European languages that have only recently been recognised as languages in their own right have this concern: Bosnian, Croatian and Serbian (in relation to each other), Galician (in relation to Spanish), Sardinian, Corsican (in relation to Italian) or Moldavian (in relation to Rumanian). It is of course easier for a linguistic variety to be recognised as a language if obvious differences can be demonstrated. Another dimension is the extension of the language into new domains, an activity that Kloss calls *Ausbau* 'elaboration, upgrade'. Languages that have not traditionally been used for communication in administration, economy and science need to be fitted for such purposes if they want to be able to compete. This is something that Catalan language planners managed especially well, because they could, on the one hand, take up an old and well-established written language tradition and, on the other, rely on the work of several visionary Catalan sociolinguists from as early as the Franco era. These circumstances allowed Catalonia to take a leading position in terminology science and practical terminology work on the Iberian Peninsula (cf. the reference work by Cabré Castellví 1993).

It is often neglected that one has to carefully distinguish between language planning in a general sense and terminology planning (which fits into the concept of *language engineering*). Language planning is primarily concerned with aspects of everyday language use. One example for a rather successful language planning effort in several western languages is the introduction of a gender-neutral/non-sexist language. Female versions of official as well as occupational titles have been created as part of this process, sometimes with a Latinizing suffix (there are examples that have been in use for a long time like It. *attore – attrice*, Sp. *actor – actriz*, Fr. *acteur – actrice* vs. It. *dottore – dottoressa*, Sp. *doctor – doctora*; Fr. *docteur* has a feminine form *docteure* only in Canada). In German, some titles are used in their Latin form (*Magister – Magistra*), some are created in accordance with native norms (*Doktor – Doktorin*; the Latin form *doctrix* has never been taken into consideration). In cases where symmetry is hardly possible, like with the French term for midwife, *sage-femme*, the traditional solution is to go back to the treasure of antique vocabulary: *obstétricien* (Latin) or *maïeuticien* (both terms allow the regular creation of female forms).

Terminologies for administration, economy, science and technology are nowadays usually elaborated by national or international committees. Most of the numerous standardisation organisations are included in a network of organisations from the same or a similar field and related organisations in other countries. Their umbrella organisation is the *International Organization for Standardization* (ISO) established in Geneva, which maintains its own *Technical Committee* (ISO/TC 37) dealing with the principles of creating new terms or whole terminologies. Even though linguists often criticise the theoretical foundations of this kind of standardisation, they usually accept the outcome. One reason for this acceptance is that ISO limits its work to areas where terminology is standardised along with the objects that are to be named, while terms pertaining to the various fields of the humanities usually are not subject to standardisation.

At the ISO, a proposal for standardisation needs to pass six stages (proposal, preparatory, committee, enquiry, approval, publication stage), which takes a lot of time.

In scientific literature, a list of criteria has been established that is designed to help measure the quality of a term. Some of these criteria, however, contradict each other, so that no term can fulfil all criteria at the same time (cf. discussion in Pöckl 1999: 1495). According to this list, a term should

- be biunique and understandable without context
- have no synonyms
- be as short as possible
- be transparent
- have no connotations
- conform to the system of the language
- be easy to translate (i.e. ideally be a potential internationalism).

These principles, even though they can only ever be fulfilled partially and sometimes are outright unrealistic (especially the first one), foster terminological convergence and further linguistic globalisation. At the same time, the linguistic "raw material" is taken from the classical languages, which among some speech communities is a fairly good prerequisite for their acceptance (even if the terms are still mainly circulated through the English language).

If smaller languages follow this model in the elaboration process (*Ausbau*) of their language, speakers might get the impression that the distance to the dominating languages of culture is dangerously decreasing. The alternative however – to disregard this strategy and create artificial native terms which a large part of the speakers might have difficulty identifying with – can easily lead into isolation.

6 Linguistic purism

6.1 Linguistic purism versus language planning

While both language planning and linguistic purism are activities through which people try to influence the way languages develop, they usually work on opposing goals and can therefore not be seen as two sides of the same coin.

Language planners usually work towards an *Ausbau* of the language, towards an extending of domains and the expressive potential of a language, whereas purists aim at the elimination of elements seen as foreign or, prophylactically, at the protection of their language from any non-native linguistic signs, an aim which basically means a reduction of linguistic resources.

Nearly all languages have seen periods in their history when linguistic purism was especially prevalent. In the 19th century, Europe was a place of deep political nationalism, and this mindset penetrated into national languages in almost all countries. As the idealist world view spread, even words that were formed from native elements but used the patterns of another language were regarded with suspicion, as they were seen as a threat to the "spirit of the language" (French *génie de la langue*). In 19th century Czech, for example, compound nouns were disapproved of as being too "German" (cf. Woldt 2010). Today, linguistic purism often takes place in the context of postcolonial discourse.

Nowadays, however, purists tend to concentrate on words and – less frequently – on sounds or on phraseology, but only very rarely on word-formation. The table of contents in Thomas' (1991) classic work on purism shows that word-formation is not an established category in the discussion about the purity of language. The chapter on morphology at least mentions not only inflectional but also derivational morphology. The examples from Slavic and Germanic languages discussed in the paragraph dedicated to derivation show the concern about maintaining a proper distance – a sufficient *Abstand* – to genetically related languages. "It is instructive that in all these instances the morphemes to be rejected belonged to closely related languages. The separate identity and autonomy of the language were threatened if it followed the word-building elements of a related idiom too closely" (Thomas 1991: 64). On the other hand, there do not seem to be too many serious reservations left about word-formations based on confixes from classical languages. This is even more surprising if we take into account the steady decline of Greek and even Latin in the curricula of Europe's schools.

6.2 A comparison of major languages

If we compare the role of linguistic purism in the major European languages, there is one detail that stands out: the English language, which is by far the most widespread language in our modern world, has never seen a strong purist movement and still entertains no institution that might be comparable in its importance to the language academies on the continent (Löffler 2002).

The enrichment of the English vocabulary in the Middle English period through complex words from Latin (often transmitted through French) founded a tradition of linguistic openness. This tradition could be shaken neither by the *inkhorn controversy* of the 16th century, which was mainly concerned with arguments about the comprehensibility of the bible translations, nor by the impetus of initiatives for the education of the people in the 19th century (Fill 1988). The history of linguistic purism can be seen as a chronicle of vain efforts, filled with anecdotes such as that of William Barnes, a figurehead of the British purist movement, who is said to have complained about the word *bicycle*, which he wanted to exchange with *wheel-saddle*, when he was already on his deathbed (Fill 1988: 231).

On the other side of the spectrum we find French, which has always been a classic example of unyielding linguistic purism, partly because this purism has been very thoroughly documented from the inside as well as the outside (cf. article 9 on word-formation and purism in French). The most striking characteristic of French purism is the casuistic approach to problems which was founded by Vaugelas and the *Académie Française* in the first half of the 17th century. Vaugelas' way of introducing a rule for every single case led to a permanent insecurity for the speakers (*insécurité linguistique*), which also put a stop to any kind of linguistic creativity. Vaugelas himself, whose ideal was the use of language at court, made the rather authoritative pronouncement that no one, not even the king, was allowed to coin new words. Technical terms were strictly banished from conversation at court and, consequently, did not find their way into the Academy's dictionary. It was only in the first half of the 20th century that the presence of technical terms in everyday language could no longer be held at bay. This linguistic change and the favourable attitude of many speakers towards a modernisation of the language provoked the so-called "crise du français". As a reaction to this crisis, foreign elements were fought by purists with a passion, especially when they originated from the English language and particularly if they looked likely to become productive in the word-formation process. Temporary linguistic fashions such as the suffixes *-ing* (*footing* [as in *jogging*], *caravaning*) or *-rama* prompted long and heated discussions among linguists and non-linguists alike. The latter suffix is of course not based on the Greek ὅραμα, but is an etymologically erroneous segmentation of the word *panorama* in imitation of the English use. The magazine *Défense de la langue française* (the voice of a purist organisation of the same name) expressed its outrage about this formation as follows: "Ce qui est le plus cocasse, c'est que jamais *rama* n'a rien signifié en grec: C'est *horama* qui veut dire spectacle. Mais on ne sait pas le grec et on veut parler grec: de là les monstres tirés d'un *panorama* mal coupé qui sont *cinérama*, et même *drapeaurama*" (cited in Klein-Zirbes 2001: 201) [The most comical is that *rama* has never meant anything in Greek: *horama* means show. But people don't know Greek and want to speak Greek all the same. It leads to monsters such as *cinérama* and *drapeaurama* coming from a *panorama* that was badly cut]. The vehement defender of the French language René Etiemble took the same line in his famous book *Parlez-vous franglais?*, where he listed many well documented examples (*babyrama, discorama, télérama*, etc.) (Etiemble 1964: 149–150).

When at the beginning of the 1970s it became clear that the modern world with its increase of technical equipment in every home and in the professional world could not be kept free of technical terminology, the French government decided to create a dedicated terminology committee in each ministry which was to create French words to replace the English terms that were already rather commonly used in France. The *Dictionnaire des termes officiels de la langue française* (1994) is the result of two decades of terminological work. Interestingly enough, many of these terms violate the principles of French word-formation once so fiercely defended by works of normative grammar. The dictionary includes compounds whose first elements are the result of an apocope, such as *gravidéviation* (< *gravité*; English *swing by*), *hélistation* (plateforme destinée à recevoir exclusivement des hélicoptères; English *helistop*), *mémomarque* (mesure de la mémorisation d'une marque, English *brand name recall*), which could be seen in a similarily critical light to *-rama*, but also a high number of formations using confixation, reversing the traditional order of morphemes in French compounds: *génothèque, géocodage, scannoscope, hydrocraquage, limbosondage, hydrodynamique, hydrorésistant, hémotoxique*. Notwithstanding the fact that the French language had developed predetermining traits as early on as the change from Middle French to Modern French, we have to note that the terminology committees (always supported by the *Académie Française*!) made a considerable contribution to the typological shift from the "Romance" practice of postdetermination to predetermination (which increased international convergence).

This is exactly the process that is in full swing now – it was confirmed as early as 1993 by the editors of the most popular dictionary in their introduction. Under the keyword *mots composés* they diagnosed (and predicted) something that did not come as a surprise for many users of the dictionary, but obviously still needed to be worded in a diplomatic way:

> Les mots savants sont traditionnellement formés avec des radicaux latins (*octogénaires*) ou grecs (*stéthoscope*), parfois hybrides (*monocle*) et autrefois critiqués par les puristes. Aujourd'hui on va plus loin: un très grand nombre de mots mêlent le grec ou le latin au français, et ce modèle est de plus en plus productif (*stratosphère, agroalimentaire* [...] *pochothèque* [...]). Parfois même, on compose de cette façon avec deux mots français ([...] *filoguidé, vagotonique, riziculture*). Cette composition des mots reste 'savante' dans la mesure où l'ordre des mots est inversé par rapport à la désignation ordinaire ([...] *riziculture: culture du riz; filoguidé: guidé par un fil*). Nous pouvons donc maintenant, comme les anglophones, produire des composés courants de ce type en disposant du système sans inversion [...].
>
> On voit comment, partie de règles très contraignantes, la composition des mots s'est libérée au profit de la néologie. Il n'est plus possible aujourd'hui de dire que la morphologie lexicale du français est une entrave à la créativité. Ce point de vue puriste est dépassé par les faits, et il faut accepter qu'une langue vivante change de normes. (Rey-Debove and Rey 1993b: XIV)
>
> [Learned words are traditionally formed with Latin stems (*octogénaire*) or Greek stems (*stéthoscope*), sometimes hybrid (*monocle*) and therefore once criticized by the purists. Nowadays, one goes further: many words mix Greek or Latin with French, and this model is more and more productive (*stratosphère, agroalimentaire* [...] *pochothèque* [...]). Sometimes,

> one even makes up in this way with two French words ([...] *filoguidé, vagotonique, riziculture*). This composition of words remains "learned" insofar as word order is reversed in comparison with the ordinary construction ([...] *riziculture: culture du riz; filoguidé: guidé par un fil*). Thus we can now, like English speakers, make this kind of common compositions by using the system without inversion [...].
>
> We see how word-formation has rid itself from the restrictive rules to which it was once submitted. Nowadays, it is not possible anymore to say that French lexical morphology is a hindrance to creativity. This purist point of view is exceeded by the facts and one has to accept that the norms of a modern language change.]

It can therefore be stated that neoclassical confix formations have served as a model for predetermined native French compounds. Lexicographers are normally the first ones to recognise new tendencies (cf. for Italian Adamo 2013).

In Germany, purism began to play an important role in the 17th century (cf. article 8 on word-formation and purism in German). The two most important chroniclers of German linguistic purism, Kirkness (1975) and Schiewe (1988), made it clear that the more perspicacious representatives of the movement between the Baroque period and the 19th century not only strove for reasonable goals, but were also quite successful in achieving them. The bad reputation of German linguistic purism stems, on the one hand, from the exaggerations of fanatics, and, on the other, from a generally negative attitude toward all prescriptive tendencies in language that has prevailed since the end of the Second World War.

In the 17th century, it was hoped that a unified German language would pave the way for the political union of a divided nation. France, having successfully completed its linguistic and politic unification a long time ago, was a good model for this endeavour. At the same time, and perhaps especially because of its success, it was felt to be important to reduce the influence of the French language on German vocabulary and word-formation. For many purists, the most important idea was an improvement in levels of education. They tried to reduce barriers to education by replacing Latin or French terms in school books and in public life (this is the reason why, for example, grammatical terms such as *Substantivum* or *Partizipium* were substituted by their German equivalents *Hauptwort* and *Mittelwort*).

During the Enlightenment, Latin was slowly replaced by German as the language of instruction at universities and the question arose as to whether scientific terminology should be Germanised as well. Joachim Heinrich Campe, whose dictionary of German terms (1801) contains many successful word-formations (*Rechtschreibung* for *Orthographie*, *Fernglas* for *Teleskop*), advocated a more radical solution than Christian Thomasius and Christian Wolff before him and Carl Gustav Jochmann after him. Jochmann argued against a total elimination of the neoclassical vocabulary by explaining that those terms constituted arbitrary signs which not only facilitated international communication but also made the integration of new scientific findings into the language easier (Schiewe 1988: 81). A modern example for this problem is the creation of the German word *Atomspaltung* 'atomic fission', which was created after the first successful act of atom-splitting and would not have been allowed because of its semantic *contradictio in adiecto* if such strict rules had been obeyed.

To be able to judge these endeavours to achieve a purely German language of science fairly, one has to take into account that in the 19th century French was seen as the language of politics and diplomacy, English as the language of trade and German as the language of humanities and science.

Generally it can be said that since the end of the 19th century no productive initiatives have been launched by the German purist movement. The *Allgemeiner Deutscher Sprachverein* [General Association for the German Language], founded in 1885 and initially moderate, provoked its own end by becoming more and more hostile towards foreign words, a tendency which irritated the National Socialists, who liked to use foreign words for their manipulations and therefore banned the association in 1940 (cf. Steinhauer 2002: 38). German linguistic purism, having definitely lost its credibility after 1945, therefore had to give way to more or less scientifically based language cultivation.

6.3 Purism in less widely used languages

In general, there is greater approval for the pursuance of purist activities in defence of "smaller" languages, which are often in competition with major ones, than of official languages that are not in danger of extinction and have a large number of speakers. This fact is the result of sociolinguistic research and today's generally positive attitude towards linguistic diversity and multilingualism.

But a deeper look into the topic shows that there are practically no universal rules to be detected, because every language is situated in an individual context: it has a specific history, a specific politico-linguistic situation, and it belongs to a specific genetic family and typological group.

It is difficult to draw comparisons between a small language with a good socio-demographic position and a tradition of self-sufficiency, such as the Icelandic language, and a language like Latvian, which has had a turbulent history and only became the language of an independent state in 1991 (except for a short period of Latvian political independence between the two world wars). A relatively short time later (May 1, 2004), Latvia became a member of the European Union and had to translate huge amounts of text with an extremely large number of terms which, before, had only been available in Russian or – because of the different economic system – not at all (this is explained in more detail in Landrø 2008: 383–474). Latvia's solution to these linguistic challenges was a network of state commissions that was about as changeable and intricate as the French system.

Looking at discussions of language purism in diverse small languages, one can get the impression that the use of neoclassical elements (if they even occur in significant numbers) is rather widely accepted. The main problem for such languages is normally the elimination of or protection from elements coming from the (formerly) dominant language (like Russian for Baltic languages), the overpowering (co-)official language (like Castilian Spanish for Catalan, Galician and Basque; French for Occitan, Corsican, Breton) or the global lingua franca, English.

7 Conclusion

If we want to name common tendencies for different languages in the area of foreign word-formation, it can be said that the suspicion towards hybrid formations of all kinds, which once were strongly criticised, has diminished to the same extent as the occurrence of such formations has increased.

During the last century, there has certainly been a growing number of foreign languages that are a source for elements used in foreign word-formation. This helps to mask the fact that the frequency of use has probably increased in all types of text.

A higher level of acceptance of such word-formations is also due to the fact that linguistic creativity (especially in the advertising business and in the press) is highly regarded today and even expected by readers and consumers of media in general.

And finally there is the rapid technical and scientific progress in which the majority of the population wishes to participate. This social development leads to the dissemination of new words following well-established patterns of foreign word-formation and to the adoption of "modular" elements such as confixes. Today, both categories are entered in general dictionaries by lexicographers, making them in the eyes of the speakers an official part of the vocabulary.

8 References

Adamo, Giovanni (2013): Neologismi italiani degli anni Duemila: Tipi, fenomeni e tendenze più recenti rilevati nella stampa quotidiana. In: Joachim Born and Wolfgang Pöckl (eds.), *„Wenn die Ränder ins Zentrum drängen ...". Außenseiter der Wortbildung(sforschung)*, 85–99. Berlin: Frank & Timme.

Adamo, Giovanni and Valeria Della Valle (2003): *Neologismi quotidiani. Un dizionario a cavallo del millennio*. Firenze: Olschki.

Alisyahbana, S. Takdir (1976): *Language Planning for Modernization. The Case of Indonesian and Malaysian*. The Hague: Mouton.

Baiandina, Natalia (2010): *La confixation en russe moderne*. http://www.e-sorbonne.fr/sites/www.e-sorbonne.fr/files/theses/these-BAIANDINA.pdf [last access 4 Dec 2014].

Bloomfield, Leonard (1970): The structure of learned words. In: Charles F. Hockett (ed.), *A Leonard Bloomfield Anthology*, 252–256. Bloomington: Indiana University Press. [First published 1933].

Bradley, Henry (1904): *The Making of English*. London/New York: Macmillan.

Cabré Castellví, M. Teresa (1993): *La terminologia. La teoria, els mètodes, les aplicacions*. Barcelona: Editorial Empúries.

Campe, Joachim Heinrich (1801): *Wörterbuch zur Erklärung und Verdeutschung der unserer Sprache aufgedrungenen fremden Ausdrücke*. Braunschweig: In der Schulbuchhandlung.

Díaz-Negrillo, Ana (2014): Neoclassical compounds and final combining forms in English. *Linguistik Online* 68(6): 4–20.

Dictionnaire des termes officiels de la langue française (1994): Paris: Journal Officiel de la République Française.

Duden (2009): *Duden. Die deutsche Rechtschreibung*. 25th ed. Mannheim: Bibliographisches Institut.

Eckkrammer, Eva Martha (2007): Papiamentu, cultural resistance, and socio-cultural challenges: The ABC islands in a nutshell. *Journal of Caribbean Literatures* 5(1): 73–93.

Elsen, Hilke (2013): Zwischen Simplex und komplexem Wort – eine holistische Sichtweise. In: Joachim Born and Wolfgang Pöckl (eds.), *„Wenn die Ränder ins Zentrum drängen ...". Außenseiter der Wortbildung(sforschung)*, 25–42. Berlin: Frank & Timme.

Etiemble, René (1964): *Parlez-vous franglais?* Paris: Gallimard.

Fill, Alwin (1988): Purism and word formation: Word substitution in 16th and 19th century English. In: Manfred Markus (ed.), *Historical English*, 231–244. Innsbruck: Institut für Sprachwissenschaft.

Ganslmayer, Christine and Peter O. Müller (2021): Historische Fremdwortbildung. Forschungsstand und Perspektiven. In: Christine Ganslmayer and Christian Schwarz (eds.), *Historische Wortbildung. Theorien – Methoden – Perspektiven*, 105–144. Hildesheim: Olms (= Germanistische Linguistik 252–254).

Haarmann, Harald (1990): Sprache und Prestige: Sprachtheoretische Parameter zur Formalisierung einer zentralen Beziehung. *Zeitschrift für romanische Philologie* 106: 1–21.

Haugen, Einar (1987): Language planning. In: Ulrich Ammon, Norbert Dittmar and Klaus J. Mattheier (eds.), *Sociolinguistics. An International Handbook of the Science of Language and Society*. Vol. 1, 626–637. Berlin/New York: de Gruyter.

Kirkness, Alan (1975): *Zur Sprachreinigung im Deutschen 1789–1871. Eine historische Dokumentation*. Vol. 2. Tübingen: Narr.

Klein-Zirbes, Anja (2001): *Die* Défense de la langue française *als Zeugnis des französischen Sprachpurismus*. Frankfurt/M.: Lang.

Kloss, Heinz (1978): *Die Entwicklung neuer germanischer Kultursprachen seit 1800*. 2nd ed. Düsseldorf: Schwann.

Kocourek, Rostislav (1982): *La langue française de la technique et de la science*. Wiesbaden: Brandstetter.

Landrø, Judith (2008): *Purismus als Strategie europäischer Sprachpolitik. Eine Untersuchung am Beispiel der "Kleinsprachen" Sardisch, Isländisch, Lettisch*. Hamburg: Kovač.

Lardschneider McLean, Margareth (1994): Die ladinische Verwaltungssprache zwischen Italienisch und Deutsch. In: Bernhard Pöll (ed.), *Fachsprache – kontrastiv*, 9–26. Bonn: Romanistischer Verlag.

Lindner, Thomas (2002): *Lateinische Komposita. Morphologische, historische und lexikalische Studien*. Innsbruck: Institut für Sprachwissenschaft.

Löffler, Marion (2002): Britisches Englisch. In: Nina Janich and Albrecht Greule (eds.), *Sprachkulturen in Europa*, 19–26. Tübingen: Narr.

Marchand, Hans (1969): *The Categories and Types of Present-Day English Word-Formation. A Synchronic-Diachronic Approach*. 2nd ed. München: Beck.

Martinet, André (1979): *Grammaire fonctionnelle du français*. Paris: Crédif/Didier.

Mattiello, Elisa (2018): Paradigmatic Morphology: Splinters, combining forms and secreted affixes. *SKASE Journal of Theoretical Linguistics* 15(1): 2–22.

Mattiello, Elisa (2022): *Transitional Morphology. Combining Forms in Modern English*. Cambridge: Cambridge University Press.

Melloni, Chiara (2023): Neoclassical Word Formation. In: Peter Ackema, Sabrina Bendjaballah, Eulàlia Bonet and Antonio Fábregas (eds.), *The Wiley Blackwell Companion to Morphology*. Hoboken, NJ: Wiley-Blackwell [Online available at: https://onlinelibrary.wiley.com/doi/10.1002/9781119693604.morphcom053]

Moliner, María (1998): *Diccionario de uso del español*. 2nd ed. Madrid: Gredos.

Müller, Peter O. (2005): Einführung. In: Peter O. Müller (ed.), *Fremdwortbildung. Theorie und Praxis in Geschichte und Gegenwart*, 11–45. Frankfurt/M.: Lang.

Müller, Peter O. (ed.) (2009): *Studien zur Fremdwortbildung*. Hildesheim: Olms.

Pace, Lara (2011): The adventure of Maltese: From a spoken vernacular to one of the official working languages of the European Union. *Moderne Sprachen* 55(2): 109–121.

Plank, Frans (1981): *Morphologische (Ir-)Regularitäten. Aspekte der Wortstrukturtheorie*. Tübingen: Narr.

Pöckl, Wolfgang (1999): Die französischen Fachsprachen im 20. Jahrhundert und ihre Erforschung: Eine Übersicht. In: Lothar Hoffmann, Hartwig Kalverkämper and Herbert Ernst Wiegand (eds.), *Languages for Special Purposes. An International Handbook of Special-Language and Terminology Research*. Vol. 2, 1491–1503. Berlin/New York: de Gruyter.

Pöckl, Wolfgang (2009): Unser tägliches Griechisch: Scherzbildungen mit Morphemen griechischer Herkunft in germanischen und romanischen Sprachen. In: Konstantina Glykioti and Doris Kinne (eds.), *Griechisch – Ελληνικά – Grekiska. Festschrift für Hans Ruge*, 185–192. Frankfurt/M.: Lang.

Pöllmann, Magdalena (2011): *Handy*, *castingshow* und *public viewing*: Pseudoanglizismen als Internationalismen – ein Vergleich in vier Sprachen. Ph.D. dissertation, Universität Innsbruck.

Raag, Virve (2015): Word-formation and language planning in Estonian. In: Peter O. Müller, Ingeborg Ohnheiser, Susan Olsen and Franz Rainer (eds.), *Word-Formation. An International Handbook of the Languages of Europe*. Vol. 3, 1730–1744. Berlin/Boston: De Gruyter Mouton.

Rainer, Franz (1993): *Spanische Wortbildungslehre*. Tübingen: Niemeyer.

Rey, Alain (dir.) (2001): *Le Grand Robert de la langue française. Dictionnaire alphabétique et analogique de la langue française*. Paris: Dictionnaires Le Robert.

Rey-Debove, Josette and Alain Rey (1993a): *Le nouveau Petit Robert. Dictionnaire alphabétique et analogique de la langue française*. Paris: Dictionnaires Le Robert.
Rey-Debove, Josette and Alain Rey (1993b): Préface du *Nouveau Petit Robert*. In: Josette Rey-Debove and Alain Rey, *Le nouveau Petit Robert. Dictionnaire alphabétique et analogique de la langue française*, IX–XIX. Paris: Dictionnaires Le Robert.
Scheller-Boltz, Dennis (2010): *Präponeme und Präponemkonstrukte im Russischen, Polnischen und Deutschen. Zur Terminologie, Morphologie und Semantik einer Wortbildungseinheit und eines produktiven Kompositionstypus*. Frankfurt/M.: Lang.
Schiewe, Jürgen (1988): *Sprachpurismus und Emanzipation. Joachim Heinrich Campes Verdeutschungsprogramm als Voraussetzung für Gesellschaftsveränderungen*. Hildesheim: Olms.
Schmidt, Günter Dietrich (1987): Das Kombinem: Vorschläge zur Erweiterung des Begriffsfeldes und der Terminologie für den Bereich der Lehnwortbildung. In: Gabriele Hoppe, Alan Kirkness, Elisabeth Link, Isolde Nortmeyer, Wolfgang Rettig and Günter Dietrich Schmidt (eds.), *Deutsche Lehnwortbildung. Beiträge zur Erforschung der Wortbildung mit entlehnten WB-Einheiten im Deutschen*, 37–52. Tübingen: Narr.
Steinhauer, Anja (2002): Deutsch. In: Nina Janich and Albrecht Greule (eds.), *Sprachkulturen in Europa*, 36–44. Tübingen: Narr.
ten Hacken, Pius and Renáta Pancová (eds.) (2020): *The Interaction of Borrowing and Word Formation*. Edinburgh: Edinburgh University Press.
Thomas, George (1991): *Linguistic Purism*. London/New York: Longman.
Tošović, Branko (2015): Word-formation and purism in Croatian. In: Peter O. Müller, Ingeborg Ohnheiser, Susan Olsen and Franz Rainer (eds.), *Word-Formation. An International Handbook of the Languages of Europe*. Vol. 3, 1720–1730. Berlin/Boston: De Gruyter Mouton.
Trésor de la langue française (1971–1994): Publié sous la direction de Paul Imbs. Paris: Editions du CNRS. Le TLF informatisé: http://atilf.atilf.fr [last access 4 Dec 2014].
Woldt, Claudia (2010): *Sprache als Wert – Werte in der Sprache. Untersuchungen zu Bewertungen von Sprache allgemein und Komposita im Besonderen in der tschechischen Sprachgeschichte*. München: Sagner.

Thomas Lindner and Franz Rainer

3 Word-formation in Neo-Latin

Abstract: The present article is the first comprehensive attempt at describing the innovations that occurred in word-formation during the Neo-Latin period (from around 1300 up to the present day). It is shown that, contrary to a widely held belief, Neo-Latin word-formation differs from Classical and Medieval Latin word-formation not only at the level of individual words, but also to some extent with respect to patterns of word-formation.

1 Introduction

Neo-Latin (henceforth: NL; cf. Neuhausen 2003) has its origins around 1300 with Italian humanists such as Petrarch (1304–1374), who were critical of their contemporaries' usage of Latin – what is now called *Medieval Latin* (henceforth: ML; on word-formation in ML, cf. Stotz 2000) – and sought to revive the high standards of Classical Latin (henceforth: CL). Some extremists advocated for considering Cicero as the only legitimate model, but generally other authors of the Golden and Silver Age were also admitted. For some, the NL period ends around 1800, which is when, in their terminology, Contemporary Latin is said to begin. But this division is quite arbitrary from a linguistic point of view. Our use of the term will therefore also include the contemporary period. What is important to bear in mind, however, is that NL does not constitute a homogeneous state of language.

If the humanists and their followers had stuck consistently to the program outlined above, the present article would be a tedious undertaking. In fact, it

Thomas Lindner, Salzburg, Austria
Franz Rainer, Vienna, Austria

https://doi.org/10.1515/9783111420530-003

would have to limit itself to an enumeration of new words coined according to the word-formation patterns of CL. Per definition, there could be no such thing as NL word-formation in the sense of a set of patterns of word-formation distinct from those of CL. This seems to be essentially Neuhausen's view who observes that NL authors did indeed coin numerous new words, but always on the basis of the principle of analogy (cf. pp. 928–929). However, as will become apparent from the following description, which is the first of its kind, NL word-formation contains not only words, but also patterns which were unknown to CL as well as to ML.

In the previous paragraphs we have used the existence of novel patterns – as opposed to words – as a necessary condition for speaking of NL word-formation. This certainly constitutes the fundamental criterion, but we think that it should be made somewhat more flexible and contain the following four degrees of innovation. At the lowest level, we would also like to take into consideration patterns which differ markedly from CL or ML in their frequency of use. The next type of pattern which we would want to include differs from CL or ML with regard to the domain of application, i.e. the kind of bases to which the pattern may be applied. Both of these aspects are often referred to indistinctly as differences in the productivity of a pattern. While some might want to quibble about whether differences in productivity should really be considered as sufficient conditions, it will be easier to achieve unanimity about the fact that a pattern which differs in meaning from a formally identical pattern of CL or ML must be counted as a NL innovation. The fourth and last type of pattern which will be taken into consideration are those which differ from CL or ML even in form. Of course, many innovative patterns will combine more than one of the four aspects distinguished here for analytical purposes.

A dimension orthogonal to the ones mentioned in the last paragraph is the degree of conventionalization. Innovative patterns invariably start out with one deviant coinage. But one swallow does not make a summer, as the proverb goes. If this deviant coinage remains isolated, it should not be equated with an established pattern. In order to qualify for the latter, the original coinage must have given rise to analogical creations. In an overview of NL word-formation, the emphasis should of course be on established patterns, but since occasionalisms and patterns form a cline, we will also to some extent take into consideration one-off formations, where this seems of interest.

A word is also in order concerning our delimitation of the field of word-formation. Though we are well aware that in theories such as construction morphology such a move is considered to be unwarranted, we will exclude what is often called "syntagmatic" word-formation. That is, we will omit terms – taken from Helfer's dictionary – such as *conductus electricus* 'electrical conductor' (← *conductus* 'conductor', *electricus* 'electrical') or *sectio cadaveris* 'autopsy' (← *sectio* 'dissection', *cadaveris* 'corpse'+GEN.SG), which follow the rules of Latin syntax, even though such combinations clearly have a lexical function. This does not mean that in in-depth studies of NL word-formation it could not be interesting to take them into consideration as well in order to assess under what conditions authors resort to syntagmatic composition rather than compounding proper or affixation. The choice of affixation or compounding proper normally seems to be the more marked option, sounding more refined if not stilted, as when 'brain-washing' is rendered as *cerebrilavium* (← *cerebr-* 'brain' + linking vowel *-i-* + *lav-* 'to wash' + action suffix *-ium*) instead of the more straightforward syntagmatic compound *lavatio cerebri* (← *lavatio* 'washing', *cerebri* 'brain'+GEN.SG), or 'lymph node' as *lymphonodus* (Nomina anatomica Jenensia; ← *lymph-* 'lymph' + linking vowel *-o-* + *nodus* 'node') instead of *nodus lymphaticus* (← *nodus* 'node', *lymphaticus* 'lymphatic').

Another branch of word-formation that will not be taken into account in this article are artificial NL taxonomies which are used in some sciences such as botany up to the present day. In phytosociology (cf. Weber, Moravec and Theurillat 2000), for example, it has been agreed upon that the name of an 'association' of plants should be formed by attaching the suffix *-etum* to the stem of the genus name of the plant in question, the name of an 'alliance', i.e. an association mixed with a similar association or similar associations, by attaching *-ion*, the name of an order by attaching *-etalia*, and that of a class by attaching *-etea*. A wood – or, to be precise, an association – consisting of alders (Latin *alnus*) is therefore called *Alnetum*, a word Cicero would not have objected to. But beyond that level, designations become rather arbitrary, though they use Latin (or Greek, in the case of *-ion*) building blocks. If the association consists of grey alders, for example, it must be called *Alnetum incanae*, whose second member is the genitive of *Alnus incana*, the NL name of the grey alder (*incanus* meaning 'grey'). An historical study of the introduction and further elaboration of NL taxonomies of this kind would certainly be interesting in itself, but lies beyond the scope of the present article, which will be restricted to innovations which originated from more or less "natural" mechanisms of language change.

As a first comprehensive approximation to NL word-formation, the present article could not but limit itself to a relatively small corpus. As far as the – predominately literary – sources from humanism and the Renaissance are concerned, we could rely on the excellent dictionaries of Hoven (henceforth: Ho) and Ramminger (R). For scientific Latin terminology, which was conspicuously expanded especially in the 17th and 18th centuries, there is no comprehensive modern dictionary, which is a very unfortunate lexicographic lacuna. However, Helfer (He) also constitutes a valuable source, albeit of very limited coverage, for that period. In order to round off the picture, we had to delve into some primary sources from the realm of medicine (Blancard), natural history (Linné), and philosophy (Bruckner). The 19th and 20th centuries are represented almost exclusively by Helfer's dictionary.

A final word concerning the presentation of the examples: In order to save space, bases in non-final position are represented only by the relevant word-formation stem, not by the corresponding lexeme (represented by a citation form). That is, we say that *conductor* is derived from *conduct-* and not from *conducere*, *anuminis* from *numin-*, not from *numen*, etc.

2 Latin and Greek

Beginning with the first extant literary documents dating from the 3rd century BC, Latin has benefitted from a constant flow of loan words and loan translations from Greek (cf. Biville 1990–95). With the advent of humanism, which re-established the study of Greek in Western Europe, this flow gained new momentum to the point of making of the high proportion of Greek words an outstanding characteristic of many NL texts. Any Greek word, one could say, became potentially Latin as long as it was adapted orthographically and grammatically to the Latin host language.

For the present article, which is dedicated to word-formation, only morphologically complex Greek words are of interest. And even among these, some are more relevant than others. In fact, morphologically complex Greek words which are not at least partially transparent for those who do not know Greek may safely be omitted, in analogy to simplex loan words. *Autopsia* 'autopsy', for example, would seem to be a case in point: It is morphologically complex from a Greek perspective (*aut-* 'self' + *ops-* 'to look' + abstract suffix *-ía*), but this structure remains impenetrable for those who do not know Greek. The issue in fact is quite tricky. Since many NL writers knew at least some Greek, even such words were transparent to them, and they were also able to coin Greek neologisms on the basis of their knowledge of *Greek* word-formation, adapting them to the orthographical and grammatical conventions of Latin only at the end of the process. Such cases, however, should better be considered as acts of word-formation in a foreign language followed by borrowing, both taking place in the head of one and the same individual. *Agatharchia* 'rule of the good', composed of *agath-* '(the) good' + *arch-* 'to rule' + abstract suffix *-ía*, or *bibliotaphium* 'book-grave', composed of *bibli-* 'book' + linking vowel *-o-* + *-taphion* 'grave', could represent pertinent examples, since they do not figure either in Liddell and Scott's dictionary of Ancient Greek nor in dictionaries of Byzantine Greek. As far as their structure and meaning are concerned, they are perfectly Greek, following the model respectively of *oligarkhía* 'rule of the few' (from *olígos* '(the) few', *arkhé* 'government' + suffix *-ía*) and *kenotáphion* 'empty grave' (from *kenós* 'empty' + *taphos* 'grave' + suffix *-ion*). Nevertheless, such words could hardly have been coined by a writer only familiar with Latin (including transparent loan words from Greek).

The point at which Greek word-formations occurring in NL texts in Latin orthography definitely become relevant for our purpose is when we have sufficient clues to believe that they were created exclusively on the basis of lexical material that was already part of the Latin language at the moment of their creation plus the common analogical mechanisms of word-formation. However compelling this criterion may sound in theory, in concrete cases it is not always easy to apply. Hybrid formations which contain elements of both Greek and Latin origin are generally valuable, though not infallible, indicators that the Greek element in question was beginning to be integrated into the word-formation system of the host language. When *orthopontifex* 'rightful pope' (R; ← Greek *ortho-* 'right(ful)' + Latin *pontifex* 'pope') was coined in the 14th century, its creator, Jean de Rocquetaillade, may have isolated the first element from well-established loan words such as *orthodoxus* 'orthodox' or *orthographia* 'orthography', but it is equally possible that he activated his knowledge of Greek (if, indeed, he had such knowledge). The same doubt remains in many early hybrids: *chrysodoctor* 'excellent teacher' (R, b. 1533; ← Greek *chrys-* 'gold' + Greek linking vowel *-o-* + Latin *doctor* 'id.'), *speculitheca* (R, 16th c.; ← Latin *specul-* 'mirror' + Latin linking vowel *-i-* + Greek *-theca* 'receptacle'), *ossilatra* (R, 16th c.; ← Latin *oss-* 'bone' + *-i-* + Greek *-latra* 'worshipping/er'), etc.

The same doubts, by the way, still apply with respect to many modern scientific terms, such as *myofibra* 'muscle fibre' (← Greek *my-* 'muscle' + *-o-* + Latin *fibra* 'fibre'), with the additional complication that in these cases the genesis of the term could also have taken place in a vernacular language such as English and its result then have been borrowed into NL. Normally, only a painstaking study of the history of the term in question in all relevant languages will allow us to gain certainty in such cases. Unfortunately, existing historical and etymological dictionaries are of little help in this task. In some rare cases, purely formal clues allow us to establish with confidence the priority of the vernacular languages, as when *ionosphere* was adapted as *iontosphaera* (He; the word-formation stem of Greek *ion* being *iont-*) or *kilogram* as *chiliogrammum* (He; the numeral for '1000' in Greek being *kilioi*) by some puristically-minded contemporary Neo-Latinist.

3 Composition

3.1 Latin-based composition

NL compounds, as Latin compounds in general (cf. Lindner 1996, 2002), are almost exclusively nouns and adjectives. Most verbal compounds follow the regular pattern with a second member *-ific-* '-ify', the few innovative formations remaining isolated: *animipendere* 'to think about' (R; ← *anim-* 'mind' + *-i-* + *pendere* 'to weigh'), *fabresculpere* 'to chisel artfully' (R; ← *fabr-* 'artist' + (*ex*?)*sculpere* 'to chisel'), and few more.

3.1.1 Nominal compounds

New synthetic compounds abound, but almost exclusively with second members already established since CL.

Most such formations are agent nouns. One series contains bound second members created by conversion – *-a* and *-us* representing inflectional endings –, such as *-cen* 'player', *-cida* 'murderer', *-fex* 'maker', *-gena* 'person born in X', *-mimus* 'imitator', etc. Innovative second members only appear in *centonifur* 'one who plagiarizes a *cento*' (R; ← *centon-* 'a type of poem' + *-i-* + *fur* 'thief', a free form), *scholirega* 'headmaster' (R; ← *schol-* 'school' + *-i-* + *reg-* 'to manage'), *quisquilivenda* 'trash-seller' (R; ← *quisquili-* 'trivialities' + *-i-* + *vend-* 'to sell'). Other agentive second members contain explicit deverbal suffixes. Again, most of these compounds follow established patterns in *-cipulum* 'trap', *-cultor* 'cultivator', *-gerulus* 'carrier', etc. But some are innovative in the choice of the second member or the linking vowel (*-o-* instead of *-i-*): *fumivenditor* 'smoke-seller' (Ho; ← *fum-* 'smoke' + *-i-* + *venditor* 'seller'), *Lutherozelator* 'admirer of Luther' (Ho; ← *Luther-* + *-o-* + *zelator* 'admirer'), *tabacobibulus* 'tobacco-smoker' (R; ← *tabac-* 'tobacco' + *-o-* + *bibulus* 'drinker'), *herbisectrum* 'lawn mower' (He, 20th c.; ← *herb-* 'grass' + *-i-* + *sec-* 'to cut' + instrumental suffix *-trum*).

Synthetic action nouns mostly end in the suffix *-ium*. Again, almost all of these formations follow patterns with second members already attested in CL, such as *-cidium* 'murder', *-cinium* 'singing', *-ficium* 'making', *-fragium* 'braking', *-fugium* 'flight', etc. The only formation with a new second member which we have found is *labellitorquium* 'lip-puckering' (R; ← *labell-* 'lip' + *-i-* + *torqu-* 'to pucker' + action suffix *-ium*), coined by Caspar Barth (1587–1658). Ramminger contains a number of rather extravagant synthetic action nouns with second members in *-io*, but these are also all taken from the work of this same author:

animambulatio 'walk of the souls' (← *anim-* 'soul' + *ambulatio* 'walk'), *animimistio* 'union of souls' (← *anim(a)* 'soul' + *-i-* + *mistio* 'union'), etc. In Contemporary Latin we find compounds such as *astronavigatio* 'space travel' (← *astr-* 'star' + *-o-* + *navigatio* 'travel'), *vasodilatatio* 'vascular dilatation' (← *vas-* 'vessel' + *-o-* + *dilatatio* 'dilatation') or even *tendovaginitis* 'tendinitis; lit. inflammation of the vagina of a tendon' (← *tend(in/on)-* + *-o-* + *vaginitis* 'inflammation of the vagina'), which may have been influenced by a vernacular language.

Root compounds – in the modern sense of 'compounds where no noun is an argument of the other noun' – were rare in CL and continue to be so in NL: *dentiforceps* 'dental forceps' (R; ← *dent-* 'tooth' + *-i-* + *forceps* 'id.'), *navidominus* 'admiral' (R; ← *nav-* 'ship' + *-i-* + *dominus* 'master'), *pedifollis* 'football' (He, 20th c.; ← *ped-* 'foot' + *-i-* + *follis* 'ball'), *burgomagister* 'Lord Mayor' (Ho; ← *burg-* 'town' + *-o-* + *magister* 'master'), etc. Some of these root compounds betray a Germanic background. Sometimes it is unclear whether we are dealing with a root compound or a synthetic compound: since Latin *-i* is not only a linking vowel, but also a genitive ending; Contemporary Latin words like *oleiductus* 'pipeline' or *ferrivia* 'railway' could also be analysed as *olei ductus* lit. 'oil+GEN conduit' and *ferri via* lit. 'iron+GEN way'.

Adjective-noun compounds have also remained rare, generally following the few established patterns such as *omni-* 'all' + noun: *omnimaiestas* 'all-embracing majesty', etc. Occasionally, however, more innovative formations have been ventured: *comicotragoedia* (Ho; ← *comic-* 'comic' + *-o-* + *tragoedia*), *tragicocomoedia* 'tragicomedy' (R; ← *tragic-* 'tragic' + *-o-* + *comoedia*; a remake of Plautinian *tragicomoedia*), *Anglocalvinismus* 'English Calvinism' (R; ← *Angl(ic)-* 'English' + *-o-* + *Calvinismus*), *Graecobarbarismus* 'a barbarism in Greek' (R; ← *Graec-* 'Greek' + *-o-* + *barbarismus*), *electromagnetismus* 'electromagnetism' (He, 19th c.; ← *electr(ic)-* 'electric' + *-o-* + *magnetismus*), etc.

Copulative compounds are extremely rare: *iuristotheologus* 'lawyer (*iurista*) and theologist (*theologus*) at the same time' (R), *gallopavo* 'turkey' (R; ← *gall-* 'cock' + *-o-* + *pavo* 'peacock'). Formations without a linking vowel such as *vir lupus* 'werewolf' (← *vir* 'man' + *lupus* 'wolf'), also written as *vir-lupus* or *virlupus*, are better viewed as appositions, and hence syntagmatic compounds. A case interpretable in both senses is *caropanis* 'flesh (*caro*) and bread (*panis*) at the same time' (R). A special kind of copulative compound is constituted by the innovative type *Lutheropapismus* 'belief in Luther and the pope at the same time' (R), which looks like a conflation of *Lutherismus* and *papismus*.

3.1.2 Adjectival compounds

Adjectival compounds, which abound in NL, fall into three main groups.

The first one is constituted by synthetic compounds closely related to those seen in the previous paragraph. Some noun compounds, in fact, could probably also be analysed as conversions of adjectival compounds. Again, most neologisms follow established patterns with second elements such as *-bibus* 'drinking', *-cola* 'adoring, inhabiting', *-crepus* 'clashing', *-fer(us)* 'bearing, producing', etc. But one also finds a sizeable number of innovative second elements, especially in poetry: *animiclepa* 'sense-stealing' (R; ← *anim-* 'sense' + *-i-* + *clep-* 'to steal'), *auricreus* 'gold-creating' (R; ← *aur-* 'gold' + *-i-* + *cre-* 'to create'), *multicubus* 'having many mistresses' (Ho; ← *multi-* 'many' + *cub-* 'to lie down'), *artidocus* 'art-teaching' (R; ← *art-* 'art' + *-i-* + *doc-* 'to teach'), *omnidomus* 'all-taming' (R; ← *omni-* 'all' + *dom-* 'to tame'), *radiineca* 'ray-killing' (R; ← *radi-* 'ray' + *-i-* + *nec-* 'to kill'), *auripluus* 'gold-raining' (R; ← *aur-* 'gold' + *-i-* + *plu-* 'to rain'), *fortipremus* 'hard-pressing' (R; ← *fort-* 'hard' + *-i-* + *prem-* 'to press'), *radiispuus* 'ray-spewing' (*radi-* 'ray' + *-i-* + *spu-* 'to spew'), *grandistrepus* 'making much noise' (Ho; ← *grand-* 'big' + *-i-* + *strep-* 'to make noise'), *oculitega* 'covering the eyes' (R; ← *ocul-* 'eye' + *-i-* + *teg-* 'to cover'). While these second elements are derived from verbs by conversion, in others we find an explicit suffix (normally the present participle suffix *-ns*, or *-ax*). Again, most neologisms follow established patterns, but there are also some innovative second elements: *undifremens* 'wave-raging' (R; ← *und-* 'wave' + *-i-* + *freme-* 'to rage'), *soporiacens* 'asleep' (R; ← *sopor-* 'sleep' (+ *-i-*) + *iace-* 'to lie'), *tergisequens* 'running behind' (R; ← *terg-* 'back' + *-i-* + *seque-* 'to follow'), *iuristudens* 'studying law' (R; ← *iur-* 'law' + *-i-* + *stude-* 'to study'), *omnivorans* 'all-devouring' (R; ← *omni-* 'all' + *vora-* 'to devour'), *urinificax* 'diuretic' (R; ← *urin-* 'urine' + *-i-* + *fic-* 'to make'). *Saccogerulus* 'wearing a sack dress' (R; ← *sacc-* 'sack (dress)' + *-o-* + *ger-* 'to wear' + *-ulus* '-ing') is notworthy for its linking vowel *-o-*.

A second group of adjectival compounds which is well represented both in CL and in NL are possessive compounds (*bahuvrīhi*, in the Indian terminology). Their first element can be anything except a verb, their second element is invariably a noun, and the whole sequence is converted into one of the adjectival declension-classes. Most neologisms again follow established patterns, but some show innovative second elements: *polycarmen* 'rich in verses' (R; ← *poly-* 'many' + *carmen* 'poem'), *tauricerebrus* 'with the brains of a bull' (R; ← *taur-* 'bull' + *-i-* + *cerebr-* 'brain'), *flexilicollus* 'with an agile neck' (R; ← *flexil-* 'agile' + *-i-* + *coll-* 'neck'), *tricoronis* 'with three crowns' (R; ← *tri-* 'three' + *coron-* 'crown'), *multicubitus* 'many cubits long' (R; ← *multi-* 'many' + *cubit-* 'cubit'), *quinquelobus* 'five-lobed' (Linné p. 20; ← *quinque* 'five' + *lob-* 'lobe'), *multinominus* 'with many names' (R; ← *multi-* 'many' + *nomin-* 'name'), *anuminis* 'godless' (Ho; ← *a-* 'without' +

numin- 'god'), *enummis* 'without money' (Ho; ← *e* 'out' + *numm-* 'coin'), *multitalentus* 'rich' (R; ← *multi-* 'many' + *talent-* 'talent'), *univalvis* 'univalve' (Linné p. xxvii; ← *uni-* 'one' + *valv-* 'valve'), *avenis* 'without veins' (Linné p. xxiv; ← *a-* 'without' + *ven-* 'vein'). *Aenochordus* 'with metallic strings' (R; ← *aen-* 'made of ore' + *-o-* + *chord-* 'string') is noteworthy for its linking vowel *-o-*. With some nouns, an explicit suffix indicates the feature 'possession': *arcuferreus* 'with an iron bow' (R; ← *arc-* 'bow' + *-u-* [the choice of *-u-* as a linking vowel being due to the fact that *arcus* pertains to the forth declension with a thematic vowel *u*] + *ferreus* 'of iron'), *tetrarotatus* 'with four wheels', etc. (← *tetra-* 'four' + *rot-* 'wheel' + possessive *-atus*), etc.

It must also be mentioned that some second elements, though not unknown to CL and ML, witnessed a spectacular rise in productivity when they were adopted in scientific terminologies with a great need of descriptive adjectives. This is especially true of *-florus* 'with X flowers' and *-folius* 'with X leaves' (cf. Selosse 2006) in botany, and *-fer(us)* 'X-bearing, producing' (cf. Rainer 2013) and *-formis* 'having the form of X' (cf. Rainer 2009) in medicine and natural history. For the latter, only 3 examples are attested in CL, while at present they outnumber 150. This increase in number was also accompanied by semantic and formal diversification, for example the use of *-ae-* as a linking vowel with feminine first members in *-a*, where *-ae* is the genitive ending (*crateraeformis* 'crateriform' ← *crater-* 'cup' + *-ae-* + *-formis*, etc.). Apparently the linking vowel *-i-* has been reanalysed as a genitive ending. Innovations regarding meaning and domain were subtler, as when *-formis* was added to mass nouns (*gummiformis* 'rubber-like' ← *gumm-* 'rubber' + *-i-* + *-formis*, etc.), denoting consistency rather than form, or in the 19th century to names of diseases (*herpetiformis* 'herpetiform' ← *herpet-* 'herpes' + *-i-* + *-formis*, etc.).

The remaining non-copulative compounds are few in number and do not form a homogeneous set. Some of the more innovative neologisms must suffice here as an illustration of what was deemed possible: *prosocarmineus* 'combining prose and verse' (R; ← *pros-* 'prose' + *-o-* + *carmineus* 'pertaining to poetry', itself a neologism), *cordintimus* 'heartfelt' (*cord-* 'heart' + *intimus* 'innermost'), *nimicredulus* 'too credulous' (R; ← *nimis* 'too' + *credulus* 'credulous'). Compounds such as *spumagenitus* 'foam-born' (R; ←*spumā* 'from foam' + *genitus* 'born') or *auriplenus* 'rich' (R; ← *auri* 'of gold' + *plenus* 'full') are to be considered syntagmatic.

By far the most important innovation in the realm of adjectival compounding, however, is constituted by the third type, the novel pattern of copulative compounds of the type *politico-moralis* 'politico-moral' with a linking vowel *-o-*, already studied in depth by Hatcher (1951: 54–132). According to Hatcher, this type of compound, unknown both to CL and to ML, has been attested sporadically in German NL texts since the middle of the 16th century and "by the middle of the seventeenth century [...] has become an international type" (p. 87). Among the CL forerunners she points to nominal compounds of the type *Gallo-Graeci* 'Gauls who settled in Greece', which, however, were semantically determinative. The link to our adjectival compounds seems to have been constituted by names of dictionaries such as *Lexicon Graeco-Latinum* (1530), which involved "the metaphorical application of the immigration-pattern to the theme of translation" (p. 62). The semantics is more clearly coordinative in *editio Graeco-Latina* 'Greek and Latin edition' (1546), *monomachia Hungaro-Turcica* 'duel between Hungary and Turkey' (1590), or *Tychonico-Kepleriana* [*nova*] 'new findings by Tycho and Kepler' (1629). The oldest toponymic example from our corpus is *Ecclesia Belgiogermanica* 'Belgian-German Church' (R, 1572), the Latin name of the Dutch-speaking "Duyddsch-Nederlandische Gemeine" at London. This example suggests that Germanic influence could also have been at stake. It also attests to the possibility of using the corresponding noun as the first member of the compound instead of the adjective (*Belgium*, in our example, instead of the adjective *Belgicus*, which would yield *Belgicogermanica*), a feature inherited from the *Gallo-Graeci* pattern. This subtype with a nominal first element became very popular in medical terminology in the 17th century (Hatcher 1951: 91–92): *sterno-thyroidalis* (← *stern-* 'breastbone' + *-o-* + *thyroidalis* 'thyroidal'), etc. It can also be found with personal names: *Lutheropuritanus* 'concerning pure Lutheran doctrine' (R; ← *Luther(us)* 'Luther' + *-o-* + *puritanus* 'puritan'), *philosophia Leibnizio-Wolfiana* 'the philosophy of Leibniz and Wolf' (Bruckner p. 394; ← *Leibnizi(us)* 'Leibniz' + *-o-* + *Wolfianus* 'Wolfian'), etc.

Another, apparently less important source for our copulative type was constituted by the adjectival compound *comico-tragicus* 'tragicomic' (1540), which involves the common nouns *comoedia* and *tragoedia* – *tragicomoedia* was already used by Plautus – and was "tied up with the rise of the dramatic form called 'tragicomedy'" (Hatcher 1951: 71). The adjective *sacrosanctus* 'sacrosanct' (← *sacr-* 'sacred' + *-o-* + *sanctus* 'holy'), which already existed in CL, does not seem to have had any influence.

Adjectives participating in our type of copulative compounds are mostly relational adjectives. Nevertheless, some combinations of qualitative adjectives also occur. Ancient *dulcacidus* 'soursweet' (← *dulc-* 'sweet' + *acidus* 'sour') and Medieval *dulcamarus* 'bittersweet' (← *dulc-* 'sweet' + *amarus* 'bitter'; cf. Hatcher 1951: 18), both translated from Greek, paved the way. This non-relational subtype witnessed a sharp rise in productivity in natural history: *folii oblongo-ovati* 'elongated and oval leaves' (Linné p. 17; ← *oblong-* 'elongated' + *-o-* + *ovatus* 'oval'), *iris caeruleo-violacea* 'dark blue-purple iris' (Linné p. 50; ← *caerule-* 'dark blue' + *-o-* + *violaceus* 'purple'), etc.

As a consequence of their origin, our copulative compounds have always had a very strong predilection for first members of the Latin second declension with a thematic vowel *o*. First members of the third declension with a stem vowel *i* have remained rare, but do occasionally occur. The linking vowel then must be *-i-* (which coincides with the thematic vowel): *levidensis* 'light and dense' (R, 16th c.; ← *lev(is)* 'light' + *-i-* + *densis* 'dense'), *viridi-argenteus* (Linné p. 77; ← *virid(is)* 'green' + *-i-* + *argenteus* 'silver (adj.)'), *clavipectoralis* 'of the collarbone and the breast' (← *clav(is)* 'collarbone' + *-i-* + *pectoralis* 'of the breast'), *nationalisocialisticus* 'national-socialist' (He, 20th c.; ← *national(is)* 'national' + *-i-* + *socialisticus* 'socialist'), etc.

3.2 Greek-based composition

As argued in section 2, compounds only interpretable on the basis of the rules of Greek word-formation may safely be omitted from a description of Neo-Latin word-formation. We will therefore only take into consideration here types of compounds with first and second members which were already on the way to being integrated into the system of (Neo-)Latin word-formation. Some of them, by the way, could be classified with good reason as prefixes from the point of view of NL.

Among the first members, we may distinguish different semantic subgroups.

Numeral first members of Greek origin were commonly used, especially with bases of Greek origin, as witnessed for example by Linné's series *monoandria, diandria, triandria, tetrandria, pentandria, hexandria, heptandria, octandria, enneandria, decandria,* etc. When introducing these neologisms, Linné (cf. p. xxxii), however, still felt obliged to translate the constituents into Latin: "μόνος unicus, & ἀνδρ maritus. Maritus unicus in matrimonio. Stamen unicum in flore hermaphrodite" [μόνος one, & ἀνδρ husband. One husband only in the marriage. One stamen only in a hermaphrodite flower]. The integration was facilitated by formations readily interpretable on a Latin basis, such as *monocentricus* 'monocentric', whose base can not only be referred to Greek *kentron* 'centre' but also to Latin *centrum* 'id.'. Its antonym *poly-* was also attached to Latin bases: *polycarmen* 'rich in verses' (*carmen* 'poem'), etc. *Chilio-* 'thousand', as in *chiliometrum* 'kilometer', was not directly taken from Greek, but constituted an attempt at making vernacular *kilo-* sound more Greek.

Another group of first members has an adjectival or adverbial meaning. A first subgroup equally relates to quantity and measurement. Many of the more recent uses of the dimensional first members *micr(o)-* 'small' (*micros-*

copium 'microscope', *microelementum* 'trace element', with a Latin second member, etc.), *macr(o)-* 'big' (*macrologus* 'boastful; lit. big-speaking'; cf. German *großsprecherisch*, etc.), and *mega-* 'big' (from Greek *megas* 'big'; *megavattium* 'megawatt', etc.) have clearly been influenced by the vernacular languages. Furthermore, we should also mention *is(o)-* 'same' (*isoperimetria* 'same perimeter', etc.), *hom(o)-* 'same' (*homocentricus* 'having the same centre', etc.), *heter(o)-* 'different' (*heteroglossus* 'speaking a different language', etc.), and *pan-* 'all' (*panharmonia* 'harmony among all members', etc.). Spatial dimensions are expressed by *endo-* 'inside' (*endolympha* 'lymph contained in the inner ear', etc.) and *epi-* 'above' (*epidermis* 'outer layer of the skin'), *hyper-* 'above' (*hyperphysicus* (R) 'beyond the body', etc.) and *hypo-* 'below' (*hypothalamus* 'that part situated below the thalamus', etc.), *mes(o)-* 'middle' (*mesotendineum* 'the connective tissue sheath attaching a tendon to its synovial sheath', etc.), *peri-* 'around' (*peritendineum* 'any of the fibrous sheaths surrounding the primary bundles of fibers in a tendon'), *tele-* 'far, away' (*telescopium* 'telescope', *televisorium* 'TV', backtranslated from a vernacular language, etc.), and others. The temporal dimension is present in the couple *prot(o)-* 'original' (*protomater* (R) 'first mother', etc.) vs. *ne(o)-* 'new, recent' (*neopropheta* 'new prophet', *neochristianismus* (R) 'neo-christianity', etc.; on *neo-* cf. Rainer 2008). The first of these is also used in a hierarchical sense: *protoepiscopus* (R) 'first, i.e. highest-ranked bishop', etc. Another subgroup is evaluative in character: *eu-* (*euloquium* (R) 'eloquence', with a Latin base, etc.), *chrys(o)-* (*chrysodoctor* (R) 'excellent teacher', from *chrys-* 'gold', with a Latin basis, etc.), and *orth(o)-* 'right' (*orthotypographia* (R) 'correct printing', etc.) represent the positive pole, *cac(o)-* 'bad' (*cacomedicus* (R) 'bad physician', etc.) the negative one. Highly productive *pseudo-* 'false' (*pseudo-philosophia* (Bruckner p. 456), etc.), as well as *crypt(o)-* 'hidden' (*Crypto-Iudaei* 'crypto-jews' (Bruckner p. 779), etc.) should also be mentioned here. The same meaning was also expressed occasionally by *par(a)-* (*parepiscopus* 'false bishop', *paradiatriba* (R) 'pseudophilosophical diatribe', etc.). Last but not least, one should mention privative *a-* (*achristianus* (Ho) 'non-christian', etc.) and reflexive *aut(o)-* (*automobilis* (He, 19th c.) 'self-propelling', probably a backtranslation from a vernacular language, etc.).

A third, largely open subgroup is constituted by nominal first members such as *hydr(o)-* 'water' (*hydrophobus* 'scared of water', etc.), *psych(o)-* 'soul' (*psychotyrannus* 'tyrant of the soul', etc.), *zo(o)-* 'animal' (*zoophytum* (He, 17th c.) 'an animal that visually resembles a plant', etc.), etc.

Last but not least, we should mention two very productive first members of verbal origin, *phil(o)-* 'loving' (*philerasmius* 'one loving Erasmus', where *-ius* represents a Latin adjectival ending), and its antonym *mis(o)-* (*misobarbarus* (Ho) 'one hating the barbarians', etc.).

A very similar situation obtains with respect to second members, of which we can also only mention the most important which were on the way of becoming established parts of Neo-Latin word-formation, as witnessed by hybrids or combinations with well-integrated first members of Greek origin: *-archa/us* 'chief' (*Austriarchus* (R) 'chief of Austria', etc.), *-cratia* 'government' (*gynaecocratia* (He, 17th c.) 'government of women', etc.), *-gamia* 'marriage' (*clerogamia* (R) 'marriage of priests', etc.), *-gamus* 'married' (*unigamus* 'married only once', with Latin *uni-* instead of Greek *mono-*, etc.), *-graphia* 'description' (*hydrographia* (Ho) 'hydrography', etc.), *-graphus* 'writer' (*calendariographus* (R) 'writer of calendars', etc.), *-latra* 'adorer' (*daemonilatra* (R) 'adorer of the demon', with the Latin linking vowel, *lutherolatra* (Ho) 'adorer of Luther', etc.), *-latria* 'adoration' (*astrolatria* 'adoration of the stars', etc.), *-logia* 'science' (*tabacologia* (R) 'science of tobacco', *terrelogia* 'science of the earth', remarkable for its linking vowel *-e-* – originally a genitive ending – copied from *terremotus* 'earthquake', etc.), *-machia* 'fight' (*monachomachia* (Ho) 'fight among monks', etc.), *-mania* 'mania' (*papimania*, with the Latin linking vowel, and *papomania* 'popemania', etc.; on *-mania* cf. Höfler 1972), *-mastix* 'basher' (*erasmiomastix* (Ho) 'Erasmus-basher', etc.), *-metria* 'measurement' (*longimetria* 'measurement of the length', etc.), *-metrum* 'measuring instrument' (*barometrum* 'id.' (17th c.), *gasometrum* 'id.' (20th c.), etc.), *-phagus* 'eating' (*porrophagus* (Ho) 'leek-eating', from Latin *porrum* 'leek', etc.), *-philus* 'loving' (*nummophilus* (He, 20th c.) 'collectionist', from Latin *nummus* 'coin', etc.), *-scopia* 'examination' (*uroscopia* (He, 19th c.) 'examination of urine', etc.), *-scopus* 'watcher' (*fatoscopus* (Ho) lit. 'fate-watcher', from Latin *fatum* 'fate', etc.), *-theca* 'depot' (*metallotheca* 'receptacle for keeping metallic objects', etc.), etc.

4 Derivation

CL derivation (cf. Leumann 1977; Kircher-Durand 2002) in all its ramifications continued to be used abundantly in NL. Again, only innovative aspects will be highlighted in the following paragraphs.

4.1 Nominal derivation

4.1.1 Denominal nouns

Personal nouns are formed both by prefixes and suffixes.

In the domain of prefixes, NL expanded the use of *co-/com-* (*co-elector* 'co-Elector' (R), *comprofessor* 'colleague (said of a teacher)' (R), etc.), *ex-* (*exiesuita* 'ex-Jesuit' (R), etc.) and *non-* (*non-fumator* 'non-smoker' (He, 20th c.), etc.), which all reach back to Late Latin (for *non-*, cf. Stotz 2000, § 131). Of the prefixes indicating hierarchy, the most current ones go back at least to ML: *praeconsul* 'Lord Mayor' (R), *procancellarius* 'vice-chancelor' (R), *subgubernator* 'vice-governor' (Ho), *vicebibliothecarius* 'deputy librarian' (R), etc. *Super-* and *supra-* seem to be new in this function, but are only attested sporadically: *superarbiter* 'higher arbiter' (Ho), *supracoquus* 'head cook' (R). A NL innovation is constituted by the intensive use of *sesqui-* lit. 'one and a half', which must have been transferred from the figurative use of *sesquipedalis* 'very long; lit. one and a half feet long': *sesquiCato* 'a person stricter than Cato' (R), *sesquihaereticus* 'an arch-heretic' (R), etc.

Among the suffixes, one group denotes professionals. The productivity of *-arius* continues unabated, while *-erius*, a Medieval loan-suffix from vernacular languages, becomes rare (but cf. *musquetterius*, besides *musquetarius* 'musketeer' (R)). The suffix *-ista*, as in ML, is used for denoting experts of all kind (*Dantista* 'Dante scholar' (R), etc.). The use of *-aster* in this sense – to be distinguished from pejorative *-aster*! – could be an innovation: *arabicaster* 'scholar of Arabic' (Ho), *scholaster* 'head master, student' (Ho, R; ← *schol-* 'school'), etc. Isolated innovations: *emporiandus* 'merchant' (R; ← *empori-* 'staple'), *caeremoniasta* 'performer of ceremonies' (R), *epitomastes* 'author of epitomes' (R), *symphoniscus* 'member of an orchestra' (R), *aeroplaniga* 'captain of an aircraft' (He, 20th c.; after *auriga* 'driver'). Though relatively rare, the playful use of *-ista* in words like *colaphista* 'someone giving punches' (Ho; ← *colaph-* 'punch') or *potista* 'drunkard' (Ho; ← *pot-* 'drink') is worth mentioning, since it seems to constitute a semantic innovation. A use of *-ista* which gets a remarkable boost in the Renaissance is that for designating followers: *Calvinista* (Ho), *Reuchlinista* (Ho), *Romanista* 'papist' (Ho), etc. The paradigmatic relationship to nouns of doctrines in *-ismus* (see below) was already firmly established: *anabaptismus* ↔ *anabaptista*, *atheismus* ↔ *atheista*, etc. In the 'follower' meaning, *-ista* was rivalled by *-ita*, which was not yet used in this sense in CL: *Vuyclevita* 'follower of Wyclyff' (Ho), *Calvinita* 'calvinist' (R), *Machiavellita* 'machiavellist' (R), etc. Much rarer was *-icanus*, which constitutes an innovation in this sense: *Apellicanus* 'follower of Apelles' (Ho). The suffix *-aster* added a pejorative tinge: *Calvinaster* 'calvinist' (R), *Machiavellaster* 'Machivellist' (R). For the designation of descendants, several Greek suffixes were imported: *Gonzagiades* 'descendant of the Gonzaga' (R), *Gonzagida* 'id.' (R), *angelida* 'descendant of an angel' (R), *Iesuides* 'descendant of Jesus' (R). Erroneously, *-ita* was also sometimes used in this meaning: *angelita* 'descendant of an angel' (R), *Danita* 'descendant of Dan' (R). *Quitoita* 'inhabitant of Quito' (R) probably follows the Classical locative type *eremita*. The hierarchical use of *-issimus* in *ministrissimus* 'highest-ranked minister' (R) is to be considered innovative, but seems to have remained isolated.

In the realm of status nouns, *-atus*, *-ia* and *-ura* (substituted for *-or*) continue to dominate the picture. An innovation seems to be constituted by the use of *-itas* in this function: *admiralitas* 'rank of an admiral (*admirali(us)*)' (Ho), *gentilhominitas* 'rank of a *gentilhomme* (latinized as *gentilhomo*, stem: *gentilhomin-*)' (R), *landsassitas* 'status of a *Landsasse* (latinized as *landsassius*)' (R), etc. This use is of course based on the suffix's use in denominal abstract nouns such as *asinitas* 'ass-hood' (← *asin-* 'ass'), already known from ML.

Place nouns continue to be coined with *-arium*, *-etum*, *-ia* and *-ile*, in their respective semantic domains. More noteworthy are several neologisms in *-(a)eum* (cf. already Classical *mausoleum*, name for the grave of king *Mausolus*): *alphabeum* 'lower school' (R), *typograph(a)eum* 'printery' (R; ← *typograph-* 'printer'), *cafeum* 'café' (He, 20th c.; ← *cafe-* 'coffee'). Equally interesting, some denominal formations in *-orium: armamentorium* 'depot for arms' (R; ← *armament-* 'arms'), *eremitorium* 'hermitage' (Ho; ← *eremit-* 'hermite').

A suffix which witnessed a spectacular rise in use in NL was *-ismus*. Originally forming action nouns corresponding to verbs in *-izein* in Greek, it has been reanalysed as denominal and deadjectival in Latin. The choice of a nominal or adjectival base is arbitrary up to a certain point: *Calvinismus* = *Calvinianismus*, *Epicurismus* = *Epicureismus*, *Lutherismus* = *Lutheranismus*, all taken from Hoven's dictionary. Since the names of followers were derived with the same suffix as the relational adjectives (cf. *Cartesianus* 'of Cartesius/Descartes' / *Cartesiani* 'the followers of Cartesius'), by reanalysis – along the lines of the hypothetical example *Cartesianismus* 'the doctrine of the *Cartesiani*' > 'the doctrine of Cartesius' – the relational adjective could eventually also be used as a base.

From a semantic point of view, we must distinguish several subpatterns. One set, which is relatively small and still reflects the original Greek 'action' meaning, designates a behaviour characterized by what the base refers to: *echetismus* 'cruelty worthy of Echetos' (Ho), *italismus* 'imitation of the Italians' (Ho), *egoismus* 'id.' (He, 18th c.), etc. Medical terms such as *priapismus*, derived from the name of the Greek god Priapos, or *strabismus* (R; ← *strab-* 'cross-eyed') come close to this behavioural set, though at a closer look 'condition, disease', in the absence of intentionality, is a more correct classification than 'behaviour'. Such medical terms reach back to Antiquity, but where greatly expanded in NL times: *alcoholismus* (19th c.), etc. Some words of the behavioural set, such as *Asiatismus*/*Asiaticismus* 'Asian, i.e. elaborated style' form a smooth transition to the following two linguistic sets. In the first one, already present in CL (cf. *iotacismus* 'id.', etc.), *-ismus* refers to a linguistic peculiarity: *cappacismus* 'the peculiarity of pronouncing Latin *c* as *k* [Greek: *kappa*]' (Ho), *Germanismus* 'germanism' (Ho), etc. In a closely related set, which seems to be a NL innovation directly influenced by Greek, the suffix designates a language: *Anglicismus* 'the English language' (R), *Germanismus* 'the German language' (R), etc. The most important subset, however, which saw its productivity soar beginning with the Renaissance, is constituted by names of all kinds of doctrines. The base denotes a crucial ingredient of the doctrine in question, such as its founder, its followers, or simply some salient feature: *absolutismus* (Bruckner p. 156), *atheismus* (Ho), *Cartesianismus* (Bruckner p. 5), *Deismus* (Bruckner p. 384), *fatalismus* (Bruckner p. 427), *materialismus* (Bruckner p. 155), *optimismus* (Bruckner p. 385), *papismus* (Ho), *Spinozismus* (Bruckner p. 38), *Zuinglianismus* (Ho), etc. In some cases, the meaning has been extended metonymically, referring to the corresponding period of time: *saeculo Islamismi secundo* 'in the second century of Islamism' (Bruckner p. 807).

Occasional innovations can also be found in other denominal categories. The temporal meaning of *pro-* in *propascha* 'day before Easter' (R) and *prosabbathum* 'day before Sabbath' (R) has been borrowed from Greek. Occasionally, Medieval *-(ist)ria* (cf. Stotz 2000, § 46) is still used in NL times: *papistria* 'papistry' (R; ← *pap-* 'pope' or *papist-* 'papist'), *theologistria* 'theological speculation' (R; ← *theolog-* or *theologist-* 'theologist'). *Maiorascum* 'right of primogeniture' (R; ← *maior-* 'older') is a loan-word, either from Italian *maiorasco* or from Spanish *mayorazgo*. In botany, names of plants began to be coined by adding *-ia* to a proper name: *Adansonia* (← *Michael Adanson*), etc. In pharmacy and chemistry, names of substances were coined with *-inum* or *-ina: chininum* 'quinine' (19th c.; ← *Chin-* 'Quina-tree'), *gelatina* 'gelatine' (17th c.; ← *gelat-* 'frozen (stuff)'), etc. Names of chemical elements were formed by attaching *-ium: silicium* (19th c.; ← *silic-* 'flint'), etc.

Diminutives of all kinds continued to be coined in great abundance, following CL patterns. One aspect worth mentioning is that scientists frequently had recourse to diminutives for terminological purposes: just think of *areola* 'id.; lit. small area', *cerebellum* 'id.; lit. small brain', *funiculus* 'umbilical cord; lit. small rope', *malleolus* 'id.; lit. small hammer', etc. in medicine. Occasionally, we find loans from Italian, some in *-et(t)us* and one in *-ucius*/*-utius: coffinetus* 'small chest' (R; ← *cophin-* 'chest', cf. It. *cofanetto*), *lancetta* 'lancet' (Blancard; ← *lance-* 'lance'; cf. It. *lancetta*), *epistolucia* or *epistolutia* 'unimportant letter' (R; ← *epistol-* 'letter'; cf. It. *epistoluccia*).

4.1.2 Deadjectival nouns

The most important group of deadjectival nouns in Latin are quality nouns, which continue to be very frequent in NL, but mostly along CL lines. The only remarkable fact in this area from a NL perspective is that authors continued to form abstract nouns in *-itas* or *-etas* from adverbs and other unorthodox bases in the style of the Scholastic philosophers, despite the ridicule poured on this usage by some humanists: *alicubietas* (Bruckner p. 483; ← *alicubi* 'somewhere'), *nullibietas* (R; ← *nullibi* 'nowhere'), *ubiqueitas* (R; ← *ubique* 'everywhere'), *aseitas* (Bruckner p. 485; ← *a se* 'from himself'), etc. On deadjectival nouns in *-ismus* see section 4.1.1.

4.1.3 Deverbal nouns

Action nouns continued to be coined productively, sometimes using even relatively unproductive CL suffixes: *ludibulum* 'play' (R; ← *ludi-* 'to play'), *divinaculum* 'soothsaying' (R; ← *divina-* 'to foretell'), *deceptela* 'deception' (R; ← *decept-* 'to deceive'), *allegorismus* 'use of allegory' (R; ← *allegor(iz)-* 'to use allegory', if it was not a loan from Greek), *respirium* 'pause' (Ho; ← *respir-* 'to breathe'), *blateramen* 'chattering' (R; ← *blatera-* 'to chatter'), etc. The most productive suffixes, however, were *-io* (*allegorisatio* 'use of allegories' (R), etc.), conversions of the type *cantus*, *-ura* and *-mentum*. The latter suffix retained the high productivity it had already acquired in ML (cf. Stotz 2000, § 64): only a detailed textual analysis of the many doublets (*aberramentum* (Ho) instead of Classical *aberratio* [← *aberr(at)-* 'to go astray'], etc.) could show whether there were semantic or stylistic differences with respect to *-io*. The type *cantus* seems to have gained new momentum in NL following the model of CL, after its relative neglect in ML (cf. Stotz 2000, § 56).

Agent nouns stick to Classical patterns: *clamitator* 'bawler' (Ho; ← *clamitat-* 'to bawl'), *Protestans* 'protestant' (← *protesta-* 'to testify'), *connugo* 'one who makes jokes together' (R; ← *connug-* 'to make jokes together'), etc. The only noteworthy innovation is the extension, apparently beginning with Vesalius, of agent nouns in *-or* to designate muscles: *supinator* 'id.' (← *supinat-* 'to supinate'), etc. A substantial increase of neologisms is found with gerundival nouns in *-ndus: graduandus* 'one who is going to get a degree' (Ho; ← *gradua-* 'to confer a degree'). It seems that this type has been reanalysed as denominal, the suffix becoming *-andus: baccalaureandus* 'bachelor candidate' (Ho; ← *baccalaure-* 'bachelor'), *magistrandus* 'master candidate' (Ho; ← *magistr-* 'master'), etc.

Much more interesting was the fate of instrument nouns in NL. Here, the scientific revolution of the 17th century and the industrial revolution of the 18th and 19th centuries created a great demand for new designations. All instrumental suffixes of CL were put to work, the choice depending on the availability of analogical models or simply the discretion of the coiner: *retinaculum* 'vice' (He, 18th c.; ← *retin-* 'to hold back'), *lactisugium* 'milking machine' (He, 20th c.; ← *lact-* 'milk' + *-i-* + *sug-* 'to suck' + instrumental suffix *-ium*), *adglutinamen* 'adhesive' (R;

← *adglutina-* 'to stick'), *irretimentum* 'net, trap' (Ho; ← *irreti-* 'to capture with a net'), *extinctorium* 'extinguisher' (He, 20th c; ← *extinct-* 'to extinguish'), *accelera-trum* 'accelerator' (He, 20th c.; ← *accelera-* 'to accelerate'), etc. The most striking innovation in this semantic category was the use of agentive *-or* to form instrument nouns, unknown to CL. The oldest attested example is *conductor fulminis* 'lightning conductor' (He, 1782; ← *conduct-* 'to conduce'). With high probability, this new function, which Helfer regards as "non commendabilis" in his dictionary, was due to loan-translations from English, where *-or* had inherited the instrumental meaning from homophonous *-er* (cf. Hales' *ventilator*, 1744). The new pattern then became established in NL: *exsiccator* 'id.' (*exsiccat-* 'to dry'), etc.

Place nouns remained within the limits of CL.

4.2 Adjectival derivation

4.2.1 Denominal adjectives

By far the biggest group of denominal adjectives in NL are relational adjectives, which enjoyed greater popularity than in CL. Most of those derived from common nouns follow the established patterns in the choice of suffix. This is also true of the combinations with prefixes, adverbs, prepositions, or numerals, of the type *retropubicus* 'situated behind the pubis' (← *retro* 'behind', *pub-* 'pubis'), which also became more frequent. Among the most noteworthy aspects one can mention the continued use of the pleonastic form *-icalis*, which goes back to Late Latin and was greatly expanded in ML: *rhetoricalis* 'rhetorical' (R) beside *rhetoricus* 'rhetoric', etc. The suffix *-isticus* received a new boost thanks to the popularity of both *-ista* and *-ismus*, to which it can be related via suffix substitution: *systema atomisticum* 'atomistic system' (Bruckner, p. 38), for example, can be analysed either as 'of the atomists [*atomistarum*]' or as 'of atomism [*atomismi*]'). A final remarkable feature, which remains to be studied in detail, is the relational use of adjectives in *-trix*. Hoven's dictionary contains many such – formally deverbal – adjectives which are glossed referring to the corresponding noun: *auditrix* 'qui concerne l'ouïe (concerning hearing)', *commutatrix* 'qui concerne les échanges de marchandises (concerning the exchange of goods)', etc. Blancard contains *facultas retentrix* and similar expressions, which are also more naturally paraphrased by a noun than by a verb: 'the capacity of retention, of retaining, *which retains'. The same reanalysis had already occurred in CL with *-ivus* and *-orius*.

Deonymic relational adjectives, i.e. adjectives derived from proper names, enjoyed enormous popularity in NL times. With names of persons, the relative abundance of synonyms seems to indicate that stylistic factors were at stake here (the following are all attested in R): *Ciceronianus* = *Ciceronicus* = *Ciceronius* = *Ciceron(a)eus* = *Ciceroniacus*, *Erasmianus* = *Erasmicus* = *Erasminus* = *Erasmiacus*, etc. In more sober texts, *-ianus* predominates, except where special conditions dictate another choice. With place names, *-ensis* and *-icus* were the favorite suffixes in NL times, followed by *-anus* and *-inus: Dresdensis* ← *Dresda*, *Suecicus* ← *Suecia*, *groeninganus* ← *Groeninga*, *Altendorfinus* ← *Altendorf*, etc.

There were hardly any innovations in the rest of denominal adjectives which express possession or resemblance. Some, like *-aceus* or *-atus* witnessed a sharp rise in scientific terminologies, for example in botany: *setaceus* 'silky', *petiolatus* 'provided with a stalk', etc. The only noteworthy innovation seems to be constituted by the pleonastic suffixes *-oideus* and *-oidalis*, which in part replaced the less well integrated Greek suffix *-oides: os ethmoides* 'ethmoid bone (having the form of a sieve)' > *os ethmoideum*, *os ethmoidale*, etc.

4.2.2 Deadjectival adjectives

In the realm of deadjectival adjectives, there is a wealth of diminutive, intensive and negative adjectives following established patterns. Among diminutive formations we noted extravagant *nosterculus* and *nostrollus* 'our' (R; ← *noster* 'our' + diminutive *-culus* and *-ulus*), with a pejorative overtone. New intensive prefixes were *archi-* and *sesqui-*: *archicatholicus* 'arch-catholic' (R), *sesquifuriosus* 'very furious' (Ho), etc. *Super-* continues the rise witnessed already in ML (Stotz 2000, § 138): *superinfelix* 'very unhappy' (R), etc. With respect to *-issimus*, only its combination with possessive adjectives commands attention: *meissimus* 'completely mine' (Ho; ← *meus* 'my, mine'), etc. As far as negative prefixation is concerned, *non* retained its popularity gained in ML (Stotz 2000, § 131): *nonperemptorius* 'non-compulsory' (R), etc.

4.2.3 Deverbal adjectives

Both new active and passive adjectives were formed quite frequently, but almost exclusively along Classical lines. The relational use of *-trix* has already been mentioned in section 4.2.1.

4.3 Verbal derivation

4.3.1 Denominal and deadjectival verbs

Prefixed verbs were productively formed, but apparently only according to Classical patterns. Among neologisms by suffixation, there are many inchoative formations in *-ascere* and *-escere: adverbiascere* 'to become an adverb' (Ho, R), *aerescere* 'to become a gas' (R; ← *aer-* 'air'), *obscurascere* 'to become dark' (R; ← *obscur-* 'dark'), *meliorescere* 'to become better' (R; ← *melior-* 'better'), etc. The suffix *-izare* (also written *-isare* or *-issare*) continued to be highly productive. It was mainly intransitive (*Calvinizare*/*Calvinianizare* 'to follow Calvin's doctrine' (R), etc.) in literary texts, but transitive in scientific texts (*alcoholisare* 'to add alcohol' (R), *saecularisare* 'to secularize' (He, 17th c.), etc.). In the following verb, the suffix *-ito* is used like *-izo: graecitare* 'to study, use Greek' (R; ← *graec-* 'Greek').

4.3.2 Deverbal verbs

CL had a very rich system of prefixed deverbal verbs – some of which could also be analysed as compounds, following the Latin tradition –, which was also exploited in full in NL times. Since there is no comprehensive classification of the plethora of subpatterns, it is difficult to say whether among the many NL neologisms there are any innovations. As a pis aller, we must content ourselves here with providing some examples of the more unexpected kind: *contraconcupiscere* 'to have an opposed wish' (R; ← *contra-* 'against' + *concupiscere* 'to wish'), *dispotare* 'to drink twice' (R; *dis-* 'away' + *potare* 'to drink'), *exbaptizare* 'to recall christening' (R; ← *ex-* 'out' + *baptizare* 'to christen'), *interoblivisci* 'to forget in the meantime' (R; ← *inter-* 'between' + *oblivisci* 'to forget'), *introexistere* 'to be inside' (R; ← *intro-* 'in(to)' + *existere* 'to exist'), *semiambire* 'to revolve around half-way' (R; ← *semi-* 'half' + *ambire* 'to revolve around'), etc.

Suffixed deverbal verbs are rarer and are mainly formed by frequentative *-itare* (*erratitare* 'to err again and again' (R) ← *errat-* 'to err', etc.), or desiderative *-urire* (*bibiturire* 'to want to drink' (R) ← *bibit-* 'to drink', etc.). This latter pattern seems to have been a favorite of the humanists, since Hoven's dictionary alone contains more neologisms than there are attested formations in CL.

4.4 Adverbial derivation

New adverbs were formed abundantly in NL, but normally with full respect for the intricacies of Classical patterns, which in part allowed multiple solutions and had evolved over time: *Epicuriter* 'in the manner of Epicurus' (R; denominal!), *deitus* 'from God' (Ho; ← *De-* 'God'), *concisim* 'concisely' (R; ← *concis-* 'concise', vs. CL *concise*), *guttulatim* 'in dribs and drabs' (R; ← *guttul-* 'small drop'), *promiscuo* 'promiscuously' (Ho; ← *promiscu-* 'promiscuous', vs. CL *promisce* or *promiscue*), etc.

5 Conversion

There is nothing noteworthy with respect to noun-noun conversion expressing feminization: *burggrafia* 'wife of a Burgrave' (R; ← *Burgrafius* 'Burgrave'), etc.

Adjective-noun conversions were very frequent, just like in CL, especially for denoting followers (*Cartesiani*, etc.), inhabitants (*Canadenses*, etc.), or medicines (*vomitorium* 'emetic', etc.). The latter group, which involved ellipsis of *medicamen* or *medicamentum*, was at least initially highly productive in pharmacy and medicine. Another originally elliptical pattern which gained autonomy over time and was boosted by scientific progress was the one designating a field (*res*), art (*ars*) or science (*scientia*): *horologica* 'horology' (R), *aeronautica* (He, 17th c.), *rhinoplastica* 'rhinoplasty' (He, 19th c.), etc. With adjectives of Greek origin, *-ice* (genitive *-ices*) could be used alternatively: *botanica* 'botany' = *botanice*, etc.

The only aspect worth mentioning with respect to adjectival conversion, which is marginal anyway in Latin, are some relational adjectives where the suffix-like ending of the base inhibits explicit derivation: *Calixtinus* 'of Calixtinus' (Ho), *Franciscanus* 'of *Franciscani*, i.e. Fransciscan friars'), etc. This phenomenon, however, existed already in CL.

Verbal conversion, both from nouns and from adjectives, was much more important, but there do not seem to be any innovations with respect to CL, where the semantics of noun-verb conversion was already quite flexible: *adverbiare* 'to use as an adverb' (Ho), *haereticare* 'to declare a heretic' (R), *haereticari* 'to be a heretic' (R), *dialecticari* 'to argue dialectically' (R), *divitare* 'to make rich' (R; ← *divit-* 'rich'), etc.

6 Blending

As a potentially universal technique, blending is also occasionally practiced in NL: *Daemonicanus* (Ho; ← *daemon* 'demon' x *Dominicanus* 'Dominican friar'), *philosophistoricus* 'someone who is at the same time a philosopher (*philosophus*) and an historian (*historicus*)' (Ho). *Lutheropapismus*, already mentioned at the end of section 3.1.1, could also be analysed as a case of blending.

7 References

Biville, Frédérique (1990–95): *Les emprunts du latin au grec*. 2 Vol. Louvain: Peeters.

Blancardus, Stephanus (1683): *Lexicon medicum Graeco-Latinum*. Jena: Müller.

Bruckner, Jakob (1744): *Historia critica philosophiae*. Vol. 4: *Pars altera*. Leipzig: Breitkopf.

Hatcher, Anna Granville (1951): *Modern English Word-Formation and Neo-Latin. A study of the origin of English (French, Italian, German) copulative compounds*. Baltimore, MD: John Hopkins Press.

Helfer, Christian (1982): *Lexicon auxiliare. Ein deutsch-lateinisches Wörterbuch*. Saarbrücken: Societas Latina.

Höfler, Manfred (1972): *Zur Integration der neulateinischen Kompositionsweise im Französischen. Dargestellt an den Bildungen auf* -(o)manie, -(o)mane. Tübingen: Niemeyer.

Hoven, René (1994): *Lexique de la prose latine de la Renaissance*. Leiden: Brill [2nd ed. 2006].

Kircher-Durand, Chantal (ed.) (2002): *Création lexicale. La formation des noms par dérivation suffixale*. Louvain: Peeters.

Leumann, Manu (1977): *Lateinische Laut- und Formenlehre*. München: Beck.

Lindner, Thomas (1996): *Lateinische Komposita. Ein Glossar vornehmlich zum Wortschatz der Dichtersprache*. Innsbruck: Institut für Sprachwissenschaft.

Lindner, Thomas (2002): *Lateinische Komposita. Morphologische, historische und lexikalische Studien*. Innsbruck: Institut für Sprachen und Literaturen.

Linné, Carl von (1785): *Systema plantarum Europae. Tomus III*. Colonia: Piestre and Delamolliere.

Neuhausen, Karl August (2003): Neulatein I. Sprache. In: Manfred Landfester (ed.), *Der neue Pauly. Enzyklopädie der Antike*. Vol. 15/I, 926–931. Stuttgart/Weimar: Metzler.

Rainer, Franz (2008): *Neo-* and Neo-Latin. *Word Structure* 1: 53–64.

Rainer, Franz (2009): Die Integration des lateinischen Kompositionstyps *tauriformis* im Französischen und Italienischen. *Zeitschrift für romanische Philologie* 125: 45–84.

Rainer, Franz (2013): L'intégration des composés latins du type *aurifer* en français. In: Georgette Dal and Dany Amiot (eds.), *Repères en morphologie*. Lille: http://stl.recherche.univ-lille3.fr/textesenligne/Reperes-Morphologie/Rainer-Reperes_morphologie_p182-214.pdf [last access 30 Apr 2015].

Ramminger, Johann (2003–): *Neulateinische Wortliste. Ein Wörterbuch des Lateinischen von Petrarca bis 1700*. [Online available at: www.neulatein.de]

Selosse, Philippe (2006): La traduction française des "bahuvrīhi" du néo-latin botanique de la Renaissance. *Le français préclassique* 9: 85–118.

Stotz, Peter (2000): *Handbuch zur lateinischen Sprache des Mittelalters*. Vol. 2: *Bedeutungswandel und Wortbildung*. München: Beck.

Weber, Heinrich E., Jaroslav Moravec and Jean-Paul Theurillat (2000): International code of phytosociological nomenclature. *Journal of Vegetation Science* 11(5): 739–768.

Peter O. Müller

4 Foreign word-formation in German

Abstract: The article first offers an overview of research on foreign word-formation in German. Subsequently, the main features of the historical development of foreign word-formation are traced. A presentation of foreign word-formation follows, which offers an overview of the inventory of central elements of foreign word-formation and addresses problems of categorization and analysis. Subsequently, possibilities of and restrictions on the combinability of exogenous and indigenous morphemes in the context of hybrid formations are presented.

1 Current state of research

The investigation of foreign word-formation in the framework of research on German word-formation was for a long time virtually ignored. A glance in traditional handbooks such as Wilmanns (1899) or Henzen (1965) confirms this finding. There, foreign elements of word-formation are at best marginally attended to. Thus, Hans Marchand can as late as 1955 rightly ascertain: "Books on German word-formation systematically omit treatment of foreign-coined words, obviously on the assumption that only morphemes of Germanic origin have a legitimate claim to a place in word-formation" (Marchand 1955 [1974: 182]). This great degree of abstinence with respect to the topic of research "foreign word-formation", which subsisted until the 60s of the 20th century, turns out to be the result of a scholarly tabu: This developed in the context of a purism with respect to foreign words (see article 8 on word-formation and purism in German), which had developed in German speaking areas since the 17th century and which in lexicography led to a great dichotomy between the documentation of the native vocabulary and the foreign vocabulary. Accordingly, tendencies toward a stigmatization of

Peter O. Müller, Erlangen, Germany

https://doi.org/10.1515/9783111420530-004

products of foreign word-formation can also be found in descriptions of word-formation. Thus, for example, Wilmanns declares with respect to verbs with *-ieren* that they "wie Schlingenkraut den ebnen Boden unserer Rede [überziehen]" [cover the even ground of our speech like strangleweed], and sees it as "Missbrauch" [abuse], "die Endung *-ieren* auch deutschen Stämmen anzuhängen" [to hang the ending *-ieren* on German stems as well] (Wilmanns 1899: 114).

Foreign word-formation was first subjected to greater scrutiny during the transition from a more diachronic research tradition oriented towards individual means of word-formation to a theory of word-formation focused on the contemporary language, which puts the systematic interaction of the means of word-formation in the center of attention and also emphasizes the function of non-native elements of word-formation. Added to this was the criticism of the traditional (purist) concept of foreign word, which Peter von Polenz (1967) combined with the requirement to systematically include productive, non-native elements of word-formation in German research on word-formation and to describe this as "Lehnwortbildung" [loan word-formation]. Within the framework of the research project on "Lehnwortbildung" (cf. Hoppe et al. 1987) carried out since 1985 at the Institut für deutsche Sprache (Mannheim), which was proposed by Polenz, the non-native word-formation of German became its own field of research. Even though the actual goal of this project, the compilation of a lexicon of German loan word-formation, could not be realized – only individual studies on foreign morphemes were published (overview in Müller 2005b and 2009b, most recently the papers by Hoppe 2009, 2010) – this research project forms an important base for further investigation. An overview of the state of research up to the year 2005 is provided in Müller (2005b). This volume (Müller 2005a) traces the history of German research on foreign word-formation on the basis of 31 reprinted articles. Among more recently published contributions are the dissertations by Banholzer (2005) on *-(i)tät*, by Eins (2008) on the concept of confix, by Seiffert (2008) on word-formation with numerals, by Heimbecher (2008) on reanalysis and integration of foreign elements as well as by Scheller-Boltz (2010) on the use of "preponemes" (i.e. initial confixes which cannot occur as bases) in German, Russian and Polish. The "Studien zur Fremdwortbildung" [Studies on foreign word-formation] (Müller 2009a) also contain important contributions on problems of morphological analysis (Seiffert 2009), on the concept of confix (Donalies 2009; Eins 2009; Michel 2009; Ronneberger-Sibold 2009), on the analysis of individual confixes such as *phob* (Trunkwalter 2009), *man* (Feine 2009), *drom* (Fließ 2009), *krat* and *naut* (Heimbecher 2009), on the linking element *-s-* in N+N compounds with exogenous determinant (Nübling and Szczepaniak 2009) as well as hybrid formations (Munske 2009). Eisenberg (2012) discusses foreign word-formation in the context of his description of foreign words in German. While research long concentrated on such non-native elements of word-formation as represent the Greco-Latin heritage and are designated as "neoclassical" (Lüdeling, Schmid and Kiokpasoglou 2002) or "Euro-Latin" (Kirkness 1996), there has recently been an increasing interest in "Euro-Anglicisms" (Scott 2007; Barz 2008; Feine 2008; Dargiewicz 2013 on hybrid formations), of which the *Anglizismen-Wörterbuch* (AWB 1993–96) documents a selection.

Even though research on the long neglected area of foreign word-formation is currently making progress, the publications available to date don't yet offer a full and complete picture. There still remain larger differences of opinion regarding the analysis of products of foreign word-formation and the concept of confix (cf. section 3.2), and for numerous bound foreign morphemes – Schmidt (1987: 48) unites these under the general term "Kombineme" [combinemes] (= affixes and confixes) – knowledge about the path by which they were borrowed, about processes of morphological-semantic development, combinatory behavior, radius of use and productivity is still too limited. German is also lacking a specialized dictionary of foreign word-formation as an important research instrument, since even relevant works such as the *Deutsches Fremdwörterbuch* (DFWB 1913–88, ^{2}DFWB 1995 ff.) or the *Anglizismen-Wörterbuch* (AWB 1993–96) offer only a selection of lemmatized borrowed combinemes (affixes, confixes) (cf. Müller 2016). Thus no broad-based comparison with corresponding works in other languages is currently possible (cf. Cottez 1988 for French; Stein 2007 for English) and a "paneuropäische lexikographische Dokumentation eurolateinischer Wortbildungseinheiten" [pan-European lexicographical documentation of Euro-Latin elements of word-formation] (Kirkness 1996: 272) remains a long-term goal.

2 Historical development of foreign word-formation

The historical development of German foreign word-formation mirrors the history of German language contact. For a long time, this was characterized by the dominant influence of Latin as early as the early Middle ages, as well as of French since the 12th century. Other languages such as Italian or Spanish have, since the early modern period, been far less influential and English played virtually no role before the 18th/19th century.

A prerequisite for foreign word-formation is borrowing. Borrowings into German predominantly involve Greco-Latin vocabulary, which partly come from Greek or Latin, but partly also from other European languages (French, Italian and English dominate as contact languages). Also involved are products of foreign word-formation from living foreign languages, which likewise demonstrate the far-reaching Greco-Latin foundation of the languages of Europe. The origin of these words cannot always be unambiguously clarified. Since reciprocal influence and polygenesis can be expected as well, these are then frequently internationalisms with "euromorphemes". Borrowing occurs partly without formal adaptation (Lat. *luxus* > *Luxus* 'luxury'), partly with shortening (Lat. *elementum* > *Element* 'element') or with further morphological integration. From the very beginning, borrowing takes place partly with integrational suffixes which guarantee adaptation to the morphological system of German (cf. Lat. *canin-us* > Old High German *kanin-isc* 'dog-like; lit. doggish'; Lat. *congel-are* > Early New High German *congelieren* 'to freeze; lit. congeal'). As long as such lexemes are morphologically unmotivated within German, they must be viewed as simplex forms. This is, for example, valid for the noun *Stupidität* 'stupidity', which was borrowed from French *stupidité* in the 17th century, and which only secondarily, after the borrowing of the adjective *stupid* 'stupid' in the 18th century, can be grasped from a synchronic perspective as a morphologically-semantically motivated product of word-formation with the suffix *-ität*, albeit – diachronically seen – not as German foreign word-formation, since the formation was not coined in German.

The formal assimilation of loan words, which makes it difficult to discern their origin (cf. Lat. *musica* > *Musik* 'music' with final word stress following Fr. *musique*, Fr. *polémique* > *Polemik* 'polemic'), forms at the same time the foundation for their further use in the context of German foreign word-formation. This is because the products of German foreign word-formation – diachronically understood as the products of word-formation which were created in German from borrowed morphemes – are a consequence of the borrowing of (complex) words, the structural shapes of which could provide a model for the coinage of further lexemes (neologisms). At the same time, two different operations underlie foreign word-formation: the activation of foreign morphemes (lexemes, prefixes, suffixes) as well as morphematization, a process by which foreign lexeme segments acquire the status of morphemes. In the first case, foreign lexemes are made usable for new formations on the basis of foreign words (cf. Lat. *luxus* > *Luxus* 'luxury' → *Luxusartikel* 'luxury article', *Luxusauto* 'luxury car', *Luxusweibchen* 'spoiled woman; lit. luxury female dim.') or foreign affixes (prefixes such as Lat. *re-*: *resozialisieren* 'to resocialize' or suffixes such as Lat. *-ismus: Darwinismus* 'Darwinism'). Whereby morphemes that can occur as words in the contact language often only occur as bound forms in German (cf. Lat. *post* 'after, behind': *postmodern* 'postmodern'). In the second case, the use of foreign word material as a source of elements for word-formation results from a reanalysis. In the process, those components of foreign words generally undergo morphematization which in the language of origin (contact language) do not constitute affixes, but which also have not been adopted as foreign words in German. To the class of corresponding morphemes, which are usually designated as "confixes" in German research on word-formation (cf. section 3.2) and only occur as bound forms, belong, for example, *meter* (in Gr. *métron* 'measure': *Barometer* 'barometer', *Gasometer* 'gasometer', *Thermometer* 'thermometer') and *therm* (in Gr. *thermós* 'warm': *Thermostat* 'thermostat', *thermophil* 'thermophilic', *isotherm* 'isothermal').

The history of German foreign word-formation has not yet been adequately investigated. Thus only for individual foreign morphemes have there been detailed analyses regarding which loan words serve as the model for new formations (key words such as *Anti-Christ* 'Antichrist', *Post-Moderne* 'post-modernism' or *Ex-Jesuit* 'ex-Jesuit'), what productivity quota and what morphological, semantic or pragmatic developmental processes are exhibited. Furthermore, it must be considered that in many cases the delimitation between borrowing and German foreign word-formation proves to be difficult, and indeed is not always possible, not even on the basis of detailed analyses. Even today, the most important resource can be considered to be the *Deutsches Fremdwörterbuch* (DFWB, ²DFWB) and in particular the index volume (with indexes based on regular and reverse spelling, chronology, and origin). Admittedly though, only preliminary conclusions can be based on this work because of its age, since the volumes 1 and 2 (A–P, 1913–1942) clearly fall quantitatively and qualitatively behind the section of the alphabet R–Z, compiled in 1977–1988. Additionally, it must be considered that hybrid formations (cf. section 4) are also counted as "deutsche Fremdwortbildungen" [products of German foreign word-formation] in which native morphemes drive word-formation, which therefore do not belong to the subject area of foreign word-formation (e.g., *ent-nerven* 'to enervate', *Reformier-ung* 'reformation'). Example analyses can be found in several descriptions, for example, in Polenz (1999–2013) or Eisenberg (2012).

Altogether, it appears that only since the early modern period has the phenomenon "deutsche Fremdwortbildung" [German foreign word-formation] led to sustained changes in German word-formation, even though the beginnings lie as early as the early Middle Ages with the foreign suffix *-āri* (< Lat. *-ārius, -ārium,* New High German *-er: Lehr-er* 'teacher'; cf. Müller 2011) and are continued in the 12th/13th century with further suffixes of French or Latin origin (*-ier-*: NHG *add-ier-en* 'to add up sth.', *-ier*: NHG *Bank-ier* 'banker', *-(er)īe*: NHG *Lauf-erei* 'running around', *-lei*: NHG *vieler-lei* 'all kinds of') (cf. the papers by Öhmann in Müller 2005a). Only between 1500 and 1800 did the deciding change occur, which transformed German word-formation in the long term (see article 15 on historical word-formation in German). While only sporadic instances of foreign suffixes can be found during the beginning of the modern period, their occurrence increases rapidly during the following three centuries and around 1800 they are used on a par with native affixes. Humanism, the courtly culture of the Baroque, and the Enlightenment bring about an extensive attachment to Greco-Latin (Neo-Latin) or French bases of borrowing and thus create requirements for their further effects in the framework of German foreign word-formation. Thus, according to an evaluation by Polenz (1999–2013 Vol. 2: 102), "until 1350 only 18, by 1500 a further 68, by 1600 a further 216, by 1700 a further 266, by 1800 a further 596 products of German loan word-formation" (English translation) are recorded in the chronological index of the *Deutsches Fremdwörterbuch* (DFWB), and "the 'foreign words' first attested in the 19th and 20th centuries are for the most part loan word-formations with the index marking 'G'" (English translation). While the use of the verbal suffix *-ier-* as well as nominal suffixes for the designation of persons (e.g., *-ist*, *-ant*) are already on the increase in the 17th century, only since about 1700 does an initial rise in the use of adjectival suffixes ensue (*-abel*/*-ibel*, *-al*/*-ell*, *-ant*/*-ent*, *-är*/*-ar*, *-iv*, *-ös*/*-os*). At the end of the 18th century first outlines of foreign word-formation with confixes appear (e.g., *graph*, *log*, *meter*, *phil*, *therm*) as well as a gradual increase in foreign prefixes of Euro-Latin origin (cf. Polenz 1999–2013 Vol. 3: 396): *anti-*, *de(s)-*, *ex-*, *extra-*, *hyper-*, *in-*, *inter-*, *para-*, *post-*, *prä-*, *pseudo-*, *re-*, *sub-*, *trans-*, *ultra-*. In the 19th and 20th century further confixes (*audio*, *bio*, *geo*, *öko*, *phon*, *tele*, *thek*, *video*, etc.) and prefixes (for example the augmentative prefixes *mega-* und *super-*) are added (examples for the use of all these combinemes in section 3.2). "Chronologically [...], the majority of the Latin borrowings are situated in the 16th/17th centuries, the French borrowings in the 17th/18th centuries, the products of German loan word-formation in the late 18th, 19th and 20th centuries" (Polenz 1999–2013 Vol. 2: 104; English translation). This finding reflects as well the emancipation of German as a language of science, together with its gradual replacement of the humanistic Neo-Latin as a scholarly lingua franca.

The relationship between borrowing and German foreign word-formation is quantitatively and qualitatively developed to very different degrees and also associated with considerable divergence in their chronological order, so that generalizations are hardly possible. The examples *-thek* and *ex-* shall make this clear (cf. Hoppe 1999, 2000):

The confix *-thek* can initially be attested in the 16th century in Greco-Latin loan words (1511 *Bibliothek* 'library', 1548 *Pinakothek* 'pinacotheca'). Only much later – beginning in the early 19th century – was it sporadically used in products of German word-formation: 1816 *Glyptothek* 'glyptotheque', 1905 *Kartothek* 'place of a collection of index cards', 1927 *Pianothek* 'place of a collection of pianos'. But as a productive foreign morpheme, *-thek* has only recently been documented – since the 60s of the 20th century – the numerous new formations diverging with regard to currency, connotation and radius of use, e.g., 1960 *Filmothek* 'film library', *Phonothek* 'place of a collection of phonograph records', 1975 *Hobbythek* 'place of a collection related to a hobby', 1981 *Spielothek* 'place of a selection of games', 1988 *Quatschothek* 'place where one can chat', *Salatothek* 'place of a selection of salads', 1994 *Puffothek* 'brothel', *Schnapsothek* 'place where one can drink/buy schnaps'.

Another picture arises, on the other hand, with the foreign prefix *ex-* 'former': Initially, it is only sporadically documented in Neo-Latin loan words (e.g., 1746 *Excalvinist* 'ex-Calvinist'), but then very soon undergoes, originating with the key word *Exjesuit* 'ex-Jesuit' (coined in 1773 in the context of the dissolution of the Jesuit order) an increase in productivity and is documented, still in the 18th century, in many new formations with exogenous or native bases (*Exgeneral* 'ex-general', *Exminister* 'ex-minister', *Exnonne* 'ex-nun', *Exschuster* 'ex-shoemaker', *Exfrau* 'ex-wife', *Exnachtwächter* 'ex-night-watchman', etc.). This productivity has been preserved until today, when *ex-* is used more and more as a free morpheme (e.g., *mein Ex* = 'ex-boy, ex-husband, ex-lover, ex-partner, etc.').

In contrast to words formed with *-thek* and *ex-*, which make clear the productivity of both combinemes, there are also patterns of word-formation, which display no or only very limited activity in the context of word-formation in German. They are components of loan words which can be morphologically-semantically motivated in German via related words and are thus analyzable. Among these are quite a few of the prefixes and suffixes which have been assembled in section 3.2 such as *-and* (*Habilitand* 'person qualifying as a university lecturer') or *-esse* (*Baronesse* 'baroness'), which can usually only be attested in a few formations and probably also for this reason remain inactive with respect to word-formation. With regard to the quantitative proportion of both groups of morphemes, the observation by Munske (2009: 247) is doubtlessly accurate, that the "Zahl der auch im Deutschen motivierten Entlehnungen (im Sinne analysierbarer Muster) [...] um ein Vielfaches höher [ist] als die der produktiv im Deutschen entstandenen Lehnwortbildungen" [number of borrowed forms which are also motivated in German (in the sense of an analyzable pattern) [...] is many times higher than the number of loan words formed productively in German]. I will return to this in the context of the synopsis of bound foreign morphemes in German (cf. section 3.2).

3 Principles of foreign word-formation

Even if native and non-native word-formation in German partially bear isonomic traits, interact and, in the framework of hybrid word-formation, converge (cf. section 4), foreign word-formation exhibits multiple particularities which lead to questions and problems. These concern the domain of study, the terminology, the status and the categorization of non-native elements of word-formation as well as the potential for modeling foreign word-formation and types of word-formation. I will elaborate on these aspects in the following.

3.1 Synchronic vs. diachronic perspective

The domain of foreign word-formation encompasses all morphemes which are not assimilated in terms of form, that is which show phonological, graphematic or morphological foreign features and in particular are combined with foreign morphemes. As this does not apply to borrowed, but assimilated, word-formation morphemes such as *-er* (< Lat. *-ārius*, e.g., *Lehr-er* 'teacher') or *erz-* (< Late Latin *archi-*, e.g., *Erz-Bischof* 'archbishop'), they also do not belong to the domain of research on foreign word-formation oriented towards the contemporary language. This speaks against the term *Lehnwortbildung* [loan word-formation] which is used alongside *Fremdwortbildung* [foreign word-formation], and whose proponents – in my opinion without foundation – reject the term *Fremdwortbildung* [foreign word-formation] as a "stigmatisierenden Begriff" [stigmatizing term] through which "aus Gründen der fachsprachlichen Plausibilität eine unselige puristische Tradition wiederbelebt [wird]" [for reasons of plausibility of technical vocabulary an unfortunate puristic tradition [is] revived] (Munske 2009: 251).

If one considers foreign word-formation under synchronic or diachronic aspects, then differences in the domain of research on foreign word-formation ensue, which will be illustrated on the basis of formations with the foreign suffix *-(i)tät* in (1):

(1) *-(i)tät* in loan words and products of foreign word-formation
  a. *Rigorosität* 'rigorousness; lit. rigorosity', *Synonymität* 'synonymy', *Vertikalität* 'verticality'
  b. *Laszivität* 'lascivity', *Naivität* 'naivety', *Neutralität* 'neutrality'
  c. *Gravität* 'gravity', *Kapazität* 'capacity', *Pietät* 'piety'

According to the *Deutsches Fremdwörterbuch* (DFWB 7: 416–418) this series of examples involves lexemes, some of which were formed in German (a), others borrowed from other languages (b, c). From a diachronic perspective, only those lexemes which were formed in German belong to the domain of German foreign word-formation, that is *Rigorosität* 'rigorousness; lit. rigorosity' (← *rigoros* 'rigorous'), *Synonymität* 'synonymy' (← *synonym* 'synonymous') and *Vertikalität* 'verticality' (← *vertikal* 'vertical'). The crucial opposition is then: borrowed vs. formed in German. From a synchronic perspective, on the other hand, the domain of German research on foreign word-formation has been interpreted more broadly, as in principle all formations are taken into account which can be motivated at a particular time by word-formation bases, that is also those which were borrowed but are analyzable within the word-formation system of German. This is the case for the lexemes in (b), which were borrowed from Latin/French, but are also motivated in German through the (equally borrowed) adjectives (*lasziv* 'lascive', *naiv* 'naive', *neutral* 'neutral') and are thus classifiable as derivatives with *-ität* (quality nouns). In the descriptions of German (foreign) word-formation, the use of foreign affixes and confixes has been documented precisely on the basis of examples from this group (and not from group a). This is in contrast to borrowings such as the lexemes in (c), as they are not motivated by a word-formation base in German, but only in the language of origin, Latin (*Gravität* 'gravity' < *gravitas* ← *gravis*, *Kapazität* 'capacity' < *capacitas* ← *capax*, *Pietät* 'piety' < *pietas* ← *pius*). A result of this generally practiced procedure is that, for example, the inventory of foreign affixes in the contemporary language includes on the one hand those affixes which occur in analyzable formations but are not productive, and on the other hand those which are productively used in German foreign word-formation and thus serve as models (cf. section 3.2). The determining factor is thus not the diachronic criterion "formed in German" (and not borrowed), but rather the synchronic criterion of morphosemantic motivation (relation to a base, morpheme status of a word's components).

3.2 Elements and types of foreign word-formation

Besides foreign morphemes which can occur as words such as the noun *Ruin* 'ruin' or the adjective *real* 'real', prefixes (*a-sozial* 'asocial', *ir-real* 'irreal') and suffixes (*Marx-ist* 'Marxist', *verbal-isier-en* 'to verbalize'), research in German word-formation has introduced the morpheme category "confix" (Konfix), the definition of which, and its differentiation from affixes are, however, associated with an ensemble of problems. This term was introduced by Schmidt (1987) following a French model, who uses it to differentiate bound morphemes such as *therm-*/*-therm* (e.g., *therm-al* 'thermal', *iso-therm* 'isothermal') from affixes according to the criteria "ability to function as a base" (Basisfähigkeit) or "ability to function as an element of a compound" (Kompositionsgliedfähigkeit). This is, however, in many cases not so easily possible, which is the reason why a good number of publications dealing with the concept of "confix" have in the meantime become available (cf. Eins 2008 as well as corresponding papers in Müller 2005a or 2009a).

As a general rule, the criteria "being bound" (Gebundenheit) (in contrast to free morphemes) as well as "lexical-conceptual meaning" (lexikalisch-begriffliche Bedeutung) (in contrast to affixes) are seen as being particularly relevant, but precisely the semantic differentiation from affixes poses problems, so that elements of word-formation such as *auto-* (e.g., *Auto-krat* 'autocrat'), *mikro-* (e.g., *Mikro-skop* 'microscope'), *mono-* (e.g., *mono-gam* 'monogamous'), *neo-* (e.g., *neo-klassisch* 'neoclassical') and *pseudo-* (e.g., *Pseudo-Kritik* 'pseudocriticism') are sometimes classified as prefixes, sometimes as confixes (i.e. bound bases). And *-itis*, which is customarily classified as a "suffix" (e.g., *Gastr-itis* 'gastritis', *Hepa-t-itis* 'hepatitis'), would be interpretable as a "confix" because of its meaning 'inflammation'.

A valid criterion of differentiation between "affix" and "confix" can initially be the fact that only confixes can occur both initially (= preconfix) and terminally (= postconfix), which however only applies to relatively few confixes such as *therm* (see above), *phob* (e.g., *Phob-ie* 'phobia', *hydr-o-phob* 'hydrophobic') or *phil* (e.g., *Phil-o-soph* 'philosopher', *biblio-phil* 'bibliophile' – here *-o* functions as a fixed preconfix component). The criterion "ability to function as a base" also leads – at least according to a broad concept of confix (see below) – to a morpheme category "confix" (e.g., *psych-isch* 'psychic, psychological', *Polem-ik* 'polemic'), but this feature also does not apply to all "confixes". A further distributional criterion which presents itself is the ability to combine with other confixes, which as a rule is not possible for prefixes. It therefore follows that bound pre-elements, which are combined with a postconfix, are not prefixes, but rather preconfixes (e.g., *Mikro-skop* 'microscope'). Thus also *mega-* would be a confix, as it combines with other confixes as in *Mega-lith* ('megalith, a large block of stone from prehistoric tombs'). In words such as *mega-cool* ('especially cool') or *mega-schlau* ('especially clever'), *mega-* is used augmentatively however, and thus fulfills a typical function of prefixes, but in which it doesn't combine with postconfixes, so that in this case one could postulate two foreign morphemes for semantic as well as distributional reasons. At least at the edges, the concept of confix remains blurry, which is true in the same way for its English counterpart "combining form" (cf. Kastovsky 2009).

Differentiating between postconfixes and suffixes is, on the other hand, not distributionally possible. One could accordingly dispense with the category "confix" and consistently classify elements such as *-ik* (e.g., *Therm-ik* 'thermal') and *-phil* (e.g., *therm-o-phil* 'thermophilic') as suffixes (terminal bound morphemes) in the context of a foreign word-formation type "affix combination" (Affixkombination) (cf. Müller 2000: 127–129) – understood as a "combination of bound morphemes". (Also the distinction between preconfixes and prefixes would be unnecessary if one were to dispense with semantic or distributional criteria; *thermophil* 'thermophilic' would thus be a prefix-suffix combination.) If one wishes to retain a differentiation between both morpheme categories, then only semantics remain as a deciding criterion: If a terminal bound foreign morpheme displays functions typical of affixes (cf. section 3.2), then it is a "suffix", otherwise a "postconfix". Accordingly, elements such as *-itis* (medical: 'inflammation', e.g., *Hepatitis* 'hepatitis, inflammation of the liver'; non-medical: 'exaggerated behavior perceived as sick', e.g., *Computeritis* 'computeritis, exaggerated usage of a computer, perceived as sick') or *-ose* ('illness'; e.g., *Psychose* 'psychosis, mental illness') would however also be confixes, despite their etymology as Greek suffixes.

A further problem with respect to the morpheme status of exogenous elements of word-formation stems from the fact that some bound foreign morphemes are increasingly used as free morphemes (lexemes). Such a – perhaps temporary – process of degrammaticalization, which is not characteristic for the native domain (here only processes of grammaticalization (lexeme > affix) usually occur), has already been lexicographically documented for morphemes such as *video*, *top*, *super*, *ex* and *mini*. In other cases, such as *neo* or *pseudo*, at least occasionalisms show that the morpheme status of foreign elements of word-formation is not a stable dimension and synchronic findings in foreign word-formation represent snapshots even more than in the native domain. Whether the product of degrammaticalization is a change in the morpheme category (combineme > lexeme) or whether a morpheme split results from this (combineme vs. lexeme), can only be decided semantically, and yet here differences between free and bound usage often become apparent. Two examples of this: *top* is used as a prefix in augmentative function ('very, to a high degree'; e.g., *top-aktuell* 'very current', *top-modisch* 'very fashionable'), but as an adjective it has in contrast the meaning 'first class, outstanding' (e.g., *Diese Leistung ist top* 'This performance is outstanding'). And *extra* also exhibits different meanings: As a prefix it performs a spatial function in technical terminology ('outside'; e.g., *extra-zellulär* 'extracellular', *extra-mental* 'extramental'), in general language it is augmentative ('very, exceedingly'; e.g., *extra-kommunikativ* 'very communicative'), but is also used as a polysemous lexeme: 'separated from others', e.g., *etwas extra einpacken* 'to pack something separately'; 'more than the usual', e.g., *Dies kostet extra* 'This costs more than usual'; 'only for a particular purpose', e.g., *Dies ist extra für dich* 'This is only for you'.

On the basis of the above categorization of foreign morphemes, the following models of composition (2) and derivation (3) result for foreign word-formation in German:

(2) Composition
  a. lexeme (stem) + lexeme (stem): *Luxus-Suite* 'luxury suite'
  b. confix + lexeme (stem): *Bio-Gas* 'biogas'
  c. lexeme (stem) + confix: *Kosm-o-naut* 'cosmonaut'
  d. confix + confix: *therm-o-phil* 'thermophilic'

(3) Derivation
   a. prefix + lexeme (stem): *in-aktiv* 'inactive'
   b. lexeme (stem) + suffix: *Hotel-ier* 'hotel keeper'
   c. confix + suffix: *Polem-ik* 'polemic'

According to this combinatorial analysis, German foreign word-formation exhibits both confix compounds (2b–d) and confix derivatives (3c). In the case of a narrower concept of confix, such as the one supported by Eisenberg (2012: 310), there are in contrast only confix compounds as the "confix" is seen here as a "morphologische Einheit, die als Erstglied eines Kompositums mit Fugenelement oder als Zweitglied eines Kompositums auftritt und kein Stamm ist" [morphological element which appears as the first member of a compound with a linking element or as the second member of a compound and is not a stem]. On this view, neither *therm* (e.g., *therm-isch* 'thermic') nor *graph* (e.g., *Graph-ie* 'spelling') and *naut* (e.g., *naut-isch* 'nautical') are confixes, since these elements are seen as bound stems based on their combinability with affixes. Accordingly, confixes are also ruled out in the case of anglicisms, since no linking elements occur here. Correspondingly, the combineme *allround* (e.g., *Allround-Talent* 'all-round talent', *Allround-Manager* 'all-round manager') is also a "bound stem".

In the following I will present, on the basis of a broad concept of confix, an overview of the central combinemes of foreign word-formation in contemporary German. The affixes are grouped by word class, the confixes according to their status as initial and/or terminal elements of word-formation. There is, as stated, no consensus regarding the classification of particular morphemes as "affix" or "confix". For the following classification, the criteria named above are decisive. Only combinemes are taken into consideration which have a certain relevance for the general language, whereby here as well the demarcation is difficult.

(4) Foreign prefixes
   a. Nouns:
      a-/an- (*Amoral* 'amorality'), *anti-* (*Antithese* 'antithesis'), *bi-* (*Bimetall* 'bimetallic strip'), *de-/des-* (*Desinteresse* 'disinterest'), *dis-* (*Disharmonie* 'disharmony'), *ex-* (*Ex-Monarch* 'ex-monarch'), *hyper-* (*Hyperproduktion* 'hyper-production'), *inter-* (*Interdisziplin* 'interdiscipline'), *ko-/kol-/kom-/kon-/kor-* (*Koautor* 'co-author'), *mega-* (*Mega-Hit* 'mega-hit'), *meta-* (*Metakommunikation* 'meta-communication'), *non-* (*Nonexistenz* 'nonexistence'), *pan-* (*Paneuropa* 'Pan-Europe'), *post-* (*Postmaterialismus* 'post-materialism'), *prä-* (*Präexistenz* 'pre-existence'), *pro-* (*Prorektor* 'prorector'), *re-* (*Reimport* 're-import'), *semi-* (*Semifinale* 'semifinal'), *sub-* (*Subkultur* 'subculture'), *super-* (*Supertalent* 'supertalent'), *supra-* (*Suprasystem* 'suprasys-

tem'), *top-* (*Topagent* 'top agent'), *trans-* (*Transaktion* 'transaction'), *ultra-* (*Ultrafaschist* 'ultra-fascist'), *vize-* (*Vizepräsident* 'vice president')

b. Adjectives:
a-/an- (*asozial* 'asocial'), *anti-* (*antiliberal* 'anti-liberal'), *bi-* (*bilateral* 'bilateral'), *de-/des-* (*dezentral* 'de-central'), *dis-* (*disproportional* 'disproportional'), *ex-* (*exradikal* 'ex-radical'), *extra-* (*extrakommunikativ* 'extra-communicative'), *hyper-* (*hypernervös* 'hyper-nervous'), *in-/il-/im-/ir-* (*irregulär* 'irregular'), *inter-* (*interaktiv* 'interactive'), *intra-* (*intrafamiliär* 'intrafamilial'), *mega-* (*megacool* 'mega-cool'), *meta-* (*metakommunikativ* 'meta-communicative'), *non-* (*nonverbal* 'non-verbal'), *pan-* (*panarabisch* 'pan-Arabic'), *post-* (*postpubertär* 'post-pubescent'), *prä-* (*pränatal* 'prenatal'), *pro-* (*proenglisch* 'pro-English'), *semi-* (*semiprofessionell* 'semi-professional'), *sub-* (*subnormal* 'subnormal'), *super-* (*superintelligent* 'superintelligent'), *supra-* (*supranational* 'supranational'), *top-* (*topaktuell* 'cutting-edge'), *trans-* (*transsexuell* 'transsexual'), *ultra-* (*ultrakonservativ* 'ultraconservative')

c. Verbs:
de-/des- (*deaktivieren* 'to deactivate'), *dis-* (*disqualifizieren* 'to disqualify'), *in-* (*inaktivieren* 'to inactivate'), *ko-/kol-/kom-/kon-/kor-* (*koexistieren* 'to co-exist'), *re-* (*resozialisieren* 'to resocialize')

As this overview shows, numerous prefixes are used across word classes for the modification of base nouns, adjectives and verbs. The degree of productivity of foreign prefixes is – and this is also true for suffixes and confixes (see below) – not always easy to determine. It can stay stable over a longer period of time, but can also be subject to fluctuations which are reflected in the proliferation or decline of neologisms and in extreme cases can lead to inactivity. Other foreign morphemes have, in contrast, never developed an appreciable productivity. They are analyzable within the framework of products of foreign word-formation which are motivated in German, but do not serve as models for new formations. The at times very specific links to particular text types which can be observed in foreign morphemes with a preference for texts from (special) branches of science or for journalistic texts must also be taken into consideration. A disparate picture results for foreign prefixes which range from elements which are inactive or only sporadically used for new formations to significantly productive elements. These include the prefixes *anti-*, *ex-*, *mega-*, *super-* and *top-*, whereby word-class-specific differences result as in the case of *ex-*, which in the meaning 'former' of the general language is only productive with nouns, and not with adjectives.

From a semantic perspective, the foreign prefixes can essentially be assigned to the categories 'negation' (*a-/an-*, *de-/des-*, *dis-*, *in-/il-/im-/ir-*, *non-*), 'augmentation' (*extra-*, *hyper-*, *mega-*, *super-*, *top-*, *ultra-*), 'temporal relation' (*ex-*, *post-*, *prä-*, *re-*), 'spatial relation' (*meta-*, *extra-*, *inter-*, *intra-*, *pan-*, *sub-*, *supra-*, *trans-*) and 'quantification' (*bi-*). Beside these groups we find the prefixes *anti-* ('against'), *ko-/kol-/kom-/kon-/kor-* ('together with'), *pro-* ('instead of'), *semi-* ('half') und *vize-* ('deputy'). Not only quantitatively, but also qualitatively, differences thus ensue compared to the small group of native prefixes, in which augmentation plays a much lesser role – this function being filled primarily by prefixoids (e.g., *mords-*: *Mordshunger* 'very great hunger; lit. murder-hunger'; *sau-*: *saukalt* 'very cold; lit. sow-cold'; *tod-*: *todtraurig* 'very sad; lit. death-sad') – and functions of spatio-temporal modification are lacking.

(5) Foreign suffixes

a. Nouns:

-ade (*Robinsonade* 'robinsonade'), *-age* (*Kartonage* 'cardboard packaging'), *-aille* (*Journaille* 'journalists who conduct smear campaigns with their articles'), *-alien* (*Archivalien* 'documents in/from an archive'), *-ament/-ement* (*Bombardement* 'bombardment'), *-and/-end* (*Doktorand* 'doctoral candidate'), *-aner* (*Afrikaner* 'African'), *-ant/-ent* (*Fabrikant* 'factory owner'), *-anz/-enz* (*Dominanz* 'dominance'), *-ar/-är* (*Revolutuionär* 'revolutionary'), *-arium* (*Planetarium* 'planetarium'), *-at* (*Konsulat* 'consulate'), *-ee* (*Resümee* 'résumé'), *-ese/-iese* (*Vietnamese* 'Vietnamese'), *-ess* (*Stewardess* 'stewardess'), *-esse* (*Delikatesse* 'delicacy'), *-ette* (*Operette* 'operetta'), *-erie* (*Galanterie* 'gallantry'), *-eur* (*Boykotteur* 'boycotter'), *-euse* (*Friseuse* 'hair dresser'), *-ie* (*Aristokratie* 'aristocracy'), *-ine* (*Blondine* 'blonde'), *-ing* (*Coaching* 'coaching'), *-ier* (*Bankier* 'banker'), *-iere* (*Garderobiere* '(female) dresser'), *-ik* (*Problematik* 'difficulty'), *-iker* (*Alkoholiker* 'alcoholic'), *-ion* (*Diskretion* 'discretion'), *-ismus* (*Aktivismus* 'activism'), *-ist* (*Terrorist* 'terrorist'), *-it* (*Israelit* 'Isrealite'), *-ität* (*Banalität* 'banality'), *-ness* (*Fairness* 'fairness'), *-or* (*Illustrator* 'illustrator'), *-ur* (*Architektur* 'architecture')

b. Adjectives:

-abel/-ibel (*diskutabel* 'debateable; lit. discussable'), *-al/-ell* (*regional* 'regional'), *-ant/-ent* (*charmant* 'charming'), *-ar/-är* (*atomar* 'atomic'), *-esk* (*clownesk* 'clownish'), *-iv* (*instinktiv* 'instinctive'), *-oid* (*faschistoid* 'fascistic'), *-os/-ös* (*medikamentös* 'medicinal')

c. Verbs:

-ier- (*asphaltieren* 'to asphalt'), *-ifizier-* (*personifizieren* 'to personify'), *-isier-* (*stabilisieren* 'to stabilize')

Just as in the area of native word-formation, it is also the case in foreign word-formation in German that the proportion of nominal suffixes is considerably higher than of adjectival and especially verbal suffixes. Unlike prefixes, suffixes are not only combinable with lexemes, but also with confixes, which can lead to problems and varying solutions with respect to assumed motivating bases (cf. section 3.3). From a semantic perspective, as in the case of prefixes, monosemic suffixes such as *-oid* ('similar', e.g., *faschistoid* 'fascistic', *snoboid* 'snobby', *grippoid* 'influenzal', i.e. 'behavior or illness, which is similar to a fascist/snob or influenza') must be differentiated from polysemous suffixes. Thus derivatives with *-or* designate both agent nouns (e.g., *Illustrator* 'somebody who illustrates something') as well as instrument nouns (e.g., *Isolator* 'substance, with which one insulates something').

The word-formation meanings of foreign suffixes generally correspond to those of the native domain. Among the nouns we find personal nouns (e.g., agent nouns such as *Kompon-ist* 'composer'), place nouns (e.g., *Konsul-at* 'consulate'), status nouns (e.g., *Monarch-ie* 'monarchy'), quality nouns (e.g., *Naiv-ität* 'naivety'), action nouns (e.g., *Mass-age* 'massage'), result nouns (e.g., *Filtr-at* 'filtrate'), instrument nouns (e.g., *Gener-ator* 'generator'), gender marking (e.g., *Baron-esse* 'baroness'), collective nouns (e.g., *Archiv-alien* 'documents in/from an archive') and diminutive nouns (e.g., *Oper-ette* 'operetta'). In the domain of adjectives, relational adjectives motivated by base nouns (e.g., *region-al* 'concerning the region'), comparative adjectives (e.g., *clown-esk* 'like a clown') and ornative adjectives (e.g., *charm-ant* 'furnished with charm') dominate as well as derivatives motivated by verbs with a passive-modal meaning (e.g., *diskut-abel* 'can be discussed'). The verbal suffixes *-ier-*, *-ifizier-* and *-isier-*, to some extent seen as allomorphs, prove to be decidedly polysemous. Among the formations motivated by nouns, we find especially ornative verbs (e.g., *asphalt-ier-en* 'to asphalt'), factitive verbs (e.g., *pulver-isier-en* 'to turn into powder') and agentive verbs (e.g., *spion-ier-en* 'to work as a spy'). Derivatives motivated by adjectives are usually factitive verbs (e.g., *legal-isier-en* 'to make legal'). When verbs are formed from confixes, then *-ier-*, *-ifizier-* and *-isier-* are, as verbalizers, inherent parts of such formations (e.g., *stud-ier-en* 'to study', *elektr-ifizier-en* 'to electrify', *polit-isier-en* 'to politicize'). The suffix *-ier-*, though, functions not only as a derivational suffix, but has also been used since the 12th century as an integrational suffix, which incorporates foreign verbs into the German inflectional system. Not all of these verbs constitute products of word-formation which are motivated in German (e.g., *edieren* 'to edit, to publish books' < Lat. *edere* 'to put forth' ← *ex* + *dare*).

Great differences in productivity result in the case of foreign suffixes as well, and here too it is the case that the majority of suffixes are not significantly productive. The inventory of lexemes is to some extent very limited, and apart from borrowed, but synchronically motivated formations, hardly any neologisms are documented. Among the exceptions are the nominal suffixes *-ismus*, *-ist*, *-ität* und *-ion*, adjectival *-abel* as well as verbal *-isier-*.

Most affixes belong to the Greco-Latin heritage of German, which in some cases was transmitted via relay languages (French, Italian, English). Only a few morphemes of word-formation are of French (*-ade*, *-age*, *-ee*, *-esse*, *-ette*, *-eur*, *-euse*, *-ier*), Italian (*-esk*) or English (*-ing*, *-ness*) origin.

(6) Confixes

a. Preconfixes/Postconfixes:

drom-/*-drom* (*Dromomanie* 'pathological urge to wander', *Hippodrom* 'riding arena'), *graph-*/*-graph* (*Telegraph* 'telegraph', *Graphologe* 'graphologist'), *log-*/*-log* (*Logik* 'logic', *Monolog* 'monologue'), *man-*/*-man* (*Manie* 'mania', *monoman* 'monomaniacal'), *naut-*/*-naut* (*Nautik* 'nautics', *Astronaut* 'astronaut'), *phil-*/*-phil* (*Philosoph* 'philosopher', *bibliophil* 'bibliophile'), *phob-*/*-phob* (*Phobie* 'phobia', *anglophob* 'anglophobe'), *phon-*/*-phon* (*Phonograph* 'device for recording tones', *anglophon* 'anglophone'), *therm-*/*-therm* (*thermophil* 'thermophilic', *isotherm* 'having the same temperature')

b. Preconfixes:

aero- (*Aeronaut* 'aeronaut'), *agrar-* (*Agrarhandel* 'agricultural trade'), *allround-* (*Allround-Talent* 'all-round talent'), *astro-* (*Astronaut* 'astronaut'), *audio-* (*Audiometer* 'device for measuring the ability to hear'), *auto-* (*autonom* 'autonomous'), *bio-* (*Biotop* 'habitat characterized by particular plants/animals'), *biblio-* (*Bibliothek* 'library'), *chem-* (*Chemie* 'chemistry'), *cyber-* (*Cybernaut* 'someone who is currently in an illusory world created by computers'), *elektr-* (*elektrifizieren* 'to electrify'), *euro-* (*Eurokrat* 'politician who advocates for the interests of the European Union'), *fanat-* (*Fanatiker* 'fanatic'), *gastr(o)-* (*Gastronom* 'gastronomer'), *geo-* (*Geologe* 'geologist'), *hetero-* (*heterogen* 'heterogeneous'), *homo-* (*homogen* 'homogeneous'), *hydr(o)-* (*Hydroskop* 'water meter'), *makro-* (*Makroglossie* 'enlargement of the tongue'), *mechan-* (*Mechanismus* 'mechanism'), *mikro-* (*Mikroskop* 'microscope'), *mono-* (*monogam* 'monogamous'), *mont-* (*Monteur* 'fitter, mechanic, electrician'), *multi-* (*Multitalent* 'versatile person'), *neo-* (*Neologismus* 'neologism'), *öko-* (*Ökonom* 'economist'), *optim-* (*Optimist* 'optimist'), *polem-* (*Polemik* 'polemic'), *polit-* (*Politik* 'politics'), *poly-* (*polygam* 'polygamous'), *pseudo-* (*Pseudonym* 'pseudonym'), *psych(o)-* (*Psychopath* 'psychopath'), *retro-* (*retrophil* 'having a preference for things from a bygone era'), *tele-* (*Telekratie* 'excessive influence of television'), *techn-* (*Technik* 'technology')

c. Postconfixes:
-a/-oholic (*Smartaholic* 'person who is addicted to the Smart Car'), *-gate* (*Kofigate* 'political scandal relating to the UN General Secretary *Kofi* Annan'), *-gen* (*telegen* 'telegenic'), *-ical* (*Jazzical* 'an effective work (performance, film) which targets the emotions, for which *Jazz* is characteristic'), *-itis* (*Computeritis* 'excessive use of a *computer*, experienced as pathological'), *-krat* (*Demokrat* 'democrat'), *-kratie* (*Expertokratie* 'rule by experts'), *-lekt* (*Soziolekt* 'sociolect'), *-mat* (*Automat* 'machine'), *-meter* (*Thermometer* 'thermometer'), *-nom* (*autonom* 'autonomous'), *-nym* (*Pseudonym* 'pseudonym'), *-ose* (*Psychose* 'mental illness'), *-skop* (*Teleskop* 'telescope'), *-thek* (*Videothek* 'video store')

Unlike affixes, in the case of confixes it is impossible to even come close to reaching completeness. The compilation in (6) offers a selection of confixes, oriented towards descriptions of word-formation, to which a certain importance in the general language is attached. The overview is subdivided according to distributional criteria: Confixes of group (a) occur both initially (bound to the right) as preconfixes – bound to lexemes, postconfixes or suffixes – as well as terminally (bound to the left) as postconfixes, combined with lexemes or preconfixes. Confixes of group (b) occur only initially (preconfixes), those of group (c) only terminally (postconfixes). The overview shows that preconfixes clearly predominate with respect to postconfixes, which is perhaps related to their wider radius of action (also combining with affixes). The parallels with respect to native word-formation are also greater, in which the combination "base + suffix" is indeed encountered, but to which the terminal usage of bound base morphemes is alien. While preconfixes are in many cases applicable across word classes (e.g., *Thermometer* 'thermometer', *thermal* 'thermal'; *Bibliothek* 'library', *bibliophil* 'bibliophile'), only a few postconfixes are documented which constitute nouns and adjectives (e.g., *Pseudonym* 'pseudonym', *antonym* 'antonymous').

Confixes behave differently with respect to their ability to combine with other items: Some can only function as members of compounds and combine with other confixes or lexemes (e.g., *astro-*: *Astronaut* 'astronaut', *Astro-Show* 'astro show'), others can function as members of compounds and as bases (e.g., *techn-*: *Technik* 'technology', *Technokrat* 'technocrat') and some can only function as bases, and thus combine neither with confixes nor with lexemes, but rather only with suffixes (e.g., *polem-*: *polemisch* 'polemical', *Polemik* 'polemic', *polemisieren* 'to polemicize', *Polemiker* 'polemicist'). The analysis of this last group as products of word-formation via confixes is however controversial, as here both a stem-based as well as a word-based analysis is possible, so that confixes must not necessarily be assumed as bases, but rather lexemes can also be seen as bases of word-formation (e.g., *Polemik*: 'polemical attitude/position'). I will elaborate on this aspect in section 3.3.

In the case of confixes as well, which in their majority embody the Greco-Latin heritage of German, a difference in productivity can be attested: Here as well, the spectrum ranges from elements which in the context of the German system of foreign word-formation are not or only marginally used for new formations, despite their status as morphemes, to productive elements such as *bio-*, *cyber-*, *euro-*, *öko-*, *retro-* or *tele-*, which are in vogue and in some cases have developed a considerable degree of activity in word-formation. This is not (yet) the case for the more recent anglicisms *-a/-oholic*, *allround-*, *-gate* and *-ical*, but nevertheless these confixes are used for neologisms. Several are distilled out of source words (E. *alcoholic*, *watergate*, *musical*) as splinters (just as in the case of *cyber-* from *cybernetics* 'cybernetics'). They function as confixes because they exhibit an individual meaning which is atypical of affixes.

Besides compounding and derivation, foreign word-formation also has a share in further types of word-formation. These include conversion (e.g., *Google* → *googlen/googeln* 'to google', *E-Mail* 'email' → *emailen* 'to email', *scannen* 'to scan' → *das Scannen* 'the scanning'), backformation (e.g., *Powerwalking* 'power walking' → *powerwalken* 'to power walk', *Windsurfing* 'wind surfing' → *windsurfen* 'to windsurf'), blending (e.g., *Magalog* 'journal which is a mix of magazine and catalogue', *Bistrorant* 'public house which is a mix of bistro and restaurant'), formation of short forms (e.g., *Homo* 'homo' ← *Homosexueller* 'homosexual', *inlinen* 'to inline' ← *inlineskaten* 'to inline skate') and word-creation. The focus of this is in the domain of such (international) company and brand names which do not have parts that can be (clearly) etymologically analyzed, so that they must be classified as morphologically unmotivated (e.g., *Elmex* 'toothpaste', *Biskin* 'frying oil', *Exxon* 'mineral oil').

3.3 Problems of morphological analysis

Beside the inconsistent classification of confixes and the demarcation between confixes and affixes, which has an effect on the classification of products of foreign word-formation (cf. section 3.2), the morphological analysis of products of foreign word-formation also causes problems which lead to different approaches towards solutions. This is the case for the question of motivation via bases of word-formation as well as the demarcation of the components of word-formation "base lexeme/confix", "linking element" and "affix/confix".

A first point concerns the relation to a base of products of foreign word-formation of the combination "confix + suffix" (e.g., *Polem-ik* 'polemic'). Here, there are two suggested solutions, depending on whether one prefers a stem-based or a word-based solution (cf. Plank 1981: 204 ff.: sign-based vs. lexeme-based analysis). This concerns relations to a base which are synchronically motivated, not etymological or having to do with a source language. Here as examples are formations containing the preconfix *polem-*:

(7) stem-based vs. word-based analysis
  a. *Polem-ik* 'polemic', *Polem-iker* 'polemicist', *polem-isch* 'polemical', *polem-isier-en* 'to polemicize'
  b. *Polemik* 'polemic' ↔ *polemisch* 'polemical', *polemisieren* 'to polemicize' ← *polemisch* 'polemical', *Polemiker* 'polemicist' ← *polemisch/Polemik/polemisieren*

The analysis in (7a) leads to a stem-based word-formation analysis with the confix *polem-* as motivating base. It has the advantage that a search can be omitted for source words which do not always lead to unambiguous classification (see below). On the other hand, problems of semantic motivation arise, as the meaning of *polem-* is synchronically rather vague, the more so as the Greek source meaning of *pólemos* 'war, battle, struggle' is no longer clear. This problem does not arise with a word-based analysis. Thus *Polemik* 'polemic' can be paraphrased by *polemisch* 'polemical' (*polemische Haltung* 'polemical stance') and *polemisieren* 'to polemicize' by *polemisch* 'polemical' (*sich polemisch äußern* 'to express oneself polemically'). The word-based analysis though does not lead to base morphemes, but rather to (bimorphemic) base lexemes. While in German native word-formation suffixation takes place as suffix addition (e.g., model X → X*heit: neu* 'new' → *Neuheit* 'novelty'), suffix substitution follows for foreign word-formation (e.g., model X*isch* → X*ik: polemisch* → *Polemik*; model X*isch* → X*isier: polemisch* → *polemisieren*). However, multiple strands of motivating relations regularly follow, which leads to the assumption of double or multiple motivation or rather to reversible (i.e. invertible) relations of motivation. Thus *Polemiker* 'polemicist' can be motivated both by *polemisch* 'polemical' ('somebody who acts polemically') as well as by *Polemik* 'polemic' ('somebody who tends to polemics') and *polemisieren* 'to polemicize' ('somebody who polemicizes'), and the motivational relation between *polemisch* 'polemical' ('in the manner of a polemic') and *Polemik* 'polemic' ('polemical stance') is reversible.

A further problem of the morphological analysis of products of foreign word-formation concerns the demarcation of the morphological components "base lexeme/confix", "linking element" and "affix/confix". Cf. in (8) the examples *Chinese* 'Chinese', *Afrikaner* 'African', *Demonstration* 'demonstration' and *Filmothek* 'film library' (individual attestations and further examples in Müller 2005b: 32 f.; Seiffert 2009: 24–38):

(8) Structural analyses of products of foreign word-formation
   a. *Chin-es-e* vs. *Chines-e* vs. *Chin-ese* 'Chinese'
   b. *Afrika-ner* vs. *Afrika-n-er* vs. *Afrikan-er* vs. *Afrik-aner* 'African'
   c. *Demonstr-at-ion* vs. *Demonstra-tion* vs. *Demonstr-ation* 'demonstration'
   d. *Film-o-thek* vs. *Film-othek* vs. *Filmo-thek* 'film library'

The different analyses for *Chinese* 'Chinese' (8a) lead to two suffixes, the native suffix *-e* in *Chin-es-e* (with linking element *-es-*) and *Chines-e* (with derivational stem form *chines-*) as well as the foreign suffix *-ese* (< Lat. *-ensem*, transmitted via It. *-ese*) in *Chin-ese.*

The same holds for *Afrikaner* 'African' (8b), in which the different analyses even lead to three suffixes, two native and one foreign. The analysis *Afrika-ner* yields the native suffix *-ner*, the structuring in *Afrika-n-er* (with linking element *-n-*) and *Afrikan-er* (with *afrikan-* as derivational stem form) the suffix *-er* (i.e. the oldest loan suffix of German, cf. section 2), while the interpretation *Afrik-aner* leads to the foreign suffix *-aner* (from Lat. *-(i)ānus*), which – as is characteristic for non-native suffixes – carries main word stress.

The noun *Demonstration* 'demonstration' (8c), which can be interpreted both in a word-based manner (as an action noun based on the verb *demonstrieren* 'to demonstrate') as well as in a stem-based manner (as a formation based on the confix *demonstr-*), exhibits in the various approaches a differing suffix form: in the case of *Demonstr-at-ion* it is *-ion* with the linking element *-at-*, in the case of *Demonstra-tion* it is *-tion* with *demonstra-* as (questionable) base form, and in the case of *Demonstr-ation* it is *-ation* with *demonstr-* as derivational stem form (similarly as well in *Demonstr-ant*, *demonstr-ieren*). While the assumption of a uniform suffix form *-ion* requires base allomorphy or interspersed linking elements, the assumption of suffix allomorphy leads in many, but not in all cases to uniform derivational stem forms (e.g., *stagn-ieren*, *Stagn-ation*; *interven-ieren*, *Interven-tion*, *diskut-ieren*, *diskut-abel*, *Diskut-ant* vs. *Diskuss-ion*). The stem form allomorphy is etymologically justified and only explainable with reference to the morphology of the source language (e.g., Late Lat. *discutere* 'to investigate, debate' and G. *diskutieren* 'to discuss' vs. Late Lat. *discussio* 'investigation' and G. *Diskussion* 'discussion').

Among the characteristics of foreign word-formation we also find, alongside the morpheme category "confix" and foreign suffixes with main word stress, the linking elements *-o-* and (rarely) *-i-* (e.g., *Stratigraphie* 'stratigraphy'), which can be traced back to the compounding vowels of Greek (*-o-*) or Latin (*-i-*). They generally occur in nominal and adjectival products of foreign word-formation which contain at least one Greco-Latin confix. The interpretation of corresponding confix compounds occurs inconsistently, which is why a three-way structuring is possible for the noun *Filmothek* 'film library' (8d): with the linking element *-o-* (*Film-o-thek*), with the compounding stem form *filmo-* (*Filmo-thek*) and with the postconfix allomorph *-othek* (*Film-othek*). The use of *-o-* depends fundamentally on the presence or absence of a final vowel of the first element or an initial vowel of the second element. This is why *-o-* is lacking in *Hobbythek* '[place of a] collection related to a hobby' (vowel-final initial element) and in *thermal* 'thermal' (vowel-initial foreign suffix *-al*), and why *-o-* is also generally lacking in combinations of preconfixes with verbs, since here the vowel-initial and main word stress carrying suffix *-ier-* (*-ifizier-*, *-isier-*) is an integral part (e.g., *hydr-ieren* 'to hydrate' vs. *Hydr-o-phobie* 'hydrophobia', *Hydr-o-skop* 'hydroscope', *hydr-o-phil* 'hydrophile'). In formations such as *Filmothek* 'film library', the linking element *-o-* guarantees a stress shift to the postconfixes (further examples in Kempf 2010: 135–139), which carry main word stress, just as do the neoclassical foreign suffixes. Indigenous initial elements are thus adapted to the stress pattern of postconfix formations. This is, however, not the only function of *-o-*, since in hybrid formations with the pattern "preconfix + indigenous lexeme" (e.g., *Thermo-Hose* 'thermal pants'), the stress pattern of native determinative compounds is preserved. The use of the linking element *-o-* is apparently right or left driven, depending on the confix, with the result that it clearly differs in its function from the native linking elements.

4 Hybrid formations

Hybrid formations (mixed formations) are products of word-formation which develop from combinations of exogenous and native morphemes. The following overview offers a compilation of the possible combinations, which are subdivided according to the word-formation types compounding (9a–d) and derivation (9e–j):

(9) Hybrid compounds and derivatives
   a. exogenous lexeme + indigenous lexeme: *Luxus+wohnung* 'luxury apartment'
   b. indigenous lexeme + exogenous lexeme: *Glas+manufaktur* 'glass manufactory'
   c. indigenous lexeme + confix: *Grün+itis* ('preference for the color green, experienced as pathological')

d. confix + indigenous lexeme: *Hydro+werk* 'hydroplant'
e. exogenous prefix + indigenous lexeme: *Ex+König* 'ex-king'
f. indigenous prefix + exogenous lexeme: *ab+montieren* 'to dismantle'
g. indigenous lexeme + exogenous suffix: *hof+ier-en* 'to pay court to'
h. exogenous lexeme + indigenous suffix: *Autor+schaft* 'authorship'
i. exogenous confix + indigenous suffix: *stat+isch* 'static'
j. indigenous prefix + exogenous lexeme + exogenous suffix: *ver+absolut+ier-en* 'to make into an absolute'

Large differences in frequency can be attested for these subtypes. For compounding (9a–d) there are no restrictions for the models (a) and (b); they are used on a massive scale. The combinations of foreign confixes with indigenous lexemes (types c, d) count, on the other hand, among the rarely used models, whereby in recent years stylistically conspicuous combinations with *-thek* (e.g., *Quatsch-o-thek* 'place where one can chat') and *-itis* (model c) are on the increase (cf. Hoppe 2000; Feine 2003).

While, apart from hybrid confix compounds, hardly any restrictions on formation exist in the domain of nominal and adjectival compounding stronger restrictions can be observed for derivation. In the domain of suffixation, hybrid formations correspond predominantly to the structural types (h) and (i) – although the latter require a stem-based analysis (cf. section 3.3). The indigenous suffix appears here to have an assimilating function. The following suffixes are very productive: *-ung* (e.g., *Klassifizier-ung* 'classification'), *-in* (e.g., *Sekretär-in* '(female) secretary'), *-isch* (e.g., *elektr-isch* 'electric') and *-bar* (e.g., *praktizier-bar* 'practicable'). The reverse case (model g), in which the exogenous suffix "alienates" the indigenous base, is to the contrary rare. To these belong formations with *-ist* (e.g., *Lager-ist* 'warehousman'), *-ität* (e.g., *Schwul-ität* 'embarrassing situation') and *-ier-* (e.g., *gast-ier-en* 'to make a guest appearance').

Divergence can also be observed with prefix derivatives: While in the case of verbs, hybrid formations of the type "indigenous prefix/particle + exogenous lexeme" (model f) are common, (e.g., *ent-tabuisieren* 'to free from tabus', *ab-montieren* 'to dismantle', *um-sortieren* 'to sort in a different manner'), partly also as denominal formations with prefix-suffix structure (model j, e.g., *ver-absolut-ieren* 'to make into an absolute'), in the nominal domain only formations with *un-* are familiar, especially with adjectives (e.g., *un-exakt* 'inexact', *un-präzise* 'imprecise'). Instead, many examples for model (e) can be found in the nominal domain, among them many augmentative formations with *mega-* (e.g., *Mega-Stau* 'mega-traffic jam'), *hyper-* (e.g., *hyper-genau* 'hyper-accurate') and *ultra-* (e.g., *ultra-stark* 'ultra-strong') as well as derivatives with *ex-* (e.g., *Ex-Fußballer* 'ex-footballer') and *anti-* (e.g., *anti-deutsch* 'anti-German').

There are large differences not only with respect to the frequency of the individual models of hybrid word-formation, but also relating to the degree of activity of native and exogenous affixes in word-formation. Thus, verbal foreign prefixes (*de-*, *dis-*, *in-*, *ko-*, *re-*, cf. section 3.2) are not used at all for hybrid formations, while in the nominal domain, prefixes with a high productivity are encountered (e.g., *ex-*, *hyper-*, *mega-*). Munske (2009: 253) explains this in saying "daß Lehnbildungsmodelle in morphologisch und semantisch eindeutigen Nischen besonders erfolgreich sind und hier auch Modelle der indigenen Wortbildung verdrängen und ersetzen können" [that loan formation models are particularly successful in morphologically and semantically explicit niches, and here can also suppress and replace models of indigenous word-formation]. However, frequency presumably also plays an important role, as precisely the analyzable, but unproductive, structural patterns are generally only represented by a few loan words (e.g., *-ast: Gymnasiast* 'high school (gymnasium) student', *Enthusiast* 'enthusiast'; *-ee: Gelee* 'jelly', *Odyssee* 'Odyssey', *Resümee* 'résumé').

Hybrid formations make clear the manner in which both subsystems of German word-formation, native and foreign word-formation, are interwoven. This convergence has its limits though, which are revealed by various factors. Among these are restrictions in the combinability of native and exogenous morphemes, but also differences relating to the morpheme status and word-formation structures ("confix", combination of bound morphemes), problems of unambiguous mapping to non-native bases of word-formation, individual rules of allomorphy (e.g., *in-aktuell* 'not current', *il-legal* 'illegal', *im-materiell* 'immaterial', *ir-regulär* 'irregular'; *explodieren* 'to explode' and *Explosion* 'explosion'), the existence of parallel word-formation patterns (e.g., *immigrieren* 'to immigrate' and *einwandern* 'to immigrate; lit. in-wander', *kooperieren* 'to cooperate' and *zusammenarbeiten* 'to work together', *renovieren* 'to renovate' and *erneuern* 'to renew') as well as domain-specific distribution: The frequency of products of foreign word-formation decreases from technical language through academic to non-academic everyday language, and the proportion of foreign morphemes in the word-formation of spoken language is considerably lower than in the written language. In this respect, German is much less of a "mixed language" than for instance English (cf. Lutz 2008). Foreign word-formation and native word-formation turn out to be, in German, fundamentally separate but complementary systems. Much still remains to be clarified relating to their historical relationship and their manifestation in the contemporary language.

5 References

AWB (1993–96): *Anglizismen-Wörterbuch. Der Einfluß des Englischen auf den deutschen Wortschatz nach 1945. Begründet von Broder Carstensen, fortgeführt von Ulrich Busse unter Mitarbeit von Regina Schmude.* 3 Vol. Berlin/New York: de Gruyter.

Banholzer, Iris (2005): *-(i)tät. Vom lateinischen Suffix zum deutschen Fremdsuffix.* Marburg: Tectum.

Barz, Irmhild (2008): Englisches in der deutschen Wortbildung. In: Ludwig M. Eichinger, Meike Meliss and María José Domínguez Vázquez (eds.), *Wortbildung heute. Tendenzen und Kontraste in der deutschen Gegenwartssprache*, 39–60. Tübingen: Narr.

Battefeld, Malte, Torsten Leuschner and Gudrun Rawoens (2016): Konstruktionsmorphologie – echt *top*? Neue Perspektiven auf den kategorialen Status einer entlehnten Wortbildungseinheit. In: Elke Hentschel (ed.), *Wortbildung im Deutschen. Aktuelle Perspektiven*, 280–308. Tübingen: Narr Francke Attempto.

Buchmann, Franziska (2021): *-ität*-Wörter zwischen 1600 und 1800. Ein Fall von Fremdwortintegration ins Deutsche. In: Christine Ganslmayer and Christian Schwarz (eds.), *Historische Wortbildung. Theorien – Methoden – Perspektiven*, 319–348. Hildesheim: Olms (= Germanistische Linguistik 252–254).

Cottez, Henri (1988): *Dictionnaire des structures du vocabulaire savant. Éléments et modèles de formation.* 4th ed. Paris: Robert.

Dargiewicz, Anna (2013): *Fremde Elemente in Wortbildungen des Deutschen. Zu Hybridbildungen in der deutschen Gegenwartssprache am Beispiel einer raumgebundenen Untersuchung in der Universitäts- und Hansestadt Greifswald.* Frankfurt/M.: Lang.

DFWB (1913–88): *Deutsches Fremdwörterbuch. Begonnen von Hans Schulz, fortgeführt von Otto Basler, weitergeführt im Institut für deutsche Sprache.* 7 Vol. Straßburg: Trübner, later Berlin/New York: de Gruyter.

²DFWB (1995 ff.): *Deutsches Fremdwörterbuch. Begonnen von Hans Schulz, fortgeführt von Otto Basler. 2. Auflage, völlig neu bearbeitet im Institut für deutsche Sprache.* Vol. 1 ff. Berlin/New York: de Gruyter.

Donalies, Elke (2009): *Stiefliches Geofaszintainment* – Über Konfixtheorien. In: Peter O. Müller (ed.), *Studien zur Fremdwortbildung*, 41–64. Hildesheim: Olms.

Eins, Wieland (2008): *Muster und Konstituenten der Lehnwortbildung. Das Konfix-Konzept und seine Grenzen.* Hildesheim: Olms.

Eins, Wieland (2009): Alter Wein in neuen Schläuchen? Zum Konfix. In: Peter O. Müller (ed.), *Studien zur Fremdwortbildung*, 65–90. Hildesheim: Olms.

Eisenberg, Peter (2012): *Das Fremdwort im Deutschen.* 2nd ed. Berlin/New York: de Gruyter.

Feine, Angelika (2003): *Fußballitis, Handyritis, Chamäleonitis*: *-itis*-Kombinationen in der deutschen Gegenwartssprache. *Sprachwissenschaft* 28: 437–466.

Feine, Angelika (2008): Wortbildungen mit Euroanglizismen. *Studia Germanistica* 3: 47–57.

Feine, Angelika (2009): Das Konfix *-man-*. In: Peter O. Müller (ed.), *Studien zur Fremdwortbildung*, 317–349. Hildesheim: Olms.

Finkbeiner, Rita (2023): *Brilleria, Hipsteria, Schlamperia*: Hybride Suffigierung, Expressivität und Konstruktionsmorphologie. *Zeitschrift für Wortbildung / Journal of Word Formation* 7(2): 150–190.

Flach, Susanne, Kristin Kopf and Anatol Stefanowitsch (2018): Skandale und Skandälchen kontrastiv: Das Konfix *-gate* im Deutschen und Englischen. In: Rita Heuser and Mirjam Schmuck (eds.), *Sonstige Namenarten. Stiefkinder der Onomastik*, 239–268. Berlin/Boston: De Gruyter.

Fließ, Silke (2009): Das Konfix *-drom*. Bedeutungswandel eines griechisch-stämmigen Fremdwortbildungsmorphems. In: Peter O. Müller (ed.), *Studien zur Fremdwortbildung*, 351–372. Hildesheim: Olms.

Ganslmayer, Christine and Peter O. Müller (2021a): Historische Fremdwortbildung. Forschungsstand und Perspektiven. In: Christine Ganslmayer and Christian Schwarz (eds.), *Historische Wortbildung. Theorien – Methoden – Perspektiven*, 105–144. Hildesheim: Olms (= Germanistische Linguistik 252–254).

Ganslmayer, Christine and Peter O. Müller (2021b): Diskurse im Spiegel der Wortbildung. *-ismus* und *Ismen*. In: Jochen A. Bär (ed.), *Historische Text- und Diskurssemantik*, 90–118. Berlin/Boston: De Gruyter.

Gräfe, Karen (2017): *Zur Fremdwortbildung bei den Adjektiven am Beispiel von* al, ell, iv, ant *und* ent. Tübingen: Stauffenburg.

Gredel, Eva (2018): *Itis*-Kombinatorik auf den Diskussionsseiten der Wikipedia: Ein Wortbildungsmuster zur diskursiven Normierung in der kollaborativen Wissenskonstruktion. *Zeitschrift für angewandte Linguistik* 68(1): 35–72.

Heimbecher, Jessica (2008): Reanalyse fremdsprachlicher Elemente und ihre Integration in das Wortbildungssystem des Deutschen. Ph.D. dissertation, Universität Leipzig.

Heimbecher, Jessica (2009): Integration unterhalb der Wortebene: Die Wortbildungselemente *-krat/-crat* und *-naut* im Englischen und Deutschen. In: Peter O. Müller (ed.), *Studien zur Fremdwortbildung*, 373–396. Hildesheim: Olms.

Henzen, Walter (1965): *Deutsche Wortbildung*. 3rd ed. Tübingen: Niemeyer.

Hoppe, Gabriele (1999): *Das Präfix* ex-. *Beiträge zur Lehn-Wortbildung. Mit einer Einführung in den Gegenstandsbereich von Gabriele Hoppe und Elisabeth Link*. Tübingen: Narr.

Hoppe, Gabriele (2000): *Aspekte der Entlehnung und Lehn-Wortbildung am Beispiel* -(o)thek. *Mit einem Verzeichnis französischer Wörter auf* -(o)thèque *und Anmerkungen zu Eingangseinheiten von* -(o)thek-*Kombinationen*. Mannheim: Institut für deutsche Sprache.

Hoppe, Gabriele (2009): Umdeutung, Fehldeutung, Mode: Neue Medizin und Entwicklung von *ant(i)*- + [Krankheit]*icus* im Neulateinischen, Französischen und Deutschen des 17. Jahrhunderts. In: Peter O. Müller (ed.), *Studien zur Fremdwortbildung*, 397–433. Hildesheim: Olms.

Hoppe, Gabriele (2010): *"Reinigung und Fixierung" – Etablierung neoklassischer Lehn-Wortbildung. Etymologisch-korrekte Wiederherstellung von fachsprachlichen* |itis|*-Lehnwörtern und ihren Ableitungen seit der Frühen Neuzeit. Herausbildung einer fachsprachlichen Lehn-Wortbildungseinheit* -itis. Mannheim: Institut für deutsche Sprache.

Hoppe, Gabriele, Alan Kirkness, Elisabeth Link, Isolde Nortmeyer, Wolfgang Rettig and Günter Dietrich Schmidt (eds.) (1987): *Deutsche Lehnwortbildung. Beiträge zur Erforschung der Wortbildung mit entlehnten WB-Einheiten im Deutschen*. Tübingen: Narr.

Hüning, Matthias (2018): Foreign Word-Formation in Construction Morphology: Verbs in *-ieren* in German. In: Geert Booij (ed.), *The Construction of Words. Advances in Construction Morphology*, 341–371. Cham: Springer.

Kastovsky, Dieter (2009): *Astronaut, astrology, astrophysics*: About combining forms, classical compounds and affixoids. In: R[oderick] W. McConchie, Alpo Honkapohja and Jukka Tyrkkö (eds.), *Selected Proceedings of the 2008 Symposium on New Approaches in English Historical Lexis (HEL-LEX 2)*, 1–13. Somerville, MA: Cascadilla.

Kempf, Luise (2010): Warum die Unterscheidung fremd – nativ in der deutschen Wortbildung nicht obsolet ist. In: Carmen Scherer and Anke Holler (eds.), *Strategien der Integration und Isolation nicht-nativer Einheiten und Strukturen*, 123–142. Berlin/New York: de Gruyter.

Kirkness, Alan (1996): Zur lexikographischen Dokumentation eurolateinischer Wortbildungseinheiten: Vergleichende Beobachtungen am Beispiel *aero-*. In: Horst Haider Munske and Alan Kirkness (eds.), *Eurolatein. Das griechische und lateinische Erbe in den europäischen Sprachen*, 236–274. Tübingen: Niemeyer.

Lüdeling, Anke, Tanja Schmid and Sawwas Kiokpasoglou (2002): Neoclassical word formation in German. In: Geert Booij and Jaap van Marle (eds.), *Yearbook of Morphology 2001*, 253–283. Dordrecht: Kluwer.

Lutz, Angelika (2008): Types and degrees of mixing: A comparative assessment of Latin and French influences on English and German word formation. *Interdisciplinary Journal for Germanic Linguistics and Semiotic Analysis* 13(2): 131–165.

Marchand, Hans (1955 [1974]): Synchronic analysis and word-formation. *Cahiers Ferdinand de Saussure* 13: 7–18. [Reprint in: Dieter Kastovsky (ed.), *Studies in Syntax and Word-Formation. Selected Articles by Hans Marchand. On the Occasion of his 65th Birthday on October 1st, 1972*, 171–184. München: Fink].

Michel, Sascha (2009): Das Konfix zwischen Langue und Parole: Ansätze zu einer sprachgebrauchsbezogenen Definition und Typologie. In: Peter O. Müller (ed.), *Studien zur Fremdwortbildung*, 91–140. Hildesheim: Olms.

Michel, Sascha (2023): Remotivierung und Wortbildung. Strukturell-morphologische, semantische und angewandt-linguistische Analysen am Beispiel der sogenannten „Konfixremotivierung". In: Igor Trost (ed.), *Remotivierung. Von der Morphologie bis zur Pragmatik*, 65–98. Berlin/Boston: De Gruyter.

Müller, Peter O. (2000): Deutsche Fremdwortbildung: Probleme der Analyse und der Kategorisierung. In: Mechthild Habermann, Peter O. Müller and Bernd Naumann (eds.), *Wortschatz und Orthographie in Geschichte und Gegenwart. Festschrift für Horst Haider Munske zum 65. Geburtstag*, 115–134. Tübingen: Niemeyer.

Müller, Peter O. (ed.) (2005a): *Fremdwortbildung. Theorie und Praxis in Geschichte und Gegenwart.* Frankfurt/M.: Lang.

Müller, Peter O. (2005b): Einführung. In: Peter O. Müller (ed.), *Fremdwortbildung. Theorie und Praxis in Geschichte und Gegenwart*, 11–45. Frankfurt/M.: Lang.

Müller, Peter O. (ed.) (2009a): *Studien zur Fremdwortbildung*. Hildesheim: Olms.

Müller, Peter O. (2009b): Fremdwortbildung: Eine Einführung in diesen Band. In: Peter O. Müller (ed.), *Studien zur Fremdwortbildung*, 1–17. Hildesheim: Olms.

Müller, Peter O. (2011): The polysemy of the German suffix *-er*: Aspects of its origin and development. *STUF – Language Typology and Universals* 64: 33–40.

Müller, Peter O. (2016): Historische Lexikographie und Fremdwortbildung. In: Anja Lobenstein-Reichmann and Peter O. Müller (eds.), *Historische Lexikographie zwischen Tradition und Innovation*, 187–212. Berlin/Boston: De Gruyter.

Müller, Peter O. (2025): Das Hybridsuffix *-isierung*. In: Sara Matrisciano-Mayerhofer, Hannes Schnitzer and Elisabeth Peters (eds.), *Patterns, variants and change: Through the prism of morphology. Studies in honor of Franz Rainer*, 167–180. Strasbourg: ELiPhi.

Munske, Horst Haider (2009): Was sind eigentlich 'hybride' Wortbildungen? In: Peter O. Müller (ed.), *Studien zur Fremdwortbildung*, 223–260. Hildesheim: Olms.

Nübling, Damaris and Renata Szczepaniak (2009): *Religion+s+freiheit, Stabilität+s+pakt* und *Subjekt(+s+)pronomen*: Fugenelemente als Marker phonologischer Wortgrenzen. In: Peter O. Müller (ed.), *Studien zur Fremdwortbildung*, 195–222. Hildesheim: Olms.

Plank, Frans (1981): *Morphologische (Ir-)Regularitäten. Aspekte der Wortstrukturtheorie*. Tübingen: Narr.

Polenz, Peter von (1967): Fremdwort und Lehnwort sprachwissenschaftlich betrachtet. *Muttersprache* 77: 65–80.

Polenz, Peter von (1999–2013): *Deutsche Sprachgeschichte vom Spätmittelalter bis zur Gegenwart.* Vol. 1: *Einführung - Grundbegriffe - 14. bis 16. Jahrhundert.* 2nd ed. 2000. Vol. 2: *17. und 18. Jahrhundert.* 2nd ed. 2013. Rev. by Claudine Moulin in collab. with Dominic Harion. Vol. 3: *19. und 20. Jahrhundert.* 1999. Berlin/New York [Boston]: de Gruyter.

Ronneberger-Sibold, Elke (2009): *Thermodur, Blend-a-med, Sivitrex.* Konfixe in deutschen Markennamen: Typen - Geschichte - Funktionen. In: Peter O. Müller (ed.), *Studien zur Fremdwortbildung*, 141–193. Hildesheim: Olms.

Scheller-Boltz, Dennis (2010): *Präponeme und Präponemkonstrukte im Russischen, Polnischen und Deutschen. Zur Terminologie, Morphologie und Semantik einer Wortbildungseinheit und eines produktiven Kompositionstypus.* Frankfurt/M.: Lang.

Schmidt, Günter Dietrich (1987): Das Kombinem. Vorschläge zur Erweiterung des Begriffsfeldes und der Terminologie für den Bereich der Lehnwortbildung. In: Gabriele Hoppe, Alan Kirkness, Elisabeth Link, Isolde Nortmeyer, Wolfgang Rettig and Günter Dietrich Schmidt (eds.), *Deutsche Lehnwortbildung. Beiträge zur Erforschung der Wortbildung mit entlehnten WB-Einheiten im Deutschen*, 37–52. Tübingen: Narr.

Scott, Alan K. (2007): Englische Wortfamilien im Deutschen. *Deutsche Sprache* 35: 119–137.

Seiffert, Anja (2008): *Autonomie und Isonomie fremder und indigener Wortbildung am Beispiel ausgewählter numerativer Wortbildungseinheiten*. Berlin: Frank & Timme.

Seiffert, Anja (2009): *Inform-ieren, Informat-ion, Info-thek*: Probleme der morphologischen Analyse fremder Wortbildungen im Deutschen. In: Peter O. Müller (ed.), *Studien zur Fremdwortbildung*, 19–40. Hildesheim: Olms.

Stein, Gabriele (2007): *A Dictionary of English Affixes. Their function and meaning*. München: LINCOM Europa.

Trunkwalter, Julia (2009): Das Konfix *-phob-*: Ein Überblick über Etymologie, Morphologie, Semantik und Pragmatik der Wortbildungseinheit *-phob-*. In: Peter O. Müller (ed.), *Studien zur Fremdwortbildung*, 261–315. Hildesheim: Olms.

Wilmanns, Wilhelm (1899): *Deutsche Grammatik. Gotisch, Alt-, Mittel- und Neuhochdeutsch. Zweite Abteilung: Wortbildung*. 2nd ed. Straßburg: Trübner.

Klaus Dietz

5 Foreign word-formation in English

Abstract: This article offers a concise and yet comprehensive survey of the historical development of foreign word-formation in English. It commences with a definition of foreign word-formation in English, an overview of research on foreign word-formation in English and of the state of the art in this field. Subsequently, the main features of the historical development of foreign word-formation in English are presented. Then the principles of foreign word-formation in English are explained. This includes a survey of the inventory of central elements of foreign word-formation which is combined with an illustration of the problems of analysis and categorization. Then the combinability of foreign and native morphemes and possible restrictions on forming hybrids are presented. Finally, the new category of combining forms is discussed.

1 Introduction

As the expression "foreign" has not been used in combination with English word-formation so far, it is necessary to begin with a description and a definition. From a synchronic as well as from a diachronic point of view, the English vocabulary represents a huge collection of native and of originally foreign words borrowed from different languages at different times as a result of language contact. The oldest strata consist of Latin, Celtic and Scandinavian loanwords which were first interpreted as foreign words, later – after having been integrated into the lexicon – as loanwords and, finally, were treated as a part of the native vocabulary. French loanwords, whose transfer began already shortly before the Norman Con-

Klaus Dietz, Berlin, Germany

https://doi.org/10.1515/9783111420530-005

quest and ended in Modern English, represent the next important layer. After the end of the 14th century, loanwords from other Romance languages began to flow in. Spanish, Portuguese and Oriental words were borrowed together with the colonial products they referred to. And especially during the 16th and 17th centuries thousands of new Latin and – via Latin – Greek loanwords were transferred for the use of educated people.

There were not only monomorphemic coinages amongst these loanwords but also words with prefixes, suffixes or both and even compounds. When integrated into the English morphological system these loanwords or loanword-elements could participate in native processes of word-formation such as zero-derivation, or they could be combined with native morphemes to form hybrids. Hence foreign English word-formations can be defined as formations which either exclusively contain foreign lexical elements of any kind or combine foreign and native lexemes or foreign affixes and native lexemes or vice versa. Normally these combinations are created according to the rules of English and not of foreign word-formation because exogenous rules are rarely if ever borrowed. This can be demonstrated with the following example. As the French language makes very restrictive use of compounding English *lily-flower* must be interpreted as a loan translation of *fleur de lis*.

2 History of research and state of the art

Research in the field of foreign word-formation in English has – to put it mildly – a rather short-lived tradition. A glance at modern handbooks such as Adams (2001), Carstairs-McCarthy (2002), Plag (2003) or Schmid (2011) implicitly conveys the idea that foreign word-formation in English, if at all, does not represent a problem the reader should be molested by. The same is true of scholarly articles; none deals with this topic explicitly, not even in the context of, for example, zero-derivation. There are only two exceptions: Marchand (1969) and Koziol (1972) which still represent the state of the art and are in urgent need of revision, all the more since recently the first contributions dealing with French affixes borrowed in the context of language contact have appeared. Monographs, articles and dictionaries which are relevant to foreign word-formation in English are listed in section 7.

3 Historical development of foreign word-formation

3.1 Foreign word-formation in Old English

The first historical period of the English language, comprising the epoch of literary Old English (OE), began with the first texts written in the form of glosses c. 700 and ended with the Norman Conquest when OE was replaced as a written language by Anglo-French. In the course of this period of nearly four centuries, loanwords from four different languages were borrowed. The Germanic tribes who began to settle Britain from the early 5th century onward brought with them a substantial number of Latin loanwords which they had borrowed on the Continent. From the 7th century onwards, Christianization brought a new layer of Latin loanwords. Latin loanwords continued to spread from the monasteries as centres of learning and were integrated into the English language. This was not, however, true of the learned late OE borrowings from Latin: they vanished with the Norman Conquest. The total number of OE loanwords of Latin origin amounts to 500 to 600 words.

The majority of these loanwords consist of mono- and dissyllabic nouns (Kastovsky 1992, 2006a). Words containing prefixes are rare: *insegel* ~ *insigle* < *sigillum* 'seal'. As the Latin etymon does not contain the prefix the loanword is a hybrid formation. Suffixation occurs more often. The following examples include loanwords whose suffixes Anglo-Saxons were capable of identifying, provided that they had at least a limited knowledge of Latin: *abudesse* 'abbess' < *abbatissa, cetel* 'kettle' < *catillus, cycene* 'kitchen' < *coquina, læden* 'Latin' < *latinus*. More evident are cases such as *antefnere* 'gradual', *butere* 'butter', *fullere* 'fuller', *mangere* 'trader', *mortere* 'mortar' and *sūtere* 'shoemaker' as the suffix *-ārius, -a, -um* had been borrowed into the Germanic languages earlier, whereas *cerfelle, -fille* 'chervil' < *cerefōlium* or *petersilie* 'parsley' < *petroselinum* could not be identified as compounds in contrast to *cesten-bēam* 'chestnut tree' and *sæter(n)-, sæter(n)es-dæy* 'Saturday' which moreover represented hybrid formations. Several loan translations occur in the religious vocabulary: *fulwian* < **full-wīhan* 'to baptize', *gōdspell-bōc* 'gospel-book', *hǣlend* 'Saviour', *þrēness* 'trinity'. They were created to make central religious concepts intelligible to the simple faithful. Finally there are a handful of verbs, but not a single adjective: *campian* 'to fight', *cēapian* ~ *cīepan* 'to buy', *diht(i)an* 'to set in order', *lafian* 'to bathe', *mangian* 'to trade', *scrīfan* 'to decree', *predician* 'to preach'.

Despite the fact that the Anglo-Saxons eventually conquered substantial parts of Britain that had previously been Celtic, only gradually did they succeed in establishing a number of small and larger kingdoms which, during the 7th century, were organized in the so-called heptarchy. Nevertheless, language contact between the Anglo-Saxons and Celts resulted only in comparatively few borrowings. A mere handful survive in contemporary English. This low grade of efficency in the Anglo-Saxon – Celtic language contact did not affect the large number of Celtic place and river names the Anglo-Saxons did, in fact, adopt.

Like Latin loanwords, the small number of Celtic loanwords fall into three strata. The first is of continental origin and includes *rīce* 'reign', as in *bisceoprīce* 'diocese', and *ambiht* ~ *embiht* ~ *-beht* 'servant, service' < Gallo-Latin *ambactus*. The number of insular loanwords is greater: *assen* 'she-ass', *bannuc* 'a small piece', *binn* 'bin', *bratt* 'cloak', *broc(c)* 'badger', *carr* 'rock', *cumb* 'deep valley', *dunn* 'dun', *luh* 'lake' and *torr* 'rock, peak'. Other alleged Celtic loanwords cited by Kastovsky (1992: 318 f.) are at least problematical. On the other hand, Kastovsky (1992) does not mention *w(e)alh* 'foreigner, stranger, slave, Briton' (cf. OHG *walah* 'member of the Romance people', ON *Valir* 'Frenchmen'), nor compounds and derivations such as *wealhstod* 'interpreter, translator' and *wī(e)len* < **walhīn* 'foreign woman'. Finally there are a few Celtic loanwords which were probably introduced by Irish missionaries: *cross* which had not superseded native *rōd* yet and *drȳ* 'magician' along with *drȳicge* ~ *-ecge* 'witch'. The majority of OE loanwords of Celtic origin consist of monosyllabic nouns. Hybrid formations like *drȳicge* and *wī(e)len* containing native suffixes demonstrate the integration into the OE vocabulary.

From the second half of the 9th to the middle of the 11th century, the Anglo-Saxons borrowed a great number of Old Norse (ON) loanwords from Scandinavian (some Norwegian, though predominantly Danish) invaders who had settled in the Danelaw, an area east of a line roughly between London and Chester, and who later ruled over the whole of Anglo-Saxon England. In spite of this intensive language contact, the Anglo-Scandinavian language the Scandinavian settlers spoke became extinct at the end of the 11th century so that the import of ON loanwords came to an end. There is therefore a chronological discrepancy between the comparatively modest number of about 150 Scandinavian loanwords attested in OE documents and the substantial number of loanwords certified by the *Middle English Dictionary* (Kurath, Kuhn and Lewis 1952–2001). The bulk of everyday words of Scandinavian origin began to become visible only with the revival of the Middle English (ME) vernacular literature towards the end of the 12th century.

The Scandinavian loanwords sometimes differ from their ON etyma because the OE forms either resulted from younger Scandinavian sound-changes or from adaptation to the OE phonological system. The main semantic fields the loanwords belong to are exemplified with the following examples which constitute a representative selection:

a) seafaring, e.g., *barð(a) ~ barda* 'stem' < ON *barð(i)* 'kind of ship'; *cnearr* 'small ship' < ON *knïrr*; *flēge ~ flǣge* 'little ship' < ON *fløy*; *hæfene* 'port' < ON *hǫ̌fn*, the loan translations *wederfæst* 'weatherbound' < *veðerfastr*, *butsecarl* 'boatsman' < ON *búza* 'boat' + *carl* 'man', *stēor(es)mann* 'helmsman' < *stýrismaðr* 'steersman' and the compounds *æsc-here* 'Viking army' < ON *askr* 'ship', *æscman* 'Viking pirate' < ON *askmaðr*.
b) legal terms, e.g., *fēo-laga* 'fellow' < ON *félagi*, *formāl(a)*, *formǣl* 'negotiation, agreement' (cf. ON *formáli*, *-mæli* 'stipulation' and *for* 'pre-'), *friðmal* 'article of peace' < ON *friðmál* 'words of peace', *grið* 'truce' < ON *grið*, *husting* 'court' < ON *húsþing* 'meeting of an earl with his followers', *lagu* 'law' < ON *lïg*, the adjectives *sac* 'guilty' < ON *sekr*, *wrang* 'wrong' < ON *vrangr* and the compounds *lahbreca* 'law-breaker', *lahbryce* 'breach of the law' < ON *lǫ̌gbrót* along with *saclēas* 'innocent' < ON *saklauss* and *ūtlaga* 'outlaw'.
c) social ranks, e.g., *eorl* 'nobleman' < ON *jarl*, a semantic loan, *(hūs)bonda* 'householder' < ON *bóndi*, a hybrid formation, *līesing* 'freedman' < ON *leysingr*, *þrǣll* 'slave' < ON *þrǣll*.
d) war terms, e.g., *brynige* 'mail-shirt' < ON *brynja*, *cnīf* 'knife' < ON *knífr*, *genge* 'troop' < ON *gengi*, *targe* 'small shield' < ON *targe*.
e) coins and measures, e.g., *īere* 'Öre' < ON *eyrir*, *marc* 'half a pound' < ON *mǫ̌rk*, recognizable by the absence of breaking, *sceppe* 'measure of wheat or malt' < ON *skep* 'bushel', *scoru* 'score' < ON *skor*.
f) other semantic areas. In contrast to Latin or Celtic loanwords, the Scandinavian loanwords of OE include not only nouns but also adjectives and verbs: a) *becc* 'brook' < ON *bekkr*, *brȳdh(l)op* 'wedding-ceremony' < ON *brúðhlaup*, *hofding* 'chief' < ON *hofþingi*, *læst* 'fault, sin' < ON *lǫ̌str*, *mǣl* 'speech' < ON *mál* 'speech', *mæla* 'to speak', *rǣdesmann* 'steward' < ON *ræðismaðr*, *sala* 'sale' < ON *sala*, *scinn* 'skin' < ON *scinn*, *wǣpentæc* 'district' < ON *vápnatak* 'weapon-grasping', *taperæx* 'small ax' < ON *taparøx*. The list includes several compounds. b) *dearf(lic)* 'bold', *dearfscipe* 'bold(ness)' < ON *diafr*, *ræggig* 'rough' < ON *raggigr*, *goldwrecen* 'inlaid with gold', a loan-translation (cf. ON *gullrekin*). c) *farnian* 'to prosper' < ON *farnask*, *geeggian* 'to incite' < ON *eggia*, *hittan* 'to hit' < ON *hit*, *tacan* 'to take' < ON *taka*. Because of the particular linguistic relationship of OE to ON, the morphological variety of English loanwords of ON origin is greater than that of borrowings from Latin. The former comprise nouns, adjectives and verbs, compounds, prefixations and suffixations as well as hybrid formations and loan translations. Two verbs need special discussion: ME *mistrŏuen* 'to distrust', evidenced since c. 1225, originates from ON *mistrūa*, whereas ME *mistāken* 'to do wrong' reflects neither

ON *mistaka*, nor is it a hybrid, but rather a combination of a fully integrated Scandinavian loanword and a native prefix as the first attestations date from c. 1380–1390.

Finally, in later OE quite a few words were borrowed from Old French (OFr.). They represent the harbingers of the influx following the Norman Conquest: *capon* 'capon', *castle* 'castle', *prūd, prūt* 'proud' along with *oferprūt*, modelled upon synonymous *ofermōd*, the internal derivatives *prūtlīce* 'proudly', *prȳt(o), prȳte* 'pride' and *tur* 'tower'.

3.2 Foreign word-formation in Middle English

3.2.1 Introduction

The literary effect of the Norman Conquest consisted in the temporary absence of vernacular texts. With the exception of the second continuation of the *Anglo-Saxon Chronicle*, ME literary texts began to be produced again only towards the end of the 12th century. In the course of the 13th century, the first literary texts of Anglo- or Continental French origin were adapted for English audiences or native readers. At first, translations into English were made which were later on replaced by adaptations. Then original ME literary texts, often designed according to French models, were produced. This new tradition of vernacular texts mirrors the increasing number of French loanwords which had enriched the ME vocabulary from the beginning.

There are two layers of French loanwords which were both integrated into spoken and written ME. The first comprises the Anglo-French vocabulary consisting of everyday words which everybody had to learn. The second layer represents the more sophisticated, dialectally less marked vocabulary which since the later 13th century was used in the French capital and became the basis of standard French which developed a century earlier than Standard English. Later Middle English loanwords, especially, no longer show the characteristic traits of insular French. The sociolinguistic stratification of both layers still survives today. After c. 1350 the number of new French loanwords decreased by the same ratio as the borrowing of Latin loanwords increased.

3.2.2 French word-formation

Morphologically, French words may be classified into prefixation, suffixation and compounding according to the processes they result from. Prefixes and suffixes may be combined with nouns, adjectives and verbs. The rules of compounding show certain restrictions. Two nouns are connected with a preposition: *gendarme* 'country constable', *hôtel de dieu* 'hospital'. In noun phrases consisting of adjective and noun the latter is placed behind the adjective as in English: *aubépine* 'white-thorn', *rouge-gorge*, Pl. *rouges-gorges* 'robin redbreast'. Other examples show the reverse sequence: *eau-bénite* 'holy water', *cul-luisant* 'glow-worm'. Combinations consisting of a verb mostly in the imperative mood and a noun in postposition are often used as names: *Chauntecleer,* the name of the cock in Chaucer's *Nun's Priest's Tale*, *Taillefer* 'old campaigner', the name of a hero of the *Battle of Hastings*, and with semantic transfer to objects: *garderobe* ~ Anglo-French *warderobe* > ME *warde-rǫ̆be.*

More marked are formations with prefixes and suffixes combined with nouns, adjectives and verbs. In comparison with suffixation, Old French prefixation is of limited importance. If we disregard Latinized prefixes like *co(m)-*, *con-* the number of nominal prefixes is rather small whereas there are more than a dozen verbal suffixes from *a-* < *ad-* to *r(e)-* ~ *ré-*: *avenir* 'to arrive', *ramasser* 'to gather'. Nominal suffixes include abstracts (*-age* < *-aticus*), collectives (*-aille* < *-ālia*) and personal designations (*-ier* < *-ārius*). Adjectival and verbal suffixes mostly give rise to abstracts: *-eur* < *-ōre*; *-ment* < *-mentum: message* 'message', *bataille* 'battle', *charbonnier* 'charcoal-burner'; *chaleur* 'heat', *vêtement* 'clothes'.

Historical French word-formation has remained a neglected field of research up to this day. There are two older handbooks (Nyrop 1935 and Meyer-Lübke (2nd ed. by Piel 1966)). Lüdtke's article of 1996 is organized from a pan-Romance point of view. Article 19 of this handbook presents an overview from Old French to Modern French.

3.2.3 Middle English word-formation and French loanwords

a) Foreign prefixation

Koziol's title "Borrowed Prefixes" (1972: 127) is wrong insofar as prefixes were not borrowed separately at first, but rather taken into the language in a loanword combination. Only if a critical number of French words with the same prefix were borrowed was the English user able to perceive that the first lexical element of such a loanword was a prefix. This process of perception was the prerequisite for combining a foreign prefix with a native lexeme and creating a hybrid. This perception came more easily where the simple word had been borrowed too: *(dis)arm, (pre)caution, (re)claim, (sur)mount*. More often however, the prefix was no longer identifiable because it had fused with the appertaining lexeme: *abhor, absorb, accept, admit, agree, contain, prefer, recede, remit, repeat, resist, retain.*

The relatively small number of French prefixes was reduced even more by the Early Modern English (EModE) process of relatinization; e.g., ME *parfĭt* > EModE *perfect*. The following list is an alphabetically arranged selection of prefixed ME loanwords. It excludes examples which may have been influenced by Latin: cf. *reward* n. 'fee' < Anglo-French *reward* and/or Medieval Latin *rewardum*.

a) Lat. *ad-* resulted in various assimilated forms according to the initial consonant of the following lexeme: *agrẹ̄en* 'to agree', *abŏunden* 'to exist', *ac(c)ŏunten* 'to account', *af(f)ermen* 'to fix', *allīen* 'to join', *an(n)oien* 'to annoy', *ap(p)ẹ̄sen* 'to appease', *aqueinten* 'to become acquainted', *ar(r)ẹ̆sten* 'to stop', *ascrīen* 'to cry out', *atteinen* 'to attain'.
b) The same is true of Lat. *co-*: *collẹ̆ge* 'college', *cŏmfort* 'encouragement', *conceiven* 'to conceive', *corrump-āble* 'subject of decay'.
c) Lat. *contra*: *cŏuntrefẹ̆ten* 'to imitate'.
d) Lat. *de-*: *debonaire* 'mild'.
e) Lat. *dis-*: *discŏmfĭten* 'to defeat', *dẹ̆speir* 'to despair'.
f) Lat. *in-* 'in': *embushen* 'to ambush', *enchauntœur* 'sorcerer', *implīen* 'to include'.
g) Lat. *in-* 'not': *impācience* 'inability to bear wrongs', *impossĭble* 'impossible'.
h) Fr. *mes-* < Lat. *minus-*, merges phonologically with OE *mis-* 'bad, wrong': *misadventūre* 'mishap', *mischẹ̄f* 'misfortune', *misẹ̄se* 'discomfort'.
i) Lat. *ob-*: *obeien* 'to obey', *occupāciŏn* 'ownership', *offĭcẹ̆r* 'retainer'.
j) Lat. *re-*: *receiven* 'to take into one's possession', *reconcīlen* 'to reconcile', *remūen* 'to take away', *repairen* 'to revert', *reteinen* 'to retain', *revel* 'joy', *revers(e)* 'opposite'.

Two of these ten prefixes, *countre-* and *de-*, occur so rarely that their productivity must be doubted. The remaining ones may be combined with adjectives, nouns or verbs as well, though verbs are decidedly in the majority. On the whole, this presentation by Marchand (1969: 139–208) agrees with Koziol's (1972: 127–177) though Marchand does not distinguish between native and foreign prefixes.

b) Foreign suffixation

Koziol (1972: 12 f.) lists about seventy foreign, allegedly borrowed suffixes, and registers just as many foreign prefixes. The majority consists of learned Greek, Latin or French elements. If we confine ourselves to French suffixes which probably were not only productive but also more often available in English loanwords of French origin which, in addition, were first recorded during the 13th and 14th centuries, their number decreases in about the same proportion as to prefixation. The principle of selection is the same.

a) *-āble*: most of the adjectives in *-āble* are formed on the stems of transitive verbs with reference to the object of the action or with reference to the action itself, some of the adjectives are derived from nouns: *acceptāble, agrę̄āble, chaungĕāble, honŏurāble*; *comfortāble, deceivāble*; *fāvŏurāble, merciāble.*
b) *-āge*: derived from nouns denoting actions, concrete things, rights and services: *avauntāğe, cariāğe, corāğe, villağe.*
c) *-al ~ -ail(le): spŏusaille* 'marriage', *suppǭsaile* 'opinion'.
d) *-ain: certain, capitain, chevetain(e), vilein* n. 'unfree tenant', *vilein* adj. 'evil'. In words like *humain(e)* and *Romain* the French form was later frequently replaced with its Latin counterpart.
e) *-ance, -ence*: The suffix (< Lat. *-antia, -entia*) creates abstract nouns which designate a quality, an action or a state. Latin *e* + *n* and *a* + *n* merged with French *an: allīa(u)nce, finaunce* 'ending', *grę̄vaunce* 'offense', *instaunce* 'insistence', *penaunce, voidaunce* 'emptiness of the stomach'. Many examples are formally influenced by Latin.
f) *-ant*: the Anglo-French participial suffix has the invariant form *-aunt: ardaunt* 'ardent', *attenda(u)nt*, adj., n. 'careful; subject to sb.', *erraunt* 'an itinerant bailiff'.
g) *-ard: bastard, cŏuard* n., adj. The suffix has a derogatory connotation.
h) *-ary*: the regular French form *-aire* normally was superseded by Latin *-ary.*
i) *-(e)ry: avŏu(e)rīe* 'acknowledgement', *bǭcherīe* 'slaughterhouse', *chevalrīe, panetrīe* 'storeroom', *robberī(e), trecherīe* 'faithlessness'.
j) *-ess: abbess, cŏuntes(se), duches(se), emperesse.*
k) *-ment*: the suffix is usually added to verb stems to create nouns of state or condition: *agrę̄ment, chaungĕment, excītement, juğement.*
l) *-o(u)r*: this derivational suffix forms agent nouns: *barbŏur* 'barber', *jŏgelŏur* 'minstrel', *joinŏur, limnŏur* 'illuminator'.
m) *-ty*: The OFr. suffix *tę̄* designates a condition, an office or a dignity. Latinized, it appears in the form *-(i)ty < -tātem: bruntę̄* 'goodness', *citę̄* 'city', *honestę̄, loialtę̄, pīetę̄, plentę̄* 'abundance', *sāvetę̄* 'safety'.
n) *-ure*: The Old French suffix *-ure < -ūra* serves to form nouns and to characterize a condition, an action or its result. Koziol's remark (1972: 259) according to which a special feature consists in the fact that many Old French nouns combined with this suffix have no Latin equivalents does not hold true: *brisūre* 'a wound', *clǭsūre, fę̄tūre* 'feature', *jointūre, nortūre* 'nourishment', *peintūre* 'the act of painting'.

Two of these fourteen suffixes, *-ail(le)* and *-ard*, occur so rarely that their productivity in connection with French loanwords before c. 1400 must be doubted. The portion of French loanwords provided with French suffixes shrinks after c. 1400 in favour of Latinized formations which refer both to the words and to the suffixes. As with prefixes, the descriptions by Koziol (1972: 212–262) and Marchand (1969: 209–355) correspond to each other, although Marchand again does not discriminate foreign from native suffixes.

3.3 Foreign word-formation in Early Modern English

3.3.1 Introduction

Whereas foreign word-formation during the ME period was characterized by the borrowing of a large number of French loanwords and its various consequences, among them the development of hybrid formations, the distinguishing feature of foreign word-formation in EModE is the transfer and the integration of thousands of learned Latin and Greek loanwords which were borrowed via Latin or – more rarely – through the intermediary of French and other Romance languages.

The principal period of borrowing began c. 1530 and ended c. 1660. The decades from c. 1580 to c. 1620 constitute the crucial time frame, during the 16th century 15,000 and in the course of the 17th century 16,000 new loanwords were introduced. That means that from c. 1550 to c. 1650 about 20,000 new loanwords were attested, 12,000 of them between c. 1580 and c. 1620. However, not every new word was integrated into the English vocabulary. Some of them were abandoned later. Among the new words registered between c. 1550 and c. 1650 55 % to 60 % were of Latin and 5 % of Greek origin, 25 % were borrowed from French and 5 % came from Italy or Spain. In contrast to the borrowing of new Latin loanwords, the influx of Italian, Portuguese and Spanish loanwords began as early as c. 1400. The aim of the transfer of educated Latin and Greek loanwords in the age of the Renaissance and Humanism was the enrichment and the refinement of the English language so that, as a result, it would be of equal rank and quality. Thus her diversity and her expressiveness had to be increased and improved by the adaptation and integration of Latin loanwords. This process occurred by way of the written language exclusively. As most of the learned Latin loanwords could only be understood by people with a certain knowledge of Latin, these so-called "hard words" were the essential motive for explaining them in dictionaries. That is why the first English dictionaries were dictionaries of hard words.

3.3.2 Early Modern English word-formation and Latin loanwords

As more and more texts were translated from Latin it became evident that the English language needed to undergo a process of lexical emancipation. Hence new loanwords were integrated by formal adaptation and adjustment to native structures. These processes of integration followed patterns which had been developed previously in comparable situations when large numbers of loanwords had to be integrated into the English language. Two types of treatment were used: 1. cutting off the endings: *conjectural* < *conjecturalis, consult* < *consultare, exotic* < *exoticus, terrific* < *terrificus, extend* < *extendere.* 2. replacement by native suffixes, mainly of French provenance: *brevity, celerity, considerable, conspicuous, external, susceptible.* Verbs are often derived from the perfect participle: *conduct* beside *conduce, construct* beside *construe* with differing semantic development; *animate, create, incarnate, exterminate,* adj. and verb respectively, supported by the process of conversion.

Frequently, it is therefore impossible to decide whether a new loanword is of Latin or of French origin. Verbs like *consist* and *explore* may go back either to Latin *consistere* and *explorare* or to French *consister* and *explorer.* EModE *consist* is first attested in 1526, French *consister* since 1540, whereas EModE *explorer* has been testified since 1546, about forty years earlier than EModE *explore* (1585). The same is true of adjectives like *affable, audible, consequent, jovial, modest* or *sublime.* The only loaned word from Latin the *Barnhart Dictionary of* [*English*] *Etymology* (Barnhart 1988) accepts as such is *audible.* Nevalainen (1999) does not discuss this problem which requires attention to the contexts of the first attestations because these supply evidence as to the original word classes.

3.3.3 The Latinization of French affixes

One of the consequences of the borrowing of numerous Latin loanwords which has not been perceived so far was the Latinization of French affixes. The vast majority of present-day foreign prefixes is of Latin provenance. Under the influence of humanistic aspirations, the Latin form was favoured over the French alternative. The preference for Latin forms resulted in a process of Latinization of French prefixes and of introducing new Greek and Latin prefixes. This process already began in ME (the abbreviations indicate the source language): *abissus* (Lat.) 'abyss', *amphibologīe* (MLat.) 'ambiguity', *analempsie* (MLat.) 'a form of epilepsy', *apocalips(e)* (Lat.), *arche-prẹ̄st* (OFr., MLat.) 'dean', *cataracte* (OFr., Lat.), *dīadę̆me* (OFr., Lat.), *discrāsīe* (OFr., MLat.) 'disorder', *emispę̄r(i)e* (OFr., Lat.) 'our sky', *encenni(a)* (Lat.) 'the Jewish festival of the dedication of the temple at Jerusalem', *epitaph(e), -ie* (OFr., Lat.), *eukarist* (OFr., Lat.) 'the sacrament of the Lord's Supper', *ipocrite* (OFr., Lat.) 'a hypocrite', *metaphisik* (OFr., MLat.), *mīcrocǭsmos* (Lat.), *mono-corde* (OFr.) 'a musical instrument', *pantę̆r(e)* (OFr., Lat.) 'a leopard', *parăble* (OFr., Lat.) 'an allegorical narrative', *periode* (OFr., MLat.), *polipodī(e)* (Lat.)

'polypody', *problę̆m(e)* (OFr., Lat.), *prosǭdī(e)* (Lat.), *sinǭneme* (Lat., OFr.) 'synonym'. The list demonstrates that scientific vocabulary with Greek prefixes was at first imparted not only by Latin but also by Old French. Later on, Old and Middle French were replaced with Latin.

The same development can be observed with suffixation: *armoniak* (MLat.) 'ammoniac', *astrologĭ̄e* (Lat., OFr.), *astronomīe* (Lat.), *fleobotomĭ̄e* (OFr., MLat.) 'bloodletting', *frenetĭ̄k* (OFr., Lat.), *ğę̄metrīe* (OFr.) 'geometry', *ĭ̄dŏ̄latrī(e)* (OFr., MLat.), *sĭ̄mŏ̄niak* adj., n. (OFr., MLat.) 'guilty of simony', *pŭ̄blik(e)* adj. (OFr., Lat.), *monarchī(e)* (OFr., Lat.), *topographī(e)* (Lat.). Though there are fewer suffixes, their borrowing takes place according to the same structures observable with the prefixes. In no case were the Greek etyma borrowed directly into Middle English, but they came exclusively via Old French or Latin.

3.3.4 Early Modern English word-formation and Romance loanwords

a) French loanwords

While the process of borrowing thousands of learned and scientific loanwords of Latin and Greek provenance was transpiring, loanwords from several other languages were borrowed too. Primarily but by no means exclusively, the borrowing consisted of Romance loanwords of French, Italian, Spanish and Portuguese provenance. In addition, a considerable number Arabic and Oriental contributions to the English language were integrated.

French loanwords were borrowed during the whole EModE period. The latest stratum originates from the Enlightenment during the 18th century. These younger loanwords mostly represent vocabulary which English travellers brought back from their educational journeys to France. The semantic fields include military terms like *ambuscade, brigade, brigadier, cartridge* (< French *cartouche*), *colonel, combat, dragoon, parade, pilot, pioneer, platoon*, art and culture: *elegant, esprit, m(o)ustache, promenade*, trade loans: *cordon, indigo, vase*, social loans: *bourgeois, liaison, metier, naïve, class* as well as dress and food: *bouillon, cravat, denim* (< *serge* de *Nîmes*), *soup*. Especially some of the military terms still preserve the stress of the source language. The same is true of later borrowings of the 18th century like *critique, liqueur, police* and *ragout* while contemporary loans such as *brochure, casserole* and *croquet* are stressed as if they were native words. The same effect can still be seen in the case of *garage* (since 1902) [gærɪdʒ] ~ [gərɑː(d)ʒ]. Irrespective of the position of stress, these later French loanwords were treated as monomorphemic. Some of them were borrowed several times: *gentle, genteel* 'refined', *jaunty* 'self confident'. Nearly all of them are nouns or adjectives and represent either simple forms or have suffixes. In addition there is a series of loan translations such as *marriage of convenience* (< *mariage de convenance*), *that goes without saying* (< *ça va sans dire*) or *reason of state* (< *raison d'État*).

b) Loanwords from other Romance Languages (Italian, Spanish, Portuguese)
Nearly every modern handbook of the history of the English language hesitates to deal independently with loanwords borrowed from other Romance languages than French. This is primarily due to the authors' lack of expert knowledge of the field – a deplorable situation not exactly recent. In addition, Serjeantson's 1935 monograph – a study now largely outdated – may to a certain extent be responsible as well. For example, due to their reliance on this monograph, neither Barber (1997: 219–232) nor Nevalainen (1999: 372–376) offers a better account as they are based on the same source. Because French often served as transit stage for Romance loanwords, it is often difficult to determine the way in which Romance loanwords from other languages travelled to England; see, for example, *brigade* < Fr. *brigade* < It. *brigata* 'crew', *cartridge* < Fr. *cartouche* < It. *cartuccia*, *colonel*, originally *coronel* < Fr. *coron(n)el* < It. *colonello*.

In contrast to the misconceptions of current handbooks like Baugh and Cable (2013: 225 f.) or Algeo (2010: 259), who still maintain that the first Italian loanwords were borrowed during the Renaissance not before the 16th century, the transfer of Italian loanwords actually began shortly after c. 1400, only gradually increased after c. 1550 and died out a century later (Dietz 2005). Most of these loanwords belong to the cultural and educational vocabulary of Western Europe. Its international dissemination and its common Latin origin complicates the etymological analysis. Especially difficult to ascertain is the role that lexical migration from one Romance language to another may have played, e.g., from French to Italian.

Among the earliest Italian loanwords there are several cases like ME *alarm(e)* 'a call to arms' < Fr. *(crier) à l'arme* ~ *allarme* < It. *all'arme*, ME *brigaunt* 'a bandit' < Fr. *brigand* < It. *brigante* and ME *miliŏun* 'million' < Old Fr. *mill(i)on* < It. *millione* where an Italian loanword was borrowed by means of Old or Middle French. Early and moreover directly transferred Italian loanwords are ME *banke* 'bank' < It. *banca, -o*, *camerelle* 'a small room' < It. *camerella* and ME *cremesin* 'a deep purplish red' adj., n. < It. *crèmisi*. All in all, three dozen ME and about fifty-five EModE loanwords of Italian origin can be safely identified up to c. 1650. They include quite a number of nouns, adjectives and verbs with prefixes or suffixes and sometimes with both: *algebra, ambassāde, ambassadŏur, archipelago, contraband, disnatūren, dispatch, imbrate, impaste(d), incastellate, incrustament, pervivacy, rescounter*; *ambassāde, -ado, arsenal, assassin, bagantīn, brigaunt, camerelle, cancrŏus, celest(r)īn(e), ceriāl, coralline, cornodo, cramoisy, cremesin, cremesye, datary, herbelāde, incastellate, incrustament, janizary, lazarett(o), milanois, mockado, pervivacy, piquant, signiory, staffette, tartorary, tavelin*. The loanwords *incastellate, incrustament* and *pervivacy* contain both prefixes and suffixes. Compounds are lacking. Yet, English speakers without knowledge of Italian were unable to understand the morphological structure of these words. Later Italian loanwords such as *cameo, grotto, piazza, stanza, stucco* and *trill* are uninteresting as far as morphology is concerned.

English loanwords from the Ibero-Romance languages have Catalan, Portuguese and Spanish as source languages. As most of these loanwords exist in more than one Romance language the phonological, morphological and semantic comparison in connection with the relative chronology of the earliest attestations and the historical background are of special importance. In addition, unlike Italian loanwords, a good number of Ibero-Romance equivalents are derived from Arabic or came to Europe through Arabic mediation. There are at least three linguistic trails for Arabic loanwords to Europe: firstly via Sicily to Italy, secondly via Andalusia and thirdly via Byzantium. After the era of voyages of discovery, loanwords from the languages of the New World and from the colonies were imported along with the products, they referred to.

The earliest Ibero-Romance loanwords, ME *algarbe* 'wine from Algarve', *alkanne(t)* 'the plant alkanet' < Oldcat. *alquenat, cordewān* 'Cordovan leather' and *cork* < Astur. *corco* ~ *corque* mirror the linguistic diversity of Ibero-Romance which provides eleven ME loanwords altogether: *alconde* 'grandee', *bastard* 'wine from the grape called *Bastardo*', *fustik* 'fustic', *jennet* 'light Spanish saddle horse', *osei(e)* 'wine from port Azoia', *pley* < Sp. *playa* 'sea-shore' and *tamarinde* 'fruit of the tamarind tree'.

The EModE lexical imports of Ibero-Romance, mostly of Spanish origin, until c. 1560 consist of about two dozen loanwords. The most important include *armada, -o, cacao* < Sp. *cacao, gabardine* 'raincoat', *guaiacum* 'Guayak', *hurricane* < Sp. *huracán, maize* < Sp. *maiz, marmalade* < Port. *marmelada, morisco* 'moorish', *nigro* < Sp. *negro* influenced by Latin *niger, sago* < Port. *sagu, tarragon*. Among the later loanwords are *alligator* < Sp. *el lagarto* 'the lizard', *banana* < Sp., Port. *banana, barricade* < Sp. *barricada, brocade* < Sp. *brocade, canoe* < Sp. *canoa, corral* 'enclosed yard', *desperado* 'reckless criminal', *embargo* 'order forbidding ships to enter or leave a port', *mosquito* 'little gnat', *potato* < Sp. *patata, sombrero* and *tobacco* < Sp. *tabaco*. With the sole exception of *to encompass* < Span. *encompasar* 'to surround a ship' and of *morisco* adj. the Ibero-Romance loanwords consist of nouns. Apart from the Arabic article *al* which may function as prefix there are only suffixes like *-ada, -ade, -ado* but it is doubtful whether they were interpreted as such.

3.3.5 Early Modern English word-formation and Arabic loanwords

Handbooks of the history of the English language sadly neglect Arabic loanwords badly although their influx began already in Early ME. Only Algeo (2010: 262 f.) mentions a few examples in his short list of loanwords from the Near East. Among the earliest borrowings are *almenāk* < MLat. *almanāch*, *amirāl* 'a Saracen lord' < OFr. *amira(i)l*, *borāğe* 'borage' < OFr. *bourache*, *-age*, *caumfre* 'camphor' < OFr. *canfre*, *cotŏun* 'cotton' < OFr. *coton*, *hazard* 'a game played with dice' < OFr. *hasart*, *maumet* 'a pagan god' < OFr. *mahomet*, *orangĕ* 'an orange' < OFr. *pomme dorange*, *papejai(e)* 'parrot' < OFr. *papegai*, *saf(f)rŏun* 'saffron' < OFr. *saf(f)ran*, *satī̆n* 'satin' < OFr. *sat(t)in*, *setewāle* 'setwall' < OFr. *zedewale*, *sirup* 'a thick viscous liquid' < OFr. *sirop*, *soudan* < OFr. *soudan* 'the Sultan', *sugre* 'sugar' < OFr. *çucre*, *sucre*.

Until c. 1500 Arabic loanwords were mostly borrowed via OFr. or via Medieval Latin. Later on, Italian replaced OFr.: EModE *artichoke* < It. *articiocco*, *carafe* < It. *caraffa*, *coffee* < It. *caffè*, *baldachin* < It. *baldacchino*, *marchpane* < It. *marzapane*, *mockado* < It. *mocaiardo*. Spanish, too, served as a conduit of Arabic loanwords: *alcohol* < Sp. *alcohol*, *alcove* < Sp. *alcoba*, *algar(r)oba* < Sp. *algarroba* 'carob'.

Whereas ME loanwords from the Near East came in via France the lexical transit traffic of EModE borrowings went through Italy and Spain. More relevant borrowings need not be discussed here because they mostly represent scientific terms.

4 Principles of foreign word-formation

The historical development of foreign word-formation in English reflects the history of English language contact which was first dominated by Latin and later on by Old Norse, whereas Celtic influence was negligible outside those areas where Celtic languages were spoken instead of Old English. The language contact with Latin was intensified with Christianization. From the Norman Conquest until the revival of English as a literary language and the evolution of a late Middle English Standard as the spoken language of educated people, a great number of French loanwords were borrowed and integrated into the English language without affecting its principles of word-formation, its morphology or its syntax. As a consequence of Humanism and of the Renaissance, thousands of new Latin and Greek loanwords were transferred within a short period of time. They were integrated only partly insofar as their use was and still is today the privilege of the educated people. Meanwhile new cultural loanwords not only from Romance languages like Italian and Spanish but also from the discovery of the New World were imported along with the products they referred to. They neither changed the structure of the English vocabulary nor its sociolinguistic stratification, nor the rules of English word-formation. The consequences are manifold. English does not distinguish in the same way as German between loanwords and foreign words and, therefore, does not require separate dictionaries of foreign words. The English language did not have to develop and to differentiate the conception of affixoids and combining forms (German: "Konfix") except for scientific terminology; e.g., *astrophysics, astrophysicist.*

Foreign word-formation in English began in OE with the Christianization, i.e. the integration of Christian loanwords and the coining of hybrid formations: *bisceopdōm* 'bishopric', *bisceophād* 'bishophood', *bisceoplic* 'episcopal', *bisceoprīce* 'bishopric', *bisceoprōd* 'bishop's cross', *bisceopscīr* 'diocese', *bisceopstōl* 'episcopal see'; *crīstendōm* 'Christendom', *crīstenmann* 'a Christian', *crīstenness* 'christianity', *crīstnian* 'to baptize'; *martyrdōm, martyrhād* 'martyrdom'. The main effects of foreign word-formation in English began in ME with the borrowing and integration of numerous Anglo- and Central-French loanwords and continued in EModE with the transfer of thousands of educated Latin and Greek loanwords, so-called hard words, which were integrated morphologically as well. The transfer of scientific vocabulary of Latin and Greek origin continued into the period of Late Modern English (LModE), whereas, during the early modern period, the process of borrowing Romance (French, Italian, Portuguese and Spanish) and Arabic loanwords had only minor consequences, if at all.

Because they belonged to the first stratum of borrowings from French, early Anglo-Saxon loanwords provide an especially helpful example of the consequences of morphological integration. It is only during the last 30 years that historical English word-formation has become a field of systematic linguistic study. Hans Sauer's research into ME nominal compounds (1985, 1988, 1992) characterizes the beginning. Meanwhile a series of studies on the word-formation of French affixes in ME and on their productivity are in existence but a general survey is still lacking. In addition, four new reference works have become available that facilitate the study of English historical lexical morphology: the *Helsinki Corpus of English Texts* (HCET 1984–91), the *Anglo-Norman Dictionary* (Gregory, Rothwell and Trotter 2005), the *Dictionary of Medieval Latin from British Sources* (Latham and Ashdowne 1975–2013) and *The Middle English Dictionary* (Kurath, Kuhn and Lewis 1952–2001). In view of this state of the art, any attempt to determine the effects of the adoption and integration of French loanwords for the lexical morphology of ME has to be content with a survey of the problems by exemplifying them with some precedents of recurrent types of word-formation so that at least the main outlines of the development and its results become evident.

French affixes could only become productive in combination with native lexemes, namely when there were a sufficient number of pairs of mono- and heteromorphemic loanwords that made it possible for native speakers of English to distinguish between formations with and without affixes: OFr. *seignier* > ME *sīgnen*, OFr. *consigner* > Late Middle English (LME) *consīgn*, EModE *consignment*, OFr. *designer* > ME *dẹ̄sīgnen*. Obviously *consignment* is an English formation without a French counterpart. When a critical mass of such formations has been borrowed the affix can be separated as such and combined with native lexemes – provided that the underlying formations are morphologically analyzable. Native processes of word-formation, especially zero-derivations such as LME *oilen* vb. ← *oil(e)* n. or LME *brǭken* vb. ← *brǭkŏur* n. demonstrate not only the lexical integration of loanwords but also mirror English rules of word-formation and therefore do not require detailed discussion.

Hybrid formations can be grouped into three main types. Type 1 represents the combination of a native prefix or suffix with a foreign lexeme, type 2 combines a foreign affix with a native lexeme and type 3 represents a new native combination of two foreign elements. The Early Middle English (EME) type 1 has been attested since c. 1200, type 2 since c. 1300 and the LME type 3 since c. 1400. Their respective morphological consequences are not equally important. Whereas type 1 indicates the lexical naturalization of the loanword, type 2 demonstrates that a foreign affix has become productive and type 3 furnishes evidence for the productivity of the combination of foreign lexemes according to native rules of word-formation. Yet, the documentation of type 1 shows certain limitations as the number of native prefixes which preserved their productivity in ME is rather small, i.e. comprises no more than six: *a-*, *be-*, *fore-*, *mid-*, *mis-* and *un-*. Moreover, *a-*, *fore-* and *mid-* later lose their productivity and *mis-* reflects native *mis-* as well as foreign *mis-* (< OFr. *mes-*); cf. ME *mischẹ̄f* 'mischief', *mischẹ̄ven* 'to mischieve'. In addition, like *un-*[2], ME *be-/bi-* combines only with verbs; cf. *bicacchen* 'to catch', *unclǭsen* 'to open'.

A comparable typology can be observed with hybrid compounds. Type 1 is represented by EME *castel-toun* 'town with a castle', *castel-werk* 'construction of a castle' and *marble-stǭn* 'marble pavement'; representatives of type 2 are *mẹ̄te-grāces* 'graces', *prive-thirles* 'cesspools', *world-riches(se)* 'worldly riches', and type 3, which was fully expanded at the end of the 14th century, is identifiable in *chen-lange* 'dog's tongue' (OFr. *chienlaingue*), *haunche-turn* 'hip-swing', *castel-tour* 'keep', *forest-plain* 'clearing', *lilīe-flŏur* 'lily', *norīce-chaumbre* 'nursery', *quẹ̄r-cǭpe* 'choral-vestment' and *renge-tāble* 'ledge'. The so-called "imperative" and "invertive" compounds like *cache-pǭl* 'sheriff's officer' (OFr. *cachepole*, Anglo-Latin *cachepollus* 'catch the chicken') do not represent French loanwords but must be seen as native formations as they are first attested in late OE (Dietz 2002: 398 f.).

5 Hybrid formations

Hybrid formations are products of word-formation which result from combinations of exogeneous and native morphemes. The following list of hybrid compounds and derivatives offers an overview of possible combinations:

a) exogenous lexeme + indigenous lexeme: *cedar-tree*
b) indigenous lexeme + exogenous lexeme: *steam-engine*
c) exogenous prefix + indigenous lexeme: *dislike*
d) indigenous prefix + exogenous lexeme: *besiege*
e) exogenous lexeme + indigenous suffix: *falsehood*
f) indigenous lexeme + exogenous suffix: *eatable*

5.1 Hybrid compounds

Like English compounds in general, hybrid compounds normally consist of two nouns, one of them is native, the other borrowed. Thus the types *cedar tree* and *steam-engine* will be discussed together. With regard to form, content and function of the elements, hybrid compounds can be classified into several subtypes.

5.1.1 Type Noun + Noun

a) Dvandva compounds: have existed since LME: *giant-dwarf, aunt-mother, uncle-father, king-cardinal, emperor-king*. The order of the elements is not fixed.
b) Tautological formations: have existed since ME: *citẹ̄-tūn* 'city', *wŏnder-mervaille* 'wonder'.
c) kind + race: OE *cederbēam, cedertrēow* 'cedar', *lāwerbēam* 'laurel', EModE: *pumice-stone*.
d) Designations of persons and animals: have existed since ME: *maid-servant, man-servant, servant-man, woman-poet, women-saints, hen-partridge, cock-oyster, peacock*.
e) Comparison of the elements: EModE *bell-flower, dragon-fly, jelly-fish, mouse-colour*.
f) Spatial or temporal relation: have existed since ME: *countryman, water-lily, rope-dancer; day-labour, winter-cherry*.
g) The determiner designates the means or the tool: has existed since ME: *pen-craft, mouth-organ, steam-engin*.

h) Type *breast-plate*: has existed since ME: *bird-cage, ink-horn, pen-knife, vine-yard.*

5.1.2 Other nominal types

a) Type noun + agent noun: This type has existed since OE: *mēter-wyrhta* 'poet', *pistol-rǣdere* 'epistel-reader', *sealm-sangere* 'psalmist'; ME and later: *cup-bearer, hair-dresser, money-maker, shop-keeper, story-teller.*
b) Type noun + verbal noun: This type has existed since OE as well: *mynster-timbrung* 'building of a minster'; ME and later: *painstaking, top-dressing, picture-writing; frying-pan, landing-place.*
c) Type adjective + noun: This type has existed since OE, too. ME: *common-room, gentleman, ill-humour, nobleman.*
d) Bahuvrihi-compounds: This type has also existed since OE; later examples: *brazen-face, redcoat, whitecoat.*
e) Type present participle + noun: This type has existed since ME: *dancing girl, serving maid, serving woman, flying squirrel, moving picture.*
f) Type imperative + noun: This type has existed since ME: *catchfly, cuttepurse, makepiece, pinchpenny.* ME *garderǭbe* and *warde-rǭbe* are French loanwords.
g) Type adverb + present participle: This type which had already existed in OE was revived in ME: *wel conditiouned, wel governed, wel norished, wel ordained*; EModE: *far-fetched, ill chosen, new coined, well-dressed.*

5.1.3 Borrowed compounds?

As the rules of creating compounds in (Old) French were limited, the few English examples such as ME *lily-flower, merchant-(ad)venturer, common sense* and the tautological compound *love-amour* can scarcely have been borrowed as such. On the contrary, they, too, represent native formations consisting of newly combined loanwords.

5.2 The type *dislike*

The number of Latin and Greek prefixes in English word-formation by far exceeds that of French prefixes. As a consequence of the return to classical values in EModE, most French prefixes were Latinized and not used for new formations any longer, so that most hybrid combinations were coined with Latin prefixes.

From LME onwards, the Latin prefix *ante-* is combined with French and Latin nouns, adjectives and, rarely, verbs. The prefix became productive during the 16th century. Hybrid coinages are LModE *antedawn, antehall, anteroom* (cf. Fr. *antichambre*), *antesunrise, antewar.*

The originally Greek prefix *arch-* has been used for neologisms with a negative connotation since LME: *archfiend, archfoe, archwife.*

The French verbal prefix *en-, em-* has existed since ME: *enfold, enharden, enlighten, ennew; embetter, embitter, embody.*

Since LME the French negative prefix *non-* has combined with native abstract nouns: *non-being, non-freedom, non-knowledge, non-truth.*

The Latin and French verbal prefix *re-* 'back' and 'again' has been attested since LME in combination with native verbs and their nominal derivations: *rebuild, recall, refill, remind, renew, retake.*

Since LME the Greek and Latin suffix *tri-* 'three' has combined with nouns and adjectives. Hybrid formations began to appear during LModE: *tridaily, trilegged, trimonthly, triweekly.*

Compared with the large number of hybrid formations with foreign suffixes the number of comparable combinations with foreign prefixes is rather small. It even includes Greek prefixes such as *arch-* and *tri-*. Some formations, such as *tridaily*, appear rather late.

5.3 The type *besiege*

During the ME period the nominal prefix *after-* begins to combine with loanwords: *aftercast, afterchaunce, afterdiner, afterperil, afterreward. Aftercourse, afterpain, afterpiece* are EModE formations.

The verbal prefix *be-* 'about' has been used in hybrid formations since ME: *bedaub, becharm, beguile, besoil, betray.*

The verbal prefix *for-* 'off' has been attested in combination with loanwords since ME: *forbruise, forpine, forwaste.* At the end of the 16th century the prefix lost its productivity.

The prefix *fore-* 'before' combines with adjectives, verbs and nouns and has formed hybrid combinations since ME: *foreconceive, foredestine, foreordain; forecastle, forepart, foreguard.*

The nominal prefix *half-* has formed hybrids since EModE: *half-crown, half-round, half-faced, half-hour, half-measure.*

The nominal as well as verbal and adjectival prefix *mis-* has two sources, OE *mis-* and *mis-* < OFr. *mes-* (cf. *mischief*). New hybrid formations have been coined since ME: *mischance, misdemeanour, misgovernment, misrule, misuse; misguided, miscontent; misadvise, misconceive*. The prefix is still productive.

The nominal, adjectival and verbal prefix *out-* did not begin to form hybrid combinations before c. 1600: *outface, outtravel, outrival, outmove, outnumber; outguard, out-post*.

At first the nominal, adjectival as well as verbal prefix *over-* formed hybrid verbs and adjectives in ME: *overcarry, overcharge, overjoy, overpraise; overnice*. Nouns were not coined before c. 1600: *overcharge, overvalue*.

The negative prefix *un-*[1] (type *unfair*) has combined with adjectives since ME: *unable, unapt, uncertain, undue, ungentle; unfailing*. The homonymous prefix *un-*[2] (type *untie*) adheres to the same pattern of word-formation: *unbrace, uncharge, unclose, uncover*.

The nominal and verbal prefix *under-* begins creating hybrids in ME: *underjoinen, underravishen; underpeinted; underbaili, under-garment*.

The nominal and verbal prefix *up-*, too, has combined with hybrid nouns and verbs since ME: *upariven, updressen, upboilen; upfixed*. This prefix is unproductive in Modern English.

Of the almost fifty native prefixes only twenty per cent are capable of combining with loanwords.

5.4 The type *falsehood*

The great majority of native suffixes consists of nominal suffixes which belong to certain semantic fields: diminutives, feminine words, personal and factual designations.

Since the OE period the denominal suffix *-dom* (< OE *dōm*) has combined with loanwords: *bisceopdōm, campdōm, cristendōm, martyrdōm*. ME coinages are *caitī̆fdō̆m* 'captivity', *dūkdọ̄m* 'dukedom', *falsdọ̄m* and *victurdọ̄me* 'victory'. Later on, *heirdom, peerdom* and *princedom* were added.

Analogous to the forms of the past participle, the suffix *-ed* has formed hybrids since ME: *fortuned, moneyed, piked*. In addition there are EModE adjectival compounds consisting of two nouns: *coal-faced, dog-faced, rose-lipped, lily-livered* and contemporary combinations of adjective and noun: *round-sided, sharp-pointed, noble-minded, good-natured*.

The suffix *-er* (< OE *-ere* < Lat. *-ārius*) which formed agent nouns behaved like a native suffix and was used for derivations from loanwords: *attender, commander, commoner, denier, jester*. These derivations must not be confused with French words borrowed with the suffix *-(i)er* such as *butler, jeweller, messenger*.

Since the 15th century, the suffix *-ful* has combined with loanwords: *pitiful, deceitful, delightful, useful.*

The abstract suffix *-hood* has been used to derive hybrid formations since ME: *Christ(en)hood, falsehood*; *chāsthę̄de* 'chastitiy', *ğentilhę̄de* 'kindness', *lechŏurhę̄̆de* 'sodomy', *povrehę̄de* 'poverty', *sotilhę̄̆d(e)* 'cunning', *spŏushę̄̆d* 'marriage', *vīlehę̄̆de* 'ignobility' (all with the same suffix variant *-hę̄d*) and after c. 1500: *sainthood, bachelorhood.*

The nominal suffix *-ish* has been tacked on to adjectives and nouns since OE. Some few hybrid formations have existed since ME: *gŏutish* 'afflicted with the gout'. Their number increases after c. 1500: *cityish, dragonish, gluttonish, modish, hippish* (< *hip* 'hypochondria'), *stylish.*

The privative suffix *-less* has derived adjectives from foreign nouns since ME: *blameless, causeless, comfortless, defaultless, joyless, moneyless, pitiless.*

Since the ME period the nominal abstract suffix *-ness* has formed nouns from borrowed adjectives, too: *ableness, certainness, chastness, cŏuardnes(se), debonairne(se), gentlenes(se), humbleness, jelousness, joliness.*

Since the ME period the suffix *-ship* has been used to derive abstract nouns from borrowed nouns designating persons or groups of persons: *bailiffship, captainship, protectorship, scholarship*. Some formations alternatively can be derived from adjectives denoting a quality: *cŏardscipe, culvertscipe, debonairshipe, rę̄̆stīscipe* 'rancidness'. ME *prīvshipe* 'denial' is a deverbal coinage.

From the ME period onward, the denominal and rarely deverbal suffix *-y* has been used to derive adjectives from borrowed nouns, too: *spicy, noisy; catchy.*

Koziol (1972) lists more than three dozen native suffixes. Only nine of them combine with loanwords.

5.5 The type *eatable*

The French suffix *-able* combines with verbs and nouns to form adjectives. Hybrid formations have existed since ME: *answerable, bearable, eatable, knowable, speakable, wilnable*; in addition there are derivatives with the prefix *un-*: *unbearable, unshrinkable, unspeakable, unthinkable, unteachable, untearable.* In ModE the suffix is added to phrasal verbs: *come-at-able, (un)get-at-able.*

Since LME, the French nominal suffix *-age* has been used to form hybrid nouns: *dotage, drainage, faldage, steerage, tillage.* Some examples denote types of tenure: *hidage, poundage.*

The adjectival suffix *-al*[1] (< Lat. *-ālis*) has since the EModE period produced a few hybrid formations: *shrieval, tidal.* The same is true of *-al*[2] (Fr. *-ail(l)e*): *bestowal, upheaval, withdrawal.*

Since ME, the French suffix *-ance, -ence* has created abstract nouns with native verbs: *forbearance, furtherance, hindrance, riddance, utterance.*

Disparaging designations of persons have been formed with the French suffix *-ard* since ME and are often used attributively: *dotard, dullard, niggard* (ON *hnøggr* 'stingy'), *shreward, sluggard.*

The suffix *-ee* is based on the French participial ending *-e(e),* was part of the English legal terminology from ME to LModE and designated persons affected by legal acts: *befriendee, borrowee, (co)trustee, drawee, followee.* Mühleisen (2010) makes no distinction between loanwords and native derivatives.

Since the 13th century, the French suffix *-ment* has combined with deverbal nouns: *botment, cursement, groundement, hongement, murtherment.*

The suffix *-(i)an* (< Lat. *-(i)ānus,* Fr. *-ain, -ien*) was added to nouns and adjectives with the designation 'inhabitant, follower': *Chaucerian, Lancastrian, Shakespearian.*

The French suffix *-ance, -ence* denotes states, attitudes and activities and produced several English formations: *abidance, furtherance, hinderance, utterance.*

The French suffix *-(e)ry* creates nouns, some of them with contemptuous meaning: *aldermanry, Englishry, foolery, husbandry, outlawry, tannery, yeomanry.*

The French suffix *-(e)resse, -esse* forms nouns denoting female agents or persons: *hunteresse, seamstress, stewardess.*

The diminutive suffix *-let* of French origin (< Fr. *-elet*) has been combined with native words since EModE: *armlet, booklet, leaflet, ringlet, starlet, streamlet.*

Since ME, the French abstract suffix *-ment* has usually been added to verbal stems to derive nouns: *cursement, fulfilment, groundement, murtherment, onement.*

Only certain French suffixes were added to native lexemes, but this never happened with Latin suffixes.

6 Combining forms

Combining form represents a new English morphological term which is the equivalent of the German morpheme category "Konfix" (cf. article 4 on foreign word-formation in German). The latter was introduced to differentiate bound morphemes such as *Anglo-* in *Anglo-Saxon* from affixes on the basis of the following criteria: 1. an ability to function as a root or as an element of a compound, 2. an ability to possess a lexical-conceptual meaning, and 3. an ability to occur initially as well as finally. A "Konfix" may therefore be combined with stems, with affixes or with another "Konfix".

Accordingly, combining forms, which can be divided into initial and final combining forms, represent a special category of borrowed lexical elements. They carry scholarly or scientific meanings and occur solely in so-called neoclassical compounds, mostly consisting of Latin or Greek elements. As a further criterion must be added that combining forms are only rarely construed with affixes.

As a systematic study is still lacking the following selection gives a provisional survey of the range of this relatively new category: *Anglo- + Celtic, Irish, Latin; arch- + bishop, enemy; archaeo- + logical; auto-, bio- + -graphic(al), -graphy; bi- + annual; bio- + centrism, chemical, -graphy, -morph, -scope; chrono- + -logy, -metry; demo- + -cracy, -crat, cratic(al), -cratize, graphic; di- + -ode; dia- + chronic, -meter, phragm; dys- + -trophic; electro- + magnet; geo- + -metry; hetero- + -morph, -onym; holo- + -gram; homo- + -phobe, phone; hydro- + -lysis; hyper- + market; melo- + drama; micro- + chip, -(o)logy; mon(o)- + -arch; neuro- + -osis; oro- + -geny; osteo- + -path; penta- + dactyle, -gon, -gram; psycho- + -metrics, -path; retro- + -(o)nym, grade; seismo- + -graph, -logy, logical; tauto- + -logy, -logize; tele- + -graph, -scope; theo- + -cracy, -crat; uni- + corn; xeno- + biotic; xylo- + -phone.*

7 References

Adams, Valerie (2001): *Complex Words in English*. Harlow: Pearson Education.

Algeo, John (1996): Spanish loanwords in English by 1900. In: Félix Rodriguez González (ed.), *Spanish Loanwords in the English Language. A Tendency towards Hegemony Reversal*, 13–40. Berlin: de Gruyter.

Algeo, John (1998): Vocabulary. In: Suzanne Romaine (ed.), *The Cambridge History of the English Language*. Vol. 4: 1776–1997, 71–82. Cambridge: Cambridge University Press.

Algeo, John (2010): *The Origins and Development of the English Language*. 6th ed. Boston: Wadsworth.

Arveiller, Raymond (1999): *Addenda au FEW XIX*. Ed. Max Pfister. Tübingen: Niemeyer.

Barber, Charles (1997): *Early Modern English*. New ed. Edinburgh: Edinburgh University Press.

Barnhart, Robert K. (ed.) (1988): *The Barnhart Dictionary of Etymology*. New York: Wilson.

Baugh, Albert C. and Thomas Cable (2013): *A History of the English Language*. 6th ed. London: Routledge.

Bongetta, Davide (2003): The development of the English suffix '-dom'. *Linguistica e filologia* 17: 57–92.

Burnley, David (1992): Lexis and semantics. In: Norman Blake (ed.), *The Cambridge History of the English Language*. Vol. 2: *1066–1476*, 414–450. Cambridge: Cambridge University Press.

Burnley, David (1994): Word-formation in fourteenth-century London: Problems and opportunities. In: Rolando Bacchielli (ed.), *Historical English Word-Formation. Papers read at the Sixth National Conference of the History of English*, 79–92. Urbino: Edizioni Quattro Venti.

Cannon, Garland (1994): *The Arabic Contributions to the English Language. An Historical Dictionary*. Wiesbaden: Harrassowitz.

Carstairs-McCarthy, Andrew (2002): *An Introduction to English Morphology*. Edinburgh: Edinburgh University Press.

Ciszek, Ewa (2004): On some French elements in Early Middle English word derivation. *Studia Anglica Posnaniensia* 40: 111–119.

Ciszek, Ewa (2005): The development of *-schip(e)* in Early Middle English. In: Marcin Krygier and Liliana Sikorska (eds.), *Naked Wordes in English*, 27–46. Frankfurt/M.: Lang.

Ciszek, Ewa (2006a): *-dōm* in medieval English. In: Nikolaus Ritt, Herbert Schendl, Christiane Dalton-Puffer and Dieter Kastovsky (eds.), *Medieval English and its Heritage. Structure, Meaning and Mechanisms of Change*, 105–124. Frankfurt/M.: Lang.

Ciszek, Ewa (2006b): LME *-ship(e)*. *Studia Anglica Posnaniensia* 42: 179–187.

Ciszek, Ewa (2008a): *Word Derivation in Middle English*. Frankfurt/M.: Lang.

Ciszek, Ewa (2008b): On competition between OE *-estre* and OF *-esse* in Early Middle English. *Kwartalnik Neofilologiczny* 55: 23–31.

Corominas, Joan and José A. Pascual (1980–1991): *Diccionario crítico etimológico castellano e hispánico*. 6 Vol. Madrid: Gredos.

Coromines, Joan (1980–2001): *Diccionari etimològic i complementari de la llengua catalana*. 10 Vol. Barcelona: Curial.

Corriente, Federico (2003): *Diccionario de arabismos y voces affines en iberoromance*. 2nd ed. Madrid: Gredos.

Corriente, Federico (2008): *Dictionary of Arabic and Allied Loanwords. Spanish, Portuguese, Catalan, Gallician and Kindred Dialects*. Leiden: Brill.

Cortelazzo, Manlio and Paolo Zolli (1999): *DELI – Dizionario Etimologico della Lingua Italiana*. 2nd ed. Bologna: Zanichelli.

Dalton-Puffer, Christiane (1994): Productive or not productive? The Romance element in Middle English derivation. In: Francisco Fernández, Miguel Fuster and Juan José Calvo (eds.), *English Historical Linguistics 1992. Papers from the 7th International Conference on English Historical Linguistics, Valencia, 22–26 September 1992*, 247–260. Amsterdam/Philadelphia: Benjamins.

Dalton-Puffer, Christiane (1996): *The French Influence on Middle English Morphology. A Corpus-based Study of Derivation*. Berlin: Mouton de Gruyter.

Díaz-Negrillo, Ana (2014): Neoclassical compounds and final combining forms in English. *Linguistik Online* 68(6): 4–20.

Dietz, Klaus (2002): Lexikalischer Transfer und Wortbildung am Beispiel des französischen Lehngutes im Mittelenglischen. In: Mechthild Habermann, Peter O. Müller and Horst Haider Munske (eds.), *Historische Wortbildung des Deutschen*, 381–405. Niemeyer: Tübingen.

Dietz, Klaus (2005): Die frühen italienischen Lehnwörter des Englischen. *Anglia* 123: 573–631.

Dietz, Klaus (2006): Das frühe iberoromanische Lehngut des Englischen. *Anglia* 124: 549–581.

Dubois, Jean, Henri Mitterand and Albert Dauzat (2007): *Dictionnaire étymologique et historique du français*. Paris: Larousse.

Durkin, Philip (2014): *Borrowed Words. A History of Loanwords in English*. Oxford: Oxford University Press.

Garland, Cannon (1994): *The Arabic Contributions to the English Language. An Historical Dictionary*. Wiesbaden: Harrassowitz.

Gregory, Stuart, William Rothwell and David Trotter (eds.) (2005): *Anglo-Norman Dictionary*. 2nd ed., 2 Vol.: *A–E*. London: MHRA. Revised edition online *A–L* www.anglo-norman.net [last access 25 Jan 2015].

HCET (1984–91): *Helsinki Corpus of English Texts*. www.helsinki.fi/varieng/CoRD/corpora/HelsinkiCorpus/ [last access 25 Jan 2015].

Kastovsky, Dieter (1992): Semantics and vocabulary. In: Richard M. Hogg (ed.), *The Cambridge History of the English Language*. Vol. 1: *The Beginnings to 1066*, 301–336. Cambridge: Cambridge University Press.

Kastovsky, Dieter (2006a): Old English. In: Richard Hogg and David Denison (eds.), *A History of the English Language*, 220–226. Cambridge: Cambridge University Press.

Kastovsky, Dieter (2006b): Middle English. In: Richard Hogg and David Denison (eds.), *A History of the English Language*, 249–255. Cambridge: Cambridge University Press.

Koziol, Herbert (1972): *Handbuch der englischen Wortbildungslehre*. 2nd ed. Heidelberg: Winter.

Kurath, Hans, Sherman M. Kuhn and Robert E. Lewis (eds.) (1952–2001): *Middle English Dictionary*. Ann Arbor: Michigan University Press.

Latham, Ronald E. and Richard K. Ashdowne (1975–2013): *Dictionary of Medieval Latin from British Sources*. 2 Vol. Oxford: Oxford University Press.

Lloyd, Cynthia (2007): From denominal to deverbal: The suffix *-age*. In: Gabriella Mazzon (ed.), *Middle English. Studies in Middle English forms and meanings*, 145–164. Frankfurt/M.: Lang.

Lloyd, Cynthia (2011): *Semantics and Word Formation. The Semantic Development of Five French Suffixes in Middle English*. Bern: Lang.

Lüdtke, Jens (1996): Gemeinromanische Tendenzen IV. Wortbildungslehre. In: Günter Holtus, Michael Metzeltin and Christian Schmitt (eds.), *Lexikon der Romanistischen Linguistik*. Vol. 2,1, 235–272. Tübingen: Niemeyer.

Machado, José Pedro (2003): *Dicionário etimológico da lingua portuguesa*. 5 Vol. 8th ed. Lisboa: Confluência.

Majewski, Kerstin (ed.) (2024): Historical English Word-Formation. Sonderheft / Special Issue of *Zeitschrift für Wortbildung / Journal of Word Formation* 8(2).

Marchand, Hans (1969): *The Categories and Types of Present-Day English Word-Formation. A Synchronic-Diachronic Approach*. 2nd ed. München: Beck.

Mattiello, Elisa (2018): Paradigmatic Morphology: Splinters, combining forms and secreted affixes. *SKASE Journal of Theoretical Linguistics* 15(1): 2–22.

Mattiello, Elisa (2022): *Transitional Morphology. Combining Forms in Modern English*. Cambridge: Cambridge University Press.

Melloni, Chiara (2023): Neoclassical Word Formation. In: Peter Ackema, Sabrina Bendjaballah, Eulàlia Bonet and Antonio Fábregas (eds.), *The Wiley Blackwell Companion to Morphology*. Hoboken, NJ: Wiley-Blackwell [Online available at: https://onlinelibrary.wiley.com/doi/10.1002/9781119693604.morphcom053]

Meyer-Lübke, Wilhelm (1966): *Historische Grammatik der französischen Sprache. Zweiter Teil: Wortbildungslehre*. 2nd ed. by J. M. Piel. Heidelberg: Winter.

Miller, D. Gary (1997): The morphological legacy of French: Borrowed suffixes on native bases in Middle English. *Diachronica* 14: 233–264.

Morlicchio, Elda (ed.) (2000): *LEI Germanismi: Lessico Etimologico Italiano*. Wiesbaden: Reichert.

Mühleisen, Susanne (2010): *Heterogeneity in Word-Formation Patterns. A Corpus-Based Analysis of Suffixation with -ee and its Productivity in English*. Amsterdam/Philadelphia: Benjamins.

Nevalainen, Tertu (1999): Early Modern English lexis and semantics. In: Roger Lass (ed.), *The Cambridge History of the English Language*. Vol. 3: *1476–1776*, 358–433. Cambridge: Cambridge University Press.

Nyrop, Christopher (1935): *Grammaire historique de la langue française*. Vol. 3: *Formation des mots*. 4th ed. Copenhague: Gyldendalske Boghandel. Repr. Genève: Slatkine 1979.

Pfister, Max and Wolfgang Schweickard (eds.) (1979): *LEI: Lessico Etimologico Italiano*. Wiebaden: Reichert.

Pinnavaia, Laura (2001): *The Italian Borrowings in the* Oxford English Dictionary. Roma: Bulzoni.

Plag, Ingo (2003): *Word-Formation in English*. Cambridge: Cambridge University Press.

Pons-Sanz, Sara M. (2013): *The Lexical Effects of Anglo-Scandinavian Linguistic Contact on Old English*. Turnhout: Brepols.

Rey, Alain (ed.) (2006): *Dictionnaire historique de la langue française*. 2 Vol. Nouvelle éd. Paris: Robert.

Rothwell, William, Louise W. Stone and T. B. W. Reid (eds.) (1977–92): *The Anglo-Norman Dictionary*. London: Modern Humanities Research Association.

Sauer, Hans (1985): Laȝamon's compound nouns and their morphology. In: Jacek Fisiak (ed.), *Historical Semantics. Historical Word Formation*, 483–532. Berlin: Mouton de Gruyter.

Sauer, Hans (1988): Compounds and compounding in Early Middle English: Problems, patterns, productivity. In: Manfred Markus (ed.), *Historical English. On the occasion of Karl Brunner's 100th birthday*, 186–209. Innsbruck: Universität Innsbruck.

Sauer, Hans (1992): *Nominalkomposita im Frühmittelenglischen, mit Ausblicken auf die Geschichte der englischen Nominalkomposition*. Tübingen: Niemeyer.

Schaefer, Ursula (2012): Romance suffixation in the history of English. New ways of solving an old problem. In: Sarah Chevalier and Thomas Honegger (eds.), *Words, Words, Words. Philology and Beyond. Festschrift for Andreas Fischer on the Occasion of his 65th Birthday*, 145–164. Tübingen: Niemeyer.

Scheler, Manfred (1977): *Der englische Wortschatz*. Berlin: Schmidt.

Schmid, Hans-Jörg (2011): *English Morphology and Word-Formation. An Introduction*. 2nd ed. Berlin: Schmidt.

Serjeantson, Mary S. (1935): *A History of Foreign Words in English*. London: Routledge and Kegan Paul.

Simpson, John A. (ed.) (2000): *The Oxford English Dictionary*. 3rd ed. (in progress) http://www.oed.com [last access 20 Jan 2015].

Stevenson, Angus (ed.) (2007): *The Shorter Oxford English Dictionary on Historical Principles*. 6th ed. Oxford: Oxford University Press.

ten Hacken, Pius and Renáta Pancová (eds.) (2020): *The Interaction of Borrowing and Word Formation*. Edinburgh: Edinburgh University Press.

Terasawa, Yoshio (ed.) (1997): *The Kenkyusha Dictionary of English Etymology*. Tokyo: Kenkyusha.

Trips, Carola und Achim Stein (2008): Was Old French *-able* borrowable? A diachronic study of word-formation processes due to language contact. In: Richard Dury, Maurizio Gotti and Marina Dossena (eds.), *Historical Linguistics 2006. Selected Papers from the Fourteenth International Conferenceon English Historical Linguistics, Bergamo, 21–25 August 2006*. Vol. 2: *Lexical and Semantic Change*, 217–239. Amsterdam/Philadelphia: Benjamins.

von Mengden, Ferdinand (1999): Französische Lehnwörter im Altenglischen. In: Wolfgang Schindler and Jürgen Untermann (eds.), *Grippe, Kamm und Eulenspiegel. Festschrift für Elmar Seebold zum 65. Geburtstag*, 277–294. Berlin/New York: de Gruyter.

von Wartburg, Walther (1967): *Französisches Etymologisches Wörterbuch*. Vol. 19: *Orientalia*. Basel: Zbinden.

Wermser, Richard (1976): *Statistische Untersuchungen zur Entwicklung des englischen Wortschatzes*. Bern: Francke.

Zbierska-Sawala, Anna (1989): On the status of French derivational suffixes in Early Middle English. *Studia Anglica Posnaniensia* 22: 91–99.

Claudio Iacobini

6 Foreign word-formation in Italian

Abstract: The strong conservative features displayed by Italian with respect to its Latin origins implies greater difficulty, compared to the other European languages, in distinguishing between morphologically complex words formed by native or foreign word-formation rules. Such a distinction is less visible because Latin plays a dual role, constituting both the source of the native lexicon and the main source of loanwords which were absorbed into Italian through the mediation of other modern languages (mainly French and English). Rather than speaking of the acquisition of foreign patterns, in the case of Italian word-formation it would seem more correct to speak of the enhanced function of trends already in effect in the language or of a support effect favouring marginal formative patterns (e.g., right-headed compounds). The inclusion of completely new constructions is of minor importance.

1 Introduction

The influence of foreign patterns on word-formation in current Italian mainly concerns neoclassical compounding and other processes involving the combination of lexemes. This influence has favoured the spread of types of compounds in the common language that were formerly absent, or at least only marginally present. These are mainly right-headed and coordinate compounds (endocentric native Italian compounds are normally left-headed). The influence of foreign patterns on affixes is marginal and pertains more to prefixes than suffixes. This

Claudio Iacobini, Rome, Italy

https://doi.org/10.1515/9783111420530-006

foreign influence is the result of a convergence of loanwords and calques, taking place through inter-linguistic exchanges, and has Neo-Latin as its main source (cf. De Mauro 2005; Rainer 2008).

Italian displays strong conservative features with respect to its Latin origins and this implies greater difficulty, compared to the Germanic or Slavic languages, in distinguishing native words from loanwords and morphologically complex words formed by native or foreign word-formation rules. In Italian, such distinctions are less visible because Latin plays a dual role, constituting both the source of the native lexicon and the main source of loanwords and calques, which were absorbed into Italian in the modern age from Latin texts as well as through the mediation of other languages (mainly French and English). The distinction between native and foreign word-formation patterns and lexemes in Italian is even more blurred than in the other Romance languages. The latter exhibit phonetic changes of words directly inherited from Latin (e.g., Lat. *aqua* > It. *acqua*, Fr. *eau*, Port. *água*, Sp. *agua*) which have partially obscured the paradigmatic relationships with derived words absorbed into the Romance languages as loans from Latin in later historical periods (Lat. *aquosus*, It. *acquoso*, Fr. *aqueux*, Port. *aquoso*, Sp. *acuoso*), while in Italian, the formal and semantic relationship between the native word *acqua* 'water' and the learned loanword *acquoso* 'watery' is the same as that of many Italian derivatives (cf. *acquitrino* 'swamp' → *acquitrinoso* 'swampy'). The strong conservativeness of Italian allows for a greater integration of Latin lexemes which have entered the language in the modern and contemporary period. This has facilitated an ever greater Latinization of the Italian lexicon and permitted paradigmatic integration between the native lexicon and morphological complex words of Latin origin, reintroduced into Italian through borrowings from foreign languages.

Rather than speaking of the acquisition of foreign patterns, in the case of Italian word-formation it would seem more correct to speak of an enhanced function of trends already in effect in the language or of a support effect favouring marginal formative patterns (e.g., right-headed compounds), or even the recovery and revitalization of certain affixes. The inclusion of completely new constructions is of minor importance.

French is the language mainly responsible for mediating foreign patterns during the 18th and 19th centuries. However, until the beginning of the 20th century, few neoclassical compounds were admitted into the vocabulary of the common language. From the beginning of the 20th century, the prevalence of English as an international language of communication (not limited solely to scientific discourse) made this language become the main mediator of foreign patterns in Italian word-formation (loans from other languages play a less important role).

Foreign intake operates mainly through the language of the media, both for reasons of the prestige attached to foreign words (especially in the case of non-adapted loanwords) and due to the expediency of loan translations in situations in which there is a need to render a foreign language text in Italian but where there is little time to produce a translation in "good" Italian. This results in the so-called "hidden translations", whose main users are professionals and scholars who relay news and knowledge from foreign sources in Italian, especially from English, and who do not feel it necessary nor have time to produce an accurate translation. Limited knowledge of English by most of the Italian population heavily restricts the possibility of intimate borrowing.

2 Neoclassical compounding

Neoclassical compounding is the word-formation pattern which uses combining forms (henceforth CFs) taken from Latin and Ancient Greek with the particular aim of coining technical and scientific terms. CFs which make up neoclassical compounds (henceforth NCCs) are used in Italian as bound elements.

NCCs are also termed *internationalisms* because they maintain the same meaning and almost the same form in different languages (It. *biologia, termometro*, Engl. *biology, thermometer*, Fr. *biologie, thermomètre*, G. *Biologie, Thermometer*, Rus. *biologija, termometr*, Lit. *biologija, termometras*, Est. *bioloogia, termomeeter*, etc.) and, thus, differ in appearance from the words of the common lexicon in each language.

The integration of NCCs into the common language is due to the spread of terms designating techniques, products and aspects of social, political and intellectual life in modern industrialized society. Italian, as other languages in technologically advanced nations, interacts with elements and formative patterns which are more or less foreign to the usual word-formation rules.

Although the spread of NCCs has taken place for analogous reasons in the languages of Europe, the characteristics of the different languages determine different consequences for the lexicon and word-formation rules in each language.

The spread of NCCs in common Italian has not only led to the introduction of new lexemes with characteristics that are partially different from native lexemes, but also to new members of compounds and new compound patterns. The most important difference regarding compounding in Italian is the position of the head element. The most productive types of native compounds in Italian are verb-noun compounds (e.g., *cavatappi* extract-corks 'corkscrew', *copriletto* cover-bed 'bedspread') and left-headed noun-noun compounds (e.g., *capostazione* chief-station 'stationmaster', *vagone letto* car-bed 'wagon-lit'). NCCs, however, are characterized by the fact that the functions of the elements within the compound (modifier + head) are ordered differently in comparison to the usual Italian compounds (head + modifier): cf. *autoparcheggio* vs. *parcheggio auto* 'car parking'. The most important consequences of the spread of NCCs in the Italian lexicon are the revitalization of composition (especially of right-headed compounds), and the spread of phonological clusters which had previously been assimilated to the dominant phonological patterns in Italian. Apart from the order of elements, the main characteristics that differentiate NCCs from Italian compounds are the following (cf. Iacobini 2004a):

a) Paradigmatic relations: Neoclassical compounding makes use of CFs in series both in initial (*idrografia* 'hydrography', *idrometro* 'hydrometer', *idrostatica* 'hydrostatics', etc.) and in final position (*aerometro* 'aerometer', *altimetro* 'altimeter', *amperometro* 'amperometer', *anemometro* 'anemometer', etc.). Native elements of compounds are used in series, numerically seen, much less frequently: even the first elements of verb-noun compounds form a far fewer number of compounds than those of the most frequently used CFs (cf. Radimský 2006: 99–101).
b) Derivability: NCCs may constitute the base of a derivation (*tecnologia* 'technology' → *tecnologizzare* 'to technologize'), while native compounds usually cannot. Suffixation may also be used to show paradigmatic relationships (*fotografo* 'photographer'/*fotografia* 'photography'/*fotografico* 'photographic'; *solforico* 'sulphuric', *solforoso* 'sulphurous').
c) Number of members and their relations: NCCs have a formative flexibility which is far superior to that of native Italian compounds. It is possible for the constituent CFs to enter the compound recursively, both in a coordinated (e.g., [[*oto rino laringo*] *iatra*]) and in a subordinated relationship (e.g., [*elettro* [*encefalo gramma*]]) to the other elements of the compound. These structures are exceptional for Italian compounds which are normally formed by only two lexemes. One consequence of the greater combining facility of CFs is the length of the compounds they can form. The great majority of Italian words containing nine-syllables (or more) is represented by NCCs.
d) Stress position: Primary stress in NCCs falls typically on the penultimate syllable, never on the last syllable. Some CFs (e.g., *-filo*, *-logo*, *-metro*) assign the stress to the adjacent syllable of the preceding element (whether it is a prefix *àfono*, a CF *idròvoro*, or a word *commediògrafo*), thus forming words stressed on the antepenultimate syllable. The position of primary stress in native compounds is less predictable.
e) Anomalous clusters: The final vowel in the great majority of initial CFs creates within-word combinations that are fairly atypical of Italian phonolo-

> gy (*bioalimento, elettroencefalogramma, fotoincisione, radiooperatore, radioutente, teleelaborazione, triidrato*). Even within certain CFs themselves there are consonant clusters that are foreign to the phonology of Italian and present only in non-adapted loanwords (*gimno-*, *lepto-*, *oftalmo-*, *picno-*). Unlike other languages, such as English and especially German, which respect the phonological and graphic features of international scientific Latin more, in Italian neoclassical CFs have undergone assimilation of consonant clusters, palatalization and diphthong reduction, analogous to that of the words directly inherited from Latin. The consequence of this is the existence of formal variants (*coino-/ceno-/cheno-*; *cinesi-/chinesi-/kinesi-*; *pecilo-/poichilo-*) and cases of homography. An example of this is the enantiosemic homography of *eso-* from Gr. *éksō* 'outside' in *esocentrico* 'exocentric' and *eso-* from Gr. *ésō, eísō* 'inside' in *esotropia* 'esotropia'. From at least the second half of the 20th century, the spread of international scientific terminology in English has increased the prestige and fostered the diffusion of the Latinate written form of neoclassical CFs, determining a preference in scientific-technical Italian for forms like *nicto-*, *dictio-*, *elaio-*, *-ptero*, *-xilo*, compared to the previous *nitto-*, *dittio-*, *eleo-*, *-ttero*, *-ssilo*.

Interaction between NCCs and the lexicon of the common language poses problems both of a theoretical and descriptive nature. Firstly, there is the problem of identifying, amongst the large number of CFs used in technical and scientific terminology, which and how many have entered the language to become part of current usage in Italian, that is, whose meanings are known to most speakers and can be used to form new words which do not just have specialized uses. From amongst those that have been integrated into the language and are currently used in word-formation processes, it is furthermore necessary to distinguish between those CFs having lexematic meanings and functions and CFs whose functions and meanings are nearer to those of derivational affixes. Within the scope of this article, rather than the *vexatae quaestiones* of the delimitation between affixes and lexemes, and between derivation and compounding, what is of most interest is to single out and describe the means of integration of word-formation patterns and CFs that have been introduced into the Italian language following the spread of NCCs into common language. Scholars agree on the recent perceptible integration of NCCs into the word-formation patterns of current Italian, cf. Radimský (2006b: 13–14): "L'évolution récente du lexique italien semble relativiser la distinction entre ces deux procédés [...], et nous ammène jusqu'à repenser en théorie la distinction entre le composé indigène et savant." [The recent developments in the Italian lexicon seems to relativize the distinction between these two processes [...], and it leads us to reconsider the distinction between native and learned compounds.]

3 Neoclassical combining forms and other members of compounds

The spread of NCCs has been responsible for not only the integration of new types of compounds into the language and the revitalization of previously marginal patterns (cf. section 4), but also for the integration of CFs taken over from classical languages into endogenous word-formation patterns (cf. section 3.1), the coining of new CFs (cf. section 3.2), and also for the modified forms of words used as the first member of compounds (cf. section 3.3), enriching the lexicon and the word-formation patterns of present-day Italian.

3.1 Combining forms from classical languages

The original stock of neoclassical CFs has its origin in Greek and Latin words used in the thematic form or in the form incorporating the linking vowel used in compound words in Latin and Ancient Greek. Initial CFs of Greek origin usually end in *-o*, those originating in Latin in *-i*, but there are also CFs of Greek origin with other endings (almost always vowels: *acu-*, *ali-*, *bari-*, *deca-*, occasionally consonants: *pan-*) and many CFs of Latin origin have endings in *-o* (e.g., *balneo-*, *carbo-*, *digito-*).

An identification of the language of origin is a marginal factor, and in fact there are no behavioural differences between CFs stemming from one or the other language. This is shown by the fact that the same notion can be expressed by CFs of either Greek or Latin origin (cf. *dattilo-* and *digito-*, *ombro-* and *pluvio-*, *seleno-* and *luni-*). Furthermore, Humanistic Latin and, more broadly, Neo-Latin have both made extensive usage of elements of Greek origin, fostering the coining of mixed Greek-Latin formations. CFs stemming from classical languages are mainly used to form compounds of a technical-scientific nature and among those most frequently used for the formation of words of common usage are: *bio-*, *filo-*, *-filo*, *-foro*, *-grafia*, *-grafo*, *idro-*, *-logia*, *-logo*, *mono-*, *proto-*, *tele-*, *termo-*, *-voro*; cf. *biografia* 'biography', *filosofia* 'philosophy', *idrofilo* 'hydrophilic', *archeologia* 'archaeology', *cardiologo* 'cardiologist', *monocromo* 'monochrome', *protozoo* 'protozoan', *telefono* 'telephone', *termometro* 'thermometer', *onnivoro* 'omnivorous'.

3.2 Combining forms from modern languages

The integration of foreign patterns of neoclassical compounding also is shown in the formation of new CFs which have not been inherited from classic languages and in their use in words in the common language. The new CFs are mainly formed through shortening, both from NCCs and from current words in Italian or foreign languages (according to Radimský 2006a: 139–140 about 30 % of a corpus of about 1,000 Italian NCCs first recorded in a reference dictionary between 1980 and 1999 are formed with modern CFs).

3.2.1 Shortening

The phonological and prosodic features of the elements obtained through shortening (coinciding with those of the minimal prosodic word of the nominal class in Italian: a foot of two syllables ending in a vowel with stress on the first syllable, cf. Thornton 1996) makes such elements particularly adaptable to being used as CFs (especially in initial position). As with all shortenings, the resulting element assumes the meaning of the word from which it derives (on shortenings in the Italian language, cf. Thornton 2007).

It is possible to distinguish two types of CFs obtained by shortening depending on the segmentation of the source word.

In the first type, the result of the shortening of an NCC coincides with a CF taken from classical languages, and thus groups of two or more homonymous forms are obtained: *auto-* from *automobile* 'car' (vs. *auto-* 'self, one's own, by oneself, independently'), *bio-* from *biologia* 'biology' (vs. *bio-* 'life, course or way of living'), *eco-* from *ecologia* 'ecology' (vs. *eco-* 'house'), *foto-* from *fotografia* 'photography' (vs. *foto-* 'light'), *tele-* from *televisione* 'television' and *tele-* from *telefono* 'telephone' (vs. *tele-* 'afar, far off'). Among the numerous compounds formed with these new CFs are: *autonoleggio* 'car rental', *bioagricoltura* 'bioagriculture', *ecocompatibile* 'eco-compatible', *fotomontaggio* 'photomontage', *telespettatore* 'televiewer', *teleselezione* 'direct dialling'.

In the second type, shortening generates a CF that has no precedent in the classical languages. This happens either because the word from which it originates is not a compound: e.g., *socio-* from *sociale* 'social' (cf. *sociolinguistica* 'sociolinguistics'), *euro-* from *Europa* (cf. *eurodeputato* 'Eurodeputy'), *-trone* from *elettrone* 'electron' (cf. *positrone* 'positron'), or because the word from which it originates is a compound, but shortening does not respect etymological and morphological segmentation: *bici-* from *bicicletta* 'bicycle' (cf. *biciraduno* 'cyclist convention'), *cine-* from *cinematografo* 'cinematograph' (cf. *cineoperatore* 'cameraman'), *-rama* from *panorama* (cf. *zoorama*). There are a few cases of reduction to prefix: *sub* from *subacqueo* 'scuba diver', *trans* from *transessuale* 'transsexual'.

Lexical exchanges among modern languages play an important role in the creation and dissemination of these new CFs (cf. Kortas 2002; Mattiello 2008). It is not always possible to establish in which language shortening took place. The element *buro-* 'bureaucracy, bureaucrat' was formed probably in Italian from a word of French origin (cf. Fr. *bureau* 'office', *buraucratie* 'bureaucracy'): *burolingua* 'officialese'. Of evident English origin are *cyber-*, *e-*: (*cybercrimine* 'cybercrime', *e-libro* 'e-book') in much the same way as other CFs connected with information technology. One of the most recent cases is *wiki-*, obtained from *Wikipedia* (*wikifoto*, *wikilibro*, *wiki(di)zionario*).

There is no functional distinction between the two types of CFs obtained through shortening. Both are used prevalently in right-headed compounds in combination with words (but can also be combined with other CFs (*telecrazia* 'telecracy', *ecocidio* 'ecocide').

Some CFs obtained through shortening, which are most frequently used in the common language, can acquire a certain syntactic autonomy and be used as nouns (e.g., *auto* f., *cinema* m., *foto* f., *moto* f., *porno* m., *radio* f., *stereo* m.), normally invariable. Others can also be used as appositions in post-nominal position (*motore turbo* 'turbo engine', *patente auto* 'driving licence'), forming phrases which are semantically equivalent to right-headed compounds (e.g., *messaggio porno* and *pornomessaggio* 'porno message', cf. Radimský 2006a: 126–132). Further nominal characteristics (which may be interpreted as a clue of integration into the lexicon) consist in the possibility of being derived with suffixes (*autista* 'driver', *videata* 'screen shot'), of being final elements of prefixed words (*maximoto*, *superporno*), and of being the head of left-headed compounds (*autoblindo* 'armoured car', *autobotte* 'tanker lorry').

In the case of *moto-* (analogous with *auto-*) a process of grammaticalization and de-grammaticalization has taken place with a passage from free word to CF by shortening: *motore* 'motor' > *moto-* 'machine, device functioning by motor' (cf. *motocicletta* 'motorcycle', *motosega* 'chain saw') and then from NCC to another CF: *motocicletta* 'motorcycle' > *moto-* (cf. *motoaccessorio* 'motorbike accessory'). This last CF can also be used as a free word: *la moto* 'motorcycle, bike'. The formative history of *video-* and *audio-* differs from that of other CFs mentioned here. Both were assimilated into Italian as loanwords from English, first as autonomous words and only subsequently utilized as CFs.

3.2.2 Secretion

Secretion is a process that determines the formation of a CF whose meaning (unlike shortening) does not express the main meaning of the word from which it derives, but a secondary (often metaphorical) meaning that the word has acquired in particular contexts (cf. Warren 1990; Fradin 2000; Giannoulopoulou 2006 considers "secretion" in a much broader sense that includes the phenomenon we defined as "shortening" in previous paragraphs). From a formal point of view, as with shortening, the result of secretion can produce an element which is homonymous to a neoclassical CF, e.g., *-poli* 'a business or political scandal' (in words like *affittopoli* 'scandal concerning rentals (*affitti*)', *concorsopoli* 'scandal concerning tenders (*concorsi*)', *sanitopoli* 'scandal concerning the health service (*Sanità*)') obtained from *tangentopoli* (originally 'city of kickbacks (*tangenti*)' (said of Milan), cf. *-poli* 'city, town' in *acropoli* 'acropolis'), or operate according to primarily prosodic criteria, forming a new element, as in the case of *-thon*, from the English *marathon*, used with the meaning 'public event of much greater duration than normal' in words like *telethon*. Secretion is a process that is completely marginal in Italian in that the determining influence is foreign and has produced a very small number of elements, most of which are borrowings whose use, furthermore, is limited almost exclusively to written language in the media; cf. *-gate* 'far-reaching scandal, particularly in politics and government': *Berlusconigate*.

3.3 Nouns transformed into compound stems

A further effect of the integration of NCCs into the Italian lexicon and word-formation processes is the use of nouns transformed into compound stems in right-headed compounds. We may denominate compound stems the words (usually nouns) whose final vowel is modified to an *o* or an *i*, so as to bring them in line with the characteristic endings of neoclassical initial CFs, which are used as initial members of right-headed compounds in combination with final CFs. There are numerous examples: *alghicida* 'algaecide' (cf. *alga* 'alga'), *mafiologia* 'mafiology' (cf. *mafia*), *tendopoli* 'city of tents' (cf. *tenda* 'tent'). The *o* or *i* ending usually depends on the origin, respectively Greek or Latin, of the final formative element (cf. *parassitologo* and *parassiticida*). Modification of the word may also affect a segment larger than the final vowel (*cosmetologia* 'cosmetology' vs. *cosmetica*), producing in some cases haplology (*mineralogia* 'mineralogy' vs. *minerale*), or consists in the insertion of a vowel (*filmologia*, *islamologia*, *merceologia* vs. *film*, *islam*, *merce* 'goods').

The fact that the final vowel of the noun transformed into a compound stem normally depends on the final CF is held by some scholars to be a valid argument, from a strictly synchronic viewpoint, to attribute the vowels *o* and *i* to CFs. Such a hypothesis is justified only if forms beginning in vowels, such as *-icida*, *-ivoro*, *-ologia*, *-omane* (different from the etymological forms *-cida*, *-voro*, *-logia*, *-mane*), are considered as the effect of a process of grammaticalization toward the formation of derivational suffixes (cf. the verbalizing suffix *-ificare*). This reinterpretation must be motivated by an accurate analysis of the use of each of these elements, distinguishing between their use in compounding and in derivation (cf. Rainer 2009).

The main differences between nouns transformed into compound stems and CFs reside in the fact that the first are nouns used in the common language (and not learned elements derived from Greek or Latin) and are used only occasionally as elements of compounds and only in combination with final CFs (they cannot in fact form right-headed compounds in combination with words, cf. Antonelli 1996). Besides ending in the vowels *o* and *i*, and participating in the compound structure modifier + head, nouns transformed into compound stems share with neoclassical CFs limitations on the length of the modifier and on the position of stress: the final syllable of the modifier is never stressed and the modifier should not be longer than two or three syllables. Words that respond to these requisites and end in *o* can be used without requiring modifications: *cremlinologo* (cf. *Cremlino* 'Kremlin'), *futurologia* (cf. *futuro* 'future'), *gattofilo* (cf. *gatto* 'cat'). The fact that most masculine singular nouns end in *o* and that the final CFs are mostly of Greek origin neutralizes, in many cases, the distinction between nouns transformed into compound stems and words used in the citation form. This distinction is instead signalled by a formal indication in the case of Latin final CFs (which require an *i*, cf. *bulbiforme* from *bulbo* 'bulb', *cubiforme* from *cubo* 'cube') and in the case of words ending with another vowel (*cartografo* from *carta* 'paper', *ovaliforme* from *ovale* 'oval') or with a consonant (*filmografia* from *film*). The occasional use of nouns transformed into compound stems and the absence of a formal indication in the case of masculine nouns ending in *o* make any list of such forms particularly uncertain and variable. However, at the same time, the use of nouns transformed into compound stems in initial position of compounds together with CFs demonstrates the high degree of integration into the Italian lexicon the CFs that participate in these structures have achieved, the increasing degree of insertion in the modifier + head type within the compound system of Italian, and the instability of the borders separating words from CFs.

4 Spread of neoclassical compounds and combining forms in the common language

The integration of neoclassical CFs into the common usage of language and the consequences for the formative processes of Italian were identified in the 1930s by Bruno Migliorini (cf. Migliorini 1968). Words like *agriturismo* 'farm holidays', *autodemolitore* 'car breaker', *dermoprotettore* 'skin-protection', *ecopacifismo* 'eco-pacifism', *fotomontaggio* '(photo)montage', *idromassaggio* 'hydromassage', *telelavoro* 'telework', *videoconferenza* 'videoconference' represent an innovative factor in the morphology of the Italian language because before the beginning of the 20th century the formation of compounds in which a nominal element, acting as a modifier, precedes a noun, was absolutely marginal in Italian (as it was in other Romance languages).

The main word-formation patterns used in NCCs in no way constitute a radical novelty for Italian word-formation. Endogenous (a) and exogenous (b) factors have fostered the spread of nominal compounds with the structure modifier + head:

a) The presence (albeit restricted to technical, scientific and literary spheres) of subordinate compounds whose first member derives from adjectives or adverbs in classical languages (*pseudoprofeta* 'pseudo-prophet', *protomartire* 'proto-martyr') and coordinated adjectival compounds (*fisicomatematico* 'physico-mathematical', *politicomorale* 'politico-moral'). The former constitute a precedent for the modifier + head structure, the latter for the use of bound forms ending in *o* as initial compound elements.
b) The acceptance of compound words from Germanic languages (esp. English), whose normal order is modifier + head (*call center, car-sharing, floppy disk, personal computer, videogame*) (cf. section 6).

Following the spread of NCCs and the acceptance of Germanic compounds such patterns began reinforcing one another, due also to the fact that one and the same CF could participate in compounds in both structures (e.g., *socio-* in *sociolinguistica* 'sociolinguistics' and *socioculturale* 'sociocultural'), that many coordinate compounds also allow for a semantic interpretation of a determining type (compare the compound *franco-canadese* 'French-Canadian' in the context of *il trattato franco-canadese* which requires a coordinated interpretation 'the treaty between France and Canada', and in the context of *la cultura franco-canadese*, which requires a determining interpretation 'Canadian culture of French origin'), and that the function of modifier of the nominal element allows for a semantic interpretation of an adjectival type (*elettrotrazione* 'electric traction'). On the development of Italian coordinative adjectival compounds from Modern-Latin patterns originating from a determinative structure, cf. Hatcher (1954); Grossmann and Rainer (2009).

The spread in common usage of a NCC is not a sufficient condition for the identification of CFs and the pattern according to which the NCC is formed. Words like *emorragia* 'haemorrhage', *frigorifero* 'refrigerator', *microfono* 'microphone' are not usually analysed into meaningful constituents by the majority of people who use them.

While within technical-scientific terminology the distinction between bound and free lexical elements is not relevant, the presence of a free word within NCCs which come into common usage in current language is a factor of utmost importance for identifying components, especially in cases where the word acts as a head. Amongst the different compound structures, CF + word, CF + CF, word + CF, the first is most easily segmented and semantically interpreted by the majority of speakers.

Identification of the word facilitates comprehension of the structure of the compound, and consequently also the singling out of the CF with the function of modifier, fostering subsequent usage in analogous contexts.

This interpretation is supported by a quantitative analysis based on neologisms of the 20th century, which shows how the spread of CFs in the Italian language kept pace with their increase in use in formations of the type CF + word. The number of neo-formations of this type in common usage experienced a strong increase during the 20th century both with regard to other compound patterns that use CFs and also with regard to overall word-formation processes of Italian (cf. Iacobini and Thornton 1992; analogous trends have also been identified for French, cf. Peytard 1975).

In dictionaries of neologisms from the beginning of the 20th century, compounds formed by two CFs account for about 80 % of the compounds using CFs. As CFs gradually became more established parts of words in the common lexicon, the proportion of compounds of the CF-word type has increased at a regular rate and nowadays represents about 80 % of a corpus made up of words containing at least one CF that was published at the beginning of the 1990s. The most recent corpus and analyses (cf. Adamo and Della Valle 2003; Radimský 2006a: 135; Rati 2012) confirm that the compounds formed by initial CFs + word nowadays account for about 75 % of NCCs of new formation.

As proof of this integration of the CF-word type within common language usage, an analysis of dictionaries of neologisms published over the last thirty years shows that the initial CFs used only in combination with other CFs appeared only very rarely in more than one lexical entry, while the formative elements attached to words usually occur in more compounds. Amongst the initial CFs which are attached to words in a greater number of compounds in common usage are: *aero-*, *agri/o-*, *audio-*, *auto-*, *bio-*, *cine-*, *ciclo-*, *eco-*, *eli-*, *euro-*, *fanta-*, *filo-*, *fono-*, *foto-*, *mono-*, *narco-*, *paleo-*, *poli-*, *porno-*, *psico-*, *radio-*, *tecno-*, *tele-*, *uni-*, *video-*; cf. *audioguida* 'audioguide', *bioalimento* 'bio food', *cicloamatore* 'amateur cyclist', *ecomuseo* 'eco museum', *eurozona* 'eurozone', *fotobiografia* 'photobiography', *monouso* 'disposable', *narcotrafficante* 'drug dealer', *paleoindustriale* 'paleo-industrial', *pseudonotizia* 'pseudo news', *psicofarmaco* 'psychotropic drug', *televendita* 'TV sale', *videoconferenza* 'videoconference'.

In addition to the order of constituents, the compounds formed by CF + word have certain peculiarities that differentiate them from native left-headed compounds.

Compounds of the type CF + word have greater possibilities of being derived, and with greater number and more variety of suffixes (*biodegradabile* 'biodegradable' → *biodegradabilità* 'biodegradability'; *fotocopia* 'photocopy' converted to *fotocopiare* 'to photocopy' → *fotocopiatore*, *fotocopiatrice* 'photocopier', *fotocopiatura* 'photocopying'). Compounds of the type CF + word also differ from those which are genuinely Italian due to their greater adaptability in freely using already derived words (*aero-navigabilità*, *cardio-stimolatore*, *crio-conservazione*, *eco-conservatorismo*), and to their ability to form compound verbs (*aerotrasportare* 'to air transport', *teleguidare* 'to teleguide', *videochiamare* 'to videocall'). Although the verbs of this type are still of a limited number (and many of them might possibly be analyzed as backformation, cf. Rainer 2004), they represent quite an important novelty in the formative system of Italian and at the same time pick up from a pattern that is present, albeit marginally in Late Latin (*manūtenēre*, *fidĕicommittĕre*, *genuflectĕre*), and present also in other Romance languages (Cat. *cama-trencar* leg-break 'to break the leg(s) (of an animal)', Sp. *mani-atar* hand-bind 'to bind the hands (of a person)', cf. Klingebiel 1989; Gràcia and Fullana 2000; Iacobini 2013).

Final CFs that form compounds in combination with words are fewer in comparison to initial CFs and form a fewer number of compounds in current usage. This lower productivity probably depends on the need for nouns transformed into stems (cf. section 3.3) as first members of compounds (with consequent phonological limitations), and might also be due to the fact that the word constitutes the non-head element of the compound. Final CFs that are relatively frequent in common usage words are: *-cida*, *-colo*, *-coltore*, *-crate*, *-fago*, *-fero*, *-fobo*, *-fugo*, *-geno*, *-grafo/ia*, *-logo/ia*, *-mane/-ia*, *-metro*, *-nauta*, *-paro*, *-teca*, *-voro*. The meanings expressed by these CFs are more homogenous compared to those of initial CFs. They express almost exclusively agentive and instrumental meanings. Compounds formed with final CFs have some similarities with the synthetic compounds of the Germanic languages and with the verb-noun compounds of Romance languages (cf. *meat-eater* and *carnivoro*, *portabandiera* and *vessillifero* 'standard-bearer').

Final CFs tend to be used in paradigmatic series in which the compound nouns indicating an agent or a tool are normally without derivational suffix (*lessicografo* 'lexicographer', *sismografo* 'seismograph'; but for certain CFs, derivatives with the agentive suffix *-ista* are also possible: *ecologista* 'environmentalist', *telegrafista*), those that indicate an action, an activity or the result of an activity are suffixed with *-ia* (*lessicografia*, *fotografia*), while the adjectives referring to the *-ia* nouns are suffixed with *-ico* (*lessicografico*, *fotografico*). Amongst the words with agentive-instrumental meaning and their corresponding suffix forms in *-ia* the morphological structure does not always correspond to the semantic one; it is in fact the noun suffixed with *-ia* which normally constitutes the semantic base of the name of the agent or tool: a *paleoantropologo* is not actually an 'ancient anthropologist', but a scholar of *paleoantropologia*. The *-logo*/*-logia* pair is the one that has the densest number of words in common usage: *futurologo*/*ia* 'futurologist/y', *politologo*/*-ia* 'political scientist/science', *tuttologo* 'know-it-all' (from *tutto* 'all'); other examples of compounds formed with final CFs are: *apicoltore* 'beekeeper', *ansiogeno* 'anxiety-provoking', *esteromania* 'foreign mania', *criminogeno* 'criminogenic', *eroinomane* 'heroin addict', *fotogenico* 'photogenic', *meritocrazia* 'meritocracy', *redditometro* 'income meter', *spermicida* 'spermicidal', *vermifugo* 'vermifuge'.

The preceding CFs are to be distinguished from those that form names of places (e.g., *-dromo* in *rocciodromo* 'gym of rock'). Among these the most frequently used is *-teca*, which apart from being used with the meaning 'gathering, collection' (*cineteca* 'film library'), is used with great success in the formation of shop names whose activities are connected to the initial element in the compound (*discoteca* 'discotheque', *minestroteca* from *minestra* 'soup', *paninoteca* from *panino* 'sandwich', *scarpoteca* from *scarpa* 'shoe').

The possibility that a CF is used in combination with words in a compound of common usage depends greatly on the meaning it expresses. Productivity in the formations in current usage may therefore vary over time. For example, some CFs in use in the 1960s are no longer used for new words, while others (e.g., *bio-*, *eco-*, *fanta-*, *narco-*, *psico-*, *tecno-*) have given rise to many neologisms. Extra-linguistic influence on the spread of CFs can be noted for example in the widespread use during the 1950s and the 1960s of formations with *aero-* and *avio-* (*aerostazione* 'air terminal', *aviogetto* 'jet-plane'), which has diminished in use since the 1980s, and the recent decline in the productivity of *auto-* 'car'. Consider, as well, the strong spread of *tele-* and *video-* from the end of the 1960s and the more recent fortunes of *euro-* and CFs connected to the digital world (*e-*, *cyber-*, *wiki-*, etc.). It can therefore be concluded that compounds with CFs are by now an integral part of word-formation in contemporary Italian.

5 From combining form to affix

A clear example of the integration of foreign elements into native word-formation patterns can be seen in the passage from a CF to a derivational affix (cf. Kastovsky 2009 for the passage from lexical compound elements to affixal derivational elements in foreign word-formation). Such a passage is more frequent from initial CFs to prefixes than from final CFs to suffixes (for a detailed analysis of the integration of a final neoclassical CF in suffixal derivation of Italian, cf. Rainer 2009). The initial CFs which more closely resemble derivational prefixes are those whose meanings express space, time, qualitative and quantitative evaluation. Many scholars agree on the fact that elements such as *auto-* 'self', *iper-*, *ipo-*, *macro-*, *mega-*, *meta-*, *micro-*, *multi-*, *neo-*, *para-*, *pluri-*, *poli-* are part of the system of Italian prefixes (cf. Iacobini 2004b; Montermini 2009) despite the fact that they can be used in combination with final CFs in the formation of technical-scientific terms (*autoctono* 'autochthonous', *iperfasia* 'hyperphasia', *ipotassi* 'hypotaxis'), apart from being attached to words in common language: *autoritratto* 'self-portrait', *iperattivo* 'hyperactive', *ipocalorico* 'low calorie'.

6 Right-headed noun-noun compounds and other compounds from foreign patterns

Besides NCCs, patterns from modern foreign languages have had a strong influence on the spread of compounding within word-formation processes in Present-day Italian. Foreign influence must be seen above all as an impulse for the spread of compounding, and secondly, for the spread of new compound types and the revitalization and dissemination of marginal patterns.

The presence of foreign compounds in the Italian lexicon is particularly evident in the great number of non-adapted English compounds that are used in different contexts and varieties of the language (from the more formal context of scientific and informative prose to the colloquial language of young people). If non-adapted English compounds are the most immediately visible of foreign compounds, we must remember that their dissemination was preceded by the absorption of foreign compounds in the form of calques, of which both the lexemes and the order of compound constituents were Italianized.

The types of foreign compounds accepted into Italian can be classified according to different criteria, the main ones being head-position, and the use of native vs. foreign lexemes. According to these criteria we can distinguish three main types of loan compounds: i) adapted head-modifier compounds; ii) adapted modifier-head compounds; iii) non-adapted modifier-head compounds.

Type (i) translates lexemes and reorders the relationship between the constituents according to the order of the native compounds (in the Italian adaptation the compound becomes left-headed): *area depressa* from *depressed area*, *arrampicatore sociale* from *social climber*, *cartoni animati* from *animated cartoons*, *Casa Bianca* from *White House*, *economia sommersa* from *underground economy*, *fine settimana* from *week-end*, *sedia elettrica* from *electric chair*, *sviluppo sostenibile* from *sustainable development*, *tavola rotonda* from *round table*, *visopallido* from *paleface*. In type (ii) – a group consisting of a small number of compounds – the lexemes are native, but the order is foreign (modifier + head): *scuolabus* from *school bus*, *pubbliche relazioni* from *public relations*, *nuova economia* from *new economy*, *politicamente corretto* from *politically correct*; *madrelingua* from G. *Muttersprache*, *madrepatria* from G. *Mutterland*. Type (iii) accepts the loanword in its original form, the nouns are customarily invariable but the verbs are inflected in the productive *-are* conjugation (*bypassare*, *downloadare*, *e-mailare*, *upgradare*): *baby-sitter*, *cameraman*, *full-time*, *happy hour*, *latin lover*, *mass media*, *part-time*, *peace-keeping*, *pop music*, *self-service*, *street food*.

The ease with which Anglo-American loan compounds are borrowed in Italian in non-adapted form, besides reasons of linguistic prestige, can also be explained by the fact that many of them are, in effect, "Anglolatinisms", i.e. compounds formed from lexemes which English has borrowed from Latin (particularly as regards the intellectual, technical and abstract parts of vocabulary). This fosters the phenomenon of interlingual identification of lexemes, an extremely important factor in the acceptance of loanwords and in the formation of calques (cf. Weinreich 1953).

The main consequences of the borrowing of foreign compounds for Italian compound patterns are: the formation of right-headed nominal compounds with native elements, the formation of both right- and left-headed mixed compounds (i.e. compounds with a native and a foreign element), and the spread of attributive compounds.

Right-headed nominal compounds with native elements have a structure which is similar to that of NCCs, but they are formed with lexemes of the common language. There are not many compounds of this type. Most are formed by two nouns (*acquascivolo* 'water slide', *agopuntura* 'acupuncture', *cartamodello* 'paper pattern', *calciomercato* 'transfer market', from *calcio* 'football'), but there are also adjectival compounds (*lungimirante* 'far-sighted', *lungodegente* 'long-term patient', *telefonino-dipendente* 'cell phone addicted'). These compounds are not completely new to Italian since they are similar in structure to words of Latin origin like *terremoto* 'earthquake' or *onnipotente* 'omnipotent', a marginal pattern with respect to number and productivity. The gender of these compounds is usually determined by the gender of the right constituent; but exceptions do exist, for instance *calcio scommesse* 'illegal bets on football results' is singular masculine despite the fact that the semantic head-noun is feminine plural *scommesse* 'bets'.

Anglo-Italian mixed compounds have been described in Dardano, Frenguelli and Puoti (2005) and in Frenguelli (2005) with data extracted from the press and from dictionaries. The presence of foreign lexemes in compounds might be interpreted as an integration of such lexemes (and of the compound patterns in which they are used) into the Italian language. The number of these compounds is slightly increasing.

In mixed compounds (which are the result of Italian formations but also of the partial adaptation of calques from English compounds), all the possibilities resulting from the combination of the parameters head position and native vs. foreign origin are attested: 1) Italian head + English modifier, 2) English modifier + Italian head, 3) Italian modifier + English head, 4) English head + Italian modifier.

The combination Italian head + English modifier (type 1) is by far the most numerous and productive category and includes, apart from subordinate, also coordinate compounds. The final constituents tend to be used in paradigmatic series (e.g., *nebbia/zanzara/strada-killer* 'fog/mosquito/road that kills'): *ascolti-flop* 'unsuccessful TV or radio ratings', *caldo record* 'heat that breaks every existing record', *confessione shock* 'a confession provoking great surprise', *crescita boom* 'exceptional growth', *moda vintage* 'vintage fashion', *palla goal* 'a goal opportunity', *pensione baby* 'a pension obtained at a young age'. There are also compounds of this type with constituents that come from other languages: *cane robot* 'a mechanical toy resembling a dog and reproducing certain dog-like behaviour', *donna kamikaze* 'a woman who voluntarily lays down her life in a terrorist action', *ospizio lager* 'a hospice where inmates are treated inhumanely'.

The combination English modifier + Italian head (type 2) includes many partial calques: *baby-piscina* 'baby pool', *computer assistito* 'computer-assisted', *internet-caffè* 'internet café', *net-azienda* 'net-company', *sexy-scandalo* 'sexual scandal', *web-sondaggio* 'web poll'.

In type 3 (Italian modifier + English head) it is the head which is used in series in many compounds (e.g., *Berlusconi/rifiuti tossici/mafia-story* 'the reconstruction of events surrounding and concerning Berlusconi/toxic waste/mafia'), *calcio crack* 'financial collapse in the world of football', *papa boy* 'young man supporting the Pope', *referendum-day* 'awareness-raising day or day of a referendum'.

Predictably, type 4 (English head + Italian modifier), formed according to the native left-headed pattern, only includes well-integrated foreign words: *gol vittoria* 'a deciding goal', *film-culto* 'cult movie', *mail spazzatura* 'junk-mail'.

During the 20th century the borrowing of foreign compounds fostered the emergence in Italian of attributive compounds (cf. *carta carbone* from Engl. *carbon paper, romanzo fiume* from Fr. *roman-fleuve* novel-river 'extended sequence of novels', *guerra lampo* from G. *Blitzkrieg* 'lightning war'). This concerns left-headed noun-noun compounds, in which the final constituent specifies the initial one, serving a function similar to that of an adjective (cf. *bambino prodigio* 'child prodigy', *pesce spada* 'sword fish'). This type of nominal compound is probably the most productive in contemporary Italian. The frequency of use of some nouns in final position in formations in series (e.g., *elemento/parola/personaggio-chiave* 'key element/word/figure') has led to the formation of a secondary sense: for example, *chiave* assumes in these contexts the meaning 'very important', a type of construction which is also present in mixed compounds like *caldo record, crescita boom.* Other recent left-headed constructions that have features in common with the previous types and have been given increased vigour by foreign patterns (cf. Klajn 1972: 174–187; Lombardi Vallauri 2008) are constructions in which the first element (used in series) introduces the second: *allarme-criminalità/inflazione* lit. 'alert-criminality/inflation', *caro-affitto/benzina* lit. 'high cost rental/petrol', *emergenza-droga/freddo* lit. 'emergency drug/cold', *rischio-terrorismo/alluvione* lit. 'risk terrorism/flood', respectively paraphrasable as 'situation of alarm and danger caused by X', 'increase in price of X', 'situation of alarm and concern regarding X', 'situation of alarm and danger regarding X'.

Other consequences of a systematic nature for the Italian lexicon are the use of non-head constituents of English compounds with the meaning of the whole compound (cf. Vogel 1990): *night* ← *night club, Play* ← *PlayStation, trench* ← *trench coat, water* ← *water-closet.* This phenomenon (common also to other Romance languages) is due to the reinterpretation of compounds according to the structure of native Romance compounds (head + modifier), and reducing them to the initial constituent. In these cases, it is clear that the meaning of foreign lexemes which form the compound is unknown or deliberately ignored.

The presence and the prestige of English borrowings have contributed to the spread of compounds which, despite appearing English, are not English formations: *autostop* 'hitchhiking', *beauty case* 'vanity bag'. Attention deserves to be given to the creation of the compound 'slow food', the name of an organization founded at the end of the '80s by a group of Italian gastronomists, farmers and intellectuals whose aim is to link the pleasure of good food with a commitment to their community and the environment, and to counter the rise of fast food and fast life. The compound *slow food*, which was given birth to in Italy, has already spread across the globe, and the shortened form *slow* combines as a modifier both with English words currently in use in Italian (*slow revolution, slow design, slow life*) and in post-nominal position with Italian words: *cultura slow, città slow.*

We must finally make mention of acronyms and initialisms, processes which have developed in contemporary Italian due to the influence of foreign borrowings: *DDT, BBC, ko, NATO, ok, NASA, SOS, TV, USA, WC.*

7 Derivation

Affixes are not adopted as independent units, but can be extracted from derived lexemes. Unlike compounding, foreign patterns have not had significant effects on the spread of derivational types.

7.1 Prefixation

A general tendency which can be partially attributed to a foreign influence, is the recent emergence of the more conservative Latinate allotropic forms as opposed to the modified form, following the phonotactic rules of the Italian language. In the coinage of neologisms, there is a preference for the forms *circum-, extra-, sub-, super-, trans-*, as opposed to *circon-, estra-, so-, sopra-, sovra-, tra-, tras-*, even in contexts in which in the previous stages of the language we observe phenomena of assimilation and reduction (cf. *soccorrere* and *subconscio, suddividere* and *subdesertico, trascorrere* and *transcaucasico, trapiantare* and *transpolare*).

Prefixes whose use has increased during the second half of the 20th century, due to their presence in words circulating internationally are: *anti-, de-, inter-, pre-, post-* (cf. *antimissile* 'anti-rocket', *decodificare* 'decodify', *interattivo* 'interactive', *prenatale* 'prenatal', *postindustriale* 'postindustrial'). In these cases it is not easy to distinguish the contribution from English as opposed to other languages. For prefixation too, the recent tendency to maintain a constant and invariable form and to increase the number of consonant clusters permitted has been confirmed (*inscrutabile, interclassista, postclassico*, cf. De Mauro 1976: 408–409).

An influence from individual languages can be noted in the prefixes of French origin, *sur-* and *mis-* (*surgelare* 'to deep-freeze', *surriscaldare* 'to overheat', *miscredente* 'unbeliever', *misfatto* 'misdeed'), and in the prefix *mini-*, borrowed from English in the 1960s (*minigonna* 'mini-skirt', *minivacanza* 'mini-holiday'). The English language has strongly influenced the spread of the prefixes *co-* 'together, in common, joint/-ly, reciprocally, mutually', and *auto-* 'self, by oneself, independent/-ly'. The former, as a phonologically conditioned variant of the prefix *con-*, has become the only really productive form (so much so as to allow for the formation of word pairs with different meanings: *cogestione* 'joint management'/ *congestione* 'congestion', *corettore* 'co-rector'/*correttore* 'correcting fluid, concealer'). The latter, as an element which was present sporadically in words of classic origin (*autoctono* 'autochthonous', *autografo* 'autograph', *autopsia* 'autopsy'), have become more important during the 20th century as a productive prefix in many words in common usage. Both prefixes have experienced much greater use from the second half of the 20th century on. In the case of *co-*, the role of English has been decisive due to borrowings in current usage, as in *cobelligerante* 'co-belligerent'/*cobelligeranza* 'co-belligerency' (cf. Väänänen 1979), see also *coproduzione* 'co-production', *cofondatore* 'co-founder', *copilota* 'co-pilot'. The use of *auto-* has been enhanced by calques of English words formed with *self-*, accepted into Italian between the end of the 19th century and the beginning of the 20th century: *autogoverno* 'self-government', *autocritica* 'self-criticism', *autodifesa* 'self-defence', *autosuggestione* 'self-suggestion'.

Here we are dealing with two prefixes that derive from the classical languages and have been present in Italian words since well before the 20th century; the English language however, in this case, has acted as a catalysing factor which has operated in harmony with intrinsic tendencies of the receiving system. In the case of *co-*, English language influence fostered the elimination of combinatory variants due to assimilation processes. However, in the case of *auto-* it has allowed for the development of a morphological way of expression for a morphosyntactic relation which did not have a specific derivational form in Italian: a word prefixed by *auto-* corresponds in fact, both in the argument structure and the thematic roles, to the unprefixed reflexive verb in much the same way as the action noun corresponds to the verb in the active form. A system of correspondence which can be summed up in the following equivalence *autocontrollo* 'self-control' : *controllarsi* 'to control oneself' = *controllo* 'control' : *controllare* 'to control' (cf. Iacobini 2003).

A reinforcement effect from the English language has also occurred in the case of the use of *non-* as a prefix (cf. Bombi 1992). *Non-* is the only prefix in Italian allowing for the expression of contradictory negation, that is, a relation between two elements in such a way that the negation of one implies the affirmation of the other in mutually exclusive relationships: *non-belligeranza* 'non-belligerence', *non-docente* 'non-teacher', *non-intervento* 'non-intervention', *non vedente* 'visually handicapped person'. These formations differ from another construction, itself also deriving from English: *no cani, no foto, no autostop,* which, according to Grasso (2007: 189–196), has an elliptical origin: *no dogs* (allowed).

7.2 Suffixation

The influence of English and French borrowings has fostered over the 20th century the spread of the verbalizing suffix *-izzare: ibridizzare, liberalizzare, attualizzare, ideologizzare* (cf. Engl. *hybrydize, liberalize*, Fr. *actualiser, idéologiser*) and consequently the nominal suffix *-zione*.

The prestige of borrowings adapted from English, such as *motivazionale, promozionale*, has fostered the spread of adjectives with the suffix *-ale* even in cases in which there were pre-existing synonymous words (cf. *facoltativo/opzionale, nutritivo/nutrizionale*). Of more interest is the case of *-ese* which, originally designating the inhabitant as well as the language of the place denoted by the base noun (*Milano → milanese, Vienna → viennese*), entered the English language in loanwords, where it was then used "to coin words denoting a strangely peculiar style, a negatively characteristic jargon" (Marchand 1969: 286), as in *Americanese, officialese*. This new meaning of the suffix migrated back to Italy in the second half of the 20th century: *politichese* 'political jargon', *giovanilese* 'youth jargon' (cf. Bombi 2003: 122–123).

One suffix which is clearly of foreign origin is *-y*, which is used as the final element of bi-syllabic trochaic shortenings of proper names to form hypocorisms which particularly denote women, *Emy* from *Emanuela, Giusy* from *Giuseppina*, but also males *Tony* from *Antonio, Roby* from *Roberta/Roberto* (cf. Caffarelli 1996: 525; Thornton 2007).

Identification of English suffixes in borrowings can be seen, according to Dardano (2009: 183), in the prevalent use of the form *plottaggio* beside *plotteraggio* 'plottering', and in the circulation in Romance languages of pseudoanglicisms: *camping* 'camp, camp-site', *footing* 'jogging'. The English plural marker *-s* is sometimes erroneously extended to words in other languages: *soviets, Talibans*. English scientific prose is also responsible for the spread of the use of the plural form of Latin words, which until recently were considered invariable in Italian (*corpus/corpora, thesaurus/thesauri*), a further example of the recovery of Latin forms in Italian through foreign influence.

8 References

Adamo, Giovanni and Valeria Della Valle (2003): *Neologismi quotidiani. Un dizionario a cavallo del millennio 1998–2003*. Firenze: Olschki.

Antonelli, Giuseppe (1996): Sui prefissoidi dell'italiano contemporaneo. *Studi di lessicografia italiana* 13: 253–293.

Bombi, Raffaella (1992): Il modulo "Non+sostantivo" nell'italiano contemporaneo. *Incontri Linguistici* 15: 79–92.

Bombi, Raffaella (2003): Anglicismi come banco di prova dell'interferenza linguistica. In: Anna-Vera Sullam Calimani (ed.), *Italiano e inglese a confronto*, 101–125. Firenze: Cesati.

Caffarelli, Enzo (1996): *L'onomastica personale nella città di Roma dalla fine del secolo XIX ad oggi. Per una prospettiva di cronografia e sociografia antroponimica.* Tübingen: Niemeyer.

Dardano, Maurizio (2009): *Costruire parole. La morfologia derivativa dell'italiano*. Bologna: il Mulino.

Dardano, Maurizio, Gianluca Frenguelli and Alberto Puoti (2005): Anglofilia (para)testuale e morfologica? In: Iørn Korzen and Paolo D'Achille (eds.), *Tipologia linguistica e società*, 229–248. Firenze: Cesati.

De Mauro, Tullio (1976): *Storia linguistica dell'Italia unita.* 3rd ed. Roma/Bari: Laterza.

De Mauro, Tullio (2005): *La fabbrica delle parole. Il lessico e problemi di lessicologia.* Torino: UTET.

Fradin, Bernard (2000): Combining forms, blends and related phenomena. In: Ursula Doleschal and Anna M. Thornton (eds.), *Extragrammatical and Marginal Morphology*, 11–59. München: LINCOM Europa.

Frenguelli, Gianluca (2005): La composizione con elementi inglesi. In: Claudio Giovanardi (ed.), *Lessico e formazione delle parole. Studi offerti a Maurizio Dardano per il suo 70° compleanno*, 159–176. Firenze: Cesati.

Gardani, Francesco (2019): Morphology and Contact-Induced Language Change. In: Anthony P. Grant (ed.), *Oxford Handbook of Language Contact*, 96–122. Oxford: Oxford University Press.

Giannoulopoulou, Giannoula (2006): On the borderline between lexicon and grammar: Confixes in Modern Greek and Italian. *Sprachtypologie und Universalienforschung* 59: 270–283.

Gràcia, Lluïsa and Olga Fullana (2000): Catalan verbal compounds: Internal order and argument interpretation. In: Wolfgang U. Dressler, Oskar E. Pfeiffer, Markus A. Pöchtrager and John R. Rennison (eds.), *Morphological Analysis in Comparison*, 75–87. Amsterdam/Philadelphia: Benjamins.

Grasso, Daniele (2007): Innovazioni sintattiche in italiano alla luce della nozione di calco. Ph.D. dissertation, University of Geneva.

Grossmann, Maria and Franz Rainer (2009): Italian adjective-adjective compounds: Between morphology and syntax. *Italian Journal of Linguistics* 21: 71–96.

Hatcher, Anna Granville (1951): *Modern English Word-Formation and Neo-Latin. A study of the origins of English (French, Italian, German) copulative compounds.* Baltimore: The John Hopkins Press.

Iacobini, Claudio (2003): Due casi di interferenza dell'inglese sulla morfologia derivazionale dell'italiano. In: Anna-Vera Sullam Calimani (ed.), *Italiano e inglese a confronto*, 43–56. Firenze: Cesati.

Iacobini, Claudio (2004a): Composizione con elementi neoclassici. In: Maria Grossmann and Franz Rainer (eds.), *La formazione delle parole in italiano*, 69–95. Tübingen: Niemeyer.

Iacobini, Claudio (2004b): Prefissazione. In: Maria Grossmann and Franz Rainer (eds.), *La formazione delle parole in italiano*, 97–163. Tübingen: Niemeyer.

Iacobini, Claudio (2013): Il tipo "videoregistrare": Da retroformazione all'emergere di un nuovo processo compositivo fondato su di un vecchio modello romanzo. In: Joachim Born and Wolfgang Pöckl (eds.), *"Wenn die Ränder ins Zentrum drängen …". Außenseiter in der Wortbildung(sforschung)*, 189–212. Berlin: Frank & Timme.

Iacobini, Claudio and Anna M. Thornton (1992): Tendenze nella formazione delle parole nell'italiano del ventesimo secolo. In: Bruno Moretti, Dario Petrini and Sandro Bianconi (eds.), *Linee di tendenza dell'italiano contemporaneo*, 25–55. Roma: Bulzoni.

Kastovsky, Dieter (2009): *Astronaut, astrology, astrophysics*: About combining forms, classical compounds and affixoids. In: Roderick W. McConchie, Alpo Honkapohja and Jukka Tyrkkö (eds.), *Selected Proceedings of the 2008 Symposium on New Approaches in English Historical Lexis (HEL-LEX 2)*, 1–13. Somerville, MA: Cascadilla.

Klajn, Ivan (1972): *Influssi inglesi nella lingua italiana.* Firenze: Olschki.

Klingebiel, Kathryn (1989): *Noun + Verb Compounding in Western Romance*. Berkeley: University of California Press.

Kortas, Jan (2009): Les hybrides lexicaux en français contemporain: Délimitation du concept. *Meta* 54: 533–550.

Lombardi Vallauri, Edoardo (2008): Composti intitolativi in italiano: Un'oscillazione. In: Emanuela Cresti (ed.), *Prospettive nello studio del lessico italiano*. Vol. 2, 555–562. Firenze: Firenze University Press.

Marchand, Hans (1969): *The Categories and Types of Present-Day English Word-Formation. A Synchronic-Diachronic Approach.* 2nd ed. München: Beck.

Mattiello, Elisa (2008): From sexgate to vallettopoli: Contrasting English and Italian combining forms. In: Carla Vergaro (ed.), *Dynamics of Language Contact in the Twenty First Century*, 177–190. Perugia: Guerra.

Micheli, M. Silvia (2020): *Composizione italiana in diacronia. Le parole composte dell'italiano nel quadro della Morfologia delle Costruzioni*. Berlin/Boston: De Gruyter.

Migliorini, Bruno (1968): *Profili di parole.* Firenze: Le Monnier.

Montermini, Fabio (2009): *Il lato sinistro della morfologia. La prefissazione in italiano e nelle lingue del mondo.* Milano: Franco Angeli.

Peytard, Jean (1975): *Recherches sur la préfixation en français contemporain.* Paris: Champion.

Radimský, Jan (2006a): *Les composés italiens actuels.* Paris: Cellule de recherche en linguistique.

Radimský, Jan (2006b): Composition indigène et confixation: deux procédés concurrents en italien contemporain. *Écho des études romanes* 2: 13–25.

Rainer, Franz (2004): Retroformazione. In: Maria Grossmann and Franz Rainer (eds.), *La formazione delle parole in Italiano*, 493–497. Tübingen: Niemeyer.

Rainer, Franz (2008): Neo- and Neo-Latin. *Word Structure* 1: 53–64.

Rainer, Franz (2009): Die Integration des lateinischen Kompositionstyps *tauriformis* im Französischen und Italienischen. *Zeitschrift für romanische Philologie* 125: 45–84.

Rati, Maria Silvia (2012): La formazione delle parole nell'italiano contemporaneo: Sondaggi sui dizionari dell'uso. In: Silvana Ferreri (ed.), *Lessico e lessicologia*, 121–129. Roma: Bulzoni.

Thornton, Anna M. (1996): On some phenomena of prosodic morphology in Italian: "Accorciamenti", hypocoristics and prosodic delimitation. *Probus* 8: 81–112.

Thornton, Anna M. (2007): Phenomènes de réduction en italien. In: Elisabeth Delais-Roussarie and Laurence Labrune (eds.), *Des sons et des sens. Données et modèles en phonologie et en morphologie*, 241–268. Paris: Hermès Science/Lavoisier.

Väänänen, Veikko (1979): *Co-*: La genèse d'un préfixe. In: Manfred Höfler, Henri Vernay and Lothar Wolf (eds.), *Festschrift Kurt Baldinger zum 60. Geburtstag, 17. November 1979*, 317–329. Tübingen: Niemeyer.

Virgilio, Giulia (2023): *Parole al microscopio. I composti neoclassici nell'italiano delle scienze tra Settecento e primo Ottocento*. Firenze: Cesati.

Vogel, Irene (1990): English compounds in Italian: The question of the head. In: Wolfgang U. Dressler, Hans C. Luschützky, Oskar E. Pfeiffer and John R. Rennison (eds.), *Contemporary Morphology*, 99–110. Berlin/New York: Mouton de Gruyter.

Warren, Beatrice (1990): The importance of combining forms. In: Wolfgang U. Dressler, Hans C. Luschützky, Oskar E. Pfeiffer and John. R. Rennison (eds.), *Contemporary Morphology*, 111–132. Berlin/New York: Mouton de Gruyter.

Weinreich, Uriel (1953): *Languages in Contact. Findings and Problems*. New York: Linguistic Circle of New York.

Krystyna Waszakowa

7 Foreign word-formation in Polish

Abstract: The initial section provides an historical overview of lexical borrowings in Polish. The following two sections of this article outline important aspects of the subject matter defined in its title: the role of the word-formation system of Polish in the process of loan adaptation and the criteria for recognizing a given item as a synchronic derivative with a foreign element. The forth section presents a synthetic description of derivatives and compounds with foreign elements active in word-formation processes; it focuses on the dynamic aspects of foreign word-formation in Modern Polish. The final section discusses various types of phenomena that illustrate the impact of the tendency towards lexicon internationalization on the role played by foreign word-formation in the Polish language of the late 20th and early 21st centuries. The discussion will focus on nouns (the vast majority of which were borrowed at different times from different languages).

1 Historical aspects

The fact that the Polish language is susceptible to foreign influence is evidenced by processes observed over centuries whereby words and meanings are borrowed. Lexical borrowings appeared in Polish in the earliest stages of its development and have remained its characteristic feature throughout the ensuing centuries. Evidence for this thesis is provided by Klemensiewicz (1961–72) in his *History of the Polish Language*; the claims and examples below have been taken from this work. Elements of foreign origin (Gothic, Old High German, Latin) can be found in the vocabulary of the earliest stages of the language, before it was

Krystyna Waszakowa, Warszawa, Poland

https://doi.org/10.1515/9783111420530-007

written down; they are words borrowed at the time of the Proto-Slavic linguistic community prior to the separation of Proto-Polish dialects, for example *kupić* 'to buy' (PSl. **kǫpiti*, cf. Gothic *kaupōn* 'to engage in trade', Latin *caupo* 'stall-keeper'), *lekarz* 'doctor' (PSl. **lěkarь*, cf. Gothic *lēkeis* 'doctor'), *wino* 'wine' (PSl. **vino*, cf. Latin *vinum*). Latin is the language that has influenced Polish for the longest period of time, for as many as eleven centuries (10th–20th century); thus, the timeline of Latin-Polish linguistic contacts covers the entire history of Polish. Latin is the source of a major part of Christian terminology via Czech, including such words as: *anioł* (earlier: *ańjoł*, Old Czech *anjel*, Latin *angelus*), *ewangelia* (earlier: *ewanjelia*, Czech *ewanjelium*, Latin *euangelium*), as well as through double intermediation, first German and then Czech, e.g., *kościół* 'church' (**kost'oł* from Old High German *kástel*, which was transformed in Czech into *kostel*, and which is a continuation of the Latin *castellum*). These two languages, which served as medium of transmission, marked their presence to a different degree and in different moments: Czech (10th–16th century), German (12th–20th century); further periods of influence were from Turkish (13th–17th century), Hungarian (14th–16th century), Ruthenian languages (14th–19th century), Italian (16th–17th century), French (16th–20th century), Russian (19th–20th century) and English (since the 19th century). The many direct lexical borrowings in the Middle Polish period (16th–18th century) come above all from German (e.g., *burmistrz* 'mayor'), Latin (e.g., *rektor* 'rector'), Italian (e.g., *bank*), French (e.g., *fryzjer* 'hairdresser'). In the same period, borrowings also appear from Ruthenian languages (e.g., *znachor* 'quack doctor'), Turkish (e.g., *haracz* 'tribute'), Hungarian (*dobosz* 'drummer'). The weakening influence of Latin was replaced by strong French influence in the first half of the 19th century (Latin borrowings are common primarily in scholarly terminology and nomenclature). In addition, due to the political conditions to which the Polish nation was subjected in the 19th century, German influence became visible in the lands annexed by Prussia and Austria (the expansion of German structures was observed not merely in the vocabulary, but in syntax and word-formation as well) and Russian influence in the area annexed by Russia. The influence of English on Polish, which was very weak in the 19th century and limited prior to World War II, has been increasing since 1945 with each passing decade (primarily because linguistic internationalization processes have become more intensive), while French, German and Russian influence has been waning, cf. Bajerowa (2003).

2 Word-formational adaptation of loans

In this article, I focus on modern processes related to the word-formational adaptation of loans into Polish. It is generally accepted that it is not individual morphemes that are borrowed, but entire words, from which a given formant is then abstracted. The abstraction of formants from borrowed words typically occurs at the time when the given language is exerting the strongest influence on Polish. Therefore, we may assume the following chronology of appearance of the individual formants: a) The turn of the Old Polish and Middle Polish era (16th/17th century) brought formants of Latin and Greek origin such as *-izm* (*anachron-izm* < Latin *anachron-ismus*, Greek *anachronismós*), *-ista* (*sofista* 'sophist'), *-ita* (*jezuita* 'Jesuit'), *-ika/-yka* (*tragika, poetyka*), *-ja* (*decyzja* 'decision'), *-or* (*audytor* 'auditor'), *-ejusz* (*plebejusz* 'plebeian'). b) The Old Polish era also brought German formants: *-ierz* (subsequently *-arz*, from German *-er*, cf. *farb-ierz* 'colourer' < *Färber*), *-unk* (subsequently *-unek*, from German *-ung*, cf. *rachunek* 'account' < *Rechnung*. c) Borrowings from French (18th century) of the type *ingénieur* (Polish *inżynier*) are the source of the suffix *-inier/-ynier*, which, after a time, started to be used to form native derivatives, e.g., *uciekinier* 'deserter' ← *uciec/uciekać* 'to run away'. d) Borrowings from English of the type *trening* 'training' are the source of the suffix *-ing* (cf. Klemensiewicz 1961–72; Rospond 1971; Waszakowa 1994). According to Szymczak (1976), over the course of its history through the 1970s, Polish borrowed 49 affixal elements: 26 suffixes and 23 prefixes. Foreign derivatives, despite their separate status, co-organize the word-formation system of Polish on a par with other word-formation units, and thus constitute an integral part of it. One of the clear signs of the integration of foreign elements into Polish is "the fact that derivational formations comprising a native noun or adjective and a foreign prefix have become settled in the language for good", which Szymczak (1982: 24) considers a tendency present in the Polish language of 1918–1978, citing numerous hybrid examples such as *eks-mąż* 'ex-husband', *kontrnatarcie* 'counter-offensive', *antywojenny* (adj.) 'anti-war', *supernowoczesny* 'ultramodern'. The special status of these foreign formants is evidenced by the fact that the vast majority of them are international derivational elements that belong to the international lexicon (Waszakowa 1994, 2005).

The special role of the word-formation system in loan adaptation processes is illustrated by derivatives created from borrowed words on the one hand (such as the agent noun *grafici-arz* 'graffiti painter, graffiti artist' from the Italian *graffiti*, the adjective *internet-owy* from the English *Internet*), and, on the other hand, by the process whereby internationalisms such as *globalizm, globalista, antyglobalista* 'globalism, globalist, antiglobalist' acquire motivation in Polish.

The synchronic analysis of derivatives with foreign elements is based on the same principles as the analysis of native vocabulary. Thus, a derivative (motivated word) is a lexeme which enters into a formal and semantic relationship with another word (other words). A foreign lexeme that uses borrowed morphemes will be deemed motivated when another lexeme can be found which is formally and semantically related to it and which is basic with regard to it, i.e. formally and/or semantically simpler or identical. The preliminary effect of such an approach to foreign words is their analysis into constituent elements: the stem and the formative (the foreign element in a compound). Nouns such as *globalista*, *antyglobalista* will be described as synchronic derivatives belonging to the word-formation system of Modern Polish because they can all be divided into a stem and a formative (*global-ista*, *anty-global-ista*), given their formal and semantic relationship with the adjective *globalny*. The notion "Modern Polish" encompasses the period after World War II. The chronological verification of derivatives from the past 50 years is based on the data comprised in the six volumes of Wawrzyńczyk's work (2000–10), as well as on studies in the area of chronological lexicography, which have been developing intensively in Poland and are discussed in detail by Wierzchoń (2010).

The adaptation of foreign linguistic elements to the morphological system of Polish is not a uniform process. Thus, the adaptation of loans may reflect grammatical (syntactic) needs – the addition of a native element to the foreign word facilitates its "entry" into the Polish language. The result of this operation, which is both the simplest and the most basic one, is the development of hybrid structures (on the notion "hybrid" in word-formation studies cf. Waszakowa 2003).

The elements that are typically used in this function include: the affix *-(i/yz)ować* for verbs and the suffix *-ow-y* for adjectives, cf. *grillować* 'to grill' (from English *grill* from French *griller*), *komputeryzować* 'to computerize' (from English *computer/computerize*), *biznesowy* (from English *business*). Assimilation occurs when derivatives are created from such initially adapted constructions with the use of native word-formation means, cf., for example, prefixal formations such as *po-grillować* 'to grill for a short period of time or several times', and suffixal formations such as *grillow-anie* (action noun), *grillow-isko* (place noun). The inclusion of lexical borrowings into the word-formation system is facilitated by those native formatives that are active and capable of attaching to foreign words. In particular, this applies to the following suffixes: *-ka* (e.g., the feminine noun *singielka* from English *single*), *-owiec*, *-arz* (e.g., the agent nouns *squashowiec* 'squash player' from *squash*, *skejciarz* 'skater' from *skate*), *-stwo* (e.g., the denominal abstract noun *hakerstwo* 'hacking, hackerdom' from English *hacker*).

A separate phenomenon is the assimilation of new units to existing classes with foreign exponents. Thus, the word-formation system is expanded to include words that complement existing types, such as names of activities ending in *-izacja/-yzacja*, names of supporters, representatives of movements, views, etc. with the suffix *-ista/-ysta*, or compounds with segments such as *bio-*, *eko-*, *mikro-*, *mini-*, cf. *talibanizacja* 'talibanization' (both in the literal meaning and in the figurative meaning of 'fundamentalism'), *chomeinista* 'a follower of Khomeini', and other internationalisms such as *bioterroryzm* 'bioterrorism', *ekotechnologia* 'ecotechnology', *mikrochip*, *minimarket*.

In turn, assimilation based on the adoption of the structure of a foreign expression is illustrated by series of compounds with the elements *spec-* (e.g., *speckomisja*, *specustawa* 'a special, i.e. extraordinary, committee/law'), *seks-* (e.g., *seksbiznes* 'sexbusiness', *seksustawa* 'law which is meant to protect women from unwanted sex'), which represent the right-headed compounding pattern typical of compounds of Russian or Germanic origin. A special kind of adaptation of foreign linguistic elements occurs when a totally new element, which has not functioned as an exponent in a given language, acquires such a status. One example of this type of advanced adaptation is the way in which the Polish word-formation system acquired a new type in the 1980s: nouns with the *-gate* element, which was isolated from a series of international borrowings such as *Irangate*, *Reagangate* (modeled on the lexeme *Watergate*) and *Kulczykgate*, *Rywingate* (in which the first stem is the name of a Polish businessman).

In general, the adaptation of foreign loans does not merely enrich the Polish word-formation system with new, genetically foreign elements (both bases and exponents), but it also has an impact on the activity of existing elements (both native and foreign).

3 Synchronic indications of foreignness in derivatives

The fact that borrowed words enter into relationships of motivation in Polish makes it possible to describe a considerable portion of foreign vocabulary as synchronic foreign derivatives. They constitute an integral part of the Polish word-formation system and they usually have certain specific morphological properties that are distinct from those typical of the native vocabulary. The distinctiveness of synchronic foreign words in a given linguistic system was discussed by Baudouin de Courtenay (1894); later, the issue was taken up and developed in the context of the Czech language by Mathesius (1947 [1932]) – these and other scholarly views on the difference between foreign and native (Polish) words are discussed by Waszakowa (1994).

The main synchronic indications of foreignness in derivatives with foreign exponents are: 1) stem alternations and sound combinations in suffixes that occur in foreign derivatives only and 2) the fact that these structures with foreign formatives and compound elements belong to the international lexicon. Semantic, stylistic and inflectional idiosyncrasies that form the basis for the differentiation of foreign suffixes (*-ik/-yk, -ura, -ol, -al, -or, -aż, -atyka, -yka, -iana*) from the homonymous native affixes are of secondary importance; cf. Waszakowa (1994).

Qualitative stem alternations that occur solely in foreign formations are almost completely limited to various types of consonantal alternations. These include:

a) palatalization before the consonant *j* in the onset of the foreign suffix, e.g., *t : t'(j), d : d'(j), d : z'(j), s : s'(j)*;
b) depalatalization in stems containing *j*, e.g., *t'(j) : t, d'(j) : d, s'(j) : s, s'(j) : t*;
c) other alternations, e.g., *z : t, s : t, n : z*.

It should be noted, however, that the status of morphonological alternations, as defined by Laskowski (1981), can only be attributed to those of them that meet two conditions: they are contextually determined alternations of phonemes within one morpheme and appear in two different morphemes under identical morphonological conditions. (Alternations between hard and softened consonants cannot be considered morphonological, because these sounds are not phonologically opposed – the alternations involve positional variants of the same phoneme.) Thus, the following morphonological alternations are characteristic of nominal derivatives with foreign suffixes:

/t/ : /s/, /t/ : /c/, /d/ : /z/, /d/ : /s/, /c/ : /t/, /s/ : /t/, /s/ : /d/, /z/ : /t/, /z/ : /d/, /n/ : /z/.

Each of them appears in at least one pair of derivatives. Many irregular and nonserial truncations of stems are observed, as well as a broad range of connectives, which is not surprising inasmuch as most of these words have been borrowed from other linguistic systems as entire lexemes – cf. Waszakowa (1994: 37–42).

The following types of quantitative stem alternations are only found in derivatives with foreign suffixes:

a) regular clipping of the theme affix *-owa-* in deverbal derivatives such as: *dekomuniz-owa-ć → dekomuniz-ator* (agent noun), and *sponsor-owa-ć → sponsorat* (action noun);
b) regular clipping of the theme elements and some foreign suffixes in denominal formations such as: *-j-(a), -acj-(a), -ing, -izm-/-yzm-*, cf. the agent nouns: *aborc-j-(a) → aborter, dekomuniz-acj(a) → dekomunizator, surf-ing → surfista, global-izm → globalista.*

A comparison of foreign and native nominal suffixes with regard to their morphonological construction shows that only foreign suffixes contain the following types of sound combinations:

-cj-: *-cja, -acja, -izacja/-yzacja, -ecja, -icja, -encja;*
-dj-, -rj-, -lj-, -gj-: *-edia, -odia, -adia; -eria, -arium, -ariusz; -alia/-alie; -urgia;*
-nt-, -nd-, -s-, -ng-: *-ant, -ent; -anda, -ando; -ans, -ens; -ing;*
-zm-: *-izm/-yzm;*
-az-, -ez-, -oz-: *-aza, -eza, -oza;*
-it-, -yt-: *-ita, -itet-, -yta;*
-um-: *-atorium;*
-je-: *-jer, -inier/-ynier, -jera;*
-rd-: *-ard;*
-od-: *-oda;*
-ss-: *-essa*

as well as combinations of two vowels such as:

-ai-, -ei-, -oi-, -eu-: *-aik, -aizm; -eizm; -oid, -oida; -eum, -eusz, -euta.*

An important addition to the above-mentioned linguistic criteria for the classification of a given unit as a synchronically foreign element in Polish is, at times, an extralinguistic criterion: the membership of structures with foreign formatives and compound elements in the international lexicon. An additional argument in support of the foreign status of some suffixes is that they display morphonological idiosyncrasies (e.g., *-acja, -izm* or *-ant*). When the latter are absent, membership in the international lexicon is the main (and only) proof of the distinct nature of the given foreign element, as is the case with the *-ista/-ysta* suffix, which displays no morphonological indications of foreignness (the combination *-st-* occurs in native suffix corpora, e.g., *-stwo, -istek*). This criterion provides objective arguments supporting the foreign status of a given word or formative; it is also helpful in distinguishing foreign suffixes from homonymous native suffixes.

To sum up, it should be stressed that foreign derivatives, despite their separate status, co-organize the word-formation system of Polish on a par with other word-formation units and thus constitute an integral part of it. The share of formations with foreign exponents varies for different parts of speech: the most common, and the most formally and semantically diverse, are nominal structures with foreign elements (formatives and compound elements), a fact which is most likely related to their naming function.

4 Structures with foreign elements

The set in question comprises words which have been adapted into Polish at different times from different languages (in particular, from Latin, French, German and English) or directly from the international lexical pool. All of them are motivated, which means that a base can be identified for each of them (i.e. a motivating word, which also belongs to the lexicon of Polish).

Applying the procedure of synchronic word-formation analysis to foreign vocabulary, I isolated 147 foreign nominal suffixes, of which only 29 are active in word-formation processes (Waszakowa 1994: 215). Thus, the set of foreign suffixes is only ca. 50 % smaller than the set of native suffixes. Using similar principles, Grzegorczykowa and Puzynina (1979) isolated 268 native suffixes.

Among nominal prefixal derivatives, there are 16 active foreign elements and among compounds – 168 foreign elements; just as in the case of simple derivation, they do not play an equal role in the Polish word-formation system: only a dozen or so create long series of compounds. The description of nominal suffixal and prefixal derivatives and compounds presented below is based chiefly on my own studies, cf. Waszakowa (1994, 2005).

4.1 Derivatives

Among nominal suffixal formations, the most common group are suffixes appearing in short lexical series (i.e. numbering several words), such as: *-oida*, *-eska*, *-um*, *-essa*, *-anta*, *-aza*, *-oza*; however, these elements are not illustrative of the importance and the dynamic nature of foreign word-formation in Modern Polish. The most important suffixes are those that can be found in longer series (numbering tens and hundreds of words), and there are just 15 of these. Most of them are productive in Polish (where productivity is measured by the number of new formations, both borrowed and created with these suffixes). These include the following morphemes: *-ia*/*-ja* (and its variants, especially such as: *-acja*, *-cja*, *-fikacja*, *-izacja*/*-yzacja*), *-ista*/*-ysta* (including the variants *-alista*, *-onista*), *-izm*/*-yzm* (including the variants: *-aizm*, *-eizm*, *-alizm*, *-onizm*, *-inizm*, *-acyzm*, *-icyzm*/*-ycyzm*), *-ator*, *-at*/*-iat*, *-ika*/*-yka* (and especially its variant *-istyka*/*-ystyka*), *-ant*, *-ik*/*-yk*, *-er* (including the variants *-ier*/*-jer*), *-ura* (including the variant *-atura*), *-ada*/*-jada*, *-eria*, *-ita*/*-yta*, *-ent*, *-aż*. It should be noted that in comparison with native suffixal structures, the longest series of nouns with foreign formatives are much shorter, because the most active native suffixes, such as *-ka*, *-ek*, *-nik*, *-ówka*, *-ak*, *-acz*, *-arz*, *-ica*, *-ec*, *-ina*, *-owiec*, *-stwo*, *-arka*, *-isko*, *-two*, *-arnia*, can create series numbering between 200 to over 1,000 nouns, cf. Grzegorczykowa and Puzynina (1979).

Derivatives with foreign suffixes can be found in all categories of nominal word-formation in which the formative performs the function of transposition and mutation, although foreign suffixation is represented in the individual derivational categories to differing degrees. Modifying derivatives are the rarest. For clarity, I will use examples to illustrate the correct understanding of these types. The division of derivatives into these three basic categories defined by the function of the formative, proposed by Dokulil (1962) and related to the thinking of Kuryłowicz (1936) and Doroszewski (1928–31), is now commonly accepted in the descriptions of Slavic word-formation.

Transpositional derivatives are derivatives in which the formative only serves the transpositional function; they differ from their bases only in their syntactic function; the derivative and its derivational base are always distinct parts of speech; this type is represented, for example, by deverbal action nouns: *komputeryzacja* 'computerization' ← *komputeryzować*, *monitoring* ← *monitorować*. In mutational derivatives, the formative always serves a semantic function: the meaning of the derivative is distinct from the meaning of its base; the change in meaning may (but need not) coincide with a change in the part of speech – this type of derivation is represented, for example, by deverbal derivatives: the instrument noun *mikser* 'mixer' ← *miksować* and the personal noun *komputerowiec* 'computer freak, informatician' ← *komputer*. Finally, modifying derivatives and their bases refer to the same objects, which means that they always represent the same part of speech – what the formative does is modify the meaning of the base, e.g., by enriching its meaning with axiological features (e.g., *superelegancja* ← *elegancja* 'elegance', *megaimpreza* ← *impreza* 'show, performance') or the "femininity" feature, as in the case of derivatives with the suffix *-ka*, e.g., *biznesmenka* 'business woman' ← *biznesmen*, *blogerka* 'female blogger' ← *bloger*.

For most foreign suffixes, e.g., *-izm/-yzm*, *-ista/-ysta*, *-ita/-yta*, *-ant*, *-ent*, *-ik/-yk*, *-ator*, *-er*, *-ika/-ica*$_{\text{pl.tantum}}$, *-ana/-iana*, *-alia/-alie*, *-an*, the mutational function is the only one (except for the structural function, which, by definition, each derivative has). Only some of them (e.g., *-aż*, *-ada*, *-at*, *-ika/-yka*, *-eria*) also fulfill the transpositional function (usually to a more limited degree), cf. Waszakowa (1994). Derivatives for which transposition is the core function include, above all, deverbal action nouns with the suffixes *-acja*, *-izacja/-yzacja*. Some of them also can have a mutational effect, cf. *breżniewizacja* 'Brezhnevization' ← *Breżniew* [Brezhnev]. Due to their relatively high semantic precision, some foreign suffixes (e.g., *-ista/-ysta*, *-izm/-yzm*, *-ana/-iana*, *-id/-yd*) function as expressive exponents of certain meanings and as such are frequently used to create new structures. By way of example: the affix *-izm/-yzm* creates names of a set of views that underpin a certain doctrine (cf. *reaganizm* ← *Reagan*), while the suffix *-ana/-iana* creates names of sets such as *hlondiana, czapskiana* 'materials associated with the life and work of August Hlond, a Primate of Poland'/'... of Józef Czapski'. A broader semantic scope is characteristic of a small number of foreign exponents: the most polyfunctional element *-at/-iat* can be found, inter alia, in such categories as: names of abstract qualities (e.g., *europartneriat, sponsorat* 'the quality of being a Europartner / patron'), names of subjects (of activities, processes or states), e.g., *fascynat* 'a person who has become/is fascinated with something'), collective names, cf. the neosemantism *elektorat (wyborczy)* 'electorate'. Polyfunctionality, although not quite as rich, is also characteristic of, inter alia, the affixes *-ator* and *-er* (which occur in agent nouns of the type *euroagitator, kontestator* 'contester', *telemarketer,* and in names of means of action of the type *dejonizator* 'deionizer', *masażer* 'massager' ← *masaż*), as well as *-ada, -ura, -eria, -acja* (cf. Waszakowa 1994).

Of 16 foreign p r e f i x e s occurring in nominal derivatives, the following are active: *anty-, de-/dez-, kontr-, post-, re-* and *super-*, while *a-, arcy-, dys-, ekstra-, hiper-, ober-, pre-, pro-, proto-, sub-* have a more limited presence in Polish. The prefix *anty-*, like all of the elements listed above, can combine with both foreign and native nominal bases. In many nouns it appears with its general, well-established meaning 'one that is the converse, negation of what the derivational base names'. The derivational bases of these nouns can point to, inter alia: 1) an idea, position, stance, attitude towards somebody or something, etc., which is the opposite of what the base names (e.g., *antyglobalizm* ← *globalizm* 'globalism', *antydekomunizacja* ← *dekomunizacja* 'decommunization'); 2) a person, e.g., *antyhaker* ← *haker* 'hacker', *antygej* ← *gej* 'gay'; 3) various actions, states of affairs, e.g., *antykamuflaż* ← *kamuflaż* 'camouflage', *antyszczyt* ← *szczyt* 'summit'.

The prefix *de-/dez-* indicates the elimination or loss of some qualities of a phenomenon or process named by the base noun (less commonly adjective). It occurs mostly in combination with foreign suffixes, especially suffixes such as: *-acja* (*deregulacja* ← *regulacja* 'regulation'), *-izacja/-yzacja* (*deideologizacja, detotalitaryzacja*); many derivatives of this type are internationalisms. To a more limited extent, the prefix *de-/dez-* plays the role of a formative with the affixes *-onizm, -ator, -ista*, cf. *dekonstrukcjonizm* 'deconstructionism', *destalinizator.*

Derivatives with the prefix *kontr-/kontra-* of the type *kontrmiting* 'counter meeting', *kontrmitologizacja* 'counter mythologization' are either borrowed or created within Polish.

The prefix *post-* in derivatives such as *posthumanizm, postnowoczesność* ← *nowoczesność* 'modernity', *postpostmodernizm, posttacheryzm* 'post-Thatcherism' names phenomena that occurred after those indicated by the base noun. Structures with the prefix *post-* also function as temporal expressions: names of periods of time in which one point is defined by the phenomenon named by the base, and the other by the present, cf. *postjałta* 'post World War II period in the history of Europe following the conference of Allied leaders in Yalta', as well as 'the system of international relations in Europe resulting from this conference'. A slightly different variant of the temporal meaning: 'following what the derivational base names' is observed in the derivatives *postcastryzm* 'the period that will follow *castryzm*, i.e. Fidel Castro's rule in Cuba', *postprodukcja* 'the final stage of work on a movie, following filming'.

The formative *post-* can also be attributed the meaning 'continuing what the base names, constituting a return to an earlier state' (with the connotation that this return is seen as an undesirable development), cf. *postpeerel* – the base of the latter formation is the abbreviation *PRL* ('Polish People's Republic') and *postkomunizm, posttotalitaryzm.* Negative connotations are also carried by the names of people and various groups comprising people or countries, where the prefix *post-* introduces the meaning 'ex-', cf. *postlewica* ← *lewica* 'the Left', *postpezetpeeria* 'members of the former PZPR' (*PZPR* stands for *Polska Zjednoczona Partia Robotnicza* 'Polish United Workers' Party', which governed Poland single-handedly between December 1948 and January 1990).

The prefix *re-* usually contributes information such as 'again, anew', cf. *redefinicja* 'redefinition', *retransplantacja* 'retransplantation'. From the synchronic point of view, a major proportion of the new structures are polymotivated derivatives of the type *reewangelizacja* (N) 'reevangelization' ← *reewangelizować* (V)/ *ewangelizacja* (N), *recentralizacja* (N) 'recentralization' ← *recentralizować* (V)/ *centralny* (A). The formative *re-* preferably attaches to genetically foreign bases; hybrid structures of the type *repeerelizacja* (from *PRL* 'Polish People's Republic') are rare in this group.

The element *super-* is used to create multiple derivatives, e.g., names of people, things, phenomena which are of the highest quality, highest intensity or which exceed other people, things or phenomena on some dimension (e.g., modernity, attractiveness, scope), cf. *supercena* 'super price', *superkredyt* 'super loan', *superimpreza* 'an event which is big, involves stars, is held at a renowned location'. In combination with names of technical devices, the prefix *super-* means 'the most modern, pertaining to the newest generation of devices of the given type, with the highest technical parameters', e.g., *superbroń* ← *broń* 'weapons', *superelektronika, supernotebook, superradar.* The assessment contributed by the element *super-* usually applies to the intensity/scale of the phenomenon indicated by the base noun, the fact that a norm has been greatly exceeded, e.g., *superelegancja, superkobiecość* ← *kobiecość* 'femininity'. The prefix *super-* also indicates 'superiority in a hierarchy' (cf. *supersłużby* ← *służby* 'security services'), and, in formations such as *supermetody* ← *metody* 'methods', *superpromocja* 'super promotion' the additional, special, extraordinary nature of the designation of the derivational base. My treatment of the elements of the type *super-*, as well as *eko-*, *mini-*, *pseudo-*, *-gate* follows the decisions and findings presented in Waszakowa (2005).

The elements *arcy-*, *hiper-* and *ekstra-* function as expressers of opinions. The prefix *arcy-* in nouns of the type *arcyfirma*, *arcymanipulator* means 'unusual; exceptional, important'; in turn, the element *hiper-* signals the intensity or great size of the thing indicated by the base noun, cf. *hiperseks*, *hiperseksualizacja*, *hiperterroryzm*. There is no doubt that the borrowing *hipermarket* has provided the base for further analogical constructions, such as *hipersklep* ← *sklep* 'shop', *hipermagazyn* 'megastore'. They are mostly lexical or semantic borrowings, cf. IT terms *hiperłącze* (English *hyperconnection*), *hipertekst* (English *hypertext*). The prefix *ekstra-* has two meanings: 'of very high quality, very attractive, extraordinary', e.g., *ekstraoferta* ← *oferta* 'offer', *ekstraciuch* ← *ciuch* 'garment', and 'additional', e.g., *ekstrawyjście* 'emergency exit', *ekstrazasilanie* 'additional power supply in computers based on special wireless adaptors'. In the former meaning, the element *ekstra-* is semantically close to the prefix *super-*; both serve as intensifiers of the meanings comprised in the bases of such derivatives. The interpretation of the meanings of such formations as *ekstraoferta*, *ekstralokata* (← *lokata* 'investment'), *ekstrawyjście* is significantly affected by the context, which determines the meaning of the prefix.

The presence of such prefixes as *pre-*, *sub-*, *ober-*, *dys-*, *pro-*, *a-* in Modern Polish is illustrated by relatively few structures including, for example, *preeliminacja* 'pre-elimination', *preembrion* 'pre-embryo', *subtytuł* 'subtitle', *oberforma* 'top-form', *dysfunkcjonalizm* 'disfunctionalism', *proaborcjonista*, *proeuropejczyk*, *profederalista* 'supporter of abortion/the EU/federalism', *aliteratura* 'literature without features traditionally thought as a characteristic for literature'.

The foreign subsystem of word-formation in Modern Polish also includes adjectival and verbal derivatives with foreign elements. Information on the scope of foreign adjectival and verbal derivation and some examples come from Grzegorczykowa, Laskowski and Wróbel (1989), Kallas (1998), as well as numerous studies of lexical innovation.

In the case of both of these parts of speech, the scope of foreign derivation is relatively limited in comparison with native derivation. The following can be found here:

a) denominal adjectives with the prefixes: *anty-*, *inter-*, *kontra-*, *post-*, *pre-*, *pro-*, *sub-*, *trans-* which play the role of formatives jointly with suffixes such as, for example, *-ny* and its expanded variants: *-iczny*/*-yczny*, *-istyczny*/*-ystyczny*, *-alny*, *-owy*, *-ski* (these suffixes play an adaptive role: they are used

to form (relational) adjectives from loans, e.g., *aborcyjny, globalistyczny, marketingowy, dilerski*);
b) deadjectival adjectives with the prefixes: *a-*, *ir-*, *anty-* 'anti-', *arcy-* 'arch-; grand, very', *ekstra-* 'extra-', *hiper-* 'hyper-', *super-*, *ultra-*, as well as *ad-*, *de-*, *eks-* 'ex-', *para-*, *re-*;
c) adjectival compounds with foreign elements of the type *ero-* ← *erotyczny* 'erotic', *foto-* ← *fotografia* 'photo(graphy)', *fotograficzny* (relational adj.), *psycho-* ← *psychiczny* 'psychic' or *mono-*, *retro-*, *ultra-* (about the status of these elements in contemporary literature on word-formation cf. Waszakowa 2005: 52–58);
d) verbs with the prefixes *de-/dez-*, *re-*, *anty-*, *kontr-* 'counter'.

In denominal adjectival derivatives, the prefix occurs in combination with a suffix. Some derivatives, e.g., *antyterrorystyczny, transeurazyjski* can be formally interpreted in two ways: as denominal or deadjectival derivatives, e.g., *antyterroryst-yczny* 'anti terror' ← *terrorysta* 'terrorist', *terroryzm* 'terrorism' or *antyterrorystyczny* ← *terrorystyczny* (adj.); *trans-eurazyj-ski* ← *Eurazja* 'Eurasia', *transeurazyjski* ← *eurazyjski* 'Eurasian'.

We describe them as denominal structures, as this motivation is supported by paraphrases such as *działania antyterrorystyczne* 'actions aimed against terrorists', *trasa transeurazyjska* 'route crossing Eurasia'. The adjectives denote, e.g., a) purposive or object relations, cf. *środek antygrypowy* 'flu medication', b) spatial relations, e.g, *wyprawa transandyjska, rejs transpacyficzny* 'journey through the Andes/Pacific Ocean'; cf. also the derivative with the complex formative comprising the prefix *inter-* and the suffix *-arny: komunikacja intersatelitarna* 'communication between satellites' and c) temporal relations, e.g., *sztuka prekolumbijska* 'art from before the discovery of America by Columbus'.

The fact that foreign prefixes have become specialized in these functions is evidenced by numerous new adjectives, including *antyaborcyjny* ← *aborcja* 'abortion', *antycellulitowy* ← *cellulit* 'cellulite', *antygejowski* ← *gej* 'gay'; *postsolidarnościowy* 'occurring after "Solidarity" (Pol. "Solidarność")'; *preakcesyjny, preunijny* 'preceding accession (to the EU)/(entry into the) EU'; *prorodzinny, prozdrowotny* 'supporting, promoting family/health'; *transdyscyplinarny* 'transdisciplinary', as well as derivatives with the prefix *kontra-*, e.g., *(działanie) kontraproduktywne* 'counterproductive (action)'.

Among deadjectival adjectives, derivatives with foreign formatives can be found in two categories: negation and gradation. Kallas (1998: 502, 506–507) attributes the negating function to three prefixes: *a-* (*amoralny* 'amoral', *aspołeczny* 'asocial'), *ir-* (*irrelewantny* 'irrelevant') and *anty-* 'anti-' (*antyseptyczny* 'antiseptic', *antyintelektualny* 'antiintellectual') and the intensifying function to the prefixes:

arcy- ~ 'very' (*arcyzabawny* ← *zabawny* 'funny'), *ekstra-* 'extra-' (*ekstramocny* ← *mocny* 'strong'), *hiper-* 'hyper-' (*hiperkrytyczny* ← *krytyczny* 'critical', *hiperpoprawny* ← *poprawny* 'correct'), *super-* (*supermodny* ← *modny* 'fashionable', *superoszczędny* ← *oszczędny* 'thrifty, economical'), *ultra-* (*ultrakatolicki* 'ultracatholic', *ultraradykalny* 'ultraradical'). Adjectives with the prefix *sub-*, appearing in such collocations as *klimat subarktyczny* 'antarctic climate', *roślinność subtropikalna* 'subtropic vegetation', are not neologisms from the period after World War II.

The smallest subsystem of foreign word-formation in Polish are prefixal verbs with foreign elements such as *anty-*, *de-/dez-*, *kontr-*, *re-*. Derivatives formed by the prefixes *anty-*, *de-/dez-* and *re-* are imperfective (like their bases), which means that the role played by these elements is not aspectual change. The prefixes *anty-* and *kontr-/kontra-* indicate an action contrary to the action named by the derivational base, cf. *antypromować* ← *promować* 'to promote', *kontroddziaływać* ← *oddziaływać* 'to affect', while *re-* names repetition of an activity or reinstitution of a state, cf. *redefiniować* 'to redefine', *reewangelizować* 'to reevangelize'. The prefix *de-/dez-* denotes 'the converse of the action named by the derivational base, the loss of certain qualities', e.g., *dekodować* 'to decode' ← *kodować*, *denacjonalizować* 'to denationalize', *destalinizować* 'to destalinize'.

4.2 Compounds

Nominal compounds that belong to the foreign subsystem of Polish word-formation differ from compounds with native elements chiefly by the presence of foreign elements with the status of international units (of the type *bio-*, *eko-*, *euro-*, *krio-*, *meta-*, *mini-*, *-gate*, *-logia*, *-mania*, *-terapia*). In foreign compounds, synchronic foreignness is also indicated by morphonological features: the (regular and irregular) truncation, cf. *psychotest* 'psychological test', *psychorelaksacja* 'psychical relaxation'; *bankomat*, *parkomat* (the element *-mat* ← *auto-mat* 'automaton'). (For a more extensive list of disintegrated foreign elements, see Waszakowa 2005: 80–82.)

From the formal point of view, compounds with foreign elements represent the following types of structures:

a) affix-free compounds of the type *ekoterroryzm* 'eco-terrorism', *eurooptymizm* 'euro-optimism', *Irakgate*, *narkomafia* 'drug mafia', *minibiznes* 'minibusiness', *pseudostereo*, *seksturystyka* 'sex tourism';
b) compounds with connecting vowels of the type *bank-o-mat*, *gadżet-o-mania* 'gadget mania', *gen-o-terapia* 'gene therapy', *komputer-o-fobia* 'computer phobia';

c) compounds with connecting vowels and suffixes of the type *palestyn-o-centr-yzm* 'the tendency to focus on Palestine';
d) compounds without connecting vowels and with suffixes of the type *euro-partner-iat* 'partnership within the European Union';
e) compounds without connecting vowels, cf. *alkotest* 'a device for testing the alcohol level in the blood'.

In order to show the diversity of foreign nominal compounds with regard to their structure, I have divided them into two main groups, differentiated by the features of "independence"/"non-independence" of the building blocks of the compound. Within these two groups, I differentiate two more detailed formal classes of compounds, defined by the form of the foreign element (full or shortened) and its location within the given compound. The classification of compounds based on these criteria covers all types of compounds, cf. Table 7.1.

Tab. 7.1: Structures of foreign nominal compounds in Polish.

1.	Compounds in which both elements are autosemantic (independent)
1.1.	Structures with initial recurrent foreign elements
1.1.1.	Full form, e.g., *auto* ← *auto* 'car': *autokomis* 'consignment-based car sales', *autolaweta* 'car transporter'; *wideo-* ← *wideo* 'video-': *wideoradar, wideokamera*
1.1.2.	Shortened form, e.g., *eko-* 'eco-' ← *ekologia* 'ecology', *ekologiczny* 'ecologic(al)': *ekoenergia* 'ecological energy'; *narko-* 'drug' ← *narkotyk* 'drug': *narkotykowy* (relational adjective): *narkobiznes* 'drug business', *narkoterapia* 'drug addiction treatment'
1.2.	Structures with final recurrent foreign elements
1.2.1.	Full form, e.g., *-fan* ← *fan: chopinofan* 'Chopin fan', *rockofan* 'rock fan'; *-mania: gadżetomania* (from English *gadget*), *potteromania* 'Pottermania'
1.2.2.	Shortened form, e.g., *-bus* ← *autobus: gimbus* 'bus transporting secondary school (*gimnazjum*) students', *mammobus* 'a bus equipped for mammography'; *-mat* ← *automat: bankomat, parkomat*
2.	Compounds with one non-independent (bound) element and quasi-compounds Compounds with a bound element and quasi-compounds are considered together because in the material under analysis there are examples where the same foreign element appears in combination with an independent or bound element, cf. *aquapark* and *aqualand*. The so called quasi-compounds are structures comprising two non-independent (bound) elements, but ones that recur in other compounds.
2.1.	Structures with initial recurrent foreign elements, e.g., *mega-*: *megabiznes* 'mega business', *megaimpreza* 'mega event'; *multi-*: *multikino* 'multiplex cinema', *multiprocesor* 'multiprocessor'
2.2.	Structures with final recurrent foreign elements, e.g., *-gate: kasyn-o-gate* 'casinogate', *orlengate* (*Orlen* is one of Europe's biggest fuel distributors); *-holik: pracoholik* (a calque of *workaholic*, Polish *prac-a* 'work'), *seksoholik* 'sexoholic'.

Foreign segments differ with regard to their level of activity in Polish word-formation. The scale is very large; studies of the newest layer of vocabulary have shown that on one end of it, we find the set of units including the *euro-*[2] element (← *Unia Europejska* 'EU'), which comprises over one thousand compounds, and on the other, derivatives with segments that have been isolated in single compounds. The size of the set of derivatives with *euro-* is shaped by external factors; Jan Wawrzyńczyk, the owner of a private "eurocollection" comprising over 470 common nouns and ca. 1,500 proper names, wrote: "If the eurofication plans designed in Brussels are implemented quickly [...], the archivists of the Polish lexicon will soon have to record not hundreds or thousands, but tens of thousands of *eurocreations*" (Wawrzyńczyk 2005: 9).

Changes affecting the various technologies of information transmission are reflected in elements such as *info-*, *inter-*/*interneto-* 'Internet', *audio-*[1] 'related to sound', and *audio-*[2] 'audiovisual' and will lead to the development of fairly numerous series of derivatives with these formatives.

Adjectival compounds with disintegrated foreign elements constitute a formally less diverse group than nominal compounds. A synchronic word-formation analysis makes it possible to isolate two types of structures:

a) compounds with a shortened element such as: *elektro-* ← *elektryczność*/*elektryczny* 'electricity/electric' (e.g., *elektrogrzejny* 'using electricity to generate heat'), *psycho-* ← *psychiczny* (e.g., *psychogeriatryczny* 'psychogeriatric'), *termo-* ← *termiczny* 'thermic' (e.g., *termojądrowy* 'thermonuclear'), and
b) compounds where the first element is non-independent, such as: *krypto-* (*kryptoeutanazyjny* 'related to crypto-euthanasia'), *mono-* (*monoreligijny* 'monoreligious'), *multi-* (*multikulturowy* 'multicultural').

The vitality of compounds discussed by scholars in the context of the neologisms of the 1970s leads to a gradual revision of the view of the role of compounding in Polish, which used to be treated as a process supplementary to derivation. In the light of chronological lexicography studies, the increase in the occurrence of compounding in Polish took place earlier, between 1918–1939, cf. Wierzchoń (2010).

5 Impact of lexicon internationalization on the role of foreign word-formation

The tendency towards internationalization is seen today as one of the most basic features of the functioning and development of national languages (including

Slavic languages), cf., for example, Bosák (1999), Ohnheiser (2003), Tichá and Rangelova (2003).

In the word-formation system of the Polish language of the late 20th and early 21st century, the tendency towards internationalization has not weakened relative to the preceding decades, nor has the type of phenomena on whose basis this tendency is identified changed. The constant influx of loans (mostly anglicisms and americanisms) has not only led to an expansion of the Polish lexicon, but also to various qualitative and quantitative changes in its word-formation system. A non-negligible portion of derivatives with foreign formatives and compound elements that are highly active in contemporary Polish word-formation are words with international scope, such as, for example, *alterglobalizm, antyglobalizm, antyglobalizacja, antyhacker, aquapark, biznesplan, eurokonstytucja* 'EU constitution', *internetyzacja* 'Internetisation', *lobbing, lobbysta, seksbiznes, telemarketing.*

The appearance of a significant number of new compounds as a result of word-formational adaptation of loans has led to:

a) the development of new word-formation models in Polish, with segments such as the following isolated from a series of loans: *biznes-, cyber-, e-, fan-, info-, rock-, top-, unio-*, and *-holik, -holizm, -gate, -mat*; according to the author's estimates based on material used in her studies, the series of compounds with these elements comprise several to 50 words, cf. Waszakowa (2005);
b) an increase in the importance of existing compound types – under the influence of new loans, segments such as the following have become more active: *eko-, neo-, auto-*^{1} 'self', *tele-*^{2} (← *telewizja* 'television'), *mega-, auto-* (← *auto* 'car'), *bio-*^{2} (← *biologia, biologiczny* 'biology, biological'), *narko-, euro-*^{1} (← *Europa, europejski* (adj.) 'Europe, European'), *wideo-*^{1} (← *wideo* 'recording technique, a device for the recording of images'), *seks-*, etc., cf. Waszakowa (2005).

Some word-formation models (which currently number tens of derivatives) were merely in the inception phase in the 1970s and comprised only a few words: they included individual lexical borrowings or partial semantic calques such as *agrokultura* 'agriculture', *biorytm* 'biorhythm', *megamiasto* 'mega-city', *megastruktura* 'megastructure', *pornoshop, pornokino, seks-story, seksfilm, wideofon* 'videophone', *wideokaseta* 'video cassette'.

Borrowed international lexemes also support the stable productivity levels of foreign models that were borrowed earlier. According to my analysis, the activity of certain segments has remained at a level similar to the 1970s, including not just the segments that were particularly productive then, *mini-* and *micro-*, but also ones which had demonstrated their activity in Polish many years earlier, e.g., *pseudo-, neuro-, elektro-, techno-*^{1} 'related to technology', *termo-*, as well as *-mania,*

-logia, -terapia, -fobia, -kracja '-cracy', *-fon, -fil.* Many other foreign segments can also be described as demonstrating stable productivity – while they do not build very long series, they are used to build new structures. In particular, this applies to elements used in the development of terminology, e.g.: *aero-, angio-, antropo-, aqua-, arte-/arto-, astro-, audio-*[1] 'related to hearing, sound', *biblio-, chemo-, cyto-, chromo-, chrono-, fono-, foto-*[1] 'related to light', *gastro-*[1] 'related to the stomach', *geo-, hipo-, hydro-, immuno-, irydo-, krio-, mikro-*[2] 'a unit of measure', *nano-, penta-, petro-* or *-grafia, -iatria, -metria, -patia, -skopia.*

The word-formational adaptation of internationalisms such as: *euromarket, eurosceptycyzm* 'euroscepticism', *homofobia, homoparada* 'gay parade', *Internet, internauta, telemarketing, teleshopping, telepizza* 'pizza ordered by (tele)phone', *techno-rock, technofan* has led to the development of series of compounds where known elements appear in new meanings which are more narrow relative to those already in existence. On this basis, the following segments are considered separate: *homo-*[2] ← *homoseksualizm, homoseksualista, inter-*[3] ← *Internet, techno-*[2] ← *techno* 'a type of rhythm-based electronic music', *tele-*[3] ← *telefon, telefoniczny* (adj.) and *euro-*[2] ← *Unia Europejska* 'EU', *euro-*[3] ← *euro* 'currency of the European Union'. In some structures, it is difficult to separate the *euro-*[2] and *euro-*[3] meanings, cf. *eurofundusz* 'funds granted by the EU'/'funds in euro, usually granted as subsidies', *eurotransformacja* 'transformation within preparations before accession to the EU'/'transformation of national currencies to the euro' – cf. Waszakowa (2005). Because of the football championship scheduled for 2012 and nicknamed *Euro 2012*, the element *euro-* has become expansive in this meaning (it could be referred to as *euro-*[4]).

The activity of foreign segments that combine with native stems has led to an expansion in the scope of word-formation that is described as of a "hybrid" type. This applies in particular to prefixal structures with foreign formatives such as *anty-, super-, post-*, as well as some types of compounds, e.g., compounds with the elements *euro-*[2], *mini-, pseudo-, -mania* (*miniogródek* 'little garden', *pseudourynkowienie* 'market deregulation in name only', *małyszomania* 'the huge popularity of ski jumping in the wake of the successes of the Polish ski jumper Adam Małysz'). These elements are "keen" to combine with native bases.

A special category is the numerous group of nouns derived from names (usually of people known from the media) with the use of suffixes such as *-izacja/-yzacja, -izm/-yzm*, cf. *wałęsizacja, wałęsizm* ← *Wałęsa* (Lech Wałęsa – Polish politician; co-founder and the first leader of "Solidarity", president of the Republic of Poland in 1990–1995, Nobel Peace Prize laureate) or in combination: a suffix with a prefix, e.g., *anty-, de-* (*antywałęsizm, dewałęsyzacja*).

Although integration between the two word-formation subsystems (native and foreign) is clearly visible, there are areas where the structural distinctiveness of derivatives with foreign suffixes relative to native derivatives clearly shows that the existence of two separate word-formation subsystems, governed by specific rules concerning combinations of foreign formatives and native stems, has not lost its actuality. Thus, the following formatives, which appear in series of derivatives, today combine only or mostly with genetically foreign bases: *-ant*, *-ing*, *-ator*, *-izm*/*-yzm*, *-izacja*/*-yzacja*, *-er*, *de-*, *pre-*, *re-*, prefixal-suffixal combinations: *de-* + *-izacja*/*-yzacja*, *re-* + *-izacja*/*-yzacja*, as well as many elements of compounds, e.g., *agro-*, *chromo-*, *info-*, *narko-*, *neuro-*, *socjal-*, *-logia*, *-terapia*. Structures with the element *-logia* and foreign or native elements which are not technical terms are semantically irregular: they do not name (in earnest) a science or scholarly discipline (like, for example, *politologia* 'political science'), but a "pseudoscience" – they may express irony, flippancy, distancing or playful attitude to the object named by the first element, cf. formations such as the colloquial: *dzieciologia* 'pseudo-science of children (*dzieci*), incl. child care', *podatkologia* 'pseudo-science of taxes (*podatek*, pl. *podatki*), tax returns, etc.'.

It should be noted that the significant presence in the most modern layer of Polish analytical constructions in the form of "cluster" structures (affix-free compounds with foreign elements, such as *cyber-*, *euro-*[2], *mega-*, *mini-*, *seks-*, *-gate*, prefixal formations with such foreign prefixes as *anty-*, *arcy-*, *de-*, *ekstra-*, *hiper-*, *kontr-*/*kontra-*, *post-*, *super-*), makes the language more agglutinative, or, more generally, leads to systemic changes. As is well known, prefixal structures and compounds are more monosemic than suffixal derivatives and combine with the motivating word without alternations.

I have reasons to believe that internationalization of the word-formation system leads to an intellectualization of the language, as shown by the fact that many of the derivatives with foreign elements belong to the erudite or specialized lexicon. At the same time, today, in the early 21st century, colloquialisms or group-specific terms created from lexical or semantic loans appear more often in the media than during the fifty years following World War II. The activity of this portion of the foreign word-formation system, which usually serves an expressive function, indicates a tendency towards colloquialization, which is a mark of a broader process – democratization of language.

6 References

Bajerowa, Irena (2003): *Zarys historii języka polskiego 1939–2000*. Warszawa: Wydawnictwo Naukowe PWN.

Baudouin de Courtenay, Jan (1894): Próba teorji alternacyj fonetycznych. In: *Rozprawy Akademii Umiejętności. Wydział Filologiczny*. Serya 2. T. 5, 219–364. Kraków: Nakład Akademii Umiejętności.

Bosák, Jan (ed.) (1999): *Internacionalizácia v súčasných slovanských jazykoch. Za a proti.* Bratislava: Vydateľstvo Slovenskej Akadémie Vied.

Dokulil, Miloš (1962): *Tvoření slov v češtině.* Vol. 1: *Teorie odvozování slov.* Praha: Nakladatelství Československé akademie věd.

Doroszewski, Witold (1928–31): Monografie słowotwórcze. In: *Prace Filologiczne* 13 (1928): 1–261; 14 (1929): 34–85; 15 (1931): 275–300, 423–436.

Grzegorczykowa, Renata and Jadwiga Puzynina (1979): *Słowotwórstwo współczesnego języka polskiego. Rzeczowniki sufiksalne rodzime.* Warszawa: Państwowe Wydawnictwo Naukowe.

Grzegorczykowa, Renata, Roman Laskowski and Henryk Wróbel (eds.) (1998): *Gramatykawspół-czesnego języka polskiego.* Vol. 2: *Morfologia.* Warszawa: Państwowe Wydawnictwo Naukowe.

Kallas, Krystyna (1998): Przymiotnik. In: Renata Grzegorczykowa, Roman Laskowski and Henryk Wróbel (eds.), *Gramatykawspółczesnego języka polskiego.* Vol. 2: *Morfologia*, 469–535. Warszawa: Państwowe Wydawnictwo Naukowe.

Klemensiewicz, Zenon (1961–72): *Historia języka polskiego.* Cz. 1: *Doba staropolska.* 1961. Cz. 2: *Doba średniopolska.* 1965. Cz. 3: *Doba nowopolska.* 1972. Warszawa: Państwowe Wydawnictwo Naukowe.

Kuryłowicz, Jerzy (1936): Dérivation lexicale et dérivation syntaxique: Contribution à la théorie des parties du discours. *Bulletin de la Société de Linguistique de Paris* 37: 79–92.

Laskowski, Roman (1981): Semiotyczne funkcje alternacji morfonologicznych. *Polonica* 6: 7–18.

Mathesius, Vilém (1947 [1932]): Cizí slova ze stanoviska synchronického. In: Vilém Mathesius, *Čeština a obecný jazykopyt. Soubor statí*, 96–109. Praha: Melantrich.

Ohnheiser, Ingeborg (ed.) (2003): *Komparacja systemów i funkcjonowania współczesnych języków słowiańskich. 1.Słowotwórstwo/Nominacja.* Opole: Uniwersytet Opolski i Opolskie Towarzystwo Przyjaciół Nauk.

Rospond, Stanisław (1971): *Gramatyka historyczna języka polskiego.* Warszawa: Państwowe Wydawnictwo Naukowe.

Szymczak, Mieczysław (1976): O interferencji językowej w zakresie formantów słowotwórczych (na przykładzie języka polskiego). *Biuletyn Polskiego Towarzystwa Językoznawczego* 34: 17–23.

Szymczak, Mieczysław (1982): Język polski w sześćdziesięcioleciu naszej niepodległości (1918–1978). In: Janusz Rieger and Mieczysław Szymczak (eds.), *Język i językoznawstwo polskie w sześćdziesięcioleciu niepodległości (1918–1978)*, 17–35. Wrocław/Warszawa/Kraków/Łódź: Zakład Narodowy imienia Ossolińskich. Wydawnictwo Polskiej Akademii Nauk.

Tichá, Zdeňka and Albena Rangelova (eds.) (2003): *Internacionalizmy v nové slovní zásobě.Sborník příspěvků z konference. Praha, 16.–18. 06. 2003.* Praha: Ústav pro jazyk český Akademie věd České republiky.

Waszakowa, Krystyna (1990): Sufiks *-ant* jako formant międzynarodowy. *Język Polski* 70(1–2): 32–39.

Waszakowa, Krystyna (1994): *Słowotwórstwo współczesnego języka polskiego. Rzeczowniki sufiksalne obce.* Warszawa: Wydawnictwa Uniwersytetu Warszawskiego.

Waszakowa, Krystyna (2003): Czy w słowotwórstwie pojęcie *hybryda* jest przydatne? *Poradnik Językowy* 10: 3–11.

Waszakowa, Krystyna (2005): *Przejawy internacjonalizacji w słowotwórstwie współczesnej polszczyzny.* Warszawa: Wydawnictwa Uniwersytetu Warszawskiego.

Waszakowa, Krystyna (2015): Zjawiska słowotwórcze w zdarzeniach użycia językowego (na przykładzie compositów z segmentami *bio-* i *eko-* w języku polskim). *Poradnik Językowy Poradnik Językowy* 9: 7–27.

Waszakowa, Krystyna (2017): Composita kontaminacyjne jako rezultaty procesów analogii i anomalii. In: Przemysław Łozowski and Adam Głaz (eds.), *Route 66: from Deep Structures to*

Surface Meanings. A Festschrift for Henryk Kardela on his 66th Birthday, 93–109. Lublin: Wydawnictwo Uniwersytetu Marii-Curie Skłodowskiej.

Waszakowa, Krystyna (2019): Internacjonalizacja w słowotwórstwie polszczyzny przełomu XX i XXI w. jako przykład jednostronnych kontaktów językowych. *Biuletyn Polskiego Towarzystwa Językoznawczego* 75: 173–186.

Waszakowa, Krystyna (2021): Wybrane aspekty integralnego związku derywatu słowotwórczego z aktem komunikacji (na przykładzie nazw żeńskich). In: Paweł Kowalski (ed.), *Słowotwórstwo w przestrzeni komunikacyjnej*, 344–369. Warszawa: Instytut Slawistyki PAN.

Waszakowa, Krystyna (2022): Żywotność tendencji do internacjonalizacji w słowotwórstwie polszczyzny pierwszych dwudziestu lat XXI w. In: Martin Ološtiak, Ľudmila Liptáková and Klaudia Bednárová-Gibová (eds.), *Slovanská slovotvorba: synchrónia, inovácie, neologizácia*, 123–133. Prešov: Vydavatelstvo Prešovskej Univerzity.

Wawrzyńczyk, Jan (2000–10): *Słownik bibliograficzny języka polskiego. Wersja przedelektroniczna*. T. 1: *A–Ć*. 2000. T. 2: *D–G*. 2004. T. 3: *H–K*. 2006. T. 5: *Nid–Ó*. 2010a. T. 9: *T–Wyf*. 2010b. T. 6: *P–Prę*. 2011. Warszawa: BEL Studio.

Wawrzyńczyk, Jan (2005): *Plan eurofikacji słownictwa polskiego*. Łódź: Uniwersytet Łódzki.

Wierzchoń, Piotr (2010): *Depozytorium leksykalne języka polskiego. Nowe fotomateriały z lat 1901–2010*. Poznań: BEL Studio.

Mechthild Habermann

8 Word-formation and purism in German

Abstract: Linguistic purism has been closely linked in the history of the German language with purism in relation to foreign words. As a commonly used method in German to expand the lexicon, word-formation has played an important role in the Germanization of foreign words. However, although new word-formations are still used today to create words or to translate or transmit foreign words in the context of attempts to conserve the language, metalinguistic discourses on the role of word-formation remain largely limited to the language societies of the 17th century (Justus Georg Schottelius) and to the period around 1800 (Joachim Heinrich Campe).

1 What is purism?

In a broader sense, linguistic purism is understood as being the purity of language, a purity which is achieved not only by combatting foreign-language elements, but also by eliminating all diatopic, diastratic and diaphasic deviations from the standard: "[Purist activity is] a desire on the part of the speech community [...] to preserve a language from, or rid it of, putative foreign elements or elements held to be undesirable elements (including those originating in dialects, sociolects and styles of the same language). It may be directed at all linguistic levels but its primary goal is the lexicon. Above all, purism is an aspect of the codification, cultivation and planning of standard languages" (Thomas 1991: 12). In a narrower sense, though, language purism is restricted to the combatting of foreign-language elements based on "[t]he belief that words (and other linguistic features) of foreign origin are a kind of contamination sullying the purity of a language" (Trask 1999: 254).

Mechthild Habermann, Erlangen, Germany

https://doi.org/10.1515/9783111420530-008

Linguistic purism presupposes an awareness of the special value of a language. In the history of the German language, foreign words were first regarded as such in the period of Humanism and the Reformation, when they were consciously differentiated from the native vocabulary with their external form being largely preserved (first dictionary of foreign words: Simon Roth, 1571). Efforts to maintain the purity of the German language were closely linked in the first phase with the development and uniformization of the standard language, and in later years with the concern for the conservation and preservation of the German language. The decisive shift to foreign-word purism then came in the period between 1789 and 1819 (Kirkness 1998: 407).

Activities to protect the purity of a language are particularly common at times of political upheaval:

In the 17th century, which was particularly influenced by the Thirty Years' War, for example, the so-called language societies which came into being (in 1617, the "Fruchtbringende Gesellschaft" [Fruitbearing Society], founded by Prince Ludwig von Anhalt; in 1643, the "Deutschgesinnte Genossenschaft" [German-Minded Association], founded by Philipp von Zesen; in 1644, the "Pegnesische Blumenorden" [Pegnitz Flower Society], founded by Georg Philipp Harsdörffer and others) devoted themselves to the maintenance and purity of the German language. Many of their members, such as Philipp von Zesen and Georg Philipp Harsdörffer, had as their objective the creation of a standard language which would transcend dialects and be extensively purified of foreign words, a language committed to the rhetorical concept of the ancient *latinitas* "language correctness" and which would form the basis of a fully developed German literary language. The linguistic purism of these language societies was motivated by cultural and patriotic concerns, and did not exhibit radical characteristics, despite some oddities (e.g., Philipp von Zesen's proposals to replace *Nase* 'nose', which he wrongly considered to be a foreign word, with *Gesichtserker* 'face oriel' or *Löschhorn* 'extinguishing horn', and *Kloster* 'convent' with *Jungfernzwinger* 'virgin kennel'; see Gardt 1998).

By 1800, work to Germanize foreign words was a result of the efforts of the late Enlightenment to widen access to education. Impressed by the ideas of the French Revolution, Joachim Heinrich Campe, for example, compiled his dictionary (in 1801, the first edition; in 1813, the second) with the intention of creating a comprehensible German language free of foreign words which would thereby allow everyone access to the bourgeois ideals of education, reason and morality.

In 1885, during the German Empire, which had existed since 1871, the "Allgemeiner Deutscher Sprachverein" [General German Language Association] (ADSV) was founded. Acting from nationalistic motives, the ADSV was involved in creating in the newly founded German Empire a German language for public institutions which was purified of foreign words, an activity which finally resulted in a general hunt for foreign words in everyday language, too. During the Nazi period, the ADSV, from 1923 on renamed the "Deutscher Sprachverein" [German Language Association] (DSV), carried out the Germanization work required by Nazi ideology, work which was devoted not only to eradicating Yiddisms and to the linguistic "cleansing" of Alsace, but also to submitting suggestions for the Germanization of foreign words in Nazi discourse (e.g., *Werbe* 'advertising' for *Propaganda*). Though, in doing so, the DSV came into conflict with the Nazis, who deliberately employed foreign words for manipulative purposes. After Josef Goebbels had already criticized the activities of the DSV in the "Völkischer Beobachter" [People's Observer] in 1937 for its "trivial bourgeois attempts to improve the German language by artificial means and with unsuitable tools" (Wiechers 2004: 46; all German quotations in this article are translated in English), Hitler restricted its scope considerably in a decree of 19 November 1940, which in fact amounted to an effective dissolution of the DSV (see Schiewe 1998: 162).

2 Strategies in the Germanization of foreign words

The Germanization of foreign words can take place in three ways:

a) A German word largely corresponding in its meaning to the foreign word already exists in the general lexicon or in dialects, in specialist discourses or as a lost item of vocabulary, etc. In such cases, the German word as substitute for the foreign word in public usage only needs to be pushed more strongly into the general consciousness.
b) The meaning of a foreign word is transferred to a German word with a similar meaning (so-called "loan meaning"; for example, the similarity in meaning of the English verb *cut* and the German *schneiden* has led to a transfer of the meaning 'to cut somebody' to the German word).
c) The foreign word is transferred into German by means of word-formation processes (mostly compounding or derivation). There are three processes here:
   - Either the individual parts are translated (loan translation: *Orthographie* to *Rechtschreibung* 'spelling; lit. correct writing'),
   - or one part is translated and the other is freely transferred (loan transfer: *Patria* to *Vaterland* 'homeland; lit. father land'),
   - or there is a new formation independent of the foreign model (loan creation: *Automobil* to *Kraftwagen* 'car; lit. power car').

In Germanization through word-formation processes, the degree of adequacy of translation oscillates from a (mostly) word-for-word reproduction to a free interpretive paraphrase of the foreign word. However, the possibility of replacing a foreign word not by a word-formation but by a simplex (e.g., Campe's *walten* for *regieren* 'to rule') is one that is hardly ever taken in efforts to purify the language.

In the Germanization of foreign words, language purists have always made use of methods a) and c) because the German substitute formations were either already known (a) or could be easily understood from their individual components (c) due to their "relative motivation" (Saussure 1916: 181–184). According to Kirkness (1975: 427), linguistic purification is on the whole a "word-substitution process" which always raises questions about the kinds of words to which purists devoted special attention at particular moments in history, and about the criteria that they used to judge whether foreign words are dispensable or indispensable.

3 Linguistic purism and its effect on word-formation in the history of the German language

3.1 The language societies of the Baroque: word-formation and the root word in the work of Justus Georg Schottelius

In the tenth eulogy "to the German main language", Justus Georg Schottelius (1612–1676) wrote that the Germans

> often / make from unconsidered greed for the foreign this our innate / perfect / pure / most rich language / into a meaningless / poor / and beggarly slave / and want to eradicate it in large part / as if they may not / or do not wish to use their own so real and magnificent words: in this way, our German words (through inserted foreign chunks) become unwords / and the German language speechless / the German spirit alienated / the correct manner demannered / deformed / and poured into a quite different mould (Schottelius 1967 [1663]: 167).

For Schottelius, the use of foreign words in German was an indication of the low esteem in which the German language was held by its speakers, who considered German to be inexplicable, poor and socially low-standing – although, for Schottelius, the language was in fact distinguished by its perfection, its purity and its most rich vocabulary. The reason for this assessment, according to Schottelius, lay on the one hand in people's greed for the foreign, but also on the other in the fact that the language had always been "distant and disconnected / from its reasons and its rules" (ibid.):

> There is therefore a major difference between being able to speak or understand German and seeing the German language as supremely informative and powerful: because everyday use is instilled and accepted by itself; but the language / is learned through nothing else / but artful instruction and diligence and contemplation (Schottelius 1967 [1663]: 168).

According to Schottelius, then, the lack of knowledge of the principles and doctrines of the German language had led people to ignore its potential as a perfect, pure and rich language. Only through scholarly study of the language could it be shown to be "fundamentally correct" and its value appreciated. Schottelius saw the proof of the perfection and purity of the language as lying in the fact that the roots of German words, the so-called root words, could be seen to have a direct relationship to the object designated by them, so that the root words were not arbitrary signs, but were instead "motivated" by the things which they designated.

To justify the argument that German possessed a sufficiently large vocabulary (*copia verborum*) and did not suffer from a poverty of words, Schottelius pointed to word-formation. In more than 200 pages (pp. 317–533) of his *Ausführliche Arbeit Von der Teutschen HaubtSprache* [Comprehensive Work on the German Main Language], Schottelius provided a detailed account of the "derivation of the new word" and of the "doubling of the new word", by which he meant the derivation and compounding of the noun and adjective. Schottelius treated word-formation like many of his contemporaries in "word research", saw *derivatio* and *compositio* as accidents of word classes, and placed them next to the nominal accidents *motio* (gender change), *numerus*, *casus*, and *declinatio*. "Completely new, however, was his presentation of an autonomous word-formation doctrine which sought to be fully comprehensive" (Gützlaff 1989: 31).

For Schottelius, compared to other languages, word-formation had a special role in German. Although Varro and Quintilian may "have conceded a glory and an excellence to the Latin language due to its art of doubling", it should also be borne in mind that the "beautiful comprehensibility / the right quantity and the pleasant meaning / already exist in German" (Schottelius 1967 [1663]: 93 f.). After German comes Greek. But, according to Schottelius, the possibilities for word-formation had not yet been exhausted completely for German, since the German main language was "unstudied and unexhausted / regarding how its source-rich veins already jump into and refresh many minds" (p. 94). Nevertheless, new creations were only permitted if they arose in line with the resources available in the language, and nobody could violate the autonomy of the language. Only the language expert could therefore carry out the work of language conservation, since the language expert knew the root words and the processes of compounding and derivation in German.

How moderately Schottelius sought to conserve and purify the language can be seen in the high esteem that he had for contemporary language use. This is why he also included foreign prefixes and suffixes as part of his inventory of morphemes and mentioned them in the *Ausführliche Arbeit* (e.g., on the suffix *-ist*, see Schottelius 1967 [1663]: 320 f.; on this, Habermann 2000: 81–85).

Schottelius was not alone in dealing extensively with issues of word-formation and its significance for the structure of German vocabulary in the Baroque period. The extent to which the discovery of root words and their combination in word-formation processes were discussed can be seen, for example, in the "Fünffache Denckring der Teutschen Sprache" [Fivefold thought ring of the German language], a word-generating machine in the mechanistic sense that was created by Georg Philipp Harsdörffer. Potential root words could be generated through the mechanical compounding of root letters. These words could in turn be linked to "main endings" and "pre-syllables" through compounding to build potential word-formations whose only condition was a possible meaning attribution, and not actual use. Harsdörffer distinguished 49 "post-syllables" and 57 "pre-words". Altogether, more than 100 million word compounds could be generated. The "Denckring" developed in the tradition of Lullus's work in combinatorics was also proof of the unlimited possibilities of language generated through mechanistic means, and therefore also of thinking – possibilities that provided the basis for a subtly differentiated exploration of the world (see Hundt 2000: 281–295).

3.2 The late Enlightenment: word-formation to serve comprehensibility in the work of Joachim Heinrich Campe

Following the education-for-all principles of the late Enlightenment, Joachim Heinrich Campe (1746–1818) put forward the following conditions for the proposed new word-formations which would replace foreign words (see Schiewe 1988; Orgeldinger 1999):

- on the level of the sign: adequacy in terms of content (meaning equality) and of language use (same level of style),
- on the level of production: rule conformity through analogy with similar formations, accuracy (no "wrong" interfixes), and aesthetics,
- on the level of reception: intelligibility on the basis of rule conformity and through consideration of the "inner logic of language", of the *language spirit*.

In the fifth chapter of the "Principles, Rules and Limits of Germanization", which preceded the supplementary volume of his *Wörterbuch zur Erklärung und Verdeutschung der unserer Sprache aufgedrungenen fremden Ausdrücke* [Dictionary for the Explanation and Germanization of Foreign Expressions Forced upon our Language], Campe named under the "real sources of German language enrichment" as point seven the "inner fertilization of our language for the creation of new words from those already in existence" [original with spaced writing] (Campe 1970 [1813]: 40). In doing so, he distinguished between "word compounding", which, like Friedrich Carl Fulda (1724–1788), he also called "word unification", and "derivation". At a later point (p. 58), he also talked about "reconstruction". He anthropologized the productivity of word-formation in German by talking in terms of marriageability – for Campe, almost every German word was capable of connecting with another word to produce a new one. For Campe, German shared this capacity only with Greek, but surpassed Greek in the variety of means available to it. As "pre-words", he named *ab-*, *be-*, *er-*, *ein-*, *ent-*, *ge-*, *miß-*, *un-*, *ver-* and *zer-*; and as "end-syllables", the nominal suffixes *-ung*, *-er*, *-heit* and *-keit*, and the adjectival suffixes *-bar*, *-ig*, *-icht*, *-isch*, *-en*, *-lich*, *-sam* and *-haft*. In his eighth point, he came to deal with the "verbatim or literal translation" of figurative and compound words from another language (Campe 1970 [1813]: 41), something which had long been practiced and to which, "as long as it was similar to the German language and corresponded to German language use, the spirit of the German language could raise no objection" (ibid.).

Campe also raised the question of when and how, i.e. under what circumstances and according to which principles, use could be made at all of a new word-formation or of a literal translation in Germanization. New word-formations could always be coined if, first, there indeed existed the need for designation and no suitable equivalent existed either in older or in contemporary sources or dialects. The need for designation existed primarily with regard to new "things", since a new thing required also a new word. Second, if the German word did not "essentially" map the foreign term. Third, if the German word did not have the same stylistic quality as the foreign term. With regard to the rules to be applied here, Campe argued that care had to be taken to ensure that both the root word and all prefixes and suffixes were of "real German origin" (Campe 1970 [1813]: 60), so that a purification and a rule-based expansion of German could be ensured. Campe also intended to protect the "law of language similarity" (p. 61), this law determining that a new word-formation be built according to a pattern, with the formation finding its analogues in a number of other word-formation units. Here, Campe represented the view that word-formation elements were characterized by a dominant main function, such as, for example, *ent-* was characterized by a "physical or moral movement away" (p. 62). Campe also stressed the importance of aesthetic considerations and of avoiding undue hardship, roughness or unpleasant sounds. Campe believed that the terms to be connected also had to "fit together", and that compounds should not be allowed to become too large. In this context, Campe called for false interfixes to be avoided, since he regarded them as being inflectional morphemes, which he sought to explain in terms of semantic plausibility and word-formation analogy. Finally, he warned that, with word translations, not every image from one language could be transferred to another, and that the peculiarities of the figurative use of a language had to be ensured.

With 5,400 entries in the first edition (1801: 677–716), expanded to 11,160 words in the second edition (1813: 613–673), Campe's book provided the largest positive list of Germanizations in a language-contact dictionary (see Heier 2012: 113). A large proportion of Germanizations have their origin in Campe's work, remaining in use today as stylistic duplicates to the foreign words which are also available in contemporary German: *Hochschullehrer* for *Professor*, *Ein-* and *Mehrzahl* for *Singular* and *Plural*, *Stelldichein* for *Rendezvous*, *einschließlich* for *inklusive* 'including', *folgerichtig* for *konsequent* 'consistent', *geeignet* for *qualifiziert* 'suitable', *auswerten* for *evaluieren* 'to evaluate', etc. The Germanizations are almost exclusively compounds or derivatives which are usually formed anew and which demonstrate a high level of semantic motivation, so that their meaning can be easily worked out. Another common strategy employed by Campe to ensure the intelligibility of a foreign word in German, however, was to draw on substitute formations which were designed to replace long-naturalized foreign words or technical terms (*Kirchentisch* lit. 'church table' for *Altar*, *Zergliederungskunst* lit. 'dissection art' for *Anatomie*), or formations which were awkward (*Denkspitzsäule* lit. 'commemorate pointed column' for *Obelisk*, *Spottnachbildung* lit. 'mockery imitation' for *Parodie*), or simply biased (*Freigläubiger* lit. 'free believer' for *Protestant*, *Zwangsgläubiger* lit. 'forced believer' for *Katholik*), or which contained within them the fundamental danger of paraphrasing in such a way as not to capture the heart of the matter (*Wagesatz* lit. 'dare theorem' for *Hypothese*, *Denkkunst* lit. 'think art' for *Logik*). Such new formations have not managed to prevail in contemporary German (see Daniels 1959; Kirkness 1975: 161–167).

3.3 The 19th century: the justification of linguistic purism in the period between Campe and the "Allgemeiner Deutscher Sprachverein"

By 1800, purism had become closely caught up with educational, aesthetic, patriotic and philosophical motives (see Kirkness 1975: 185). For Campe, the predominant principle guiding Germanizations was that of analogy, which he placed before both reason (*ratio*) and use (*usus*) (Campe 1970 [1813]: 60). However, both contemporaries of Campe and language conservationists after Campe moved away from analogy as the guiding principle in favor of other criteria. For the painter Carl Wilhelm Kolbe (1757–1835), for example, aesthetic motives were of primary importance. He took the view that morphological productivity in German was affected by the influence of foreign words, with the word stress of foreign words leading most strikingly to non-German forms (since, for example, the syllable-initial stress pattern was missing: *Fri'seur* 'hairdresser' alongside *fri'sieren*), or with mixed forms coming about which did not exist in the language of origin, as, for instance, in new formations such as Goethe's coinage *extrematisch* lit. 'extrematic'.

As a prominent representative of enlightenment-rational belief, the educational theorist Christian Hinrich Wolke (1741–1825) claimed that language was based solely on reason: for Wolke, there were 320 monosyllabic root words, and, through derivation and compounding, 200,000 words had already been formed, with the prospect in the near future of a further 160,000 words coming into existence. To prove this claim, Wolke coined some hundred words with *Ort* 'place', 60 with *Geist* 'spirit' and 350 with *Wort* 'word' (see Kirkness 1975: 225). Ernst Moritz Arndt (1769–1860), though, warned against the systematic and random coinage of new words, since "language purification must be rooted for all things in the populace, and substitutes for foreign words can be found easily in the vernacular" (Kirkness 1975: 194). Carl Gustav Jochmann (1789–1830), though, was the first to place "use" clearly above analogy as the decisive criterion for German substitute formations.

Some purists subscribing to a rational extension of language suggested at a time when historical-comparative linguistic analysis was emerging that German roots be harnessed for the Germanization of foreign vocabulary as the basis of new word-formations.

In the spirit of a rationalistic view of language, the poet Jean Paul (1763–1825), for example, eliminated the interfix *s* in compounds and argued for *s*-less forms such as *Wahrheitliebe* 'love of truth', *Volkbildung* 'national education', *Geburttag* 'birthday', and *Liebedienst* 'favor'. The philosopher Karl Christian Friedrich Krause (1781–1832), co-founder of the "Berlinische Gesellschaft für deutsche Sprache" [Berlin Society for the German Language] (1815 to about 1880), wanted to avoid the inconsistencies and foreign influences encountered in High German by establishing a new, rational language, one based on German, or even on supposedly Germanic forms. Krause envisaged this new language as being initially a special language of philosophy, a language formed "from a number of analogous root words and according to established laws", so that it would denote the essential terms of the populace (Kirkness 1975: 230). For Krause, the most comprehensive were the ideal forms realized in Sanskrit, but the German came very close to these. For this reason, Krause saw it as being a moral and patriotic duty to keep the German language pure. For Krause, all necessary terms could be formed from German word stems (he took about 3,000 stems), which he derived by shortening word forms to monosyllabic words and to prefixes and suffixes. Foreign words, though, should neither be borrowed nor translated or naturalized into German. He paid particular attention to the German or Germanic roots *leb(en)* 'to live', *lieb(en)* 'to love', *Minn(e)* 'love' or *lob(en)* 'to praise', which could be combined with various prefixes and suffixes. In doing so, he ascribed a fixed meaning to morphemes used in word-formation (in particular, *-heit*, *-keit*, *-thum*, *-sam*, *-niß*, *-bar*, *-lich*, *ant-*, *ab-*, and *ur-*), and sought to revive historical morphemes such as *ant-* (e.g., in *Antlitz* 'face'), which had become unproductive (see Kirkness 1975: 231–236). The representatives of historical-comparative linguistics were also sceptical towards the new word-formations created by the language purists: Jacob Grimm (1785–1863), for example, pointed to the already existing richness of the German language and argued that substitutes for foreign words could always be found within it. For Grimm, loanwords were a fundamental enrichment, and even foreign words ending in *-isch* and *-lich* had already been largely integrated into German. According to Grimm, then, any attempt to purify the language had to be aware of the historical development of the language and also had to ensure that the development of the forms of language remained the responsibility of language itself (Kirkness 1975: 282–296).

Fundamentally, what we can observe in the nineteenth century was an increasing involvement of philologists in debates surrounding foreign words, although early national-patriotic motives (as, for example, in the work of Friedrich Ludwig Jahn (1778–1852)) were already influencing these debates, so that they became increasingly politically ideologized during discussions on the creation of a German nation state.

According to Heier (2012: 166, 168, 172), a total of 19 Germanization dictionaries, 35 dictionaries of Germanization and explanation, and 59 dictionaries with explanations were published in the period between 1800 and 1870. Pure Germanization dictionaries were therefore not as common as those with an explanatory function. In many of these works, however, no clearly identifiable intent to purify the language can be proven.

3.4 Linguistic purism in the service of the nation: from the German Empire to National Socialism

During the founding of the German Empire (1871), foreign-word purism became the task of the state and of semi-official institutions (see Kirkness 1975: 360–408; Greule and Ahlvers-Liebel 1986: 29–35). As part of new regulations on language use in the newly established nation state, the language of the post office and railway, of law, of administration and the army, and also some technical languages, underwent a thoroughgoing Germanization directed mainly against the influence of French. The Germanizations were ideologically motivated to build a nationalist sense of empire and were largely carried out by people who, although experts in the respective areas under reform, were not university-trained experts in the German language. The most important Germanization dictionaries of the period, though, were produced by philologists, such as the *Wörterbuch von Verdeutschungen entbehrlicher Fremdwörter* [Dictionary of Germanizations of Dispensable Foreign Words] (1989 [1882]) by the Dresden-based German scholar Hermann Dunger (1843–1912), and the *Verdeutschungs-Wörterbuch* [Dictionary of Germanizations] (1884) by the lexicographer Daniel Sanders (1819–1897). Chief building official Otto Sarrazin (1842–1921), who had compiled in 1886 a highly regarded dictionary of Germanizations in five editions, coined, for example, *Abteil* for *Coupé* 'compartment', *Bahnsteig* for *Perron* 'platform', *Fahrgast* for *Passagier* 'passenger', *Fahrrad* for *Velo* 'bike', *Nebenbahn* for *Sekundärbahn* 'subsidiary track', and *Stellwerk* for *Signalhäuschen* 'signal house' (see Kirkness 1975: 367). Many Germanization initiatives were directly, if not exclusively, related to the efforts to purify the language made by the "Allgemeiner Deutscher Sprachverein", whose founding members included both Dunger and Sarrazin, and which, from its inception in 1885 until its effective dissolution in 1940, pursued for national-patriotic or chauvinistic reasons the replacement of foreign words with German expressions. This work of Germanization was not accompanied by linguistic considerations, however, but was motivated in particular by the belief that a German national consciousness would be greatly enhanced by the conscious use of a German language largely purified of foreign words. "No foreign word for something that can be given in good German", or "Remember when you speak German that you are a German!". The general public participated actively for the first time in these Germanization campaigns. Hermann Dunger, amongst others, took a moderate position, giving a paper in 1887 at the annual meeting of the association in Dresden which bore the title *Die Sprachreinigung und ihre Gegner. Eine Erwiderung auf die Angriffe von Gildemeister, Grimm, Rümelin und Delbrück* [Language purification and its opponents: A response to the attacks by Gildemeister, Grimm, Rümelin and Delbrück]. Dunger was one of the few purists of the Empire period to base his arguments on structural principles in that he emphasized that dispensable foreign words be avoided "in deference to the richness and productivity of our language, in deference to good taste, in deference to clarity and linguistic accuracy, and to intelligibility for our less educated countrymen" (Dunger 1887: 44). He also saw the foreign terms as a German "hereditary defect" which had to be fought against as a national duty. Although the productivity of German was a key reason for its lexical richness, Dunger also warned against building new formations on the basis of private initiative, and he spoke in favor of using the existing vocabulary or the officially endorsed substitutes. He also took a decisive stance against loanword formations, which he termed "shapeless entities" (p. 26), "the ugliest kinds of deformity" (p. 28), and "homeless rabble" (p. 29).

Overall, there was a huge increase in the number of pure dictionaries of Germanizations in the period from 1870/71 until 1945: 81 editions (compared to 23 dictionaries on Germanization and explanation) (see Heier 2012: 225–228). Of these, though, 61 dictionaries were no more than 200 pages in length and were therefore weak in lemmas, and 47 dictionaries contained only subject-specific lemmas.

4 Neopurism in Germany after 1945?

Finally, the question arises as to whether the language-conservation tendencies found in Germany after the Second World War can be termed "purism", and how far the discourse of language conservations has dealt with the subject of the expansion of the lexicon through word-formation (see, e.g., Förster 2000).

In Germany, there are currently both state-funded language organizations, such as the "Gesellschaft für Deutsche Sprache" [Society for German Language] (GfDS) in Wiesbaden, as well as a number of associations which aim to protect the language, the best-known of which is the "Verein Deutsche Sprache" [Association of German Language] (VDS). Criticism of foreign words today means almost exclusively criticism of anglicisms; according to Pfalzgraf (2006), this criticism, has, particularly since German reunification, been characterized by neopuristic features – the more so indeed, the further its supporters are from government-funded language-conservation organizations. The discourse concerning the admission of foreign words and its consequences for the German language, as observable in the VDS, for example, is also usually accompanied by a scolding of those academics "responsible" who, from a lack of loyalty to the language, underestimate the threat to German posed by the use of foreign words (Stukenbrock 2005: 230–235). Although some Germanization campaigns since the 1990s can be seen as puristic with regard to foreign words, they are not referred to as such by their supporters for fear of echoing the nationalist motives of the foreign-word purism of the nineteenth century and of the Nazi period. Clearly not in the tradition of foreign-word purism, but rather of language conservation, is, for example, Bartsch, Pogarell and Schröder's (2009 [1999]) *Wörterbuch überflüssiger Anglizismen* [Dictionary of Superfluous Anglicisms], which offers many suggestions for Germanizations using word-formation processes. Criticism of anglicisms, however, has not given rise to a renewed debate on the role of word-formation.

5 Conclusion: word-formation and linguistic purism

Linguistic purism, understood as purism with regard to foreign words, is characterized by a close argumentative link between the need to replace foreign vocabulary and the observed richness of word-formation options in German. But there is disagreement in the debate on foreign-word purism. One issue concerns which words of foreign origin are to be Germanized. Is the integrated loan vocabulary also affected or just the "dispensable" foreign words? Are specialist vocabularies to be Germanized or only the public language used by state institutions? And a further issue concerns how the Germanization of foreign vocabulary is to be carried out. Will recourse be had to already existing German vocabulary or will new word-formations formed by means of loan translations or transfers or by loan creations be permitted? Finally, there is the question of acceptability, the criteria according to which the formation of a new word is permitted in the first place.

The basic meaning of linguistic purism as foreign-word purism is the replacement of foreign vocabulary with native words; German substitute formations are compounds or derivatives whose meaning largely emerges from the individual components due to "relative motivation". The methodological-theoretical discourse on the value of word-formation as part of activities to purify the language remains largely restricted, however, to the language societies of the Baroque and to the late-Enlightenment figure of Joachim Heinrich Campe.

6 References

Bartsch, Rudolf, Reiner Pogarell and Markus Schröder (eds.) (2009): [1999] *Wörterbuch überflüssiger Anglizismen.* 8th ed. Paderborn: IFB Verlag Deutsche Sprache.

Campe, Joachim Heinrich (1970 [1813]): *Wörterbuch der Deutschen Sprache. Ergänzungsband: Wörterbuch zur Erklärung und Verdeutschung der unserer Sprache aufgedrungenen fremden Ausdrücke. Neue stark vermehrte und durchgängig verbesserte Ausgabe.* Hildesheim/New York: Olms. [First published 1813 Braunschweig: In der Schulbuchhandlung (1st ed. 1801)].

Daniels, Karlheinz (1959): Erfolg und Mißerfolg der Fremdwortverdeutschung: Schicksal der Verdeutschungen von J. H. Campe. *Muttersprache* 69: 46–54, 105–114, 141–146. [Reprint 1979 in: Peter Braun (ed.), *Fremdwort-Diskussion*, 145–181. München: Fink].

Dunger, Hermann (1887): *Die Sprachreinigung und ihre Gegner. Eine Erwiderung auf die Angriffe von Gildemeister, Grimm, Rümelin und Delbrück*. Dresden: Albann'sche Buchdruckerei C. Teich.

Dunger, Hermann (1989): *Wörterbuch von Verdeutschungen entbehrlicher Fremdwörter. Engländerei in der deutschen Sprache.* Reprint d. Ausg. Leipzig 1882 u. Berlin 1909 mit e. Vorwort von Wolfgang Viereck. Hildesheim: Olms. [*Wörterbuch* first published 1882 Leipzig: Teubner. *Engländerei* 2nd ed. 1909 Berlin: Verlag des Allgemeinen Deutschen Sprachvereins.]

Förster, Uwe (2000): *Sprachpflege auf wissenschaftlicher Grundlage. Beiträge aus drei Jahrzehnten.* Mannheim: Dudenverlag.

Gardt, Andreas (1998): Die Sprachgesellschaften des 17. und 18. Jahrhunderts. In: Werner Besch, Anne Betten, Oskar Reichmann and Stefan Sonderegger (eds.), *Sprachgeschichte. Ein Handbuch zur Geschichte der deutschen Sprache und ihrer Erforschung*. Vol. 1, 332–348. 2nd ed. Berlin/New York: de Gruyter.

Greule, Albrecht and Elisabeth Ahlvers-Liebel (1986): *Germanistische Sprachpflege. Geschichte, Praxis und Zielsetzung*. Darmstadt: Wissenschaftliche Buchgesellschaft.

Gützlaff, Kathrin (1989): *Von der Fügung Teutscher Stammwörter. Die Wortbildung in J. G. Schottelius' 'Ausführlicher Arbeit von der Teutschen HaubtSprache'*. Hildesheim: Olms.

Habermann, Mechthild (2000): Fremde Wortbildungselemente in deutschen Grammatiken des 17. bis 19. Jahrhunderts. In: Mechthild Habermann, Peter O. Müller and Bernd Naumann (eds.), *Wortschatz und Orthographie in Geschichte und Gegenwart. Festschrift für Horst Haider Munske zum 65. Geburtstag*, 79–102. Tübingen: Niemeyer.

Heier, Anke (2012): *Deutsche Fremdwortlexikografie zwischen 1800 und 2007. Zur metasprachlichen und lexikografischen Behandlung äußeren Lehnguts in Sprachkontaktwörterbüchern des Deutschen.* Berlin/Boston: de Gruyter.

Hundt, Markus (2000): *"Spracharbeit" im 17. Jahrhundert. Studien zu Georg Philipp Harsdörffer, Justus Georg Schottelius und Christian Gueintz.* Berlin/New York: de Gruyter.

Kirkness, Alan (1975): *Zur Sprachreinigung im Deutschen 1789–1871. Eine historische Dokumentation.* 2 Vol. Tübingen: Narr.

Kirkness, Alan (1998): Das Phänomen des Purismus in der Geschichte des Deutschen. In: Werner Besch, Anne Betten, Oskar Reichmann and Stefan Sonderegger (eds.), *Sprachgeschichte. Ein Handbuch zur Geschichte der deutschen Sprache und ihrer Erforschung*. Vol. 1, 407–416. 2nd ed. Berlin/New York: de Gruyter.

Orgeldinger, Sibylle (1999): *Standardisierung und Purismus bei Joachim Heinrich Campe*. Berlin/New York: de Gruyter.

Pfalzgraf, Falco (2006): *Neopurismus in Deutschland nach der Wende*. Frankfurt/M.: Lang.

Roelcke, Thorsten (2014a): *Französisch in Barock und Aufklärung. Studien zum Sprachdenken im Deutschland des 17. und 18. Jahrhunderts*. Frankfurt/M.: Klostermann.

Roelcke, Thorsten (2014b): *Latein, Griechisch, Hebräisch. Studien und Dokumentationen zur deutschen Sprachreflexion in Barock und Aufklärung*. Berlin/Boston: De Gruyter.

Roth, Simon (1571): *Teutscher Dictionarius*. Augsburg: Michael Manger. [Ed. by Emil Öhmann 1936 Simon Roths Fremdwörterbuch. *Mémoires de la société néo-philolologique de Helsingfors* 11: 225–370].

Sanders, Daniel (1884): *Verdeutschungs-Wörterbuch*. Leipzig: Wigand.
Sarrazin, Otto (1886): *Verdeutschungs-Wörterbuch*. Berlin: Ernst & Sohn. [Further ed. Berlin 1889, 1906, 1912, 1918].
Saussure, Ferdinand de (1916): *Cours de linguistique générale*. Ed. by Charles Bally and Albert Séchehaye. Lausanne/Paris: Payot.
Schiewe, Jürgen (1988): *Sprachpurismus und Emanzipation. Joachim Heinrich Campes Verdeutschungsprogramm als Voraussetzung für Gesellschaftsveränderungen*. Hildesheim: Olms.
Schiewe, Jürgen (1998): *Die Macht der Sprache. Eine Geschichte der Sprachkritik von der Antike bis zur Gegenwart*. München: Beck.
Schottelius, Justus Georg (1967 [1663]): *Ausführliche Arbeit Von der Teutschen HaubtSprache*. 2 Vol. ed. by Wolfgang Hecht. Tübingen: Niemeyer. [First published 1663 Braunschweig: Christoph Friedrich Zilliger].
Stukenbrock, Anja (2005): Aus Liebe zur Muttersprache? Der VDS und die fremdwortpuristische Diskurstradition. *Aptum* 3: 220–247.
Thomas, George (1991): *Linguistic Purism*. London: Longman.
Trask, R. Larry (1999): *Key Concepts in Language and Linguistics*. London: Routledge.
Wiechers, Silke (2004): *Die Gesellschaft für deutsche Sprache. Vorgeschichte, Geschichte und Arbeit eines deutschen Sprachvereins*. Frankfurt/M.: Lang.

Petra Braselmann

9 Word-formation and purism in French

Abstract: For the last four decades modern French language policy has influenced the language in varying degrees by introducing official compulsory neologisms to replace unwanted anglicisms. Until the "turning point" in the mid-1990s these measures also concerned the standard vocabulary; afterwards they focused on technical language. This article aims to investigate the different types of word-formation used in the different phases by studying the official corpora (e.g., FranceTerme) and the adoption of some patterns in the standard lexicon (among others, as contained in the latest edition of the Petit Robert 2011). Two phenomena will be revealed: first, language change tendencies (e.g., asyndetic nominal compounds, portmanteau words, certain affixes that have been criticised, such as *anti-*, *cyber-*, *-ing*, *self-*, etc.) cannot be held back artificially; on the other hand, the official attitude towards anglicisms and new word-formation patterns (that have traditionally been considered "un-French") has become much more liberal.

1 Purism and language planning in France

France undoubtedly has the longest tradition of a discourse on language norm. The activities of the academy and the conception of the "bon usage" in the 17th century are still highly influential for today's prescriptive norm. At the same time it has become an anachronism because of its retrospective character which is unable to adequately describe current linguistic developments. The conservation of a retrospective norm, of a pure High French, meant that terminology and neologisms were disapproved of. More than other languages French thus had to rely on linguistic imports: anglicisms. In the 20th century French language planners concentrated on two problems: orthography and anglicisms, the latter of

Petra Braselmann, Innsbruck, Austria

https://doi.org/10.1515/9783111420530-009

which were considered the main cause of the "crise du français"; the roots of the "crise", however, lie in the conservation of a language state that was once proclaimed good (Braselmann 1999: 4–9). The attitude of traditional language cultivation, aggravated by the activities of modern language policy with its refined monitoring authorities and instruments known in no other European language, condemns French to be immobile, stagnant and unproductive (Schmitt 1978).

1.1 Modern French language cultivation and language legislation

The systematic rejection of neologisms and technical vocabulary due to their status as not belonging to the "bon usage" only changed when the state began to intervene in the early 1970s by creating the first terminology committee (1970) and publishing the first *Arrêtés* in 1973: instead of the traditional rebuke for scolding the use of neologisms, the highest authority now actually produces them. But they are special neologisms: they have to be "French", and they are intended to replace anglicisms that have often already become established in the linguistic standard. What is new is the deliberate attention to technical languages, from which the "bon usage" was once supposed to be kept free. The language cultivation institutions recognised that terminologies in particular were a source of English loan words. However, the suggested neologisms soon left the purely terminological area and the authorities attempted (with little success) to replace the anglicisms of everyday language as well.

The climax of dirigisme are the language laws of 1975 (*Loi Bas-Lauriol*) and 1994 (*Loi Toubon*) with their different decrees (see Braselmann 1999 for a description of the genesis and effect of these two language laws). The language directives and the neologisms are published in various collections by the *Journal officiel* (= JO). The last version in form of a book is the *Dictionnaire des termes officiels de la langue française* of 1994 (= DO 94) published by the highest language authority *Délégation générale à la langue française* (in 2001 it was renamed as *Délégation générale à la langue française et aux langues de France* = DGLFLF). This dictionary contains about 3,500 French neologisms, mostly substitute terms for disliked anglicisms, created by 19 terminology committees.

1.2 The "turning point" in the official attitude

In the mid-1990s, the decree of July 3, 1996 and the new use of the Internet (*Circulaire* of 15/5/1996) initiate a new phase of official language policy which leads to a restructuring of the institutional organisation, a professionalisation of the 18 newly founded terminology committees under the respective ministries and a reconsideration of all published lists of neologisms, including the DO 94 (Braselmann 2008a: 11–16).

This turning point has important consequences for the linguistic material: criteria for the formation of terminology are developed (cf. also section 2) and the committees are told to work preventively, i.e. to provide suggestions of substitutes for anglicisms before they are able to establish themselves in the standard. This preventive stance can be illustrated by the replacement of *cloud computing*, a technology that was just introduced as the major topic at the world computer fair Cebit 2011 (March 1–5) in Hannover. Already on June 6, 2010, the official French equivalent, *informatique en nuage*, was published in the *Journal officiel*. Or take, for instance, the decision to adopt the term *euro* for the European currency as early as 1997 (JO 2/12/1997), including information about its pronunciation and pluralisation, long before the currency was introduced on January 1, 2002. One had learned from past mistakes. Suggested neologisms now have to pass a number of official channels of examination and acceptance, before they are published as the officially recognised equivalent in the JO and thus become binding (Braselmann and Ohnheiser 2011: 11–25).

In 2007 the interactive data base *FranceTerme* went online: it allows searches for French neologisms or the anglicism to be replaced. This data base, which is constantly kept up to date, replaced the data base CRITER from 2001 and the other online glossary *Répertoire terminologique* from 2000 (for more on these databases, cf. also Egger 2008). The interactivity of *FranceTerme* is expressed by the link "boîte à idées" which encourages the language user to participate with their suggestions. Furthermore, *FranceTerme* also reinstates a dynamic process which existed in the printed word lists before the DO 94: the rubric of "termes recommandés", i.e. substitute words that have not become binding yet but whose acceptance and use by the speakers is still being tested (JO 9/11/1976), cf. Braselmann (1999: 57–67) on the dynamic concept of "cooperative" neologisms. Such recommendations, which usually offer several possible variations, are currently given for *beach, coach, e- (électronique), flyer, fooding, gender, live, pitch, podcasting, s'miles* and *travel retail*, words which were published in the JO between 2005 (e.g., *fooding*) and 2011 (*flyer*). However, some of these recommendations seem to be coming too late, because *coach, e-, flyer, live* and *pitch* have already been established in the standard (cf. *Petit Robert* 2011).

2 Formation of neologisms

In the following we will consider some aspects of the formation of neologisms, specifically the question of possible new developments within the paradigms of French word-formation. Particular attention is devoted to the lexical material of the DO 94 and of *FranceTerme*. A comparison of these two corpora is very informative, particularly with respect to the effects of the language-political "turning point" with respect to the linguistic material and the use of certain word-formation patterns. In order to establish whether these patterns have entered the standard lexicon, the dictionary *Petit Robert* 2011 (= PRob11) shall be consulted.

2.1 Instructions on how to form neologisms before 1994

As early as 1981 the *Conseil international de la langue française* (= CILF), a descriptively oriented language association editing dictionaries for technical languages as well as the bi-annual journal *La Banque des mots* since 1971, published some guidelines by Diki-Kidiri, Joly and Murcia on how to form neologisms to replace anglicisms. Next to types such as semantic loans (attaching a new meaning to an existing word) and borrowing the anglicism (with certain adaptations), the formal neologism, i.e. the new word-creation, is the focus of interest. They discourage a process that is very popular in terminology committees, namely the simple translation (loan translation) of the English term, a method whereby the neologist finds him/herself in a "prison psychologique" (for classification see Braselmann 2008b: 211–216). The result is said to be "mediocre". They recommend instead starting with the definition, as was done with the very successful formation *logiciel* for *software*. The new suffix *-iel* was then also employed in the official substitute term for *hardware: matériel*, cf. also the examples in section 2.2 and 2.3.

The authors also warn against formations that are too long and, hence, lead to non-acceptance, such as *prêt-à-monter* for the short word *kit*. However, formations with hybrid forms, mostly from Greek or Latin, for example *auto-(mobile)* or *termino-(logie)*, which are condemned by purists, are actually recommended. They name as the most important principle motivation, "clarté", which they do not see, for instance, in the badly formed *carburéacteur* (for *jet fuel*) (Diki-Kidiri, Joly and Murcia 1981: 11–17).

A more puristic stance is represented by Rey-Debove (1987), many years co-editor (with Alain Rey) of the revised versions of the *Petit Robert*. According to her, the Greek-Latin influence on French via English results in a suppression of French affixes: borrowings with *multi-* (Lat.) increase productivity at the cost of *poly-* (Greek), borrowings with *mono-* block the productivity of *uni-*, as in the anglicism *monolingue* (Rey-Debove 1987: 257–265). Portmanteau words (blends) and incorrect abbreviations – which have already become a model for French – would lead to a "morphologie sauvage". Rey-Debove mentions "fracto-morphèmes" such as *-(gic)iel* in *progiciel, héli-, pétro-, perma-, tele-*, etc. Such tendencies influenced by English, as well as noun-noun compounds (often with the English order modifier + head), abbreviations and acronyms increase the "lexical irregularities" of French and "disorganise" the morphology. In contrast to these, Rey-Debove believes that the affixes *-man, -ing* and *self-* will become acclimated to French.

2.2 Neologisms in DO 94

Braselmann (1999: 68–98) describes the preferred formation patterns of substitute words in DO 94. Abbreviations, acronyms and blends such as *publipostage* 'mailing', *restovite* 'fast-food restaurant' are highly frequent. The warnings by Diki-Kidiri, Joly and Murcia (1981) were not followed, as shown by the large number of translated words (*radio de poche* for *pocket radio, billet ouvert* for *open ticket*) or multi-word substitutes for monosyllabic anglicisms that resemble definitions: *syndicat de prise ferme* for *pool, message publicitaire* for *spot*. Greek-Latin affixes, transmitted via English, are highly productive, in particular *mono-, publi-, cine-, multi-, télé-, -iel* (*logiciel, matériel, progiciel, didacticiel*; *courriel* for *e-mail* was first formed in 2003; the DO 94 lists *publipostage* for *mailing*). Asyndetic compounds (noun-noun) as opposed to the more French-sounding prepositional constructions are rare. This practice of forming neologisms is a conscious effort of the terminology committees to stop an already existing, frequent and accepted tendency of language change in French. In an empirical study, Helfrich (1993: 229) shows the high level of production output of asyndetic noun compounds and their high acceptance among speakers. Furthermore, the high productivity in French of the affixes *-ing, self-* and *-man* (proven by the numerous pseudo-loans), whose integrative potential is also confirmed by Rey-Debove (1987: 260), is slowed down and consistently replaced by the committees: *-man* often by *-iste*, e.g., *perchiste, groupiste*; *-ing* usually by *-age* (*dopage, aquaplanage*), but also by *-ion* (*pression*); *-self* by *auto-* (*self help housing* → *autoconstruction*) (Braselmann 1999: 80). Helfrich (1993: 228) also shows for constructions with *-ing* that speakers already find them transparent, "simple" and thus "normal".

2.3 Current formation of neologisms

Since about 1995 the regularly published contributions "Néologie coopérative" in *La Banque des Mots* have increasingly contained formations with "fracto-morphèmes", particularly *bio-*, *télé-*, *cyber-* and *éco-* (cf. Joly et al. 1995: 3–48; Joly et al. 1996: 3–61). In particular, there is an attestation of "uncontrolled expansion" of *cyber-* (e.g., *cybermonde*, *cyberthèque*), whose productivity is particularly high in 1997 (Natallamby et al. 1998: 3–78): in that year alone we find 50 neologisms in a variety of meanings referring to animate (*cyberartiste*) and inanimate objects (*cyberboutique*). The original meaning of *cybernétique* has developed a new sense, namely 'interactivity characterised by a direct link with the internet'. This contradicts the principle of "clarté"; similarly, formations with *auto-* ('soi-même' and 'automobile'), *info-* ('informatique' and 'information') and *télé-* ('à distance' and 'télévision') also belong to two different semantic fields. The viability of such forms (as, e.g., *cyberbar*, *cybersandwicherie*, *cyberrestaurant* and *cyberfanatique*) is questionable. They are often based on English models, but there are also genuine French formations (*cybercarnet*, *cyberthécaire*), as Rüdel-Hahn (2008: 113) states in her empirical study. In 2005 the "Commission générale de terminologie et de néologie" (JO 22/7/2005) criticises the increasing use of *cyber-* (e.g., *cybercriminalité*): they encourage the use of alternatives and – in line with the new descriptive attitude after the "turning point" – only keep such formations that have been established in the "usage".

An English influence on French derivation, particularly on formations in technical languages, can be observed with *-able: pilotable* or *sauvegardable* are clearly French formations since **drivable* and **savable* are not attested in English (cf. Beciri 2000: 30). The tendency to replace the suffix *-ing* by *-age* (*listing/listage*, *zoning/zonage*, etc.), already observed in the DO 94, can also be confirmed in the new material. The nominalisation of certain English verbs (*stripping*, *testing*) is a French process that cannot be found in English dictionaries (Bossy 2000: 43). The suffix *-iel*, created for *logiciel* 'software' in 1970, continues to be productive and already forms a paradigm, as visible, for instance, in *courriel* 'e-mail', *matériel* 'hardware', *didacticiel* 'educational software', *pourriel* 'spam', *progiciel* 'package', *synergiciel* 'groupware' (Depecker 2000: 103–134; Jansen 2005: 215), cf. also *linguisticiel* (Ouellet 2007: 5–25), apparently a linguistic computer programme, which does not appear either in *FranceTerme* or in PRob11. The prefix *e-* is an interesting case and can be increasingly observed in French for internet and communication applications but also in adminstration: *e-commerce*, *e-business*, *e-book*, *e-administration*, *e-ministère*. The "Commission générale de terminologie et de néologie" recommends avoiding the prefix *e-*, whose meaning is said to be imprecise, by using *télé-* (as in *télécharger*) and *en ligne* (*apprendre en ligne* instead of *e-learning*), cf. JO 13/3/2002, JO 22/7/2005; Nicoletti (2002: 357–358).

When comparing numbers of general and technical newspaper texts, it turns out that the formation of neologisms in standard language texts relies especially on derivation (about 61 %) and in particular on Greek-Latin "fracto-morphèmes". As for compounding, asyndetic noun-noun compounds have become most frequent, particularly in non-technical texts. Technical texts, by contrast, contain a large number (43 %) of semantic neologisms (compared with 6 % in the non-technical texts), acronyms and borrowings (cf. Beciri 2000: 19–36). In an overview of "Quelques aspects des vocabulaires spécialisés de la fin de XXe siècle", which is based on approximately 10,000 official terms, Depecker (2000: 131–132) appeals to the terminology committees to reconsider whether blends such as *publipostage* 'mailing', *restovite* 'fast food restaurant', *scénarimage* 'story-board', *micromisation* 'downsizing' are morphologically correct, whether *progiciel* 'package' is a felicitous formation (or whether it is not prone to confusion with the French prefix *pro-*) and whether the tendency to form noun-noun compounds with suppression of the preposition (observable in France since the 1950s, influenced by translations of English terms) does not incur a loss of precision.

The DGLFLF itself, highest language authority in France, editor of the JO and the database *FranceTerme*, has been strictly pursuing a descriptive approach (since the language-political "turning point") in its description of the formation of neologisms ("La fabrique des mots, ou comment naissent les mots dans la langue français"; cf. http://www.culture.gouv.fr./culture/dglf/terminologie/termino_accueil.htm [last access 10 Sept 2007]; meanwhile "La fabrique des mots" has been taken offline). According to them, there are two types of neologisms: substitute words that speakers spontaneously form "in-vivo" and ones that the committees create artificially, "in-vitro". In my analysis of the DO 94 (Braselmann 1999: 68–95), I categorised replacements into these two groups: "spontaneous" and "artificial". However, even in those cases in which a spontaneously created neologism already existed, the committees put forward an artificial one: for instance, the spontaneous adaptation *tour-opérateur* for *tour operator* and replacement by *voyagiste*; rejection of the spontaneous partial lexeme substitution *surbooking* for *overbooking* and replacement by the artificially created *surréservation*. The respective article in *FranceTerme* s.v. *surréservation* still explicitly refers to this: "*Note*: Le terme 'surbooking' ne doit pas être employé." A similar reference can be found for the ban of *tour-opérateur* s.v. *organisateur de voyages* (*voyagiste* is only given as an equivalent). The PRob11 interprets the situation differently: *surbooking* features as a lemma (referring to the "wrong anglicism", *surréservation* as the "official recommendation"), and *tour-opérateur* has an entry as well. This means that in the end the "spontaneously" created substitute words have succeeded in usage.

The artificial replacements created by the committees were not accepted, despite repeated puristic interventions, the latest via *FranceTerme*.

The DGLFLF (entirely free of evaluation or warning) lists the following word-formation possibilities (among others): prefixes (such as *anti-* in *antisocial*, *e-* in *e-commerce* and *cyber-* in *cybercafé*), noun-noun compounds (such as *voiture-bélier* 'car battering ram') and blends, which are very productive in formations such as *télématique* (*télé* and *informatique*), *alicament* (*aliment* and *médicament*) or *pourriel* (*pourri* and *courriel*), cf. also Jansen (2005: 215). Of these only the substitute word *commerce en ligne* (for *e-commerce)* and *télématique*, belonging to the technical languages of computer science and telecommunications, appear in *FranceTerme*. One of the conclusions to be drawn from these facts could be that terminology committees now only deal with technical vocabulary, which then appears in *FranceTerme*. This assumption is supported by the fact that *antisocial*, *cybercafé*, *télématique*, *alicament* and *pourriel*, terms belonging to standard language, have entered PRob11.

2.4 The linguistic material

Compared with the neologisms in DO 94, the standard language has remained largely untouched since the reorientation in language policy. Instead, most substitute words in the new material have been created for technical vocabulary. Moreover, a considerably higher number of anglicisms have been permitted, even and in particular ones that had previously been banned, such as *corner*, *lifting*, *manager*, *marketing*, *spot*, etc. (Braselmann 2008a: 11–16). The number of official substitute words has increased: in 2006, for instance, almost 300 terms were published, while in 2010 (the period investigated was January 5, 2010 to February 2, 2011) more than 340 new terms were added to *FranceTerme*. In 2011 (from February 5 to October 29) 385 terms had already been published. Not surprisingly, the majority of words belong to the domains of computer science and electronics, but there are also a large number of neologisms from other fields such as aviation and nuclear technology.

The glossary published by the DGLFLF in 2004 ("Cent termes français du vocabulaire technique: sélection de termes tous domaines confondus"; access: http://www.dglf.culture.gouv.fr/publications/publications.htm), which comprises a manageable selection of 100 French terms from different technical areas will be used to carry out a systematic analysis and a comparison with the entries of the dictionary *Le Petit Robert* of 2011. The 2004 glossary was chosen because one could assume that it would contain neologisms that are more likely part of standard usage than the specific glossaries of individual domains. This expectation was fulfilled: approximately 50 % of the neologisms have entered the PRob11. Consequently, it is possible to say whether new word-formation models have been able to enter standard language. When comparing the two sources it becomes apparent that in the end usage cannot be regulated by ministerial word lists and recommendations:

a) In many cases the anglicism that is supposed to be replaced enters the dictionary as a separate lemma, for instance, *magnet, aquaplaning, raider, CD-Rom, leader, joint venture, packaging, e-mail, starter, discount, coach, crash-test, scoop, hacker, listing, check list, sponsoring, spam, spot, morphing, stock option, hit-parade, sparring partner* (in the glossary at least marked as "équiv. admis", as permitted equivalent – for this category cf. also Egger 2008: 27–41), *driver, cracker, pool, mailing, brainstorming, dispatching, turnover, airbag, web*.
b) In many cases the official neologism as well as the anglicism it is supposed to replace get separate entries in the dictionary, for example, *baladeur* (beside *walkman*), *cédérom* (beside *CD-Rom*), *coentreprise* (beside *joint venture*), *conditionnement* (beside *packaging*), *démarreur* (beside *starter*), *entraîneur* (beside *coach*), *fouineur* (beside *hacker*), *listage* (beside *listing*), *mécénat* (beside *sponsoring*), *arrosage* (beside *spam*), *palmarès* (beside *hit-parade*), *pirate* (beside *cracker*), *publipostage* (beside *mailing*), *remue-méninges* (beside *brainstorming*), *exclusivité* (beside *scoop*). This means that both the anglicism and its French equivalent have been established in usage.
c) In other cases the PRob11 only lists the official French substitute word in the article of the lemmatised anglicism with a note saying that it is the "official recommendation" (= rec.off.), such as with *magnet* (rec.off. *aimantin*), *morphing* (rec.off. *morphage*), *flash-ball* (rec.off. *arme de défense à balles souples*), *aquaplaning* (rec.off. *aquaplanage*), *discount* (rec.off. *discompte*), *scoop* (rec.off. *exclusivité*), *let* (rec.off. *filet!*), *check list* (rec.off. *liste de vérification*, but also listed s.v. *vérification*), *stock option* (rec.off. *option sur titres*, also listed s.v. *option*), *airbag* (rec.off. *sac gonflable*, also s.v. *gonflable*). This means that the dictionary fulfils its duty by referring to the official equivalent while at the same time emphasising that the prescribed anglicism (and not the official French neologism) is the more commonly used expression in standard language.
d) Further, there are cases in which only the anglicism to be replaced is entered without referring to the official French equivalent: *webmaster* or *webmestre* (instead of: *administrateur de site*, but there is a reference s.v. *administrateur*).
e) Abbreviations, also English ones (i.e. ones to be officially avoided) can be found in examples such as *URL* (instead of: *adresse universelle*), *FAQ* (*Fre-*

quently Asked Questions), *ABS* (*Anti-lock Braking System*). In the latter case the respective committee suggests *antiblocage de securité* as a French substitute construction (which is not listed in PRob11). This is very clever because *ABS* could also be a French abbreviation. Similarly successful is *PR* (for: *park and ride*, but also for the official French substitute construction *parc relais*) which, however, has not become generally accepted: PRob11 mentions neither the acronym nor the English or French construction. The French abbreviation *IRM* (and not the long version *Imagerie par Résonance Magnétique*) has its own entry in the dictionary.

f) The following are interesting exceptions that impressively show that "usage" cannot be regulated: In the glossary we investigated one official French substitute construction *conservation de numéro* (for *number portability*) with the explicit remark that the use of *portabilité de numéro* is not advised: "est déconseillée". However, it is this unpopular loan translation that has become generally accepted according to PRob11 (s.v. *portabilité*). A similar development can be observed for *flash-ball* (official French substitute construction: *arme de défense à balles souples*) in whose entry in the glossary there is an even clearer note that this "marque déposée française" must not be used. However, according to PRob11 the rejected (much shorter) anglicism has become standard usage.

g) Formations with the prefix *e-* (for *électronique*) and the equivalent prefix *cyber-* are often rejected, also in the glossary of 2004. What is interesting is their further development: while the PRob11 lists not a single formation with *e-* (neither *e-commerce*, nor *e-ministère*), *cyber-* is productive in the standard lexicon: PRob11 lists 11 formations (*cybercafé*, *cybercriminalité*, etc.). This development is finally also recognised by the authorities: the data base *FranceTerme*, which is constantly updated, introduces as official neologisms the French formations *cybercaméra* (for Engl. *webcamera*), *cybervêtement* (for Engl. *e-wear*), the (slightly adapted) anglicisms *cybernaute* (beside the French formation *internaute*), *cybersquat* (for Engl. *cybersquatting*) and *cybersquatteur, -euse* (for Engl. *cybersquatter*). Engl. *cybermarketing*, however, is replaced by *mercatique électronique*. These neologisms (apart from *cybernaute*) are not found in PRob11, which means that they have not become accepted in standard usage, probably due to the fact that they are too technical. However, apart from those mentioned above, the PRob11 has lemmatised the probably internal French formations *cyberculture*, *cyberdélinquance*, *cyberespace*, *cyberguerre*, *cybermonde*, *cyberpirate* beside the (slightly adapted) anglicisms *cybernétique* and *cybernéticien, -ienne*.

3 Selected "new" word-formation patterns

Finally, we turn to a number of other word-formation patterns, some of which have already been touched on so far. The suffix *-ing*, of which even Rey-Debove (1987: 269) (beside *self-* and *-man*) assumed that it would become acclimatised in French, indeed shows high productivity and acceptance: PRob11 lists, for instance, *aquaplaning, couponing, doping, listing, merchandising, nursing, parking, pressing, sponsoring, stripping, zoning*. This tendency toward change is further slowed down (just like in the DO 94, cf. section 2.3) by official interventions, particularly by the suffix replacement *-age: FranceTerme* prescribes the following substitute words: *aquaplanage, couponnage, dopage, listage, marchandisage, maternage, parc de stationnement, pression, mécénat* (beside *parrainage*), *stripage, zonage*. The "turning point" in language policy has not changed anything in this respect, cf. Schmitt (1978: 458), who documented the academy's strict rejection of *-ing* already more than 30 years ago.

A similar development can be shown in formations with the component *self-*: in the standard language we find, for instance, *self-control, self-government, self-made-man, self-service* (PRob11), which do not appear in the data base *France-Terme*. The respective technical terms (e.g., *self-stressing, self-consuming, self-compacting concrete, self-condensation*) continue to be replaced by authorities with *auto-*: *autocontrainte, autoconsommation, béton autoplaçant, autocondensation*.

However, *-man* does not seem to be productive: in the DO 94 *comingman, groupman, perchman, recordman, tennisman* were replaced by the neologisms *espoir, groupiste, perchiste, détenteur d'un record, joueur de tennis* (cf. also Braselmann 1999: 74); *FranceTerme* does not list these terms (which is one of the arguments for the technical orientation of this official data base) and the standard language (according to PRob11) seems to have only accepted the two criticised English forms *tennisman* and *recordman* and the partly adapted form *perchiste*.

Jansen (2005: 212) emphasises the efforts of the terminology committees to avoid the invasion of new compounding types, such as the adoption of Germanic word order through the English model, the placement of the adjective before the noun such as in *libre service*. In 1973 it was still suggested to replace the anglicism *self service*, to use *franc-jeu* instead of *fair play* and *libre-échange* instead of *free trade* (cf. Braselmann 1999: 62, 84). Since 1983, and also in the DO 94, these three anglicisms have no longer been criticised and the French substitute expressions with Germanic word order no longer proposed (*gros-porteur* for *jumbo jet*, however, is still recommended in the DO 94 and is also listed in the current *Francetерme*). In standard language the following have become accepted (PRob11): *libre-service, libre-échange* and *fair-play* (beside *gros-porteur* for *jumbo jet*).

However, in 2007 the expression *stockage en libre service* is created to replace Engl. *self storage*, thus reintroducing the English word order *libre service* into French (JO 23/12/2007). The English word order adjective + noun seems to be present in the linguistic conscience and frequent in usage.

Blends are seen as a typical English type of word-formation (Jansen 2005: 213). In *appliquette*, for instance, the terminology committees have attached the suffix *-ette*, which in French usually only combines with nouns (but cf. *grimpette* 'steep little climb'), to a verbal base (*appliqu-*). In the standard language (PRob11) *nétiquette* has been established; but this is probably a loan from Engl. *netiquette* (← *net*[*work*] + [*e*]*tiquette*).

From the perspective of language purism the cases in which English word-formation patterns become productive in French are more problematic than the adoption of an English expression, because they infringe upon the internal structure of French. The same goes for the formation of acronyms and noun-noun compounds, which can be found increasingly as a consequence of the influence of English, for instance the official technical equivalents *boîtier-système*, *puce-système*, etc. Compounds without prepositions lack the "clarté" always requested of new formations, cf. among others Goose (1975: 63–64). This is the same for the many cases of blends such as *scénarimage* (*scenario* and *image*), *alicament* (*aliment* and *médicament*), *télématique* (*télé* and *informatique*).

The "fracto-morphèmes" that Rey-Debove (1987: 263) still criticised are currently very productive, as confirmed by *FranceTerme* and PRob11, particularly formations with *anti-*, *cyber-*, *éco-*, *info-*, *mono-*, *multi-*, *télé-*.

4 Conclusion

It should have become clear that since the turning point in 1996 the terminology committees have usually dealt with technical vocabulary and, unlike in the DO 1994, rarely intervene in the standard language. In the decree of 1996, the committees were instructed to initiate preventive actions, i.e. to form substitute words before the English expression becomes established; this request is generally taken seriously (e.g., *informatique en nuage*). Occasional relapses where anglicisms have already become accepted in the "usage" while the committees offer variants that have yet to stand the test of the speakers (cf. the analyses of *coach*, *e-*, *flyer*, *live* and *pitch* in section 1.2) remain single cases and do not change the general preventive attitude.

The new lexical material still contains simple translations of English expressions (*faiseur d'argent* for *money maker*) or very long multi-word units that resemble definitions of the short anglicisms (e.g., *arme de défense à balles souples* for *flash-ball, course de pleine nature* for *trail, épreuve de figures libres* for *free style*, or *randonnée d'aventure* for *trekking*). As shown above, experts have long since warned against such word-formation types. It has become clear that these constructions rarely get accepted. In those cases in which the committees wanted to slow down language change, they were not successful and language usage gains the upper hand, as we have seen in the examples of formations with *-ing* and *self-*: they were able to become established without considering the substitute affixes *-age* and *auto-* proscribed by the ministry. Questioning the viability of formations with *cyber-* and warning against them because their semantic polysemy is said to harm the "clarté", becomes obsolete when faced with the "usage". The situation is similar for asyndetic noun compounds, for the formation of adjective-noun constructions and for blends. In general, many banned anglicisms, spontaneous adaptations and substitute words whose use is not advised (such as *surbooking, tour-opérateur*, or *portabilité de numéro*) have become established.

What, then, has changed for the language material since the turning point in French language policy? Have the formations really become more system-adequate because of the many authorities a substitute word has to pass through before becoming official? This is certainly true. However, it seems more important to me that what is seen as "system-adequate" and thus the official attitude have become more open. We can see that not least in the fact that blends, noun-noun compounds (without prepositions) and affixes such as *cyber-*, which were once denounced as "fracto-morphèmes", are now considered completely "normal" French word-formations by the highest language authority, the DGLFLF. (Note also the term *RoissyBus* – an asyndetic compound with the "un-French" determinative pattern – for the airport shuttle in Paris, which is also printed on the tickets.)

I would like to end with a quote by Goose (1975: 72), who usually sees the new word-formation tendencies in French quite critically (and partly puristically): "Il me reste à réaffirmer la force prépondérante de l'usage: là où il a choisi définitivement, même s'il a mal choisi, le théoricien n'a plus qu'à se taire. L'usage a toujours raison, même quand il a tort" [I have to reaffirm the determining force of language usage: where it has chosen, even if it was the wrong choice, the theoretician must remain silent. Usage is always right, even if it is wrong].

5 References

Beciri, Hélène (2000): Néologie générale, néologie spécialisée: Quelques observations dans le domaine de la micro-informatique. *La banque des mots* 60: 19–36.

Bossy, Jean (2000): Possibles recommandations pour l'évolution de la lexicologie de la santé. *La banque des mots* 60: 37–50.

Braselmann, Petra (1999): *Sprachpolitik und Sprachbewusstsein in Frankreich heute*. Tübingen: Niemeyer.

Braselmann, Petra (2008a): Französische Sprachpolitik. In: Petra Braselmann and Ingeborg Ohnheiser (eds.), *Frankreich als Vorbild? Sprachpolitik und Sprachgesetzgebung in europäischen Ländern*, 7–26. Innsbruck: Innsbruck University Press.

Braselmann, Petra (2008b): Anglizismen. In: Ingo Kolboom, Thomas Kotschi and Edward Reichel (eds.), *Handbuch Französisch*, 211–216. Berlin: Schmidt.

Braselmann, Petra and Ingeborg Ohnheiser (2011): Wie kontrollieren Frankreich und Polen ihre Sprachgesetze? In: Imke Mendoza, Bernhard Pöll and Susanne Behensky (eds.), *Sprachkontakt und Mehrsprachigkeit als Herausforderung für Soziolinguistik und Systemlinguistik (Ausgewählte Beiträge des gleichnamigen Workshops der 37. Österreichischen Linguistiktagung 2009)*, 11–25. München: LINCOM Europa.

Délégation générale à la langue française (ed.) (1994): *Dictionnaire des termes officiels de la langue française*. Paris: Journal officiel de la République française.

Depecker, Loïc (2000): Quelques aspects des vocabulaires spécialisés de la fin du XXe siècle: Entre créativité lexicale et parallélisation sur l'anglais. *La banque des mots* 60: 103–134.

DGLFLF = Main internet address of the DGLFLF including publications and corpora (*FranceTerme*, *Rapport au Parlement*, *Journal officiel*, etc.): http://www.dglflf.culture.gouv.fr

Diki-Kidiri, Marcel, Hubert Joly and Colette Murcia (1981): *Guide de la néologie*. Paris: Conseil international de la langue française.

Egger, Christine (2008): Neueste Tendenzen der französischen Sprachpolitik (dargestellt am Beispiel der Sportsprache). In: Petra Braselmann and Ingeborg Ohnheiser (eds.), *Frankreich als Vorbild? Sprachpolitik und Sprachgesetzgebung in europäischen Ländern*, 27–41. Innsbruck: Innsbruck University Press.

Goose, André (1975): *La néologie française aujourd'hui*. Paris: Conseil international de la langue française.

Helfrich, Uta (1993): *Neologismen auf dem Prüfstand. Ein Modell zur Ermittlung der Akzeptanz französischer Neologismen.* Wilhelmsfeld: Egert.

Jansen, Silke (2005): *Sprachliches Lehngut im* world wide web. *Neologismen in der französischen und spanischen Internetterminologie*. Tübingen: Narr.

Joly, Hubert, Pravina Nallatamby, Lay Ngo and Colette Mulder (1995): Néologie coopérative 1995. *La banque des mots* 50: 3–48.

Joly, Hubert, Pravina Nallatamby, Carine Ansart, Véronique Bayot, Colette Strous and R. Vlot (1996): Néologie coopérative 1996. *La banque des mots* 52: 3–61.

Murcia, Colette and Hubert Joly (2004): Néologie 2004. *La banque des mots* 68: 3–53.

Nallatamby, Pravina, Nicole van der Maazen, Brigitte Myr and Hubert Joly (1998): Néologie coopérative 1998. *La banque des mots* 56: 3–78.

Nicoletti, Otty (2002): Internet-Terminologie und romanische Sprachen: Beispiele aus dem Spanischen, Italienischen und Französischen. In: Wolfgang Dahmen, Günter Holtus, Johannes Kramer, Michael Metzeltin and Otto Winkelmann (eds.), *Englisch und Romanisch (Romanistisches Kolloquium XVIII)*, 341–368. Tübingen: Narr.

Ouellet, Sophie (2007): Les linguisticiels et la terminologie: Le cas de la nutrition publique. *La banque des mots* 74: 5–26.

Rey-Debove, Josette (1987): Effets des anglicismes lexicaux sur le système du français. *Cahiers de lexicologie* 51: 257–265.

Robert, Paul (ed.) (2011): *Le petit Robert. Dictionnaire alphabétique et analogique de la langue française*. Nouvelle édition du Petit Robert. (Texte remanié et amplifié sous la direction de Josette Rey-Debove et Alain Rey). Nouvelle édition millésime 2012. Paris: Le Robert: Pons (= PRob11).
Rüdel-Hahn, Martina (2008): Anglizismen im Internetwortschatz der romanischen Sprachen: Französisch – Italienisch – Spanisch. Ph.D. dissertation, Universität Düsseldorf. http://docserv.uni-duesseldorf.de/servlets/DerivateServlet/Derivate-11297/Dissertation%20Martina%20R%C3 %BCdel.pdf [last access 24 May 2011].
Schmitt, Christian (1978): Wortbildung und Purismus. In: Wolfgang Dressler and Wolfgang Meid (eds.), *Proceedings of the Twelfth International Congress of Linguists, Vienna 1977*, 456–459. Innsbruck: Institut für Sprachwissenschaft der Universität Innsbruck.

Franz Rainer

10 Mechanisms and motives of change in word-formation

Abstract: The mechanisms and motives of change in word-formation have often been treated in diachronic linguistics over the last two hundred years, but no consistent classification, nor a widely-accepted terminology, have emerged from these discussions. The present overview should be considered as a mere starting point for a more thorough treatment.

1 Introduction

Single mechanisms of change in word-formation have been discussed many times since the 19th century, but no systematic doctrine has emerged from these discussions up to the present day, nor a unified terminology. The relative neglect of the topic may partly be due to the fact that linguists tend to think that the general principles governing the evolution of the lexicon (cf. Blank 1997) will automatically cover that of complex words. It is of course true that word-formation is intimately tied to the lexicon and that similar forces are at play in both areas, but, as will become apparent, beside the many commonalities, there are also a number of phenomena that can only be found in word-formation or at least have their own distinct profile there.

The main focus in this article will be on the classification of the mechanisms of change that I have been able to identify. Motives of change will be discussed along with the mechanisms, provided any generalization in this respect is possible (for an insightful discussion of "motives of lexemic change", cf. Grzega 2002: 1029–1038). We will start with changes affecting the formal side and then proceed

Franz Rainer, Vienna, Austria

https://doi.org/10.1515/9783111420530-010

to the realms of semantics and pragmatics, as well as productivity. Language contact as a source of change will be touched upon briefly in the final section 5.

2 Change affecting the formal side

2.1 The regular action of the sound laws

The most trivial case of formal change is due to the blind action of the sound laws. Most of the time, this kind of change does not affect the system of word-formation at a deeper level. In some instances, however, it does lead to important changes.

In one such scenario the action of the sound laws makes an affix disappear physically. As a consequence, the pattern in question is sometimes simply shifted from affixation to conversion, but continues to work very much the same from the point of view of word-formation. This is what happened, for example, to Old English verbs in *-ian* – whose status as a derivational suffix, admittedly, is not uncontroversial –, e.g., *fisc-ian* (← *fisc*), whose present-day descendant *fish* 'to catch fish' is related to the noun *fish* via conversion. In other cases, such as Old English *cealf-ian* 'to give birth to a calf' (← *cealf*), the original suffix has left a formal trace in Modern English due to the sonorization of the final consonant of the base (*calve* ← *calf*). In extreme cases, however, the sound laws can do severe damage to the word-formation system by completely obliterating the morphological structure of originally complex words. Our languages are replete with simple words that etymological dictionaries show to have been complex at earlier stages.

The action of the sound laws can also lead to h o m o n y m i z a t i o n. In this case, two or more affixes continue to function as morphological entities, but are no longer distinguished formally. Latin, for example, had an agentive suffix *-tor* and an instrumental-locative suffix *-torium*, which were formally very similar (in fact, from a diachronic perspective, the latter is composed of the former plus the relational suffix *-ius*). As a consequence, in some Romance languages and dialects these two suffixes merged for purely phonological reasons (cf. Rainer 2011). In Catalan, for example, they both ended up as *-dor: caçador* 'hunter' (← *caçar* 'to hunt'), *mocador* 'handkerchief' (← *mocar-se* 'to blow one's nose'), *menjador* 'dining room' (← *menjar* 'to eat'). Another well-known case are the Latin suffixes *-arius*, forming agent nouns, and *-arium*, forming instrument and place nouns, which merged not only in all Romance languages (cf. Fr. *-ier*, It. *-aio*, Sp. *-ero*, etc.), but even in German as *-er* (cf. *telonarius* 'customs officer' > *Zöllner*, *spicarium* 'granary' > *Speicher*; cf. Müller 2011). For German, Henzen (1957, § 66) also points out that the highly multifunctional German verb prefix *ver-* is the result of a merger of three prefixes or particles which are still distinguished as *faur, fra-* and *fair-* in Gothic.

While homonymization in most cases simply leads to affixal multifunctionality from a synchronic perspective, it can also give rise at times to a secondary, orthographic differentiation. In languages where one and the same sound can correspond to different orthographic realizations, such innovations mostly occur in times characterized by a low level of literacy or a still unstable orthography. It is probably no coincidence that cases of "Suffixverkennung" (lit. 'suffix misidentification') have been reported mainly for Old French (cf. Willenberg 1881), a language that had suffered severe phonological reduction and therefore was characterized by a high degree of homophony in suffixation. French *filet* 'net', for example, whose suffix *-et* (phonologically /e/) is identical to the diminutive suffix, in reality goes back to Old French *filé*, the regular outcome of Latin *filatum*, a nominalized neuter past participle of *filare* 'to spin'. Another case in point is mentioned by Baldinger (1961: 13–14), who surmises that the unexpected use as an approximative suffix (cf. *noiraud* 'blackish' ← *noir* 'black') of *-aud* (phonologically /aut > au > o/), which goes back to the second element *-walt* of Germanic names such as *Grim-walt*, in reality conceals the diminutive suffix *-eau* (phonologically /jau > au > o/), which goes back to Latin *-ellus*.

2.2 Erosion

Regular sound change must be distinguished from cases of erosion – also called *attrition* or *mutilation* – due to grammaticalization (cf. Heine and Kuteva 2007: 42–44) or lexicalization, which may go beyond the normal action of the sound laws in fully regular morphologically complex words.

When lexemes become desemanticized in the course of grammaticalization (cf. section 3.2), this can often be seen to trigger phonological reduction processes after some time. Formal reduction here iconically mirrors prior semantic reduction. Well-known examples are English *man* /mæn/, which appears reduced to /mən/ in older compounds denoting "a member of a specified professional group or body" such as *clergyman* (cf. Marchand 1969, § 2.3.3), or the adjective *full* /fʊl/, whose vowel has been reduced or even completely elided in its use as a derivational suffix, as in *beautiful* /bju:tifəl, bju:tifᵊl/.

Lexicalized complex words also often behave differently phonologically from regular complex words. Plank (1981: 70–71), for example, observed that in the German verbs *empfangen* 'to receive' (cf. *fangen* 'to catch'), *empfehlen* 'to recommend' (cf. *fehlen* 'to miss') and *empfinden* 'to feel' (cf. *finden* 'to find') the prefix *ent-* has been assimilated to the following /f/, because in these verbs the prefix was no longer recognized by speakers as a meaningful unit, contrary to semantically transparent verbs such as *entflechten* 'to unbundle' (← *flechten* 'to weave') or *entfliegen* 'to fly away' (← *fliegen* 'to fly'), in lento style at least.

2.3 Output optimization

In a number of cases, irregular formal changes seem to be attributable to a desire to optimize the output from a phonological point of view, for example, by avoiding awkward sound repetition or by matching the syllable structure or the rhyme of the model(s) more closely.

A case illustrating the influence of dissimilation is the well-known Latin suffix *-alis*, which had a variant *-aris* that was used when the base contained an /l/ in a position defined in detail by Czer (2010). The distribution of these allomorphs was phonologically conditioned by liquid dissimilation at the beginning, but on its way to Romance the phonological conditioning was partially lost (cf. Spanish *melon-ar* 'melon field', but also *alfalf-al* 'lucerne field'). Another case can be adduced from French, where the suffix *-esque* occasionally changes into *-este* if the base ends in /k/ in order to avoid the cacophonous repetition of /k/, as in *Silvio Pellico* → *silviopelliqueste* (Verlaine); cf. Plénat (2015) on dissimilatory phenomena in French word-formation.

Cases of prosodic output optimization have sometimes been described as cases of juncture shift or reanalysis. The Latin suffix *-anus*, for example, arose as a consequence of an anti-etymological separation of words like *Romanus* 'Roman', which originally contained a suffix *-nus* attached to the theme vowel *-a* of the first declension: *Roma-nus* > *Rom-anus*. The shift of the morpheme boundary may have occurred when *-anus* was attached to bases that were not part of the first declension, such as *urbs* 'city (of Rome)' (derivational stem: *urb-*): *urbanus* (instead of **urb-nus*). If the juncture shift really took place in the pair *Roma*/*urbs*, as some Latinists think, its function could have been to attain a trisyllabic output in correspondence with the trisyllabic model *Romanus*, sacrificing morphological to prosodic faithfulness.

While the *-a* of *Rom-a* is a morphological unit, no morphology at all is involved in the next example. The rise of the related Latin suffix *-ianus* of *Caesarianus* '(follower) of Caesar' and similar formations is also considered to have been the result of a juncture shift. In derivatives such as *Aemilius* → *Aemilianus*, *Fulvius* → *Fulvianus*, *Iulius* → *Iulianus*, etc. the suffix still has the shape *-anus*, as the comparison with the corresponding proper names shows, whose *-us* is an inflectional ending. So how did the suffix variant *-ianus* then arise? Schnorr v. Carolsfeld (1884: 184) already correctly observed that "because of their sheer number they [i.e. the derivatives from names ending in the phonic sequence *-ius*] caused other stems to take on a suffix *-ianus* obviously inappropriate for them" (my translation). Derivatives with *-ianus* like *Catonianus*, from *Cato* (derivational stem: *Caton-*) have been attested since Cicero and originally had a popular tinge. The reason for this reanalysis seems to have been again the desire to make the words phonologically more similar to the dominant series of derivatives in *-i-anus*. At the same time, this output-oriented strategy allowed the Romans to avoid the repetition of two /n/s separated only by one vowel (*Catonanus*), which may have been felt as cacophonous.

Phonological adjustments of this kind are a major source of formal changes in the evolution of word-formation, as Roché et al. (2011) have shown on the basis of abundant French material. A linguistic trait typical of the region of Flandres, for example, is not called *flandrisme*, nor *flamandisme* (*flamand* is the French adjective corresponding to *Flandres*), which would be morphologically faithful derivatives, but *flandricisme*, apparently in order to make it rhyme better with *atticisme*, *anglicisme*, *belgicisme*, *gallicisme*, and similar words, where *-ic-* is part of the base (at least historically). Prosodic faithfulness may also have been at play here (all words have four syllables), but the price to pay for lexical and prosodic optimization is an awkward repetition of /s/ (<c> before <i> is pronounced /s/), which is generally avoided. This kind of process is an important source of affix variants and interfixes (cf. Roché 2015 on interfixes in Romance). The desire to match the number of syllables of the model could also have been at the origin of the English suffix variant *-nese* of *Bali-nese*, whose model could have been *Japa-nese* (Malkiel 1966: 320).

Other explanations have been proposed for suffix extensions of the kind discussed here. Plank (1981: 74), for example, argued that the passage from *-ing* to *-ling* in German (cf. *Jüngling* 'young man' ← *jung* 'young') was due to a preference for consonantal onsets. A word like Old High German *ediling* 'nobleman' (← *edil* 'noble'), whose morphological structure was *edil-ing*, was syllabified as *edi·ling*, which is how the suffix variant *-ling* arose. This explanation, however, is not uncontroversial; cf. Haspelmath (1995: 16–18). In other cases, according to Plank (1981: 74), juncture shift can be interpreted as a consequence of a previous rearrangement of form and meaning in established complex words. The passage from the suffix *-ier* to *-tier* in French (cf. *armur-ier* 'gunsmith' ← *armure* 'armour' vs. *bijou-tier* 'jeweller' ← *bijou* 'jewel') probably was due to the fact that final /t/ ceased to be pronounced in Middle French in words like *fruit* 'id.' or *pot* 'id.'; hence, *fruitier* 'fruit merchant' and *potier* 'potter' could rightfully be resegmented as *frui-tier* and *po-tier* respectively.

2.4 Contamination and affix pleonasm

Contamination is a linguistic accident during retrieval, viz. the simultaneous activation of two synonymous or otherwise semantically related lexemes. For example, on the border of the German dialect area where 'potato' is *Kartoffel* and that where it is *Erdapfel* lit. 'ground apple', a contaminated form *Erdoffel* has arisen. Apparently, this same accident can also affect synonymous affixes, though much more rarely. Rohlfs (1969, § 1147), for example, explains the origin of the feminizing suffix *-ressa* of the dialect of Venice as a contamination of the descendants of Latin *-trix*, which lost its productivity in popular speech, and the Late Latin suffix of Greek provenance *-issa*. In an analogous way, the Northern Italian adverbial suffix *-mentre*, also present as *-mientre* in Old Spanish, is explained by Rohlfs (1969, § 888) as a result of the contamination of the Classical Latin adverbial suffix *-enter*, which was doomed, and the newly grammaticalized *-mente* suffix (Detges 2015 prefers an explanation as a case of affix pleonasm, i.e. *-mente* + *-iter*).

Something very similar happens in affix pleonasm (cf. Lehmann 2005; Gardani 2015), a process which we can define with Haspelmath (1993: 297) as "the semantically vacuous addition of a transparent affix to a word that is already characterized for the morphosyntactic property expressed by this affix". Contrary to what happens in contamination, the two affixes are not fused, but stacked up. The result therefore is a longer affix variant, like the *-essin* of German *Prinzessin*, which was the result of adding the productive feminizing suffix *-in* to *Prinzess* (< French *princesse*). A direct addition to *Prinz* 'prince' would have yielded regular, but unusual *Prinzin*.

2.5 Ellipsis

One further type of change concerning the formal side is ellipsis, which however also often leads to semantic change (absorption) in a second step; cf. section 3.4.4. In cases of ellipsis, part of a complex word is dropped, while the meaning remains constant. The motive behind ellipsis normally is economy of expression, as when German *Atomkraft(werks)gegner* 'anti-nuke; lit. atom power (station) enemy' was shortened to *Atomgegner* lit. 'atom opponent'. Note that an *Atomgegner* still opposes nuclear energy or nuclear power plants, not atoms in general. Ellipsis is even more frequent with lexemes of a phrasal nature, as when Latin *faber ferrarius* 'blacksmith; lit. craftsman iron-REL' was shortened to *ferrarius*. Clippings, acronyms and abbreviations are other notorious manifestations of this same tendency towards economy of expression.

3 Change affecting the semantic side

3.1 General considerations

The analysis of semantic change in word-formation has not attracted excessive attention up to the present day, neither at the descriptive nor at the theoretical level. Fundamental issues remain unsettled.

Among these, there is the question of whether affixes are signs or not. Those who, like Lehrer (2000), answer in the affirmative should expect affixes to evolve semantically like ordinary signs. This contention, however, was already rejected over 100 years ago by Jaberg (1905), who claimed that affixes have no independent existence and hence can only change their meaning as a by-product of semantic change in one or some of their host words. This scenario of lexical semantic change followed by a reanalysis that ties the new meaning to the affix undoubtedly is an important one in the evolution of word-formation, but not the only possibility, as we will see in section 3.5.

Another fundamental divide in semantic studies of word-formation concerns the very notion of meaning. Most morphologists agree that it is useful to make an analytical distinction between the referential meaning of a morphologically complex word, i.e. the category of objects in the world that the word refers to or the corresponding concept in the mind, and its relational meaning, i.e. the semantic relationship between base and affix in the case of a derivative, or between the bases in the case of a compound. From a referential perspective, one would say that *writer* and *mixer* belong into two different categories, viz. persons and kitchen appliances, while some linguists have claimed that from the relational viewpoint both are instances of one and the same semantic category, since both can be paraphrased by 'an *x* that Vs' (the writer writes, the mixer mixes). Whether you adopt one or the other perspective also has important consequences for the study of semantic change. When the English suffix *-er*, which originally could only designate persons, came to be used for appliances such as mixers, a referentialist would say that a significant semantic change had happened. Those who focus on the semantic relation between base and affix, on the contrary, might contend that nothing of interest has happened, since the relation has remained the same. This latter stance has been particularly popular among European structuralists. It seems to me that neither the referential nor the relational perspective can be neglected if we want to gain a full understanding of what is going on in semantic change in word-formation.

Intimately tied to this problem is the distinction between linguistic meaning and encyclopedic meaning. While for most psychologists and cognitive linguists meanings and concepts are one and the same thing, many linguists continue to think and speak of them as separate entities. (Admittedly, attempts to come up with hard and fast criteria for distinguishing the two have not been very successful up to the present day.) In studies on word-formation, the distinction is often presented as one between the lexical meaning of a complex word as opposed to its "word-formation meaning" (*Wortbildungsbedeutung*, in German). Bréal (1868) already argued that languages tend to express only relatively general meanings which are then fleshed out by our "intelligence", i.e. by general cognitive processes. This was particularly evident for him in suffixation. The French suffix *-ier*, for example, refers to a fruit tree in *pommier* (← *pomme* 'apple'), a receptacle in *encrier* 'inkpot' (← *encre* 'ink'), but a person in *chevalier* 'knight' (← *cheval* 'horse'). In this latter class of personal nouns, furthermore, there is considerable variation in the semantic relation between base and suffix: while a *prisonnier* 'prisoner' is kept in prison, a *geôlier* 'jalor' is in charge of the *geôle* 'jail'. How do we get the right semantics? According to Bréal, either by "tradition", i.e. because we have learned the specific meaning, or, in the case of words we have never heard before, by guessing it: "notre entendement achève ce qui est seulement indiqué par le langage" [our understanding completes what is only hinted at by the language] (p. 11). Again, this idea of distinguishing different levels of abstraction in the meaning of an affix is undoubtedly important also for the historical study of word-formation. But it would be aberrant to conclude that linguists have to limit themselves to the study of "word-formation meaning" only, to the exclusion of encyclopedic knowledge or the influence of the speech situation and context, for that matter. As will become apparent, most explanations of semantic change in word-formation involve encyclopedic knowledge, as well as context and speech situation (cf. already Paul 1880).

A fourth meaning-related issue of some importance is whether the meaning of complex words should be considered as compositional or holistic. Those who believe in compositionality see the meaning of the complex word as deducible from the meaning of the constituents plus the meaning of the pertinent word-formation rule, while for those who favour holism (cf. Plank 1981; Serbat 1983) the meaning of the whole exceeds the sum of the meaning of its parts. It seems to me that many types of change in word-formation can only be explained from a holistic perspective, i.e. by taking into account the whole lexical meaning of the model or models that constitute(s) the starting point for a new formation. The same output-orientedness has also been seen in section 2.3.2 as crucial for the explanation of some formal aspects of neologisms.

3.2 Grammaticalization

"Grammaticalization" is a cover term for processes of language change by which some unit of a language turns into a more "grammar-like" unit, to use a slightly circular definition. In the process, this unit becomes semantically more abstract ("bleached", or "desemanticized") and tends to lose phonological substance, though not necessarily so. Often it ends up as a bound form (clitic, affix). As Lindström's (2004) sobering history of this concept and term demonstrates, there is little agreement among researchers beyond this vague characterization. Some consider grammaticalization as a separate process, while others see it as an epiphenomenon of "deeper" mechanisms such as reanalysis, metaphor/metonymy, or analogy.

As far as word-formation is concerned, many cases of lexemes turning into affixes have been documented in the literature, see also articles 12–14. The pathway from lexeme to affix can be direct, as in the case of Romance adverbs in *-mente*, which go back to Latin ablative phrases of the type *clarā mente* 'with a clear mind'; cf. Detges (2015). Cases involving a passage from preposition to prefix, as in *après-guerre* 'post-war period' (← *après* 'after', *guerre* 'war'), are discussed in detail in Amiot (2015).

In many cases, however, the immediate origin of the affix is not a syntactic construction, but a member of a compound, i.e. another morphological entity. Members of compounds often form long series of similar formations, and if this process of "Reihenbildung", as it is called in German, is accompanied by semantic change the road is cleared for the progressive development of a true affix. A thorough account of the development of the English suffix *-hood* from the second member of compounds ending in *-hād* 'position, condition' and of many similar cases is contained in Dietz (2007); cf. also Trips (2009). A nice illustration of the semantic bleaching involved in grammaticalization is provided by the suffix (or clitic) *-ma* of the English-based Creole language Saramaccan (cf. *hunti-ma* 'hunter'; Bakker, Smith and Veenstra 1995), which goes back to English *man* but is applicable in present-day Saramaccan both to men and women. In English, the process can also be observed at an early stage of grammaticalization, *in fieri* as it were, in adjectives with the second member *-like*, such as *apelike*, *statesman-like*, etc. That *-like* is already on the way towards suffixhood is proven, according to Marchand (1969, § 4.80.2.), by the fact that these adjectives, contrary to real compounds, are compatible with the negative prefix *un-* (cf. *unmanlike*). Such elements half-way between lexemes or members of compounds and affixes, which abound in natural languages, are generally called s e m i - a f f i x e s or a f f i x o i d s.

When a lexeme or member of a compound has become a derivational affix, this normally constitutes the end of their morphological career. Some cases, however, of derivational affixes turning into inflectional affixes have been documented in Panagl (1987: 134–136): the Indo-European agentive *-lo-*suffix, for example, appears as a formative of participles in Armenian and Old Church Slavonic, in Sanskrit the agent noun in *-tar* has become part of the periphrastic future, the individualizing *-n-*suffix has become a formative of the weak declension of adjectives in Germanic, in Latin the locative of *s*-stems (action nouns) has turned into an active infinitive (**legesi* > *legere* 'to read'), the dative into a passive infinitive (**legei* > *legi* 'to be read'). Not all of these examples, however, are equally pertinent in our context: in some cases, a derivational form is only used as part of an inflectional periphrasis, with no direct change from derivational to inflectional affix involved, while the rise of the Latin infinitives is better viewed as a case of affix coalescence. The boundary between derivation and inflection seems to be more permeable in Uralic languages. Hamari (2014), for example, presents an interesting case study of a privative – or "caritive", as Uralists say – adjectival suffix ('-less') that has acquired a new function as an abessive case marker ('without') in Mordvin. Meul (2013) is an interesting study of two Latin derivational suffixes, *-sc(ere)* and *-idi(are)*, which in some Romance varieties developed into meaningless stem extensions (cf. Latin *flor-ēre* 'to flourish' / *flor-ēsc-ere* 'to begin to flourish' vs. French *fleur-ir* 'to flourish' / *ils fleur-iss-ent* 'they flourish').

3.3 Degrammaticalization

Some linguists (e.g., Lehmann 1982) have claimed grammaticalization to be a unidirectional process. Under this view, lexemes may develop into ever more abstract grammatical markers, but there is no way back, no "degrammaticalization". This contention sparked a huge debate, which has been just as much about substance as about terminological issues (cf. Norde 2009, 2010). In our present context, two types of change could possibly be subsumed under such a heading.

First, it is not uncommon to observe derivational affixes acquire the status of free lexemes over time (a process sometimes called debonding). Intensifying prefixes, for example, seem to be particularly prone to become intensifying adverbs. As is well-known, the French adverb *très* 'very' goes back to the Latin prefix *trans-*. As a reminiscence of its prefixal origin, it is still restricted to a position immediately to the left of its base, and well into the 19th century it was attached to its base with a hyphen. Similarly, in the last decades, the prefix *ur-*, which only occurs in a few formations in standard German (cf. *uralt* 'very old'), has become an unrestricted intensifying adverb in the dialect of Vienna, where younger speakers say things like *ur viel Geld* 'very much money' or even *das taugt mir ur* 'I enjoy that very much'. Note, however, that in both cases the meaning has remained more or less unchanged. A comparable case is also reported from the realm of suffixation, where the English attenuative suffix *-ish* has become debonded in certain registers: *Can you swim well? – Ish.*

A second type of change that one might want to subsume under degrammaticalization is constituted by inflectional endings that end up as derivational suffixes (or clitics), a process also called d e i n f l e c t i o n a l i z a t i o n. Norde (2009: 179–181), for example, reports that in Swedish the suffix *-er* has evolved from an inflectional ending realizing the features MASCULINE, SINGULAR and NOMINATIVE into an attributive nominal suffix with the meaning 'person with attribute *x*': *en dummer* 'a stupid one', *en slarver* 'a messy one' (← *slarv* 'mess'), a change in the opposite direction of that of the "individualizing *n*-suffix" mentioned in section 3.2. Contrary to the intensifiers treated in the last paragraph, in this case the resulting affix has clearly been "enriched" semantically. In German, the genitive ending *-s* has become an adverbial suffix: *flugs* 'quickly' (← *Flug* 'flight'), *mittags* 'at midday' (← *Mittag* 'midday'), etc. Another case in point is constituted by the fate of the "long" infinitive in Romanian (cf. article 18 From Latin to Romanian, section 4.4) that developed into a true action-noun suffix.

3.4 Reanalysis

Reanalysis, also sometimes called "metanalysis" with a term coined by Jespersen, is a cover term for a family of processes that make a complex word or series of complex words change the relationships it/they entertain(s) with other words or series of words (paradigmatic perspective) or its constituency (syntagmatic perspective) without changing the surface form of the word or series of words. The phenomenon has been well-known since the 19th century under labels such as "falsche Abtrennung" (lit. 'false separation'), "Gliederungsverschiebung" (lit. 'constituency shift'), "Präfix-/Suffixverkennung" (lit. 'prefix/suffix misidentification'), or "Umgruppierung" (lit. 'regrouping'; cf. Leumann 1973 [1944]). This conceptual and terminological indeterminacy unfortunately is still with us, the same phenomenon receiving different labels by different authors, and the same label often covering different sets of phenomena (for a recent overview, cf. Igartua 2012). Some types of change that have traditionally been considered cases of reanalysis have already been treated in section 2.3.

3.4.1 Paradigmatic realignment

Under this heading, I will assemble some well-known cases of reanalysis which have in common that a new paradigmatic anchoring is chosen by the speaker or hearer for some type of complex words; cf. also article 21 on historical word-formation in Slavic. This paradigmatic realignment may be due to the fact that the original alignment has become opaque or that the new alignment seems more plausible or desirable to the speaker or hearer.

The phenomenon now often dubbed affix telescoping has been well-known since the 19th century under a variety of designations, e.g., "Affixverschmelzung" 'affix coalescence'. It can be defined as a process "where a secondary derivate is related by speakers not to its immediate base (the primary derivate), but to the base of the primary derivate" (Haspelmath 1995: 3–4). In other words, a derivative of the structure [[[X]A]B] is reanalyzed as [[X]AB], giving rise to a new affix AB that fuses both the form and the meaning of the formerly independent affixes A and B. A well-known example is the French locative suffix *-erie*, which goes back to the fusion of agentive *-ier* (also *-eur*) and locative *-ie: tuile* 'tile' → *tuil-ier* 'tile maker' → *tuil-er-ie* 'tile-maker's shop/factory' > *tuil-erie* 'tile shop/factory'. As one can see, the agentive feature has been integrated into the new suffix, which means something like 'place where *x* is made or sold'. The importance of affix telescoping in the history of word-formation is underlined by Henzen's (1957: 114) contention that the majority of German suffixes arose at some moment in history from the coalescence of two elements.

A set of affixes such as A and B in the example above which tend to co-occur and may eventually coalesce into one affix, is often referred to as affix chain (German *Affixkette*). In affix chains, it is normally the outer affix which constitutes the semantic head; *-erie*, for example, is a locative suffix like *-ie*, not an agentive one. This however, is not necessarily the case. The Italian agentive suffix *-aiolo* (Fanfani 1985) of *pizz-aiolo* 'pizza chef' and similar formations, for example, is the result of the coalescence of agentive *-aio* (< Lat. *-arius*) and diminutive *-olo* (< Lat. *-olus*). The original semantic-pragmatic contribution of the now unproductive diminutive suffix has faded away over time or manifests itself at most at the connotative level in a way difficult to pin down exactly.

In affix telescoping, a new paradigmatic relationship is established with the base of the base. Speakers, however, can also target another member of the word family of the base: A derivative of the structure [[X]A], instead of being referred to X, is referred to a derivative [[X]ø], i.e. a word derived from the same base via conversion and therefore formally identical to X. This was what happened in the reanalysis of originally exclusively deverbal French nouns in *-eur* as denominal. Since some verbs were flanked by action nouns derived via conversion, the agent noun could also be directly linked to this action noun which was formally identical to the verb stem. *Chasseur* 'hunter', for example, instead of being related to the verb stem *chass-* 'to hunt', could also be related directly to the action noun *chasse* 'hunting'. This, according to Meyer-Lübke (1966 [1921], § 43), is how denominal *-eur* arose in French: *chasse* : *chasseur* = *chronique* 'chronicle' : *chroniqueur* 'chronicler', etc. In a similar way, German verb-noun compounds are said (cf. Osthoff 1878: 15) to have originated historically through the reanalysis of noun-noun compounds whose first member was formally identical as a verb stem and as an action noun (*Schlaf*$_{N}$*zimmer* 'room for sleep' > *Schlaf*$_{V}$*zimmer* 'room for sleeping').

The same process can also involve a co-radical derivative with an explicit suffix, of the structure [[X]B]. In this case, the result is a pattern of affix substitution, where A and B are directly related. In German, for example, there are many synthetic compounds with an agent noun in second position that are flanked by analogous synthetic compounds with an action noun. *Schulleitung* 'school management', for example, is flanked by *Schulleiter* 'school manager', and similarly for hundreds of other pairs. Though both are derived from *Schule* 'school' and *leiten* 'to manage', respectively by the action noun suffix *-ung* and the agentive suffix *-er*, at a certain point speakers must have established a relationship between such action and agent nouns, considering the latter to be based directly on the former. Semantically, this makes sense: a school manager, after all, is a 'person engaged in school management'. Once this reanalysis had been carried out, words in *-er* could be directly derived from a corresponding synthetic compound in *-ung*: *Territorialverteidigung* 'territorial defense' → *Territorialverteidiger* 'person practicing t. d.; lit. territorial defender', *Koalitionsverhandlungen* 'coalition negotiations' → *Koalitionsverhandler* 'member of the c.-n. team', *Völkerverständigung* 'international understanding; lit. peoples' understanding' → *Völkerverständiger* 'person working for i. u.', *Unschuldsvermutung* 'presumption of innocence' → *Unschuldsvermuter* 'person granting p. of i.', etc. Many such formations can be found in newspapers nowadays, sometimes with a jocular overtone, but Henzen (1957: 15) already quotes *Selbstbeschränker* 'person practicing self restraint' from Nietzsche, which he considers to be derived from *Selbstbeschränkung* 'self restraint' via the non-attested backformed verb **selbstbeschränken* (this verb can in the meantime also be found on the internet). The action noun that serves as a base, by the way, need not necessarily end in *-ung*: *Geschäftsessen* 'business lunch' → *Geschäftsesser* 'participant in a b. l.', *Seitensprung* 'infidelity; lit. side leap' → *Seitenspringer* 'person guilty of an i.', etc.

3.4.2 Secretion

"Secretion" is a term due to Jespersen (1922: 384), who defined it in the following way: "By secretion I understand the phenomenon that one portion of an indivisible word comes to acquire a grammatical signification which it had not at first, and is then felt as something added to the word itself." In other words, it is the process whereby a formerly purely phonological sequence acquires the status of a morpheme. The phenomenon, by the way, had already been identified by Ludwig (1873), who called it "Adaptation" (cf. also Bloomfield 1891), while more recently one variety of it has been dubbed "exaptation" (Lass 1990).

One example from the realm of word-formation is described in detail in Jespersen (1939). He shows that the final sequence *-en* was purely phonologically conditioned in older stages of English: *harden* was a variant of the verb *hard* just as in present-day English *often* still is a distributional variant of *oft* and *drunken* of *drunk*. At a certain point, however, possibly when the verb *hard* dropped out of use, *harden* was reinterpreted as derived from the adjective *hard*, and in that way the sequence *-en*, originally void of meaning, was reinterpreted as a causative or inchoative suffix.

Nowadays the notion of secretion is also frequently used to refer to the extraction of new morphemes such as *-gate* 'scandal', which comes from *Watergate*, the name of the building where the headquarters of the Democratic Party bugged by the Republicans were located. In Haspelmath (1995: 8–10), it is applied to cases of "affix extensions by incorporation of a root element", which have been treated in section 2.3 as cases of juncture shift.

3.4.3 The patternization of morphologically heterodox complex words

For the lack of an established term, by "patternization of morphologically heterodox complex words" I refer to a process that creates a new word-formation pattern out of a complex word whose structure does not correspond to any established word-formation pattern in the language. Such words seem to originate essentially from two processes, univerbation and backformation.

U n i v e r b a t i o n, i.e. the fusion of two or more originally independent words into one lexeme, most of the time yields phraseological units or simplex words (cf. German *heute* 'today' < *hiu dagu* 'on his day') in the long run, but occasionally univerbated lexemes are reanalyzed as compound types. German noun-noun compounds, for example, originated from a reanalysis of univerbated phrases consisting of a noun preceded by a genitive, which is still reflected in present-day German in the linking elements of some compounds (cf. *Sonnenschein* 'sunshine'

< Middle High German *sunnen schīn* lit. 'sun-GEN shine'; in Modern German the genitive of *Sonne* 'sun' is *Sonne*).

Another scenario involves backformation. In English, for example, it has become quite common to backderive verbs from synthetic compounds: *babysitter → to babysit, stage manager → to stage-manage, vacuum cleaner → to vacuum-clean*, etc. These backderived verbs, at least at the beginning, did not correspond to any established pattern: English had no productive pattern of noun-verb compounding. Whether it has one now as a consequence of the reanalysis of such backderived verbs, is still disputed among Anglicists.

In other languages, on the contrary, there can be no doubt that such a reanalysis of backderived verbs has taken place. For example, from German adjective-noun compounds involving an ordinal adjective and an action noun such as *Erstaufführung* 'first performance', *Erstbegutachtung* 'first assessment', etc. complex verbs such as *erstaufführen* 'to give the first performance; lit. to first-perform' or *erstbegutachten* 'to give the first assessment; lit. to first-assess' have been derived by backformation. The adjective-verb structure of these verbs did not correspond to an established compound type in German. Nevertheless, neologisms like *zweitaufführen* 'to give the second performance', *drittaufführen* 'to give the third performance', or even *fünftbegutachten* 'to give the fifth assessment', can now easily be formed directly on the model of these back-formed verbs by joining an ordinal adjective and a verb, without necessarily starting from the corresponding adjective-noun compounds.

This same kind of scenario can also give rise to new uses of prefixes. The German prefix *ur-* with the meaning 'original, first' is a denominal prefix (cf. *Ursprache* 'proto-language'). From the derivative *Uraufführung* 'first performance', a verb *uraufführen* 'to give the first performance; lit. to first-perform' has been created through backformation. As a result, *ur-* can be reanalyzed as a deverbal prefix if referred directly to *aufführen* 'to perform'. Though the prefix does not seem to be much used in this new function, a neologism like *urinterpretieren* 'to interpret for the first time' is certainly conceivable. The same kind of reanalysis can be observed with other originally non-deverbal prefixes, e.g., *gegen-* 'counter-' (cf. Klosa 2003).

3.4.4 Conventionalization of lexical features

The conventionalization of semantic features originally attached to a single complex word or a set of words is one of the most frequent processes leading to new semantic uses of patterns of word-formation. In this process, a feature that was originally lexical becomes directly attached to a pattern of word-formation that is automatically passed on to all neologisms formed according to this new pattern. As already mentioned in section 3.1, according to Jaberg (1905), this should even be the only mechanism of semantic change observable in word-formation. Different scenarios may be distinguished depending on the origin of the lexical feature.

In section 2.5 we already alluded to the fact that the semantic features corresponding to the part suppressed through ellipsis can eventually become associated with the pattern corresponding to the remaining part of the word. Following Darmesteter's (1904 [1886]: 54–60) suggestion, we can call this process absorption. After Latin *faber ferrarius* 'blacksmith; lit. craftsman iron-REL' had been shortened to *ferrarius*, this noun, originally a relational adjective, received the whole semantic load. Since the base noun of *ferrarius*, i.e. *ferrum*, was firmly linked to the meaning 'iron', the meaning 'craftsman' eventually became associated with the suffix, which then became highly productive in the formation of personal nouns. In Romance, ellipsis and absorption in connection with relational adjectives were among the most frequent sources of new suffixes. Another notorious case is Greek *-itis* 'inflammation', originally the feminine form of the relational suffix *-ites* that absorbed its new meaning from the elided feminine base noun *nosos* 'disease'. But ellipsis can also be observed in compounding, as we have already seen in section 2.5. When in German overly long *Atomkraft(werks)gegner* 'anti-nuke; lit. atom power (station) opponent' was shortened to *Atomgegner*, *Atom-* as the first member of compounds came to mean 'nuclear energy' – *Atomgegner* oppose nuclear energy, not atoms – and is now freely available for analogical coining on the basis of this pattern as in *Atomminister* 'minister for nuclear energy', not 'for atoms' (cf. Matussek 1994).

Bréal (1892) described a similar mechanism under the label irradiation, characterized as follows: "a suffix with a general and vague meaning seems to acquire a more specialized and precise sense thanks to the word to which it is joined" (p. 20; my translation). By "irradiation", he referred to cases where semantic features of base words are eventually attached to the suffix. As a consequence of its being attached to bases with a negative connotation, the originally neutral Latin collective suffix *-alia* for example acquired itself a negative connotation in Romance (cf. *prêtraille* 'clergy-PEJ' ← *prêtre* 'priest'). In a convincing explication of this mechanism of change, Serbat (1983: 534), however, observed that the new sense does not migrate directly from the base to the affix, as Bréal's wording might suggest, but is always mediated by the holistic meaning of a lexeme or lexemes. A "floating" semantic feature of a complex word, i.e. one with no immediate counterpart on the formal side, becomes firmly attached to the pattern itself, just like in the case of absorption considered above.

The "floating" lexical feature can also arise as a consequence of metonymic extension. One example of this kind among many is constituted by the rise of the collective meaning of the Spanish suffix *-ado* (cf. Rainer 1993: 392). The central function of this suffix, which goes back to Latin *-atus*, has always been that of forming status nouns. But like many other status nouns, those in *-ado* also developed secondary uses referring to the building or territory where the relevant function is exerted (e.g., *el consulado está cerrado* 'the consulate is closed', *el electorado de Tréveris* 'the Electorate of Trier'), to the period of time when it was exerted (e.g., *durante su papado* 'during his popeship'), or to a group of persons with that status (e.g., *patriciado* 'the class of patricians' ← *patricio* 'patrician'). At a certain point in time, however, the collective meaning became directly associated with the suffix, which then could give rise to neologisms in *-ado* of the collective type even when no corresponding status nouns were in actual use (e.g., *alumnado* 'pupils, student body' ← *alumno* 'pupil, student', *campesinado* 'peasantry' ← *campesino* 'peasant', *empresariado* 'business community' ← *empresario* 'businessman', etc.).

The same general mechanism can also be seen at work in compounding. One case whose development can be observed practically *in fieri* are compounds referring to what Benczes (2006: 156–157) dubbed "gadget-related illnesses". The earliest example of this kind seems to have been *tennis elbow* (also referred to as *shooter's elbow* or *archer's elbow*), which metonymically refers to the pain felt in the elbow as a consequence of excessive tennis playing. This leader word then sparked off a whole series of similar metonymic compounds which by now constitute a small, but firmly established lexical series: *Nintendo thumb, phone neck, mouse wrist, tetwrist* (caused by playing too much Tetris), etc.

3.5 Semantic extension

Semantic change in word-formation can also come about as a consequence of an operation that changes the meaning of an existing pattern directly, at the very moment of the creation of a neologism. Two such scenarios can be distinguished.

3.5.1 Extending the meaning of a pattern

In Rainer (2005) I argued that, contrary to Jaberg's claim, patterns of word-formation could also undergo direct semantic change. In that case, a pattern of word-formation is combined with a semantic extension, generally of a metaphoric nature, at the very moment of creating a neologism. (Since in this case, a word-formation pattern is not followed one to one, but only approximately, I dubbed this kind of change "approximation".) The case of *tennis elbow* treated in the last section could possibly be a case in point, but we cannot exclude that this compound was first used in its literal sense, referring to an elbow, and only then metonymically applied to the related pain. I therefore prefer the more conservative solution of considering it as a kind of Jabergian change.

A clear case of direct semantic extension of a pattern is provided by the origin of the metaphorical use of the suffix *-itis*. In the language of medicine, *-itis* refers to inflammations, as in *tonsillitis, bursitis*, etc. During the 19th century, in a language still to be determined (for once, it does not seem to have been English), this suffix came to be used with a jocular intention for metaphorical "diseases", such as *telephonitis, adjectivitis, Wagneritis*, etc. It is important to stress that the passage from 'inflammation' to 'addiction, excessive fondness' was not mediated by the lexical semantic change of one of the medical terms in use at that time. *Tonsillitis*, for example, never came to mean 'excessive fondness for tonsils', nor did any other of the medical terms develop a similar meaning. Rather, the very first figurative word of this kind – which, by the way, remains to be identified – already came into being as a consequence of a figurative use of *-itis*, i.e. of the word-formation pattern itself.

3.5.2 Changing the semantic relation between base and complex word

As already mentioned in section 3.1, complex words differ from simplex words semantically in that they often contain a relational meaning. In the study of the semantic evolution of word-formation patterns we therefore have to take into consideration not only the referential and pragmatic aspects of meaning, but also this word-internal relational meaning. It is quite often the case, in fact, that a certain pattern remains constant from a referential point of view, while at the same time the relational meaning changes.

The change in the relational meaning can be a simple side effect of a more general semantic change. When *-itis* was first used metaphorically, for example, the relational meaning also changed automatically from 'of' (*tonsillitis* 'inflammation of the tonsils') to 'to' or 'for', depending on the periphrasis you prefer (*Wagneritis* 'addiction to, excessive fondness for Wagner'). But the relational meaning can also change independently. Spanish, for example, has a productive type of verb-noun compounds, where the semantic relation between V and N is overwhelmingly one of verb to direct object. A *guardabosque* 'ranger', for example, literally is 'one who protects (*guarda*) a forest (*bosque*)', and a *guardamuebles* 'storeroom for furniture' literally 'a place where you keep (*guarda*) furniture (*muebles*)'. Now, there is a series of words that does not fit into this picture semantically. Just like other *guarda*-words, these words refer to objects with a certain function, but the N, instead of the thing(s) protected, refers to the thing(s) that the object in question protects from, as in *guardabarros* 'mud guard' (← *guarda-* 'protect', *barros* 'mud-PL'). This kind of metonymic switch, as I prefer to call it, is one way in which word-formation patterns diversify semantically over time. The same kind of cognitive process, by the way, is also frequently observed in changes affecting the valency of verbs.

Change concerning the semantic relation between base and derivative often goes hand in hand with a change of the part-of-speech of the base, a process sometimes referred to as affix generalization. The jocular suffix *-itis* for metaphorical "diseases", for example, was originally applied only to nouns in German (type *Telefonitis*), as was its medical model. Since *Telefonitis* is just as much about the gadget, *Telefon*, as about the related activity, *telefonieren*, the extension to verbal bases was quite straightforward: *Abkürzitis* 'abuse of acronyms' ← *abkürzen* 'to use an acronym', etc. The choice of a verbal base in *Abkürzitis* had the additional advantage of making the output more easily pronounceable, as compared with a hypothetical denominal *Abkürzungitis* (← *Abkürzung* 'acronym'). Ease of pronunciation may even have been the decisive factor in the coining of *Neutralitis*, which is derived from the adjective *neutral*, but refers to Austrians' excessive attachment to political neutrality. A hypothetical denominal *Neutralitätitis* (← *Neutralität* 'neutrality'), in fact, would sound decidedly cacophonous.

4 Change in productivity

Concerning "change in productivity" (cf. article 11 for a general perspective) two cases can be distinguished, at least in principle: change in the number of neologisms per time span and change in domain size.

In reality, these two aspects are often inextricably intertwined, as the case of the evolution of the Latin suffix *-unus* in Romance (Malkiel 1950–51, 1959) shows. In Latin, this adjectival suffix was only present in *aprunus* (← *aper* 'boar') and *caprunus* (← *caper, capra* 'goat'), of which the latter became the leader word. While in most Western Romance languages the suffix remained confined to a few formations or died out, in Spanish *-uno* gave rise to a numerous progeny. The origin of the suffix is still reflected in the fact that in its central use Spanish *-uno* continues to attach to bases denoting animals. The formation of such a semantic niche is, of course, a straightforward consequence of the analogical nature of the process (cf. Hüning 2009). Two domain-extensions, however, have occurred. On the one hand, bases denoting human beings have come within the reach of *-uno* (e.g., *frailuno* 'monkish' ← *fraile* 'monk'), generally in formations with a derogatory overtone because of the implicit comparison of human beings to animals, and, on the other, in some regions *-uno* is also used to derive ethnic adjectives from toponyms (this use was possibly an offspring of *montuno* ← *monte* 'mountain', a word strongly associated with animals). In Colombia, furthermore, adjectives in *-uno* are also derived from the names of farmers (e.g., *la finca moraluna* 'Morales' farm'). This extension could either be a side line of the ethnic branch or originally have been due to the fact that some names of animals such as *lobo* 'wolf' are also family names.

While in the case of Spanish *-uno* it is not too difficult to imagine the logic behind the different domain extensions, it must remain more or less mysterious why the rise in productivity and the concomitant extensions of the domain of this suffix occurred only in Spanish. In some privileged cases, however, the external causes for the change in productivity can be pinned down with a high probability. In many European languages, for example, instrumental suffixes denoting tools and machines witnessed a spectacular rise in the wake of the Industrial Revolution, which created the need for many new denominations in this lexical field. In another notorious case, that of the prefix *mini-*, its spectacular rise in the sixties of the 20th century can safely be attributed, not to a sudden demand for denominations for new small objects, but to the enormous emotional impact of the miniskirt on the speech community.

As has already been pointed out by scholars in the second half of the 19th century (e.g., Bahder 1880), the rise and fall of word-formation patterns is best studied in the context of a word-formation category, i.e. the set of patterns with the same function, since the rise of one pattern is often causally connected to the demise of its rival(s). Frequently, rare suffixes or suffixes subject to phonological attrition are replaced by more productive or phonologically conspicuous ones: Latin *-ulus*, for example, as in *an-ulus* 'ring-DIM', doomed very much like other unstressed suffixes of that language, was replaced by stressed *-ellus* (cf. *anellus* > French *anneau*). But the study of c o m p e t i t i o n or r i v a l r y b e t w e e n p a t t e r n s has to look even beyond word-formation proper, since word-formation often competes with syntax. In Latin, for example, relational adjectives were in competition with the genitive (cf. Wackernagel 1908), which eventually won the contest. Similarly the formation of material adjectives in *-eus* (*aureus* 'golden' ← *aurum* 'gold') competed with prepositional phrases (headed by past participles), e.g., *poculum ex auro* (*factum*) 'a bowl (made) of gold'. On the way to Romance, the suffix *-eus* was lost, while the preposition *de*, as a substitute for *ex*, and in French later also *en*, took over the expression of material (It. *un bicchiere d'oro*, Fr. *une coupe en or*).

5 Borrowing

Up to now, we have concentrated on endogenous mechanisms of change. In real life, however, all languages are in more or less intense contact with other languages, and such language contact is a major source of change in word-formation just like in other language domains (cf. articles 1–7 and Müller et al. 2015–2016, chapters VIII and IX, as well as the monographic descriptions of single languages in volumes 4 and 5).

Languages can take over foreign word-formation patterns, normally as a consequence of the borrowing, along with their bases, of a sizeable number of complex words formed according to the relevant pattern. Strictly speaking, in such cases only the complex words are borrowed (lexical borrowing), while the pattern is extracted language-internally from the borrowed words in a second step. We can only be sure that pattern extraction has taken place when the pattern in question begins to be applied to native bases. Notorious cases of borrowed suffixes are the numerous reflexes of the Latin agentive suffix *-arius* in European languages or its Turkish equivalent *-ci* in the areas once dominated by the Ottoman Empire. Borrowed patterns of compounding in Slavic languages are described in several of the articles in volume 4 of Müller et al. 2015–2016 dedicated to these languages; see also article 7, section 4.2. A scenario particularly frequent in European languages is the creation of combining forms – now often called confixes – as a consequence of the borrowing of Latin or Greek compounds. When a compound is borrowed, but not its constituents or only one of them, these constituents become bound elements in the receiving language but often retain a meaning typical of lexemes (cf. *hydro-* 'water' < Greek *hydor* 'id.'). But in some cases, such combining forms can also turn into real affixes in the receiving language, if their meaning is of the relational kind typical of affixes. This, for example, is what happened to the second element *-fer* of Latin compounds of the type *aurifer* 'auriferous, containing gold' in Romance (cf. French *pétrolifère* 'oil-bearing' ← *pétrole* 'oil'), since the verb *ferre* 'to bear, contain' died out and the meaning 'containing *x*' of compounds in *-fer* is very close to that of derivational suffixes with a possessive meaning.

Borrowing need not concern a pattern as a whole, form and meaning. Sometimes, it is only a new meaning which is imported. This happens when the receiving language only has an equivalent for one of two senses of a polysemous foreign pattern. In standard French, for example, the suffix *-(at)eur* was (almost) exclusively agentive until the 18th century, just like its Latin ancestor *-ator*. The functionally equivalent English suffix *-er* and its orthographic variant *-or*, on the contrary, had already developed an instrumental sense at that time (cf. *poker*, *ventilator*). As argued in Rainer (2011), the instrumental use of *-(at)eur* arose in French mainly as a consequence of calques such as *ventilateur* (< Engl. *ventilator*) or *condens(at)eur* (< Engl. *condenser*). In this case, the formal side of the suffix was already part of the language and could be infused with a new meaning (calque).

Last but not least, borrowing can also influence productivity. Latinists, for example, agree that the productivity of the Latin suffix '-*icus* was greatly enhanced by the adoption of many Greek adjectives in *-ikós*.

6 References

Amiot, Dany (2015): The grammaticalization of prepositions in French word-formation. In: Peter O. Müller, Ingeborg Ohnheiser, Susan Olsen and Franz Rainer (eds.), *Word-Formation. An International Handbook of the Languages of Europe*. Vol. 3, 1811–1824. Berlin/Boston: De Gruyter Mouton.

Arkadiev, Peter and Franz Rainer (eds.) (forthc.): *The Oxford Handbook of Historical Morphology*. Oxford: Oxford University Press.

Bakker, Peter, Norval Smith and Tonjes Veenstra (1995): Saramaccan. In: Jacques Arends, Pieter Muysken and Norval Smith (eds.), *Pidgins and Creoles*, 165–178. Amsterdam/Philadelphia: Benjamins.

Bahder, Carl von (1880): *Die Verbalabstracta in den germanischen Sprachen ihrer Bildung nach dargestellt*. Halle/S.: Niemeyer.

Baldinger, Kurt (1961): Entstehung und Entwicklung der Suffixe *-ard* und *-aud* im Französischen (im Hinblick auf die Methodologie der Wortbildungslehre). *Sitzungsberichte der Heidelberger Akademie der Wissenschaften*, Jahresheft 1959/60, 12–14.

Benczes, Réka (2006): *Creative Compounding in English*. Amsterdam/Philadelphia: Benjamins.

Blank, Andreas (1997): *Prinzipien des lexikalischen Bedeutungswandels am Beispiel der romanischen Sprachen*. Tübingen: Niemeyer.

Bloomfield, Maurice (1891): *On Adaptation of Suffixes in Congeneric Classes of Substantives*. Baltimore: Johns Hopkins Press.

Bréal, Michel (1868): *Les idées latentes du langage*. Paris: Hachette.

Bréal, Michel (1892): De l'irradiation grammaticale. *Mémoires de la Société de Linguistique de Paris* 7: 20–23.

Czer, András (2010): The *-alis/-aris* allomorphy revisited. In: Franz Rainer, Wolfgang U. Dressler, Dieter Kastovsky and Hans Christian Luschützky (eds.), *Variation and Change in Morphology. Selected papers from the 13th International Morphology Meeting, Vienna, February 2008*, 33–51. Amsterdam/Philadelphia: Benjamins.

Darmesteter, Arsène (1904 [1886]): *La vie des mots étudiée dans leurs significations*. 7th ed. Paris: Delagrave.

Detges, Ulrich (2015): The Romance adverbs in *-mente*: a case study in grammaticalization. In: Peter O. Müller, Ingeborg Ohnheiser, Susan Olsen and Franz Rainer (eds.), *Word-Formation. An International Handbook of the Languages of Europe*. Vol. 3, 1824–1842. Berlin/Boston: De Gruyter Mouton.

Dietz, Klaus (2007): Denominale Abstraktbildungen des Altenglischen: Die Wortbildung der Abstrakta auf *-dōm*, *-hād*, *-lāc*, *-r¢den*, *-sceaft*, *-stæf* und *-wist* und ihrer Entsprechungen im Althochdeutschen und im Altnordischen. In: Hans Fix (ed.), *Beiträge zur Morphologie. Germanisch, Baltisch, Ostseefinnisch*, 97–172. Odense: University Press of Southern Denmark.

Fanfani, Massimo L. (1985): Storia e funzioni del suffisso *-aiolo*: Su *crisaiolo* e termini analoghi. *Lingua Nostra* 46: 15–25, 64–79, 113–119.

Fertig, David (2013): *Analogy and morphological change*. Edinburgh: Edinburgh University Press.

Gardani, Francesco (2015): Affix pleonasm. In: Peter O. Müller, Ingeborg Ohnheiser, Susan Olsen and Franz Rainer (eds.), *Word-Formation. An International Handbook of the Languages of Europe*. Vol. 1, 537–550. Berlin/Boston: De Gruyter Mouton.

Grzega, Joachim (2002): Some aspects of modern diachronic onomasiology. *Linguistics* 40(5): 1021–1045.

Hamari, Arja (2014): Inflection vs. derivation: The function and meaning of the Mordvin abessive. In: Franz Rainer, Wolfgang U. Dressler, Francesco Gardani and Hans Christian Luschützky (eds.), *Morphology and Meaning. Selected papers from the 15th International Morphology Meeting (Vienna, February 2012)*, 163–175. Amsterdam/Philadelphia: Benjamins.

Haspelmath, Martin (1993): The diachronic externalization of inflection. *Linguistics* 31(2): 279–309.

Haspelmath, Martin (1995): The growth of affixes in morphological reanalysis. In: Geert Booij and Jaap van Marle (eds.), *Yearbook of Morphology 1994*, 1–29. Dordrecht: Kluwer.

Heine, Bernd and Tania Kuteva (2007): *The Genesis of Grammar. A Reconstruction*. Oxford: Oxford University Press.

Henzen, Walter (1957): *Deutsche Wortbildung*. 2nd ed. Tübingen: Niemeyer.

Hüning, Matthias (2009): Semantic niches and analogy in word formation: Evidence from constrastive linguistics. *Languages in Contrast* 9(2): 183–201.

Igartua, Iván (2012): Para una tipología del reanálisis morfológico. *Revista de la Sociedad Española de Lingüística* 42(1): 109–144.

Jaberg, Karl (1905): Review of Max Roediger: *Die Bedeutung des Suffixes* -ment. Diss. Berlin 1904. *Archiv für das Studium der neueren Sprachen und Literaturen* 114: 458–462.

Janda, Richard D. and Brian D. Joseph (2003): On language, change, and language change – or, Of history, linguistics, and historical linguistics. In: Richard D. Janda and Brian D. Joseph (eds.), *The Handbook of Historical Linguistics*, 3–180. Malden, MA: Blackwell.

Jespersen, Otto (1922): *Language. Its Nature, Development and Origin*. London: Allen & Unwin.

Jespersen, Otto (1939): The history of a suffix. *Acta Linguistica* 1: 48–56.

Klosa, Annette (2003): *gegen*-Verben – ein neues Wortbildungsmuster. *Sprachwissenschaft* 28: 467–494.

Lass, Roger (1990): How to do things with junk: Exaptation in language evolution. *Journal of Linguistics* 26: 79–102.

Lehmann, Christian (1982): *Thoughts on Grammaticalization. A Programmatic Sketch*. Vol. I. Köln: Institut für Sprachwissenschaft. (Revised edition, Erfurt: Seminar für Sprachwissenschaft 2002.)

Lehmann, Christian (2005): Pleonasm and hypercharacterisation. In: Geert Booij and Jaap van Marle (eds.), *Yearbook of Morphology 2005*, 119–154. Dordrecht: Springer.

Lehrer, Adrienne (2000): Are affixes signs? The semantic relationships of English derivational affixes. In: Wolfgang U. Dressler, Oskar E. Pfeiffer, Markus A. Pöchtrager and John R. Rennison (eds.), *Morphological Analysis in Comparison*, 143–154. Amsterdam/Philadelphia: Benjamins.

Leumann, Manu (1973 [1944]): Gruppierung und Funktion der Wortbildungssuffixe des Lateins. In: Klaus Strunk (ed.), *Probleme der lateinischen Grammatik*, 131–161. Darmstadt: Wissenschaftliche Buchgesellschaft.

Lindström, Therese A. M. (2004): The history of the concept of grammaticalisation. Ph.D. dissertation, University of Sheffield.
Ludwig, Alfred (1873): *Agglutination oder Adaptation? Eine sprachwissenschaftliche Streitfrage*. Prag: Calve.
Malkiel, Yakov 1950–51 The Latin background of the Spanish suffix *-uno*. *Romance Philology* 4: 17–45.
Malkiel, Yakov (1959): Nuevas aportaciones para el studio del sufijo *-uno*. *Nueva Revista de Filología Hispánica* 13: 241–290.
Malkiel, Yakov (1966): Genetic analysis of word formation. In: Thomas A. Sebeok (ed.), *Current Trends in Linguistics*, 305–364. Den Haag: Mouton.
Marchand, Hans (1969): *The Categories and Types of Present-Day English Word-Formation. A Synchronic-Diachronic Approach*. 2nd ed. München: Beck.
Matussek, Magdalena (1994): *Wortneubildung im Text*. Hamburg: Buske.
Meul, Claire (2013): *The Romance Reflexes of the Latin Infixes -I/ESC- and -IDI̯-. Restructuring and remodeling processes*. Hamburg: Buske.
Meyer-Lübke, Wilhelm (1966 [1921]): *Historische Grammatik der französischen Sprache. Zweiter Teil: Wortbildungslehre*. Zweite, durchgesehene und ergänzte Auflage von J. M. Piel. Heidelberg: Winter.
Müller, Peter O. (2011): The polysemy of the German suffix *-er*: Aspects of its origin and development. *Language Typology and Universals* 64(1): 33–40.
Müller, Peter O. (2016): Wortbildungswandel oder Bedeutungsbildung? – Zur Entstehung und Interpretation sekundärer Wortbildungsbedeutungen. In: Sarah Kwekkeboom and Sandra Waldenberger (eds.), *PerspektivWechsel* oder: *Die Wiederentdeckung der Philologie*. Bd. 1: *Sprachdaten und Grundlagenforschung in der Historischen Linguistik*, 309–332. Berlin: Schmidt.
Müller, Peter O. (2017): Wortbildungsbedeutungswandel. In: Florentine Oehme, Hans Ulrich Schmid and Franziska Spranger (eds.), *Wörter. Wortbildung, Lexikologie und Lexikographie, Etymologie*, 184–208. Berlin/Boston: De Gruyter.
Müller, Peter O., Ingeborg Ohnheiser, Susan Olsen and Franz Rainer (eds.) (2015–2016): *Word-Formation. An International Handbook of the Languages of Europe*. 5 Vol. Berlin/Boston: De Gruyter Mouton.
Norde, Muriel (2009): *Degrammaticalization*. Oxford: Oxford University Press.
Norde, Muriel (2010): Degrammaticalization: Three common controversies. In: Katerina Stathi, Elke Gehweiler and Ekkehard König (eds.), *Grammaticalization. Current Views and Issues*, 123–150. Amsterdam/Philadelphia: Benjamins.
Osthoff, Hermann (1878): *Das Verbum in der nominalcomposition im deutschen, griechischen, slavischen und romanischen*. Jena: Costenoble.
Panagl, Oswald (1987): Productivity and diachronic change in morphology. In: Wolfgang U. Dressler, Willi Mayerthaler, Oswald Panagl and Wolfgang U. Wurzel (eds.), *Leitmotifs in Natural Morphology*, 127–151. Amsterdam/Philadelphia: Benjamins.
Paul, Hermann (1880): *Prinzipien der Sprachgeschichte*. Halle/S.: Niemeyer.
Plank, Frans (1981): *Morphologische (Ir-)Regularitäten. Aspekte der Wortstrukturtheorie*. Tübingen: Narr.
Plénat, Marc (2015): Dissimilatory phenomena in French word-formation. In: Peter O. Müller, Ingeborg Ohnheiser, Susan Olsen and Franz Rainer (eds.), *Word-Formation. An International Handbook of the Languages of Europe*. Vol. 2, 945–956. Berlin/Boston: De Gruyter Mouton.
Rainer, Franz (1993): *Spanische Wortbildungslehre*. Tübingen: Niemeyer.
Rainer, Franz (2005): Semantic change in word formation. *Linguistics* 43(2): 415–441.
Rainer, Franz (2011): The agent-instrument-place "polysemy" of the suffix -TOR in Romance. *Language Typology and Universals* 64(1): 8–32.

Roché, Michel (2015): Interfixes in Romance. In: Peter O. Müller, Ingeborg Ohnheiser, Susan Olsen and Franz Rainer (eds.), *Word-Formation. An International Handbook of the Languages of Europe*. Vol. 1, 551–568. Berlin/Boston: De Gruyter Mouton.

Roché, Michel, Gilles Boyé, Nabil Hathout, Stéphanie Lignon and Marc Plénat (2011): *Des unités morphologiques au lexique*. Paris: Lavoisier.

Rohlfs, Gerhard (1969): *Grammatica storica della lingua italiana e dei suoi dialetti. III. Sintassi e formazione delle parole*. Torino: Einaudi.

Schnorr v. Carolsfeld, Hans (1884): Das lateinische Suffix ânus. *Archiv für lateinische Lexikographie und Grammatik* 1: 177–194.

Serbat, Guy (1983): *Turibulum*: Esquisse d'une théorie sur le signifié des suffixes de dérivation. In: Hubert Zehnacker and Gustave Hentz (eds.), *Hommages à Robert Schilling*, 525–536. Paris: Les Belles Lettres.

Trips, Carola (2009): *Lexical Semantics and Diachronic Morphology. The Development of* -hood, -dom *and* -ship *in the History of English*. Tübingen: Niemeyer.

Wackernagel, Jakob (1908): Genetiv und Adjektiv. *Mélanges de linguistique offerts à M. Ferdinand de Saussure*, 125–152. Paris: Champion.

Willenberg, Gotthold (1881): Review of Ismar Rothenberg: *De suffixarum mutatione in lingua francogallica*. Berolini: Haber 1880. *Zeitschrift für neufranzösische Sprache und Literatur* 3: 558–582.

Carmen Scherer

11 Change in productivity

Abstract: The temporal dimension has long been neglected in the study of morphological productivity. This is all the more remarkable as productivity is inherently a diachronic notion. The present article provides an overview of the main theoretical and methodological questions that arise in diachronic research on productivity.

1 Introduction

Productivity is often claimed to be one of the most used and most debated notions in morphology. As even linguists studying productivity from a synchronic point of view do not agree on an exact definition of the concept of productivity, it comes as no surprise that studying change in productivity only intensifies the problems at hand by adding further problems related to a diachronic approach. As the understanding of productivity is central to the study of its change, some basic questions regarding productivity will be tackled in section 2. The sections 3 and 4 are dedicated to theoretical and methodological aspects of the study of change in productivity. Section 3 addresses the diachronic aspect of productivity, discusses the causes for change in productivity, and illuminates its consequences. Section 4 is concerned with the methodological questions that arise when empirically investigating change in productivity.

2 Productivity

The central problem when discussing change in productivity is that *productivity* is still one of the most debated notions in morphology. Rainer (1987) specifies six

Carmen Scherer, Mainz, Germany

https://doi.org/10.1515/9783111420530-011

types of definition of productivity based, e.g., on the frequency of the output, on the proportion of actual words to potential words, or the probability of encountering new forms. Still today, the term *productivity* is used in a number of different ways in the literature (for an overview see Bauer 2005 and Gaeta and Ricca 2015). Nevertheless, most linguists agree that the potential of a morphological process to create new forms is central to the concept of productivity.

Section 2.1 addresses the question of what kind of linguistic entity is productive. Section 2.2 deals with two major concepts of productivity, the qualitative and the quantitative one.

2.1 What kind of entity is productive?

One of the first questions that arise when talking about productivity is what kind of linguistic entity it is that is actually productive. Yet, a look at the literature reveals that productivity is assigned to different linguistic entities. For some authors it is affixes that are productive, for others it is morphological processes or groups of processes. Some authors attribute productivity to rules, categories, or word types, while others see it as a feature of a language system as a whole or parts of it. However, these different views reflect different approaches to morphological productivity rather than serious theoretical incompatibility (cf. Koefoed and van Marle 2000: 303). Actually, as Bauer (2001: 32) states, productivity can always be conceived as a feature of individual word-formation processes.

2.2 Quantitative and qualitative approaches

Two main concepts of productivity can be found in the literature, a qualitative and a quantitative one, corresponding, by and large, to the concepts of *availability* and *profitability* (Dal 2003; Plag 2006). Unfortunately, there is no clear distinction between the qualitative and the quantitative understanding that all linguists agree on.

The qualitative concept of productivity refers to the potential of a word-formation process "for repetitive rule-governed morphological coining" (Bauer 2001: 211). This potential is defined in terms of domains, i.e. the totality of linguistic entities that could serve as input to a particular word-formation process. The domain of a process may be more or less restricted by constraints (Rainer 2000, 2005; Romaine 2004). For example, the domain of the German *-in* suffixation, deriving words that denote female individuals, is restricted to nouns designating persons or, to a lesser extent, animals: NHG *König* 'king' → *Königin* 'queen', *Lehrer* 'teacher' → *Lehrerin* 'female teacher', or *Löwe* 'lion' → *Löwin* 'lioness'. According to the qualitative concept of productivity, productivity is basically understood as a binary property. This means that a morphological process is either available and therefore productive or not, with nothing else in between. Still, a process may be productive in one domain, such as with verbal bases, and unproductive in another, such as with nominal bases. The adjective-deriving German suffix *-bar*, e.g., used to take nominal bases in Middle High German (MHG *vruht* 'fruit' + *-bære* → *vruhtbære* 'fruitful'). Nowadays, it is productive with verbal bases only (NHG *machen* 'to make' + *-bar* → *machbar* 'feasible'). Contrary to the binary nature of qualitative productivity, some linguists take the number and scope of constraints imposed upon a word-formation process as an indicator for varying degrees of productivity, e.g., Demske (2000).

The quantitative concept of productivity refers to the profitability of a word-formation process, i.e. to "the extent to which its availability is exploited in language use" (Bauer 2001: 211). As a consequence, productivity can be measured – given that adequate forms of measures can be found. In the past decades, several measures have been suggested, which vary depending on the theoretical and/or empirical approach chosen (e.g., Baayen 1989, 1992; Gaeta and Ricca 2006). The measures proposed either rely on type frequency (V) – a special case being *new* types –, token frequency (N), hapax legomena (n_1) or a combination of them, e.g., productivity in the narrow sense (*P*), which is defined as the relation between the total number of tokens with a particular affix and the hapax legomena with that affix in a representative corpus. For an overview of the field, see Baayen (2009), Plag (2006), and Gaeta and Ricca (2015).

However, there are a number of theoretical and empirical problems regarding these measures. On the one hand, type or token frequency does not necessarily correlate with the potential of a word-formation process to create new forms, as stated, e.g., by Baayen (1992). Especially token-frequent processes are often only marginally productive, the high token frequency resulting from lexicalized formations. On the other hand, hapax legomena are not necessarily new coinings by themselves, even though it has been argued that their number largely correlates with the number of new coinings (Baayen and Lieber 1991: 809–820, esp. 813). For further discussion, see van Marle (1992), Plag (1999), Bauer (2001).

Finally, it has to be kept in mind that productivity as such is an abstract phenomenon that cannot be grasped directly. Therefore, what is called *productivity measures* in the literature are indicators of qualitative or quantitative productivity only.

3 Theoretical issues

In this section some main theoretical issues connected to change in productivity will be debated: the diachronic side of productivity in section 3.1, the causes for change in productivity in 3.2, and the consequences of this change in section 3.3.

3.1 Productivity and diachrony

A fundamental prerequisite for change in productivity to take place is that productivity is not only a synchronic, but also a diachronic phenomenon (cf. Romaine 2004; Trips 2009: 33–37). After all, if productivity were a solely synchronic phenomenon, change in productivity would be excluded and discussing change in productivity would be meaningless. However, evidence for the diachronic nature of productivity comes from at least two different sources.

First of all, as soon as a word-formation process is investigated at two different points of time, changes in productivity become manifest. For example, the English suffix *-th* forming nouns from adjectives is productive in Old and Middle English (*depth*, *length*, *truth*). Today, new coinings bearing the suffix *-th* are no longer possible, i.e., the process is no longer productive. Thus, as soon as the productivity of a given process has been observed for more than one point in time, productivity is interpreted diachronically.

Secondly, if productivity is perceived as the potential of a word-formation process to give rise to new words, the concept of time is inevitably included in the concept of productivity, as the coining of new words refers to the future. Therefore, regardless of the diachronic perspective provided by comparing different points of time, productivity is, at least inherently, a diachronic concept.

In addition, it has to be stressed that a clear-cut distinction between synchrony and diachrony is rather a theoretical construct than a fact (e.g., Bauer 2001: 29). Neither does investigating short time spans necessarily imply a synchronic perspective, nor does examining long time spans necessarily correspond with a diachronic one. Examining empirical studies on word-formation clearly reveals the problem. The corpus-based study of Baayen and Renouf (1996), for example, comprising four volumes of the *Times* (1989–1993), shows clearly diachronic aspects, whereas Doerfert (1994) analyzes her corpus covering 350 years from a synchronic perspective. Hence, to put it in the words of Cowie and Dalton-Puffer (2002: 421), "what counts as synchronic and a time-point and what as diachronic and a time-stretch is ultimately a matter of definition and methodological necessities".

Finally, the way in which change in productivity manifests itself depends upon the underlying concept of productivity. From a qualitative point of view, productivity is a matter of yes or no. Therefore, the only change possible is the change from productive to unproductive or vice versa. In contrast, a quantitative understanding of productivity provided, productivity may change gradually.

3.2 Causes

So far, causes as well as consequences of change in productivity have only rarely been addressed. Still, as language change is generally initiated either by language internal or language external factors, the same should apply to change in productivity.

The most important language internal factor causing change in productivity is change in competition. Competition may surface in different forms, such as competing lexical, morphological, and syntactic devices. For example, the emergence or loss of synonymous words blocking individual word-formation products may result in a slight decrease or increase of the productivity of the word-formation process concerned. The emergence or loss of rival word-formation processes, however, affects the productivity of the competing process to a much greater extent, cf., e.g., the competition of *-ation* and *-ment* in English (Lindsay and Aronoff 2013). Yet, also smaller increases or decreases in the productivity of rival processes may lead to changes in the productivity of the competing process. For German, the competition of the Germanic suffix *-e* (OHG *-(e)o* > MHG/NHG *-e*) and the suffix *-er* (OHG *-ari* > MHG *-ære/-er* > NHG *-er*), which goes back to Latin *-arius*, is attested. In Old High German, both suffixes derived person nouns from verbal bases (OHG *geban* 'to give' → *geb-o* 'giver, donor' vs. *geb-ari* 'giver, donor'). In Middle High German, the number of new coinings bearing the suffix *-e* diminished, whereas the number of derivatives with the suffix *-ære/-er* increased. Today, *-er* is the most productive suffix deriving personal nouns, whereas the suffix *-e* has become unproductive (Wilmanns 1896: 194–197; Weinreich 1971). As to the influence of competing syntactic constructions, an interesting example is provided by the German language. In German, the complexity of syntactic constructions decreased between the 15th and 18th century, whereas the complexity of word-formation products rose (Pavlov 1983: esp. 88–103). In this case, the loss of possibilities for expressing complex structures syntactically may have advanced the productivity of word-formation processes, either in general or at least for individual processes. Another important case of competition is the competition between different domains of an individual affix, such as the competition between the different semantic patterns of polysemous affixes, e.g., as the English suffixes *-age* and *-ery*. Changes in the availability of the potential lexical input, i.e. the domain, may also result in changes in productivity. If, for example, all potential bases in the domain of a derivational process have been derived, the process itself is no longer productive.

Besides language internal factors, language external factors have to be taken into account as well. In recent diachronic studies, the influence of sociolinguistic factors, such as register, social status, and gender, on word-formation processes has been investigated (Cowie 1999; Palmer 2009). Still, even though the authors show that productivity varies depending on the factors investigated, sociolinguistic factors may be excluded as triggers of change up to this point. It seems rather that register and other sociolinguistic factors influence the subjects' readiness to use a given process. Generally speaking, "words are only formed as and when there is a need for them" (Bauer 2001: 143). If new words of a certain type are no longer needed, new coinings will not occur. Hence, if the need for words of a particular type increases or decreases, the productivity of individual word-formation processes deriving such words may be affected.

Scherer (2005), in her study on nominal *-er* derivation in German, gives two examples for language external factors leading to change in morphological productivity. For object designations such as NHG *Bohrer* 'borer, drill' ← *bohren* 'to bore, drill', Scherer detected a rise of productivity by the end of the 19th century, which she attributes to the industrialization and the need to label new products and machines. On the other hand, productivity decreased in the deonymic domain between the 17th and 20th century. Scherer attributes this to social changes from the medieval feudal society to the modern globalized world. Whereas the former type of society emphasizes regional and personal relations, thus giving rise to a large number of nouns based on geographic (NHG *Schweizer* 'person from Switzerland, Swiss' ← *Schweiz* 'Switzerland') and personal names (NHG *Calviner* 'calvinist' ← *Calvin*), this kind of noun is much less needed in a society emphasizing personal autonomy.

3.3 Consequences

Change in productivity is one of the major factors resulting in changes in the word-formation system and its inventory (Scherer 2007). Some of the most important consequences of change in productivity concern constraints on word-formation processes, i.e. changes in the domain of a process. These changes arise if the productivity of a given process increases or decreases considerably more in one domain than in another. An example is the change from nominal to verbal bases in German adjective derivation using the suffix *-bar* (OHG *-bâri*, MHG *-bære*, NHG

-bar). According to Flury (1964), in Middle High German more than 60 % of all new coinings are based on nouns, such as MHG *vruhtbære* 'fertile' ← *vruht* 'fruit' + *-bære*, whereas the proportion of deverbal new coinings, such as MHG *ëȥbære* 'edible' ← *ëȥȥen* 'to eat' + *-bære*, is rather small (11 %). However, from the 13th century on, the number of deverbal new coinings rises and the number of denominal ones falls. By the late 20th century, the suffix *-bar* is one of the most productive German suffixes with 98 % of all new coinings derived from verbal bases. This development displays an increase in productivity of deverbal *-bar* derivation that is paralleled by a decrease of productivity of denominal *-bar* derivation, the latter one finally leading to the loss of the denominal domain, thus implementing the change from denominal to deverbal bases.

Similarly, the extension of word-formation meaning, such as the emergence of concrete *-ung* derivations in German, or the focusing of particular meanings are the result of gains in productivity of a given output category. Moreover, further changes in word-formation given by Müller (2002) and Munske (2002), such as the diminution of competing semantic word-formation products (ENHG *abschneiden* 'to cut off' → *Abschneidung* 'segment' vs. *Abschnitt* 'segment') or the diminution of word-formation products with pleonastic affixes (ENHG *Feldung* 'field' ← *Feld* 'field' + *-ung*), may be explained in terms of change in productivity. The decrease of pleonastic marking, e.g., may be interpreted as a consequence of decreasing productivity in particular, namely pleonastic, contexts.

However, change in productivity may not only affect individual word-formation processes, it may also result in changes in the word-formation system or parts of it. Scherer (2005) argues that global tendencies in the word-formation system, such as the diachronic tendency to concretize nouns and to abstract verbs in German as reported by Habermann (2002: 48–52), go back to a number of local changes affecting individual word-formation processes. According to Scherer (2005: 18), the tendency of verbs to gain a more abstract meaning by means of affixation, e.g., results – amongst others – from the diachronic development of the prefixation with *be-*. Whereas *be-* used to add a local meaning in Old High German, its main function today is the syntactic modification of verbs (NHG *lügen* + NOM 'to lie' → *belügen* + NOM + ACC 'to lie to somebody'). This kind of functional change in the word-formation system can be traced back to productivity change in individual processes. Thus, the consequences of change in productivity are not limited to individual processes. Change in productivity may also lead to changes in the inventory of the word-formation system. Moreover, even the very first stage of analogical coining can be explained as a new process becoming productive, and the loss of existing processes can be interpreted as the result of productivity approaching zero.

4 Methodological issues

Methodologically, two major questions arise when dealing with change in productivity. First, what empirical methods can be used to investigate change in productivity? And, second, as productivity cannot be captured directly, what means are available to determine change in productivity? The first question will be addressed in section 4.1, the second one in sections 4.2 and 4.3. Whereas section 4.2 is concerned with the question of how change in productivity can be captured at all, section 4.3 discusses quantitative and qualitative indicators used to detect change in productivity.

4.1 Empirical approaches

Empirical techniques used in synchronic research on productivity include the study of dictionaries, corpora, and experiments (Schröder and Mühleisen 2010). As for diachronic research, the earliest empirical studies are based on dictionaries, e.g., Dubois (1962), Neuhaus (1973), Kiesewetter (1987), Anshen and Aronoff (1989). However, as dictionaries provide only information about type frequency, conclusions on productivity are either limited to qualitative indicators or to type-based quantitative indicators. Nevertheless, quite elaborate ways of interpreting the information provided by dictionaries have been found (cf. Anderson 2000; Pounder 2000).

Since the late 1990s, when electronic corpora became available to historical linguists, a number of corpus-based investigations on change in productivity have been carried out, e.g., Dalton-Puffer (1996), Cowie (1999), Palmer (2009), Schröder (2011). Still, as the studies by Romaine (1985), Demske (2000) and Scherer (2005) demonstrate, the availability of electronic corpora is not a prerequisite of corpus-based research.

Experimental techniques, such as elicitation tests, seem to be unavailable for diachronic studies traditionally covering several decades or even centuries. However, the study by Baayen and Renouf (1996) clearly shows that change in productivity may take place within a few years, so experimental work on change in productivity is by no means excluded. The main problem consists rather in the delimitation of synchrony and diachrony, cf. section 3.1.

4.2 Capturing change

Regardless of the theoretical and empirical approach chosen, studies concerned with change in productivity have to deal with the problem of how change in productivity may be determined. The simplest way to do this is to compare the productivity of a process or, to be more precise, some indicator of its productivity for two periods or points in time (t_1, t_2). This approach has been pursued by a number of authors in the past, e.g., Demske (2000), Lüdeling and Evert (2005). Yet, comparing productivity for two points in time only allows one to confirm that change actually took place. In order to trace ongoing changes, further points in time (t_1, ..., t_n) have to be considered. Therefore, in the past, studies comparing productivity indicators covering three (Dalton-Puffer 1996), four (Palmer 2009), and even more periods of time (Cowie 1999; Scherer 2005) have been carried out. Strictly speaking, however, it would be necessary to examine an infinite number of points in time in order to be able to retrace ongoing change. The study that comes closest to this ideal, so far, is the study by Baayen and Renouf (1996).

Comparing indicators of productivity at different points in time is a method that can be used with any of the empirical techniques mentioned. Even data originating from different sources may be matched if the information on productivity provided is comparable, e.g., Demske (2000); Schröder (2011). Furthermore, some dictionaries, such as the *Oxford English Dictionary* (OED), provide the possibility to investigate changes in productivity by means of first attestation dates (Romaine 2004), cf. the studies of Anshen and Aronoff (1989), Aronoff and Anshen (1998), Anderson (2000), Schröder (2011) and Lindsay and Aronoff (2013).

4.3 Indicators of change

Unfortunately, morphological productivity is a phenomenon that cannot be accessed directly. Researchers have therefore developed a broad range of instruments meant to capture productivity. These indicators are derived from the properties attributed to productivity and differ with respect to the qualitative or quantitative concept of productivity.

Central to qualitative indicators of productivity is that they refer to the availability of a word-formation process and its domain. Therefore the basic indicator of productivity in terms of a qualitative understanding of productivity is the availability of a process in a given domain. More elaborate qualitative indicators refer to the delimitation of the domain, assuming, e.g., that productive word-formation processes are less restricted in terms of domains. The emergence of hybrid coinings, i.e. word-formation products consisting of native and borrowed entities, as proposed by Anderson (2000) and Palmer (2009), also belongs to the qualitative indicators of productivity since they refer to specific domains, namely native and/or borrowed lexical input.

Quantitative indicators of productivity, on the other hand, refer to the extent to which a given word-formation process gives rise to new words. Quantitative indicators are often called productivity measures, as they are based on word counts that can be found in dictionaries or corpora, cf. section 2.2. Changes in quantitative and/or qualitative indicators may be used to detect change in productivity. Whereas some linguists rely exclusively on quantitative or qualitative indicators of productivity (e.g., Scherer 2005; Demske 2000), others, such as Anderson (2000) and Pounder (2000), use quantitative as well as qualitative indicators.

Most indicators proposed have been developed and used, first of all, for synchronic research, an exception being the rate of increase, as proposed by Bauer (2001). However, as studies on change in productivity show, these indicators may easily be adapted for diachronic research. An example is Scherer's (2005) diachronic study on productivity changes in three different domains of nominal *-er* derivation in New High German, namely the word class of the base, the complexity of the base, and the concept of the derived noun. The study investigated nine periods of time covering four centuries (1609–2000). In order to detect changes in productivity, for each domain the number of types, tokens, and hapax legomena per period as well as productivity in the narrow sense (*P*) were investigated. The data not only proved that the productivity of *-er* derivation was continuously rising, but also showed that change in productivity differs depending on the domain investigated. For example, the productivity of deverbal *-er* nominals, such as NHG *Leser* 'reader' ← *lesen* 'to read', increased to a greater extent than the productivity of denominal ones, such as NHG *Handballer* 'handball player' ← *Handball* 'handball', and the productivity of object designations, such as NHG *Bohrer* 'borer, thrill', grew faster than the productivity of person designations (NHG *Leser*, *Handballer*).

Yet, there are some characteristic problems that arise when applying the indicators developed for synchronic research to the diachronic study of productivity. These are due to the fact that synchronic and diachronic studies in productivity differ fundamentally in the availability and accessibility of data. One important problem is that historical corpora are usually much smaller than corpora of present-day language. As a consequence, research on change in productivity has to be especially mindful of effects typical for small corpora, such as an extraordinary high number of hapax legomena (Cowie and Dalton-Puffer 2002: 424–425). Still, linguists have found different ways to deal with the problem of small-sized corpora. In her study, Cowie (1999) adapts the method developed by Baayen and Renouf (1996), namely counting *newwords*, for historical corpora. To compensate for the small corpus size she checks her corpus against a so-called starting lexicon of established words and eliminates types appearing in the starting lexicon.

Another problem characteristic for diachronic work on productivity that is based on dictionary studies only is the lack of information on token frequency, since the number of tokens or at least the number of hapax legomena is central to many quantitative indicators of productivity. However, as the study of Anderson (2000) shows, this lack of information may be compensated for by using other productivity indicators. Anderson combines in her study based on first attestation dates quantitative and qualitative indicators of productivity. As for quantitative indicators, she uses a benchmarking method, comparing for each period the percentage of new words formed with the suffix under consideration with the percentage of new words of the base category. As for qualitative indicators, she analyzes changes in the domain upon which the process operates (Anderson 2000: 54–55).

5 Conclusion

The aspect of time has long been neglected in research on productivity. However, in the past years, research on diachronic aspects of productivity has been intensified due to technological progress enabling linguists to conduct empirical studies more easily and on a larger scale. The number of studies focusing on change in productivity is still limited, though. Furthermore, studies widely differ concerning their theoretical and methodological approaches. As a matter of fact, many questions concerning change in productivity are still open. Especially central theoretical questions, such as the causes and consequences of change in productivity, have hardly been investigated so far.

6 References

Anderson, Karen Elisabeth (2000): Productivity in English nominal and adjectival derivation, 1100–2000. Ph.D. dissertation, University of Western Australia.

Anshen, Frank and Mark Aronoff (1989): Morphological productivity, word frequency, and the Oxford English Dictionary. In: Ralph W. Fasold and Deborah Schifferin (eds.), *Language Change and Variation*, 197–202. Amsterdam/Philadelphia: Benjamins.

Aronoff, Mark and Frank Anshen (1998): Morphology and the lexicon: Lexicalization and productivity. In: Andrew Spencer and Arnold M. Zwicky (eds.), *The Handbook of Morphology*, 237–247. Oxford: Blackwell.

Baayen, R. Harald (1989): A corpus-based approach to morphological productivity. Statistical analysis and psycholinguistic interpretation. Ph.D. dissertation, Vrije Universiteit, Amsterdam.

Baayen, R. Harald (1992): Quantitative aspects of morphological productivity. In: Geert Booij and Jaap van Marle (eds.), *Yearbook of Morphology 1991*, 109–149. Dordrecht: Kluwer.

Baayen, R. Harald (2009): Corpus linguistics in morphology: Morphological productivity. In: Anke Lüdeling and Merja Kytö (eds.), *Corpus Linguistics. An International Handbook*, 899–919. Berlin/New York: Mouton de Gruyter.

Baayen, R. Harald and Rochelle Lieber (1991): Productivity and English derivation: A corpus-based study. *Linguistics* 29: 801–843.

Baayen, R. Harald and Antoinette Renouf (1996): Chronicling the times: Productive lexical innovations in an English newspaper. *Language* 72: 69–96.

Bauer, Laurie (2001): *Morphological Productivity*. Cambridge: Cambridge University Press.

Bauer, Laurie (2005): Productivity: Theories. In: Pavol Štekauer and Rochelle Lieber (eds.), *Handbook of Word-Formation*, 315–334. Dordrecht: Springer.

Berg, Kristian (2020): Changes in the productivity of German word-formation patterns. Some methodological remarks. *Linguistics* 58(4): 1117–1150.

Berg, Kristian (2021): Produktivität in der historischen Wortbildung. Neubelege als Produktivitätsmaß. In: Christine Ganslmayer and Christian Schwarz (eds.), *Historische Wortbildung. Theorien – Methoden – Perspektiven*, 53–79. Hildesheim: Olms (= Germanistische Linguistik 252–254).

Cowie, Claire S. (1999): Diachronic word-formation: A corpus-based study of derived nominalizations in the history of English. Ph.D. dissertation, University of Cambridge.

Cowie, Claire S. and Christiane Dalton-Puffer (2002): Diachronic word-formation and studying changes in productivity over time: Theoretical and methodological considerations. In: Javier E. Díaz Vera (ed.), *A Changing World of Words. Studies in English Historical Lexicography, Lexicology and Semantics*, 410–437. Amsterdam: Rodopi.

Dal, Georgette (2003): Productivité morphologique: Définitions et notions connexes. *Langue française* 140: 3–23.

Dalton-Puffer, Christiane (1996): *The French Influence on Middle English Morphology. A Corpus-Based Study of Derivation*. Berlin: Mouton de Gruyter.

Demske, Ulrike (2000): Zur Geschichte der *ung*-Nominalisierung im Deutschen. Ein Wandel morphologischer Produktivität. *Beiträge zur Geschichte der deutschen Sprache und Literatur* 122: 365–411.

Doerfert, Regina (1994): *Die Substantivableitung mit* -heit/-keit, -ida, -î *im Frühneuhochdeutschen*. Berlin/New York: de Gruyter.

Dubois, Jean (1962): *Étude sur la dérivation suffixale en français moderne et contemporain. Essai d'interprétation des mouvements observés dans le domaine de la morphologie des mots construits*. Paris: Larousse.

Flury, Robert (1964): *Struktur- und Bedeutungsgeschichte des Adjektiv-Suffixes -bar*. Winterthur: Keller.

Gaeta, Livio and Davide Ricca (2006): Productivity in Italian word formation: A variable-corpus approach. *Linguistics* 44: 57–89.

Gaeta, Livio and Davide Ricca (2015): Productivity. In: Peter O. Müller, Ingeborg Ohnheiser, Susan Olsen and Franz Rainer (eds.), *Word-Formation. An International Handbook of the Languages of Europe*. Vol. 2, 842–858. Berlin/Boston: De Gruyter Mouton.

Habermann, Mechthild (2002): Sprachwandel im Licht diachroner und synchroner Wortbildung. In: Mechthild Habermann, Peter O. Müller and Horst Haider Munske (eds.), *Historische Wortbildung des Deutschen*, 41–57. Tübingen: Niemeyer.

Kempf, Luise (2016): *Adjektivsuffixe in Konkurrenz. Wortbildungswandel vom Frühneuhochdeutschen zum Neuhochdeutschen*. Berlin/Boston: De Gruyter.

Kempf, Luise (2021): Methoden der Produktivitätsmessung in diachronen Korpusstudien. In: Christine Ganslmayer and Christian Schwarz (eds,), *Historische Wortbildung. Theorien – Methoden – Perspektiven*, 23–52. Hildesheim: Olms (= Germanistische Linguistik 252–254).

Kiesewetter, Jutta (1987): Entwicklungsprozesse in der deutschen Wortbildung, in Ausschnitten verfolgt und dargestellt an den verbalen Bildungen mit den Elementen bei-, dar- und ob-. Ph.D. dissertation, Universität Leipzig.

Koefoed, Geert and Jaap van Marle (2000): Productivity. In: Geert Booij, Christian Lehmann and Joachim Mugdan (eds.), *Morphology. An International Handbook on Inflection and Word-Formation.* Vol. 1, 303–311. Berlin/New York: Mouton de Gruyter.

Lindsay, Mark and Mark Aronoff (2013): Natural selection in self-organizing morphological systems. In: Nabil Hathout, Fabio Montermini and Jesse Tseng (eds.), *Morphology in Toulouse. Selected Proceedings of Décembrettes 7 (Toulouse, 2–3 December 2010)*, 133–153. München: LINCOM Europa.

Lüdeling, Anke and Stefan Evert (2005): The emergence of productive non-medical *-itis*: Corpus evidence and qualitative analysis. In: Stephan Kepser and Marga Reis (eds.), *Linguistic Evidence. Empirical, Theoretical, and Computational Perspectives*, 351–370. Berlin/New York: Mouton de Gruyter.

Müller, Peter O. (2002): Historische Wortbildung im Wandel. In: Mechthild Habermann, Peter O. Müller and Horst Haider Munske (eds.), *Historische Wortbildung des Deutschen*, 1–11. Tübingen: Niemeyer.

Munske, Horst Haider (2002): Wortbildungswandel. In: Mechthild Habermann, Peter O. Müller and Horst Haider Munske (eds.), *Historische Wortbildung des Deutschen*, 23–40. Tübingen: Niemeyer.

Neuhaus, H. Joachim (1973): Zur Theorie der Produktivität von Wortbildungssystemen. In: Abraham P. ten Cate and Peter Jordens (eds.), *Linguistische Perspektiven. Referate des VII. Linguistischen Kolloquiums Nijmegen, 26.–30. September 1972*, 305–317. Tübingen: Niemeyer.

OED = *Oxford English Dictionary.* http://www.oed.com [last access 8 Feb 2015].

Palmer, Chris C. (2009): Borrowings, derivational morphology, and perceived productivity in English, 1300–1600. Ph.D. dissertation, University of Michigan.

Pavlov, Vladimir M. (1983): *Zur Ausbildung der Norm in der deutschen Literatursprache (1470–1730). Von der Wortgruppe zur substantivischen Zusammensetzung*. Berlin: Akademie Verlag.

Plag, Ingo (1999): *Morphological Productivity. Structural Constraints in English Derivation*. Berlin/New York: Mouton de Gruyter.

Plag, Ingo (2006): Productivity. In: Bas Arts and April McMahon (eds.), *The Handbook of English Linguistics*, 537–556. Malden, MA: Blackwell.

Pounder, Amanda (2000): *Processes and Paradigms in Word-Formation Morphology*. Berlin/New York: Mouton de Gruyter.

Rainer, Franz (1987): Produktivitätsbegriffe in der Wortbildungstheorie. In: Wolf Dietrich, Horst Geckeler and Hans-Martin Gauger (eds.), *Grammatik und Wortbildung romanischer Sprachen. Beiträge zum Deutschen Romanistentag in Siegen, 30. 9.–3. 10. 1985*, 187–202. Tübingen: Narr.

Rainer, Franz (2000): Produktivitätsbeschränkungen. In: Geert Booij, Christian Lehmann and Joachim Mugdan (eds.), *Morphology. An International Handbook on Inflection and Word-Formation.* Vol. 1, 877–885. Berlin/New York: Mouton de Gruyter.

Rainer, Franz (2005): Constraints on productivity. In: Pavol Štekauer and Rochelle Lieber (eds.), *Handbook of Word-Formation*, 335–352. Dordrecht: Springer.

Romaine, Suzanne (1985): Variability in word formation patterns and productivity in the history of English. In: Jacek Fisiak (ed.), *Papers from the 6th International Conference on Linguistics*, 451–466. Amsterdam/Philadelphia: Benjamins.

Romaine, Suzanne (2004): Change in productivity. In: Geert Booij, Christian Lehmann and Joachim Mugdan (eds.), *Morphology. An International Handbook on Inflection and Word-Formation.* Vol. 2, 1636–1644. Berlin/New York: Mouton de Gruyter.

Säily, Tanja (2014): *Sociolinguistic Variation in English Derivational Productivity: Studies and Methods in Diachronic Corpus Linguistics*. Helsinki: Société Néophilologique.

Scherer, Carmen (2005): *Wortbildungswandel und Produktivität. Eine empirische Studie zur nominalen* -er-*Derivation im Deutschen*. Tübingen: Niemeyer.

Scherer, Carmen (2007): The role of productivity in word-formation change. In: Joseph C. Salmons and Shannon Dubenion-Smith (eds.), *Historical Linguistics 2005*, 257–271. Amsterdam/ Philadelphia: Benjamins.

Schröder, Anne (2011): *On the Productivity of Verbal Prefixation in English. Synchronic and Diachronic Perspectives*. Tübingen: Narr.

Schröder, Anne and Susanne Mühleisen (2010): New ways of investigating morphological productivity. *Arbeiten aus Anglistik und Amerikanistik* 35: 43–59.

Trips, Carola (2009): *Lexical Semantics and Diachronic Morphology. The Development of* -hood, -dom *and* -ship *in the History of English*. Tübingen: Niemeyer.

van Marle, Jaap (1992): The relationship between morphological productivity and frequency: A comment on Baayen's performance-oriented conception of morphological productivity. In: Geert Booij and Jaap van Marle (eds.), *Yearbook of Morphology 1991*, 151–163. Dordrecht: Kluwer.

Weinreich, Otto (1971): *Die Suffixablösung bei den Nomina agentis während der althochdeutschen Periode*. Berlin: Schmidt.

Wilmanns, Wilhelm (1896): *Deutsche Grammatik. Gotisch, Alt-, Mittel- und Neuhochdeutsch. Zweite Abteilung: Wortbildung*. Straßburg: Trübner.

Mechthild Habermann

12 Grammaticalization in German word-formation

Abstract: Grammaticalization denotes the process whereby lexical units of a language become grammatical units or less grammatical units develop into more grammatical units. Word-formation, on the other hand, denotes the process of creating new words, i.e. new lexical units. These two processes, while appearing to run counter to one another, share a large number of parameters. Historically, several German word-formation affixes have arisen from autonomous lexemes, the great majority of which have not been preserved. Only diachronic research can trace the grammaticalization processes undergone by German collective suffixes, adjectival suffixes in *-bar*, *-haft*, *-lich*, *-sam* and German prefix verbs. Present-day German is characterized by a co-existence of free lexemes and homonymous bound word-formation elements, with different degrees of desemanticization between free lexemes and word-formation elements. The degree of grammaticalization of some particular item can be determined on the basis of the parameters of semantic abstraction, low paradigmatic variability and closed class membership. It appears that word-formation elements (which have arisen from grammaticalization processes) occupy different positions on the grammar-lexis continuum. The only element to enter the grammar of German is verbal *ge-*, which has evolved from a word-formation morpheme into an inflectional morpheme, now serving to mark the passive perfect participle of unprefixed verbs.

1 Definition

Grammaticalization is a process whereby lexical units of a language become grammatical units or less grammatical units develop into more grammatical units.

Mechthild Habermann, Erlangen, Germany

https://doi.org/10.1515/9783111420530-012

The notion of grammaticalization is predicated on a view of lexis and grammar as opposite poles on a continuum; in the course of grammaticalization the units in question lose some of their lexical properties, thus mutating into increasingly grammatical elements. The degree of grammaticalization of linguistic signs can be assessed by means of prototypical criteria: loss of autonomy, i.e. paradigmatic independence (open choice) and syntagmatic independence (relatively free movement of constituents); loss of integrity or "weight" due to phonological erosion and desemanticization, or "attrition" (cf. Lehmann 1995 [1982]: 121–178).

According to Givón (1979: 109), grammaticalization takes the following path:

discourse > syntax > morphology > morphophonemics > zero

Processes of grammaticalization can be observed both diachronically and synchronically. They are posited to be unidirectional, meaning that grammatical elements which have emerged from grammaticalization will not develop back into lexical elements along the same path. Grammaticalization is essentially set in train by the cognitive processes of reanalysis and analogy. "Reanalysis and analogy are the major mechanisms in language change. They do not define grammaticalization, nor are they coextensive with it, but [...] grammaticalization does not occur without them. The subset of processes that are particular to grammaticalization are those that over time render more independent elements less independent" (Hopper and Traugott 1993: 61 f.). By reanalysis is meant the reinterpretation of a linguistic structure, by analogy the transfer or extension of a rule. While reanalysis and analogy describe mechanisms which set repair processes in motion when structures are no longer transparent, they cannot explain under what conditions some particular structure is re-interpreted or some rule is transferred or extended (on unsolved questions concerning grammaticalization, see Diewald 2004; on grammaticalization and reanalysis, see Eckardt 2012).

In Givón's cycle, the morphological stage, which gives rise to new affixes, is situated between the stage of syntactic bonding within the syntagm and the stage of phonological attrition. The term "new affixes" is used primarily to refer to inflectional affixes, which are almost universally considered to be elements of grammar, their function being to change the grammatical form of a word. By contrast, the status of word-formation affixes remains a subject of controversy in research on grammaticalization.

2 Extent of overlap between grammaticalization and lexicalization

Whilst grammaticalization is centred around the development of new grammatical elements, word-formation is a process whereby new words are created. Grammaticalization entails a move towards the grammatical pole of the aforementioned continuum, word-formation entails a strengthening of the lexical pole (cf. Wischer 2011: 356).

It has been known for some time, however, that a number of word-formation affixes, namely prefixes/particles and suffixes, have evolved from free lexemes in a long diachronic process involving derivation, one of the central word-formation procedures apart from compounding. This kind of evolution is considered to be a prime example of the initiation of a grammaticalization process whereby previously independent lexemes give rise to bound morphemes (on the grammaticalization of English prefixes, cf. Wischer 2008).

The question then arises as to the extent to which word-formation affixes exhibit grammatical properties in moving towards the grammatical pole of the continuum and the extent to which they have moved away from the lexical pole. Wischer (2011: 359) points out the close diachronic relationship between derivational affixes and inflectional morphemes, which is due to their going through similar processes (provided they derive from independent lexemes): "semantic abstraction, phonetic reduction, paradigmaticization, decategorialization, and fusion; hence, their evolution has traditionally been characterized as a process of grammaticalization [...]."

From a synchronic perspective, not all word-formation affixes are located at the same point between the extremes of lexicon and grammar, regardless of whether or not they can be traced back to independent lexemes. This is why bound elements may also be more or less lexicalized or grammaticalized and may be positioned on a cline.

Tab. 12.1: Criteria for bound lexical and grammatical categories (cf. Wischer 2011: 359).

	Lexicon	←	→	**Grammar**
Semantic abstraction	low	←	→	high
Paradigmatic variability	high	←	→	low
Class	open	←	→	closed

Prefixes and particles with a purely modifying function are closer to the lexicon than suffixes, which may change word class. While suffixes may also be purely modificatory, they invariably determine word class and, in the case of nouns, gender. Prefixes and particles, by contrast, may occasion changes in the valency of the base verb, especially transitivization. In addition, suffixation creates abstract semantic classes. In the case of prefixes and particles, these semantic classes are closer to the lexicon. Both initial and terminal affixations go hand in hand with semantic change through metaphorization and metonymization.

For German word-formation affixes, the cline between lexicon and grammar can be characterized as follows:

a) Prefixes with a low degree of semantic abstraction and high paradigmatic variability (i.e. a number of variant formal elements with the same function), purely modifying in function; examples are *Haupt-* ('main; lit. head') in *Hauptproblem* 'most important problem' alongside *Grund-* (lit. 'ground') in *Grundproblem* 'most important problem' and *Kern-* (lit. 'core') in *Kernproblem* 'id.'. These are often classified as prefixoids on the borderline between compounding and derivation.
b) Suffixes with a low degree of semantic abstraction and high paradigmatic variability, leading to semantic modification and determining word class; examples include the diminutive suffixes *-chen* and *-lein* (*Tellerchen* or *Tellerlein* 'small plate') or gender suffixes such as *-in* (*Wirtin* 'landlady'), *-ess* (*Stewardess*), *-essin* (*Prinzessin* 'princess'), *-euse* (*Friseuse* 'female hairdresser'), etc.
c) Prefixes/particles and suffixes with a high degree of semantic abstraction and of paradigmatic variability due to metaphorization and metonymization. Thus, prefix verbs, for example, undergo lexicalization, giving rise to secondary features which may in turn develop into productive patterns: 'spatial-dimensional: upward movement + local-directional base verb', as with intransitive particle verbs such as *aufsteigen* 'to rise; lit. up-rise' (of *Dampf* 'steam') > 'temporal-dimensional: beginning + dynamic base verb', as with intransitive *aufblühen* 'to start to blossom; lit. up-blossom' (inchoative); 'relational: on(to) a surface', e.g., *etw. auf etw.* resp. *jmdm. aufkleben* 'to stick sth on a surface; lit. on-stick' > 'relational: on a person in a negative manner', e.g., *jmdm. etw. aufschwatzen* 'to talk sb into sth; lit. on-talk', etc.
d) Prefixes/particles with a high degree of semantic abstraction and low paradigmatic variability as well as a change in valency patterning; transitivization, e.g., through (semantically empty) applicative verbal prefix *be-*, as in *bedienen: x dient jmdm.* ('to serve: x serves sb'; intransitive verb *dienen*) > *x bedient y* (transitive verb *bedienen*: 'x serves y'); change of syntactic function and semantic role for objects and adverbials: *x hängt y in/an/auf z* ('x hangs y in/on z') with accusative object y as patient and obligatory adverbial z as direct-

ive > *x behängt z* (*mit y*) with accusative object z (as patient) and y (as instrument).

e) Suffixes with a high degree of semantic abstraction and low paradigmatic variability, leading to changes in word class; e.g., abstract suffixes such as *-ung* and *-ion*/*-tion*/*-ation*, as in *Renovierung* and **Renovation* 'renovation', but *Variation* and **Variierung* 'variation'.

All word-formation affixes differ from inflectional affixes in exhibiting a lower degree of semantic abstraction and a higher degree of paradigmatic variability as well as in forming less closed classes. Viewed from this perspective, inflectional affixes are always more grammaticalized than word-formation elements.

In German, however, one word-formation prefix has entered the grammar of the language, namely the verbal prefix *ge-*, which, together with *-en* (and historical Ablaut) or *-(e)t*, forms the passive perfect participle, as in *ge-ritt-en* ('ridden'; from *reiten* 'to ride') or *ge-koch-t* ('cooked'). There are various reasons for this. According to Wischer and Habermann (2004: 281) *ge-* is "the only prefix which cannot be traced back to an adverb with a local meaning" (my translation). Its basic meaning is sociative and hence partly abstract, allowing it to combine with nouns (*Ge-birg-e* 'mountains'), adjectives (*ge-mein* 'common, mean') and verbs (*ge-leiten* 'to accompany, escort'). Complex words like *Geschlecht* 'gender', *geschwind* 'fast', and *gewinnen* 'to win' formed with the word-formation prefix *ge-* have now been completely idiomaticized.

What remains of the originally sociative meaning and the polysemy which it gives rise to is the ability of *ge-* to specify the temporal limits of verbal events, with the result that it has become "the only grammatical perfectivity marker in German" (ibid.). As late as Middle High German *ge-* showed higher paradigmatic

Tab. 12.2: Passive perfect participles in Middle High German and in present-day German.

Passive perfect participles	
Middle High German	**present-day German**
brâht	*gebracht* 'brought'
funden	*gefunden* 'found'
komen	*gekommen* 'come'
worden	*geworden* 'become'
troffen (often)	*getroffen* 'met, hit'
lâzen (often)	*gelassen* 'let'
geben (sometimes)	*gegeben* 'given'
nomen (sometimes)	*genommen* 'taken'

variability in that it was not used with verbs with perfective meaning, i.e. verbs which in themselves describe a complete or punctual action. This is why in Middle High German the passive perfect participles were formed without *ge-* by verbs with perfective meaning, while in present-day German *ge-* is also appended to perfective verbs (cf. Paul et al. 2007: 247, § M 73, see Table 12.2).

It does not attach to verbs that have an inseparable prefix (e.g., *begonnen* 'begun', *erfunden* 'invented', *verliehen* 'lent') or foreign suffix *-ier-* (e.g., *probiert* 'tried, tasted').

To what extent the term grammaticalization can be applied to nominal, adjectival and verbal word-formation is the subject of the next section. For diachronic data on word-formation elements which span the entire period from Old High German to Middle High German, research in word-formation still has to rely on older standard works such as Wilmanns (1899) and Henzen (1965) (see also article 15 on historical word-formation in German).

3 Grammaticalization in nominal word-formation

Turning now to nominal word-formation, we find that since Old High German the suffixes *-heit* (cf. English *-hood*), *-schaft* (cf. English *-ship*) and *-tum* (cf. English *-dom*) have evolved from autonomous lexemes into word-formation affixes. The elements *-werk* (lit. 'activity, work, the product of work') and *-wesen* (lit. 'essence of a person or object, living individual') are usually classified as suffixes, although free lexemes exist which have the same form. The same goes for most augmentative elements such as *Affe(n)-* (lit. 'monkey'), *Bombe(n)-* (lit. 'bomb'), *Spitze(n)-* (lit. 'top'); cf. English *dead-* with adjective as in *dead-tired*, *dead-wrong*. This begs the question as to whether and to what extent they can be regarded as word-formation affixes.

3.1 Grammaticalization of *-heit*

The suffix *-heit* can be traced back to the free lexeme *heit* which is attested in Old High German and Middle High German with the meaning 'shape, person, estate, rank, being, manner'. Its development into a suffix starts from compounds whose modifier is a person noun (e.g., *magadheit* f. 'girlhood, virginity'). In Western Germanic compounds involving *-heit* and a person noun give rise to *-heit* as a collective suffix as in Old High German *kristanheit* 'Christianity'. In German in

Tab. 12.3: Grammaticalization of *-heit*: from compound element to suffix.

Compound	Compound > Collective derivative	Abstract derivative
OHG *gotheit*	OHG *kristanheit*	OHG *wīsheit*
got 'god' + *heit* 'state, being'	*kristan* 'Christians' + *heit* 'state, being' > 'totality'	*wīs* 'wise' + *-heit* ('quality of being wise')

particular, the suffix combines with adjectives and participles forming abstract nouns which designate a quality or a state (e.g., OHG *frīheit* 'freedom' or *trunkanheit* 'drunkenness'; cf. Pfeifer 2005: 527, s. v. *-heit, -keit*). The use of *-heit* that was once productive in Middle High German and Early New High German to form new nouns designating actions and processes is no longer available in New High German. When there is a shift in the syllabic boundary, suffixal variants (*-keit* or *-igkeit*) result from the phonetic assimilation at the juncture between the suffix and the base word in cases where adjectives end in *-ec/-ic* (*-ig*). The path of grammaticalization may be sketched as seen in Table 12.3.

In case of the suffix *-heit*, grammaticalization cannot be conceived of as a strictly diachronic sequence, since both compounds and derivatives formed with *-heit* have been attested from the time of the earliest written records. It is nonetheless possible to model the path of grammaticalization by reconstructing minimal developmental stages:

a) The initial stage involves a noun with a relatively abstract meaning combining with a person noun.
b) If the modifier is a person noun which can be interpreted as a collective, a reanalysis occurs, i.e. a re-interpretation of its linguistic structure. Thus, *Christenheit* 'christianity' may be interpreted in two different ways: either as a compound 'estate consisting of the group of Christians' or as a collective derivative 'Christians which act as a group or collective'. The need for a repair process (i.e. a re-interpretation) may be due to the noun *heit* gradually passing out of use. Particular word-formations assumed collective meanings at different times: thus, *Menschheit* 'mankind' has been primarily a collective noun only since the 18th century; well into the early 19th century it was still common in the sense of 'human being' (cf. Paul 2006: 653 f., s. v. *Mensch*). The establishment of new collective suffixes may be linked to the fact that the old **ga-...-ja* (OHG *gi*-BN [base noun]-*(i)* as in *Gebirge* 'mountains') or OHG *-ahi* (BN-*ahi*, NHG *-icht* as in *Röhricht* 'reed') patterns for deriving collectives became unproductive. Denominal word-formations with *-heit* in its collective

meaning are now unproductive, but the present-day German vocabulary has retained a number of such units (cf. Fleischer and Barz 2012: 213).

c) Another commonality between collective abstract nouns and compounds is the presence of a nominal modifier or derivational base. At the next stage adjectives or participles can serve as the derivational base, giving rise to abstract nouns which refer to a quality and bestowing an abstract meaning on the derivational suffix (e.g., OHG *tumbheit* 'stupidity, ignorance' ← *tumb* 'stupid, ignorant'; cf. Wilmanns 1899: 384, § 289). Such new abstract nouns referring to a quality gradually replace their predecessors ending in OHG *-ī* and MHG *-e*, which, in the High German area, were subject to morphological erosion from a full vowel via a schwa [ə], in the Upper German dialects, to zero. Some lexicalized derivatives (e.g., *Güt-e* 'goodness' ← *gut* 'good', *Mild-e* 'mildness' ← *mild* 'mild', etc.) have remained in use to the present day.
d) Verbal extensions resulting in abstract nouns denoting actions and processes are abandoned, since derivatives in *-heit* are in competition with those in *-ung* (cf. Ring 2008: 232, who provides additional references).
e) Through metonymization, abstract nouns denoting qualities develop into person nouns ('state of being BA [base adjective]' > 'sb/sth who is BA'); consider, for example, *Sie hat sich zu einer Schönheit* (= 'a person who is beautiful') *entwickelt* 'she has developed into a beauty'.
f) The formation of the allomorphs *-keit*, *-igkeit* is the result of reanalysis. Assimilation of preceding *-ig* with *-heit* produces the suffixal variant *-keit* and readjustment of syllable boundaries leads to a shift in the interpretation of derivatives, as from *Traurig-keit* 'sadness' to *Leicht-igkeit* 'lightness'. The variant ending in *-keit* is not found with nominal bases (cf. Oberle 1990). According to Kluge (1925: 20), *-keit* achieved currency from the 12th century.
g) The suffixal variant in *-keit*, which, according to Wilmanns (1899: 386, § 290), is always preceded by an unstressed syllable, is invariably attached to multisyllabic, usually derived adjectives serving as derivational bases. These are no longer restricted to *-ig*; consider, for example, *Ewig-keit* 'eternity' vs. *Heiter-keit* 'cheerfulness'. Independently of their stress pattern, derivations which have passive perfect participles as their base have *-heit* only (cf. Fleischer and Barz 2012: 209–214).

3.2 Derivation with *-schaft* and *-tum*

Common to the nominal suffixes *-schaft*, *-tum* and *-heit* is that they can be traced back to an autonomous lexeme with a comparatively independent meaning: *-schaft* belongs etymologically to *schaffen* 'to make, create, produce', derived from

OHG *(gi)scaf(t)* and MHG *schaft* 'creature, shape, formation, quality' (Pfeifer 2005: 1177, s. v. *-schaft*); similarly, *-tum* belongs to OHG/MHG *tuom* 'judgment, court, power, rule, dignity, living conditions, possessions, curious state' (Pfeifer 2005: 1473, s. v. *-tum*).

Although, in spite of various lexicalizations (e.g., *Eigenschaft* 'quality', *Eigenheit* 'characteristic', *Eigentum* 'property'), *-schaft* overlaps somewhat in function with *-tum* (cf. *Bürgerschaft* 'citizenry' vs. *Bürgertum* 'citizenship') and also with *-heit*, statistical evidence suggests a frequency cline, with derivatives ending in *-heit* being most common, *-schaft* less common and *-tum* least common (on *scaf(t)* in Old High German, see Meineke 1991; on the grammaticalization of *-tum* from a cognitive perspective, see Lightfoot 2005). Derivatives ending in *-schaft* and *-tum* show a clear preference for nominal bases, usually person nouns (e.g., *Beamten-schaft* 'civil servants', *Beamten-tum* 'civil servant status'). With both suffixes, nouns other than person nouns are rare: *Land-schaft* 'landscape' (as early as Middle High German), *Schrift-tum* 'writings'.

There are also a few isolated examples of adjectival bases (*Bereit-schaft* 'readiness', *Reich-tum* 'riches') and verbal bases (*Beleg-schaft* 'staff, personnel', *Wachs-tum* 'growth'; see Fleischer and Barz 2012: 221–224). However, the relationship between *Wachstum* and *wachsen* 'to grow' is the result of reanalysis: *Wachstum* derives etymologically from the Old High German noun *wahst* 'growth' (see Wilmanns 1899: 393, § 295), whose loss made it possible to reinterpret *Wachstum* as being derived from the verb *wachsen*. With both suffixes, adjectival and verbal bases are unproductive. With *-schaft* we find formations involving passive perfect participles or infinitives, which are also quite rare (cf. *Gefangen-schaft* 'captivity', *Machen-schaft* 'machinations').

Like *-heit* the suffixes *-schaft* and *-tum* form collective derivatives, with the difference that the latter have stopped evolving towards prototypical abstract suffixes. This is because *-schaft* and *-tum* serve a predominantly modifying function (in combination with base nouns), while their word-changing function, in combination with adjectival and participial bases, is almost non-existent and remains the province of *-heit*.

3.3 Collective derivation with *-werk* and *-wesen*

Unlike *-heit*, *-schaft* and *-tum*, which are usually classified as nominal suffixes in the literature, there are some suffixes whose autonomous counterpart still exists, albeit not in the original sense it had when the suffix emerged. In this class belong *-werk* which meant 'activity, work, the product of work' in Old High German, while the additional New High German meaning 'factory, production unit' did not arise until the 17th century (Pfeifer 2005: 1558, s. v. *Werk*), and *-wesen*, which can be traced back to the nominalized infinitive of *sein* 'being', OHG *wesan*. The present-day noun *Wesen* 'essence of a person or object, living individual' has evolved quite far from its original meaning 'staying in a place, sojourn, existence' (Pfeifer 2005: 1560, s. v. *Wesen*). Bound elements such as *-werk* und *-wesen* are usually described as affixoids (also: suffixoids), a term denoting the transition from an autonomous word into a word-formation affix. Both these suffixes serve to form collective nouns. *-werk* does so mainly with bases that designate plants, parts of plants or substances (*Astwerk* 'boughs', *Zuckerwerk* 'confectionery'), while there is a complete absence of person nouns and a comparative paucity of abstract nouns (*Regelwerk* 'rules'); the suffix *-wesen* exhibits a preference for abstract nouns from the world of administration (e.g., *Rechnungswesen* 'accounting'), more rarely also for nouns denoting persons or objects. With *-werk* and *-wesen* one occasionally finds verbal bases such as *Backwerk* 'that which has been baked; baked goods' (patient noun) and *Meldewesen* 'communications' (cf. Fleischer and Barz 2012: 231 f.). The DWB records a large number of lemmas ending in *-wesen* (e.g., *Gerichtswesen* 'judiciary', DWB 4,1/2: 3685, *Staatswesen* 'state system', DWB 10,2/1: 327, etc.) which date from the 19th century.

3.4 Collective suffixes in present-day German

Table 12.4 shows how present-day German uses collective suffixes productively; there is a clear tendency here to avoid competing forms as far as possible.

The status of second elements of compounds such as *-gut* (lit. 'property; estate'; e.g., *Leergut* 'empties'), *-kram* (lit. 'odds and ends'; e.g., *Papierkram* 'paperwork'), and *-zeug* (lit. 'stuff'; e.g., *Nähzeug* 'sewing utensils') is controversial. Like *-werk* and *-wesen*, these have a very general meaning and form series in present-day German, but their semantic and functional specificity is often not deemed sufficient to grant them the status of suffixes (Fleischer and Barz 2012: 133). If

Tab. 12.4: Productivity of collective suffixes (denominal formations) in present-day German.

<table>
<tr><th colspan="4">Collective suffixes in present-day German</th></tr>
<tr><th>unproductive</th><th>weakly productive</th><th>productive</th><th>productive in specific areas only</th></tr>
<tr><td>Ge-BN-(e)</td><td>BN-heit</td><td>BN-schaft</td><td>BN-werk</td></tr>
<tr><td>BN-icht</td><td colspan="2">BN-tum</td><td>BN-wesen</td></tr>
</table>

anything, therefore, they may be regarded as marking the onset of grammaticalization.

3.5 Augmentation

Alongside collective nouns, there are a number of augmentatives which have recently been formed from nominal first elements such as *Jahrhundert-* lit. 'century', *Mammut-* lit. 'mammoth', *Monster-* lit. 'monster', *Rekord-* lit. 'record', *Riesen-* lit. 'giant', *Grund-* lit. 'ground', *Herzens-* lit. 'heart', *Kern-* lit. 'core', *Schwerpunkt-* lit. 'focal point', *Spitzen-* lit. 'top', *Affen-* lit. 'monkey', *Bullen-* lit. 'bull', *Hunde-* lit. 'dog', *Sau-* lit. 'sow', *Bären-* lit. 'bear', from nominal second elements such as *-flut* lit. 'flood', *-lawine* lit. 'avalanche', *-riese* lit. 'giant', *-sturm* lit. 'storm', and from adjectival first elements such as *Groß-* lit. 'big, great', *Hoch-* (*Höchst-*) lit. 'high, highest', *Voll-* lit. 'full'. Diminutives are formed from nouns such as *Teil-* lit. 'part', *Zwerg(en)-* or *-zwerg* lit. 'gnome' and adjectives such as *Klein-* (*Kleinst-*) lit. 'small, smallest', *Schmal-* lit. 'slim', *Schwach-* lit. 'weak', *Halb-* lit. 'semi, half'; cf. English 'mini-', etc. (Fleischer and Barz 2012: 261 f.). These elements are employed to suggest that the noun in question, functioning as either head or modifier, is big or small in size or significance. Since many elements, such as *Riesen-* lit. 'giant' in *Riesenkonzern* 'giant concern', *Riesenschwindel* 'colossal fraud' and *Riesenskandal* 'huge scandal' have become highly productive, the question arises as to whether they may be classified as word-formation affixes. Here too, though, the semantic and functional specificity of the forms in question may not be sufficient, so that they hardly differ from metaphorical compounds such as *Flussknie* 'river bend', *Kopfbahnhof* 'terminus; lit. head-railway-station' or *Presselandschaft* 'press landscape'.

A partial exception is the augmentative prefix *Haupt-* 'main', as found in derivatives of the type *Hauptbahnhof* 'main station', *Hauptperson* 'central character, protagonist' or *Hauptstadt* 'capital'. This prefix is a synchronic homonym of the autonomous noun *Haupt* 'head' from which it derives etymologically but is functionally separate (Fleischer and Barz 2012: 257 f.).

In the case of affixoids or "semi-affixes", Römer (2000: 37) suggests that the grammaticalization process leading from the syntagm via the complex word to the derivative has not yet been completed, since there is no lexicalization. Androutsopoulos (1999: 160) considers the following formations from youth languages as "'serially productive' (*reihenhaft produktiv*) formatives rather than affixes", cf. *Killerband* 'killer band', *Killersongs* 'killer songs', *Killer-Keller* 'killer basement', *Scheißjob* 'crap job; lit. shit job', *Scheißkaff* 'crap place; lit. shit place', *Scheißbullen* 'bloody police; lit. shit police', *Scheißleben* 'crap life; lit. shit life';

Intyp 'hip guy; lit. in guy', *Machotypen* 'machos', *Schrotttypen* 'crap guys; lit. scrap guys', *Soundfreaks* 'sound freaks', *Drogenfreaks* 'drug freaks', *Computerfreaks* 'nerds'. Potential reasons for categorizing such elements as affixoids are "generalization of meaning, generalization of distribution" and the higher frequency of use of formatives as compared to free lexical morphemes (Androutsopoulos 1999: 161).

4 Grammaticalization in adjectival word-formation

4.1 Suffixation

Coming now to adjectival word-formation, we note that, here too, free lexemes have developed into word-formation suffixes such as *-bar*, *-haft*, *-lich* and *-sam*. Such adjectival suffixes have been well researched. *-bar* derives from OHG *-bāri*, which in turn was based on the free lexeme **bāri* 'carrying' formed from OHG *beran* 'to bear'. The old verb has been preserved in the formations *gebären* 'to bear, give birth to' and *entbehren* 'to dispense with'. The suffix first combined with concrete and abstract nouns (e.g., *fluahbāri* 'curse-bearing') before becoming associated with adjectives and, finally, with verbs in Early New High German through reanalysis. While the OHG *-bāri* compounds have an active verb and an accusative noun, this is reversed in formations such as MHG *ahtebære* 'remarkable' which has a passive verb: 'worthy of being remarked'. Since Early New High German *-bar* has been combining with verbs to produce word-formations which have a passive-modal meaning: *trinkbar* 'that can be drunk' (cf. Flury 1964; Nübling et al. 2013: 77–80).

The suffix *-haft* derives from the verbal adjective *haft* 'bound, captured' (Pfeifer 2005: 493, s. v. *-haft*) which in modern German is attested as the noun *Haft* 'custody; detention'. Since Middle High German *-haft* has given rise to denominal derivations with an ornative ('equipped with'; e.g., *prunkhaft* 'magnificent') or similative meaning ('in the manner of'; e.g., *greisenhaft* 'like a very old man/woman'). Deverbal formations do not, as a rule, appear until New High German (e.g., *naschhaft* 'having a sweet tooth'), while modern deadjectival formations can be historically related to nouns (cf. *krankhaft* 'pathological' in present-day German, derived from *krank* 'sick', whose historical predecessor is the Middle High German noun *kranc* 'weakness, shortcoming, damage'; cf. Wilmanns 1899: 503, § 381; also Fleischer and Barz 2012: 336 f.).

One of the most productive adjectival suffixes is *-lich*, which combines with nouns as well as with adjectives and verbs. Historically, it can be traced back to Germanic **līka-* 'body, shape', OHG *līh* 'body' and NHG *Leiche* 'corpse'. Killie (2007) discusses several different hypotheses on the origin of the suffix. The long vowel /i:/ of the suffix was shortened in Early New High German times, thus preventing the diphthongization which occurred in the noun. Formally, the suffix differs from its now homonymous base *Leiche*; semantically, it has undergone a process of abstraction, resulting in a) relational (*herbstlich* 'autumnal') or ornative (*leidenschaftlich* 'passionate') meanings close to those of adjectives in *-ig* when it combines with nouns, and b) in a meaning which signals the actual occurrence of an event when it combines with verbs, in contradistinction to *-bar*; cf. *beachtlich* 'remarkable' vs. *beachtbar* 'to be noted'. From the outset adjectives and adverbs ending in OHG *-līh* and *-līhho* had been in competition (cf. Schmid 1998). *-līch(e)*/ *-līch(en)* was highly frequent in Middle High German as an adverb-forming suffix. While in English *-ly* has prevailed as an adverb marker, German has only retained some lexicalized relics such as *bitterlich* 'slightly bitter', *freilich* 'however', *gänzlich* 'complete', *kürzlich* 'recently', *schwerlich* 'hardly', *sicherlich* 'certainly' (cf. Fleischer and Barz 2012: 342–345; here: 344 f.).

The suffix *-sam* is close to OHG *samo* 'the same' and is used to form adjectives with the meaning 'inclined to do sth' from nominal stems. In recent times it has also combined with verbal stems as in *gehor-sam* 'obedient' (Pfeifer 2005: 1162, s. v. *-sam*; on *-sam* in Old High German, see Möllmann 1994).

As with nominal word-formation, the views expressed in the literature concerning the second elements of adjectival formations are not entirely unproblematic. Olsen (1986) views *-arm* 'poor', *-fest* 'resistant', *-frei* 'free', *-leer* 'empty', *-reich* 'rich', *-sicher* 'safe', *-voll* 'full' as compositional elements rather than adjectival suffixes (cf. also Fandrych 1993). According to Fleischer and Barz (2012), similar considerations hold true for *-aktiv* 'active', *-bereit* 'ready', *-dicht* 'dense', *-echt* 'real', *-eigen* 'own', *-fertig* 'finished', *-fremd* 'foreign', *-froh* 'happy', *-gerecht* 'adequate', *-gleich* 'equal', *-intensiv* 'intensive', *-müde* 'weary', *-nah* 'close', *-reif* 'ripe', *-schwach* 'weak', *-schwer* 'heavy', *-stark* 'strong', *-tüchtig* 'able', *-weit* 'wide', *-wert* 'worth'. On the other hand, *-los* 'without; lit. loose' (e.g., *sprachlos* 'without language') and *-mäßig* 'with regard to; lit. mediocre, moderate' (e.g., *gefühlsmäßig* 'by instinct'), which have undergone a functional and semantic shift away from the still existing base lexemes, are regarded as suffixes (Fleischer and Barz 2012: 345–347; on the diachrony of *-mäßig* cf. Inghult 1975).

4.2 Prefixation

Turning now to gradation, we find a number of elements marking the highest degree, such as *stock-* 'ultra; lit. stick' (*stockkonservativ* 'ultraconservative'), *brand-* 'brand' (*brandneu* 'brand new'), *tod-* 'dead' (*todlangweilig* 'deadly boring') and *blitz-* '(like) lightning' (*blitzgescheit* 'brilliant') which are restricted to specific lexemes, as are elements expressing a low degree (e.g., *halb-* 'semi, half' (*halbblind* 'half-blind') or *zart-* 'tenderly' (*zartrosa* 'carnation pink')) (Fleischer and Barz 2012: 310–314). There is considerable lexical overlap here with nouns (*grund-* lit. 'ground', *hoch-* lit. 'high', etc.), with both categories usually comprising metaphorical compounds. It should be noted that comparative compounds are subject to restrictions to the extent that they do not support any degrees of comparison in Standard German: *neu – neuer – am neuesten* 'new, newer, newest', but: *brandneu* 'brand new' – **brandneu-er – *am brandneuesten*; they share this feature with other uncomparable adjectives: *ledig* 'unmarried' – **lediger, lila* 'purple' – **lilaner.* Superlatives, however, accumulate easily (e.g., non-standard *bildschönst* lit. 'most picture-perfect'), especially in new media.

The evolution of comparative adjectival compounds can be described as a lexicalization process since the augmentative elements in question are more strongly tied to specific words than is the case with nominal compounds. Thus, for example, the use of *ober-* lit. 'upper' as an augmentative element in *oberfaul* ('incredibly lazy') cannot be replaced with *bitter-* 'bitter' (*bitterböse* 'furious'), *blut-* 'bloody' (*blutjung* 'very young'), *haupt-* 'main' (*hauptverantwortlich* 'mainly responsible') or *tief-* 'deep(ly)' (*tieftraurig* 'deeply sad'). Compounds like *blutjung* and *tieftraurig* may have arisen from constructions imbued with a certain degree of idiomaticity, such as *junges Blut* ('young blood = young person') and *tiefeTrauer* ('deep grief = profound grief'). Seen from this perspective, the process whereby a more or less fixed syntagm turns into a fixed compound is one of lexicalization. In "freezing" elements within the compound, however, it also has certain characteristics of grammaticalization. "Both lexicalization and grammaticalization are reductive processes which constrain the freedom of the speaker in selecting and combining the constituents of a complex expression. Thus, both processes can be regarded as a transition of an expression from *parole* into *langue.* [...] Grammaticalization reduces the autonomy of a unit, shifting it to a lower, more strictly regulated grammatical level [...]. Lexicalization reduces the inner structure of a unit, shifting it into the inventory [...]" (Lehmann 2002: 15). According to Lehmann (ibid.) grammaticalization stands in an orthogonal relationship to lexicalization. Harnisch (2004: 211) provides a brief discussion describing the process of grammaticalization (characterized by reduction in status and desemanticization) as the opposite process of de-grammaticalization (characterized by an increase in status and specialization of meaning). Orthogonal to the axis of grammaticalization and de-grammaticalization is the axis of lexicalization (characterized by desegmentation and demotivation) and de-lexicalization (characterized by resegmentation and remotivation, i.e. folk etymology; see Michel 2025 on word-formation and folk etymology).

5 Grammaticalization of prefix and particle verbs

In verbal morphology the age of some particular unit can be determined on the basis of a variety of factors: (1) degree of morphological erosion, (2) degree of desemanticization, (3) stress pattern, (4) the fact that the word-formation element may be segmented.

Morphological erosion has evolved furthest in the case of the verbal prefixes *be-*, *ent-*, *er-*, *ver-*, *zer-* which originated in local adverbs/prepositions and developed into bound morphemes. These also show the highest degree of desemanticization in that they neither bear stress nor can be segmented within the sentence. The prefix verbs formed from them can be traced etymologically to adverbs/prepositions.

a) The prefix *be-*, with a short vowel, exists alongside OHG/MHG *bī* and NHG *bei* 'at, near'. It "starts out as a preposition, but loses its independence as early as Old High German, with the Old High German adverb *bī* assuming the prepositional function" (Pfeifer 2005: 107, s. v. *be-*; my translation). The original meaning is a local one, signalling an effect on an object, as, e.g., 'um ... herum' ('around') (e.g., MHG *belegen* 'to surround, encircle').
b) *ent-* is assumed to be traceable to a Proto-Germanic prefix **and(a)-* probably related to Old Indo-Aryan *ánti* 'opposite, in front of, near', whose original meaning 'against' is still discernible in NHG *entbieten* 'to offer' (Pfeifer 2005: 286 f., s. v. *ent-*).
c) The prefix *er-* can be traced back to OHG *ur-* (also *ar-*, *ir-*, *er-*) which is based on a Germanic preposition (OHG *ur*) that corresponds to the preposition/adverb *aus* 'from, out of'. The original local meaning 'out' or 'upwards' is still present in NHG *erheben* 'to raise', *erwachsen* 'to arise' (cf. Pfeifer 2005: 292, s. v. *er-*).
d) *ver-* derives from OHG *fir-*, *far-*, MHG *ver-*, combining three Gothic prefixes: got. *fra-* 'away', *faír-* and *faur-*. The meaning underlying these prefixes is an Indo-Germanic root noun **per* 'going beyond' which occurs in prepositions and adverbs (Pfeifer 2005: 1497 f., s. v. *ver-*). The local meaning is still discerni-

ble in NHG *verrücken* 'to push sth somewhere', *verschwinden* 'to disappear' or *verführen* 'to seduce'.

e) *zer-* is based on OHG *za-*, *zi-* and *zar-*, *zir-* whose meaning 'apart' belongs to Latin *dis-*, Indo-Germanic **dis-*, **du̯is-* 'apart' or **du̯is* 'twice' and can be seen in formations such as NHG *zerteilen* 'to cut up', *zerreißen* 'to tear apart' (cf. Pfeifer 2005: 1602 f., s. v. *zer-*).

Fritz (2011: 45 f.) outlines the history of language change pertaining to the system of prepositions, adverbs, prefixes and/or particles (or preverbs). The local meaning of what were originally free-standing prepositions has been preserved in a number of prefix verbs (see above). This pattern of word-formation has now ceased to be productive; in present-day German, the main function of prefix verbs is to signal aktionsart by specifying the temporal limits of verbal events. Thus, *er-* and *ver-* serve mainly to mark perfective or resultative aktionsart, as the case may be with *er-* (e.g., *etw. erarbeiten* 'to work on sth until it is successfully completed') and *ver-* (*etw. verändern* 'to change sth completely'); the same is sometimes true of *be-* (*jdn. besiegen* 'to defeat sb'). *ent-* and *zer-*, on the other hand, occupy semantic niches such as the meanings '(local) movement away from sth' (e.g., *enteilen* 'to hasten away'), 'repealing effect' (e.g., *entbinden* 'to release'), 'destruction' (e.g., *zerbrechen* 'to break') or 'damage' (e.g., *zerkratzen* 'to scratch').

In present-day German there are also a number of prefix verbs which are motivated by nominal or adjectival bases, but can be traced historically to verbal bases. Examples are *vergiften* 'to poison' with the base noun *Gift* which is historically related to the Middle High German verb *giften* 'to give, make a gift; poison' (DWB 4,1: 7444 f., s. v. *giften*); *zerkleinern* 'to cut up' with the adjectival base *kleiner* in the comparative degree, which is historically related to MHG/ENHG *kleinern* 'to make smaller' (DWB 5: 1107, s. v. *kleinern*). This means that, from a historical perspective, there has been no change in word class, although the loss of the unprefixed base verbs has resulted from a synchronic perspective in word class shifts between the base lexemes and the prefix verbs.

In addition, prefix verbs lead to changes in the valency patterns of the base verb via (1) transitivization (*über jmdn./etw. lächeln* 'to smile about sb/sth' > *etw. belächeln*), (2) syntactic incorporation involving changes in semantic roles (*Beeren* [patient] *auf den Kuchen* [directive] *legen* 'to put berries on the cake' > *den Kuchen* [patient] *mit Beeren* [instrument] *belegen*) or (3) reflexivization entailing a reduction in valency (*jmdn. in/an/auf/nach x fahren* 'to drive sb to x' > *sich verfahren* 'to lose one's way').

There are prefix verbs in German whose first element is composed of an unstressed particle which is inseparable from the verb in the sentence. Examples are verbs with *durch-* 'through', *über-* 'over', *um-* 'round', *unter-* 'under', *wider-*

'against' (e.g., *übersétzen* 'to translate', *unternéhmen* 'to undertake'). If the first element is stressed and separable, they belong to the class of particle verbs (e.g., *úmkehren* 'to turn round; lit. round-turn', *úntergehen* 'to go under; lit. under-go; to set; to be destroyed').

Particle verbs are less grammaticalized than prefix verbs. As late as Early New High German it was still common to separate the adverb/preposition and the verb in writing. In the literature on word-formation, particle verbs are sometimes referred to as "particle compounds" or "prefixoid formations".

Particle verbs with *ab*- 'off', *an*- 'on', *auf*- 'up', *aus*- 'from' (etc.) share some properties with prefix verbs but differ from them in other respects. Like prefix verbs, they are characterized by desemanticization, and they can form deadjectival or denominal derivatives and contribute to a restructuring of the base. Particle verbs too have a first element which can etymologically be traced back to an adverb or a preposition. But in contrast to prefix verbs, the prepositions are preserved in present-day German in an identical form (exception: particle *ein*- vs. preposition *in*).

For a while, adverbs, prepositions and particles were identical in form (e.g., *aus(-)* 'out; from' being a local adverb, a preposition and a bound morpheme representing a particle). In cases where adverbs, prepositions and bound particles are difficult to distinguish, "the word class 'adverb' undergoes formal re-marking by means of deictic derivation, with the deixis highlighting the local meaning" (Fritz 2011: 45; my translation). Deictic derivation is expressed by means of *her*- and *hin*- plus preposition (e.g., *her/hin* + *aus* → *heraus, hinaus* 'out of', etc.), resulting in directional adverbs which give rise to new verbal formations (e.g., *herauskommen* 'to come out; lit. out-come', *hinausgehen* 'to go out; lit. out-go').

In present-day German more or less homonymous prepositions exist alongside the bound particles of particle verbs (e.g., the preposition *aus* and the particle *aus*-); there is no morphological erosion of form here. In particle verbs the stress is on the particle which is separable and serves to form the verbal bracket. It is a reasonable assumption that the grammaticalization of particle verbs relates to the wider use of the verbal bracket in German.

Unlike prefix verbs, whose main function is to mark aktionsart, particle verbs continue to have a primarily local meaning (e.g., *anblinzeln* 'to blink at; lit. at-blink', *aufblicken* 'to glance up; lit. up-glance', *ausschlüpfen* 'to hatch out; lit. out-hatch', *nachrennen* 'to run after; lit. after-run'), so that the process of desemanticization has not progressed as far as in the case of prefix verbs. Furthermore they mark aktionsart (perfective or resultative, e.g., *abschätzen* 'to estimate', *auslernen* 'to finish learning'; inchoative or ingressive, e.g., *anreißen* 'to begin to rupture; lit. on-tear', *aufheulen* 'to begin to screech; lit. on-howl') and serve other functions

Tab. 12.5: Prefix verbs, particle verbs and verbs with a directional adverb and their functions.

Function/meaning of verbal derivative	Prefix verbs	Particle verbs	Particle verbs with a directional adverb
local meaning	no longer productive, few lexicalized formations	main function, with a tendency towards idiomatization	main function, with little idiomatization (as yet)
marking aktionsarten	main function	less frequent	rare
synchronic change in word-class	frequent	less frequent	rare
change in valency pattern	yes	yes	rare
separability (brace construction)	no	yes	yes
semantic niches	frequent	frequent	rare

which have arisen as a result of semantic processes such as metaphorization and metonymization.

With regard to the signalling of local functions, we can observe processes of idiomatization which have been at work since the Early New High German period when the particle verbs *ausgehen* and *umkommen*, used with personal subjects, meant, respectively, 'to go outside' and 'to get around somewhere' (cf. Habermann 2002: 48–52). Today the particle verb *ausgehen* has the additional semantic feature 'for a particular purpose, for pleasure', and *umkommen* has been fully idiomatized as 'to meet a violent death'. The purely local meaning 'out' is now realized by means of particle verbs in conjunction with directional adverbs: *heraus-gehen* 'to go out; lit. out-go', *herum-kommen* 'to get around; lit. around-get'. It was only during the Early New High German period that this process gradually got under way.

In present-day German, prefix verbs, particle verbs, and particle verbs with a directional adverb (such as *heraus-*) perform the range of functions exemplified in Table 12.5.

6 Conclusion

Countless word-formation elements found in present-day German have arisen historically from free lexemes which are no longer present today. The co-existence of free lexemes with their more or less homonymous corresponding bound forms can be observed in the present-day language. Even though new word-formation elements enrich a language's lexicon, the process of lexicalization is inextricably connected with grammaticalization. The use of word-formation elements for particular grammatical functions is of particular relevance in the area of particle-verb formation where particle-verbs are used to form a verbal bracket, while prefix verbs are not.

There are many open questions concerning the evolution of word-formation elements in German. Providing answers requires adequate data which reliably document the broad range of variation found at each of the various periods in the history of German. One of the major tasks of the diachronic corpora of German that are currently under compilation will be to help remedying the existing shortcomings in diachronic research.

7 References

Androutsopoulos, Jannis K. (1999): Grammaticalization in young people's language: The case of German. *Belgian Journal of Linguistics* 13: 155–176.

Diewald, Gabriele (2004): Entwicklungen und Fragen in der Grammatikalisierungsforschung. *Zeitschrift für germanistische Linguistik* 32: 137–151.

DWB = *Deutsches Wörterbuch von Jacob Grimm und Wilhelm Grimm*. 16 Vol. 1854–1971. Leipzig: Hirzel.

Eckardt, Regine (2012): Grammaticalization and semantic reanalysis. In: Claudia Maienborn, Klaus von Heusinger and Paul Portner (eds.), *Semantics. An International Handbook of Natural Language Meaning.* Vol. 3, 2675–2701. Berlin/Boston: De Gruyter Mouton.

Fandrych, Christian (1993): *Wortart, Wortbildungsart und kommunikative Funktion. Am Beispiel der adjektivischen Privativ- und Possessivbildungen im heutigen Deutsch*. Tübingen: Niemeyer.

Fleischer, Wolfgang and Irmhild Barz (2012): *Wortbildung der deutschen Gegenwartssprache.* 4th ed. Berlin/Boston: de Gruyter.

Flury, Robert (1964): *Struktur- und Bedeutungsgeschichte des Adjektiv-Suffixes -bar.* Winterthur: Keller.

Fritz, Matthias (2011): Verbalkomposition oder Präfixverb? In: Maurice Kauffer and René Métrich (eds.), *Verbale Wortbildung im Spannungsfeld zwischen Wortsemantik, Syntax und Rechtschreibung.* 2nd ed., 37–48. Tübingen: Stauffenburg.

Ganslmayer, Christine and Christian Schwarz (eds.) (2021): *Historische Wortbildung. Theorien – Methoden – Perspektiven*. Hildesheim: Olms (= Germanistische Linguistik 252–254).

Givón, Talmy (1979): *On Understanding Grammar.* New York: Academic Press.

Habermann, Mechthild (2002): Sprachwandel im Licht diachroner und synchroner Wortbildung. In: Mechthild Habermann, Peter O. Müller and Horst Haider Munske (eds.), *Historische Wortbildung des Deutschen*, 41–57. Tübingen: Niemeyer.

Habermann, Mechthild (2018): Gradation bei Adjektiven. Gradationselemente in Adjektivkomposita unter historischem und gegenwartssprachlichem Aspekt. In: Kerstin Kazzazi, Karin Luttermann, Sabine Wahl and Thomas A. Fritz (eds.), *Worte über Wörter. Festschrift zu Ehren von Elke Ronneberger-Sibold*, 143–164. Tübingen: Stauffenburg.

Harnisch, Rüdiger (2004): Verstärkungsprozesse: Zu einer Theorie der "Sekretion" und des "Re-konstruktionellen Ikonismus". *Zeitschrift für germanistische Linguistik* 32: 210–232.

Hartmann, Stefan (2016): *Wortbildungswandel. Eine diachrone Studie zu deutschen Nominalisierungsmustern*. Berlin/Boston: De Gruyter.

Henzen, Walter (1965): *Deutsche Wortbildung*. 3rd ed. Tübingen: Niemeyer.

Hopper, Paul and Elizabeth Traugott (1993): *Grammaticalization*. Cambridge: Cambridge University Press.

Inghult, Göran (1975): *Die semantische Struktur desubstantivischer Bildungen auf* -mässig. *Eine synchronisch-diachronische Studie*. Stockholm: Almqvist & Wiksell.

Killie, Kristin (2007): On the source(s) and grammaticalization of the Germanic *-lik* suffix. *Neuphilologische Mitteilungen* 108: 659–682.

Kluge, Friedrich (1925): *Abriß der deutschen Wortbildungslehre*. 2nd ed. Halle/S.: Niemeyer.

Kopf, Kristin (2018): *Fugenelemente diachron. Eine Korpusuntersuchung zu Entstehung und Ausbreitung der verfugenden N+N-Komposita*. Berlin/Boston: De Gruyter.

Lehmann, Christian (1995): [1982] *Thoughts on Grammaticalization*. München: LINCOM Europa.

Lehmann, Christian (2002): New reflections on grammaticalization and lexicalization. In: Ilse Wischer and Gabriele Diewald (eds.), *New Reflections on Grammaticalization*, 1–18. Amsterdam/ Philadelphia: Benjamins.

Lightfoot, Douglas (2005): Gestalt derivation in German. In: Torsten Leuschner, Tanja Mortelmans and Sarah De Groodt (eds.), *Grammatikalisierung im Deutschen*, 59–70. Berlin/New York: de Gruyter.

Luxner, Bernhard (2022): *Die althochdeutschen Adjektive auf* -aht(i)/-oht(i). *Eine diachron- und synchron-vergleichende Untersuchung*. Berlin/Boston: De Gruyter.

Meineke, Birgit (1991): *Althochdeutsche* -scaf(t)-*Bildungen*. Göttingen: Vandenhoeck & Ruprecht.

Michel, Sascha (2025): Word-formation and folk etymology. In: Peter O. Müller, Susan Olsen and Franz Rainer (eds.), *Word-Formation – Semantics and Pragmatics*, 21–42. Berlin/Boston: De Gruyter Mouton.

Möllmann, Ulrich (1994): *Die althochdeutschen Adjektive auf* -sam. Göttingen: Vandenhoeck & Ruprecht.

Nübling, Damaris, Antje Dammel, Janet Duke and Renata Szczepaniak (2013): *Historische Sprachwissenschaft des Deutschen. Eine Einführung in die Prinzipien des Sprachwandels*. 4th ed. Tübingen: Narr.

Nübling, Damaris, Antje Dammel, Janet Duke and Renata Szczepaniak (2017): *Historische Sprachwissenschaft des Deutschen. Eine Einführung in die Prinzipien des Sprachwandels*. 5th ed. Tübingen: Narr.

Oberle, Brigitta E. (1990): *Das System der Ableitungen auf* -heit, -keit *und* -igkeit *in der deutschen Gegenwartssprache*. Heidelberg: Winter.

Olsen, Susan (1986): "Argument-Linking" und produktive Reihen bei deutschen Adjektivkomposita. *Zeitschrift für Sprachwissenschaft* 5: 5–24.

Paul, Hermann (2006): *Deutsches Wörterbuch. Bedeutungsgeschichte und Aufbau unseres Wortschatzes*. 10th ed. by Helmut Henne, Heidrun Kämper and Georg Objartel. Revised and adapted for CD-ROM by Helmut Rehbock. Tübingen: Niemeyer.

Paul, Hermann, Thomas Klein, Hans-Joachim Solms and Klaus-Peter Wegera (2007): *Mittelhochdeutsche Grammatik*. 25th ed. *Mit einer Syntax von Ingeborg Schöbler* [!], *neubearbeitet und erweitert von Heinz-Peter Prell*. Tübingen: Niemeyer.

Pfeifer, Wolfgang (2005): *Etymologisches Wörterbuch des Deutschen. Erarbeitet im Zentralinstitut für Sprachwissenschaft, Berlin, unter der Leitung von Wolfgang Pfeifer.* 8th ed. München: Deutscher Taschenbuchverlag.

Pfeifer, Wolfgang et al.: *Etymologisches Wörterbuch des Deutschen* (1993). Digitalisierte und von Wolfgang Pfeifer überarbeitete Version im Digitalen Wörterbuch der deutschen Sprache. [Online available at: https://www.dwds.de/wb/etymwb/]

Ring, Uli (2008): *Substantivderivation in der Urkundensprache des 13. Jahrhunderts. Eine historisch-synchrone Untersuchung anhand der ältesten deutschsprachigen Originalurkunden*. Berlin/New York: de Gruyter.

Römer, Christine (2000): Processes of grammaticalization and lexicalization in Modern German word-formation. *Logos and Language* 1: 35–47.

Schmid, Hans Ulrich (1998): -lîh-*Bildungen. Vergleichende Untersuchungen zu Herkunft, Entwicklung und Funktion eines althochdeutschen Suffixes*. Göttingen: Vandenhoeck & Ruprecht.

Wilmanns, Wilhelm (1899): *Deutsche Grammatik. Gotisch, Alt-, Mittel- und Neuhochdeutsch. Zweite Abteilung: Wortbildung*. 2nd ed. Straßburg: Trübner.

Wischer, Ilse (2008): Zum kategorialen Status von Derivationsaffixen im Rahmen von Grammatikalisierungsprozessen. In: Thomas Stolz (ed.), *Grammatikalisierung und grammatische Kategorien*, 135–146. Bochum: Universitätsverlag.

Wischer, Ilse (2011): Grammaticalization and word formation. In: Heiko Narrog and Bernd Heine (eds.), *The Oxford Handbook of Grammaticalization*, 356–364. Oxford/New York: Oxford University Press.

Wischer, Ilse and Mechthild Habermann (2004): Der Gebrauch von Präfixverben zum Ausdruck von Aspekt/Aktionsart im Altenglischen und Althochdeutschen. *Zeitschrift für germanistische Linguistik* 32: 262–285.

Krystyna Kleszczowa

13 Grammaticalization in Slavic word-formation

Abstract: The processes of grammaticalization in the word-formation systems of the Slavic languages are triggered by intralinguistic determinants and the influence of foreign languages. The article presents an evolutionary approach to grammaticalization as a linguistic phenomenon of the past, present and predictable stages of languages.

1 Introduction

Grammaticalization is traditionally described as a process consisting in the transition of a lexical element (morpheme, word or word group) from the lexical to the grammatical system of language. Most monographs and encyclopedias (in Poland, e.g., Perlin 2004: 309) refer to Meillet's (1912) definition of grammaticalization as "the attribution of grammatical character to an erstwhile autonomous word" (cited in: Hopper and Traugott 2003: 19), or to Kuryłowicz (1975: 52): "Grammaticalization consists in the increase of the range of a morpheme advancing from a lexical to a grammatical or from a less grammatical to a more grammatical status, e.g., from a derivative formant to an inflectional one". As example from Slavic languages Kuryłowicz mentions "the evolution *collective* (*derivative*) > *plural* (*inflectional*)", as reflected, e.g., in the "fate of the collective suffix *-ja*, *-je*" (Russ. plur. *druz'-ja* from *drug* 'friend'). Hopper and Traugott (2003: 145–148) – with reference to Andersen (1987) – regard the evolution of the contemporary Polish past tense forms as a distinct example of morphologization. In this case parts of forms of the postponed auxiliary verb *być* 'to be' had become attached to the active past tense *l*-participle, cf., e.g., *mówiłem* 'I spoke' (1st pers. masc. sg.) < *mówił jeśm*, *mówiliśmy* < *mówili jesmy* (1st pers. masc. personal pl.).

Krystyna Kleszczowa, Katowice, Poland

https://doi.org/10.1515/9783111420530-013

When it comes to grammaticalization in word-formation, the phenomenon becomes even more complicated, since an ostensibly simple definition cannot provide information explicit enough to clarify it, requiring further specification. This stems from the specific character of word-formation, particularly Slavic word-formation (cf. Kleszczowa and Pastuchowa 2009), and also from the way in which the term *grammaticalization* is understood in the different linguistic approaches (Closs Traugott and Heine 1991; Hopper and Closs Traugott 2003; Molencki 2012). An element which has undergone the process of grammaticalization mostly does not change its lexical meaning, rather, what can be observed is a change in the status of its components: an originally autonomous component of the word-formation base or the underlying syntactic expression (e.g., prepositions or autosemantic lexemes) starts to be perceived as a formative (prefix or suffix) or an inflectional morpheme acquires the function of a derivational affix. It needs to be mentioned, however, that in Slavic studies, grammaticalization in word-formation is a rarely studied topic or rather a topic which is not referred to under this term. Here we see a significant difference compared to works on grammaticalization in the fields of aspect, modal words or definiteness/non-definiteness in the Slavic languages (cf., e.g., Bisang, Himmelmann and Wiemer 2004).

A grammatical rule is instantiated by a number of similar phenomena: only when a particular phenomenon is repetitive in either form or meaning we can refer to it as a case of grammaticalization. This statement may seem uncomplicated, however, it instantly provokes questions: How many elements must a series minimally consist of to be considered a series? Is each series a manifestation of grammaticalization? No one searches for grammaticalization in examples like Russian *spasibo* 'thank you' (← *spasi Bog* 'God save [you]') or Polish *bodaj(że)* 'probably; at least' and Slovak *bodaj(že)* 'may; introduction of an optative clause' (← *Bóg*/*Boh daj* 'God give') as these are isolated facts. Nonetheless, grammaticalization does not do justice to the Ukrainian series *probi*, *spasibi*, *magajbi*, *pomagajbi*, *dasťbi*, *prostybi* 'By God! May Heaven grant your attempt, God willing', because the morpheme *bi-* (← *Big*, with the variant *Bog*) does not contribute anything to these expressions by way of category values. Here we observe only lexicalization.

Independently of how we understand the term word-formation, whether it is "creating words" in a diachronic sense or "understanding words" in synchronic analyses, grammaticalization is a *process*, and what we experience is a change in a linguistic sign (a lexeme or a morpheme). As is customary for every process, grammaticalization too can be presented in the form of a scale – where the process from the initiation through all of its different stages including the end may be observed. Such a perspective serves a good purpose for all considerations made in this article. In the same manner, phenomena undergoing grammaticalization in the individual Slavic languages consist of various developmental stages.

Their analysis, without indicating in which language we have an initial stage and in which we find a considerably advanced or even a completed one, presents a general potential existing in all the Slavic language systems; it provides not only the results, but also the possibilities.

Since this article is concerned with linguistic change, the factors that trigger grammaticalization processes need to be addressed. Typically, they are part of the very nature of natural languages (which will be discussed in section 2) or have to do with the influence of foreign languages (analyzed in section 3). However, it needs to be emphasized that such a division serves only an organisational purpose since, in actual fact, language is constantly influenced by external factors (such as language contact). In turn, a reaction to external conditions is strictly dependent on the internal structure of the language.

Space limitations make it impossible to present the complete characteristics of grammaticalization at the word-formation level in the Slavic languages. For this reason we focus on the *processes* of grammaticalization and illustrate them with selected examples.

2 Intralinguistic determinants stimulating grammaticalization

One of the tasks which structuralists assigned to themselves was defining clear borderlines between linguistic levels. More careful consideration of this particular concept reveals that these borderlines in natural languages are blurred, that there exist gradual transitions between them which generate tension, and that this circumstance may stimulate shifts between two levels. It is of no surprise then that the source of new word-formation means may take its origin in phenomena occurring at various levels, particularly at the lexical and inflectional levels, or even at the level of word-formation itself. Let us investigate some relevant examples from the history of the Slavic languages.

2.1 From syntax to word-formation

A convincing example of the lexicalization of semantic constructions is the emergence of the numerals 11 to 19. As other languages belonging to the Indo-European group (compare: Lat. *quattuordecim*, It. *quattordici*, E. *fourteen*, *fifteen*, *sixteen*), the Slavic languages also experienced the fusion of Proto-Slavonic prepositional structures into one word: **dъva na desętе* '12; lit. two on ten', **tri na desętе* '13',

**četyre na desętе* '14', etc. Since the process occurred in a series composed of a number of elements, one may assume the emergence of a new formative, i.e. grammaticalization. Compare: Cz. *dvanáct, třináct*, Slk. *dvanásť, trinásť*, Pol. *dwanaście, trzynaście*, Kashubian *dwanôsce*, Lower Sorbian *dwanasćo*, Upper Sorbian *dwanasće*, Polabian *dvenədist/dvenədicti/dvenocte/dvenəcte*, Russ. *dvenadcať, četyrnadcať*, Ukr. *dvanadcjať, trinadcjať*, Serb. and Croat. *dvanaest, trinaest, četrnaest*, Sln. *dvanajst, trinajst*. In Bulgarian, the following official forms exist: *dvanadeset, trinadeset* along with the common forms *dvanajset, trinajset* (in careless pronunciation: *dvanajse, trinajse*).

It is obvious that the rule is not productive. We are dealing here with a closed series; however, it is a fact that out of the initial combination of the preposition *na* and the locative from **desętь* '10', the final parts of the numerals 11 to 19 have been reanalyzed as suffixes in the majority of Slavic languages. It needs to be noted that phonetic phenomena facilitated the grammaticalization in that the initial relations between the components were blurred. The role of phonetic change in the process of grammaticalization is clearly visible in the development of decimal numerals. Some Slavic languages have maintained the Proto-Slavonic pattern **dъva/tri/četyre desęti* lit. 'two/three/four ten', cf. Pol. *dwadzieścia* '20', *trzydzieści* '30', Serb. and Croat. *dvadeset, trideset*, Macedonian *pedeset* '50'. In others, phonetic changes have lead to the separation of the decimal numerals from their genetic background, the changes being obviously scalar, cf. Slk. *dvadsať, tridsať*, Russ. *dvadcať, tridcať*, Ukr. *dvadcjať, tridcjať*, Cz. *dvacet, třicet*. Note that these changes are still in progress and this is observable in common Bulgarian: along with official forms such as *petdeset* there exist forms of decimal numerals accompanied by elision of the final *-t* as in *dvajse, trijse, četirese, pedese, šejse* '60', *sedemdese* '70', *osemdese* '80', *devedese* '90', and, as a consequence, the (formal) relation to the basic numeral *deset* '10' has become opaque.

The negative prefix *ne-/nie-*, common in the Slavic languages, also has a syntactic origin. In comparison with a particle, the connectivity of a prefix is limited. What is more, the meaning of a lexeme newly created with the prefix does not always constitute a straight negation of the meaning of the stem (cf. Stramljič Breznik 2010: 70–79). For example, Ukr. *nedurnyj*, Russ. *neglupyj*, Pol. *niegłupi* are not antonyms of the adjectives *durnyj, glupyj, głupi* 'silly', since they mean 'not that silly, but not necessarily clever'; they may be interpreted as a kind of euphemism (Krysin 2000). Russ. *nemudryj* ('NEG-wise') means 'not too clever, simple-hearted' (euphemism), but Pol. *niedobry* ('NEG-good') and *niemądry* ('NEG-wise') are synonymous with *zły* 'evil' and *głupi* 'stupid'. The asymmetry between adjectives with and without the prefix *ne-* is confirmed by the following Ukrainian adjectives: *nesportyvna povedinka* 'unfair behaviour', *neordynarna ljudyna* 'unusual man', *nevytravnyj slid* 'indelible trace', in light of unacceptable combinations like: **sportyvna povedinka, *ordynarna ljudyna, *vytravnyj slid* (Karpilovs'ka 2007), similarly in Serbian, Croatian, Bosnian and Montenegrin: *neophodan* (cf. also German *unumgänglich*) 'inevitable', *neosporan* (cf. German *unbestreitbar*) 'indisputable' in comparison to such unacceptable forms as **ophodan, *osporan.*

One of the grammatical categories specific to the Slavic languages is aspect. There are verbs which signal an action continuing in time, no matter what grammatical tense is considered. That is why in Polish we have *piszę, pisał, będzie pisał*; Ukr. *pyšu, pysav, budu pysaty/pysatymu* 'I am writing, I was writing (m.), I will be writing'; on the other hand, there are perfective verbs (e.g., Russ. *na-pišu, na-pisal* (*pis'mo*) 'I will have written, I have written (m.) (a letter)'). The meaning of the perfective aspect is introduced by prefixes, e.g., Slk. *za-viazat* 'to tie', Cz. *při-nést* 'to bring', Kashubian *pòd-chòdzëc* 'to come', Serb. *za-braniti* 'to prohibit'. Prefixation (and perfectivization) is often accompanied by a lexical-semantic modification (e.g., Russ. *nadpišu, nadpisal* 'I will have superscribed, inscribed; he has superscribed; lit. over-written'; *vpišu, vpisal* 'I will have inserted/inscribed, he has inserted/inscribed'. Most of the verbal prefixes have the same form as prepositions. Hence, in the literature on the Slavic languages there is an approach that regards verbal prefixes as the result of the grammaticalization of prepositions (Słoński 1937; Horecký 1957; Bajec 1959; Böttger 2004; Tabačenko 2011). Here we have an example of the emergence of word-formation affixes on the basis of syntactic (prepositional) constructions (*pisat' v, nad* 'to write in, over', etc.).

2.2 From inflection to word-formation

The relations between inflection and word-formation have always been at the centre of attention in morphology, and the status of some categories is debatable. For example, regular deverbal formations such as Cz. *psaní* 'writing', *myšlení* 'thinking', Pol. *czytanie* 'reading', *chodzenie* 'walking', Kashubian *gôdanié, prawienié, gòwarzenié* 'telling/talking', are perceived by some scholars as an inflectional category (gerunds), whereas others treat them as a word-formation category (action nouns).

Another example of derivational suffix that goes back to inflection is the development of the Proto-Slavonic nominal declension with the stem -*ęt*. As early as in the Proto-Slavonic era, the words **telę*, genitive **telęte* 'calf', **jagnę*, gen. **jagnęte* 'lamb', **porsę*, gen. **porsęte* 'piglet', **žerbę*, gen. **žerbęte* 'colt' shared a common semantic feature – 'immaturity', however, the names were not derivationally correlated with the names of grown up or mature animals: **korva* 'cow', **ovьca/*baranъ* 'sheep/ram', **svinьji* 'pig', **konь* 'horse'. The inflectional type -*ę*/-*ęte* gained a word-formative value only when motivational relations appeared, e.g., Cz. *slon* 'elephant' → *slůně* 'baby elephant', *lev* 'lion' → *lvíče* 'baby lion', Slk. *kozol* 'goat' → *kozľa* 'goatling', Sln. *pès* 'dog' → *psè* 'puppy'. Out of this process, a new word-formation type emerged – converted nouns denoting offsprings (Kleszczowa 2008: 29–31), cf. Slk. *vlk* 'wolf' → *vľč-a* 'young wolf', *vnuk* 'grandson' → *vnúča* 'grandchild', Pol. *osioł* 'donkey' → *oślę* 'young donkey', *orzeł* 'eagle' → *orlę* 'young eagle', *wnuk* 'grandson' → *wnuczę* 'grandchild', Upper Sorbian *kurjo* 'chicken', *wjelčo* 'young wolf', *wroblo* 'young sparrow', *baćonjo* 'young stork', Lower Sorbian *zwěrjeśa* 'young animal', Ukr. *oslja* 'young donkey', *vnuča* 'grandchild', *vedmedja/medveža* 'young bear', Sln. *oslè* 'young donkey', *psè* 'puppy', *svinè* 'piglet', Serb. *siròče* 'orphan', *ùnuče* 'grandchild', Croat. *djevojče* 'young girl', *momče* 'boy', Bulg. *orle* 'young eagle', *petle* 'rooster', Macedonian *kozle*, *kote* (plural *koteta*) 'kitten' (Bernstein 1985: 239–259).

In Ukrainian, along with the examples of grammaticalization presented above (e.g., *vedmedja*, gen.sg. *vedmedjaty*; nom.pl. *vedmedjata*), stem extension by the morpheme *-(ь)n-* has occurred: *vedmed-en-ja* 'young bear'. In works on contemporary Ukrainian word-formation (cf. Žovtobrjux 1979: 98 ff.), this element is described as the suffix *-en-(ja)* which primarily derived nouns designating young animals, e.g., *ptašenja* 'young bird' ← *ptax* 'bird', *kozenja* 'billy-goat' ← *koza* 'she-goat' (the nouns in *-en-ja* are also inflected according to the paradigm of the old *t*-stems, e.g., *vedmedenja*, gen.sg. *vedmedenjaty*; nom.pl. *vedmedenjata*); similarly Belarus. *medzvedzjanja* 'young bear' (gen.sg. *medzvedzjanjaci*; *c* < *t*) ← *mjadzvedz* 'bear', *ptušanja* 'young bird' ← *ptuška* 'bird', *kazljanja* (nom.pl. *kazljanata*) ← *kazël* 'billy goat'. As stated in Žovtobrjux (1979: 99), Ukr. *-en-ja* also derived designations of children according to their ethnic or social affiliation (e.g., *turčenja* 'child of a Turk', *popenja* 'child of an orthodox priest'; also as surname *Popenja*), later it obtained a diminutive meaning in derivatives from inanimate nouns (e.g., *garbuz-enja* 'small pumpkin').

In Russian, the primary inflection of *t*-stems is preserved only fragmentarily in the plural (e.g., **telęta* > *teljata* 'calves'; *žerebjata* 'colts', etc.). In the singular (*telenok* 'calf', *žerebenok* 'colt'), however, the semantic value of 'young' was reinforced by the addition of the diminutive suffix *-ъkъ-* > *-ok-* (i.e. **telę-ъkъ* > *telenok*) which confirms that in Russian the grammaticalization did not develop on the base of an inflectional suffix alone, but was aided by a derivational suffix. Rarely, we find the suffix *-enok/-onok* also attached to personal nouns (*popenok* 'child of an orthodox priest'; as surname, e.g., *Pastušenok* lit. 'child of a shepherd'), cf. also the sovietism *oktjabrenok*, pl. *oktjabrjata* 'October Children' (a communist organization of young schoolchildren) ← *Oktjabr'* in the metonymic meaning of 'October Revolution'.

In the previous paragraphs we have presented a word-formation category that developed before the break-up of Proto-Slavonic. In this connection it is essential to mention an inflectional type which was subject not only to derivational changes, but also to inflectional ones already in the historic period. This is the Proto-Slavonic participle with the *-l-* suffix which became the base for inflectional forms of the past tense. The addition of new functions to the preterite active participle II was undoubtedly one of the initiating factors for the adjectivization of its complex inflection. This resulted in an elaborate array of forms for which opinions vary among linguists. Some perceive them as participles (as Pol. *posiwiały* 'grizzled' ← *posiwieć* 'to turn grey', *zeschły* 'dried' ← *zeschnąć* 'to dry (up)', *zsiadły* (*-e mleko*) 'sour (milk); lit. set (milk)'), while others consider them adjectives (e.g., Cz. *zamrzlý* 'frozen' ← *zamrznout* 'to freeze'), *uplynulý(rok)* 'last (year)' ← *uplynout* 'to flow away'; Ukr. *puxlyj* 'swollen' ← *puxnuty* 'to swell', *rozm'jaklyj* 'softened' ← *rozm'jaknuty* 'to soften', *zdyčilyj* 'wild' ← *zdyčity* 'to become wild', *skamenilyj* 'fossil' ← *skamenity* 'to change to stone, fossilize'; Russ. *okamenelyj* 'fossil', *odičalyj* 'wild', *razmjaklyj* 'softened', also Belarus. *akamjanely, zdzičely, razmjakly*; Bulg. *zaspal* 'asleep, sleepy, slow' ← *zaspja* 'to fall asleep', *xlătnal* 'concave' ← *xlătna* 'to cave in', *zakăsal* 'being in trouble' ← *zakăsam* 'to get into trouble'). There are also Slavic languages in which the original *l*-participle in attributive-adjectival function is only rudimentarily preserved, for instance, in those South Slavic languages which are based on Shtokavian dialects (that extend over the greater parts of the Bosnian, Serbian, Croatian and Montenegrin territory). What remains is: Serb. *prošla godina* 'last year; lit. having-passed-by year', *spožutelo lišće* 'yellow leaves; lit. having-become-yellow leaves', Croat. *spožutjelo lišće* 'id.' (Gugulanova 2005).

2.3 From compounding to affixation

The grammaticalization process may also consist in changing the grammatical status of elements in derivatives. A case in point are compounds formed in Proto-Slavonic with the first components **zъlo* 'evil' and **kolo* 'wheel' and the second deverbal component **dějь*, an agent noun (← **dějati* 'to do, act'); hence, we have **zъloděјь* 'malefactor', **koloděјь* 'wheelmaker, wheeler'. The following words were formed in this way: Pol. *dobrodziej* 'benefactor', Russ. *zlodej* 'malefactor', Ukr. *dobrodij*, Bulg. *zlodej, čarodej* 'magician; lit. magic-doer', *čudodej* 'miracle worker', Cz. *zloděj*, Slk. *čarodej, zlodej*. The next stage includes a change of status in the second part of the compound. Due to the fact that suffixation is the basic derivative process in Slavic, language change is triggered – the final fragment of a compound is understood at first as a "semi-suffix" (Kovalyk 1958) and subsequently as a true suffix. It is worth mentioning that in closely related languages we can observe the different stages of grammaticalization of this particular linguistic sign. And so, in the Russian words *lixodej* 'evildoer', *zlodej* 'malefactor', *čarodej* 'magician', *licedej* obsolete 'actor; lit. person-maker'; Ukr. *zlodij*, *čudodij* 'magician', *lycedij*, Belarus. *lixadziej*, *zlodzej*, *čaradzej*, the element *-dej/-dij/-dzej* is still considered part of a compound, because the verbs *dejat'*, *dijaty*, *dzejac'* 'to do, make' are still used (in colloquial language and dialects). In Bulgarian, *-dej* is interpretable only via the noun *dejstvie* 'action'. But in Polish the element *dziej-* functions only in words whose meaning differs from Proto-Slavonic **dějati* 'to do, act', cf. *dzieje* 'events, history', *dziejowy* 'referring to history', *dziejopis* 'historian, annalist'; that is why in the lexemes *dobrodziej* 'benefactor', *złodziej* 'malefactor, thief', *kołodziej* 'wheelmaker, wheeler', *bartodziej* 'bee-keeper' the final *-dziej* is considered a suffix.

The grammaticalization of a part of a compound is a process which operates in the following sequence: part of a compound > suffixoid > suffix, and its stages are determined by the functioning of the second part of a compound in the lexical system, as exemplified by **dějь*. Frequency and function are also significant for what can be observed in Russian compounds with *-obráznyj* and *-vidnyj* (the corresponding autonomous adjective *óbraznyj* means 'figurative', both go back to *obraz* 'shape, form; image'; *vidnyj* has the meaning 'conspicious; eminent', referring to *vid* 'appearance', but not to other meanings of the polysemous noun, like 'shape, form'). There are numerous lexemes where these parts acquire the meaning 'similar, having the form of, -like', e.g., *zigzagoobraznyj*, *zigzagovidnyj* 'in the form of a zigzag', *šaroobraznyj*, *šarovidnyj* 'globe-shaped, ball-shaped', *zmeevidnyj* 'serpentine, sinuous'. (They can be regarded as "the result of an as yet incomplete grammaticalization from independent items into affixes", similar to Engl. *-like*, cf. Shopen 2007: 58.) In words like *zmee-podobnyj* 'serpentine, sinuous' the second element is semantically identical with the adjective *podobnyj* 'similar'. In Polish we also observe formations with *-podobny*; however, there are not many of them, and the element is regarded as part of a compound; the meaning 'similar' in the equivalents of the above mentioned Russian examples is expressed by the suffix *-owaty* (*zygzak-owaty* 'in the form of a zigzag', *żmij-owaty* 'serpentine', cf. also *grušk-owaty* 'pear-shaped', but Russ. *gruševidnyj*).

Different rules apply to the grammaticalization process in negative-privative derivatives with *bez-/brez-*. This morpheme belongs genetically to the motivating word-formation base (it represents the preposition 'without'), and hence is also part of a syntactic construction, cf. Cz. *bez-bolest-ný* 'painless; lit. without-pain-ADJ' (← *bez bolesti* 'without pain'), *beznadějný* 'hopeless' (← *bez naděje* 'without hope'), Slk. *bezdetný* 'childless' (← *bez detí* 'without children'), *bezdomovský* 'homeless' (← *bez domova* 'without home'), Serb. and Croat. *bezbrižan* 'carefree' (← *bez brige* 'without care'), *bezdiman* 'smokeless' (← *bez dima* 'without smoke'), *bezdrvan* 'treeless' (← *bez drva* 'without trees'), Sln. *brezgotovinski* 'non-cash'

(← *brez gotovine* 'without cash'), *breznamenski* 'nameless' (← *brez namena* 'without name'), Macedonian *bezgrižen* 'careless' (← *bez griži* 'without care'), *bespaten* 'pathless' (← *bez pat* 'without road'), *bezmesen* 'meatless' (← *bez meso* 'without meat') (Sokołowski 2000). Having been constructed on the base of a prepositional phrase, the derivative is involved in relations with other lexemes in a word family, which may result in a double motivation. As a result of such processes, correlated pairs are produced, cf. Pol. *bezcelowy* ↔ *celowy* 'aimless – purposeful'; *bezczynny* ↔ *czynny* 'inactive – active'; similarly, the morpheme *bez* has with increasing frequency become understood as a prefix *bez-* meaning 'negation, absence of sth.', cf. Cz. *bezalkoholický* (= *nealkoholický* 'non-alcoholic'), *bezčinnost* (= *nečinnost* 'inactivity'), Slk. *bezúčinný* (= *neúčinný* 'ineffective'), Russ. *besporjadok* (= *neporjadok* 'mess, disorder'), *bezgramotnyj* (= *negramotnyj* 'illiterate'), Ukr. *bezsmak* (= *nesmak* 'disgusť), *bezščastja* (= *neščastja* 'misfortune, bad luck'), *bezčesť* (= *nečesť* 'dishonour'), Sln. *brezgotovinski* (= *negotovinski* 'non-cash'), Bulg. *bezsmislen* lit. 'without.sense-ADJ' (= *nesmislen* 'stupid'). We also observe the emergence of a new meaning of *bez-*/*bèz-*/*brez-*: initially belonging to the base it begins to be understood as a word-formative element (prefix). A different stage of grammaticalization can result in a different realization of the same meaning in closely related languages, cf. Russ. *bespokoiť* and Belarus. *nepokoic'* 'to bother; lit. to unquiet (trans.)' (Lukašanec 2010: 83).

3 Grammaticalization as a result of the influence of foreign languages

It is difficult to imagine a natural language free from the influence of other languages. Throughout their history, languages have absorbed foreign, mostly lexical, elements (usually such elements only). It is a well-known fact that over 90 % of the lexemes in the Slavic languages are involved in word-formation relations. Word-formation then can be considered as a mechanism arranging the multiplicity and diversity of the elements at the lexical level. If a language adopts foreign lexemes, it is therefore natural that mechanisms will emerge which organize their inordinate dispersion. Grammaticalization is one process whereby foreign lexemes are adapted to the word-formation system of the recipient language and integrated into existing word-formation categories. In other words, intralinguistic forces exist which influence the process of borrowing.

3.1 Strengthening of existing categories

Although there are no clear boundaries between word-formation and other levels of language, Slavic word-formation – like that of other languages – has given rise to a set of categories, e.g., place nouns, collective nouns, personal nouns, female nouns, etc. Therefore, when dealing with grammaticalization we can take into account the grammaticalization of those components of foreign words that correspond to the existing derivational and morphological categories of the Slavic languages.

The absorption of foreign elements, morphemes or parts of lexemes, and grammaticalization are conditioned by two factors: serial occurrence and the specific character of the recipient language system. The category "female" in Slavic languages is strongly linked to the morphemes *-ka*, *-ini*/*-yni*, *-ova* which are attached to masculine nouns. There is little chance then that the Slavic languages would form more words denoting females with the use of borrowed formatives, e.g., the English feminine suffix *-ess* (*actress*, *waitress*, *lioness*). Even if a lexeme appears which is patterned on this model, e.g., the Polish humorous *pisuardesa* 'a woman who collects charges for a public toilet', Bulg. *mutresa* 'gangster's concubine' (← *mutra* 'gangster'), such occasionalisms do not influence the word-formation system.

By contrast, the elements of loanwords which bear the agent noun meaning 'someone who does sth.' undergo the process of grammaticalization easily. Personal nouns belong to the most appropriately specified categories in the Slavic languages, including both distinct formatives going back to Proto-Slavonic and borrowed ones like *-ator*, *-ar*, *-er*, *-ant*, *-ent*. However, not only foreign suffixes have been adopted to express this category. The pressure of the system was so strong that parts of borrowed compounds were gradually reanalyzed as suffixes, e.g., the elements *-man*/*-men* in such lexemes as Slk. *barman* 'barman', *fachman* 'specialist', *finišman* 'finalist', *kameraman* 'camera operator', Pol. *biznesmen* 'buzinessman', *sportsmen* 'sportsman', *jazzmen* 'jazzman', Russ. *barmen* 'barman', *kongresmen* 'congressman', *sportsmen* 'sportsman', Belarus. *jaxtsmen* 'yachtsman', *džazmen* 'jazzman', Ukr. *rekordsmen* 'record holder', *šoumen* 'showman', Bulg. *kongresmen*, *jaxtsmen*. English borrowings are above all influential here, however earlier German loans have functioned as the source as well (e.g., Pol. *fachman* 'specialist' < Germ. *Fachmann*; *furman* 'carter' < Germ. *Fuhrmann*). The fact that female words are formed on the basis of words in *-man* '-man' + suffix *-k-a*, which is in contradiction to the origin of these elements, proves that they are considered suffixes. However, Slavic speakers have already shifted the meaning of *man* 'male human' to '(male) agent/person', therefore the corresponding female nouns are formed by adding the suffix *-ka* to the masculine word, cf. Pol. *sportsmenka*, *biznesmenka*, Slk. *barmanka, kongresmanka*, Ukr. *rekordsmenka, šoumenka*, Belarus. *spartsmenka, rekardsmenka*, Bulg. *biznesmenka, sportsmenka*, Croat. *kongresmenka*.

The element *-olog* is on the way to grammaticalization in such lexemes as Cz. *farmakolog* 'pharmacologist', *astrolog* 'astrologer', Pol. *filolog* 'philologist', *dermatolog* 'dermatologist', Ukr. *politolog* 'political scientist', *radiolog* 'radiologist', Serb. and Croat. *alergolog* 'allergologist', *kardiolog* 'cardiologist', Bulg. *anesteziolog* 'anaesthesiologist', *sociolog* 'sociologist'. Although it is still assumed that they are derived from words designating special fields of knowledge (e.g., Slk. *farmakológ* 'pharmacologist' ← *farmakológia* 'pharmacology', *alergiológ* 'allergologist' ← *alergiológia* 'allergology', *bakteriológ* 'bacteriologist' ← *bakteriológia* 'bacteriology'), such words function in large word-formation families, consequently next to the word *farmakológ* there are words such as *farmácia* 'pharmacy', *farmaceut* 'pharmacist', *farmaceutka* (f.), *farmaceutský* (relational adj.); next to Slk. *alergiológ* we find such words as *alergia* 'allergy', *alergický* (adj.); next to *bakteriológ – baktéria* 'bacterium', *baktériový* 'bacterial', *bakteriálny* 'id.', etc. Consequently, another possible motivation appears: *farmakológ* ← *farmácia, alergiológ* ← *alergia, bakteriológ* ← *baktéria*, where the element *-ológ* is regarded as agent noun suffix, similar to the above-mentioned *-men/-man* (Walczak-Mikołajczykowa 2000: 51–53). It is evident then that grammaticalization sometimes results from the involvement of some lexemes in word-families where new motivational relations appear, e.g., Bulgarian hybrid neologisms *pazarolog* 'expert in marketing' (← *pazar* 'market'), *čovekolog* 'expert in human nature' (← *čovek* 'man, human being'), occasional *ženolog* 'expert in women' (← *žena* 'woman').

An example of the grammaticalization of a part of a borrowed compound within the category of the collective nouns is *-teka*. The meaning of the Greek *thēkē* 'repository' has faded away, all that is left is the value 'collection of the objects designated by the base'. Examples are found in different Slavic languages, e.g., Slk. *videotéka*, Cz. *fonotéka*, Russ. *kartoteka* 'card index', Bulg. *biblioteka, videoteka*, Serb. and Croat. *filmoteka, videoteka*. Particularly telling are derivatives in which *-teka* introduces the collection of objects named in the base with native lexemes, e.g., Cz. *pivotéka* 'collection of beers' (← *pivo* 'beer'), Pol. *płytoteka* 'record library' (← *płyta* 'disc, record'), or borrowed lexemes other than internationalisms, e.g., Bulg. *čalgoteka* 'disco, club' (← *čalga* 'music', borrowed from Turkish *çalgı* 'musical instrument, music'), or Pol. *taśmoteka* 'collection of tape recordings' (← *taśma* 'tape' from Turkish *tasma* 'neckband').

In the above-mentioned examples we have dealt with final components of borrowed compounds which in the Slavic languages have turned into suffixes. At the same time, there is an inflow of new prefixes (as, e.g., *auto-/avto-* or *anti-/anty-*) which either displace original elements of Slavic compounds (*samo-* or *sebe-* 'self') or original prepositions (belonging to the motivating base, as, e.g., Cz. *proti*, Pol. *przeciw* 'against'), or may contribute to their grammaticalization.

3.2 Formation of new word-formation categories?

Grammaticalization does not duplicate existing meanings, but creates word-formation elements for new ones, as in the following types: 1) *-gate*/*-gejt*, e.g., Pol. *schnapsgate* 'alcohol scandal' containing the German loanword *schnaps* 'hard liquor', *ropagate* 'petrol scandal; lit. petrol-gate', Russ. *Kreml'gejt*, *Irangejt* 'scandals connected with the Kremlin, Iran', Bulg. *Kozlodujgejt* 'scandal connected with the atomic power station near Kozloduj', *telefongejt* 'scandal connected with the bugging of politicians' phones'; 2) *-manie*/*-mania*/*-manija*, e.g., Cz. *beatlemanie* 'admiration for the Beatles', *Havlomanie* 'admiration for Václav Havel', Pol. *zakupomania* 'shopmania'; Bulg. *cicomanija* 'admiration for women's breasts'; 3) *-holik*, e.g., Cz. *jablkoholik* 'lover of apples', *pivoholik* 'lover of beer', Slk. *čokoholik* 'chocaholic', Pol. *pracoholik* 'workaholic', *zakupoholik* 'shopaholic', Bulg. *rabotoholik* 'workaholic', *seksoholik* 'sexaholic'; 4) *-fil*, e.g., Cz. *amerikanofil* 'admirer of America', *čechofil* 'Czechophile', Bulg. *kinofil* 'film-fan', *natofil* 'advocate of NATO' (Avramova 2009; Waszakowa 2009).

Are we dealing in these cases with new word-formation categories? Are they word-formation phenomena (since they appear in long series) or merely lexical phenomena (Pastuchowa 2011)? It has happened in the past that initial elements with lexical features have formed a word-formation category. Therefore, such a possibility should not be disregarded either for final elements. The repeated use of such foreign patterns can result in the formation of new word-formation categories, or – as in the case of personal nouns – in new word-formation types with a specialized meaning, such as that of *-fil* '-lover' (e.g., Russ. *knigofil* 'bibliophile') as compared to the potential meaning of '-lover' in already existing types (e.g., *kniž-nik* 'id.').

5 References

Avramova, Cvetanka (2009): Projavi na internacionalizacija v slovoobrazuvaneto na bălgarskija knižoven ezik. In: Elena Koriakowcewa (ed.), *Przejawy internacjonalizacji w językach słowiańskich*, 77–88. Siedlce: Wydawnictwo Akademii Podlaskiej.

Bajec, Anton (1959): *Besedotvorje slovenskega jezika*. Vol. 4: *Predlogi in predpone*. Ljubljana: Slovenska akademija znanosti in umetnosti.

Bernstein, Samuel (1985): *Zarys gramatyki porównawczej języków słowiańskich. Alternacje. Tematy imienne*. Warszawa: Państwowe Wydawnictwo Naukowe.

Bisang, Walter, Nikolaus P. Himmelmann and Björn Wiemer (eds.) (2004): *What makes Grammaticalization? A Look from its Fringes and its Components*. Berlin/New York: de Gruyter.

Böttger, Katharina (2004): Grammaticalization the derivation way: The Russian aspectual prefixes *po-*, *za-*, *ot-*. In: Walter Bisang, Nikolaus P. Himmelmann and Björn Wiemer (eds.), *What makes Grammaticalization? A Look from its Fringes and its Components*, 187–212. Berlin/New York: de Gruyter.

Closs Traugott, Elizabeth and Bernd Heine (eds.) (1991): *Approaches to Grammaticalization*. Amsterdam/Philadelphia: Benjamins.

Gugulanova, Ivanka (2005): *Bălgarskite pričastija i deepričastija v slavjanski kontekst*. Sofija: Universitetsko izdatelstvo "Sv. Kliment Ohridski".

Hopper, Paul J. and Elizabeth Closs Traugott (2003): *Grammaticalization*. 2nd ed. Cambridge: Cambridge University Press.

Horecký, Ján (1957): O tvorení slovies predponami. *Slovenská Reč* 23: 141–155. http://www.juls.savba.sk/ediela/sr/1957/3/sr1957-3-lq.pdf [last access 15 March 2015].

Karpilovs'ka, Jevgenija (2007): Pryxovani (zgornuti) ta vidkryti vybirni leksemni kategoriї: Dynamika slovotvirnyx markeriv. In: Hanna Burkhardt and Alicja Nagórko (eds.), *Sprachliche Kategorien und die slawische Wortbildung*, 45–59. Hildesheim: Olms.

Kleszczowa, Krystyna (2008): Destrukcyjne skutki produktywności znaków i reguł słowotwórczych. In: Jevgenija Karpilovs'ka (ed.), *Dynamika ta stabil'nisť leksyčnyx i slovotvirnyx system slov'jans'kyx mov. Tematyčnyj blok. XIV Mižnarodnyj z'їzd slavistiv. 9.–16. 9. 2008, Ohrid, Respublika Makedonija*, 23–36. Kyїv: Viddrukovano u naukovo-vydavnyčomu centri Nacional'noї biblioteky Ukraїny imeny V. I. Vernads'kogo.

Kleszczowa, Krystyna and Magdalena Pastuchowa (2009): Word formative grammaticalization. *Issledovanija po slavjanskim jazykam* 14(1): 63–72.

Kovalyk, Ivan (1958): *Pytannja imennykovogo slovotvoru v sxidnoslov'jans'kyx movax u porivnjanni z inšymy slov'jans'kymy movamy*. L'viv: Vydavnictvo L'vivs'kogo universytetu.

Krysin, Leonid P. (2000): Evfemizmy v sovremennoj russkoj reči. In: Elena A. Zemskaja (ed.), *Russkij jazyk konca XX stoletija (1985–1995)*, 384–408. Moskva: Jazyki russkoj kul'tury.

Kuryłowicz, Jerzy (1975): The evolution of grammatical categories. In: Jerzy Kuryłowicz, *Esquisses linguistiques*. Vol. 2, 38–54. München: Fink.

Lukašanec, Aleksandr A. (2010): O nekotoryx aspektax sopostavitel'nogo izučenija slovoobrazovanija v blizkorodstvennyx jazykax. In: Elena Koriakowcewa (ed.), *Aktualne problemy komparatystyki słowiańskiej. Teoria i metodologia badań lingwistycznych*, 81–88. Siedlce: Wydawnictwo Akademii Podlaskiej.

Molencki, Rafał (2012): *Causal Conjunctions in Mediaeval English. A corpus-based study of grammaticalization*. Katowice: Uniwersytet Śląski: WW Oficyna Wydawnicza.

Pastuchowa, Magdalena (2011): Lexicalization and grammaticalization – similarities and differences. *East European Studies* 27: 185–207.

Perlin, Jacek (2004): *Metodologia językoznawstwa historycznego*. Warszawa: Dialog.

Shopen, Timothy (ed.) (2007): *Language Typology and Syntactic Description*. Vol. 3: *Grammatical Categories and the Lexicon*. 2nd ed. Cambridge: Cambridge University Press.

Słoński, Stanisław (1937): *Funkcje prefiksów werbalnych w języku starosłowiańskim (starobułgarskim)*. Warszawa: Nakład Towarzystwa Naukowego Warszawskiego.

Sokołowski, Jan (2000): *Słowiańskie derywaty imienne z przyimkiem negacji w podstawie słowotwórczej*. Wrocław: Wydawnictwo Uniwersytetu Wrocławskiego.

Stramljič Breznik, Irena (2010): *Tvorjenke slovenskega jezika med slovarjem in besedilom*. Maribor: Univerzitetna knjižnica.

Tabačenko, Ludmila V. (2011): O kompleksnom podxode k issledovaniju dinamiki vnutriglagol'noj prefiksacii. *Vestnik PSTGU III: Filologija* 2(24): 72–79.
Walczak-Mikołajczykowa, Mariola (2000): *Słowotwórstwo agentywnych nazw osobowych w języku polskim, rosyjskim i bułgarskim*. Poznań: Publishing House of the Poznan Society for the Advancement of the Arts and Sciences.
Waszakowa, Krystyna (2009): Internacjonalizacja polskiej leksyki – stan obecny, prognozy na najbliższą przyszłość. In: Elena Koriakowcewa (ed.), *Przejawy internacjonalizacji w językach słowiańskich*, 11–28. Siedlce: Wydawnictwo Akademii Podlaskiej.
Wischer, Ilse (2011): Grammaticalization and word formation. In: Bernd Heine and Heiko Narrog (eds), *The Oxford Handbook of Grammaticalization*, 356–364. Oxford: Oxford University Press.
Žovtobrjux, Myxajlo A. (ed.) (1979): *Slovotvir sučasnoï ukraïns'koï literaturnoï movy*. Kyïv: Naukova dumka.

David Pharies

14 The origin of suffixes in Romance

Abstract: The following is meant to be an exhaustive account of the categories of suffix origins in the Romance languages. It will be shown that the Romance inventory of suffixes is primarily based on the large number of patrimonial Latin suffixes which have, in many cases, served as points of departure for the development of new suffixes, mostly through reanalysis and semantic or grammatical change. Borrowed suffixes – an important secondary source – have likewise continued to evolve according to the same principles once they are accepted into the inventory.

1 Previous works on suffix typology

Most accounts of Romance suffixation are organized on the basis of phonological criteria rather than according to type of origin. Rohlfs' (1969) account of Italian word-formation, for example, is organized alphabetically according to consonantal nuclei. Moll (1952) and Tekavčić (1980) respectively list Catalan and Italian suffixes alphabetically by Latin etymon, while Alemany Bolufer (1920) lists suffixes alphabetically in Spanish. Only Nyrop's (1979) study of French suffixes is organized according to rudimentary etymological criteria. Among the sections that make up his chapter on nominal suffixes, for example, are the following: Latin suffixes of popular formation (*raisonn-able* 'reasonable'), Latin suffixes of learned formation (*ador-ation* 'adoration'), suffixes of foreign origin (*vieill-ard* 'old codger'), suffixes formed in French *napp-eron* 'doily'), and suffixes of unknown origin (*sal-igaud* 'filthy pig').

Aside from Marchand's (1969) account of English, which offers a section entitled "origins of suffixes" alongside an alphabetic presentation, the earliest typology is that of Stein (1970). The article is difficult to follow given Stein's employment of Coseriu's theory of word-formation, whose terminology Trips (2009: 10) aptly

David Pharies, Gainesville, USA

https://doi.org/10.1515/9783111420530-014

describes as "more than confusing and not very helpful". Nevertheless, one eventually gleans the following list of possible suffix origins: 1) degradation of a lexeme to a lexical morpheme, i.e. grammaticalization (Engl. *king-dom* whose final element reflects earlier *doom* 'jurisdiction'), 2) transformation of an inflectional ending into a derivational suffix (Germ. *tags* 'during the day' from the genitive *des Tages* 'of the day'), 3) borrowings from modern languages (Engl. *-kin* < Dutch *-kîn*), 4) borrowing from older stages (Fr. *-tion* < Lat. *-tiō, -ōnis*), 5) combinations of suffixes (Fr. *chevalerie* 'cavalry' ← *cheval* 'horse' + *-ier* + *-ie*), 6) irradiation (an idiosyncratic use of this term, see Rainer 2002: 116 for discussion), through which a part of a word becomes a suffix (Engl. *cafeteria*, hence *washateria*), 7) a poorly defined category called "spontaneous origin" (Engl. *Jack-y*, Germ. *Hans-i*), 8) grammatical expansion to formerly inadmissible stems (Fr. *-eur*, originally verbal, as in *flatteur* 'flatterer' ← *flatter* 'flatter', which expands to admit nominal stems, cf. *chroniqueur* 'chronicler' ← *chronique* 'chronicle'), 9) morphological reanalysis (Engl. *tricks-y* 'playful', reanalyzed as *trick-sy*, analogically motivating *tip-sy*), 10) change in the grammatical category of the derivative, typically through ellipsis (Lat. *faber ferr-ārius* 'iron artisan' > *ferrārius, -iī* 'id.') and 11) semantic change (Germ. *Dichter-ling* lit. 'small poet' > 'unskilled poet').

Haspelmath (1994: 1) recognizes only two overall suffix-generating processes, one syntagmatic, i.e. "the reduction of a previously free word and its attachment to a non-reduced word" (a process that he calls "agglutination" but which would now be called "grammaticalization"), the other paradigmatic, i.e. "a new way in which speakers understand the structure of a word by relating it to other words in a different, novel way" (called "reanalysis"). Haspelmath focuses entirely on the latter, subdividing it into three subcategories. The first two of these, "affix telescoping" and "conglutination", are poorly distinguished from each other, as shown by the fact that the development of Fr. *-erie* is cited as an illustration of both types. In affix telescoping, according to Haspelmath, a secondary derivative is related by speakers to a primary base rather than to an immediate base, as when, on the pattern of *tuile* 'tile' → *tuilier* 'tilemaker' → *tuil-er-ie* 'tile-making works', the word *conserv-erie* 'canned food factory' is created directly from *conserve* 'canned food'. In conglutination, an inner affix and an outer affix are combined in such a way that the inner affix becomes formally if not semantically a part of the outer affix, as when, on the pattern of (*bijou* 'jewel' →) *bijout-ier* 'jeweler' → *bijout-er-ie* 'jeweler's shop', the new derivative *orfèvr-erie* 'goldsmith's shop' is formed directly from *orfèvre* 'goldsmith'. Whatever their supposed semantic differences, both phenomena depend on the misidentification of the primary base, and the additional examples cited do not clarify the distinction he is trying to make. Haspelmath's third category is called "secretion", whereby a part of a root is reanalyzed as part of an affix, cf. Fr. *fruit-ier* 'fruit grocer' is reanalyzed as *frui-tier*, making possible *bijou-tier* 'jeweler' (← *bijou* 'jewel').

In 2004, thirty-four years after the appearance of Stein's article, Heidermanns published an article with the same title ("Zur Typologie der Suffixentstehung" [On the typology of suffix origins]) in the same journal (*Indogermanische Forschungen*). Heidermanns's primary interest is the degree to which lexemes, inflectional endings and derivational affixes may trade categories (2004: 6–11). He discovers that the great majority of changes proceed in the direction of lost autonomy and greater integration, i.e. from lexeme to affix (Engl. *kingdom*, cited above) and lexeme to inflection (Lat. *cantāre habeō* 'I must sing' > Fr. *chanterai* 'I will sing').

Rainer's (2002) article is meant as a study of the ways in which the Romance languages converge and diverge among themselves in terms of word-formation, but as such it makes abundant reference to affix origins. Most importantly, he focuses on semantic change, offering considerable expansion and refinement of the category in that he distinguishes among three overall types, each with its own internal structure. The first type, called "reinterpretation", has four subtypes: semantic extension (the augmentative suffix *-azo*, as in *cochazo* 'large car', from *coche* 'car', is extended to loud sounds, as in *trompetazo* 'trumpet blast', from *trompeta* 'trumpet', ellipsis (as in *ferrārius*, cited above), folk etymology (Fr. *prieur*, descendent of Lat. *prior*, *-ōris* 'the first', is interpreted as an agentive derivative of *prier* 'to pray', i.e. as 'one who prays') and reanalysis (Fr. *chasseur* 'hunter', a derivative of the verb *chasser* 'to hunt' is associated instead with the noun *chasse* 'hunt', creating the pattern for deriving *chroniqueur* from *chronique*, in the absence of a verb **chroniquer*). The other two types of semantic change cited by Rainer are "approximation", through which the suffix of *lobezno* 'wolf cub', applied originally only to wild animals (as here, to *lobo* 'wolf'), is extended to certain undesirable humans, e.g., *rufezno* 'young ruffian' (← *rufián* 'rogue'), and grammaticalization, exemplified by *-mente*.

Besides semantic change, Rainer also mentions, among other possible suffix origins, resegmentation (Fr. *fruit-ier* 'fruit grocer', from *fruit* 'fruit', is interpreted as *frui-tier*, hence *cocotier* 'coconut tree', from *coco* 'coconut'), contamination or blend, cf. the Friulian feminine agentive ending *-trissa*, a blend of *-trice* and *-issa*), apophony (Sp. *-ungo*, patterned on pre-existing *-engo*, *-ango*, and *-ongo*), and borrowing, both learned and vernacular.

Rainer's analysis is unusual in classifying reanalysis as a form of semantic change. It may be true that associating *chasseur* with *chasse* rather than *chasser* involves a change in the semantic interpretation of the word, but if so, it is an exceedingly subtle change. Conversely, it is interesting that Rainer views contamination and blending of suffixes to be a category separate from semantic change.

As I show below, contamination and merger of suffixes are often accompanied by semantic changes.

In a subsequent article, Rainer (2005) further develops the categories of semantic change. To the category of "reinterpretation" mentioned above, he adds both "adaptation", whereby a semantically void or archaic formative is infused with a new meaning (the Latin distributive suffix *-(e)nus* is adapted to designate ordinals, cf. Sp. *catorceno* 'fourteenth' and Old Lombard *setén* 'seventh' < *septēni*), and also "regrouping", whereby the constituents of a word are syntactically recategorized, a phenomenon for which Rainer gives no suffixal examples. Similarly, "approximation" is divided into two subtypes, according to whether the semantic change is located at the level of pattern or base. The best example of the former is the prefix *mega-*, which according to Rainer was assigned the meaning 'one million *x*' at a scientific conference in 1960, a change that took place independently of any specific derivative in *mega-*. Exemplifying change at the level of base – the normal arrangement – is Sp. *-era*, whose base may designate either the thing contained in a receptacle (*chequera* 'checkbook', which contains *cheques* 'checks'), or the carrier of the receptacle (*mariconera* 'man's purse', carried by a *maricón* 'homosexual man').

2 Typology of Romance suffix origins

The catalog of suffix origins presented below is based largely on the list I developed for Pharies (2004), but with some modifications and clarifications. The main difference resides in the selection of examples, which are no longer limited to Spanish but taken from a variety of Romance languages. Another difference is that, while I still aim to identify all possible suffix origins, no attempt is made to identify all possible examples of each origin. As we shall see, most Romance suffixes turn out to be continuations of Latin suffix ancestors, sometimes preserving their original traits largely unchanged, but more often exhibiting more or less significant changes, whether in formal, semantic, or grammatical parameters. We will also identify a large number of borrowed suffixes – both learned and vernacular – and make the discovery that many of these, too, have continued to evolve within Romance.

2.1 Patrimonial suffixes

The Romance languages are merely the current forms of a linguistic entity that has existed for thousands of years, and which was first documented a little over two millennia ago when it was commonly known as Latin. The question of Romance suffix origins, then, is defined for a purely practical reason, i.e. the lack of documentation before the Latin stage, as an etymological account of the suffix inventory of the current forms of this entity as compared with the Latin inventory. The first step in this comparison is to consider the degree to which contemporary inventories include patrimonial suffixes, i.e. continuations of Latin suffixes.

Most patrimonial suffixes undergo significant changes in the course of their transmission into Romance, but a very few can be said to have suffered no changes or very minor changes other than regular phonological change. Some Latin suffixes seem to have survived both grammatically and semantically intact, for example, *-aster* (Sp. *hermanastro* 'step-brother', It. *figliastro* 'step-son', Fr. *marâtre* 'step-mother'), *-menta* (It. *vestimenta* 'women's attire', OFr. *ossemente* 'bones', Sp. *cornamenta* 'horns') and *-ōsus* (Sp., It. *amoroso*, Fr. *amoureux* 'amorous').

2.1.1 Grammatical change

Many patrimonial suffixes undergo grammatical changes, especially in terms of input and output categories, in the course of the evolution of the Romance languages.

The Latin adjective suffix *-ānus*, for example, which admits primarily noun stems (*urbānus* 'urban' ← *urbs*, *-bis* 'city'), differs from its Romance reflexes in their expanded list of admissible input categories, cf. Ital. *sottano* 'inferior' from the adverb *sotto* 'under' and Sp. *lejano* 'distant', from the adverb *lejos* 'far'. Another example: Lat. *-tor*, used in Latin primarily to derive agent nouns from verbs (*victor*, *-ōris* 'victor' ← *vincō*, *-ere* 'to emerge victorious'), has evolved in its Spanish reflex such that it now admits noun stems (*agua* 'water' → *aguador* 'water carrier'). In the Romance reflexes of Lat. *-āneus*, conversely, there has been a change in permissible output. Whereas the suffix was employed in Latin to derive adjectives from a variety of stems, including nouns (*oppidāneus* 'pertinent to a town' ← *oppidum*, *-ī* 'town'), in Romance it has evolved to produce nouns as well, as shown by Sp. *cestaño* 'small basket' (← *cesta* 'basket'), *picaño* 'rogue' (← *picar* 'to bite, sting').

In the evolution of Fr. *-aie* 'planted area', there is a reinterpretation of a Latin suffix in terms of gender and number, as its Latin etymon *-ēta* is a neuter plural that is reinterpreted in French as a feminine singular, cf. *olivaie*, *oliveraie* 'olive grove' (← *olive*), *oseraie* 'osier or willow plantation' (← *osier* 'osier, willow').

2.1.2 Semantic change

We find semantic changes among Romance patrimonial suffixes corresponding to many of the categories spelled out by Rainer. In several cases, for example, it appears that, after an ellipsis has the effect of deriving nouns from adjectives, suffixes take on meanings associated with their bases. Thus, the Latin adjectival suffix *-alis* (as in *nāvālis* 'nautical, naval' ← *nāvis, -is* 'ship'), acquires in Spanish the meaning 'area populated by a certain kind of plants' through the following sequence of associations: *junco* 'rush' → *juncal* 'relative to rushes' → *campo juncal* 'rush bed' → *juncal* 'id.'. Also through ellipsis, the suffix of pertinence, color and material *-ineus* (as in *lactineus* 'milk-colored' ← *lac, lactis* 'milk'), extends its reach to inhabitant names in *cacereño* '(person) from Cáceres' through the association 'pertinent to Cáceres' → 'inhabitant of Cáceres'. This change is also documented in Italian, cf. *mornesigni* 'inhabitant of Mornese' (← *Mornese*).

Another notable case whereby a suffix takes on the meaning of its base through ellipsis is that of Sp. *-azo*. Originally augmentative (*plumazo* 'large pillow' ← *pluma* 'feather'), the suffix takes on the secondary meaning 'blow with an object' when it is inserted into collocations such as *dar azotes* lit. 'give whips', an ellipsis of *dar golpes de azote* 'to give blows with a whip'. Initially, the effect of adding the augmentative suffix *-azo* (*dar azotazos*) is to suggest giving blows with a large whip. Subsequently, the meaning 'blow' is transferred from the base to the suffix, such that *dar azotazos* comes to mean 'to give violent blows with a whip'.

Another mechanism of semantic change is metonymy. Spanish, for example, inherited the patrimonial meaning 'offices and titles' from Lat. *-ātus* (*consul-ātus, -ūs* 'consulate'), then extended this meaning metonymically to include the territory pertaining to the title (*cond-ado* 'county' ← *conde* 'count'), the duration of the office (*rein-ado* 'reign' ← *reino* 'reign') and the collective of persons holding the office (*profesor-ado* 'faculty' ← *profesor* 'teacher'). Another example is the suffix of quality nouns *-itiēs, -ēi* (*amār-itiēs, -ēi* 'bitterness' ← *amārus* 'bitter'), which in Spanish metonymically expanded its range from the quality itself (*rojo* 'red' → *roj-ez* 'redness') to status nouns that entail the quality derived on noun bases, including age (*niñ-ez* 'childhood' ← *niño* 'child') and social standing (*viud-ez* 'widowhood' ← *viudo* 'widow'). Finally, the presence of the augmentative Latin suffix *-ūtus* in derivatives referring to parts of the body (*nas-ūtus* 'having a large nose' ← *nāsus, -ī* 'nose') leads analogically to Italian derivatives denoting 'undesirably large' body parts, as in It. *corp-uto* 'corpulent' (← *corpo* 'body') and *panci-uto* 'potbellied' (← *pancia* 'belly'). In general, both diminutive and augmentative suffixes may be expected to develop pejorative overtones through metonymy, as they are applied to bases that are not expected to be small (*profesor-cito* 'inconsequential little teacher' ← *profesor* 'teacher') or large (*orej-ón* 'ridiculously large ear' ← *oreja* 'ear').

Also representing the metonymic category is It. *-ino*, Port. *-inho*, diminutive suffixes that derive from Lat. *-īnus*, whose function was to derive relational adjectives from noun bases (*equīnus* 'concerning horses' ← *equus, -ī* 'horse'). Meyer-Lübke (1923, § 452) explains the semantic change as follows: "Mais alors le sens de 'ressemblance' exprimé par l'adjectif s'est développé dans une direction toute différente; un objet analogue à un autre fut considéré comme inférieur à lui, comme plus petit, et voilà comment *-inu*, dans l'italien et le portugais notamment, est devenu un suffixe diminutif très employé." [But then the sense of 'similarity' expressed by the adjective developed in a completely different direction; an object similar to another was considered inferior to it, as smaller, and this is how *-inu*, notably in Italian and Portuguese, became a commonly employed diminutive suffix.] Examples: It. *bandierina* 'pennant' (← *bandiera* 'flag'), *tavolino* 'small table' (← *tavola* 'table'); Port. *copinho* 'small cup' (← *copo* 'cup'), *filhinho* 'little son' (← *filho* 'son').

In the two articles summarized above, Rainer provides excellent examples for three of the remaining categories, i.e. folk etymology (Fr. *prieur*), approximation (Sp. *lobezno*), and adaptation (Lat. *-(e)nus*). Another example of approximation is Sp. *-uno*, from Lat. *-ūnus*, formerly *-ūgnus*, a rare suffix forming adjectives of pertinence to animals, cf. *caprū(g)nus* 'pertinent to goats' (← *caper, -prī* 'goat'), in Spanish extended pejoratively to persons, cf. *hombruna* 'said of a mannish woman' (← *hombre* 'man'). There is an additional source of suffixal semantic change not mentioned by the theorists cited above, i.e. interaction between or among suffixes in the form of contamination or even merger. The case of It. *-aggine*, for example, might be characterized as semantic change through contamination. A reflex of Lat. *-āgō, -āgine*, It. *-aggine* was originally employed as a phytonymic suffix (*piantaggine* 'plantain' < Lat. *plantāgō, -āginis* 'id.' ← *planta -ae* 'seedling'), only to be mysteriously extended to the derivation of names of negative qualities and defects, as in *balordaggine* 'stupidity' (← *balordo* 'stupid'), *testardaggine* 'stubbornness' (← *testardo* 'stubborn'). As both Rohlfs (1969, § 1058) and Meyer-Lübke (1923, § 428) recognize, this transformation is due to contamination by the apophonic cousin of *-āgō*, namely *-īgō*, which has precisely this function in *vertīgō, -inis* 'dizziness' (← *vertō, -ere* 'to spin') and *impetīgō, -inis* 'scaly skin eruption' (← *petō, -ere* 'to attack'). Another possible case of semantic contamination is that of the Spanish action-noun suffix *-zón*, i.e. the popular result, beside learned *-ción*, of Lat. *-tiō, -ōnis* (cf. *laudātiō, -ōnis* 'act of praising'). This verbal ending may have taken on a connotation of intensity in some derivatives due to contamination with the nominal augmentative suffix *-ón* (< *-ō, -ōnis*), cf. *virazón* 'sudden change of wind' (← *virar* 'to turn'), *tragazón* 'gluttony' (← *tragar* 'to swallow').

Semantic change through actual merger is exemplified by Fr. *-aille*, which as a result of Lat. *-āculum* designates instruments (*tenailles* 'pliers'), places and objects, but also designates collectives (*funérailles* 'funeral rites') as a result of a merger with Lat. *-ālia*, the neuter plural form of the adjective suffix *-ālis* (here, Church Lat. *funeralia* 'id.'). Another example is Port. *-ão*, which as a reflection of *-ānus* designates inhabitants, as in *castelão* 'castellan' (< *castellānus*), and as a reflection of *-ō, -ōnis* large size or intensity (*abelhão* 'bumblebee' ← *abelha* 'bee'). Notably, when two merging suffixes are synonymous, no semantic change is detectable. This is the case of It. *-igiano* (as in the inhabitant name *parmigiano* 'from Parma'), of which Rohlfs (1969, § 1071) states: "Questo suffisso è sorto dalla fusione di due elementi di derivazione, precisamente *-ensis* (> *-ese*) ed *-anus*." [This suffix arose from the fusion of two derivational elements, namely *-ensis* (> *-ese*) and *-anus*.]

Finally, Malkiel (1988: 238) reports a case of semantic change through borrowing, i.e. the acquisition of a locative sense by Sp. *-dor* (*mirador* 'overlook', *comedor* 'dining room') through the influence of Provenzal, where it originated in the coalescence of agentive *-tor* and locative *-tōrium*.

2.1.3 Reanalysis

As indicated in our review of the literature, the term *reanalysis* refers to a paradigmatic reinterpretation of the internal structure of words. This process typically involves the addition of material to a pre-existing suffix to produce a new, longer suffix.

A number of Spanish suffixes result from the reanalysis of the Latin unstressed diminutive suffix '*-ulus* and its allomorph '*-culus*. In the case of *-ancho*, the source of new material is the rare and archaic suffix *-anco*, such that the compound suffix *-anc-ulus* produces the pejorative suffix *-ancho*, cf. *corp-ancho* 'body' (< **corp-anc-ulu* < *corpus, -oris* 'cuerpo'). In the remaining cases, the allomorph '*-culus* is combined with stem material to produce a new suffix. For example, '*-culus* is reanalyzed as *-iculus* in such words as *ovi-cula, -ae* 'little sheep' (← *ovis, -is* 'sheep') and *vermi-culus, -ī* 'little worm' (← *vermis, -is* 'worm'), creating the suffix seen in *rufian-ejo* 'punk' (← *rufián* 'rogue') and *caball-ejo* 'small horse' (← *caballo* 'horse'). Similarly, when '*-culus* is combined with the endings of words such as *corpus, -oris* 'body' and *opus, -eris* 'work' to produce *corpus-culum, -ī* 'small body' and *opus-culum, -ī* 'small work' respectively, the suffix seen in modern *cas-ucha* 'hovel' and *animal-ucho* 'critter' is created. The apparently similar case of Sp. *-ijo* actually differs markedly in that the reanalyzed element in this case is the Latin instrumental suffix '*-culum*. Thus, from such examples as *vehi-culum, -ī* 'cart' (← *vehere* 'to transport in a cart') and *sedi-culum, -ī* 'seat' (← *sedēre* 'to sit'), the suffix *-ijo* arises from a reanalyzed segment *-iculum*, as in Cast. *casqu-ijo* 'gravel' (← *cascar* 'to crack') and *acert-ijo* 'riddle' (← *acertar* 'to get something right').

Haspelmath's example of the reanalysis of Fr. *fruit-ier* 'fruit grocer' (← *fruit* 'fruit') as *frui-tier*, thus creating an allomorph *-tier* for the derivation of *bijou-tier* 'jeweler' (← *bijou* 'jewel') is in fact indicative of a large number of such "secretions" in this language. These are catalogued systematically by Nyrop (1935, see especially pp. 54–62), who terms them "formes élargies" ('widened forms', cf. additional terms such as Fr. *mécoupure* and Germ. *falsche Abtrennung*, both of which imply a false analysis or separation). Thus, on the model of *bavard* 'talkative' → *bavard-er* 'to chat' we have the derivation *bazar* 'junk' → *bazar-der* 'to get rid of'; on the model of *saut* 'jump' → *saut-er* 'to jump' we have *chapeau* 'hat' → *chapeau-ter* 'to supervise'. Another example is *numéro-tage* 'numbering' (← *numéro* 'number') and *cano-tage* 'canoeing' (← *canoë* 'canoe'), perhaps on the model of *pilot-age* 'piloting' (← *pilot* 'pilot') and *rabot-age* 'planing down' (← *rabot* 'plane').

The case of *-ura* is notable in that the reanalysis that gives birth to this suffix results in a shorter rather than a longer suffix. When Lat. *-tūra, -ae,* used to derive nouns naming actions and results from verbal bases (*coctūra, -ae* 'cooking' ← *coquī, -ere* 'to cook'), is obscured in Spanish derivatives such as *derechura* (< *directūra, -ae* ← *dīrīgere* 'to direct') and *estrechura* (< *strictūra, -ae* ← *stringere* 'to compress'), speakers begin to associate them with the corresponding adjectives *derecho* and *estrecho*, thereby creating a new suffix through reanalysis to be used in quality nouns: *angostura* 'narrowness' (← *angosto* 'narrow'), *dulzura* 'sweetness' (← *dulce* 'sweet'). According to Meyer-Lübke (1923, § 466), this same process of reanalysis also explains the origins of OFr. *hauture* 'height' (← *haut* 'high'), *blanchure* 'whiteness' (← *blanc, blanche* 'white'), and It. *altura* 'height' (← *alto* 'high; tall'), *freddura* 'cold(ness)' (← *freddo* 'cold'). Note that Rohlfs (1969, § 435–46) has a different explanation for the evolution of It. *-ura* in Italian: "Per affinità fonetiche e semantiche è giunto a confondersi con il suffisso *-ore* […] cfr. *paura* (per **paore*), *calura* (per *calore*), *freddura* (per un antiquato *freddore*), *grossura* (per l'antiquato *grossore*), *verdura* (per l'antiquato *verdore*)." [Through phonetic and semantic affinities it came to be confused with the suffix *-ore* […] cf. *paura* (for **paore*), *calura* (for *calore*), *freddura* (for obsolete *freddore*), *grossura* (for obsolete *grossore*), *verdura* (for obsolete *verdore*).]

One fascinating subcategory of reanalysis involves the creation of a suffix from the non-suffixal (i.e. non-morphemic) ending of a single word, a category that seems to correspond to Stein's "irradiation" but which clearly involves reanalysis. A good example of this in Spanish is the ordinal suffix *-avo*, whose sole etymon is Lat. *octāvus*, whence Old Sp. *ochavo* 'eighth' (mod. *octavo*) and the series *doce-avo* 'twelfth', *trece-avo* 'thirteenth', etc. Rohlfs (1969, § 1127-a) claims that dialectal It. *-ustello* derives through suffix telescoping from the single word **arbust-ello* 'young shrub' (← *arbustum, -ī* 'shrub'), analyzed as **arb-ustello* and revealing its productivity in Sic. *ram-isteḍḍa* and Calabr. *ram-usteḍḍu*, both 'twig' (← *ramo* 'branch') and Sic. *lag-usteḍḍu* 'small lake' (← *lagu* 'lake'). Rohlfs (1969, § 1127-a) remarks: "Questi esempi dimostrano come, partendo da una parola unica, d'analogia in analogia, possa diffondersi una nuova forma suffissale." [These examples demonstrate how, on the basis of a single word, through multiple analogies, a new suffix can be diffused.] Finally, Moll (1952: 293–294) claims that the pejorative and collective suffix *-orum* found in Balearic Cat. *llatin-òrum* 'macaronic Latin' (← *llatí* 'Latin') and *robat-òrum* 'larceny' (← *robar* 'to steal') derives from the final word in the liturgical phrase *per omnia saecula saeculorum*.

2.1.4 Grammaticalization

We explained above that the adverbializing suffix Sp., Port., Ital. *-mente*, Fr., Cat. *-ment* is the only clear case of suffix origin through grammaticalization in Romance. The process occurs when phrases such as *tranquillā mente* 'with a tranquil mind' (where *mente* is the ablative singular form of *mens, mentis* 'mind'), are interpreted as referring to manner generally (here, 'in a tranquil way'), thus opening the door for the formative to be attached to any adjective whatever, e.g., Sp. *afortunada-mente* 'fortunately', which cannot refer to a state of mind.

There is no indication that any of the legitimate compounding patterns in the Romance languages are undergoing a process of grammaticalization in such a way that a suffix might arise from them. There are preliminary indications, however, that something akin to grammaticalization may be occurring with some of the final elements of learned Latin and Greek compounds. These compounds, which are composed of two learned roots, differ from normal compounds in that neither of their constituents is an actual independent word: compare Sp. *tocadiscos* 'record player; lit. plays records' (← *tocar* 'to play' + *discos* 'records'), with *fructífero* 'fruit-bearing, fruitful', whose parts are *fruct-* (< Lat. *fructus, -ūs* 'fruit'), the connecting vowel *-i-*, and *-fero* (< Lat. *-(i)fer* < *ferō, ferre* 'to bear'). I would posit that since the final segment *-ífero* has a distinctive meaning, is not independent, and is not internally analyzable in Spanish, the possibility exists of reinterpreting it as a suffix and adding it to non-learned stems. This is supported by examples such as Sp. argotic *plum-ífero* 'bureaucrat; lit. pen-bearer' (← *pluma* 'pen'), and Rainer's (1993: 534) neologism *(artículos) roll-íferos* 'bothersome (articles)' (← *rollo* 'hassle'). Other possible candidates: *-ólogo* 'student of', cf. Grk. *astrológos* 'astrologer', whence *timbr-ólogo* 'stamp collector' (← *timbre* 'stamp'), *chinólogo* 'expert on China', also *-ódromo* 'race-track', cf. Grk. *hippódromos* 'track for horse-races', whence Sp. *can-ódromo* 'dog-racing track' (← *can* 'dog'), and jocular *me-ódromo* 'latrine' (← *mear* 'to piss'). This last suffix is also quite productive in Brazilian Portuguese, cf. *namor-ódromo* 'drive-in motel for illicit trysts' (← *namorado* 'lover'), *samb-ódromo* 'place for samba parades' (← *samba*), and *camel-ódromo* 'place for street vendors' (← *camelô* 'street vendor'). Evidently the same phenomenon occurs in Italian, cf. *dolorifero* 'involving pain' (← *dolore* 'pain'), *zuccherifero* 'sugar-bearing' (← *zucchero* 'sugar'), *piovifero* 'rain-bearing' (← *piovere* 'to rain') and others found in an on-line reverse Italian dictionary (http://www.culturitalia.info/wb1/wb_it.asp).

Two objections of a theoretical nature can be adduced against designating formations such as *-ífero*, *-ólogo*, and *-ódromo* as suffixes. The first of these is the lexical nature of their semantic content. Most suffixes have fairly abstract meanings such as 'pertaining to', 'diminutive', and 'abundant'. However, given that the inventory of Spanish suffixes includes such meanings as 'blow' (*cuchill-ada, cuchil-lazo, pal-iza*), 'tax' (*pont-aje, pont-azgo, mensual-idad, arrenda-miento*) and 'illness' (*anquilostom-iasis, apendic-itis, fibr-oma, tubercul-osis*), this objection is unlikely to be decisive. The second is the fact that certain constituents of Greco-Latin learned compounds can occur initially as well as finally, e.g., *geólogo* 'geologist' vis-à-vis *logo-terapia* 'speech therapy'. This objection is neutralized by the fact that the newly grammaticalized suffix being posited is not *-logo* but *-ólogo*, which is unlikely to be associated with the first element in *logoterapia*. In my view, this legitimizes Rainer's (1993) inclusion of productive formants of this type in his suffix inventory, as they are invariably associated with a connecting vowel, cf. *-iforme* (*punt-iforme*), *-ífugo* (*calor-ífugo*), *-ófilo* (*soviet-ófilo*), *-ómetro* (*aplaus-ómetro*).

2.1.5 Apophony

I have argued on several occasions (e.g., Pharies 2002) that an analogical process based on apophony has been used to supplement the suffix inventory of Spanish. This is evident in the cases of Sp. *-incho* and *-encho*, which arise as complements to the pre-existing series *-ancho*, *-oncho* and *-uncho*, just as the pre-existence of the series *-ajo*, *-ejo*, *-ijo* and *-ojo* explains the coining of *-ujo*.

Meyer-Lübke (1923, § 418) resorts to the apophonic argument in seeking the origin of It. *-uccio* and Rum. *-uţ*:

> *Uceus -a* ne se présente en latin que dans *pannuceus*, qui manque à son tour au roman. Or, si le roumain et l'italien connaissent néanmoins un suffixe marquant la diminution (*-uţ* en roum., *-uccio* en ital.), où faut-il en chercher l'origine? C'est que, probablement, la langue a fait passer dans d'autres suffixes aussi la variété de voyelles qui se trouvait dans *-ame*, *-ime*, *-ume*; *-atus*, *-itus*, *-utus*; *-ago*, *-igo*, *-ugo*.
> [*Uceus -a* is only present in Lat. *pannuceus*, which in turn is missing in Romance. Now, if Romanian and Italian nevertheless have a suffix indicating diminution (*-uţ* in Rumanian, *-uccio* in Italian), where should its origin be sought? Most likely, the language has transferred into other suffixes the variety of vowels found in *-ame*, *-ime*, *-ume*; *-atus*, *-itus*, *-utus*; *-ago*, *-igo*, *-ugo*.]

Similarly, Rohlfs (1969, § 1040), considering the origin of It. *-occio*, *-ozzo*, muses: "Un presumibile *-ŏceus* non è attestato in latino. Probabilmente esso è sorto soltanto nel latino volgare tardo, per completare la serie di alternanze *-accio*, *-eccio*, *-iccio*, *-uccio*." [A presumed *-ŏceus* is not attested in Latin. Probably this form first arose in Late Vulgar Latin, in order to complete the series of alternations *-accio*, *-eccio*, *-iccio*, *-uccio*.] Again in the case of *-atto*, Rohlfs (1969, § 1142) states: "Come *-otto* anche *-atto* sembra essere una forma di alternanza ('Ablautform') del suffisso primario *-etto*." [Like *-otto* also *-atto* seems to be an alternating form ('Ablautform') of the primary suffix *-etto*.]

2.2 Borrowing

Like borrowed words, borrowed suffixes in the Romance languages exist on two lexical tiers: learned, i.e. absorbed from ancient Latin and Greek, and vernacular, i.e. adopted from all other sources.

2.2.1 Learned borrowing

Rainer (2002: 123–24) remarks that the massive presence of shared learned borrowings is the most important element in the convergence of the Romance languages, to the point that he sanctions the use of such terms as "euromorfología" and "europeización morfológica" to describe this convergence. Indeed, it is the case that to a large extent the various suffixes borrowed from ancient, medieval and modern Latin – many of them originally Hellenisms – are present, with local alterations, in most or all of the Romance languages. Further, it is also the case that the inventory of borrowings incorporating these suffixes is also largely identical from language to language. This is primarily true of the elements of Greek and Latin scientific compounds that are frequently called suffixoids: *-derm-* 'skin'

(Sp. *paquidermo*, It. *pachiderma*, Fr. *paquiderme* 'pachyderm'), ˈ*-fag-* 'eating': Sp. *antropófago*, It. *antropofago*, Fr. *antropophage* 'cannibalistic'), *-lit-* 'stone' (Sp. *megalito*, It. *megalite*, Fr. *mégalithe* 'megalith'), etc. However, the list of learned suffixes and corresponding borrowings is also fairly uniform, cf. *-āceus* (Sp. *gallináceo*, It. *gallinaceo*, Fr. *gallinacé*), *-ārius* (Sp. *honorario*, It. *onorario*, Fr. *honoraire*) and *-ficāre* (Sp. *modificar*, It. *modificare*, Fr. *modifier*), etc.

2.2.2 Vernacular borrowing

The term *vernacular borrowing* is used here to denote the adoption of a suffix from any language other than classical Greek or the various stages of Latin (classical, medieval, modern), whether the borrowing entered through intense bilingualism or through scientific, artistic, economic, military, or literary influence. Defining the phenomenon broadly in this way, we find that numerous foreign suffixes have made their way into the Romance languages.

Borrowing between and among the Romance languages has been particularly intense. Thus, we find the Italian suffix *-esco* throughout Romance (Sp. *-esco*, Fr. *-esque*), while several additional Italian suffixes have passed into French, including It. *-asco* (> Fr. *-asque*) and *-iccio* (> Fr. *-ice*). The French suffix *-age* has been very widely borrowed (Sp. *-aje*, It. *-aggio*, Port. *-agem*, Rom. *-aj*), and Fr. *-ise* also appears in Italian as *-igia*. It is often the case that a foreign suffix has more than one source, as is the case with Fr. *-ade*, whose inventory includes words adopted from Provenzal, Italian, Portuguese, and Spanish.

A subcategory here is interdialect borrowing, as in the case of Sp. *-aina*, an Aragonese borrowing that reflects Lat. *-āgō*, *-āginis* in the same meanings found in It. *-aggine*, cf. Sp. *plantaina* 'plantain', a phytonym, and *colaina* 'wood defect', which shows the admixture of *-īgō*. In Italian, the forms *-azzo*, *-izzo*, *-uzzo* are considered to be southern Italian dialectal variants of Tuscan *-accio*, *-iccio*, *-uccio* (Rohlfs 1969, § 1037–1041).

The number of non-Romance borrowed suffixes is also considerable. The diminutive suffixes in *-it-* (Sp. *-ito*) or *-et-* (Fr. *-ette*) found in many Romance languages are considered to be borrowed from pre-Latin linguistic strata. Borrowings from Germanic are numerous as well. Of particular interest here are two Germanic words used as the second element in compound anthroponyms and analyzed as suffixes in French and Italian. These are *-hart* 'strong', which produces Fr. *-ard* and Italian *-ardo*, and *-wald* 'ruler' (cf. Germ. *walten* 'to rule'), whence Fr. *-aud*, It. *-aldo*. As mentioned above, the Germanic patronymic suffix *-engo* (more specifically, East and West Gothic *-ingôs*) also passes into Spanish and Italian. More recently, we find Engl. *-ing* playing a role in Modern French (*footing* 'jogging'). Further afield, it is thought that the *-rr-* suffixes in Ibero-Romance derive from Basque, and several suffixes in Romanian are attributed to non-Romance languages, including Hungarian *-aş* (Rom. *arcaş* 'archer' ← *arc* 'bow'), and Bulgarian *-iş* (Rom. *măritiş* 'marriage' ← *mărita* 'to marry') and *-işte* (*porumbişte* 'cornfield' ← *porumb* 'corn'). Also from Slavic is the gentilic *-ean* (*sătean* 'villager' ← *sat* 'village').

Notably, once a suffix has been accepted into a language, it is free to begin evolving in precisely the way patrimonial elements do. As a result, we find examples of many of the categories cited above in the histories of many borrowed suffixes. On the one hand, a borrowed suffix may undergo grammatical changes, as in the case of *-ista*, originally applied only to verbal bases to produce nouns (*baptízo* 'to baptize' → *baptistēs* 'baptizer'), but which can also accept noun bases in Romance (Sp., It. *arab-ista, marx-ista*, Fr. *arab-iste, marx-iste*). Exemplifying semantic change is the Greco-Latin suffix *-ía*, originally employed in Spanish to form quality nouns (*cobard-ía* 'cowardice' ← *cobarde* 'coward'), which takes on more concrete meanings (*alevos-ía* 'act of treason' ← *alevoso* 'premeditated'), and is extended to names of titles and offices (*alcald-ía* 'mayoralty' ← *alcalde* 'mayor'), places where these duties are carried out (*escriban-ía* 'office of a scribe' ← *escribano* 'scribe') and collectives (*burgues-ía* 'citizenry' ← *burgués* 'citizen'). Curiously, several of these same semantic fields are also developed by the Greco-Latin suffix *-aticus*, originally used to derive adjectives of pertinence from nouns (*herb-āticus* 'herbivorous' ← *herba, -ae* 'grass, seedling'), but extending to titles and offices (Sp. *alguacil-azgo* 'office of sheriff' ← *alguacil* 'sheriff') as well as the place (Sp. *alcald-azgo* 'mayoralty' ← *alcalde* 'mayor') and duration (Sp. *pap-azgo* 'papacy' ← *papa* 'pope') of these offices. The development of *-āticus* into French *-age* is even more wide-ranging, as described by Fleischman (1977).

The process of reanalysis can be seen in the Hellenic suffix *-osis*, as it derives not from the from the suffix *-sis* but from *-ōsis*, where *-ō-* forms part of the base in several verbal abstracts denoting diseases, cf. Gr. *hélkōsis* 'ulceración' (← *helkóō* 'to ulcerate'), whence it is adopted to designate maladies in Spanish, cf. *triquin-osis, neur-osis, tubercul-osis*. This process is also observable in the histories of other disease suffixes of Greco-Latin origin such as *-itis* and *-oma*.

3 References

Alemany Bolufer, José (1920): *Tratado de la formación de palabras en la lengua castellana*. Madrid: Suárez.

Fleischman, Suzanne (1977): *Cultural and Linguistic Factors in Word Formation. An Integrated Approach to the Development of the Suffix* -age. Berkeley: University of California.

Gibert-Sotelo, Elisabeth and Isabel Pujol Payet (2020): Derivación verbal y cambio tipológico: a propósito del latín *-izāre*. *Lingue antiche e moderne* 9: 107–130.
González Saavedra, Berta (2010): Procesos de gramaticalización. Estudio de la formación adverbial latina y romance. Los sustantivos en ablativo *mente y modo* como sufijos para la formación de adverbios. *Diálogo de la Lengua* 2: 86–97.
Haspelmath, Martin (1995): The growth of affixes in morphological reanalysis. In: Geert Booij and Jaap van Marle (eds.), *Yearbook of Morphology 1994*, 1–29. Dordrecht: Kluwer.
Heidermanns, Frank (2004): Zur Typologie der Suffixentstehung. *Indogermanische Forschungen* 109: 1–20.
Malkiel, Yakov (1988): Las peripecias españolas del sufijo latino *-ōriu*, *-ōria*. *Revista de filología española* 68: 217–255.
Marchand, Hans (1969): *The Categories and Types of Present-Day English Word-Formation. A Synchronic-Diachronic Approach*. 2nd ed. München: Beck.
Merz, Giuliano (On-line): *Dizionario inverso dell'italiano moderno*. http://www.culturitalia.info/wb1/wb_it.asp.
Meyer-Lübke, Wilhelm (1923): *Grammaire des langues romanes. Tome deuxième: Morphologie*. Paris: Welter.
Mihatsch, Wiltrud (2021): Collectives in Romance Languages. In: Mark Aronoff (ed.), *Oxford Research Encyclopedia of Linguistics*. Oxford: Oxford University Press [Online available at: https://doi.org/10.1093/acrefore/9780199384655.013.682]
Moll, Francesc de Borja (1952): *Gramática histórica catalana*. Madrid: Gredos.
Nyrop, Christopher (1979): *Grammaire historique de la langue française*. Vol. 3: *Formation des mots*. 4th ed. Genève: Slatkine.
Pharies, David (2002): Historia de los sufijos españoles *-ajo*, *-ejo*, *-ijo*, *-ojo* y *-ujo*. In: Joaquín García-Medall (ed.), *Aspectos de morfología derivativa del español*, 95–101. Lugo: Tris Tram.
Pharies, David (2004): Tipología de los orígenes de los sufijos españoles. *Revista de filología española* 84: 153–167.
Rainer, Franz (1993): *Spanische Wortbildungslehre*. Tübingen: Niemeyer.
Rainer, Franz (2002): Convergencia y divergencia en la formación de palabras en las lenguas románicas. In: Joaquín García-Medall (ed.), *Aspectos de morfología derivativa del español*, 103–133. Lugo: Tris Tram.
Rainer, Franz (2005): Semantic change in word formation. *Linguistics* 43: 415–441.
Rainer, Franz (2011): The agent-instrumental-place "polysemy" of the suffix *-tor* in Romance. *STUF – Language Typology and Universals* 64(1): 8–32.
Rainer, Franz (2017): Patterns and niches in diachronic word formation: the fate of the suffix *-men* from Latin to Romance. *Morphology* 28(4): 397–465.
Rainer, Franz (2018): La descendencia colectiva, aumentativa e intensiva del sufijo latino *-aria* en las lenguas románicas. *Verba* 45: 225–264.
Rainer, Franz (2020): Nombres de acción en -ŌRIU/-ŌRIA Y -ARIA en las lenguas románicas. *Revue de linguistique romane* 84: 429–468.
Rainer, Franz (2021): I suffissi *-AROLO e -ARELLO* e il problema dell'interfisso *-AR-* nelle lingue romanze. *Revue de linguistique romane* 85: 447–506.
Rainer, Franz (2022): Origin and development of the suffix -ARIA in Romance. *Zeitschrift für romanische Philologie* 138(1): 1–64.
Rainer, Franz (2024): El desarrollo de los sufijos *-ĭcius* e *-īcius* en la Iberorromania. *Lletres asturianes* 130: 6–32.

Rasmussen, Jens (2004): On the typology of Indo-European suffixes. In: James Clackson and Birgit Anette Olsen (eds.), *Indo-European Word Formation*, 269–282. Copenhagen: Museum Tusculanum Press.
Rohlfs, Gerhard (1969): *Grammatica storica della lingua italiana e dei suoi dialetti*. Vol. 3: *Sintassi e formazione delle parole*. Turin: Einaudi.
Stein, Gabriele (1970): Zur Typologie der Suffixentstehung (Französisch, Englisch, Deutsch). *Indogermanische Forschungen* 75: 131–165.
Tekavčić, Pavao (1980): *Grammatica storica dell'italiano*. Vol. 3: *Lessico*. Bologna: Il Mulino.
Trips, Carola (2009): *Lexical Semantics and Diachronic Morphology. The Development of* -hood, -dom *and* -ship *in the History of English*. Tübingen: Niemeyer.

Peter O. Müller

15 Historical word-formation in German

Abstract: This article offers a description of the historical development of German word-formation and the forms of change in word-formation which are thereby revealed. Following an overview of the history of research, general developmental tendencies are initially explained. Subsequently, a description is presented of the important processes of change for the areas of compounding, derivation and conversion which reaches from the beginnings to the present. A brief overview of further types of word-formation concludes the article.

1 Current state of research

The investigation of historical word-formation in German (for an overview cf. Müller 1993, 2002 and Solms 1998) has its roots in the 19th century. Jacob Grimm's treatment of word-formation in the second and third volume of his *Deutsche Grammatik* [German Grammar] (1819–37) became formative for a long period of time. Grimm's description which was primarily diachronic and more oriented towards etymological criteria, more morphologically than semantically, and more oriented toward the single word than the system of word-formation, also remained fundamentally influential for the later work of Wilmanns (1899), Paul (1920), Kluge (1925) and Henzen (1965) which was indebted to the neogrammarian tradition.

Since the mid-1980s this line of research has been supplemented by "research on historical-synchronic word-formation" in the course of a theoretical and methodological paradigm shift. Characteristic of this approach are the following goals

Peter O. Müller, Erlangen, Germany

https://doi.org/10.1515/9783111420530-015

which constitute a contrast to the traditional diachronic view of word-formation: (i) The reconstruction of historical systems of word-formation in order to understand the functional interaction of morphemes and patterns of word-formation. The analysis is thus undertaken primarily from a synchronic perspective, i.e. with regard to a particular period of time, revealing the morphological-semantic motivation of word-formations present at that point in time. (ii) The analysis of word-formation is developed on the basis of the evaluation of large text corpora, not examples from dictionaries or chance discoveries, and the results are based on an exact percentual evaluation of a corpus, not on estimates of frequency. (iii) The diachronic comparison of historical-synchronic analyses of word-formation makes statements possible about change in systems of word-formation, about shifts in the functional potential of models of word-formation, competition and opposition, as well as the functional interaction of models of word-formation in the establishment of functional classes (i.e. categories of word-formation such as action nouns, agent nouns, collective nouns, etc.; cf. sections 3–5), so that lines of development become visible from the medieval to the Early Modern and New High German system of word-formation.

Corresponding studies of word-formation were initially presented for Early New High German (ENHG, 1350–1650) (cf. Müller 1993a; Döring and Eichler 1996; Brendel et al. 1997; Russ 2004 for derivation of nouns; Habermann 1994, and Prell and Schebben-Schmidt 1996 for word-formation of verbs; Thomas 2002 for derivation of adjectives). In recent years, Middle High German (MHG, 1050–1350) has become the center of attention (cf. Herbers 2002; Leipold 2006 for word-formation of verbs; Ring 2008 and Ganslmayer 2012 for derivation of nouns and adjectives in the MHG language of documents as well as the comprehensive description of derivation and compounding in nouns, adjectives and verbs in volume III of the *Mittelhochdeutsche Grammatik* [Middle High German Grammar] (= Mhd. Gr. III). Old High German (OHG, 750–1050) has, on the other hand, not yet been made accessible in the same way via historical-synchronic studies of word-formation (for an overview of research cf. Meineke 2009). Splett's (1993) word-family dictionary represents an important tool for future studies of OHG word-formation. Research on word-formation in OHG presents specific problems, however, due to the limited written record (slightly exceeding 28,000 lexemes), the dominance of glossing vocabulary (ca. two thirds) as well as the high proportion of (partially apocryphal) hapax legomena. All this makes a comparison of OHG word-formation with later systems of word-formation difficult.

In addition to word-formation in OHG, word-formation in recent stages of German (17th–20th century) has also not yet been sufficiently studied. Only a few newer studies can be found (cf. Bentzinger 1991 on adjective suffixes, Stricker 2000 on terms referring to persons in Goethe, Pounder 2000 on adjectival derivation from the 16th to the 19th century, Heinle 2004 on word-formation of adverbs, Scherer 2005 on the productivity of *-er-* derivatives in newspaper language).

Brief overviews of research on word-formation in historical stages of German are presented in Splett (2000) on OHG, Meier and Möhn on Old Low German/Old Saxon (ca. 800–1200), Zutt (2000) on MHG, Cordes and Niebaum (2000) on Middle Low German (13th–16th century), Wegera and Prell (2000) on ENHG, Heinle (2000) on NHG (17th–20th century) as well as Wellmann (1997), Habermann (2002), Müller (2002), Munske (2002), Erben (2003a) and Scherer (2006) on general developmental tendencies and on change in word-formation.

As this overview shows, previous studies of historical word-formation in German have placed an emphasis in the area of derivation of nouns, adjectives and verbs. Studies on compounding, which are always confronted with the problem of differentiating between a syntagma and a product of word-formation (cf. Pavlov 1983; Solling 2012) are by comparison in the minority, and the historical development of conversion is also only partially captured. For other types of word-formation, on the other hand, independent studies are completely missing. A comprehensive description of the historical word-formation of adverbs is provided by Heinle (2004), although it is largely compiled from dictionaries. Article 4 on foreign word-formation in German provides an overview of the roots of German foreign word-formation. Thus, for German an outline of historical word-formation and change in word-formation can be sketched, whereas the development of a comprehensive description on a historical-synchronic basis which can supplement the traditional handbooks will presumably remain a long-term objective for some time.

2 General developmental tendencies

The developmental tendencies discussed below involve partly change in word-formation in a narrow sense, in which models of word-formation undergo change with respect to the affinity for a base (i.e. morphological-semantic characteristics of the word-formation base) and word-formation function, and partly change in interface phenomena, in which phonological, lexical, morphological and syntactic change affect word-formation. These tendencies lead to situations in which models of word-formation become unproductive or morphologically opaque and new models arise, and they also determine formal or functional change in models of word-formation. In the course of language history, particularly important tendencies of word-formation in German have been (i) univerbation (word group > product of word-formation), (ii) grammaticalization (lexeme > affix), (iii) the development of German foreign word-formation (morphematization of foreign-language elements) as well as (iv) standardization, together with the reduction of allomorphs, competing formations, idiomaticized word-formations and formations with a pleonastic (i.e. non-functional) affix. Such changes have served to increase the efficiency of the system of word-formation. Reanalysis plays a central role in many phenomena of change.

In the following, I give examples for these general tendencies of development in the area of German word-formation, whereby the exposition is divided into the sections 2.1. Development of models of word-formation, 2.2. Development of archaism in models of word-formation and 2.3. Change in models of word-formation.

2.1 Development of models of word-formation

a) Univerbation: In the course of the history of the German language, the univerbation of syntactic groups to word-formations has been of particular importance. That German has today become a language with a particular affinity for compounding is to a large degree the result of the development of compounds from word groups, through which new models of word-formation have developed. A special role has been played here by corresponding changes in the area of nominal N+N compounds: Ever since OHG there have been two types of compounds inherited from (Indo-)European (cf. Lindner 2011: 15 ff., 50 ff.), stem compounds (traditionally: proper ("eigentliche") or genuine ("echte") compounds (= "Zusammensetzung")) and case compounds (traditionally: improper ("uneigentliche") or non-genuine ("unechte") compounds (= "Zusammenrückung")). In the case of stem compounds, which are seen as historically older, the determining first member is a nominal stem (e.g., OHG *hunt-fliaga* lit. 'dog-fly'). Sometimes the first and second member are joined by a linking vowel (OHG *-a-*, *-e-*, *-i-*, *-o-*, *-u-*), which is historically a stem-forming suffix (e.g., OHG *tag-a-lioht* 'day-light', *spil-i-hūs* 'theatre; lit. play-house'). To some extent these Germanic stem-forming suffixes were already abandoned in OHG, or appear in altered form and in variants, depending on quantity and quality of the noun stem, but also depending on time period, region, or specific words (e.g., alongside *spil-i-hūs* also *spil-o-hūs*, *spil-e-hūs* and *spil-hūs*; overview in Gröger 1911). In the development towards MHG they are weakened to *-e-* and (later) partially abandoned (cf. OHG *bot-a-scaf* > MHG *bot-e-schaft* > NHG *Bot-schaft* 'news'). Only a few of the NHG compounds with the linking element *-e-* can be traced back to OHG formations with a linking vowel (e.g., NHG *Tag-e-werk* 'day's work'), so that the development of linking elements from stem-forming suffixes in German is unimportant (cf. Nübling and

Szczepaniak 2013: 69–72). The stem compounds still clearly predominate in OHG and MHG in comparison to the second type of so-called case compounds in which the first member exhibits a genitive inflectional marker (e.g., OHG *tages-zīt* 'time; lit. (of) day-time', *sunnūn-tag* '(of) sun-day', a loan translation of Lat. *dies solis*). The demarcation between case compounds and syntagmas is however often not straightforwardly possible due to frequency of the open spelling, so that structural ambiguity results (e.g., OHG *huntes zunga* 'tongue of a dog; lit. dog's tongue' as a noun phrase with a prenominal genitive attribute [[*huntes*] *zunga*] or as a genitive compound [*huntes zunga*]; this example is taken from Nübling and Szczepaniak 2013: 73). Neither is a differentiation between stem compounds and case compounds always unambiguously possible (e.g., OHG *hell-e-wazer* 'river of underworld; lit. hell-water' with genitive *e* or weakened stem vowel *-i-*; example following Splett 2000: 1214). Only in ENHG from the 16th/17th century (cf. Demske 1999: 151) does the frequency of case compounds rise sharply, leading to the development of a very productive model of composition. This is associated with a syntactic change effective in ENHG, i.e. the restructuring from prenuclear to postnuclear genitive attributes (cf. *der sunnen schein* > *der Schein der Sonne* lit. 'the shine (of) the sun'). During the course of this change, the boundaries between a syntagma and a compound become fluid – Pavlov (1983) speaks here of half-compounds ("Halbkomposita") –, and lexicalized syntactic combinations (noun phrases) could be reanalyzed as compounds (cf. [[*der tohter*] *man*]$_{\mathrm{NP}}$ > [*der* [*tohter man*]]$_{\mathrm{COMP}}$ 'son-in-law; lit. (of) daughter-man'), whereby the genitive inflectional markers could be refunctionalized (grammaticalized) as linking elements and then also used unparadigmatically (cf. NHG *Geburt-s-tag* 'birth-day', although *Geburt* does not exhibit an *-s-* as inflectional marker). Many new, even multi-member case compounds developed by analogy. In the 17th century their status as compounds was graphically marked in different ways (e.g., *RechtsSachen* 'legal matters', *Kenn=Zeichen* 'mark; lit. know mark'). Nevertheless, there is a clear preponderance of compounds in the contemporary German language which are constructed without a linking element (according to DWb 4: 54: 72.8 % noun compounds, 69.2 % adjective compounds).

For other word classes as well, univerbation (also: "incorporation") plays an important role. It is of central importance for adverbial word-formation (for an overview cf. Heinle 2004). Corresponding formations, especially with adverbial, prepositional and nominal final members are already attested in OHG and have been on the increase since MHG (e.g., NHG *da-durch* 'so; lit. there-through', *dort-hin* 'there', *der-zeit* 'at present'). Formations with adverbial or prepositional final members are classified as compounds (cf. section 3.4), those with nominal final members as conversions (cf. section 5.4).

In the case of adjectives, univerbation leads to the large group of participial compounds, in which the final member is an adjective in the form of the participle I or II (e.g., NHG *preis-gekrönt* 'award-winning', *ohren-betäubend* 'ear-splitting'). Corresponding formations, which cannot always be clearly differentiated from syntagmas and are highly frequent in the contemporary language, constitute a phenomenon of recent language history. There are hardly any examples from the Middle Ages.

From a diachronic perspective, prefix or particle verbs are also examples of univerbation, which is why these word-formations are referred to in the traditional handbooks as prefix or particle compounds (cf. Wilmanns 1899: 115 ff.; Meid 1967: 35 ff.). They originated in the merger of adverbs/prepositions with verbs. As early as OHG, some of them were frozen as prefixes (e.g., OHG *int-ērēn* 'to dishonour'), some of them are still encountered today as independent words (e.g., OHG *miti-loufan* 'to run; lit. with-run'). In the case of all these verbal pre-elements (cf. section 4.3.1), univerbation is linked to grammaticalization. Since the particle verbs are morphologically and syntactically separable, just as are the rare adjective-verb or noun-verb combinations (e.g., NHG *fest-binden* 'to tie; lit. fast-bind', *stand-halten* 'to hold out; lit. position-hold') – these are also partly subsumed under the particle verbs (cf. Fleischer and Barz 2012: 424 ff.) – (e.g., *ich beschloss mitzulaufen* lit. 'I decided with-to-run'; *ich lief mit* lit. 'I ran with'), their status as word-formations is, however, questioned to some extent, and an interpretation as syntagmas is preferred (cf. Lindner 2011: 38). In this case, leftwards-extending verbal word-formation would be limited to the prefix derivatives as well as a few examples of fixed compounds (e.g., NHG *grins-keuchen* 'to gasp with grin' or coordinative: 'to grin and gasp; lit. grin-gasp').

b) Grammaticalization: The grammaticalization of members of compounds has played a central role in the extension of the affix inventory in the history of the German language (cf. article 12 on grammaticalization in German word-formation). In this way formations with nominal compounding suffixes ("Kompositionssuffixe") as well as verbal prefix compounds ("Präfixkomposita") developed as early as OHG (Meid 1967: 36, 218). The corresponding elements of word-formation can be found with a more or less clear loss of concrete meaning alongside the nouns, adjectives, adverbs and prepositions out of which they developed. This is true in OHG, e.g, for nominal *-tům* (< *tům* 'judgement, dignity, reign, status'), *-scaf(t)* (< *scaf* 'rules', *scaft* 'creation'), and *-heit* (< *heit* 'person, family, status, nature'), for adjectival *-līh* (< *līh* 'body, corpse, figure'), *-sam* (< *sama*/*samo* 'just as, the same'), *-haft* (< *haft* (verbal adjective) 'marked with, bound'), *-lōs* (< *lōs* 'loose, outside') and *-bāri* (< *bāri* (verbal adjective from *beran* 'to produce, carry')) as well as the verbal prefix elements *ir-* (< *ir* (preposition) 'out, outside') and *bi-*

(< *bi* (preposition) 'on, at, around'). While in these cases the process of grammaticalization has generally been completed since the late Middle Ages and free lexemes can no longer be found alongside these affixes, the separable verbal particles retain their free counterpart (e.g., OHG *nāh-loufan* 'to run after; lit. after-run', *bī-stān* 'to stand by; lit. by-stand') and are referred to as particle verbs – from a diachronic perspective also as particle compounds – and are thus terminologically differentiated from the prefix verbs.

In the nominal and adjectival domain too, the later (E)NHG grammaticalization causes no abandonment of the original lexemes, for example in the case of the nominal collective suffixes *-werk* (< *Werk* 'work'; e.g., *Laub-werk* 'all the foliage; lit. foliage-work') and *-wesen* (< *Wesen* 'being, nature'; e.g., *Schul-wesen* 'school system'), the relational adjectival suffix *-mäßig* (< *mäßig* 'moderate, mediocre'; e.g., *vorschrift-s-mäßig* 'according to the regulations') or the adverbial suffix *-weise* (< *Weise* 'kind, way'; e.g., *gruppe-n-weise* 'in groups'). For this reason, the corresponding elements are sometimes referred to as affixoids (prefixoids, suffixoids) and conceptually differentiated from the affixes which only occur in bound form.

c) Foreign word-formation: German foreign word-formation also plays a central role in the development of new models of word-formation and has likewise had considerable consequences for the system of German word-formation (cf. article 4 on foreign word-formation in German). Even though the beginnings of German foreign word-formation with the foreign suffix OHG *-āri* (< Lat. *-ārius*; cf. Müller 2011) are situated as early as the early Middle Ages, and in the 12th/13th century further suffixes of French or Latin origin are added (cf. MHG *-(er)īe: voget-īe* 'bailiwick'; *-ier-*: *kurz-ier-en* 'to shorten'), a differentiated foreign word-formation has only taken shape since the early modern period. Nominal suffixes lead the way (cf. *-ismus, -ist, -ant*), adjective suffixes follow in the 18th century (cf. *-abel/-ibel, -iv, -ös/-os*), and the beginnings of foreign word-formation with confixes (cf. *graph, log, meter*) and prefixes (cf. *anti-*, *ex-*, *re-*, *ultra-*) are situated around 1800. Through the adoption and activation of foreign morphemes or the morphologization of foreign language morpheme segments, German is not only enriched by additional affixes and confixes, but also by new, partly hybrid models of word-formation: confix compounds (e.g., NHG *Therm-o-hose* 'thermal trousers') and confix derivatives (e.g., NHG *polem-isch* 'polemical'). With respect to their productivity, the foreign morphemes are however very different: Many are analyzable in the context of foreign word-formation in German but do not serve as models (e.g., *non-*: *non-verbal*; *-ess: Steward-ess*), while the number of foreign morphemes with significantly high productivity is rather low (cf. the confixes *bio-*, *euro-* and *öko-*, the prefixes *anti-*, *ex-*, *mega-*, *super-* and *top-* as well as the nominal suffixes

-ismus, *-ist*, *-ität* and *-ion*, adjectival *-abel* and verbal *-(is)ier*). A few bound foreign morphemes are becoming increasingly able to occur as words (cf. *video*, *top*, *super*, *mini*). Such a process of degrammaticalization is atypical for native morphemes and remains the exception (cf. *-zig* as suffix for the formation of multiples of ten such as *neun-zig* '90' > *zig* as numeral 'indefinite, very high number').

d) Phonetic change: Phonetic change has had a great influence on word-formation in German and has led to the development of new models of word-formation. Thus formations with the nominal suffix *-e* prove etymologically to be on the one hand word-formations determined by declension types (stem-forming suffixes) such as *Sprache* 'language' (former *-ō*-stem), but on the other hand also as lexemes formed with various word-formation morphemes, such as *Glaube* 'belief' (former deverbal derivation based on *-ni-* from *glauben* 'to believe') or *Länge* 'length' (former derivative based on *-ī-* from *lang* 'long') (cf. Henzen 1965: 170 ff.).

While in these cases suffix syncretism occurs as a result of the reduction of unstressed syllables ("Nebensilbenabschwächung"), the phonetic levelling leads in the case of verbs with formerly weak *-jan-*, *-ōn-* and *-ēn-* (> *-en*) to a change in model from suffixed verbs to conversion. The late OHG weakening of the suffixes Germ. *-jan* (> OHG *-en*; e.g., *zūn-en* 'to fence around' ← *zūn* 'fence'), *-ōn* (e.g., *fisc-ōn* 'to fish' ← *fisc* 'fish') and *-ēn* (e.g., *alt-ēn* 'to get old' ← *alt* 'old'), the status of which as inflectional markers (stem-forming suffix) or word-formation morpheme is however not undisputed (cf. Wilmanns 1899: 44–86 vs. Meid 1967: 230 f.), turns the formation of verbs by means of denominal conversion (cf. section 5.3) into the second central area of the formation of verbs alongside prefix derivation and particle-verb formation (cf. section 4.3.1).

Also in the case of many nominal formations, which even in OHG were only classifiable synchronically as conversions (cf. section 5.1), the levelling of Germanic stem-forming suffixes leads to a corresponding change in models, such as in OHG *tranc* 'drink' (< Westgerm. **drank-i*, Gothic as *-a*-stem *dragk*). From a diachronic-etymological perspective they are, however, assigned to the suffixal formations by authors such as Meid (1967: 56).

e) Suffix transference and suffix fusion: A further form of the development of new models of word-formation consists in a reanalysis of the linking of morphemes, whereby two different cases – suffix transference and suffix fusion – must be differentiated.

An example of suffix transference ("Suffixübertragung", Henzen 1965: 114) is the development of the verbal suffix *-ig*. It originated from denominal adjectives ending in *-ig*, which were verbalized by conversion (e.g., *Kraft* 'strength, power' → *kräft-ig* 'strong, powerful' → *kräftig-en* 'to strengthen'). While in OHG corresponding verbs were generally formed from adjectives ending in *-ig* (but not, for example, *krūz-ig-ōn* 'to crucify' ← *krūzi* 'cross'), as early as MHG a number of verbs with the reanalyzed verbal suffix *-ig* developed, which were not formed in a deadjectival, but rather in a denominal manner, and were thus not conversions, but rather suffix derivatives. Thus, out of MHG *pīn* 'punishment, agony', the suffix derivative *pīn-ig-en* 'to punish, torture' developed, which on the way to NHG displaced the older competing form *pīn-en* (< OHG *pīn-ō-n*). Circumfix derivatives also develop as a result of this reanalysis, (e.g., NHG *Nachricht* 'notification' → *be-nachricht-ig-en* 'to notify'; *Absicht* 'intention' → *be-absicht-ig-en* 'to intend').

While the development of the verbal word-formation morpheme *-ig* involves a change in the type of word-formation, this is not the case for suffix fusion ("Suffixverschmelzung" Henzen 1965: 113 f.). Here, the (phonetic syllable) boundary between the word-formation base and the suffix is moved via reanalysis such that the suffix is extended to include the final elements of the base word. In this way, new suffixes or suffix allomorphs develop. This includes the following examples:

- suffix *-ling* from derivatives with the suffix *-ing* (e.g., OHG *edil-ing* 'nobleman' ← *edili* 'noble' > reanalysis: *edi-ling*; later also MHG *vrisch-linc* (alongside *vrisch-inc* 'young animal' ← *vrisch* 'young'; NHG *Roh-ling* 'brute, blank' ← *roh* 'rough, crude');
- suffix *-ner* from derivatives with the suffix *-er* (e.g., MHG *wagen-er* 'wagon maker, wagoner' ← *wagen* 'wagon' > reanalysis: *wage-ner* > *Wagner*; later also NHG *Glöck-ner* 'bell-ringer, sexton' ← *Glocke* 'bell'; *Rent-ner* 'pensioner' ← *Rente* 'retirement pension');
- suffix *-ler* from derivatives with the suffix *-er* (e.g., MHG *gürtel-er* 'girdle maker' ← *gürtel* 'belt' > reanalysis: *gürte-ler* > *Gürtler*; later also NHG *Sport-ler* 'sportsman' ← *Sport* 'sport'; *Künst-ler* 'artist' ← *Kunst* 'art');
- suffix (allomorph) *-keit* from derivatives with the suffix *-heit* (e.g., MHG *üppec-heit* 'abundance, transience, triviality, high spirits' ← *üppec* 'useless, trivial, thoughtless, high-spirited' > reanalysis: *üppe-cheit* > *üppe-keit* > NHG *Üppig-keit* with restitution of the adjective ending *-ig*; later also NHG *Wirksam-keit* 'effectiveness' ← *wirksam* 'effective'; *Betulich-keit* 'fussiness' ← *betulich* 'fussing' or *Dreist-igkeit* 'brazenness' ← *dreist* 'brazen'; *Genau-igkeit* 'exactness, meticulousness' ← *genau* 'exact, meticulous').

Henzen (1965: 114, 159, 200) also speaks in such cases of secondary suffixes ("Sekundärsuffixe") or – metaphorically – of rampant suffixes ("Wuchersuffixe").

f) Double motivation: Another important factor for the development of new models of word-formation is double motivation. In these cases, certain word-formations seem ambiguous with respect to their relation to their bases or their type of word-formation (cf. Müller 1993: 52).

Thus, the possibility of double motivation in OHG favored the development of V+N compounds, beginning with N+N compounds, the first member of which could be interpreted both nominally as well as verbally: e.g., *beto-man* 'prayer; lit. prayer-man' (from *beta* 'prayer' or *betōn* 'to pray'), *strīt-louft* 'race' (from *strīt* 'quarrel' or *strītan* 'to quarrel'), *slāf-kamara* 'bedroom' (from *slāf* 'sleep' or *slāfan* 'to sleep').

Such a reinterpretation also took place in the case of formations with the adjectival suffix *-bar*. The change from initially exclusively denominal formations to the currently predominating deverbal formations occurs here as well via the possibility of reanalyzing nominal bases as verbal (e.g., MHG *ēr-bœre* 'respectable' from *ēre* or *ēren*, *wandel-bœre* 'changeable' from *wandel* or *wandeln*). Here, again, double motivation functions as a hinge facilitating change in word-formation, in the course of which *-bar* is currently used primarily for deverbal formations with a passive-modal character (e.g., *erklär-bar* 'explicable') (cf. section 2.3).

That double motivation can also lead to the development of word-formation morphemes is demonstrated by the element *gegen-* which has only been used as a verb particle since end of the 20th century (cf. Fleischer and Barz 2012: 412). It is initially a component of backformations from nouns (e.g., *Gegendarstellung* 'reply' → *gegendarstellen* 'to dispute'), which can be reanalyzed as a verb-forming particle due to double motivation (*gegen-darstellen*) and then also occurs in formations which cannot be interpreted denominally (as backformations) (e.g., *gegen-lesen* 'to check through', *gegen-kehren* 'to sweep in the opposite direction'). This type of development has also become apparent for *zwischen-* 'in between' (cf. Fleischer and Barz 2012: 417) and *ur-* 'for the first time' (cf. article 10 on mechanisms and motives of change in word-formation, section 3.3).

g) Word-formation morphemes from inflectional markers: The development of word-formation morphemes from inflectional markers (deinflectionalization) is not very pronounced in German. Among the word-formation morphemes which are also still used in the contemporary language, only the adverbial suffix *-s* along with the adjectival circumfixes *ge-...-t* and *be-...-t* have an inflectional foundation.

The adverbial suffix *-s* developed from the genitive-singular form of strong masculine/neuter nouns, which as early as OHG are already attested in adverbial use (cf. *des abends* > *abends* 'evenings'). The inflectional marker *-s* was then reanalyzed as an adverbial suffix and can be found as early as OHG with feminine nouns, not licensed by inflection (*naht-es* > *nacht-s* 'nights'). It then develops into an adverbial marker, which in combination with other final members of adverbs also forms characteristic suffixes (e.g., NHG *-mals* in *nie-mals* 'never'; cf. section 4.4).

The adjectival circumfix formations with *ge-...-t* and *be-...-t* (e.g., NHG *ge-blüm-t* 'furnished with a flower pattern', *be-brill-t* 'furnished with glasses') are also reanalyzed based on the pattern of the participle II of weak verbs. On a formal level, they function like departicipial conversions, yet they cannot be assigned to any verb paradigm. They are thus referred to as pseudo-participles. They are ornative denominal circumfix formations, of which Riecke (1999) lists over 60 examples from OHG (e.g., *gi-hār-it* 'hairy' ← *hār* 'hair', *bi-rent-it* 'furnished with a rim' ← *rant* '(shield) rim').

2.2 Development of archaism in models of word-formation

Archaization in models of word-formation begins with a loss of productivity: A means of word-formation is no longer used for new formations. For some elements of word-formation, this process begins as early as Germanic, in other cases much later. In some cases, erstwhile models of word-formation are already no longer transparent even at the beginning of the history of German and corresponding formations have the status of simplex forms, since their word-formation structure is no longer recognizable. This is the case for the lexemes NHG *Saum* 'hem' (← Indo-European **sjeu-* 'to sew') and *Zaum* 'bridle' (← Germ. **teuh-a-* 'to pull'), which etymologically prove to be formations with the Indo-European suffix *-mo* (cf. Henzen 1965: 119). Side effects of the gradual archaization are the elimination of numerous formations from the vocabulary, the increasing lack of clarity of the morphological or semantic relation to a base, as well as the large number of lexicalized and idiomaticized formations. In other cases, the models of word-formation inherited from (Indo-)European are still transparent, although they were already no longer productive in OHG. This is, for example, the case for the adjectival *bahuvrīhi* formations with a nominal head (cf. sections 4.2.1, 5.2), among which only NHG *bar-fuß* 'having a bare foot' has been preserved. In the case of the nominal suffix *-t* (< Indo-European **-ti/-tu*) on the other hand, which was also already unproductive in OHG, more formations have remained productive. As early as MHG, the number of formations with *-t* which were still motivated is low (cf. Mhd. Gr. III: 120). In the contemporary language a small number of lexemes have been preserved which are still recognizable as corresponding derivations (e.g., *Fahr-t* 'driving' ← *fahren* 'to drive', *Fluch-t* 'escape' ← *fliehen* 'to escape'), but alongside these there are also numerous formations which have a relation to a morphological-semantic base which has become more or less unclear, and which have taken on the character of simplex forms (e.g., *Vernun-f-t* 'reason' <

OHG *firnum-f-t* ← *firneman* 'to perceive, understand', *Kluf-t* 'gap' ← *klieben* 'to split'). In these cases the *-t* already has the character of a pseudomorpheme (for further examples of archaizing morphemes cf. Simmler 2002).

In many cases, a decline in productivity or a loss of models of word-formation becomes apparent in MHG, generally in connection with a phonetic weakening of the affix structure. This is the case for the following examples:

- abstract nouns with the OHG suffix *-ōd*/*-ōt*, from which in NHG only a few formations have been preserved (cf. *Heimat* 'home', *Armut* 'poverty', *Zierat* 'decoration');
- agent nouns with the OHG suffix *-o* (> MHG *-e* > NHG *-e*/∅; e.g., OHG *erb-o* 'heir' > MHG *erb-e* > NHG *Erb-e*, OHG *beck-o* 'baker' > MHG *beck-e* > NHG *Beck* as a dialectal variant of the standard *Bäcker* which has also been preserved in family names), which in most cases succumb to the competition of the loan suffix OHG *-āri* (> MHG *-ere* > NHG *-er*; e.g., OHG *iagāri* 'hunter' > MHG *jeg-er(e)* > NHG *Jäg-er*);
- the nominal abstract suffix OHG *-ida* (> MHG *-(e)de* > NHG *-de*), which in NHG is only documented in a few formations (e.g., OHG *gimein-ida* 'general public' (← *gimeini* 'general') > MHG *gemein-de* > NHG *Gemein-de* 'municipality'), and which was primarily replaced by the suffix *-heit* (cf. MHG *gemein-heit* 'general public');
- the adverbial suffix *-o*, which in OHG had been the central means of word-formation for the formation of deadjectival adverbs (e.g., OHG *lang* 'long' → *lang-o*, *snel* 'rapid' → *snell-o*). As a result of the MHG reduction of final syllables (*-o* > *-e*; cf. *lang-e*, *schnell-e*) as well as the deletion of *-e* (cf. *schnell-e* > *schnell*) the suffix lost its productivity. Adverbs with the suffix *-līhho*, which initially continued as a replacement form, developed by means of reanalysis from formations with *-o* into adjectives with *-līh* in OHG (e.g., OHG *meister-līhh-o* 'masterful' > reanalysis: *meister-līhho*). At this point, *-līhho* could secondarily also be bound to simplex adjectives (e.g., OHG *gern-līhho* 'with pleasure, careful' ← *gern*) but eventually also lost its final *-o*. As a result, differentiation with respect to adjectives ending in *-lich* was no longer possible, so that this adverbial suffix also became unproductive in ENHG (cf. section 4.4);
- the nominal negation and valuation prefix *ā-*, which is disadvantageous from the perspective of syllabic structure (cf. MHG *ā-maht* 'powerlessness' ← *maht* 'power', further developed into *omacht* and folk-etymologically reinterpreted as (E)NHG *Ohn-macht* = 'without power'), which as early as MHG was hardly productive anymore and was replaced by the prefixes *ab-* and *un-* (cf. section 4.1.1);

- adjectival prefix derivatives with *ge-* (< Gothic/OHG *ga-* 'with'), which were strongly declining as early as MHG (cf. section 4.2.1). Diachronically, these are converted *bahuvrīhi* compounds (particle+noun) – Wilmanns (1899: 419) calls them mutated compounds ("mutierte Composita") –, which took on the character of prefix derivatives as early as the development of *ge-* from a particle to a prefix, which was completed in Germanic (cf. MHG *ge-hār* 'hairy' ← *hār* 'hair'). Alongside the function as a possessive prefix for base nouns it is also documented in deadjectival formations as a pleonastic prefix (cf. MHG *ge-willic* 'willing' ← *willic* 'id.'). In the development towards NHG, this model of word-formation was abandoned and replaced by patterns which mark the adjectival character more clearly (cf. MHG *ge-hār* > NHG *be-haar-t*, *ge-haz* > *ge-häss-ig* 'spiteful'). In NHG, only a few formations with *ge-* survive (cf. *ge-streng* 'stern' ← *streng* 'id.', *ge-lind(e)* 'mild, light' ← *lind* 'mild, lenient'). *ge-* is today only productive as a nominal prefix (cf. *Ge-schrei* '(continual) shouting' as an action noun from *schreien* 'to shout'); adjectival prefixes which bring about a change in the word class of the base no longer exist;
- formations with the adjectival suffix *-icht* (< OHG *-ahti*/*-ohti*, MHG *-eht*/*-oht*), for which the loss of productivity occurred considerably later than for the models named thus far, namely only after 1800, and is restricted to the NHG standard language. Here only *tör-icht* ('unreasonable, stupid' ← *Tor* 'simple-minded person') remains. In Upper German dialects, this suffix is still productive in the weakened variants *-et*/*-at* (cf. *bauch-et* 'having a belly' ← *Bauch* 'belly'). The task of this primarily ornative suffix in the standard language (cf. MHG *bart-oht* 'furnished with a beard' ← *bart* 'beard', ENHG *schnee-icht* 'furnished with snow' ← *Schnee* 'snow') cannot be explained with its phonetic structure. Crucial were presumably (cf. Wegera and Prell 2000: 1598) the phonetic and functional similarity to the adjective suffix *-ig*, with which it competed as early as OHG and by which it was finally replaced (cf. NHG *bauch-ig*, *bärt-ig*, *schnee-ig*). Also, the homonymy with the nominal suffix *-icht* (cf. NHG collective *Röhr-icht* 'reed bed' ← *Rohr* 'reed'), which in ENHG had developed via epenthesis of *-t* from MHG *-ach*/*-ech*/*-ich* (< OHG *-ahi*), proved to be a disadvantage. A clear differentiation between nominal and adjectival word-formation was attained by the transition of the adjectives ending in *-icht* to the suffix *-ig*, as had already happened with phonetically identical lexemes through the addition of the adjectival suffix *-ig* (cf. MHG *grim* 'rage' vs. *grim* 'furious' → *grimm-ic*, *undertān* 'subject' vs. *undertān* 'submissive' → *under-tænic*).

As all these examples show, the factors "phonetic change with phonological reduction" as well as "competition with other models of word-formation" play a central role for the archaization of models of word-formation. In order to be able to discover such instances of motivating competition, studies of systems of word-formation are necessary however, which have thus far only partially been made available for the history of German word-formation (cf. section 1).

2.3 Change in models of word-formation

Change in models of word-formation affects morphological as well as semantic word-formation processes.

The morphological changes in the domain of compounding encompass on the one hand the development of linking elements, which developed from stem-forming suffixes (in the case of the proper or "eigentliche" stem compounds) or from inflectional suffixes (in the case of the improper or "uneigentliche" case compounds) (cf. section 2.1 (a) as well as Lindner 1998; Nübling and Szczepaniak 2013) and which ultimately also led by analogy to compounds with unparadigmatic linking elements (e.g., NHG *Arbeit-s-zeit* 'working hours' with the linking element *-s-*, which does not occur as an inflectional marker with *Arbeit*). Further changes affect the closed spelling, which was increasing strongly in ENHG, as a graphical characteristic of compounding, the formation of polymorphemic compounds, which was also increasing in ENHG (e.g., NHG *Autobahn-raststätte* 'motorway services', *Fußballweltmeisterschaft-s-qualifikationsspiel* lit. 'football world championship-qualifying match') as well as the formation of hyphenated compounds (i.e. phrasal compounds) with word groups or sentences as first element (cf. OHG *zwei-elne-mez* lit. 'two-cubit-measure' as an early example, NHG *Erste-Hilfe-Ausrüstung* 'first-aid equipment', *Es-hat-keinen-Sinn-mehr-Gefühl* lit. 'it-has-no-sense-anymore feeling'), which is characteristic of recent German.

Word-formation suffixes are first of all subject to the general phenomena of phonetic or spelling changes in German and thus change their form (cf. OHG *-ida* > MHG *-ede* > NHG *-de*, *-āri* > *-ære*/*-ere* > *-er*, *-unga* > *-unge* > *-ung*). However alongside this, historical-synchronic variation can be observed, which is to some extent very pronounced, and which is diatopically founded. Thus for MHG a phonetic-graphic affix variation is not the exception, but the rule. In the case of the adjectival suffix *-lich*, for example, numerous other forms such as *-lih*, *-leich*, *-lig*, *-līh*, *-lik*, *-lic*, *-leh* and *-lech* are attested (cf. Mhd. Gr. III: 311). In the development towards NHG, this pronounced affix allomorphy is reduced and one form is standardized; the affix structure is thus stabilized.

The affixes are also subjected to change with respect to affinity for a base. This includes changes with respect to the word class of the base as well as the morphological or semantic characteristics of the base lexemes:

- A striking change with respect to the word class of the base is, e.g., exhibited by the grammaticalized suffix *-sam* (cf. section 2.1 (b)), which in MHG (cf. Mhd. Gr. III: 334 ff.; Ganslmayer 2012: 759 f.) still predominantly adjectivizes nouns (e.g., *tugent-sam* 'virtuous' ← *tugent* 'virtue'), whereas in NHG base verbs very clearly predominate (e.g., *einpräg-sam* 'easy to remember' ← (*sich*) *einprägen* 'to remember'); cf. section 4.2.2.
- The suffix *-ung*, on the other hand, has certainly served from the beginning as a means for forming deverbal action nouns, but exhibits in the contemporary language semantic restrictions with respect to its base and thus to its level of productivity: In contrast to MHG/ENHG (cf. Mhd. Gr. III: 133; Demske 2000), in NHG, for example, derivatives ending in *-ung* are lacking for verbs of perception and stative verbs (cf. MHG *seh-unge* 'the seeing' ← *sehen* 'to see', *wünsch-unge* 'the wishing' ← *wünschen* 'to wish').
- An example for change with respect to morphological restrictions on the base is provided by the nominal suffix *-heit* with its allomorphs *-keit* and *-igkeit* which were developed through reanalysis (cf. section 2.1 (e)), the distribution of which in the contemporary language (cf. Fleischer and Barz 2012: 209 ff.) was not yet fixed in ENHG (cf. Wegera and Prell 2000: 1595). Thus in the 14th/15th century *-heit* still combines with polysyllabic adjectives to form quality nouns (e.g., *bitter-heit* 'bitterness' ← *bitter* 'bitter', *eitel-heit* 'emptyness, cleanness, invalidity' ← *eitel* 'empty, pure, invalid'), while the allomorph *-keit* is also used with monosyllabic bases (e.g., *crank-keit* 'illness' ← *crank* 'ill', *geyl-keit* 'cheerfulness, high spirits, lecherousness' ← *geyl* 'cheerful, high-spirited, lecherous').

The processes of semantic change affect changes in the domain of the functional potential of models of word-formation, which will be explained here with the example of affixes. As a general rule, these have a primary word-formation function which is either – in the case of affixes taken from Germanic – the original one, or – in the case of affixes grammaticalized from lexemes – immediately derived from the former meaning of the lexeme. Most affixes do not remain monosemic in the course of their historical development, but rather are furnished with additional, secondary functions. The primary function remains thereby to some extent the main function, and the secondary functions remain subordinate. An example for this is the suffix *-ung*, which from the Middle Ages to the present can be attested in almost 90 % of all cases in action nouns (cf. Mhd. Gr. III: 126 f.; DWb 2: 94 f.). The secondary uses in instrument nouns (e.g., NHG *Bescheinig-ung* 'written confirmation'), agent nouns (e.g., *Regier-ung* 'people who govern') or patient nouns (e.g., *Abbild-ung* 'image') remain marginal. Here the question arises whether these secondary uses are at all linked to the productivity of the suffix, and there is thus a change in word-formation, or are not rather the result of a change in meaning (metonymization, e.g., *Regier-ung* 'the governing' > 'people who govern') (cf. Müller 2016). But in other cases, the primary function can also suffer a loss of productivity, become subordinate, and be surpassed in frequency by secondary meanings, as is the case with *-bar* (see below). The functional restructuring processes can lead to the number of affix functions increasing or decreasing, but also to individual functions being profiled or levelled. These functional changes of affixes also have consequences for their rates of productivity as well as for the system of word-formation. This will be illustrated with the example of the suffix *-bar*:

The adjectival suffix *-bar* (OHG *-bāri* > MHG *-bære* > NHG *-bar*) can be traced back to an originally independent verbal adjective (to OHG *beran* 'to carry') with the meaning 'carrying, capable of carrying'. Through processes of grammaticalization it changed from a member of a compound to a suffix. For this reason it initially only combined with nouns (cf. MHG *ēr-bære* 'carrying honor'). Still in MHG, denominal formations dominate by far (cf. Mhd. Gr. III: 273; Ganslmayer 2012: 225), among them causative-factitive adjectives (cf. *vruht-bære* 'fertile') and possessive-ornative adjectives (cf. *ēr-bære* 'honorable'). In the development towards NHG, *-bar* undergoes a fundamental functional change into a prominent suffix for the formation of deverbal passive-modal adjectives (cf. *mach-bar* 'feasible'). At the starting point of this semantic restructuring are medieval formations, which are doubly motivated and thus both denominally and also deverbally interpretable (cf. MHG *ēr-bære liute* 'people who have honor' vs. 'people who are honored; lit. honorable people'). The real shift occurs in ENHG. Since the 15th century, the proportion of deverbal formations has increased considerably; in the 17th century around two-thirds of new formations were already deverbal (cf. Flury 1964: 92 ff.), whereby the sudden increase in productivity is presumably also caused by the influence of Latin or French adjectives with *-abilis* or *-able*/*-ible*. In the contemporary language, deverbal adjectives ending in *-bar* have ultimately reached a proportion of around 95 %, whereby active-modal formations (cf. *brenn-bar* 'combustible') with fewer than 3 % play no role. With around 92 % passive-modal formations, *-bar* is a nearly monofunctional suffix. This functional change of *-bar* has also had consequences for the load of the 'passive-modal' functional domain in general. In the MHG Grammar (cf. Mhd. Gr. III: 360) the following distribution is attested: *-lich*$_9$: 44.4 %; *-ig*$_5$: 33.3 %; *-bære*$_4$: 14.8 %; *-haft*$_6$: 7.4 %. In passive-modal function, mainly adjectives with *-lich* and *-ig* are thus attested, whereby this function is subordinate for both suffixes: In the case of *-lich* it is ninth most common, in the case of *-ig* it is the fifth most common function. Adjectives with *-bære* are much less frequent, and are hardly used anymore with passive-modal meaning (fourth most common function), similarly for formations with *-haft* (sixth most common function). In the contemporary written language on the other hand, a completely different picture appears (cf. DWb 3: 398): *-bar*$_1$: 63.9 %; *-lich*$_3$: 19.8 %; *-abel/-ibel*$_1$: 9.4 %; *-ig*$_{12}$: 3.4 %; *-(at)iv*$_8$: 1.9 %; *-sam*$_3$: 1.9 %; others below 1 %. *-bar* is in its main function now by far the dominant suffix for the formation of passive-modal adjectives. Although in the case of *-lich* the function 'passive-modal' has gained prominence (MHG ninth most common > NHG third most common function), it has lost its dominant rank in this functional domain, and the same also applies to *-ig*, for which the passive-modal function is unimportant in the contemporary language (only the 12th most common function). The number of affixes which are used in passive-modal function has increased in the contemporary language, whereby now two foreign suffixes have also entered the language: *-abel/-ibel*, the main function of which is 'passive-modal' (e.g., *akzept-abel* 'acceptable') and *-(at)iv*, for which this function is unimportant (eighth most common function; e.g., *addit-iv* 'can be added; lit. additive'). This restructuring and the high productivity of *-bar* have also led to the 'passive-modal' functional domain becoming collectively more strongly weighted. While in MHG deverbal adjectives with active meaning (e.g., MHG *übertref-lich* 'surpassing' ← *übertreffen* 'to surpass') dominate with respect to those with passive meaning (cf. Mhd. Gr. III: 359 f.: 63 vs. 27 formations), the proportion in the contemporary written language has reversed (47 % : 51 %). In the contemporary spoken language, the dominance of active formations is, on the other hand, preserved (45 : 21 formations; cf. Thomas 2002: 543). This greater proximity of word-formation in the contemporary spoken language to earlier stages of the language is also apparent in other domains (cf. Müller 1993: 479 f.; Thomas 2002: 562) and makes clear that the medieval-early-modern system of word-formation exhibits a greater conceptual proximity to verbality. Ganslmayer (2011: 367 ff.) determines the differentiation between word-formation in the contemporary spoken and written language mainly on the basis of the factors "degree of complexity", "spectrum of variation" and "preferred use of word-formation rules" (in the written language: especially nominalizations with the function of condensing expression and textual interconnectedness, primarily via action/result nouns ending in *-ung*).

3 Composition

Compounding assumes a central role in German word-formation along with derivation. However, its distribution differs with respect to word classes: Nominal compounds are particularly characteristic, the proportion of adjectival or adverbial compounds clearly lags behind. Compounding is an atypical means of forming new verbs. An unequivocal demarcation between compounds and syntactic constructions is historically not always possible, since open and closed spelling fluctuates for a long period of time. Only since the 17th century has a clear tendency to closed spelling become apparent.

3.1 Nominal compounding

From the beginning the majority of German compounds are endocentric, right-headed determinative compounds which are encountered as stem compounds or case compounds (cf. section 2.1 (a)). N+N compounds clearly predominated initially, with simplexes as first and second members (e.g., OHG *bluom-garto* 'flower-garden'), as do stem compounds with respect to case compounds (e.g., OHG *tag-es-zīt* 'time; lit. day-time'). Compounds with other word classes as a first member represent exceptions. This is the case for the less important A+N compounds (e.g., OHG *junc-man* 'young man'), for P+N compounds (e.g., OHG *ūf-himil* lit. 'up-sky') as well as for V+N compounds, the beginnings of which lie in West Germanic (cf. Meid 1967: 28) and the development of which was favored by double motivation – reinterpretation of nominal first members as verbal (e.g., OHG *scelt-wort* 'swear word' from *scelta* 'trouble' or *sceltan* 'to scold'; cf. section 2.1 (f)). Further formations of low frequency are polymorphemic compounds (e.g., OHG *haselnuze-cherno* 'hazelnut-kernel') as well as exocentric *bahuvrīhi* compounds (e.g., OHG *ein-horn* 'animal with one horn; lit. one-horn', *sibin-blat* 'plant with seven leaves; lit. seven-leaf'), which in Proto-Indo-European still clearly predominate in comparison with endocentric compounds (cf. Lindner 2011: 26 f.). Due to the limitations of the written record, they are only attested as of late OHG and are almost all loan translations (cf. Splett 2000: 1215). In contrast to the converted adjectival *bahuvrīhi* formations (cf. section 5.2), they can be (slightly) productive in the contemporary language (cf. Fleischer and Barz 2012: 178 f.: *Acht-zylinder* 'motor with eight cylinders; lit. eight-cylinder').

As for coordinative compounds, which even in Germanic are only attested as relicts (cf. Meid 1967: 23 f.), unambiguous examples can be found neither in OHG nor in MHG. For the contemporary language as well, the existence of nominal coordinative compounds is controversial (cf. Fleischer and Barz 2012: 149–152), since as a rule alongside the coordinative reading a determinative reading is also possible (e.g., NHG *Spieler-Trainer* 'someone who is a player and a trainer at the same time' vs. 'trainer who trains players; lit. player-trainer').

This picture, which is characteristic of OHG (cf. Splett 1993, 2000: 2013 ff.), is also obviously true for MHG. On the other hand, the only systematic collection of MHG nominal compounds to date (cf. Mhd. Gr. III: 164–245) does not make possible an accurate comparison with other stages of the language with respect to the quantitative distribution of the word classes of the first members, the ratio between stem and case compounds, the proportion of polymorphemic compounds, or the frequency of closed or open spelling, since they are presented according to semantic groups. In each of the following compound types a proportion of more than 10 % is reached; namely around 19 % by action compounds ("aktionale Komposita"; e.g., *hals-slac* 'blow to the neck; lit. neck-blow'), around 13 % by referential compounds ("referentielle Komposita"; e.g., *helle-vürste* 'the Prince of Darkness; lit. hell-prince') and around 12 % by compounds with spatial classification ("Komposita mit räumlicher Einordnung"; e.g., *velt-bluome* 'wild flowers; lit. field-flowers'). This picture conforms roughly to the results for the contemporary written language, whereby compounds with spatial classification have a significantly lower frequency (around 6 %), and partitive/sociative compounds (e.g., *Kind-er-hand* 'hand of a child; lit. child-ren-hand') on the other hand have a slightly higher frequency (about 12 % vs. MHG 7.5 %) (cf. DWb 4: 126–141). The semantic diversity has been significantly expanded as a result of the differentiation of the spectrum of text types in the course of development towards the contemporary language.

Mainly two processes are then important for the further development of nominal compounds: On the one hand the sudden increase in productivity of case compounds beginning in ENHG as a result of the reanalysis of syntagmas as compounds with univerbation and the formation of linking elements (cf. section 2.1 (a)); on the other hand, the increase in the degree of complexity of the members of compounds, which has become increasingly apparent since the 17th century (e.g., ENHG *Vor-nennwort* 'pronoun; lit. for-nominal word', *Erb-küchenmeisteramt* lit. 'hereditary-kitchen-master-office'). Despite this development, the essential characteristics of historical nominal compounds are also preserved in the contemporary language (cf. DWb 4). Thus N+N compounds still dominate (around 80 %) with respect to V+N compounds (even if the latter are 7 % less frequent than in the Middle Ages), A+N compounds (around 5 %) and P+N compounds (less than 1 %); compounds without a linking element (around 73 %) dominate with respect to compounds with the linking elements *-s-*, *-n-*, *-en-*, *-er-*, *-e-* and *-ens*, and also the percentage of two-member compounds clearly outweighs the percentage of formations with three or more members (around 12 %; e.g., *Dreizimmer-Neubauwohnung* 'newly-built flat with three rooms; lit. three-room-new-building-flat'). Nominal compounding has furthermore experienced a model expansion in recent language history through the emergence of different forms of confix compounds (cf. article 4 on foreign word-formation in German).

3.2 Adjectival compounding

Adjectival compounding differs from nominal compounding by a significantly lower frequency as well as a less pronounced formal and semantic diversity. Both in the German of the Middle Ages – an analysis of the corpus of the MHG Grammar (= MHG corpus) provides a very good basis for this (cf. Mhd. Gr. III: 367–384) – as well as in the Innsbruck corpus of the contemporary written language (cf. DWb 5) the percentage of adjectival compounding within nominal compounding only amounts to around 16 %. There are other parallels between the two corpora as well. This is the case for the preponderance of compounds with two members with simplex components (over 90 %). Multi-member compounds with polymorphemic elements (e.g., NHG *bierflasche-n-dunkelgrün* 'dark green, that is the same as the color of beer bottles; lit. beer-bottle-dark-green') increase in the development towards the contemporary language, but remain here as well below 10 %. With respect to the word class of the first member on the other hand, a change becomes apparent: In the MHG corpus, nouns dominate (around 64 %) with respect to adjectives (around 20 %), adverbs and prepositions. In the Innsbruck corpus, the percentage of adjectives is higher (around 38 %), but nominal first members still predominate (around 55 %). This is especially due to the higher percentage of participial adjectives with a nominal first member (e.g., *speicheldrüse-n-anregend* 'stimulating the salivary gland; lit. salivary-gland-stimulating'). While in the Innsbruck corpus almost half of all adjective compounds are participial adjectives, their occurrence is negligible in the MHG corpus (4 out of 276 adjectival compounds). Verbal first members are lacking in the MHG corpus; their percentage in the contemporary language is even lower than in the nominal domain (around 6 %; cf. DWb 5: 19). As in the case of nominal compounds, the formation of adjectival compounds also predominantly occurs without linking elements. In the MHG corpus only a few examples of the linking elements *-e-* or *-s-* are documented (e.g., *künst-e-rīch* 'ornate'); in the Innsbruck corpus around 69 % are documented without a linking element (cf. DWb 4: 54); the use of linking elements thus increases in the development towards NHG, where a similar figure can be found as for nominal compounds.

From a semantic perspective the adjectival determinative compounds of the MHG corpus (cf. Mhd. Gr. III: 375) are primarily graduating formations (around 45 %; e.g., *bleich-grüene* 'pale green'), comparative formations (around 16 %; e.g., *snē-wīz* 'white as snow; lit. snow-white') and referential formations (around 16 %; e.g., *wīn-gir* 'greedy for wine; lit. wine-greedy'), which also predominate in the contemporary language (cf. DWb 5: 32–35). In general, the semantic spectrum is less diverse than is the case for nominal compounds, and as there as well, not all of the functional domains documented for the contemporary language are developed in MHG.

An important diachronic change (also in comparison with nominal compounds) appears with respect to adjectival coordinative compounds, which – apart from the numeral adjectives *drī-zēn* '13' through *niun-zēn* '19' – in OHG and MHG are not documented (cf. Splett 2000: 1215; Mhd. Gr. III: 368), but which constitute almost one third of all adjective compounds in the Innsbruck corpus of the contemporary written language, among them primarily additive formations (e.g., *rot-grün* 'red and green; lit. red-green'), but also clarifying equating compounds with an appositional second member (cf. DWb 5: 53 ff.: *rundlich-herzförmig* 'roundish, strictly speaking heart-shaped; lit. roundish-heart-shaped').

3.3 Verbal compounding

In contrast to nominal word-formation, compounding is unimportant for verbs. There is, however, no uniform conception as to the demarcation of verbal compounds. In earlier research, with a view towards the development of complex verbs through the merger of a lexeme with a verb, a broad concept of "compounding" is used, classifying verbs as prefix or particle compounds which today are classified as prefix or particle verbs (cf. section 2.1 (a)). A further point concerns the separability or inseparability of the verbal pre-elements. If one excludes separable first members of verbs, because one doesn't assume that these verbs are products of word-formation but rather syntactic constructions, or because all corresponding elements can be seen as "verb particles" ("Verbpartikeln") (cf. Fleischer and Barz 2012: 91 f.) – that is also adjectives and nouns (e.g., NHG *frei-halten* 'to keep clear, to save; lit. free-hold', *stand-halten* 'to hold out against; lit. position-hold') –, then only a small group of V+V compounds with a determinative or coordinative reading remain. These are used in technical or literary language (cf. Fleischer and Barz 2012: 440 f.; e.g., *grins-keuchen* 'to gasp with a grin' or 'to grin and gasp; lit. grin-gasp', *spül-bohren* 'to drill while rinsing' or 'rinse and drill; lit. rinse-drill'). Furthermore, verbs with a nominal first member are in most cases not formed by compounding, but rather by denominal conversion (e.g., *eislaufen* 'to ice-skate' ← *Eislauf* 'ice skating') or backformation (e.g., *notlanden* 'to make an emergency landing; lit. to emergency-land' ← *Notlandung* 'emergency landing'), and are thus "pseudo-compounds" ("Pseudokomposita" cf. Åsdahl Holmberg 1976).

The classifications in studies of historical stages of German are accordingly heterogeneous (cf. Mhd. Gr. III: 553–574; Habermann 1994: 37–40), whereby yet other problems arise as well: The often lacking closed spelling as a criterion for the demarcation between word groups and word-formations, the often unanswerable question, due to lack of evidence, whether the pre-elements are separable or not, as well as the process of the desemanticization of meaning beginning in OHG (lexeme > prefixoid > prefix/verb particle). Thus according to Splett (2000: 1216), the existence of N+V compounds is questionable for OHG, since verbs such as *hamirslag-ōn* 'to hit with a hammer; lit. hammer-hit' are also interpretable as denominal formations (← *hamerslag* 'hammer-blow'). Much the same applies to A+V compounds, which are at any rate rare. Formations with initial elements such as *eban-* (e.g., *eban-prinkan* 'to leave, to be of use' ← *eban* 'equal, just, honest' + *prinkan* 'to bring, to give') or *folla-* (e.g., *folla-ziohan* 'to complete, to carry out' ← *fol* 'full, entire' + *ziohan* 'to move, to lead') are seen by Splett (2000: 1216) as prefix formations because they occur in a series (for *vol-* cf. section 4.3.1, Table 15.5). In Mhd. Gr. III (553–574), in which "particle-verb formation" ("Partikelverbbildung") is not taken into account as a word-formation category and the criterion of inseparability plays no role, the following verbs are seen as "compounding" ("Komposition"): 74 verbs with a simplex particle (e.g., *nider-bringen* 'to ruin; lit. down-bring'), 30 verbs with a (already documented in OHG) double particle (e.g., *darum-besliezen* 'to enclose; lit. around-enclose'), 11 N+V formations (e.g., *salm-singen* 'to sing psalms; lit. psalm-sing'), 3 A+V formations (e.g., *liep-kōsen* 'to caress, to speak kindly'; lit. kind-caress) as well as 1 V+V formation (*weine-klagen* 'to moan crying; lit. cry-moan'). If one assumes a narrow view of "compounding" ("Komposition") as basic and takes existing classification problems into account – Splett (2000: 1216) sees *salmo-sang-ōn* 'to sing psalms; lit. psalm-sing' in contrast to Mhd. Gr. III as derivation from *psalmosang* 'singing of psalms; lit. psalm-singing' –, then verbal compounding from the Middle Ages to the present proves to be a marginal type of word-formation.

3.4 Adverbial compounding

The domain of adverbial compounding is seen here as involving formations with adverbial or prepositional final members. A differentiation of these elements as "adverb" or "preposition" is diachronically problematic, since many of these final members belong to both word classes. Formations with nominal final members are, on the other hand, classified as conversions (cf. section 5.4). Studies of adverbial word-formation – especially historical ones – are rare in German. For the most part, the description remains focused on nominal, adjectival and verbal word-formations. Thus in the following, only the results of the historical study by Heinle (2004) can be presented, which, however, is largely based on the evaluation of dictionaries. There, 27 adverbial/prepositional final members are collected and their development from the Middle Ages to the present is investigated. In most cases the beginnings of the formation of compounds go back as far as OHG, such as is the case for *-ab* (e.g., NHG *vor-ab* 'first'), *-an* (e.g., *hier-an* 'on here; lit. here-on'), *-aus* (e.g., *her-aus* 'out') or *-um* (e.g., *wieder-um* 'again'). Only attested in MHG are formations with *-hinter* (e.g., *da-hinter* 'behind'), *-neben* (e.g., *da-neben* 'next to'), *-nieder* (e.g., *her-nieder* 'down'), *-von* (e.g., *wo-von* 'what ... about') and *-zwischen* (e.g., *da-zwischen* 'between them; lit. them-between') and only in ENHG compounds with *-ohn(e)* (e.g., *zweifels-ohne* 'without doubt; lit. doubt-without') and *-wegen* (e.g., *des-wegen* 'therefore'). While in the middle ages primarily adverbs or prepositions function as first elements, in ENHG nouns and adjectives are also found (cf. NHG *berg-auf* 'uphill; lit. hill-up', *weit-aus* 'far; lit. wide-out'). Overall in the development towards ENHG a significant increase in productivity becomes apparent. In particular in the 16th as well as in the 18th/19th centuries, adverbial compounds evidently attain a special diversity in their formations and are even documented with numerous formations which are no longer in use in the contemporary language (cf. *dorf-zu* 'towards a village; lit. village-towards', *diesem-nach* 'therefore; lit. this-after'). In the contemporary language on the other hand, the degree of productivity of adverbial compounds, which according to Heinle (2004: 371) are primarily used in local (around 55 %), modal (around 25 %) and temporal (around 16 %) function, is rather low. The number of demotivated formations is large and a demarcation of determinative from more additive-coordinative formations is to some extent difficult (cf. Fleischer and Barz 2012: 362 f.).

4 Derivation

Derivation is the second central process of word-formation in German and plays an important role in the formation of nouns, adjectives, verbs and adverbs. For as early as OHG, Splett (1993 II: 1, 183 f.) documents 69 prefixes and 154 suffixes. There is, however, a fundamental difference in the distribution of prefix and suffix derivation: While prefix derivation/particle-verb formation is the focus of verbal word-formation, suffix derivation is fundamental for the formation of nouns, adjectives and adverbs.

4.1 Nominal derivation

4.1.1 Prefix derivation

Only a few elements of word-formation are used for the prefix derivation of nouns. In the Middle Ages these are primarily *un-* and *ge-*, the percentage of which in the MHG corpus (cf. Mhd. Gr. III: 39) very clearly outweighs (*un-*: around 63 %, *ge-*: around 20 %) that of other prefixes (*misse-*, *houbet-*, *ur-*, *ab-*, *ā-*), the percentages of which amount to less than 5 % respectively. While *un-* is used primarily for negation (e.g., MHG *un-heil* 'disaster'), but additionally also for valuation ("Taxation", e.g., MHG *un-tāt* 'bad deed') and augmentation (e.g., NHG *Un-summe* 'very large sum'), the prefix *ge-* forms mainly collective nouns (e.g., ENHG *ge-stain* 'many/all stones') and additionally also a few personal nouns with sociative components (e.g., MHG *ge-verte* 'co-traveller'). Only secondarily does it become productive as an element of word-formation, which mainly forms action nouns, partly also as a component of the circumfix *ge-...-e* (e.g., MHG *ge-brüll-e* '(continual) bellowing'). Wilmanns (1899: 244 ff.) suspects that the formation of this model is the result of a reanalysis based on doubly motivated, denominally and deverbally interpretable formations. But one can also assume that here formations with the suffix *-e* are the basis for a reanalysis of *ge*-verbs, which occurred as a result of the further grammaticalization of *ge-* (verbal word-formation morpheme > participle II-inflectional marker) (cf. Mhd. Gr. III: 71).

The negational prefix *ā-* (e.g., OHG *ā-maht* 'no power', in NHG reinterpreted as *Ohnmacht* i.e. 'without power') which was still productive in OHG and which also had a valuative function (e.g., OHG/MHG *ā-kust* 'falseness, vice' ← OHG *kust* 'state, attitude, virtue'), has fallen out of use as a prefix since ENHG. On the other hand, *ur-* remains preserved, although it loses its function as a negational prefix (e.g., MHG *ur-vēhede* 'renunciation of revenge'). Instead the percentage of formations which designate 'originality' or 'chronological antecedence' has increased significantly since the early modern period (cf. Kluge 1925: 54: ENHG *ur-heimat* 'original homeland', *ur-großvater* 'great-grandfather').

The prefix *miss-* (< MHG *misse-* < ahd. *missi-*) is also documented from OHG to the contemporary period in valuative (e.g., MHG *misse-tāt* 'bad, false act') or negating (e.g., ENHG *misse-treue* 'lack of loyalty') function.

Two further prefixes, on the other hand, experience a significant increase in productivity from OHG to NHG. This is the case for *erz-* (< Late Latin *archi-* < Gr. *archi-* 'the first, highest'), which is initially only found in Latin loan words (e.g., OHG *erzi-biscop* 'archbishop') and only in the development towards ENHG does it occur in series as an augmentative foreign prefix (e.g., ENHG *erz-bösewicht* 'particularly great villain'). Also *haupt-* (< MHG *houbet* 'head') has developed since MHG into a prefix (e.g., MHG *houbet-list* 'particularly great wisdom'), which in the development towards NHG – parallel to the more and more limited use of the noun *Haupt* – has experienced an increase in productivity and is, in the contemporary language, the most frequent prefix (over 60 %) well before *un-* (around 15 %) (cf. Müller 1993: 128).

All other prefixes documented in OHG/MHG, all with low frequency (see above), lose, as does *ā-*, at the latest in the development toward ENHG/NHG their potential for word-formation. Some are lost completely, others remain present in relict forms. Among these are the following OHG word-formation elements (cf. Splett 2000: 1217): *ab-* (e.g., OHG *ab-got* 'false, heathen God'), *aber-* (e.g., MHG *aber-list* 'repeated subterfuge'), *after-* (e.g., MHG *after-ruom* 'posthumous fame'), *ant-* (e.g., OHG *ant-dag* 'day of remembrance'), *bi-* (e.g., OHG *bi-sprācha* 'slander'), *fra-* (e.g., OHG *fra-tāt* 'misdemeanour'), *ita-* (e.g., *ita-wīz* 'disgrace, mocking'), *uo-* (e.g., OHG *uo-wahst* 'offspring' ← *wahst* 'growth').

Altogether the prefixes perform essentially four functions: negation, collectivizing, valuation and augmentation. In the course of this development, a clear diachronic shift becomes apparent: While in MHG/ENHG negative formations clearly outweigh collective, valuative and augmentative formations (cf. Mhd. Gr. III: 135; Müller 1993: 413; Brendel et al. 1997: 106), in the contemporary language we find a clear preponderance of augmentatives with respect to collectives, but especially valuatives and the negative formations which assume only forth place. This result mirrors the (early) modern emergence of numerous elements in augmentative function, partly referred to as "prefixoids" (e.g., ENHG *angst-bösewicht* 'particularly great villain; lit. fear-villain', NHG *Mords-lärm* 'particularly great noise; lit. murder-noise', *Höllen-durst* 'particularly great thirst; lit. hell-thirst', *Sau-kälte* 'particularly great cold; lit. sow-cold'). The foreign prefix *super-* (e.g., *Super-leinwand* 'particularly large screen'), which became productive after World War II, also plays a role, as the influence of foreign word-formation has generally led to a significant expansion of the means of prefixation in NHG (cf. article 15 on foreign word-formation in German).

4.1.2 Suffix derivation

In comparison to the prefixation of nouns, suffixation is much more pronounced. This is the case both for the percentual distribution as well as the number of affixes. Thus we find in the corpus of the MHG Grammar 240 prefix formations as opposed to 1,995 suffix formations and 7 prefixes as opposed to 21 suffixes (cf. Mhd. Gr. III: 39, 56 f.). Much the same applies to the ENHG corpora (cf. Müller 1993; Döring and Eichler 1996; Brendel et al. 1997), and in the contemporary language the percentage of suffix formations in the derivation of nouns amounts to around 80 %, while prefix derivatives are situated far below 10 % and even come after conversions (overview in Müller 1993: 390). In the following, I give an overview of the inventory, proportion (type frequency) and main function of the suffixes in the corpus of the MHG Grammar (cf. Mhd. Gr. III: 57–161):

Tab. 15.1: Nominal suffixes in MHG.

-heit/-keit (20.5 %): quality nouns ("Abstrakta", i.e. nomina actions and nomina acti) (68.0 %; e.g., *schœn-heit* 'beauty');
-e (20.1 %): quality nouns (38.8 %; e.g., *sterk-e* 'strength, power'); action nouns ("Abstrakta", i.e. nomina actionis and nomina acti) (33.8 %; e.g., *touf-e* 'baptism');
-unge (18.1 %): action nouns (86.4 %; e.g., *lob-unge* 'praise');
-er(e) (11.0 %): agent nouns ("Agentiva") (73.1 %; e.g., *dien-er* 'servant');
-(e)līn (> NHG *-lein*) (5.6 %): diminutives (100 %; e.g., *kind-elīn* 'small child');
-(e)de (5.3 %): action nouns (51.9 %; e.g., *beweg-ede* 'movement'); quality nouns (23.6 %; e.g., *sterk-ede* 'strength, power');
-in(ne) (4.3 %): gender marking ("Movierung") (100 %; e.g., *diub-inne* 'female thief');
-nisse (4.2 %): action nouns (45.2 %; e.g., *spreche-nisse* 'speaking');
-el (2.8 %): diminutives (54.5 %; e.g., *kind-el* 'small child'); deverbal personal names and names denoting things ("Agentiva") (27.3 %; e.g., *köuf-el* 'dealer', *stach-el* 'thorn, spine, spike'); instrument nouns (18.2 %; e.g., *sleg-el* 'drumstick');
-schaft (2.0 %): status nouns ("Abstrakta") (45.0 %; e.g., *vīent-schaft* 'hostility'); collective nouns (22.5 %; e.g., *heiden-schaft* 'many/all pagans');
-t (1.7 %): action nouns (61.8 %; e.g., *vluh-t* 'escape' ← *vliehen*);
-tuem/-tuom (> NHG *-tum*) (1.3 %): quality nouns (42.3 %; e.g., *siech-tuem* 'illness'); status nouns (42.3 %; e.g., *maget-tuem* 'virginity');
-sal (0.6 %): action nouns (75.0 %; e.g., *āhte-sal* 'pursuit' ← *āhten* 'to follow');
-(e)chīn (> NHG *-chen*) (0.6 %): diminutives (100 %; e.g., *schęf-chīn* 'small sheep');
-īe (> NHG *-ei*) (0.5 %): status nouns (80.0 %; e.g., *voget-īe* 'stewardship');
-sen (> NHG recent dialectal *-sche*) (0.5 %): gender marking (100 %; e.g., *meister-sen* 'female master');
-linc (> NHG *-ling*) (0.4 %): deadjectival personal nouns (50 %; e.g., *junge-linc* 'youth'); deverbal personal nouns (50 %; e.g., *kome-linc* 'newcomer');
-ōt (0.3 %): action nouns (100 %; e.g., *achez-ōt* 'groaning' ← *achzen* 'to groan');
-ach (0.2 %): collectives (100 %; e.g., *dorn-ach* 'thornbushes' ← *dorn* 'thornbush');
-āt (0.1 %): action nouns (100 %; e.g., *bliuw-āt* 'beating' ← *bliuwen* 'to beat');
-(e)rich (unter 0.1 %): denominal personal nouns (100 %; e.g., *wüet-erich* 'brute').

As this overview shows, the four suffixes *-heit/-keit*, *-unge*, *-e* and *-er(e)* are dominant and form around 70 % of all suffix derivatives. A similar center of gravity is also exhibited by other MHG (cf. Ring 2008), ENHG (cf. Müller 1993; Döring and Eichler 1996; Brendel et al. 1997) and contemporary (cf. DWb 2; Gersbach and Graf 1984–85) corpora.

A special case are the diminutive suffixes *-(e)līn* und *-(e)chīn*, which are also regionally distributed. The suffix *-(e)chīn*, initially only attested in Middle German, has since the 18th century developed into the primary suffix for diminution in the written language. The percentage of diminutives depends to a high degree on the text type, so that large deviations arise depending on the corpus (cf. *-(e)līn* > NHG *-lein*: Mhd. Gr. III: place 5; Ring 2008 (MHG language of documents): place 9; Gersbach and Graf 1984–85 (contemporary spoken language): place 1).

In comparison to the four dominant suffixes *-heit/-keit*, *-unge*, *-e* and *-er(e)*, the frequency of all further suffixes is significantly lower. For the suffixes *-(e)līn*, *-(e)de*, *-in(ne)*, *-nisse*, *-el*, *-schaft*, *-t*, and *-tuem* values between 5 % and 1 % are found, all 9 further affixes are below 1 %. The finding partially mirrors developments which had already begun in OHG. Thus the suffixes *-t*, *-ōt*, and *-āt* are either unproductive or of lesser importance and are abandoned in NHG. The suffix *-ach* is preserved in dialect words as well as in toponyms (cf. *Steinach* as place name) and in the standard language the variant *-icht* is contained in a few lexemes (e.g., NHG *Dickicht* 'thicket'). The OHG diminutive suffix *-īn* is only preserved in MHG in relict forms (e.g., diminutive *maged-īn* ← *maget* 'unmarried woman, virgin'). The weakening productivity of these suffixes manifests itself in a high degree of lexicalization or idiomatization in this segment of the vocabulary.

On the other hand, the MHG results show a number of new developments with respect to OHG: This is the case on the one hand, for the morphemes which have grammaticalized to suffixes, *-heit*, *-schaft* and *-tuem*, as well as, on the other, for the suffixes which have been altered by the reduction of unstressed syllables, *-(e)de* (< OHG *-ida*) and *-e*. The suffix *-ida*, which was already in retreat in OHG, succumbed to competitive pressure from *-heit*. Its use is already limited in MHG. In NHG, it becomes unproductive and is displaced by *-e* or *-heit* (quality nouns) or *-ung* (action nouns). In the case of *-e*, the reduction of unstressed syllables leads to the collapsing of several suffixes. Among others the OHG suffix for agent nouns *-o* and the very productive suffix *-ī*, which in OHG formed action/quality nouns, end up with the same form (cf. section 2.1 (d)). This leads in MHG to a polyfunctional suffix, also with the inflectional marker *-e*, which then as a result of this formal reduction increasingly ends up being in competition with the more distinctive suffixes *-er* (e.g., *becke* 'baker' vs. *becker*), *-heit* (e.g., *swach-e* 'weakness' vs. *swach-heit*) and *-ung* (e.g., *aneveht-e* 'temptation, moral conflict, contestation' vs. *aneveht-unge*) and in the development towards NHG is abandoned as a suffix for agent nouns or is reduced to an action/quality suffix. The suffix *-el* also already proves to be in retreat in MHG. In the development towards NHG, it loses its meaning as a diminutive suffix (only dialectally productive) and is replaced as a suffix for the formation of agent/instrument nouns by *-er*.

The MHG loan suffix *-īe*, on the other hand, only becomes productive in ENHG. In the overview in Ring (2008: 494 f.) on the comparative ranking of the 10 most frequent suffixes in different corpora, it is only documented beginning in ENHG (9th place) and reaches place 5 or 4 in the spoken and written contemporary language. The increasing importance of foreign word-formation since the early modern period – as can also be seen from the nascent competitive formations of native and exogenous derivatives (regarding Goethe cf. Stricker 2002) – leads ultimately to further restructuring, so that in the contemporary written language the foreign suffixes *-(at)ion*, *-ismus* and *-ität* take the places 8–10.

Alongside non-native suffixes, in ENHG indigenous suffixes are added, which arise from processes of grammaticalization, such as the collective morphemes *-werk* (e.g., NHG *Laub-werk* 'all leaves of a tree/shrub') and *-wesen* (e.g., *Schul-wesen* 'school system'). However in these cases – unlike in the case of *-heit*, *-schaft* and *-tum* – the underlying nouns are still in use (cf. *Werk* 'work, works, factory', *Wesen* 'being, nature'), the process of grammaticalization is not yet completed.

All in all it appears that, in the course of the history of German, the system of nominal suffix derivation is relatively stable in its center and experiences change more in its periphery.

With respect to the functional load of the suffixes from the Middle Ages to the contemporary period, both similarities and differences can be seen. For example *-ung*, which is predominantly documented in action nouns, proves to be stable. In the case of *-er* as well, the primary function of the formation of agent nouns is preserved, but in the development towards ENHG further functions are added (formation of instrument nouns, patient nouns and result nouns; e.g., *Entsaft-er* 'juicer', *Aufkleb-er* 'sticker', *Rülpser* 'belch'); also the suffix *-(e)rich* is only used as a gender marking suffix in NHG (e.g., *Gäns-erich* 'gander'). But also larger shifts and the reduction of functions are possible. Thus in the case of *-e* the following changes in frequency in comparison with the contemporary written language can be observed for the first four functional domains dominant in MHG (cf. Mhd. Gr. III: 61 f.) (overview in Müller 1993: 290): quality nouns: 1st place > 3rd place; action nouns: 2nd place > 1st place; patient nouns: 3rd place > 4th place; agent nouns (and further deverbal personal names and names denoting things): 4th place > 7th place. That these restructurings – also the significantly higher proportion of instrument nouns (6th place > 2nd place) is striking – can be triggered by competition with other suffixes was demonstrated above. A larger number of competing formations in the historical text corpora demonstrates that the system of word-formation is still open. Thus in MHG for example, the following competing formations (derivatives with the same bases and with identical word-formation function) are documented (cf. Mhd. Gr. III: 146–149): quality nouns: *schœn-heit* 'beauty' vs. *schœn-e* vs. *schœn-de*; action nouns: *beschouw-unge* 'sight, contemplation' vs. *beschouw-e* vs. *beschouw-ede*. In the development towards NHG, such competition is commonly reduced, either by semantic differentiation or by a loss of lexemes.

With respect to the frequency of the functional domains covered by the suffixes, the following picture emerges for the corpus of the MHG Grammar (cf. Mhd. Gr. III: 144): abstract nouns (especially action nouns and quality nouns) clearly outweigh (about two thirds) agent nouns and further personal nouns and nouns denoting things (almost one quarter). They are followed at some distance by diminutives, patient nouns, gender markings, instrument nouns and place nouns, which all lie between 8 % and 1 %. This sequence is, with similar frequency, also valid for the contemporary written language (cf. Müller 1993: 474 f.), so that there is great continuity in this domain. A few functional domains exhibit thereby a dominant suffix which clearly predominates quantitatively. For the action nouns this is *-ung*, for the quality nouns *-heit*, for the agent nouns *-er*, for the diminutives *-lein* (MHG) or *-chen* (NHG), for gender marking *-in* (OHG gender marking with *-āra* (cf. Splett 1993 II: 215 f.) to formations with the loan suffix *-āri*, e.g., *zuht-āra* 'female educator' ← *zuht-āri* 'educator' are already abandoned in MHG). The other functional domains lack such a characteristic suffix and the suffix frequencies are more balanced. This is also due to the fact that in German patient nouns, instrument nouns and place nouns are only formed with such suffixes which have a primary function in another domain. Thus we find, for example, for patient nouns in the corpus of the MHG Grammar (cf. Mhd. Gr. III: 154) the following distribution: *-e*$_3$: 42.1 %; *-unge*$_2$: 30.7 %; *-(e)de*$_3$: 13.2 %; *-nisse*$_3$: 9.6 %; *-t*$_3$: 4.4 %. This means that patient nouns are ranked second for *-ung*, and for all other suffixes they are ranked third. In this respect the question can naturally be raised whether and how much productivity the individual suffixes have in this function and what role the factor of "semantic change" plays for such secondary formations (cf. Müller 2016, 2017).

4.2 Adjectival derivation

4.2.1 Prefix derivation

Just as is the case for nouns, prefix derivation is also much less used for adjectives than suffix derivation. For MHG, a proportion of around 30 % is attested, which has decreased in the development toward the contemporary written language (around 22 %) (cf. Ganslmayer 2012: 983). Essentially the same affixes are used for adjective prefixation as is the case for nouns, whereby the prefix *un-* is significantly more frequent (407 adjectives with *un-* vs. 152 nouns with *un-* in the corpus of the MHG Grammar). In MHG it forms, together with the suffixes *-lich* and *-ig*, almost 80 % of all adjectival derivatives (cf. Ganslmayer 2012: 984 f.) and its proportion of the prefix derivatives is over 85 %. Beyond that, it is documented in combinatorial derivations with negating-passive function together with suffixes (cf. Ganslmayer 2012: 964–976), thus with *-lich* (e.g., *un-vergez-lich* 'unforgettable' ← *vergezzen* 'to forget') and *-bære/-bar* (e.g., *un-lougen-bære* 'undeniable' ← *lougenen* 'to deny'). The proportion of other prefixes, on the other hand, is low. Even the second-ranked prefix *ge-* in the MHG corpora is only just over or under 5 % (cf. Mhd. Gr. III: 249; Ganslmayer 2012: 986) and the other prefixes are even more peripheral. The following prefixes are documented in the MHG corpora:

Tab. 15.2: Adjectival prefixes in MHG.

un-: negating (e.g., *un-edel* 'not nobel, of lower provenance');
ge-: possessive (denominal; e.g., *ge-haz* 'spiteful'); pleonastic (e.g., *ge-willic* 'willingly' ← *willic* 'id.');
hōch-: intensificative ("gradativ") (e.g., *hōch-wirdic* 'particularly worthy');
eben-: similative (i.e. adjectives of resemblance) (e.g., *eben-alt* 'just as old'); intensificative (e.g., *eben-gelīch* 'just as equal');
durch-: intensificative (e.g., *durch-schœne* 'very beautiful');
misse- (> NHG *miss-*): valuative ("taxativ") (e.g., *misse-var* 'sparsely colored, pale' ← *var* 'colored');
ā-: negating (e.g., *ā-wīse* 'dumb' ← *wīse* 'smart'); privative (denominal; e.g., *ā-wicke* 'impassable, not having a path' ← *wec* 'way, path');
über-: intensificative (e.g., *über-vil* 'particularly much');
ur-: intensificative (e.g., *ur-grōz* 'very large'); privative (denominal; e.g., *ur-klege* 'without complaint' ← *klage* 'complaint, lawsuit').

This inventory of prefixes is still clearly determined by OHG traditions (cf. Splett 2000: 1217), but already indicates the change, most clearly through the reduction of formations with *ā-* and in particular with *ge-*, which in OHG were still clearly more productive (cf. Mhd. Gr. III: 251, 260). The number of the former *bahuvrīhi* compounds – cf. section 5.2 on corresponding adjectival A+N formations – is already greatly reduced in MHG. The prefixes *eben-* and *durch-* – as well as others, documented corpus externally, such as *ab-* (e.g., MHG *ab-holt* 'not weighed' ← *holt* 'weighed') or *an-* (e.g., ENHG *an-eben* 'uneven') – are also no longer productive in NHG and partially only preserved in relict forms (cf. *abhold*). Of the prefixes preserved in the contemporary language *un-* is still productive, but with a small share. The prefixes *hoch-* and *über-* increase slightly, *miss-* remains rare, and *ur-* loses on the one hand its function as a privative prefix, but distinguishes itself on the other as an intensificative morpheme (e.g., NHG *ur-gemütlich* 'very cozy'). The inventory of prefixes has been extended since ENHG especially through intensificative foreign prefixes such as *erz-*, *super-*, *hyper-* or *ultra-* (cf. article 4 on foreign word-formation in German), supplemented by intensifying initial members which are partially characterized as prefixoids, such as *hunds-* (e.g., *hunds-gemein* 'particularly mean; lit. dog-mean'), *sau-* (e.g., *sau-stark* 'particularly strong; lit. pig-strong') or *scheiß-* (e.g., *scheiß-freundlich* 'particularly friendly; lit. shit-friendly'), which are especially used colloquially. The percentage of foreign prefixes in the contemporary language amounts nevertheless to around 6 % of all prefixes (cf. Ganslmayer 2012: 986).

From a semantic perspective, adjectival prefix derivation serves primarily the purpose of 'negation'. In the corpus of the MHG Grammar (cf. Mhd. Gr. III: 340) 94.2 % of prefix formations are negating, 5.3 % intensificative and 0.5 % valuative. This relationship changes, though, in the development towards NHG, since in the contemporary written language the proportion of intensificative prefix derivatives is significantly higher: In the Innsbruck corpus (cf. DWb 3) the proportion of 'negation' and 'intensification' is 4 : 1 (cf. Ganslmayer 2012: 1066 ff.). Around one third of all intensificative formations contains a foreign prefix, while in the domain of 'negation' *un-* still clearly dominates. The proportion of foreign prefixes (cf. *a-sozial*, *anti-autoritär*, *in-adäquat*) amounts here to nevertheless around 10 %. Also, due to the increasing productivity of negating compounds with *nicht-* 'non-' (cf. Wellmann 1997: 83; e.g., *nicht-christlich* 'non-Christian'), which, in the second half of the 20th century become ever more productive, the dominance of *un-* in the modern language is relativized in comparison to MHG.

4.2.2 Suffix derivation

Adjectival suffix derivation also exhibits a concentration on a few highly frequent affixes which is even more pronounced than in the nominal domain. In the following, the suffixes from the corpus of the MHG Grammar (cf. Mhd. Gr. III: 273) are compiled with their percentage (type frequency) and main functions (see Table 15.3).

Tab. 15.3: Adjectival suffixes in MHG.

-lich (37.7 %): relational [type I] ("korrespondierend"; the base noun is a corresponding entity) (25.6 %; e.g., *brüeder-lich* 'fraternal');
-ig/-ic (27.5 %): possessive-ornative (52.9 %; e.g., *zorn-ic* 'angry');
-īn (> NHG *-en/-ern*) (7.8 %): material ("substance adjectives") (82.8 %; e.g., *sīdīn* 'silk');
-isch (7.3 %): relational [type II] ("spezifizierend"; adjectives signaling 'affiliation') (65.0 %; e.g., *bern-isch* 'from Bern (i.e. Verona)');
-haft (6.4 %): possessive-ornative (57.7 %; e.g., *zwīfel-haft* 'doubtful');
-sam (3.4 %): causative-factitive (61.5 %; e.g., *trōst-sam* 'comforting');
-bære (> NHG *-bar*) (3.3 %): causative-factitive (37.0 %; e.g., *vruht-bære* 'fertile');
-lōs (3.2 %): privative (100 %; e.g., *ende-lōs* 'endless');
-oht/-eht (with reanalyzed suffix variant *-loht/-leht* from bases ending in *-l*) (> NHG *-icht*) (1.7 %): possessive-ornative (71.4 %; e.g., *bart-oht* 'beardy');
-valt (0.7 %): multiplicative (100 %; e.g., *siben-valt* 'sevenfold');
-el (0.7 %): active(-modal) (66.7 %; e.g., *wank-el* 'swaying' ← *wanken* 'to sway');
-mæze/-mæzig (> NHG *-mäßig*) (0.2 %): similative (50.0 %; e.g., *zucker-mæzic* 'like sugar').

This MHG system of adjectival suffix derivation – similar to Ganslmayer's results (2012: 987) for the MHG language of documents – is largely consistent with the OHG affix inventory and is a combination of inherited Germanic affixes (cf. *-ig*, *-isch*, *-īn*, *-oht*) and OHG/MHG products of grammaticalization (cf. *-lich*, *-haft*, *-sam*, *-bære*, *-lōs*, *-mæze*/*-mæzig* and section 2.1 (b)). In comparison with OHG (cf. Splett 2000: 1219 f.), a decline of the suffixes which fall out of use in ENHG is already clearly visible, namely *-el* and *-valt*, the latter of which was initially replaced by the pleonastic extension *-valtig* and has been displaced since the 14th century by *-fach*. Only much later, after 1800, is the MHG suffix *-oht*/*-eht* (*-loht*/*-leht*)/NHG *-icht*, which was still productive in ENHG, abandoned (cf. section 2.2).

A comparison with the suffix frequency in the contemporary written language (cf. Ganslmayer 2012: 988) shows the following developments: While the suffix *-ig* now ranks first with almost the same proportion and is also increasingly used in the contemporary language for the derivation of word groups in the function of condensing text passages (cf. *dreifenstr-ig* 'with three windows'), the suffix *-isch* (18.9 %) experiences significant growth and takes second place with a considerably expanded functional spectrum (cf. Ganslmayer 2012: 510), still before *-lich* (12.8 %). The decline of the adjectival suffix *-lich* is also caused by the fact that in MHG, due to the deletion of the final vowel, the adverb-forming suffix

OHG *-līhho*/MHG *-līche* (cf. section 4.4) partially collapses with it formally and thus *-lich* additionally functions as a suffix for marking adverbial use and then loses this function in the development towards NHG. Among the other suffixes, *-sam* (0.9 %) and *-īn* (> NHG *-en*/*-ern*) (2.2 %) also decline slightly, on the other hand *-bære* (> NHG *-bar*) (5.3 %), *-los* (5.6 %) and *-mäßig* (2.8 %) increase to some extent. In the contemporary written language, the percentage of foreign suffixes is especially important (16 %; cf. *-al*/*-ell*, *-ar*/*-är*, *-iv*, *-abel*/*-ibel*, *-ant*/*-ent*, *-ös*; cf. article 4 on foreign word-formation in German) and the system of suffixes is also complemented by morphemes such as *-reich* (e.g., *nikotin-reich* 'containing a lot of nicotine; lit. nicotine-rich'), *-arm* (e.g., *schadstoff-arm* 'containing few harmful substances; lit. harm-stuff-poor') or *-selig* (e.g., *wein-selig* 'elevated by wine; lit. wine-blissful'), which are partially seen as suffixoids.

Incisive restructurings can be observed from MHG to NHG with respect to the word classes of the bases, as the comparison between the MHG language of documents and the contemporary written language shows (cf. Ganslmayer 2012: 999). Thus nouns (40.0 % > 79.8 %) and verbs (6.1 % > 17.0 %) increase significantly as bases of word-formation. Verbs do so due to the reinterpretation of doubly motivated, actually denominal formations (on such derivatives with *-bære* cf. section 2.3). Adjectives (27.1 % > 1.2 %), on the other hand, decrease significantly, facilitated by the fact that *-lich* loses its adverb-marking function as well as by the reduction of competing formations (e.g., MHG *ēr-haft* 'honourable' vs. *ēr-sam* vs. *ēr-bære*) and doubly suffixed adjectives in which the second suffix only makes the word class "adjective" clearer. In the latter function especially *-ig*/*-ic* develops into a prototypical adjectival suffix (e.g., MHG *ēr-bære* → *ērbær-ic*, *won-haft* 'residing' → *wonhaft-ic*, *zwi-valt* 'twice' → *zwifalt-ic*, *ge-haz* 'spiteful' → *gehäss-ig*, *-mæze* > *-mæzig*) which also attaches to suffixless adjectives that are formally identical to nouns (cf. section 2.2; e.g., MHG *grim* 'furious' → *grim-ic*). In this function it becomes a role model for further ENHG double suffixes (cf. Thomas 2002: 504: *-haftig*, *-echtig*), which are indicators of a temporary system overload (cf. Ganslmayer 2011: 371), and which are therefore later abandoned. This phenomenon already occurs in OHG (cf. Splett 2000: 1219: *forsc-al* 'curious' with the unproductive suffix *-al* → *forscal-īn*). The tendency toward the unambiguous marking of suffixes in opposition to other word classes or inflectional morphemes continues in ENHG with the development of the suffix variant *-ern* (< *-erīn*). This suffix arose through the reanalysis of the boundary between the stem forming element *-er* and the affix *-īn* (cf. MHG *lember-īn* '(belonging) to lambs' > *lemb-erīn*) and to some extent displaced older forms with *-en* (cf. Paul 1920 § 66: ENHG *hölz-en* 'wooden' > *hölz-ern*, *stähl-en* 'of steel' > *stähl-ern*).

From a functional perspective, the MHG suffix derivatives are predominantly denominal relational adjectives, which can be further subdivided semantically.

The number, naming, and demarcation of the various functional domains differentiated in the historical descriptions of word-formation (cf. Mhd. Gr. III: 342 f.; Ganslmayer 2012: 1041; Thomas 2002: 525 ff.) is, however, very heterogeneous, which makes the comparison of the results difficult (cf. the synopsis in Ganslmayer 2012: 1124–1127). For MHG, four dominant functional domains can be identified, the proportion of which is over 10 %, and which together make up slightly less than 50 % (MHG language of documents) or almost two thirds (MHG Grammar corpus) of all suffix functions (13 in Mhd. Gr. III, 20 in Ganslmayer 2012): relational [type I] (the base noun is a corresponding entity), possessive-ornative, causative-factitive and relational [type II] (adjectives signaling 'affiliation'). Comparison with the contemporary language (cf. Ganslmayer 2012: 1045) shows a few characteristic changes conditioned by the text-type: Thus the proportion of possessive-ornative formations, the most common in MHG, is still increasing (around 30 % of denominal suffix formations), while in the contemporary written language the percentage of causative-factitive (2.1 %) and relational [type I] (4.8 %) formations is decreasing significantly. In return, the percentage of similative formations (i.e. adjectives of resemblance), which in MHG was less than 4 %, increases considerably in the contemporary written language: Here they attain second place with 16.7 %, but remain, on the other hand, unimportant in the contemporary spoken language with 5.0 %.

In comparison with denominal suffix derivation, the percentage of deverbal formations in MHG is still low. Essentially, these are primarily active(-modal) or passive-modal derivatives, the percentage of which in adjectival suffix derivation in the corpus of the MHG Grammar is only 11 % (active(-modal): 7.7 %; passive-modal: 3.3 %). While this dominance of active(-modal) formations also holds for the corpus of the contemporary spoken language (Gersbach and Graf 1984–85), for the Innsbruck corpus of the contemporary written language (DWb 3) a light surplus of passive-modal adjectives can be found (cf. Ganslmayer 2012: 1051 ff.).

Apart from the monofunctional suffixes *-los* and *-valt* (see above), a pronounced polysemy is particularly characteristic for the adjectival suffixes (on average more than seven functional domains; cf. Ganslmayer 2012: 1084). Thereby from MHG to NHG, to some extent considerable changes in the functional potential and the proportion of word-formation functions result. The example *-bar* has already been pointed out (cf. section 2.3). Two further examples are *-haft* and *-sam*. In the case of *-haft* (cf. Mhd. Gr. III: 281; Ganslmayer 2012: 322), the change in word-formation from MHG to NHG leads to a fundamental functional upheaval in which the similative function, in MHG still fully peripheral (e.g., MHG *man-haft* 'brave'), has developed in the contemporary written language into the dominant primary function (71.6 %). The further functions, including the 'possessive-ornative', which in MHG was the primary function, are less than 10 %, which leads to the decline in the percentage of deverbal derivatives with *-haft*. Consequences for the distribution of functional classes also result from this functional change, since the functional domain 'similative' (i.e. adjectives of resemblance) is no longer peripheral in the contemporary written language as it was in MHG, but rather occupies the second place (see above). Alongside *-haft* (29.9 %), the suffixes *-isch* (24.6 %) and *-ig* (19.1 %) are also well represented (overview in Ganslmayer 2012: 1030), which in the MHG Grammar corpus only play a subordinate role in this function (cf. Mhd. Gr. III: 354).

In the case of *-sam*, on the other hand, a change in function takes place which is linked to a change in the word class of the base. The deverbatives with active (-modal) function, which in MHG were not yet systematically developed (cf. Mhd. Gr. III: 334; Ganslmayer 2012: 784), form the main group in the contemporary written language with a percentage of around 60 % (e.g., NHG *folg-sam* 'obedient'). However, this morphological-semantic refunctionalization in the case of *-sam* leads neither to an increase of this suffix in the adjectival system of word-formation nor to a dominance in the functional domain 'active(-modal)', since in the contemporary written language *-sam* in this case only occupies the fifth place with 6.9 % (cf. DWb 3: 385).

4.3 Verbal derivation

4.3.1 Prefix derivation and particle-verb formation

Verbal derivation is in German predominantly realized as prefix derivation or particle-verb formation. Seen diachronically, this is the result of univerbation of (local) particles (adverbs/prepositions) with verbs (particle compounds), in which the particles go through a process of grammaticalization, partly only occur as bound forms and give up their local particle meaning in favor of grammatical-functional meanings (e.g., marking of lexical aspect). (The demarcation between syntactic group, compounding and particle-verb formation is however not always unambiguously possible.) The inseparable prefixes of OHG include (cf. Splett 2000: 1216): *bi-* (e.g., *bi-grīfan* 'to clasp'), *fir-* (e.g., *fir-loufan* 'to go/run on ahead'), *gi-* (e.g., *gi-bintan* 'to tie'), *int-* (e.g., *int-ērēn* 'to dishonour'), *ir-* (e.g., *ir-scouwōn* 'to see'), *it-* (e.g., *it-peran* 'to bear again'), *missi-* (e.g., *missi-tuon* 'to commit a wrong, to sin'), *zir-* (e.g., *zir-gān* 'to pass'). Only *ir-* and *bi-* are already also attested as preposition/adverb.

Additionally, the prefix *un-* should be pointed out, which however is generally considered to be a nominal prefix. Accordingly, verbs prefixed with *un-*, which are documented from OHG up until the 18th century (cf. the overview in Henze

2010), should be seen as conversions (cf. OHG *unliumuntōn* 'to slander' ← *unliumunt* 'slander' ← *liumunt* 'reputation, fame'). Alongside verbs with *un-* which can unequivocally be seen as denominal conversions (cf. OHG *unmahten* 'to become weak' ← *unmaht* 'weakness'), doubly motivated formations can also be found, which can be interpreted denominally as well as deverbally (cf. MHG *unēren* 'to dishonour; lit. un-honour' ← *unēre* 'insult' or *ēren* 'to honour'), as well as verbs for which no nominal base exists (cf. MHG *undienen* 'to serve not; lit. un-serve' ← *dienen* 'to serve', *unbinden* 'to not oblige; lit. un-tie' ← *binden* 'to tie'). In Henze (2010: 237) at least 26 % of the roughly 180 verbs with *un-* documented from OHG up into the 18th century are classified as exclusively verbally motivated. Later, these verbs were abandoned, in contrast to English, for example (cf. *undo*, *unwrap*).

Alongside these prefixes in a narrow sense, *turuh-* (e.g., *turuh-tuon* 'to carry out, to complete'), *hinder-* (e.g., *hinder-chōsōn* 'to slander'), *ubar-* (e.g., *ubar-queman* 'to surprise') and *untar-* (e.g., *untar-fāhan* 'to stop') also occur as inseparable prefixes in OHG, which in the course of the further development of the language become separable and are thus counted among the group of verbal particles (also: "separable prefixes") (cf. *ubar-stīg* lit. 'over-climb' vs. *stīg ūf* lit. 'soar up').

In OHG, the following morphemes, which – due to the more or less clearly recognizable desemanticization of meaning – are no longer classified as forming compounds from a synchronic perspective, are counted among these morphologically and syntactically separable particles, which form particle verbs and also always occur as lexeme (preposition/adverb) (cf. Splett 1993 II: 1, 2000: 1216 f.):

Tab. 15.4: Verbal particles in OHG.

aba- (e.g., *aba-brechan* 'to break off; lit. off-break'), *after-* (e.g., *after-ruafan* 'to shout after; lit. after-shout'), *ana-* (e.g., *ana-werfan* 'to throw at; lit. at-throw'), *avur-* (e.g., *avur-pringan* 'to bring back; lit. back-bring'), *az-* (e.g., *az-wesan* 'to be here; lit. here-be'), *bī-* (e.g., *bī-stān* 'to stand by; lit. by-stand'), *dana-* (e.g., *dana-stōzzan* 'to push away; lit. away-push'), *dara-* (e.g., *dara-leiten* 'to lead there; lit. there-lead'), *fora-* (e.g., *fora-quedan* 'to predict; lit. before-speak'), *fram-* (e.g., *fram-gangan* 'to stride first; lit. first-stride'), *furder-* (e.g., *furder-sezzen* 'to move; lit. somewhere-put'), *furi-* (e.g., *furi-tragan* 'to carry on ahead; lit. on ahead-carry'), *gagen-* (e.g., *gagen-sezzen* 'to oppose with; lit. with-oppose'), *hera-* (e.g., *hera-queman* 'to come here; lit. here-come'), *hina-* (e.g., *hina-faran* 'to move there; lit. there-move'), *in-* (e.g., *in-lāzan* 'to let in; lit. in-let'), *ingagan-* (e.g., *ingagan-pellan* 'to bark towards; lit. towards-bark'), *inne-* (e.g., *inne-ligen* 'to stay inside; lit. inside-stay'), *miti-* (e.g., *miti-loufan* 'to run; lit. with-run'), *nāh-* (e.g., *nāh-loufan* 'to run after; lit. after-run'), *nidar-* (e.g., *nidar-fallan* 'to fall down; lit. down-fall'), *obe-* (e.g., *obe-sehen* 'to look down on; lit. down on-look'), *samen-* (e.g., *samen-standan* 'to stand together; lit. together-stand'), *ūf-* (e.g., *ūf-springan* 'to jump up; lit. up-jump'), *umbi-* (e.g., *umbi-sellen* 'to surround with; lit. with-surround'), *ūz-* (e.g., *ūz-spīwan* 'to bring up; lit. up-bring'), *widar-* (e.g., *widar-scouwōn* 'to look back; lit. back-look'), *zisamine-* (e.g., *zisamine-fuagen* 'to join together; lit. together-join'), *zuo-* (e.g., *zuo-legen* 'to add; lit. to-lay').

Already in OHG this large number of verbal prefixes and particles leads to a highly differentiated modification of the basic verbal vocabulary and to a considerable increase in word-family structures. For example, in the case of *geban* 'to give' almost 20 prefix and particle verbs are attested, in the case of *faran* 'to move' even more than 30 (cf. Splett 1993 I: 204 f., 292), which functionally alleviates the burden on both of these very polysemous base verbs. Most of the OHG prefixes and particles are also preserved in later stages of the language. In the MHG Grammar we find the following distribution (type frequency) of the prefixes/particles with word-formation functions (cf. Mhd. Gr. III: 391; supplemented here by the main functions of the prefixes/particles), presented in Table 15.5 below.

As this overview (in which the prefix *un-* is not taken into consideration; cf. Mhd. Gr. III: 393 f.) shows, the inseparable prefixes (*be-*, *ent-*, *er-*, *ge-*, *misse-*, *ver-*, *zer-* and *vol-*, whose prefixal status is, however, controversial) outweigh the other word-formation morphemes ("particles") which are used separably, or both separably and inseparably (around 57 % vs. 43 %). This preponderance becomes even clearer when one also takes the idiomaticized formations as well as all formations with *ge-* into account (also those with syntactic functions). Then the prefix *ge-* proves to be by far the most common prefix and the relation prefixes : particles becomes even clearer (cf. Mhd. Gr. III: 546: around 70 % : 30 %). On the other hand there is already a preponderance of particles in ENHG (cf. Habermann 1994: 252; 399 f.: 45.4 % : 54.6 %), and in the contemporary language the dominance of particles is even more pronounced (cf. DWb 1: 144–154: 29.8 % : 70.2 %). Again, this can also be linked to the processes of functional restructuring discussed above.

The ranking of prefixes remains in NHG for the most part the same. Only *ent-* increases in the contemporary written language to a good 13 % and thus reaches place 3, even ahead of the prefix *er-*, which recently has also been observed in dialects in the dentalized variant *der-*. The prefix *ge-*, on the other hand, which is also a component of double prefixations (cf. Herbers 2002: 131 ff.; e.g., *ane-ge-loufen* 'to run close up'), is a special case: In MHG it fulfils not only word-formation but also syntactic functions (for example marking the perfect and future). In the development towards NHG, it quickly loses both functions. The prefix *ge-* is in ENHG largely attested in pleonastic formations which do not fulfil word-formation functions (cf. Habermann 1994: 375). In the contemporary language it functions solely as a marker of participles.

In the cases of the particles, however, large increases in productivity take place. So for the contemporary written language the following ranking results for the six most frequent particles with a percentage of almost 10 to 16 % each (cf. Habermann 1994: 252): *ab-*, *aus-*, *an-*, *ein-*, *auf-*, *durch-*. Comparison with the findings for MHG (see below) shows a significant increase in productivity especially for *ab-*, *ein-* and *durch-*, while *wider-* (< 0.5 %) is in decline.

Tab. 15.5: Verbal prefixes and particles in MHG.

ver- (15.5 %): complete implementation ("vollständige Durchführung" = egressive) (45.0 %; e.g., *ver-ezzen* 'to eat up; lit. up-eat'); incorrect implementation ("verkehrte Durchführung") (23.1 %; e.g., *ver-leiten* 'to persuade');
be- (13.5 %): contact ("Kontakt"; including one third of the denominal ornatives): (66.3 %; e.g., *be-nemen* 'to take besides; lit. besides-take', *be-schirmen* 'to protect');
er- (12.2 %): complete implementation (= egressive) (27.7 %; e.g., *er-leschen* 'to extinguish'); beginning ("Beginn") (25.5 %; e.g., *er-lachen* 'to laugh');
ane- (> NHG *an-*) (6.2 %): contact (85.6 %; e.g., *ane-slīchen* 'to creep up; lit. up-creep');
ent- (5.8 %): distance ("Entfernung") (53.3 %; e.g., *ent-sagen* 'to renounce' (deverbal); *ent-houbeten* 'to behead' (denominal));
ūf- (> NHG *auf-*) (5.8 %): movement upwards ("Aufwärtsbewegung") (55.1 %; e.g., *ūf-blicken* 'to look upwards; lit. upwards-look');
ūz- (> NHG *aus-*) (4.9 %): distance (78.9 %; e.g., *ūz-ziehen* 'to take off (clothes); lit. off-take');
ge- (4.8 %): complete implementation (= egressiv) (32.4 %; e.g., *ge-brechen* 'to break sth into pieces'); factitive (23.0 %; e.g., *ge-starken* 'to strengthen');
wider- (3.8 %): local (= NHG *wider-*): 'back' (53.4 %; e.g., *wider-loufen* 'to come back; lit. back-come'); 'against' (25.9 %; e.g., *wider-rīten* 'to ride against; lit. against-ride'); temporal (= NHG *wieder-*): 'repetition' (20.7 %; e.g., *wider-lāzen* 'to issue again; lit. again-issue');
zuo- (> NHG *zu-*) (3.3 %): contact (82.8 %; e.g., *zuo-komen* 'to come up; lit. up-come');
vor-/vür- (> NHG *vor-*) (3.2 %): local (67.3 %; e.g., *vor-/vür-bringen* 'to bring forward; lit. forward-bring');
über- (3.1 %): local (89.6 %; e.g., *über-komen* 'to come over; lit. over-come');
abe- (> NHG *ab-*) (3.0 %): distance (87.0 %; e.g., *abe-legen* 'to put away; lit. away-put');
zer- (2.5 %): complete implementation (= egressive) (94.9 %; e.g., *zer-klieben* 'to split');
umbe- (> NHG *um-*) (2.1 %): contact (78.8 %; e.g., *umbe-gān* 'to go around; lit. around-go');
īn- (> NHG *ein-*) (1.9 %): contact (100 %; e.g., *īn-giezen* 'to pour');
vol- (> NHG *voll-*) (1.7 %): complete implementation (= egressive) (100 %; e.g., *vol-gān* 'to happen to the end');
under- (> NHG *unter-*) (1.6 %): local (100 %; e.g., *under-houwen* 'to hit between; lit. between-hit', *under-ligen* 'to be underneath; lit. underneath-be');
durch- (1.3 %): local (50.0 %; e.g., *durch-graben* 'to dig through; lit. through-dig'); complete implementation (= egressive) (50.0 %; e.g., *durch-brennen* 'to burn completely');
nāch- (1.0 %): local (93.8 %; e.g., *nāch-jagen* 'to chase after; lit. after-chase');
misse- (> NHG *miss-*) (1.0 %): incorrect implementation (100 %; e.g., *misse-sprechen* 'to speak falsely, poorly; lit. false-speak');
mite- (> NHG *mit-*) (0.8 %): contact (100 %; e.g., *mite-ligen* 'to lie together; lit. together-lie');
bī- (> NHG *bei-*) (0.7 %): contact (100 %; e.g., *bī-wonen* 'to be present at').

With respect to the word class of the base, the picture is clear: prefix and particle verbs are predominantly formed deverbally. In the MHG corpus from Herbers (2002: 169 ff.) the proportion of adjectival or nominal bases is under 5 %, whereby double motivation is often also present, so that a base verb is also possible as a motivating base. Thus in the corpus of the MHG Grammar, all formations with *ge-* which are classified as deadjectival (cf. Mhd. Gr. III: 487) can also be motivated by a base verb (cf. *ge-stark-en* 'to strengthen' vs. *ge-starken*). In the ENHG corpus from Habermann (1994: 250, 398), denominal formations are also marginal, whereby prefixes however exhibit a significantly higher affinity for nominal bases (around 13 % deadjectival, 10 % denominal) than do particles (around 2 %). These findings reflect the development of denominal prefix/particle verbs which only arise secondarily through the reanalysis of deverbal verbs as denominal. As a result of the abandonment of the non-prefixed base verbs or the restrictions emerging on their use, this double motivation is often eliminated (cf. Habermann 2002: 53: *ver-größer-n* 'to extend' vs. ENHG *größer-n*; *auf-tisch-en* 'to dish out; lit. out-dish' vs. *tisch-en* (now only in Swiss 'to set the table').

From a functional perspective, the MHG prefix and particle verbs form essentially two large groups (cf. Mhd. Gr. III: 522): formations with local functions (e.g., movement upwards/downwards, contact, distance), in which the semantic relation to the origin of the prefixes and particles in spatial preposition/adverbs is thus closer (around 54 %), and formations with which the nature of the course of action of the base verb is modified (around 44 %; e.g., ingressive, egressive, factitive, instrumental and valuative formations). There are thereby four functional classes with a percentage of over 10 % each, which together cover a good 70 % of all formations (cf. Mhd. Gr. III: 548: 'contact', 'complete implementation', 'distance', 'other local relations'; for examples see Table 15.5). These four classes, in each of which in MHG between four and eleven prefixes/particles participate, are also dominant in the contemporary language with a somewhat higher percentage of more than 75 %. In the functional development of the prefixes and particles on the other hand, differences can be observed (cf. Mhd. Gr. III: 549): Thus the respective main functions generally remain the same both in the case of prefixes and particles – deviations as in the case of *er-*, where the third most important function in MHG 'reaching a goal' (e.g., MHG/NHG *er-arbeiten* 'to work for sth') dominates in the contemporary language with 43.5 % (cf. Mhd. Gr. III: 408 f.; DWb 1: 148 f.), are exceptions. However in the case of prefixes the main function is more likely to be developed further, so that here a functional profiling is present, linked with a reduction of the functional potential (reduction of polysemy). Thus, for example, in MHG *ent-* has six functions, but in the contemporary written language only three (cf. Mhd. Gr. III: 402; DWb 1: 148). In the case of the particles, on the other hand, the percentage of the main function, which usually also remains the most frequent function in NHG, decreases in some cases considerably, whereby the functional spectrum is at the same time further developed, thus in the case of *īn-* (> NHG *ein-*) from 1 to 5 (cf. Mhd. Gr. III: 444; DWb 1: 147 f.), in the case of *ūf-* (> NHG *auf-*) from 5 to 9 (cf. Mhd. Gr. III: 454; DWb 1: 145 f.). This development mirrors the fundamental shift from a prefix to a particle verb system, since to some extent the particles take over the functions of the prefixes, which in MHG was already predictable due to the numerous competing formations (cf. 'closing', e.g., *be-sperren* 'to lock up; lit. up-lock' vs. *zue-sperren* 'id.': in NHG this function can no longer be attested for *be-*; 'opening', e.g., *ent-sliezen* 'to unlock' vs. *ūf-sliezen* 'id.': in NHG *ent-* no longer has this function; *entschließen* is only in use as a reflexive verb with another meaning 'to decide').

Just as in the case of the competing formations, in the development toward NHG pleonastic formations are reduced in which prefixes/particles cannot be given a function. The percentage of corresponding formations in which no semantic modification of the verb occurs is in MHG in the case of prefixes significantly higher (a quarter to a third, in the case of *ge-* even more than three quarters) as is the case for particles (below 10 %; cf. Mhd. Gr. III: 549 f.). The decline of such verbs is linked to a displacement of information from simplex verbs to prefix/particle verbs (cf. Solms 1990: 119). The base verb thereby surrenders one or more meaning variants completely to the derivative that it initially shares with it and which in this respect were already profiled through word-formation, and is thereby functionally unburdened. For instance, the verb *trügen* was still used transitively in ENHG just as was *be-trügen* ('to cheat'), while the prefix verb today in its function of 'transitivizing the base verb' is different from *trügen* and because of this differentiation of meaning now carries a functional load. The selection of the, initially still pleonastic, prefixes/particles is not made arbitrarily, but rather according to their functional potential. In other cases either the base verb or the derivative was abandoned (e.g., MHG *gern* 'to desire' alongside *be-gern* > NHG *begehren*; MHG *ge-sehen* 'to see' alongside *sehen* > NHG *sehen*).

4.3.2 Suffix derivation

In comparison with prefix derivation/particle-verb formation, verbal suffix derivation is only marginal. In the corpus of the MHG Grammar its percentage is less than 10 % (cf. Mhd. Gr. III: 492). This finding mirrors a fundamental change in word-formation, which began at the end of OHG as a result of the reduction of unstressed syllables, and lead to the stem forming suffixes inherited from West Germanic, *-jan* (> ahd. *-en*), *-ōn* and *-ēn*, the status of which as morphemes of word-formation is controversial (cf. section 2.1 (d)), collapsing in MHG *-en* with the result that they must be considered from there on conversions from a synchronic perspective (cf. section 5.3). Still in OHG, weak verbs constitute with these suffixes the focal point of verbal suffix formation. They are for the most part secondarily formed: verbs ending in *-jan* especially as deverbal or denominal causatives/factitives (e.g., OHG *trenk-en* (Old Saxon *drenk-ian*) 'to water' ← *trinkan* 'to drink', *full-en* 'to fill' (Old Saxon *full-ian*) ← *fol* 'full'), verbs ending in *-ōn* especially as denominal factitives or deverbal intensives (e.g., OHG *fisc-ōn* 'to fish' ← *fisc* 'fish', *bezzir-ōn* 'to improve' ← *bezzir* 'better', *greif-ōn* 'to grasp, to finger' ← *grīfan* 'to grasp, to touch') and verbs ending in *-ēn* especially as deadjectival inchoatives (e.g., OHG *graw-ēn* 'to (become) grey' ← *grāo* 'grey', *mēr-ēn* 'to become larger' ← *mēr* 'more, larger'). As a result of the leveling to *-en*, the possibility of marking these different word-formation functions with suffixes was lost. Thus as a result of the levelling, the development of prefix derivation and the formation of particle verbs was favored (cf. OHG *graw-ēn* 'to (become) grey' > NHG *er-grau-en*).

Further formations with suffixes in OHG are of lesser importance (cf. Henzen 1965: 223–227; Splett 1993 II: 183 f.). The following suffixes occur, which are also preserved in later stages of the language (cf. Splett 2000: 1220, ordered according to frequency):

Tab. 15.6: Verbal suffixes in OHG.

-al-/-il- (> NHG *-el-*): e.g., *kling-il-ōn* = diminutive-iterative of *kling-an* 'to sound';
-azz-/-ezz-/-izz- (> NHG *-e(n)z-*): e.g., *plech-azz-en* = iterative of *plecchen* 'to flash';
-in- (> NHG *-en-*): e.g., *bib-in-ōn* = intensive of *bibēn* 'to shake, tremble';
-is- (> NHG *-s-*): e.g., *michil-is-ōn* 'to glorify' = factitive of *michil* 'large, powerful';
-ar-/-ir- (> NHG *-er-*): e.g., *gang-ar-ōn* 'to wander around' = iterative of *ganggan* 'to go';
-īg-/-ag- > (NHG *-ig-*): e.g., *gimunt-īg-ōn* 'to remember' ← *gimunt* 'remembrance'. This suffix is only rudimentarily documented in OHG; it only becomes productive later (see below).

These suffixes, the emergence of which Henzen (1965: 225) sees as the result of the reanalysis of the endings of bases (for *-ig-* cf. section 2.1 (e)), are also only documented in small numbers in MHG. Table 15.7 presents the distribution of suffixes (type frequency with specification of the main function) in the MHG Grammar (cf. Mhd. Gr. III: 493).

Tab. 15.7: Verbal suffixes in MHG.

-ig- (42.6 %): factitive (44.4 %; e.g., *rein-ig-en* 'to clean' ← *rein* 'clean'); ornative (22.2 %; e.g., *pīn-ig-en* 'to torment' ← *pīn* 'pain');
-ier- (20.9 %): performative ("Abstraktionsverben", i.e. verbs formed from abstract nouns which characterize behavior) (45.2 %; e.g., *būhurd-ier-en* 'to make a *būhurt*' ← *būhurt* '(jousting) tournament'); ornative (19.4 %; e.g., *ordin-ier-en* 'to order' ← *orden* 'law, order, rule'); factitive (16.1 %; e.g., *kurz-ier-en* 'to shorten' ← *kurz* 'short');
-er- (14.2 %): factitive (61.9 %; e.g., *niuw-er-en* 'to renew' ← *niuw* 'new');
-el- (8.8 %): iterative-diminutive (76.9 %; e.g., *grüew-el-en* 'to shudder repeatedly/a little' ← *gruwen* 'to be terrified of sb/sth, to shudder');
-(e)s- (7.4 %): intensive (27.3 %; e.g., *riuw-es-en* 'to whine, to regret strongly' ← *riuwen* 'to complain, to regret'); furthermore small semantic groups from base nouns, e.g., *vürst-es-en* 'to make sb to a prince' ← *vürst* 'prince';
-(e)z- (6.1 %): intensive-iterative (80.0 %; e.g., *blec-ez-en* 'to flash repeatedly/strongly' ← *blicken* 'to flash').

In comparison with OHG, only two changes appear in MHG: On the one hand the suffix *-ig-* is now the dominant indigenous suffix, which has a higher frequency than all other native suffixes together (the peripheral suffix *-(e)n-*, cf. Table 15.6, isn't mentioned in this compilation). On the other hand, the foreign suffix *-ier-*, borrowed from French in the 12th century, is in MHG already in second place. Its productivity, to a limited degree also for derivation with indigenous bases (cf. MHG *hof-ier-en* 'to pay court to sb'), increases significantly beginning in the 17th century (cf. Prell and Schebben-Schmidt 1996: 35). In the development toward the contemporary language its functional spectrum changes: Thus the performative verbs which were dominant in MHG (see Table 15.7) are only in fourth place, while ornative (24.2 %) and factitive (22.4 %) formations dominate (cf. DWb 1: 36–39; e.g., *lack-ier-en* 'to laquer', *komplett-ier-en* 'to complete').

The suffix *-ig-* also experiences a further increase in productivity in ENHG, especially in the 15th and 17th century (cf. Prell and Schebben-Schmidt 1996: 40–53), and it often competes with conversions (e.g., ENHG *stein-ig-en* 'to stone' vs. *stein-en* 'id.' > NHG *stein-ig-en*, *sünd-ig-en* 'to sin' vs. *sünd-en* 'id.' > NHG *sünd-ig-en*, *kürz-ig-en* 'to shorten' vs. *kürz-en* 'id.' > NHG *kürz-en*). After that it quickly loses importance and becomes unproductive in NHG. The suffix *-ig-* also experiences a functional change in ENHG and NHG: Unlike in MHG (see Table 15.7), in the contemporary language (cf. DWb 1: 34 f.) ornative formations from base nouns are in first place (54.5 %), the factitive deadjectival verbs on the other hand are in second place (27.3 %). While *-ier-*, with its allomorphs *-isier-* and *-ifizier-* which developed ENHG, becomes a characteristic suffix in the contemporary written language (82.4 %), *-ig-* loses its importance (3.2 %) and even drops behind *-(e)l-* (12.5 %; e.g., *hüst-el-n* 'to cough slightly/repeatedly'). Only *-er-* (1.7 %; e.g., *blink-er-n* 'to shortly and quickly blink in succession') as well as the rarely used suffixes *-z-* (e.g., *du-z-en* 'to address with (the familiar pronoun) *du*') and *-s-* (e.g., *quiek-s-en* 'to (make a) squeak' ← *quiek* 'onomatopoeic for a sound especially by piglets, squeak') have an even lower percentage.

In contrast to the suffixes *-ig-* and *-ier-*, which only form denominal and deadjectival verbs and only occur infrequently as components of circumfix formations (e.g., NHG *ver-absolut-ier-en* 'to make sth absolute' ← *absolut* 'absolute', *be-nachricht-ig-en* 'to inform', *ver-eid-ig-en* 'to make sb swear to sth'), the suffixes which are significantly less frequent in MHG are also used for actional modification (iteration, diminution, intensification), but their percentage is even in MHG only around 20 % (cf. Mhd. Gr. III: 550). In ENHG they decline even further (cf. Habermann 1994: 420; Prell and Schebben-Schmidt 1996: 55–58), although *-enz-* develops a short-term productivity in formations such as *luther-enz-en* 'to belong to the doctrine of Martin Luther', *jud-enz-en* 'to behave like a Jew' or *öl-enz-en* 'to smell like oil'. It thus becomes clear that the marking of actional differentiation is gradually abandoned and replaced by prefix and particle models. This causes a further increase in the portion of deadjectival and – primarily – denominal verb formations with a suffix. In the contemporary written language around two thirds of all suffix derivatives are denominal, around one quarter is deadjectival and only around 6 % deverbal (overview in Habermann 1994: 421). The formation of verbs from other word classes was always an exception (e.g., OHG *ūf-ōn* 'to take sb/sth up; to glorify' ← *ūf* (adv.) 'upwards', MHG *ir-ez-en* 'to address with (the pronoun) *ir* (i.e. *ihr*)'.

How low the percentage of deverbal suffix derivation is in total is also demonstrated by a comparison with conversions (cf. section 5.3). Thus converted verbs dominate (e.g., MHG *sünd-en* 'to commit a sin') in the MHG corpus with around 90 % (cf. Mhd. Gr. III: 494), in the ENHG corpus from Habermann (1994: 488) with 92 %, in the corpus of the contemporary spoken language from Gersbach and Graf (1984–85 II: 336) with 82 % and in the Innsbruck corpus of the contemporary written language (DWb 1: 27) with 72 %. If one includes a comparison with prefix derivation and particle-verb formation (cf. the overview in Habermann 1994: 488), the following distribution results on the basis of a comparison of ENHG and NHG for the domains a) prefix derivation/particle-verb formation, b) conversion, c) suffix derivation and d) circumfix derivation:

- ENHG (authors from Nuremberg): a) 77.03 % b) 20.76 % c) 1.81 % d) 0.40 %
- spoken NHG: a) 75.61 % b) 19.29 % c) 4.18 % d) 0.92 %
- written NHG: a) 89.24 % b) 7.56 % c) 2.95 % d) 0.25 %

4.4 Adverbial derivation

In contrast to the nominal, adjectival and verbal domain, prefix formation does not play a role in adverbial derivation. Only suffix derivation is important. This occurs in OHG predominantly via the suffix *-o* for the formation of deadjectival adverbs (e.g., OHG *ernusthaft-o* 'keenly, sincerely' ← *ernusthaft*). As a result of the reanalysis of corresponding adverbs from adjectives ending in *-līh* as adverbs ending in *-līhho* (e.g., *zartlīhh-o* 'merciful, tender' > *zart-līhho*) the suffix *-līhho* developed as an alternative suffix, which was already productive in OHG: Thus for more than 70 adverbs ending in *-līhho*, no adjective ending in *-līh* is attested (cf. Heinle 2004: 137). But adverb markers were impaired in their functionality by the reduction of unstressed syllables and their subsequent deletion (OHG *-o* > MHG *-e* > MHG/ENHG *-Ø*; *-līhho* > *-līche* > *-lich*) and were ultimately abandoned. This process already began in MHG. Thus *-līche* (reanalyzed allomorphs: *-eclīche*, *-līchen*, *-līches*) was already affected by deletion in almost 50 % of cases in the MHG document corpus (cf. Ganslmayer 2012: 530), so that now also the adjective suffix *-līch* (> *-lich*) functions as an adverb marker. In this way the difference between adjective and adverb formation is lost, so that German in contrast to other languages (e.g., E. *-ly*, It. *-mente*) today has no grammatical suffix of its own for the marking of adverbs derived from adjectives. While *-lich* is still the most productive adverbial suffix in ENHG, its corresponding formations decline after the 17th century considerably (cf. Heinle 2000: 1915, 2004: 166) and today are only preserved in relicts (e.g., *schwer-lich* 'hardly', *ewig-lich* 'eternally').

Of the other, significantly less frequent, adverbial suffixes of OHG (cf. Heinle 2004: 95 f.: *-sun*/*-son* in formations such as *dara-sun* 'there', *ūfwert-son* 'upwards'), besides *-s* (see below) only *-ingūn*/*-ingōn* is preserved in NHG, in the form *-lings*. This form resulted via the reanalysis of *-l-* as part of the suffix which was supplemented with *-s* (cf. OHG *chrumbe-lingūn* > ENHG *krümm-lings* 'bended') and has prevailed since the 17th century against the MHG allomorphs *-ling*/*-lingen* (e.g., MHG *niuwe-lingen* 'recently') (cf. Heinle 2004: 172), perhaps due to the homonymy with the nominal suffix *-ling* (e.g., *Fremd-ling* 'stranger').

The expansion with *-s* was particularly appropriate since it had been developing since OHG as an independent adverbial suffix, originating from adverbial genitives (cf. section 2.1 (g)). But it only develops a certain productivity in the period after MHG (cf. Heinle 2004: 103), without being in any way a replacement for the highly frequent suffixes *-o*/*-e* or *-līhho*/*-līche* of OHG/MHG. Accordingly infrequent are also the formations found in the contemporary language which are derived from pronouns (e.g., *ander-s* 'differently'), adjectives (e.g., *öfter-s* 'more often'), participles (e.g., *eilend-s* 'immediate') and nominal syntagmas (e.g., *allerort-s* 'everywhere').

Apart from the case of *-lings*, *-s* also occurs in other cases as an expansion:

a) It expands the suffix *-en*, which in OHG initially had inflectional character (e.g., OHG *meistarlīhh-ūn* 'masterfully'), but temporarily became productive as an adverbial suffix in MHG (cf. Wilmanns 1899: 629 ff.; e.g., *klein-en* 'delicate, dainty' ← *klein* (adj.)). In NHG, it is only used in the variant expanded with *-s*, namely *-ens*, which already occurs in MHG (cf. MHG *verr-ens* 'distant' ← *verre* (adj.) alongside *verr-en*). In NHG, *-ens* adverbializes especially superlative forms (e.g., *schnellst-ens* 'as fast as possible') and is a component of numeral adverbs (e.g., *erst-ens* 'firstly').
b) It forms in *-dings* the ending variant of adverbs with final *-ding*/*-dinge*, which was developed in ENHG via univerbation and conversion from adverbially used genitive syntagmas (cf. *unverrichteterdinge* 'unsuccessful' (← *unverrichteter Dinge*) as a NHG relict form). As a result of the formation of a series and the desemanticization of meaning, *-dings* develops into a suffix (e.g., NHG *all-er-dings* 'however', *neu-er-dings* 'recently' with *-er-* as a (synchronic) linking element).
c) It forms the variant *-mals*, which is attested in adverbialized mergers with MHG *māl* ('point in time') since the MHG period together with the variant endings *-mal*/*-male*/*-malen* (cf. Heinle 2004: 178 f.; e.g., *nie-malen* > *nie-mals* 'never') and has acquired suffix character in NHG (e.g., *je-mals* 'ever', *ehemals* 'previously'). But alongside these, also conversions with *-mal* have been preserved (cf. section 5.4).
d) It forms the variant *-seits* in adverbial mergers with the MHG noun *sīt(e)* ('side of a body, direction'), which has been attested since the MHG period. Initially the form of *sīt(e)* without an ending dominates (e.g., MHG *hie-sīt* 'here'). This was replaced in the 17th century by the variant *-seits* (cf. Heinle 2004: 196 ff.) which does not occur in the inflectional paradigm of the feminine *Seite*. As shown by its open spelling, the element *-seits* was still interpreted as a noun in the 19th century (cf. 19th century *mütterlicher seits* > 20th century *mütterlicherseits* 'maternally; lit. on one's mother's side'). The development as a suffix thus occurs only late.
e) It forms since OHG the variant *-wertes* (*-wartes*) of *-wert* (an adjective attested in OHG/MHG word-formations in the sense of 'turned, gone in a direction') in adverbs of direction. While the form without an ending dominates in OHG/MHG, the form *-wärts* which goes back to the genitive singular prevails in the 16th century. After the abandonment of the underlying adjective, *-wärts* has had the character of a suffix since ENHG (cf. Heinle 2004: 212). In the development towards NHG, there is an increase especially in three-member formations (e.g., *südost-wärts* 'southeast(ern) direction', *hinaus-wärts* 'outward').

The development of further adverbial suffixes – without the involvement of *-s* – is also linked to processes of grammaticalization:

Formations with *-maßen* (< MHG *māze* 'measure, way') originate from the univerbation of syntagmas and adverbial conversion (cf. MHG *der māze* > NHG *dermaßen* 'such, in such a way'). From the beginning, the variant *-maßen* (genitive of the weak declination) was dominant (cf. Heinle 2004: 185). Since the 16th/17th century it has been increasing its productivity and combining primarily with participial bases (with the linking element *-er-*), in which the no longer existing noun *māze* has faded and the status as a suffix has been reached (e.g., NHG *versprochen-er-maßen* 'as promised'). In the contemporary language it also serves more frequently in commentary adverbs to express an evaluating attitude of a speaker (e.g., NHG *zugestanden-er-maßen* 'granted', *zugegeben-er-maßen* 'admittedly'). These uses, in which *-maßen* competes with *-weise* (see below), have been attested since the 18th century (cf. Heinle 2004: 187).

Formations with the suffix variants *-halb*/*-halben*/*-halber* trace back to nominal syntagmas with the noun OHG *halba*/MHG *halbe* '(half) side', which in NHG no longer exists. Here as well, adverbs with suffix character develop through univerbation and conversion. Up into the 20th century the variants *-halben* and especially *-halb* have dominated (cf. Heinle 2004: 124 f.). Currently the form *-halber* is in first place, initially attested in ENHG. This form is still productive today in the formation of causal denominal adverbs (e.g., *vorsicht-s-halber* 'as a precaution', *interesse-halber* 'out of interest'). Formations with *-halben* from pronouns (e.g., *seinet-halben* 'because of him') as well as with *-halb* from other word classes (e.g., *ober-halb* 'above') are unproductive today.

The suffix *-lei* (< MHG *-leie*) is based on the MHG noun *lei(e)* 'manner', which is a borrowing (< Old French *lei* 'id.'). It is found in MHG combinations such as *maneger* (gen.) *leie* 'in some manner' or *zweier* (gen.) *leie* 'in two manners', which were converted to adverbial forms (e.g., NHG *manch-er-lei* 'all sorts of', *zwei-er-lei* 'two different'). The noun is hardly used anymore in ENHG, so that the process of grammaticalization to the suffix *-lei* was completed early. In NHG, it is especially used in the formation of numbers of types (e.g., *acht-er-lei* 'eight different' ← *acht* 'eight').

The suffix *-weg* (rarely: *-wegs*) originates from medieval syntagmas with the noun OHG/MHG *wēg*/*wec* 'way, kind' (cf. Wilmanns 1899: 635: MHG *in welhen wec* 'in which way', *in all wege* 'in every respect'). Just as in the case of the adverb formed from this, *weg* 'away' is differentiated from the noun through the shortness of its vowel. In this case as well, syntagmas converted to adverbs form the starting point of the development of *-weg* (cf. Heinle 2004: 219 ff.), the suffixal character of which results from the semantic bleaching which has occurred (cf. NHG *schlank-weg* 'just like that', *durch-weg* (*durch-wegs*) 'without exception', *glatt-*

weg 'flatly'). Formations with *-wegen*, which originated in ENHG from univerbated postpositional phrases (cf. Heinle 2004: 341 ff.; e.g., NHG *des-wegen* 'therefore', *wes-wegen* 'why', *unser-(e)t-wegen* 'because of us'), must be kept distinct. They are compounds (cf. section 3.4).

The most productive NHG adverbial suffix *-weise* is also the result of a process of grammaticalization and originates from adverbially used syntagmas with the noun OHG *wīs(a)*/MHG *wīs(e)* > NHG *Weise* 'manner, form' (cf. Wilmanns 1899: 634: OHG *andra wīs* 'differently'; *maniga wīsa* 'in some way'). Products of the univerbation of adverbial genitive noun phrases emerge in MHG and until the present have been extraordinarily productive. Since the semantic connection with the noun *Weise* is still recognizable today, a classification as an adverbial conversion of a word group (as in Heinle 2000: 1915) also fundamentally comes into question for formations with *-weise* (earlier also: *-weis*). Most frequent are formations with nouns (especially quantifying; e.g., *gruppe-n-weise* 'in groups', *teil-weise* 'partly'), which are increasingly also used as attributive adjective conversions (e.g., *stunde-n-weise Beschäftigung* 'part-time job'). Formations with (modal) adjectives (e.g., *töricht-er-weise* 'stupidly', *normal-er-weise* 'normally') are younger in the history of the language and have only increased more strongly since the 19th century (cf. Kluge 1925: 50). They are often also used in the contemporary language as commentary adverbs to render an evaluating attitude of a speaker (e.g., *seltsam-er-weise* 'strangely enough', *unnötig-er-weise* 'unnecessarily').

As this overview shows, the system of adverbial derivation from OHG to NHG has changed fundamentally. For the OHG suffixes *-o* (> *-e*) and *-līhho* (> *-līche*), which already in MHG were no longer fully functional, no adequate replacement was created. The adverb marking element *-s*, which not only functions as a suffix on its own, but which also was secondarily added to a series of other suffixes as an adverb marker, also does not fill this gap. An important role in the development of newer adverbial suffixes is played by grammaticalization. At the beginning we find adverbially used nominal syntagmas (conversion of word groups), the inventory of which is expanded through analogical formations. Adverbial suffixes originate via the formation of series and the semantic bleaching of the nominal final members, partially expanded by *-s*. With the exception of *-weise*, *-maßen* and *-seits* though, none of these elements with suffixal character has its main period of productivity in the present (cf. Heinle 2004: 357). Peak frequencies predominate rather in the MHG/ENHG period (*-halben*, *-lings*) or in the 18th/19th century (*-dings*, *-mals*, *-wärts*, *-weg*), whereby the following ranking results according to the number of units of formation (cf. Heinle 2004: 354 f.): *-weise*, *-wärts*, *-halben*/*-halber*, *-lings*, *-mals*, *-maßen*, *-seits*, *-weg*, *-dings*. In keeping with this, in the contemporary language the activity of word-formation of the adverbial suffixes is not very pronounced and alongside the very productive *-weise* only *-s*, *-halben*, *-maßen* and *-wärts* exhibit significant productivity.

5 Conversion

Alongside compounding and derivation, conversion constitutes the third most common procedure of German word-formation. Nominal and verbal conversion dominate over adjectival and adverbial conversion. There are few investigations of the diachronic development of conversion in comparison with derivation. In particular, corpus-based descriptions of conversion in OHG and MHG are lacking. Beyond that, there is also no consensus with respect to the boundaries to other types of word-formation. In the following, morphological and syntactic (i.e. with the retention of inflectional markers) conversions are dealt with and alternative classifications are pointed out. Syntactic conversions (e.g., NHG *sammeln* 'to collect' → *das Sammeln* (action noun), *alt* 'old' → *der/die/das Alte* 'old being, old thing') are partially excluded from word-formation and are treated as syntactic phenomena.

5.1 Nominal conversion

In the domain of nominal conversion, which is already documented for OHG (cf. Erben 2003a: 2530), deverbal formations predominate, which are infinitive conversions (e.g., NHG *schlafen* 'to sleep' → *das Schlafen* 'sleeping' or verb stem conversions with or without change of the stem vowel (e.g., *schlafen* → *Schlaf* 'sleep', *werfen* 'to throw' → *Wurf* 'throw'). (The type of conversion with a change in the stem vowel, which became unproductive at the latest in MHG, is partially seen as "implicit derivation" ("implizite Derivation") and excluded from conversion.) In the ENHG corpora from Müller (1993: 74 ff.), Russ (2004: 250 f.), Döring and Eichler (1996: 45 ff., 106 ff.) and Brendel et al. (1997: 68 ff.), the percentage of verb stem conversions is comparatively high (in both of the latter studies, however, they are mixed with derivatives ending in *-e*). In Müller's (1993) ENHG corpus conversions are, after the formations with *-ung*, the second most common means of word-formation (in the contemporary language according to DWb 2: 96 f. in fourth place after *-ung*, *-heit* and *-er*), whereby there is a preponderance of verb stem conversions without change in the stem vowel (57 %). As is the case in the contemporary language, masculine nouns (80 %) dominate over feminine nouns (10 %) and neuter nouns (7 %). Infinitive conversions, which generally designate an occurrence as a continuum (e.g., NHG *verbieten* 'to ban, to forbid' → *das Verbieten* 'banning'), are only captured in the ENHG corpora from Döring and Eichler (1996: 45 ff.) and Russ (2004: 250 f.). There they are significantly more frequent than verb stem conversions, through which the individual act of an occurrence is designated (e.g., NHG *verbieten* → *Verbot* 'ban, prohibition'). The comparison of MHG-ENHG dictionaries by Ganslmayer (2011: 355) shows, on the other hand, a different picture with a preponderance of verb stem conversions (70 %), which however reflects more the lexicographical custom of only exceptionally recording infinitive conversions as lemmas in dictionaries (in the case of peculiarities in usage).

From a functional perspective, deverbal conversions are above all action nouns, which compete in particular with derivatives formed with *-ung*. In the course of ENHG until the 18th century, verb stem conversions often displace the formations with *-ung* (cf. Wegera and Prell 2000: 1596; e.g., ENHG/NHG *Wachs-ung* > *Wuchs* 'growth', *Genies-ung* > *Genuss* 'enjoyment', *Verbleib-ung* > *Verbleib* 'remaining'), which experience a semantic limitation in the development towards NHG (cf. section 2.3). In other cases both formations remain preserved with semantic differentiation (e.g., NHG *Reiz-ung* 'irritation' vs. *Reiz* 'appeal, stimulus'). Concrete nouns also develop secondarily, however, through meaning change, especially in the case of verb stem conversions (e.g., action noun > place noun: NHG *Abfluss* 'drainage' > 'drain'), which should not be generally misinterpreted as a sign of an increase in productivity. They are significantly more frequent in the contemporary written language than in ENHG and in the contemporary spoken language (cf. Müller 1993: 113).

The deadjectival or departicipial conversions have a significantly lower percentage than the deverbal conversions. Thus, almost 300 infinitive conversions are found in the ENHG corpus from Döring and Eichler (1996: 45, 56 ff.) as opposed to a good 160 deadjectival conversions, of which (for historical reasons) the masculine nouns (132) clearly dominate over the neuter nouns (30) and feminine nouns (5). In most of these conversions, the adjectival inflection is preserved (which is why such lexemes are not always classified as "word-formations") and personal nouns dominate (e.g., *minderiaerige* 'underage person') over nouns denoting things (e.g., *das law* 'lukewarm (water)'). In the case of participial formations, the interpretation is determined by the function of participle I or II (e.g., *geschedigte* 'harmed person' as patient noun). Converted adjectives with nominal inflection are exceptions in the corpus from Döring and Eichler (1996) (e.g., *das übel* 'evil'). This historically old pattern of formation (cf. Wilmanns 1899: 397) is currently familiar as a designation for color and language, especially in the case of neuter nouns (e.g., NHG *das Blau* 'blue color', *das Deutsch* 'the German language').

Nominal conversions from other word classes are seldom encountered. Interesting are the so-called "sentence names" ("Satznamen"), which emerge in the 12th century and occur more often in the 14th/15th century (cf. Meid 1967: 30 f.; Kunze 2004: 152 f.). They are sentences converted to nouns with mostly an imperative message (e.g., *Brechseif* 'break the soap', *Rumsland* 'leave the land'), which are partially preserved (e.g., NHG *Luginsland* 'watchtower; lit. look in the land'), also and especially as family names (e.g., *Kehrein* 'set in', *Bleibtreu* 'remain loyal').

5.2 Adjectival conversion

The oldest model of adjectival conversion is that of the so-called *bahuvrīhi* compounds with a noun as head (e.g., OHG *bar-fuoz* 'barefoot'). The method of formation is not completely clear: While Paul (1920: 29) and Henzen (1965: 79) assume an adjectivizing of originally nominal compounds, Meid (1967: 32) suspects an origin in the Indo-European period from nominal sentences, so that in modern terminology this would be a case of "word group conversion" (Meid's example: "bar (den) Fuß (geht er)" lit. 'bare (the) foot (goes he)' → *bar-fuß*). In any case, the compounding is linked to a change in word class and it is – differently from the nominal *bahuvrīhi* compounds (cf. section 3.1) – a special form of word-formation, which is why Wilmanns (1899: 419) also calls such formations "mutated compounds" ("mutierte Composita") or mergers ("Zusammenbildungen"). Even in OHG this means of formation is unproductive and the few preserved formations are predominantly loan translations (cf. Splett 2000: 1215; e.g., *gold-fahs* 'gold-haired', *mihhil-muot* 'generous'). They were already morphologically adjectivized in OHG in a number of cases – similarly to the former possessive compounds with *ge-* (cf. section 2.2) – via the addition of the suffix *-ig* (cf. Splett 2000: 1215; e.g., OHG *arm-herz* 'compassionate' → *armherz-īch*, *lang-muot* 'patient' → *langmuot-īg*) or transformed into endocentric N+A compounds via a rearrangement of the members (cf. Meid 1967: 35: Old Saxon *geil-muot* vs. OHG *muot-geil* 'arrogant'). In MHG the adjectival *bahuvrīhi* formations are only present in remnants (cf. Mhd. Gr. III: 366); in NHG only *bar-fuß* is in use, but alongside that also the extension *barfüß-ig*.

The newer adjectival conversions are predominantly departicipial formations (from participle I/II). These are still rare in OHG/MHG (cf. Wilmanns 1899: 508), but increase considerably toward ENHG/NHG (e.g., Albrecht Dürer: *Unterweisung der Messung*, 1525: *die beleybenden eck* 'remaining corners (at a geometric figure)'; *forgemachts ding* 'shown thing').

Denominal conversions, on the other hand, remain peripheral. The conversion of simplex nouns (e.g., ENHG/NHG *angst* 'afraid' ← *Angst* 'fear') is a rarely used model. The MHG-ENHG comparison of dictionaries from Ganslmayer (2011: 357) produces a preponderance of departicipial syntactic conversions (73 %) as opposed to denominal morphological conversions (10 %).

5.3 Verbal conversion

With the reduction of the suffixes forming verb stems completed since the MHG period (cf. sections 2.1 (d), 4.3), weak verbs develop via morphological conversion with *-en*. This inflectional marker is partially interpreted as a word-formation morpheme, so that corresponding verbs are then classified as derivatives (cf. DWb 1: 20; Mhd. Gr. III: 494; Prell and Schebben-Schmidt 1996: 23 f.). This interpretation is, however, not generally followed, since, in contrast to suffixes, *-en* is not inherent in the verb stem and is also a component of verbs not formed by word-formation. With respect to the word class of the base, in all stages of the language a preponderance of denominal as opposed to deadjectival formations is apparent. The percentage of denominal formations increases considerably from MHG (cf. Mhd. Gr. III: 495: over 50 %) through ENHG (cf. Habermann 1994: 477: two thirds) to NHG (cf. DWb 1: 26 f.: 85 %), while the deadjectival formations decrease from MHG/ENHG (a quarter or a third) to 15 % in the contemporary written language. Other base word classes (e.g., NHG *miau-en* 'to meow') are peripheral.

The denominal and deadjectival verbal conversions, the percentage of which is significantly higher than that of the verbal suffix formations (cf. section 4.3.2), have a broad functional spectrum at their disposal (cf. Mhd. Gr. III: 494 ff., but exact frequency values are lacking; Habermann 1994: 454, 475). In Habermann (1994: 454) eight functional domains for denominal conversions are given for ENHG (authors from Nuremberg) with the following distribution (rounded type frequency) differentiated:

- performative ("Abstraktionsverben", cf. Table 15.7) (48 %): e.g., *scharmützel-n* 'to skirmish';
- ornative (26 %): e.g., *tadel-n* 'to reprimand';
- causative ("effektiv") (6 %): e.g., *teil-en* 'to share';
- instrumental (3 %): e.g., *nagel-n* 'to nail';
- imitative (2 %): e.g., *meister-n* 'to master';
- locative (2 %): e.g., *knie-n* 'to kneel';
- eventive ("aktualisierend") (2 %): e.g., *hagel-n* 'to hail';
- privative (1 %): e.g., *köpf-en* 'to behead'.

A significant restructuring is apparent in the development towards the contemporary language, as the dominance of the performative and ornative conversions is only preserved in the corpus of the contemporary spoken language from Gersbach and Graf (1984–85), in which, however, the instrumental formations take second place. In the Innsbruck corpus of the contemporary written language (DWb 1) there is, on the other hand, a relative equilibrium of 16–18 % for the first six functional domains with a different order (instrumental, ornative, performative, imitative, causative). The percentage of ornative formations, but especially performative formations is thus in decline, while instrumental, causative and imitative verbs have increased.

The deadjectival conversions are also polysemous. For the comparison between ENHG (authors from Nuremberg) and the contemporary language (cf. Habermann 1994: 475) the following four functional domains are important (in parentheses the rounded type frequencies for a) ENHG, b) spoken NHG and c) written NHG):

- factitive: e.g., ENHG *pesser-n* 'to improve'; a) 68 % b) 70 % c) 51 %;
- behavioral ("verhaltenscharakterisierend"): e.g., ENHG *gehorsam-en* 'to be obedient'; a) 13 % b) not registered c) 6 %;
- durative: e.g., ENHG *gleich-en* 'to be like sb/sth'; a) 5 % b) 11 % c) 10 %;
- inchoative: e.g., ENHG *trückn-en* 'to get dry'; a) 5 % b) 18 % c) 31 %.

In contrast to the denominal formations, the dominance of the factitive conversions remains preserved in NHG (but in the contemporary written language in reduced form). The other groups exhibit here as well larger differences in frequency, whereby especially the significant increase of inchoative formations is apparent. It can't always be decided clearly to what extent here, as in general with comparable changes in frequency variation, text specific or pragmatic developments are in play or – as could be partly shown – system internal restructurings are being reflected.

5.4 Adverbial conversion

The domain of adverbial conversion includes primarily formations with a nominal final member. Initially nominal syntagmas are thereby used adverbially and in a second step are developed by analogy into word-formation patterns. These conversions have developed since MHG/ENHG – just as the adverbial compounds which likewise originated in univerbation (cf. section 3.4) – into a characteristic phenomenon of formation of adverbs, which after the 17th century displays clear signs of solidification (cf. Heinle 2004: 364). In contemporary German mostly only (often demotivated) remnants remain. Among these are formations with the following nominal final members: *-art* (only attested since the 19th century; e.g., *der-*

art 'to such an extent'), *-gestalt* (e.g., *der-gestalt* 'thus'), *-hand* (e.g., *kurzer-hand* 'there and then'), *-weile* (e.g., *mittler-weile* 'meanwhile'), *-zeit* (e.g., *der-zeit* 'at present'). Only *-mal* occurs often, because it forms numbers of repetition (e.g., *drei-mal* 'three times'). Such conversions were partly further developed into derivatives, in that the nominal final member – partially by the addition of the adverb marker *-s* – assumed suffixal character (cf. section 4.4). Formations with non-nominal final members (e.g., *trotz-dem* 'nevertheless', also in use as a concessive conjunction; *bis-lang* 'until now') are just as rare as denominal conversions (e.g., *Morgen* 'morning' → *morgen* 'tomorrow'). Adjectives used as adverbs are considered in Germanic word-formation theory – unlike for example in Romance studies – to not be converted adverbs, but rather to be adjectives, since the morphological criterion of inflectability is more highly valued than the syntactic criterion of adverbial position. According to this, a deadjectival conversion only occurs in the few cases in which lexemes originally used as adjectives are only used adverbially, as is, for example, the case for *zweifellos* ('without doubt').

6 Further types of word-formation

In comparison with compounding, derivation and conversion, the other types of word-formation such as reduplication, backformation, blending and clipping are peripheral in German (cf. Barz 2025). From the Middle Ages and early modern period only a few examples are known.

Wilmanns (1899: 22) names as OHG examples for reduplication the nouns *fi-faltra* ('butterfly' > NHG *Falter* 'id.') and *wi-wint* ('whirlwind') as well as the adverb *selb-selbo* ('equal to oneself'). Reduplications remain until the present marginal forms of word-formation, which have a rather colloquial character (e.g., NHG *Larifari* 'rubbish').

Backformations appear to be newer. In ENHG deadjectival nouns are documented (e.g., *Sanftmut* 'gentleness' ← *sanftmütig* 'gentle', *Allmacht* 'unlimited power' ← *allmächtig* 'all-powerful'). This form of backformation is rare in the contemporary language in comparison to the productive formation of denominal verbs (e.g., NHG *zwangsräumen* 'to make an eviction' ← *Zwangsräumung* 'eviction', *notlanden* 'to make an emergency landing; lit. to emergency-land' ← *Notlandung* 'emergency landing'), for which no clear examples can be found in older German (cf. Åsdahl Holmberg 1976; Erben 2003b).

Blending as a consciously employed stylistic device is initially documented in broad use in ENHG. A number of examples can be found in the 16th century used by Johann Fischart ("Geschichtklitterung"), who thus follows his French role model François Rabelais (cf. Müller and Friedrich 2011: 75, e.g., the personal nouns *Sau-zius* ← *Sau* 'pig' + *Sozius* 'partner, mate' and *Tumb-her* ← *tumb* 'stupid' + *Domherr* 'canon'). Alongside the focus in the language of literature (numerous examples can also be found in the works of Heinrich Heine in the 19th century), blending is also popular in journalism and in advertising and has developed a clearly increasing productivity in these domains only recently (models of formation in Müller and Friedrich 2011).

The origins of clipping reach back to the Middle Ages and are linked to the shortening of two-member Germanic first names (cf. Kunze 2004: 20 f.). From these, unisegmental short names develop (as head or final words; e.g., *Folc* ← *Folc-rad*, *Brand* ← *Hilde-brand*), but also bisegmental names (e.g., *Alf* ← *Adal-wolf*, *Rolf* ← *Rud-olf*) as well as so-called "slur forms" ("Lallformen") (e.g., *Beppo* ← *Bern-hart*, *Ditto* ← *Diet-rich*). Acronyms, on the other hand, have a significantly more recent history than these short forms which are characteristic of the spoken language. The former have only become more frequent since the second half of the 19th century, developing due to processes of language economy in the natural sciences/technology, politics/business and journalism (e.g., NHG *TÜV* ← *Technischer Überwachungsverein* 'Technical Inspection Agency', *ÖNV* ← *öffentlicher Nahverkehr* 'local public transport'/*Österreichischer Naturistenverband* 'Austrian nudist association'). In particular, acronyms have been continually increasing since the second half of the 20th century, strengthend by internationalisms and the so-called *AKÜ-Sprache* (shortening of *Abkürzungssprache* lit. 'abbreviation language') of the internet (cf. Balnat 2011).

7 References

Åsdahl Holmberg, Märta (1976): *Studien zu den verbalen Pseudokomposita im Deutschen*. Lund: Blom.

Balnat, Vincent (2011): *Kurzwortbildung im Gegenwartsdeutschen*. Hildesheim: Olms.

Barz, Irmhild (2025): German. In: Peter O. Müller, Susan Olsen and Franz Rainer (eds.), *Word-Formation – European Languages*, 1–27. Berlin/Boston: De Gruyter Mouton.

Bentzinger, Rudolf (1991): Zur Verwendung von Adjektivsuffixen in der deutschen Literatursprache (1570–1730). In: Joachim Schildt (ed.), *Aspekte des Sprachwandels in der deutschen Literatursprache 1570–1730*, 119–225. Berlin: Akademie Verlag.

Brendel, Bettina, Regina Frisch, Stephan Moser and Norbert Richard Wolf (1997): *Wort- und Bergriffsbildung in frühneuhochdeutscher Wissensliteratur. Substantivische Affixbildung*. Wiesbaden: Reichert.

Carr, Charles T. (1939): *Nominal compounds in Germanic*. London: Milford.

Cordes, Gerhard and Hermann Niebaum (2000): Wortbildung des Mittelniederdeutschen. In: Werner Besch, Anne Betten, Oskar Reichmann and Stefan Sonderegger (eds.), *Sprachgeschichte. Ein Handbuch zur Geschichte der deutschen Sprache und ihrer Erforschung*. 2nd ed. Vol. 2, 1463–1469. Berlin/New York: de Gruyter.

Demske, Ulrike (1999): Case compounds in the history of German. In: Matthias Butt and Nanna Fuhrhop (eds.), *Variation und Stabilität in der Wortstruktur. Untersuchungen zu Entwicklung, Erwerb und Varietäten des Deutschen und anderer Sprachen*, 150–176. Hildesheim: Olms.

Demske, Ulrike (2000): Zur Geschichte der *ung*-Nominalisierung im Deutschen. Ein Wandel morphologischer Produktivität. *Beiträge zur Geschichte der deutschen Sprache und Literatur* 122: 365–411.

Denkler, Markus and Stefan Mähl (eds.) (2022): *Beiträge zur historischen Wortbildung des Niederdeutschen*. Wien/Köln: Böhlau.

Döring, Brigitte and Birgit Eichler (1996): *Sprache und Begriffsbildung in Fachtexten des 16. Jahrhunderts*. Wiesbaden: Reichert.

DWb = *Deutsche Wortbildung. Typen und Tendenzen in der Gegenwartssprache. Eine Bestandsaufnahme des Instituts für deutsche Sprache. Forschungsstelle Innsbruck.*

(1973): 1. Hauptteil: Ingeburg Kühnhold and Hans Wellmann: *Das Verb. Mit einer Einführung von Johannes Erben*. Düsseldorf: Schwann.

(1975): 2. Hauptteil: Hans Wellmann: *Das Substantiv*. Düsseldorf: Schwann.

(1978): 3. Hauptteil: Ingeburg Kühnhold, Oskar Putzer and Hans Wellmann: *Das Adjektiv*. Düsseldorf: Schwann.

(1991): 4. Hauptteil: Lorelies Ortner, Elgin Müller-Bollhagen, Hanspeter Ortner, Hans Wellmann, Maria Pümpel-Mader and Hildegard Gärtner: *Substantivkomposita – Komposita und kompositionsähnliche Strukturen 1*. Berlin/New York: de Gruyter.

(1992): 5. Hauptteil: Maria Pümpel-Mader, Elsbeth Gassner-Koch, Hans Wellmann and Lorelies Ortner: *Adjektivkomposita – Komposita und kompositionsähnliche Strukturen 2*. Berlin/New York: de Gruyter.

Erben, Johannes (2003a): Hauptaspekte der Entwicklung der Wortbildung in der Geschichte der deutschen Sprache. In: Werner Besch, Anne Betten, Oskar Reichmann and Stefan Sonderegger (eds.), *Sprachgeschichte. Ein Handbuch zur Geschichte der deutschen Sprache und ihrer Erforschung*. 2nd ed. Vol. 3, 2525–2539. Berlin/New York: de Gruyter.

Erben, Johannes (2003b): Zur Frage der 'Rückbildung' (retrograden Ableitung) als Möglichkeit der Wortbildung. *Zeitschrift für deutsche Philologie* 122: 93–100.

Fischer, Hanna (2024): Von der Flexion in die Wortbildung und darüber hinaus. Zur diachronen Entwicklung des *s*-Suffixes im Deutschen. *Zeitschrift für germanistische Linguistik* 52(2): 257–286.

Flury, Robert (1964): *Struktur- und Bedeutungsgeschichte des Adjektiv-Suffixes -bar*. Winterthur: Keller.

Ganslmayer, Christine (2011): Wortbildungswandel in frühneuhochdeutscher Zeit: Zur Etablierung des Deutschen als wortbildungstypische Sprache. In: Anja Lobenstein-Reichmann and Oskar Reichmann (eds.), *Frühneuhochdeutsch – Aufgaben und Probleme seiner linguistischen Beschreibung*, 317–382. Hildesheim: Olms.

Ganslmayer, Christine (2012): *Adjektivderivation in der Urkundensprache des 13. Jahrhunderts. Eine historisch-synchrone Untersuchung anhand der ältesten deutschsprachigen Originalurkunden*. Berlin/Boston: de Gruyter.

Ganslmayer, Christine and Peter O. Müller (2021): Historische Fremdwortbildung. Forschungsstand und Perspektiven. In: Christine Ganslmayer and Christian Schwarz (eds.), *Historische Wortbildung. Theorien – Methoden – Perspektiven*, 105–144. Hildesheim: Olms (= Germanistische Linguistik 252–254).

Ganslmayer, Christine and Christian Schwarz (eds.) (2021): *Historische Wortbildung. Theorien – Methoden – Perspektiven*. Hildesheim: Olms (= Germanistische Linguistik 244–245).

Gersbach, Bernhard and Rainer Graf (1984–85): *Wortbildung in gesprochener Sprache. Die Substantiv-, Verb- und Adjektiv-Zusammensetzungen und -Ableitungen im "Häufigkeitswörterbuch gesprochener Sprache"*. 2 Vol. Tübingen: Niemeyer.

Grimm, Jacob (1819–37): *Deutsche Grammatik*. 4 Vol. Göttingen: Dieterichsche Buchhandlung.
Gröger, Otto (1911): *Die althochdeutsche und altsächsische Kompositionsfuge mit Verzeichnis der althochdeutschen und altsächsischen Composita*. Zürich: Zürcher & Furrer.
Habermann, Mechthild (1994): *Verbale Wortbildung um 1500. Eine historisch-synchrone Untersuchung anhand von Texten Albrecht Dürers, Heinrich Deichslers und Veit Dietrichs*. Berlin/New York: de Gruyter.
Habermann, Mechthild (2002): Sprachwandel im Licht diachroner und synchroner Wortbildung. In: Mechthild Habermann, Peter O. Müller and Horst Haider Munske (eds.), *Historische Wortbildung des Deutschen*, 41–57. Tübingen: Niemeyer.
Habermann, Mechthild (2023): Diachrone Wortbildung und Konstruktionsgrammatik. In: Alexander Lasch and Alexander Ziem (eds.), *Konstruktionsgrammatik VII. Wandel im Sprachgebrauch*, 27–50. Tübingen: Stauffenburg.
Hartmann, Stefan (2016): *Wortbildungswandel. Eine diachrone Studie zu deutschen Nominalisierungsmustern*. Berlin/Boston: De Gruyter.
Heinle, Eva-Maria (2000): Wortbildung des Neuhochdeutschen bis zur Mitte des 20. Jahrhunderts. In: Werner Besch, Anne Betten, Oskar Reichmann and Stefan Sonderegger (eds.), *Sprachgeschichte. Ein Handbuch zur Geschichte der deutschen Sprache und ihrer Erforschung*. 2nd ed. Vol. 2, 1911–1917. Berlin/New York: de Gruyter.
Heinle, Eva-Maria (2004): *Diachronische Wortbildung unter syntaktischem Aspekt. Das Adverb*. Heidelberg: Winter.
Henze, Daniela (2010): Verben mit *un*-Präfix im älteren Deutsch. *Sprachwissenschaft* 35: 219–245.
Henzen, Walter (1965): *Deutsche Wortbildung*. 3rd ed. Tübingen: Niemeyer.
Herbers, Birgit (2002): *Verbale Präfigierung im Mittelhochdeutschen. Eine semantisch-funktionale Korpusanalyse*. Tübingen: Niemeyer.
Kempf, Luise (2016): *Adjektivsuffixe in Konkurrenz. Wortbildungswandel vom Frühneuhochdeutschen zum Neuhochdeutschen*. Berlin/Boston: De Gruyter.
Kloocke, Helga (1974): *Der Gebrauch des substantivierten Infinitivs im Mittelhochdeutschen*. Göppingen: Kümmerle.
Kopf, Kristin (2018): *Fugenelemente diachron. Eine Korpusuntersuchung zu Entstehung und Ausbreitung der verfugenden N+N-Komposita*. Berlin/Boston: De Gruyter.
Kunze, Konrad (2004): *dtv-Atlas Namenkunde. Vor- und Familiennamen im deutschen Sprachgebiet*. 5th ed. München: Deutscher Taschenbuch Verlag.
Leipold, Aletta (2006): *Verbableitung im Mittelhochdeutschen. Eine synchron-funktionale Analyse der Motivationsbeziehungen suffixaler Verbwortbildungen*. Tübingen: Niemeyer.
Lindner, Thomas (1998): Zur Geschichte und Funktion von Fugenelementen in Nominalkomposita am Beispiel des Deutschen. *Moderne Sprachen* 42: 1–10.
Lindner, Thomas (2011): *Indogermanische Grammatik*. Ed. by Thomas Lindner. Vol. 4/1: *Komposition*. Lieferung 1. Heidelberg: Winter.
Luxner, Bernhard (2022): *Die althochdeutschen Adjektive auf* -aht(i)/-oht(i). *Eine diachron- und synchron-vergleichende Untersuchung*. Berlin/Boston: De Gruyter.
Meid, Wolfgang (1967): *Germanische Sprachwissenschaft. III. Wortbildungslehre*. Berlin: de Gruyter.
Meier, Jürgen and Dieter Möhn (2000): Wortbildung des Altniederdeutschen (Altsächsischen). In: Werner Besch, Anne Betten, Oskar Reichmann and Stefan Sonderegger (eds.), *Sprachgeschichte. Ein Handbuch zur Geschichte der deutschen Sprache und ihrer Erforschung*. 2nd ed. Vol. 2, 1270–1275. Berlin/New York: de Gruyter.
Meineke, Eckhard (2009): Wortbildungsmorphologie. In: Rolf Bergmann and Stefanie Stricker (eds.), *Die althochdeutsche und altsächsische Glossographie. Ein Handbuch*. Vol. 2, 1030–1076. Berlin/New York: de Gruyter.

Meineke, Eckhard (2016): *Substantivkomposita im Mittelhochdeutschen*. Heidelberg: Winter.
Mhd. Gr. III = Klein, Thomas, Hans-Joachim Solms and Klaus-Peter Wegera (2009): *Mittelhochdeutsche Grammatik. Teil III: Wortbildung*. Tübingen: Niemeyer.
Müller, Peter O. (1993a): *Substantiv-Derivation in den Schriften Albrecht Dürers. Ein Beitrag zur Methodik historisch-synchroner Wortbildungsanalysen*. Berlin/New York: de Gruyter.
Müller, Peter O. (1993b): Historische Wortbildung: Forschungsstand und Perspektiven. *Zeitschrift für deutsche Philologie* 112: 394–419.
Müller, Peter O. (2002): Historische Wortbildung im Wandel. In: Mechthild Habermann, Peter O. Müller and Horst Haider Munske (eds.), *Historische Wortbildung des Deutschen*, 1–11. Tübingen: Niemeyer.
Müller, Peter O. (2011): The polysemy of the German suffix *-er*: Aspects of its origin and development. *STUF – Language Typology and Universals* 64: 33–40.
Müller, Peter O. (2016): Wortbildungswandel oder Bedeutungsbildung? – Zur Entstehung und Interpretation sekundärer Wortbildungsbedeutungen. In: Sandra Waldenberger and Sarah Kwekkeboom (eds.), *PerspektivWechsel* oder: *Die Wiederentdeckung der Philologie*. Vol. 1: *Sprachdaten und Grundlagenforschung in der Historischen Linguistik*, 309–332. Berlin: Schmidt.
Müller, Peter O. (2017): Wortbildungsbedeutungswandel. In: Florentine Oehme, Hans Ulrich Schmid and Franziska Spranger (eds.), *Wörter. Wortbildung, Lexikologie und Lexikographie, Etymologie*, 184–208. Berlin/Boston: De Gruyter.
Müller, Peter O. and Cornelia Friedrich (2011): Kontamination. In: Hilke Elsen and Sascha Michel (eds.), *Wortbildung im Deutschen zwischen Sprachsystem und Sprachgebrauch. Perspektiven – Analysen – Anwendungen*, 73–107. Stuttgart: ibidem.
Munske, Horst Haider (2002): Wortbildungswandel. In: Mechthild Habermann, Peter O. Müller and Horst Haider Munske (eds.), *Historische Wortbildung des Deutschen*, 23–40. Tübingen: Niemeyer.
Nübling, Damaris and Renata Szczepaniak (2013): Linking elements in German: Origin, change, functionalization. *Morphology* 23: 67–89.
Pavlov, Vladimir M. (1983): *Zur Ausbildung der Norm der deutschen Literatursprache (1470–1730). Von der Wortgruppe zur substantivischen Zusammensetzung*. Berlin: Akademie Verlag.
Pounder, Amanda (2000): *Processes and Paradigms in Word-Formation Morphology*. Berlin/New York: Mouton de Gruyter.
Prell, Heinz-Peter and Marietheres Schebben-Schmidt (1996): *Die Verbableitung im Frühneuhochdeutschen*. Berlin/New York: de Gruyter.
Riecke, Jörg (1999): Pseudopartizipien im Althochdeutschen: Ein Beitrag zur Geschichte eines Wortbildungstyps. *Sprachwissenschaft* 24: 157–193.
Ring, Uli (2008): *Substantivderivation in der Urkundensprache des 13. Jahrhunderts. Eine historisch-synchrone Untersuchung anhand der ältesten deutschsprachigen Originalurkunden*. Berlin/New York: de Gruyter.
Russ, Charles V. J. (2004): Nominalization in Martin Luther's word formation. *Journal of Germanic Linguistics* 16(3): 245–268.
Scherer, Carmen (2005): *Wortbildungswandel und Produktivität. Eine empirische Studie zur nominalen* -er-*Derivation im Deutschen*. Tübingen: Niemeyer.
Scherer, Carmen (2006): Was ist Wortbildungswandel? *Linguistische Berichte* 205: 3–28.
Simmler, Franz (2002): Pseudomorpheme. Ermittlungsmethoden, Typologie und Sprachgeschichte. In: Mechthild Habermann, Peter O. Müller and Horst Haider Munske (eds.), *Historische Wortbildung des Deutschen*, 75–103. Tübingen: Niemeyer.
Solling, Daniel (2012): *Zur Getrennt-, Zusammen- und Bindestrichschreibung von Substantivkomposita im Deutschen (1550–1710)*. Uppsala: Elanders.

Solms, Hans-Joachim (1990): Das System der Präfixverben in der frühesten Überlieferung des Hartmannschen 'Gregorius' (Hs. A aus dem Alemannischen des 13. Jahrhunderts). In: Werner Besch (ed.), *Deutsche Sprachgeschichte. Grundlagen, Methoden, Perspektiven. Festschrift für Johannes Erben zum 65. Geburtstag*, 115–128. Frankfurt/M.: Lang.

Solms, Hans-Joachim (1998): Historische Wortbildung. In: Werner Besch, Anne Betten, Oskar Reichmann and Stefan Sonderegger (eds.), *Sprachgeschichte. Ein Handbuch zur Geschichte der deutschen Sprache und ihrer Erforschung*. 2nd ed. Vol. 1, 596–610. Berlin/New York: de Gruyter.

Splett, Jochen (1993): *Althochdeutsches Wörterbuch. Analyse der Wortfamilienstrukturen des Althochdeutschen, zugleich Grundlegung einer zukünftigen Strukturgeschichte des deutschen Wortschatzes*. 2 Vol. Berlin/New York: de Gruyter.

Splett, Jochen (2000): Wortbildung des Althochdeutschen. In: Werner Besch, Anne Betten, Oskar Reichmann and Stefan Sonderegger (eds.), *Sprachgeschichte. Ein Handbuch zur Geschichte der deutschen Sprache und ihrer Erforschung*. 2nd ed. Vol. 2, 1213–1222. Berlin/New York: de Gruyter.

Stricker, Stefanie (2000): *Substantivbildung durch Suffixableitung. Untersucht an Personenbezeichnungen in der Sprache Goethes*. Heidelberg: Winter.

Stricker, Stefanie (2002): Konkurrenzen im Wortbildungssystem um 1800: Aufgezeigt an der Wortbildung Goethes. In: Mechthild Habermann, Peter O. Müller and Horst Haider Munske (eds.), *Historische Wortbildung des Deutschen*, 315–339. Tübingen: Niemeyer.

Thomas, Barbara (2002): *Adjektivderivation im Nürnberger Frühneuhochdeutsch um 1500. Eine historisch-synchrone Analyse anhand von Texten Albrecht Dürers, Veit Dietrichs und Heinrich Deichslers*. Berlin/New York: de Gruyter.

Wegera, Klaus-Peter and Heinz-Peter Prell (2000): Wortbildung des Frühneuhochdeutschen. In: Werner Besch, Anne Betten, Oskar Reichmann and Stefan Sonderegger (eds.), *Sprachgeschichte. Ein Handbuch zur Geschichte der deutschen Sprache und ihrer Erforschung*. 2nd ed. Vol. 2, 1594–1605. Berlin/New York: de Gruyter.

Wellmann, Hans (1997): Wortbildung im Sprachwandel. In: Rainer Wimmer and Franz-Josef Berens (eds.), *Wortbildung und Phraseologie*, 65–87. Tübingen: Narr.

Werner, Martina (2020): Korpuslinguistische Perspektiven auf die sprachhistorische Entwicklung der nominalisierten Infinitive im Deutschen. *Linguistik online* 102(2): 155–181.

Werner, Martina (2023): The diachronic increase in morphological complexity in German infinitive nominalizations. In: Martina Werner and Wolfgang U. Dressler (eds.), *Between Derivation and Inflection*, 261–276. Wien: Verlag der Österreichischen Akademie der Wissenschaften.

Wilmanns, Wilhelm (1899): *Deutsche Grammatik. Gotisch, Alt-, Mittel- und Neuhochdeutsch. Zweite Abteilung: Wortbildung*. 2nd ed. Straßburg: Trübner.

Zutt, Herta (2000): Wortbildung des Mittelhochdeutschen. In: Werner Besch, Anne Betten, Oskar Reichmann and Stefan Sonderegger (eds.), *Sprachgeschichte. Ein Handbuch zur Geschichte der deutschen Sprache und ihrer Erforschung*. 2nd ed. Vol. 2, 1358–1365. Berlin/New York: de Gruyter.

Klaus Dietz

16 Historical word-formation in English

Abstract: This article presents a succinct and yet comprehensive survey of the historical development of English word-formation. After summing up the history of research and the state of the art, the account first discusses the inherited patterns of Old English word-formation (affixing and compounding) which have not only been preserved but also extended their productivity up to the present. The next section centres on the multi-stage process of morphological integration of French loanwords, on the rise of zero-derivation in Middle English, on their typology and on their specific preconditions. The Early Modern English period is characterized by the morphological incorporation of a great number of learned Latin loan-words borrowed in the wake of the Renaissance and humanism, by the coexistence or rivalry of native and foreign affixes and by the development of minor word-formation processes such as backformation, blending and clipping. The concluding section summarizes the development of late Modern and Present-Day English. It comprises the strengthening of older patterns, the increase in productivity of, e.g., the zero-derivation of phrasal verbs and ends with a few innovations such as the use of acronyms.

1 Introduction

Historical English word-formation not only comprises the major and minor word-formation patterns and processes and their development from the beginning of the Anglo-Saxon period (c. 700) to the present but also the Germanic heritage in the form of certain inherited types of word-formation which made possible the

Klaus Dietz, Berlin, Germany

https://doi.org/10.1515/9783111420530-016

creation of complex words by affixation and compounding. In Middle English zero-derivation or conversion was added to the inventory as an important new productive type. Whereas the transfer of Latin and Scandinavian loanwords had no consequences for the lexical morphology of Old English (OE), the influx of French and, later on, of Latin loanwords in Middle English (ME) had serious consequences and in the long run led to the restructuring of native affixation. The process was reinforced by the adoption of learned Latin loanwords during the sixteenth and seventeenth centuries. In Early Modern English (EME) at the latest minor patterns of word-formation such as backformation and blending evolved and completed the morphological inventory. As studies on word-formation in Late Modern English (LME) are still lacking, this desideratum conveys the wrong impression that Modern English word-formation has not been developing at all since c. 1700.

Future research work will profit by two kinds of new instruments: firstly, by the *Dictionary of Old English* (DOE) and its *Web Corpus*, by the *Middle English Dictionary* (MED) and by the nascent third edition of the *Oxford English Dictionary* (OED), and secondly, by new corpora of historical English.

2 History of research and state of the art

Research in the field of English lexical morphology started in Germany during the first decade of the twentieth century. In the beginning it took the shape of dissertations which mostly dealt with individual or groups of Old English suffixes and more rarely with Old English prefixes and with Middle English affixes. Several of these early dissertations were supervised by Ferdinand Holthausen and published in the series of *Kieler Studien zur englischen Philologie*. In the course of the next half century the new field of research developed more slowly than steadily. Yet a small number of important studies and handbooks appeared at that time. Some of them have not been superseded till today; cf., for example, Carr (1939) on Germanic compounds, Lindelöf (1938) and Biese (1941) on zero-derivation and, with certain reservations, Jespersen, who in 1942 produced the first standard history of English word-formation after Koziol had presented in 1937 the first edition of his survey. After c. 1960 the development gradually gathered speed and the area of research widened as it was no longer confined to diachronic studies but eventually began to include synchronic aspects which finally lead to the enquiry into word-formation of Present-Day English (PDE).

Already at the beginning of the modern period of research three compendia and an introduction were published: Meid (1967) on Germanic word-formation,

Marchand (1969) and Koziol (1972 [1937]) with comprehensive surveys on historical word-formation in English, whereas Adams (1973) confined herself to Modern English. Koziol's and Marchand's surveys complement one another, as Koziol offers a strictly historical description, whereas Marchand, starting from Present-Day English, traces the development back to Old English, where necessary. Meanwhile each of these three handbooks needs thorough revision as long as no replacement exists, for the existent modern outlines (Faiß 2004 and Kastovsky 2006b) are unable to fill the gap. The relevant articles in volumes I–IV of the *Cambridge History of the English Language* (Kastovsky 1992; Burnley 1992; Nevalainen 1999; Algeo 1998), where word-formation was subsumed under lexicology, offer a better alternative, even if the rather short articles by Burnley and Algeo are less informative than they should be, so that the periods of Middle English and of Late Modern English are covered only provisionally.

At the same time a series of both diachronic and of synchronic studies were published; cf. Thun (1963) on lexical reduplication, Pennanen (1966) on backformation and again (1971) along with Irmer (1972) on zero-derivation in Modern English. In addition Seymour presented a bibliography of word-formation in the Germanic languages including English in 1968. Yet it was over another decade before the first detailed study of Present-Day English word-formation, Bauer (1983), was available. Meanwhile the emphasis of research has shifted from diachrony to synchrony. Several surveys of Present-Day English word-formation are available by now, which greatly profit from the progress of modern theoretical research: Adams (2001), Carstairs-McCarthy (2002), Lipka (2002), Plag (2003), Schmid (2011), and Bauer, Lieber and Plag (2013). Nowadays even comprehensive English grammars include full chapters on word-formation in contrast to their predecessors (cf. Bauer and Huddlestone 2002), whereas handbooks of historical English and of Germanic grammar as well still tend to lack a chapter on word-formation. At the same time more than a dozen monographs have appeared dealing with morphological aspects and patterns which had been neglected so far: Plag (1999) and Bauer (2001) on productivity, Benczes (2006) on creative or ad-hoc-compounding, Karius (1985), Bauer and Valera (2005) as well as Balteiro (2007a, b) on zero-derivation, Kunter (2011) on compound stress, Mühleisen (2010) on suffixation with *-ee*, Reischer (2008) on blending, Ryder (1994), Fernández-Domínguez (2009) and Pastor-Gómez (2011) on noun + noun compounding and Schneider (2003) on diminutives. Finally two shorter surveys must be added: Bauer (2006) on compounds and minor word-formation types and Lieber (2005) on word-formation processes.

A nearly comparable number of contemporary studies in book form deal with themes and problems of historical English word-formation: cf. Koma (2000) on deverbal nouns in Old English, Niwa (1991–95) on Old English prefixes and particles, Terasawa (1994) on nominal compounds in Old English, Ciszek (2008) on word-derivation in early Middle English, Lloyd (2011) on five Middle English suffixes of French origin, Sauer (1992) on nominal compounds in early Middle English, Zbierska-Sawala (1993) on affixation in early Middle English, Haselow (2011) on the history of Old English and Middle English noun suffixes, Faiß (1992) on the aspects of morphological loss and enrichment and, with certain reservations, Dalton-Puffer (1996) on the French influence on Middle English morphology (cf. Miller 1997) and Trips (2009) on the development of three noun suffixes. In addition there are two important miscellanies: Fisiak (1985) and Bacchielli (1994). Again two shorter surveys must be mentioned: Kastovsky (2006a) on typological changes in derivational morphology and Lutz (1997) on the history of the prefix verbs. Moreover, during the last forty years an increasing number of articles have appeared which cannot be surveyed here.

There is only one short and, by the way, rather sketchy article on the state of the art (Lipka 2000). Štekauer (2000) can be subsumed in the same category. His personalized history of research from 1960 to 1995 is organized by authors and their significant works in order to show their contributions to the development of the theory of general linguistics and of English linguistics in particular, though only six of twenty-four chapters, beginning with Hans Marchand and ending with Laurie Bauer, deal with representatives of word-formation in English and even include Valerie Adams who stated that her book is chiefly concerned with data and their classification and not with theories (Adams 1973: vii).

3 Affixation and compounding in Old English and their Germanic heritage

3.1 The Germanic heritage

A comparison with other Germanic languages, especially with Gothic, Old High German, and Old Norse demonstrates that Old English inherited from Common Germanic three major processes of word-formation: prefixation, suffixation and compounding (Meid 1967). Their typological origins go back to Indo-European and their structure is uniform insofar as the modifier always precedes the head. This holds for compounds as well as for affixations.

Germanic prefixation normally originated from the combination of deictic particles having local sense (< adverbs and prepositions) with verbs or nouns. At first prefixation was restricted to nouns, later on, after the Indo-European movable stress had been fixed on the first syllable, prefixation was extended to verbs with the result that prefixed verbs were stressed on the root because verbal prefixes developed from former proclitic particles. The co-existence of OE *andswárian* 'to answer' and *ándswaru* 'answer' n. reflects this difference. By contrast, suffixation was widely confined to the domain of nouns and adjectives. Here we must distinguish between suffixes which functioned as stem-formation elements and determined the inflectional class of a noun and suffixes in a narrow sense which were added to the stem or to an inflected form; cf. OE *ciefes* 'concubine' < Germanic **kaƀ-isjō-*, OE *hleahtor* 'laughter' < **hlah-tra-*, OE *morþor* 'murder' < **mur-þrō-*; OE *glæd-lic* 'gladly' < **glað-līka-*. Contrary to Meid's opinion (1967: 226–229) Old English possessed only two Germanic adjectival suffixes: *-lic* '-ly' and probably *-sum* '-some'. Combinations with **-fasta-* > OE *-fæst*, **-kunða-* > OE *-cund* and **-wandja-* > OE *-wende* as in OE *hell-cund* 'hellish', *wīs-fæst* 'wise' and *lēof-wende* 'kind' are doubtless compounds (cf. Dietz 2007).

Compounding in Germanic concerns nouns and/or adjectives only. Nevertheless there are examples like OE *here-toga* 'commander, who marches in front of the army', whose head consists of a deverbal noun derived from the past participle of the strong verb OE *tēon* 'to draw'. Germanic compounds are always two-membered with a pure nominal stem as determiner independent of the grammatical relation existing between both elements. Determiners as a rule appear in the form of their stems, whose final vowels survive in the oldest layer of personal names including examples from early runic inscriptions. Old English preserves a few relics: *hago-steald* 'unmarried', *hilde-rinc* 'warrior'. Later on the linking vowels were syncopated. The stem-formation of heads, however, not infrequently deviates from the respective word: OE *ān-daga* 'appointed day' vs. *dæg* 'day'.

Germanic nominal compounds may be divided into three groups according to the semantic and syntactic relations of their elements. The largest group comprises determinative or endocentric compounds. Their characteristic feature consists in the determination of the head by the modifier. Determinative compounds represent combinations of nouns, of adjectives or of both. The second group embraces copulative or dvandva compounds. They are characterized by the fact that two different but semantically equal concepts are linked together. Except for numerals of the type OE *þrēo-tīene* ~ *-tēne* 'thirteen' dvandvas occur rarely in Germanic; cf. OE *āþum-swēoran* 'son-in-law and father-in-law', *suhtor-fædran* 'nephew and uncle'. The third group includes exocentric or bahuvrīhi compounds, whose semantic head is located outside the compound and therefore is not part of the compound itself. Exocentric compounds most frequently denote people by giving prominence to salient characteristics which stand metonymically for the whole person. Morphologically they are composed either of two nominal members or of a particle and a noun: OE *bær-fōt* 'barefoot', *twelf-wintre* 'twelve years old'.

3.2 Prefixation in Old English

Old English affixation and its Germanic origin are relatively well documented and explored. Prefixation is originally characterized by two important distinctions. The first refers to the differing word accent of stressed nominal prefixes, weakly stressed verbal prefixes and their respective derivatives. It manifests itself in pairs like *ándsaca* 'adversary' – *onsácan* 'contest' or *bīgenga* 'inhabitant' – *begān* 'occupy'. Remains of this stress pattern survive in early Old English. Later on most of the stressed prefixes were lost and the allomorphic variation largely disappeared, a development which did not apply to *ge-*, *for-* and *mis-* (Dietz 2004; Minkova 2008). The second distinction concerns the difference between primary and secondary prefixes. While the first group was inherited from Germanic, the second consists of prefixes which exist side by side with the lexical or grammatical morphemes (adverbs; prepositions) from which they developed. Still unsolved is the problem of separable verbal prefixes like *ūt* 'out' as in *ūt-gān* – *ic gā ūt* '(I) go out'. Since they are always stressed they are better interpreted as verbal compounds (Kastovsky 1992: 374 ff., 2006b: 236 ff.). The problem of multiple prefixation likewise awaits a solution (cf. *ofadrincan* 'to drain', *ingefeoht* 'internal war'). Finally, formal convergence, semantic bleaching and lexicalization caused the far-reaching decay of the inherited system of primary prefixes in late Old English (Hiltunen 1983). The process of attrition applies to *a-* and *ge-* especially and, to a lesser degree, to *be-* as is confirmed by the missing semantic difference between simple and prefixed forms.

The late Old English system of productive prefixes, including those like *for-*, *of-* and *on-*, which made themselves functionally independent from their adverbial or prepositional equivalents, consists of no more than three primary prefixes: *be-*, *mis-* and *un-*. The partially lexicalized (de)verbal prefix *be-* (cf. *becnāwan* 'to know', *bedīglian* 'to hide') has a mainly intensifying and transitivizing function: *bebrecan* 'to break to pieces', *besprengan* 'to besprinkle'. The prefix *for-* (< **fur*) occurs with adjectives, verbs and their derivatives. In adjectives it may have an emphasizing function. In verbs it may have the meaning 'loss, destruction' or it may signify intensification and perfectivity: *formanig* 'very many', *foroft* 'very often'; *fordōn* 'to destroy', *forbærnan* 'to burn up'. The negative prefix *mis-* (< **missa-*) occurs with nouns and verbs: *misdōn* 'to do evil', *misdǣd* 'misdeed'. The prefix *of-* combines with verbs and supplies the meaning 'off, away': *ofcuman* 'to descend', *offlēogan* 'to fly away'. The prefix *on-* forms chiefly verbs and verbal derivations with local meaning: *onhebban* 'to pick up', *onfeohtan* 'to attack', *onwadan* 'to break in(to)'. The prefix *un-* represents two older, etymologically distinct types. The negative and pejorative type joins adjectives and nouns: *unbrād* 'narrow', *unlīf* 'death', *unlagu* 'injustice'. The reversative type combines with verbs only: *unbindan* 'to unbind', *unfealdan* 'to unfold'.

3.3 Suffixation in Old English

The number of Germanic suffixes which were added, not to roots, but to stems and which remained productive even in later Old English is comparatively small. The principal nominal suffixes are *-end*, *-ere*, *-estre*, *-(l)ing*, *-ness*, *-scipe*, *-þ(o)-* ~ *-t-*, *-ung-* ~ *-ing-*. They formed either agent nouns or had abstract function.

The suffix *-end*, which is based on the present participle of verbs, predominantly serves to derive strong masculine agent nouns: *hǣlend* 'saviour', *lǣrend* 'teacher'. It competes with the originally denominal suffix *-ere* (< lat. *-ārju*) which forms primarily masculine agent nouns but was subsequently extended to produce deverbal derivations: *scipere* 'sailor', *scō(h)ere* 'shoemaker'; *bæcere* 'baker' (Kastovsky 1971). OE *-estre* (< **-striōn*) derives mainly deverbal but also denominal agent nouns of feminine as well as of masculine gender: *bæcestre* 'female baker', *þēamestre* 'sempstress; sewer' (Bammesberger 2003). The suffix *-ing* ~ *-ung* (< **-ingō-/*-ungō-*) forms deverbal feminine action, agent, instrumental, locative, and object nouns. The first variant rarely combines with strong and normally with weak class 1 verbs, the latter with weak class 2 verbs: *binding* 'binding', *huntung* 'hunting', *gaderung* 'assembly', *beorning* 'incense', *lācnung* 'medicine', *cīeping* 'market'. The originally complementary distribution begins to loosen in late Old English (Knappe-Maas 1998). In contrast to this the suffix *-(l)ing* (< **-inga-/*-unga-*) produces masculine concrete nouns derived from adjectives and nouns with the notion 'derived from or associated with the meaning of the root': *æþeling* 'prince', *cyning* 'king'. It often has patronymic function: *Centingas* 'people of Kent'. The variant *-ling* results from reanalysis of derivatives like *æþel-ing* → *dēor-ling* 'favourite' (← *dēor* 'brave'). While *-ness* (< **-nissi-*) forms feminine abstract nouns of action and state from adjectives and verbal stems or participles (Suzuki 1990), the likewise very productive suffix *-scipe-* (< **-skapi-*) derives deadjectival or denominal masculine abstract nouns with the meanings 'state, act, condition': *æþelness* 'nobility', *costness* 'temptation', *forgivenness* 'forgivenness'; *frēondscipe* 'friendship', *hwætscipe* 'activity, boldness', *lēodscipe* 'nation, people'. The suffix *-þ(o)* ~ *-t* (< **-iþo-*) forms deadjectival feminine abstract nouns (with and without *i*-mutation): *drūgoþ* 'drought', *sihþ* ~ *gesiht* 'sight', *hīehþ(o)* 'height' (Čermák 2002).

Some Old English nominal suffixes, e.g., the feminine agent noun suffixes West Saxon *-estre*, Anglian *-icge* and the diminutive suffix *-incel*, lost their productivity in the course of Old English. Alleged suffixes like *-dōm*, *-hād* or *-lāc* had not yet developed a word-formation meaning of their own but still functioned as head of compounds (Dietz 2007).

The list of a dozen or more adjectival suffixes discussed, e.g., by Kastovsky (1992: 389–391 and 2006b: 241 f.) must be reduced considerably because several suffixes lost or had lost their productivity in Old English or already in pre-Old English, and other supposed suffixes had not yet made themselves independent from the corresponding lexemes. The corrected list includes *-ig*, *-isc*, *-lic* and probably *-sum*.

The suffix *-ig* '-y' produces adjectives meaning 'characterized by, having' which are mainly derived from nouns but also from adjectives and verbs: *blōdig* 'bloody'; *untrymmig* 'infirm, sick', *cēorig* 'querulous'. The suffix *-lic* '-ly' (< **-līka-*) is a morphological and semantic rival of *-ig: dēoplic* 'deep', *cīeplic* 'vendible'. The originally long vowel /ī/ was shortened under weak stress. The suffix *-isc* '-ish' derives denominal adjectives with the meaning 'characterized by, having': *cildisc* 'childish', *Englisc* 'English'. The presumable suffix *-sum* (< **-suma-*) 'characterized by' has the same morphological range as *-ig* and *-lic: friþsum* 'peaceful', *ānsum* 'whole', *(ge)hīersum* 'obedient'.

As in Germanic, Old English verbal suffixation with other than stem-formation elements was weakly developed. Old English inherited only a few verbal suffixes which, however, soon lost their productivity. The sole example worth mentioning is the complex suffix *-ettan* (< **-atjan-*). It has iterative and intensifying meaning and primarily occurs with verbal bases: *blicettan* 'glitter, quiver', *droppettan* 'drop, drip'.

3.4 Compounding in Old English

The structure of Old English compounds depends on the Germanic heritage of the Old English language. Old English determinative compounds are strictly nominal as far as the head is concerned and as a rule consist of two, occasionally of more than two lexemes, if the modifier itself is a compound: *dēofol-gyld-hūs* 'heathen temple', *god-spell-bodung* 'gospel preaching'. Historically, two types exist according to the grammatical form of the modifier. The older type consists of compounds which are more or less lexicalized and whose modifier appears in the form of the stem or with a linking vowel: *gōd-spell* 'gospel', *cyne-helm* 'crown'. Originally, the younger type differed from the older in two ways, firstly in terms of the inflected form of the modifier and secondly by the lack of lexicalization.

In Old English the difference is often confined to the form of the modifier which usually appears in the genitive or, occasionally, with a linking vowel: *dæges-ēage* 'daisy', *sunnan-dæg* 'Sunday'; *hilde-calla* 'war-herald'. Every possible combination of nouns and adjectives is attested: N + N, N + A, A + N, A + A; cf. *ceder-bēam* 'cedar', *cniht-hild* 'boy'; *ellen-rōf* 'renouned for strength', *snāw-hwīt* 'snow-white'; *cwic-seolfor* 'mercury', *middan-geard* 'world, mankind'; *eal-mihtig* 'allmighty', *sām-cwic* 'half-dead'. Verbal elements are confined to modifiers: *bærn-īsen* 'branding iron', *scear-seax* 'razor'. According to the semantic relations which exist between modifier and head, determinative compounds are divided into several groups: e.g., attributive compounds like *wīf-mann* 'woman', subsumptive compounds such as *gold-finc* 'goldfinch' (for details see Kastovsky 1992: 365 ff.). Tautological compounds which represent combinations of two synonyms are typical of Old English poetry: *mægen-cræft* 'great strength', *holt-wudu* ~ *wudu-holt* 'forest, wood'. Copulative compounds are not productive in Old English, but exocentric compounds occur in verse as well as in prose texts: OE *gamol-feax* 'grey-haired', *idel-hende* 'empty-handed'. Inverse exocentric compounds emerge from exchange of the elements: *glæd-mōd* → *mōd-glæd* 'cheerful'.

The question of whether zero-derivation was already a productive process of word-formation in Old English, as Kastovsky (1992: 392–396, 2006b: 242 f.) maintains, needs further investigation, for as long as the principles of Germanic stem-formation, including the feasibility of deriving different stems from the same root, were valid, the precondition for zero-derivation was lacking.

4 Affixation, compounding and zero-derivation in Middle English

4.1 General remarks

During the Middle English Period (c. 1100 – c. 1500) the English language experienced major changes. While early Middle English to a large extent preserved the grammatical and morphological structure inherited from Old English, from the first half of the thirteenth century onwards Middle English developed from a synthetic into an analytical language so that its structure took on increasingly more features of Modern English including a fixed word order. Most of these developments commenced in the Northern dialects and afterwards advanced via the East Midlands into the capital and eventually into the more conservative Southern and West Midland dialects. The progressive loss of inflectional endings, which ended in the loss of nominal and verbal inflection classes as well as in the abandonment of adjectival inflection and of grammatical gender, affected not only grammar but also word-formation. Compared to Old English word-formation, Middle English word-formation is still a largely unexplored area.

4.2 Affixation in Middle English

Middle English affixation is characterized in three different ways: firstly by the loss of inherited elements, secondly by the development of new native affixes and thirdly by the consequences of the morphological integration of French and Latin loanwords, which, however, did not lead to the borrowing of foreign rules of word-formation.

The integration of French loanwords took place in several stages. The precondition for their utilization was the existence of a sufficient number of loanwords with and without a given affix. If the number of such pairs was great enough, even native speakers without any knowledge of French were able to analyse the affixed partners as having a meaningful affix which later on could become productive in combination with native or with borrowed words, notwithstanding the morphophonemic alternations featured by separately borrowed members of Romance word families; cf. *innocent – innocence – innocencī(e).*

In the first stage, native affixes combined with foreign bases. The second stage produced reverse combinations of foreign affixes with native bases. In the last stage, combinations of borrowed affixes and bases were created according to native rules of word-formation which had no equivalent in the borrowing language. Phase 1 started c. 1200 at the earliest, phase 2 began well after 1300 and phase 3 not before c. 1400 (Dietz 2002). The details need further investigation. As a result of the growing influx of Latin loanwords after c. 1350, French affixes were often Latinized: *des-* > *dis-*, *en-* ~ *em-* > *in-* ~ *im-*.

While the native Old English prefixes *a-* and *ge-* > *i-* (~ *y-*) lost their morphosemantic transparency and were lexicalized in early Middle English, *be-*, *for(e)-*, *mis-* and *un-* continued to be productive. In addition, the Old French equivalent *mes-* (< **missi*) converged with *mis-*: *mischę̄f* 'mischief'. Hybrid examples are attested from c. 1200: *bicacchen* 'to catch', *unblāmed* 'unblamed'. With the help of the verb-second rule, the Old English coexistence of separable and inseparable prefixes was transformed in such a way that the former developed into the new category of phrasal verbs with consistent postpositioning of the erstwhile prepositional or adverbial element. Prefixes of Romance or Latin origin do not seem to have become productive before c. 1380: *debreiden* 'to rend', *enwrappen* 'to cover', *reneuen* 'to renew'. New formations of phase 3 appear after c. 1400: *disappę̄ren* 'to disappear'.

Compared to native prefixes the percentage and the continuity of native Middle English suffixes was greater. On the one hand, most Old English suffixes survived into Middle English, and on the other, newly developed suffixes like *-dọ̄m* and *-họ̄d*, which had previously functioned as heads of compounds, were added. Along with *-nes(se)* and *-ship(e)*, Middle English had no fewer than four competing native abstract suffixes available. After the loss of grammatical gender ME *-nes(se)* and *-ship(e)* became functionally equivalent: *freshnes(se)*, *hard-nes(se)* ~ *-scip(e)*. Meanwhile *-dọ̄m* and *-họ̄d* developed limited productivity: *họ̄redọ̄m* 'harlotry', *brọ̄therhọ̄d* 'brotherhood'. In addition four other suffixes, two old ones and two new, should be mentioned. After the variant *-ung* had been lost, early ME *-ing* continued deriving verbal nouns and *-som* kept forming adjectives: *clọ̄thing*, *drinkinge*; *buxom*, *handsom*. Like its antonym *-les*, ME *-ful* produced denominal adjectives and nouns: *blisful*, *armles*.

Hybrid combinations with foreign bases appear soon after c. 1200: *angerful* 'fearful', *joyful*; *culvertshipe* 'villainy', *hardishipe* 'bravery'. A century later coinages on *-les* and *-nes(se)* follow: *pẹ̄rles* 'matchless'; *clẹ̄rnesse* 'clearness'. Reverse combinations, some of which are contemporary comprise the adjective suffix *-āble*, the pejorative suffix *-ard* and the feminine suffix *-esse*: *ẹ̄tāble* 'eatable'; *Ballard* 'bald head', *shreuard* 'scoundrel'; *goddess(se)* 'goddess'. Coinages of type 3 have come into existence since c. 1400: *bauderīe* 'bawdry', *repayment*, *scantitẹ̄* 'meagreness'.

4.3 Compounding and zero-derivation in Middle English

The patterns of early Middle English compounding generally correspond to their Old English predecessors (Sauer 1992). Some of them, e.g., N + deverbal agent noun, increased their productivity later on. Owing to the generalization of *-ing* as the form of the present participle, formations of verbal noun + *-ing* were reinterpreted as representing the new pattern V + N: *chēpeing-toun* 'market-town'; *draue-briǧǧe* 'draw-bridge'. Among the rare late Old English/early Middle English innovations of native origin rank the so-called imperative words. They represent nouns derived not from imperative but from transitive clauses. They first appear as nicknames and were reinforced later on by French: *Cunne-bried* (< OE *cunnian* 'to test' + *brēad* 'bread'), *cæce-pole* 'tax collector' (< OFr. *cach(i)er* 'to catch' + *p(o)ul* 'hen'). Reduplicative compounds with and without gradation are evidenced later: *gāle-gāle* 'chatterbox', *handī-dandī* 'the conveying of a bribe', *finter-fanter* 'name of a herb' whereas the sex-denoting type *hē asse*, *shē asse* '(fe)male ass' and the adjectival type *rẹ̄d-hot* 'red-hot', *leuk-warm* 'luke-warm' represent late Middle English innovations. Burnley (1992: 443) misinterpreted early Middle English compounds such as *lẹd(e)-folk* 'people' or *stān-roche* 'rock' as copulative. In fact, they are tautological formations whose elements express the same semantic concept and which may have had interpretative function. Bahuvrīhi compounds are not uncommon in early Middle English: *stǭn-stikel* 'stickleback', *thorn-bak* 'thornback ray'. All three stages of hybrid compounding are supported by documentary evidence: 1) *castel-toun* 'town with a castle', *marble-stǭn* 'marble flooring'; 2) *mix-maumes* 'filthy idols', *privẹ-thirles* 'holes of the latrine'; 3) *lilie-flour* 'fleur-de-lis', *renğe-tāble* 'stringcourse'.

The precondition for zero-derivation in Middle English is the conformity of the non-inflected forms of adjectives, nouns and verbs. The progressive loss of inflectional endings started with the early Middle Englisch loss of final *-n* and came to an end with the loss of primary and secondary final *-e* c. 1400. There are three main types of such derivations: deadjectival and denominal verbs and deverbal nouns: *belt* n. → *belt* v., *bettre* a. → *bettre* v., *walke* v. → *walke* n. The derivational connections were supported by closely resembling pairs of Middle English strong verbs and nominal derivatives from the same root: *drink(e)* 'drink' n. (< OE *drinc, -a*) – *drinke* 'drink' v., *fāre* 'journey' n. (< OE *fær* ~ *faru*) – *fāre* 'travel' v. Middle English zero-derivation began to develop on a larger scale soon after c. 1200 (Biese 1941). The coexistence of separately borrowed pairs like *anoi* n. – *anoie* v. 'annoy' or *blāme* n., v. 'blame' facilitated the transfer of zero-derivation to French loanwords. As no earlier examples exist as yet, it is doubtful whether the zero-derivation of French loanwords was as firmly rooted after c. 1300 as Marchand (1969: 365) asserts. The zero-derivation of verbs came to be the most productive type of verbal derivation for two reasons. Functionally comparable native verbal suffixes were lacking not only in Middle English but also later on, and the suffixes *-ate*, *-ise* and EModE *-ify* combined with Romance loanwords only. So, zero-derivation of verbs filled a gap.

5 Early Modern English word-formation processes

5.1 General remarks

There is no comprehensive account of Early Modern English word-formation, which is why Nevalainen's (1999) and Kastovsky's (2006b) short surveys are largely based on Marchand (1969) and Koziol (1972 [1937]). The word-formation of this period urgently needs further research, including the unsolved problem of multiple affixation. In addition, both Marchand and Koziol neither distinguished consistently between newly borrowed loanwords and new internal English formations nor did they use the *Middle English Dictionary* which often gives older references for supposed Early Modern English loans. The existence of only one recent monograph dealing with Early Modern English word-formation, Sundby (1995), who treated the evidence of contemporary grammarians, characterizes the situation.

The adoption and integration of a great number of learned Latin loanwords during the 16th and 17th centuries had far-reaching consequences for the word-formation of Early Modern English. As the morphological incorporation was modelled on the treatment of French loanwords in Middle English, the new vocabulary was adapted to native rules of word-formation, too. The idea that Middle English loan patterns borrowed from French enabled further non-native word-formation processes to become productive in Early Modern English is erroneous. As far as new formations were created they had no counterpart in the source languages. Accordingly, the transfer of French, Italian and Iberoromance loanwords later on had no morphological consequences worth mentioning.

5.2 Affixation in Early Modern English

Early Modern English affixation is characterized by the coexistence and sometimes by the rivalry of native and foreign prefixes and suffixes. Affixes of French as well as of Latin origin developed increasing productivity despite their morphophonemic variations. However, while the former often freely combined with native bases, the latter combined with Romance bases only.

The single native negative prefix *un-* deriving antonymous adjectives and nouns was complemented by French and Latin *dis-*, *in-* (~ *il-*) and by Latin *non-*, which originated in the legal domain: *uncommon, ungratitude*; *dislike, dissimiliar, disorder*; *illegal, incivility*; *non-ability*. *In-* and *non-* are restricted to foreign bases. In addition, *un-* and *dis-* have reversative and privative functions: *unmount, unballast*; *dishearten, disburden*. Still larger is the number of locative and temporal prefixes. The first group consists of three native and at least three foreign prefixes: *a-*, *fore-* and *mid-*, *inter-*, *sub-* and *super-*: *ajar*; *forename, forecourt*; *mid-season, mid-air*; *inter-marry, intermit*; *sublet, subcommittee*; *superstructure*. The Latinate prefixes *sub-* and *super-* do not combine with native bases. Just as numerous is the group of temporal prefixes: *fore-* and *mid-*, *ante-*, *post-*, *pre-* and *re-*: *forecourt, foreshadow* v.; *midnoon, mid-season*; *antedate, anti-masque*; *post-date* n., v.; *preconceive, pre-existence*; *reconsider, refill, reprint*. The Latinate prefixes *ante-*, *post-* and *pre-* combine with foreign bases only. The same is basically true of other foreign prefixes, e.g., of *anti-* and *counter-*, *co-* and *pro-* denoting opposition or support respectively.

The pattern of suffixation is similar, for the majority of Early Modern English suffixes are of foreign origin. While a good deal of them had gained their productive force in late Middle English, others were beginning to become productive in Early Modern English. Nevertheless, the most productive suffixes employed to form adjectives and nouns were of native origin: *-ed* and *-y*, *-ness* and *-er*. Some foreign suffixes involve stress shifting as against the pattern of the base. The main stress may be transferred to the syllable immediately preceding the suffix or to the suffix itself: cf. *ˈ-ary*, *ˈ-ious*, *ˈ-ity* vs. *-átion*, *-ée*, *-éer*, *-étte*.

In view of the great number of suffixes, the following list will concentrate merely on the word class they form and on the word class they combine with. The largest group consists of noun suffixes which are semantically either abstract or concrete. Abstract denominal nouns are mostly derived by *-dom*, *-ful*, *-hood*, *-ing*, *-ship* as well as by *-age*, *-ate*, *-cy*, *-ery*. Concrete denominal nouns are formed by *-er*, *-ling*, *-y* and by *-ess*, *-et(te)*. The suffixes *-er* and *-ant*/*-ent*, *-ee* derive personal nouns from verbs, whereas *-ing* and *-age*, *-al*, *-ance*/*-ence*, *-ation*, *-ment* and *-ure* produce deverbal nouns which are mostly abstract. The main suffixes deriving abstract nouns from adjectives are native *-ness* and French *-ity*; *-acy* was used in derivations of words ending in *-ate*, and most of the coinages with *-ancy*/*-ency* had deadjectival function. The next group comprises at least four non-native suffixes which form adjectives and nouns derived from members of the same word classes: *-(i)an*, *-arian*, *-ist* and *-ite*. Finally, a large group of suffixes existed in Early Modern English – half of them native, half borrowed – for deriving denominal adjectives: *-ful*, *-ish*, *-less*, *-ly*, *-some*, *-y* and *-(i)al* including variants, *-ary*/*-ory*, *-ate*, *-ous*. The second to last group includes three suffixes which form deverbal adjectives: *-y*, *-able*, and *-ive*.

Furthermore, Early Modern English inherited three productive native verb suffixes and generalized three borrowed ones, which normally did not combine with native bases: *-en*, *-er*, *-le*; *-ate*, *-ify*, *-ise*. By c. 1660 the form *-en* was used primarily to derive both causative and intransitive verbs from adjectives: *brighten*, *deafen*. The suffixes *-le*, which often combines with verbs, and *-er* have frequentative-iterative senses: *draggle*, *dribble*; *gibber*, *stutter*. The suffix *-ate* derived verbs from Latin nominal stems, from Romance nouns and verbs: *articulate*, *facilitate*. Like *-ate*, *-ify* developed a causative function in forming denominal and deadjectival derivations: *beautify*, *uglify*. The suffix *-ize* is not only the most productive of the new verb suffixes but may also be considered naturalized in view of the number of new deadjectival and denominal coinages: *bastardize*, *equalize*.

Finally there are two new, and moreover homonymous, native suffixes, nominal *-y* (~ *-ie*) and adjectival *-y*. Hypocoristic *-y*[1] first appeared in late Middle English, became productive in Early Modern English and combines with personal names such as *Charlie* and, later on, with common nouns: *daddy, jockey, monkey.* The homonymous suffix -y^2 is the only native one to produce deverbal adjectives: *slippy, sweepy.*

5.3 Compounding, zero-derivation and other word-formation processes

In general, Early Modern English compounding developed along the same lines as in Middle English and continued to be productive. The combination N + N represents the most common type of compound nouns, followed by A + N, V(*-ing*) + N, N + V-*ing* and adjective-based compounds A + A, N + A, A ~ N + V-*ing*. The number of examples of the type *self-boasting* increases. Bahuvrīhi compounds gain ground. This is especially true of attributive A + N compounds: *busybody.* Sentence names, which Nevalainen (1999: 416) confuses with exocentric compounds, occur more often: *pickpocket, spitfire.*

Zero-derivation including formations with loanwords experiences its Early Modern English culmination in the age of Shakespeare. Among the three types of deverbal nouns, denominal and deadjectival verbs, the latter two prevail due to the limited derivational range of native verbal suffixes: *contest*; *bottle, empty.*

Other, i.e. minor word-formation processes are generally much less frequently attested. The Early Modern English record of reduplicative formations shows increasing frequency but stagnant formal variety: *pooh-hooh, hocus-pocus, chit-chat.* Backformation, which began to appear in late Middle English, becomes established: *ginger* 'dainty' (← *-ly*), greed n. (← *-y*), *negate* (← *negation*), *peddle* (← *peddler*), *speckle* (← *-ed*), *soothsay* (← *-er, -ing*). Clipping, a feature of colloquial language, reduces polysyllabic words to the extreme of a monosyllabic form either by fore- or by backclipping: *cute* (← *acute*); *chap* (← *chapman*), *miss* (← *mistress*). Blending or word mixing merges two words or word-fractions in a new lexical item: *twirl* (← *twist* + *whirl*), *rariety* (← *rare* + *variety*).

6 Late Modern and Present-Day English word-formation

According to Algeo's (1999: 66–76) and Kastovsky's (2006b: 268 ff.) short and rather selective articles, which are the only ones to discuss the development of word-formation in Late Modern English and Present-Day English, there are some strengthened older patterns and only a few innovations, mostly actuated by the growing scientific and technical terminology of the 19th and 20th centuries. However, the word-formation of these registers, whose lexical components were either coined within English from existing morphemes of classical origin or represent new loanwords based on Greek and Neo-Latin formations, is not the subject of this survey which concentrates on the general vocabulary, even though it eventually incorporated elements of scientific and technical jargon.

While the established patterns of affixing and compounding remained not only in general use but also produced new combinations using elements of an expanding vocabulary, at least four types have developed increased productivity since the late 19th century: zero-derivation of phrasal verbs, backformation, clipping and blending. Zero-derivation of verb-particle combinations results in nouns: *stand-by, take-off*. Backformation most often produces verbs derived from agent nouns in *-er*, from action nouns and from participial adjectives in *-ed: edit* (← *editor*), *demarcate* (← *demarcation*), *isolate* (← *isolated* which is now regarded as the past participle of the verb). Since the 19th century nouns can be backformed from adjectives, too: *megalith* (← *megalithic*). Clipping in the form of back- and fore-clipping or of the combination of both increased in popularity: *bike* (← *bicycle*), *cello* (← *violoncello*), *flu* (← *influenza)*. The same is true of blending: *brunch* (← *breakfast* + *lunch*), *smog* (← *smoke* + *fog*).

At the same time four new patterns emerged: the suffixes *-ers* and *-esque*, acronyms and the use of trade names as generics. The suffix *-esque* 'having the style of' of both French and Italian origin comes to be productive since around 1800: *carnivalesque, statuesque*. The suffix *-ers* exists in the imaginary plural form only: *bonkers* 'crazy', *crackers* 'crazy', *jabbers* (interjection). Some examples are slangy. Acronyms appear in two forms, either as letter or as word acronyms: *Wren*, backformation of *Wrens* pl. (← *WRNS* 'a member of the Women's Royal Naval Service'), *yuppie* (← *young urban professional*). The use of trade names as generics likewise represents quite a new development. *Coke* (← *Coca-Cola*) and *escalator* (← *escalade* v. + *-ator* after *elevator*) began as American proprietary names, *Cellophane* is an example from British English.

7 References

Adams, Valerie (1973): *An Introduction to Modern English Word-Formation*. London: Longman.

Adams, Valerie (2001): *Complex Words in English*. Harlow: Pearson Education.

Algeo, John (1998): Vocabulary. In: Suzanne Romaine (ed.), *The Cambridge History of the English Language*. Vol. 4: *1776–1976*, 57–91. Cambridge: Cambridge University Press.

Bacchielli, Rolando (ed.) (1994): *Historical English Word-Formation. Papers read at the 6th National Conference of the History of English*. Urbino: Edizioni Quatro Venti.

Balteiro, Isabel (2007a): *A Contribution to the Study of Conversion in English*. Münster: Waxmann.
Balteiro, Isabel (2007b): *The Directionality of Conversion in English. A Dia-Synchronic Study*. Bern: Lang.
Bammesberger, Alfred (2003): The provenance of the Old English suffix *-stre*. *North-Western European Language Evolution* 43: 53–63.
Bauer, Laurie (1983): *English Word Formation*. Cambridge: Cambridge University Press.
Bauer, Laurie (2001): *Morphological Productivity*. Cambridge: Cambridge University Press.
Bauer, Laurie (2006): Compounds and minor word-formation types. In: Bas Aarts and April McMahon (eds.), *Handbook of English Linguistics*, 483–506. Malden, MA/Oxford: Wiley/Blackwell.
Bauer, Laurie and Rodney Huddleston (2002): Lexical word-formation. In: Rodney Huddleston and Geoffrey K. Pullum (eds.), *The Cambridge Grammar of the English Language*, 1621–1721. Cambridge: Cambridge University Press.
Bauer, Laurie, Rochelle Lieber and Ingo Plag (2013): *The Oxford Reference Guide to English Morphology*. Oxford: Oxford University Press.
Bauer, Laurie and Salvador Valera (eds.) (2005): *Approaches to Conversion/Zero-Derivation*. Münster: Waxmann.
Benczes, Réka (2006): *Creative Compounding in English. The Semantics of Metaphorical and Metonymical Noun-Noun Combinations*. Amsterdam/Philadelphia: Benjamins.
Biese, Yrjö M. (1941): *Origin and Development of Conversions in English*. Helsinki: Suomalaisen Tiedeakatemia.
Burnley, David (1992): Word formation. In: Roger Lass (ed.), *The Cambridge History of the English Language*. Vol. 2: *1066–1476*, 439–450. Cambridge: Cambridge University Press.
Carr, Charles T. (1939): *Nominal Compounds in Germanic*. London: Oxford University Press.
Carstairs-McCarthy, Andrew (2002): *An Introduction to English Morphology*. Edinburgh: Edinburgh University Press.
Čermák, Jan (2002): A diachronic perspective on Old English deadjectival nouns ending in *-þ(u)/-t(u)*. *Brno Studies in English* 28: 19–25.
Ciszek, Ewa (2008): *Word Derivation in Early Middle English*. Frankfurt/M.: Lang.
Dalton-Puffer, Christiane (1996): *The French Influence on Middle English Morphology. A Corpus-Based Study of Derivation*. Berlin/New York: Mouton de Gruyter.
Dietz, Klaus (2002): Lexikalischer Transfer und Wortbildung am Beispiel des französischen Lehngutes im Mittelenglischen. In: Mechthild Habermann, Peter O. Müller and Horst Haider Munske (eds.), *Historische Wortbildung des Deutschen*, 381–405. Tübingen: Niemeyer.
Dietz, Klaus (2004): Die altenglischen Präfixbildungen und ihre Charakteristik. *Anglia* 122: 561–613.
Dietz, Klaus (2007): Denominale Abstraktbildungen des Altenglischen: Die Wortbildung der Abstrakta auf *-dōm, -hād, -lāc, -rǣden, -sceaft, -stæf* und *-wist* und ihrer Entsprechungen im Althochdeutschen und im Altnordischen. In: Hans Fix (ed.), *Beiträge zur Morphologie. Germanisch, Baltisch, Ostseefinnisch*, 97–172. Odense: University Press of Southern Denmark.
DOE = *Dictionary of Old English*. http://www.doe.utoronto.ca [last access 25 Jan 2015].
Faiß, Klaus (1992): *English Historical Morphology and Word-Formation. Loss versus Enrichment*. Trier: Wissenschaftlicher Verlag Trier.
Faiß, Klaus (2004): From Old English to Modern English. In: Geert Booij, Christian Lehmann, Joachim Mugdan and Stavros Skopeteas (eds.), *Morphology. An International Handbook on Inflection and Word-Formation*. Vol. 2, 1668–1680. Berlin/New York: de Gruyter.
Fernández-Domínguez, Jesús (2009): *Productivity in English Word-formation. An approach to N+N compounding*. Bern: Lang.
Fisiak, Jacek (ed.) (1985): *Historical Semantics. Historical Word-Formation*. Berlin: Mouton de Gruyter.

Fisiak, Jacek and Magdalena Bator (eds.) (2013): *Historical English Word-Formation and Semantics*. Berlin: Lang.
Gardner, Anne-Christine (2014): *Derivation in Middle English: Regional and Text Type Variation*. Helsinki: Société Néophilologique.
Haselow, Alexander (2011): *Typological Changes in the Lexicon. Analytic Tendencies in English Noun Formation*. Berlin/New York: Mouton de Gruyter.
Hiltunen, Risto (1983): *The Decline of the Prefixes and the Beginnings of the Phrasal Verb. The Evidence from some Old and Early Middle English Texts*. Turku: Turun Yliopisto.
Irmer, Roland (1972): Die mit Nullmorphem abgeleiteten deverbalen Substantive des heutigen Englisch. Ph.D. dissertation, Universität Tübingen.
Jespersen, Otto (1942): *A Modern English Grammar on Historical Principles*. Vol. 6: *Morphology*. London/Copenhagen: Allen and Unwin/Munksgaard.
Karius, Ilse (1985): *Die Ableitung der denominalen Verben mit Nullsuffigierung im Englischen*. Tübingen: Niemeyer.
Kastovsky, Dieter (1971): The Old English suffix *-er(e)*. *Anglia* 89: 285–325.
Kastovsky, Dieter (1992): Word-Formation. In: Richard M. Hogg (ed.), *The Cambridge History of the English Language*. Vol. 1: *The Beginnings to 1066*, 355–400. Cambridge: Cambridge University Press.
Kastovsky, Dieter (2006a): Typological changes in derivational morphology. In: Ans van Kemenade and Bettelou Los (eds.), *The Handbook of the History of English*, 151–176. Oxford: Blackwell.
Kastovsky, Dieter (2006b): Vocabulary. In: Richard M. Hogg and David Denison (eds.), *AHistory of the English Language*, 199–270. Cambridge: Cambridge University Press.
Knappe-Maas, Meike (1998): Das Suffix germ. **-ingō/-ungō* im Alt und Frühmittelenglischen: Semantik und Wortbildung. Ph.D. dissertation, Freie Universität Berlin.
Koma, Osamu (2000): *A Descriptive Study of Deverbal Nouns in Old English*. Tokyo: Hituzi Syobo.
Koziol, Herbert (1972 [1937]): *Handbuch der englischen Wortbildungslehre*. 2nd ed. Heidelberg: Winter.
Kunter, Gero (2011): *Compound Stress in English. The Phonetics and Phonology of Prosodic Prominence*. Berlin/New York: de Gruyter.
Lieber, Rochelle (2005): English word-formation processes. In: Pavol Štekauer and Rochelle Lieber (eds.), *Handbook of Word-Formation*, 375–427. Dordrecht: Springer.
Lindelöf, Uno (1938): *English Verb-Adverb Groups Converted into Nouns*. Helsingfors: Societas Scientiarum Fennica.
Lipka, Leonhard (2000): English (and general) word-formation – The state of the art in 1999. In: Bernhard Reitz and Sigrid Rieuwerts (eds.), *Anglistentag 1999 Mainz. Proceedings*, 5–20. Trier: Wissenschaftlicher Verlag Trier.
Lipka, Leonhard (2002): *English Lexicology. Lexical structure, word semantics and word-formation*. Tübingen: Narr.
Lloyd, Cynthia (2011): *Semantics and Word-Formation. The Semantic Development of Five French Suffixes in Middle English*. Oxford: Lang.
Lutz, Angelika (1997): Sound change, word-formation and the lexicon: The history of the English prefix verbs. *English Studies* 78: 258–290.
Majewski, Kerstin (ed.) (2024): Historical English Word-Formation. Sonderheft / Special Issue of *Zeitschrift für Wortbildung / Journal of Word Formation* 8(2).
Marchand, Hans (1969): *The Categories and Types of Present-Day English Word-Formation. A Synchronic-Diachronic Approach*. 2nd ed. München: Beck.
MED = *Middle English Dictionary*. http://quod-lib.umich.edu/m/med/ [last access 25 Jan 2015].
Meid, Wolfgang (1967): *Germanische Sprachwissenschaft*. Vol. 3: *Wortbildungslehre*. Berlin: de Gruyter.

Miller, D. Gary (1997): The morphological legacy of French: Borrowed suffixes on native bases in Middle English. *Diachronica* 14: 233–264.

Minkova, Donka (2008): Prefixation and stress in Old English. *Word Structure* 1: 21–52.

Mühleisen, Susanne (2010): *Heterogeneity in Word-Formation Patterns. A Corpus-Based Analysis of Suffixation with* -ee *and its Productivity in English.* Amsterdam/Philadelphia: Benjamins.

Nevalainen, Terttu (1999): Word-formation. In: Roger Lass (ed.), *The Cambridge History of the English Language*. Vol. 3: *1476–1776*, 376–433. Cambridge: Cambridge University Press.

Niwa, Yoshinobu (1991–95): *The Function and Development of Prefixes and Particles in Three Early Old English Texts. The Beginning of the Phrasal Verb*. 2 Vol. Tokyo: Kinseido.

OED = *Oxford English Dictionary*. http://www.oed.com [last access 25 Jan 2015].

Pastor-Gómez, Iria (2011): *The Status and Development of N+N Sequences in Contemporary English Noun Phrases*. Bern: Lang.

Pennanen, Esko V. (1966): *Contributions to the Study of Back-Formation in English*. Tampere: Julkaisija Yhteiskunnallinen Korkeakoulu.

Pennanen, Esko V. (1971): *Conversion and Zero-Derivation in English*. Tampere: Tampereen Yliopisto.

Plag, Ingo (1999): *Morphological Productivity. Structural Constraints on English Derivation*. Berlin/New York: Mouton de Gruyter.

Plag, Ingo (2003): *Word-Formation in English*. Cambridge: Cambridge University Press.

Reischer, Jürgen (2008): *Die Wortkreuzung und verwandte Verfahren der Wortbildung. Eine korpusbasierte Analyse des Phänomens „Blending" am Beispiel des Deutschen und Englischen*. Hamburg: Kovač.

Ryder, Mary E. (1994): *Ordered Chaos. The Interpretation of English Noun-Noun Compounds*. Berkeley: University of California Press.

Säily, Tanja (2014): *Sociolinguistic Variation in English Derivational Productivity: Studies and Methods in Diachronic Corpus Linguistics*. Helsinki: Société Néophilologique.

Säily, Tanja (2018): Change or Variation? Productivity of the Suffixes -ness and -ity. In: Terttu Nevalainen, Minna Palander-Collin and Tanja Säily (eds.), *Patterns of Change in 18th-Century English: A Sociolinguistic Approach*, 197–218. Amsterdam/Philadelphia: Benjamins.

Sauer, Hans (1992): *Nominalkomposita im Frühmittelenglischen. Mit Ausblicken auf die Geschichte der englischen Nominalkomposita*. Tübingen: Niemeyer.

Schmid, Hans-Jörg (2011): *English Morphology and Word-Formation. An Introduction*. 2nd ed. Berlin: Schmidt.

Schneider, Klaus P. (2003): *Diminutives in English*. Tübingen: Niemeyer.

Seymour, Richard K. (1968): *A Bibliography of Word-Formation in the Germanic Languages*. Durham, NC: Duke University Press.

Štekauer, Pavol (2000): *English Word-Formation. A History of Research (1960–1995)*. Tübingen: Narr.

Sundby, Bertil (1995): *English Word-Formation as Described by English Grammarians 1600–1800*. Oslo: Novus.

Suzuki, Seiichi (1990): On the origin and development of the action noun suffix *-nis* in Old English. *Indogermanische Forschungen* 95: 184–207.

Terasawa, Jun (1994): *Nominal Compounds in Old English. A Metrical Approach*. Copenhagen: Rosenkilde and Bagger.

Thun, Nils (1963): *Reduplicative Words in English. A Study of Formations of the Type 'Tick-tick', 'Hurly-burly', and 'Shilly-shally'*. Lund: Blom.

Trips, Carola (2009): *Lexical Semantics and Diachronic Morphology. The Development of* -hood, -dom *and* -ship *in the History of English*. Tübingen: Niemeyer.

Zbierska-Sawala, Anna (1993): *Early Middle English Word Formation. Semantic Aspects of Derivational Affixation in the AB Language*. Frankfurt/M.: Lang.

Éva Buchi and Jean-Paul Chauveau

17 From Latin to Romance

Abstract: This article provides a succinct overview of the evolution of central aspects of word-formation from Latin to Romance, in particular Romanian, Italian, French, Catalan, Spanish, and Portuguese.

1 Introduction

This article deals with the principal tendencies in the evolution of word-formation – be it losses, surviving features, phenomena of restructuring, or the emergence of new structures – which took place during the transition from Latin to Romance. As the common ancestor of the Romance languages is not classical Latin as it is known from a great variety of written testimonies, but its spoken counterpart (Lausberg 1976, vol. 1: 97–99; cf. Buchi 2010), or rather its counterpart pertaining to "communicative immediateness" (Koch and Oesterreicher 2008: 2575) called *Proto-Romance* (or sometimes *Vulgar Latin*), the starting point of our account should ideally be Proto-Romance word-formation as it can mainly be reconstructed from the Romance languages. Indeed, the results of this reconstruction converge partly with what is known about word-formation in classical Latin, but they also assign some originality to the common ancestor of the Romance languages within global Latin. For instance, whereas there was a great deal of allomorphy for the Latin prefix *dis-*, its Proto-Romance correlate */dɪs-/ does not seem to have had any of it (Buchi 2009: 152). But apart from the noteworthy exception of Hall's *Proto-Romance Morphology* (Hall 1983), work in the field of

Éva Buchi, Nancy, France
Jean-Paul Chauveau, Nancy, France

https://doi.org/10.1515/9783111420530-017

Proto-Romance word-formation – as opposed to classical Latin word-formation, which has received a great deal of attention, as well as philology-inspired "Vulgar Latin" word-formation (Cooper 1975 [1895]; Olcott 1898) – is scarse (see however Heidemeier 2014 on */-'ani-a/, */-'aki-/ ~ */-'iki-/ ~ */-'uki-/, */-'agin-/ ~ */'igin/ ~ */-'ugin-/, and */-kl-/). For this reason, we adopt here a double, classical Latin *and* Proto-Romance, starting point, represented in the dual form *dis-* ~ */dɪs-/; a scientifically more convincing approach would be to go back precisely to the common ancestor of the Romance languages, but such an ambitious enterprise is still at least a generation away.

(Classical) Latin word-formation is fairly well covered by a range of trustworthy standard works (Leumann 1963; Kircher-Durand 2002; Weiss 2011: 266–324); the same holds for comparative Romance word-formation (Meyer-Lübke 1895; Anderson and Rochet 1979; Lüdtke 1996, 2007; Bauer 2011). Comprehensive reference works are available as well for some of the individual Romance languages, be they of synchronic (Pascu 1916 on Romanian; Grossmann and Rainer 2004 on Italian; Siller-Runggaldier 1989 on Ladin; Jochems 1959 on Romansh; Adams 1913 on Old Occitan; Rohlfs 1931 on Gascon; López del Castillo 2002 and Bruguera 2006 on Catalan; Rainer 1993 and Bosque and Demonte 1999 on Spanish; Sandmann 1986 and Rio-Torto 2013 on Portuguese) or diachronic essence (Rohlfs 1954 and Tekavčić 1974 on Italian; DRG Registerband 1998: 82–93 on Romansh; Nyrop 1908 and Rainer 2004 on French; Ronjat 1980 [1937] on Occitan; Badia i Margarit 1994 on Catalan; Pharies 2002 on Spanish; Williams 1962 [1938] and Viaro 2014 on Portuguese). We will consider this set of titles, as well as Hall (1983) for Proto-Romance, as our default bibliography: they will not be cited below under the different headings. In addition, the handbook *Word-Formation* (Müller et al. 2015–2016) provides detailed articles on synchronic and diachronic aspects of word-formation in several of the Romance languages.

2 General overview

Rainer (2002, 2008) offers a synthetic overview of convergence and divergence in the word-formation of the Romance languages. What differentiates word-formation of the various Romance languages is often semantics, suffixes of a common origin which present different meanings (see Rainer 2005a for some theoretical thoughts on semantic change in word-formation). Moreover, phonetic evolution gave way to much more allomorphy in (at least some of) the Romance languages than in the proto-language. Many suffixes were borrowed from (classical, medieval, and modern) Latin and from other Romance languages. This massive borrowing gave way to something one could call morphological Europeanization (Schmitt 2000), a phenomenon which exceeds Romance.

One of the most important differences between Latin and Romance word-formation lies in the development, during the 20th century, of a wide range of "affixoids". However, this and other modern phenomena like re-Latinization tendencies will not be treated in this article, which focuses on the transition from Proto-Romance to early states of Romance languages.

3 Composition

The role of composition in Latin and Romance word-formation (cf. Giurescu 1975; Lindner 1996; Moussy 2005) is relatively marginal. Romance languages have conserved some Latin compounds, but they have mainly developed this mode of formation on their own. The Latin modifier-head order is conserved in the rare N+N Latin compounds that have been maintained: *aquaeductus* ~ */akue'dʊkt-u/ ~ */akui'dʊktu/ 'aqueduct' > It. *acquedotto*, OFr. *avidotz*, Sp. *aguaducho*, but the opposite order prevailed in later formations: Lat. *comes stabuli* ~ */komes'stabol-i/ 'earl of the stable' > It. *conestabile*, Fr. *connétable*, Sp. *condestable*, Port. *condestavel*. In modern formations, the semantic relationship between the two elements is marked by a preposition: It. *infortunio sul lavoro* 'work accident', Fr. *accident de travail*, Sp. *accidente de trabajo*, Port. *acidente de trabalho*. For the noun-adjective compounds, the Latin order adjective + noun survived in ancient formations: *mediu die* ~ *media die* ~ */'mɛdi-u 'di-e/ ~ */'mɛdi-a 'di-e/ 'midday' > Rom. *miazăzi*, It. *mezzodì*, Fr. *midi*, Sp. *mediodía*, Port. *meiodia*. Later on, the reverse order prevailed: It. *cassaforte* 'safe; lit. box strong', Fr. *coffre-fort*, Sp. *caja fuerte*, Port. *caixa-forte*. Another type of composition of which first examples already appear in Latin is that of compounds formed by V+N, in which the verb appears as a stem form. A lot has been written about this type of formation (for the history of the debate cf. Villoing 1999), which has been treated either as an innovation coming from Proto-Romance or as following a Latin model (Bork 1990). The oldest attestations are nicknames that have corresponding forms in the Romance languages, such as the following type, existing in Italian, Romansh, French, Occitan and Catalan: *Bevilacqua, Bebelagua, Boileau, Boilesve, Beulaigue* (Badia i Margarit 1991: 54–65; 84–85; 103–104; 131–132). However, it is as names for professions or functions (It. *porta-bandiera* 'standard bearer', Fr. *porte-drapeau* [> Rom. *portdrapel*], Sp. *portaestandarte*, Port. *porta-bandeira*) and in the modern age especially as names for instruments or machines that this type has given rise to many new terms, numerous loanwords being formed on the same mode of formation: Rom.

portavion 'aircraft carrier', It. *porta-aerei*, Fr. *porte-avions*, Sp. *portaviones*, Port. *porta-aviões*; It. *cavatappi* 'corkscrew', Fr. *tire-bouchon* [> Rom. *tirbuşon*], Sp. *saca-corchos*, Port. *saca-rolhas*. For the compounds of the same type as Sp. *bocacalle* 'entrance into a street; lit. mouth street', cf. Dardel (1999), for the type Lat. *aurifer* 'gold-bearing', cf. Rainer (2003).

4 Derivation

4.1 Nominal derivation

4.1.1 Denominal nouns

Latin had in place a range of several types of patterns for the production of abstract nouns derived from personal nouns. Examples of such formations can be found in Romance languages, but the models, with some exceptions, have not been maintained.

In a few cases, it is the nominal base that has been lost. Nominal derivatives in *-tās, -tātis* ~ */-'tat-e/, such as Lat. *civitās* 'the citizens who constitute a town, a city' (← *civis* 'citizen') or *societās* 'society' (← *socius* 'partner'), have survived, but this type of derivation has been abandoned in favour of derivation from an adjectival base. In the same way, derivatives with the suffix *-itia* ~ */-'ɪti-a/ on a nominal base, such as *amīcitia* (← *amīcus* 'friend'), or *pueritia* (← *puer* 'child'), disappeared in favour of the derivation from an adjectival base (see section 4.1.2). Derivatives in *-tūra* denominating an action parallelled by an agent noun in *-tor* (*quaestor* → *quaestūra*) have not survived, unlike the action nouns derived on a verbal base (cf. section 4.1.3).

Most of the time, this type of suffixation itself disappeared. A derivative in *-tūs, -tūtis* has survived, e.g., *virtūs* 'virtue', but the model itself disappeared with the disappearance of the base (*vir* 'male human being'). The derivation in *-ium* has suffered a similar fate, even though, for example, the derivative *iūdicium* 'judgement' and its base *iūdex* 'judge' have been widely retained. A derivative formed with *-mōnium*, i.e. *testimōnium* 'testimony', maintained itself, but neither the base *testis* 'witness' nor its derivational model survived. The derivation model in *-ia* disappeared and the corresponding lexemes in the Romance languages are borrowings from Lat. *adulescentia* 'youth', *custōdia* 'act of guarding', *militia* 'profession of a soldier', etc.

The case of the status-noun suffix *-ātus* ~ */-'atu/ is slightly different. Roman institutions corresponding to this derivation, e.g., *consulātus* 'consulate', *principātus* 'principate' (← *princeps* 'prince'), died out with the Roman Empire. But the Church has adopted this model of derivation for its own institution and several examples have followed, more or less directly, in a few Romance languages; thus, from *clēricātus* 'state of a cleric' (← *clēricus* 'clerc'), we have It. *chiericato* and Fr. *clergé*, and from *episcopātus* 'episcopate' (← *episcopus* 'bishop'), It. *vescovado*, Fr. *évêché*, Sp. *obispado*, Port. *bispado*. During the High Middle Ages, the political administration followed the same model and built upon it Lat. *comitātus*, the denomination of the function of the *comes*, *-itis* 'earl', from which Fr. *comté*, Occit. *comtat*, Cat. *comdat*, Sp. Port. *condado* and, following the same model, It. *marchesato*, Sp. Port. *marquesado* for the function of a marquis. Nevertheless the use of this type of derivation has been fairly limited, though it was eventually expanded with scholarly borrowings from classical or medieval Latin: the ecclesiastical or academic denominations of the function of the dean (Lat. *decānus*) are often borrowed directly from the Medieval Latin *decānātus*, e.g., Rom. *decanat*, It. *decanato*, Fr. *décanat*, Sp. *decanato*, Port. *decanado*, rather than being loan-translated, as Fr. *doyenné* (< *doyen*), Port. *deado* (< *deão*). The formation of denominative nouns has been widely replaced by the nominalization of denominative adjectives in *-ārius* ~ */-'ari-u/ and *-āticus*~ */-'atik-u/ (cf. section 4.2) or by deadjectival nouns in *-ia* ~ */-i-a/ (cf. section 4.1.2).

The reduced amount of Latin diminutive formations in the Romance languages is due to the fact that only accented suffixes, such as *-ellu*, *-ella* ~ */-'ɛll-u/, */-'ɛll-a/, *-iculu*, *-icula* ~ */-'ekl-u/, */-'ekl-a/, *-īculu*, *-īcula* ~ */-'ikl-u/, */-'ikl-a/, *-uculu*, *-ucula* ~ */-'ʊkl-u/, */-'ʊkl-a/, *-eolu*, *-eola* ~ */-'iɔl-u/, */-'iɔl-a/, maintained their function as morphemes and stayed productive. During Late Latinity, suffixes such as *-īnu*, *-īna* ~ */-'in-u/, */-'in-a/ and new formations built on *-tt-* */-'att-u/, */-'att-a/, */-'ett-u/, */-'ett-a/, */-'ɔtt-u/, */-'ɔtt-a/ developed a diminutive value and eventually became the main formations. For the history of diminutive formations in Romance languages, see Hakamies (1951), Hasselrot (1957), and Dębowiak (2014).

4.1.2 Deadjectival nouns

It is not surprising that an unproductive quality-noun suffix such as *-monia* (e.g., *acer* → *acrimonia*) disappeared. But the *-tūdin-* derivation, though productive in Latin and forming common words derived from adjectives (cf. *magnus* 'great' → *magnitūdo*, *-inis* 'greatness', a far more common derivative than *magnitas* and *magnitiēs*), stopped being active in Romance languages. Its decline must have been early, considering the limited number of surviving formations of this type coming from the Latin period. Furthermore, the result of *-tūdin-* may have been conflated with that of *-ūmen*, like in the case of the derivative formed on the past participle of *consuescere* 'to accustom', *consuētūdine(m)* 'custom', which gave rise to It. *costume*, Fr. *coutume*, Sp. *costumbre*, Port. *costume*. However, the scholarly language reintroduced many Latin formations: the derivative of Lat. *longus* 'long', *longitūdo, -dinis* 'length', for example, became a geographical term (Rom. It. *longitudine*, Fr. *longitude*, Sp. *longitud*, Port. *longitude*).

The *-ia* ~ */-i-a/ suffix (e.g., Lat. *superbus* 'arrogant' → *superbia* 'arrogance') did not maintain itself in the Romance languages. Its atonicity made it unidentifiable and the link between the derived noun and the adjective has been loosened. Either the adjective did not survive, as is the case in Lat. *verecundus* 'shy' → *verecundia*, where only the latter is preserved in It. *vergogna*, Fr. *vergogne*, OSp. *vergüeña*, Sp. *vergüenza*, OPort. *vergonha*, Port. *vergonça*; or if the adjective continued to be used like Lat. *minūtus* 'small', that became Rom. *mărunt*, It. *minuto*, Fr. *menu*, Sp. *menudo*, Port. *miudo*, the derived noun, Lat. *minutiae* 'small things, small details' (especially used in the plural), subsists only with specialized and concrete meanings, such as It. *minugia* 'gut', Fr. *menuise* 'small wood pieces; small lead shots; small fish', OSp. *menuza* 'division; small piece of something', OPort. *miunças* pl. 'small dimes'. As a noun describing a quality, it has been replaced by borrowings: It. *minuzia*, Fr. *minutie*, Sp. *minucia* 'meticulousness', or by internal creations: Rom. *mărunţiş*, Port. *miudeza*. Nevertheless, this type of derivation was still productive during the Proto-Romance period. From the adjective *crassus* 'thick; fat', Latin derived the nouns *crassitūdo*, *crassitās* and *crassitiēs* meaning 'thickness; consistency', of which none has survived. It is a Proto-Romance derivative, */'kras-i-a/, that is at the origin of the Romance lexemes: It. *grasce* f.pl. 'subsistences, provisions', Romansh *grascha* sg. 'manure', Fr. *graisse* 'greasy substance', OCat. *graixa*, Cat. *greix* m., Port. *graxa* 'polish'. This type of formation gave more long-lasting products in the Gallo-Romance domain, where Lat. *lātus* 'wide' > */'lat-i-a/ 'width' has survived as Fr. *laize* f. 'width (of fabric, of paper)' and Lat. *districtus* 'tight, narrow' > */dɪ'strɪkt-i-a/ 'narrowness' has resulted in *détresse* f. 'anguish'.

The parallel suffixes *-itia* ~ */-'iti-a/ and *-itiēs* ~ */-'iti-e/ coexisted in Latin and had the possibility to compete with each other (*dūrus* 'hard' → *dūritia* f. 'hardness' and *dūritiēs* f.). The second suffix is only conserved in a few dialects from Southern Italy (Rohlfs 1954, § 1153) and especially in Spanish and in Portuguese (e.g., Sp. Port. *rápido* 'fast' → *rapidez* 'speed'). It is its rival, the *-itia* suffix, that has generally been conserved. The early vitality of this suffix can be seen in the fact that it replaced *-tūdin-*, for example, in the quality noun corresponding to *altus* 'high', viz. *altitia* 'height' (which replaced *altitudo*), from which It. *altezza*, Fr. *hautesse*, Sp. Port. *alteza*. It remained productive in some Romance languages, in which we can find, as derivatives from different representatives of the Latin adjective *teneru(m)* 'tender; young', Rom. *tinereţe*, It. *tenerezza*, Fr. *tendresse*, Sp.

terneza, while the derivatives *teneritās* and *teneritūdo*, attested in Latin, have left no trace. In this case, the learnèd language also reintroduced a form of the suffix closer to the original, but almost exclusively limited to borrowings (e.g., Rom. *justiţie*, It. *giustizia*, Fr. *justice*, Sp. *justicia*, Port. *justiça*, borrowed from Lat. *justitia* 'justice, compliance with the law'). These formations can coexist with the derivatives formed from the other suffix, but with the meaning 'correctness' (e.g., Rom. *justeţe*, It. *giustezza*, Fr. *justesse*, Port. *justeza*). The scholarly influence must have come very early, since the phonologically regular form is rarely attested in French (e.g., *riche* → OFr. *richoise* 'wealth'), while the productive forms are innovations, for example OFr. *-ece*/Fr. *-esse*, as well as the suffix *-ise* (e.g., *sot* 'stupid' → *sottise*, *traître* 'treacherous' → *traîtrise*), which has been adopted by Italian in borrowings (e.g., It. *franchigia* < Fr. *franchise* 'franchise'; OIt. *cuvidigia*, It. *cupidigia* < OFr. *covoitise*, Fr. *convoitise* 'greed; envy') as well as in native formations (e.g., It. *altero* 'haughty' → *alterigia* 'arrogance').

The most productive derivation in Latin was the one using the suffix *-tās*, *-tātis* ~ */-'tat-e/, and its productivity increased even more during Late Latinity. A good number of Latin formations have been conserved, such as *bonus* 'good' → *bonitās* 'goodness', which has been continued by Rom. *bunătate*, It. *bontà*, Fr. *bonté*, Sp. *bondad*. This is also the case of later derivatives like */amik-i'tat-e/, reconstructed from the cognates OFr. *amisté*, OOccit. *amistat*, Cat. *amistat*, Sp. *amistad*, and Port. *amizad* 'friendship'. This derivation kept being productive, as is attested by parallel formations derived from the equivalent of Lat. *lēgālis* 'legal', such as Fr. *loyauté*, It. *lealtà*, Cat. *lleyaltat*, Sp. *lealtad*, Port. *lealdade* 'loyalty', which have been formed on the model of Medieval Latin *legalitas*. A confirmation of this productivity can also be seen in derivatives coined within the different Romance languages, like the ones derived from the descendants of Lat. *misellus* (e.g., Rom. *mişel* 'poor' → *mişelătate* 'misery'), Lat. *rēgālis* (e.g., Fr. *royal* 'royal' → *royauté* 'royalty'), or Lat. *curtus* (e.g., Romansh *cuort* 'short' → *cuortadad*), etc. However, the inherited model has been remodelled by the introduction of Latinisms in the scholarly language. These have introduced variations of the suffix: Rom. *propriu* 'own' and *proprietate* 'property', It. *proprio* and *proprietà*, Fr. *propre* and *propriété*, Sp. *propio* and *propiedad*, or It. *caro* 'expensive' and *carità* 'charity', Fr. *cher* and *charité*, Sp. *caro* and *caridad*, Port. *caro* and *caridade*. These variants became autonomous and the only ones to stay productive: It. *ovvio* 'obvious' → *ovvietà*, *goloso* 'gluttonous' → *golosità*, Fr. *net* 'clean' → *netteté*, *frivole* 'frivolous' → *frivolité*, Sp. *solo* 'alone' → *soledad*, *bárbaro* 'barbaric' → *barbaridad*.

The Greek suffix -ία was first rendered as *-ia* ~ */-i-a/ in borrowings, Greek ἐκκλησία becoming Lat. *ecclesia*, with the accent placed on the last syllable of the stem, as in its Romance representatives It. *chiesa*, Fr. *église*, Sp. *iglesia*, Port. *igreja* 'church'. But the Greek accentuation */-'i-a/ imposed itself on the scholarly language, and the suffix became productive in Latin, to the point of being conserved in Romance languages, as can be seen in the parallelism between It. *cortese* 'courteous' → *cortesia*, Fr. *courtois* → *courtoisie*, Sp. *cortés* → *cortesía*, Port. *cortês* → *cortesia*. But this is not the only environment in which the suffix has been productive: it was also, very early, combined with nouns, as can be seen in formations such as Late Lat. *abbas* 'abbot' → *abbatia* 'abbey', continued in It. *badia*, Fr. *abbaye*, Sp. *abadía*, Port. *abadia*. This type of derivation became common in Romance for the formation of lexemes designating a quality or a function: It. *signoria* 'lordship', Fr. *seigneurie*, Sp. *senhoría*, Port. *senhoria*, which constitute derivatives from the descendants of Lat. *seniore(m)*, or It. *borghesia*, Fr. *bourgeoisie*, Sp. *burguesía*, Port. *burguesia* (see 4.2 for the base). This suffixation has particularly been used in combination with nouns ending in *-ārius*; thus, on the Late Latin noun *caballārius* 'stable boy', that became the name for a warrior riding a horse, the name corresponding to his function was formed: It. *cavallaria* 'chivalry', Fr. *chevalerie*, Sp. *caballería*, Port. *cavalaria*. This combination of suffixes has gained autonomy resulting in the complex suffix *-aría/-ería/-erie*, that is used to form nouns which designate places where a certain activity is carried out: from the descendant of Lat. *lacte(m)* 'milk', for example, are derived Rom. *lăptărie* 'place where dairy is sold', It. *latteria*, Fr. *laiterie*, Sp. *lechería*, Port. *leitaria*.

At a late stage Latin developed for the suffix Lat. *-or*, *-ōris* ~ */-'or-e/ a formation on an adjectival base, while before the base had been solely verbal. In parallel with Lat. *calere* 'to be warm' → *calor* 'warmth', beginning in the Classical period *calidus* 'warm' → *caldor* 'warmth' appeared. This model prevailed in Romance where there are still formations dating from Late Latinity, such as *albus* 'white' → *albor* 'whiteness' > Rom. *alboare* f. 'weak light', It. *albore* m. 'whiteness; dawn', OFr. *abor* f. 'dawn', Sp. *albor* m. On the model of these formations words designating qualities have been created, like It. *biancore* m. 'whiteness', Fr. *blancheur* f., Sp. *blancor* m.; these formations are most frequent in the Gallo-Romance territory.

4.1.3 Deverbal nouns

Action nouns: Latin possessed several possibilities for the derivation of action nouns from verbal bases, and these would meet different fates. Romance formations follow from these possibilities; however, the system has been remodelled, following changes in the morphology of the verb.

The Latin suffix *-tiō*, *-tiōnis* ~ */-'tion-e/, attached to a verb stem, was the most productive pattern for abstract nouns and has maintained itself in Romance, but the range of derivations has become limited (cf. Burdy 2013). Formations based on a stem without a thematic vowel are inherited: *cantiōne(m)* > It. *canzone* 'song', Fr. *chanson*, Sp. *canzón*. Only the formation based on a stem with a thematic vowel has remained productive, but its regularity has been restricted. While, for example, in Old Occitan, the suffix's form is dependent on the conjugation class (e.g., *donar* 'to give' → *donazon*, *batre* 'to beat' → *batezon*, *garir* 'to heal' → *garizon*), in Italian the suffix allomorphs are reduced to two, *-agione* and *-igione*, and in French only the terms formed with *-aison* persisted, apart from a few exceptions. After the 16th century, almost only the scholarly forms, like It. *-zione*, Fr. *-tion*, Sp. *-ción*, have been productive.

The fate of the two related suffixes Lat. *-men*, *-minis* ~ */'-me/ and *-mentum*, *-menti* ~ */-'mɛnt-u/, which could generate doublets such as *medicāre* 'to heal' → *medicāmen* and *medicāmentum* 'medication', was quite distinct. Whilst *-men* ~ */'-me/ survived only in parts of the domain, and mostly in the form of a denominal collective noun (cf. Rainer 2018), *-mentum* ~ */-'mɛnt-u/, which was preferred in oral language, has been widely maintained. Since the Latin era, it is seen to compete with other formations, especially with the derivatives coined with *-tiō*, *-tiōnis*. For example, to the older derivatives from *fricāre* 'to rub', viz. *fricātus* m., *fricātio* f. and *fricātūra* f., *fricāmentum* n. was added in a later period. The high productivity of this type of derivation in Romance, which has not been discontinued in the contemporary period, can be inferred from the fact that, for example, as an action noun derived from Latin *iūrāre* 'to swear, make an oath', *iūrātio* has no equivalent in Romance, while Lat. *iūrāmentum* does have them: Rom. *juramînt*, It. *giuramento*, Fr. *jurement*, Sp. *juramento*. The suffix is added to a stem with a thematic vowel, which closely corresponds to the conjugation class of the verb. Thus, for the three conjugation classes of Proto-Romance **cominitiāre* 'to begin', *accrēscere* 'to increase' and *consentīre* 'to agree', Old Occitan has *comensamen*, *acreisemen*, *consentimen*, while Italian reduces the thematic vowels to two (cf. *cominciamento* vs. *accrescimento*, *consentimento*), and French generalises the first conjugation (cf. *commencement*, *accroissement*, *consentement*). The concrete metonymic senses of abstract nouns, already known to Latin (e.g., *vestīre* 'to dress' → *vestīmentum* 'clothes'), continue in Romance: It. *armamento*, Fr. *armement*, Sp. *armamento* can either refer to the action of arming, or to the concrete means involved.

The derivation in *-tūra* ~ */-'tur-a/, also productive in Latin, even if later and on a more reduced scale, survived in the Romance languages. In this case as well, the lexemes without a thematic vowel are residual (e.g., *consuere* 'to sew' → */kosu-'tur-a/ [cf. *sūtūra* 'sewing'] > It. Sp. Port. *costura*, Fr. *couture*), in opposition to the formations with a thematic vowel, which have become productive: Rom. *țesătură* 'weaving', It. *tessitura*, Fr. *tiss(e)ure*, Sp. *tejedura*. However, as is the case in Latin, this derivative pattern has developed, in parallel to the original sense, metonymic senses, notably the one designating the result of the action. It. *lavatura* and Sp. Port. *lavadura*, for example, present both senses, 'act of washing' and 'water used to wash', while French *lavure* only conserved the second sense, as is also the case for the inherited lexeme Rom. *lătură*. Where there was competition with another derivational type it is, most of the time, the concrete meaning that has prevailed: It. *cancellatura* 'erasure' vs. *cancellamento, cancellazione* 'cancellation', Fr. *raclure* 'scrapings' vs. *raclement* 'act of scraping off'. Since the Latin era, derivatives of this type maintain a closer relationship with the nouns of the same lexical family than with the verb. Thus, Latin *armātūra* is not the action noun of the verb *armāre* 'to arm', but is linked to *arma* 'weapons', with the collective meaning 'weaponry', which has been maintained in Romance (Rom. *armătură*, It. *armatura*, Fr. *armure*, Sp. *armadura*, etc.). From the concrete meaning of the suffix a new function has developed, that of forming denominal collective nouns, such as It. *dentatura* 'teeth', Fr. *denture*, Sp. Port. *dentadura*.

Though the productivity of the Latin suffix *-or, -ōris* ~ */-'or-e/ had already faded during Latinity, it has nevertheless survived in Romance, especially in deverbal action nouns. The gender of its derivatives, which was masculine in Latin, tended to align itself to the feminine gender of the other action nouns, notably in Romanian, in the dialects of Northern Italy, in Romansh and in Gallo-Romance. But the Romance derivatives are either exceptional, like It. *bollire* 'to boil' → *bollore* 'boiling', *sentire* 'to hear' → *sentore* 'knowledge', or perceived as old or outdated, like OFr. *trembler* 'to tremble' → *tremblor* 'fear' or Fr. *sentir* 'to smell' → *senteur* 'smell'. This can be explained by the fact that the deadjectival formations that have appeared since Latin times have outnumbered the action nouns.

The *-ntia* formations, present at all times in Latin, experienced a great development in the post-classical oral language and have continued in Romance. Taking their origin in the present participle, these derivatives are constructed with *-antia* ~ */-'anti-a/ for verbs with an *-āre* ending and with *-entia* ~ */-'enti-a/ for the other verbs. Both of these types of derivatives have survived, but Romanian has not conserved the first suffix, while French has generalized it: It. *speranza* 'hope', Fr. *espérance*, Sp. *esperanza*; Rom. *credinţă*, It. *credenza*, Fr. *créance*/*croyance*, Sp. *creencia*.

A particular case concerns a derivative pattern of one Romance language which has spread to the others (cf. Fleischman 1977). The Latin suffix *-āticu* ~ */-'atik-u/ was used to form, on a nominal base, adjectives and neutral nouns to denote a relationship. It became *-age* in French, where its function changed: in the modern era it is used only to form deverbal action nouns. A noun such as OFr. *passage* m. 'place where sb. passes' can be referred to *pas* m. 'place where sb. passes' as well as to the verb *passer* 'to pass by', in which case it takes the meaning of 'action of passing'. In this sense Fr. *passage* has been borrowed as It.

passagio and Sp. *pasaje*. In fact, many cases in other Romance languages are borrowings from French: Rom. *dopaj* 'doping', It. *dopaggio*, Fr. *dopage*, Port. *dopagem* f. But formations can be independent of a French model as well: It. *pestaggio* m. 'beating' (← *pestare* 'to beat'), Sp. *almacenaje* 'storage' (← *almacenar* 'to store').

Agent nouns: Romance drastically reduced the range of processes available in Latin for forming agent nouns. It essentially kept the suffix *-tor*, *-tōris* ~ */-'tor-e/, which was the most productive one in Latin and has survived in all the Romance languages. In Latin, the suffix was added to the stem of the past participle. Stems fell into two classes, those without a thematical vowel (*docēre* → *doctor*, *vincere* → *victor*) and those which had one (*amāre* → *amātor*, *dēbēre* → *dēbitor*, *servīre* → *servītor*). As a noun of the first type we may mention *cantor* (← *canere* 'to sing', past participle: *cant-*), which was specialised in the ecclesiastical sense 'cantor' and only survived in Italian *cantore* and French *chantre*, while *cantātor* 'singer' (← *cantāre* 'to sing', past participle: *cantat-*) has descendants in all Romance languages. In some cases where the athematic stem has survived we observe a change in its form, as in Cat. Sp. Port. *pintor* 'painter', OFr. *peinteur*, whose stem has been remodelled partially on the present tense of *pinguere* 'to paint', in opposition to It. *pittore*, which continues */pɪk-tor-e/. Most of the time such formations have been abandoned in favour of formations conforming to the regular, thematic model: *victor*, for example, has been replaced by Rom. *învingător*, It. *vincitore*, Fr. *vainqueur*, Sp. *vencedor*.

Romance languages also present differences with respect to our suffix, where Romansh and Gallo-Romance, which conserve residues of the Latin nominal declension, maintain a double form of the suffix. Occitan has conserved the double forms in all three conjugations, as *-aire*/*-ador*, *-eire*/*-edor* and *-ire*/*-idor*; while in Old French the forms have been aligned on the first pair as *-ere*/*-(ë)eur*. After the loss of the syntactical value which they had in the old stages of the languages, the double forms nevertheless survived, with different varieties of a language choosing one or the other: thus, in Romansh, Vallader keeps the nominative forms (e.g., *chatscháder* 'hunter', *müráder* 'mason'), while Sursilvan preserves the oblique forms (e.g., *catschadur*, *miradur*). In Occitan, the forms of the nominative case *-aire* and *-èire* have survived the best; however, in varieties that conserve both types, a distinction, unknown to Latin, has been established between the occasional agent and the professional agent (e.g., *pescaire* 'person fishing' vs. *pescadou* 'fisherman'; cf. Ronjat 1980 [1937], § 697β). In French, on the contrary, nominative forms are maintained only in a few examples that no longer constitute a typical derivative pattern (e.g., *chantre*, *pâtre*, *peintre*); otherwise, only the oblique form *-eur* has remained productive. French therefore joins the languages which keep only the oblique form, such as It. *-tore*, Cat. Sp. Port. *-dor*, joined to the present stem. Romanian *-tor* is not the direct outcome of Latin *-tor*, but goes back to the oblique form *-tore(m)* via *-toare*.

Borrowings from Latin reintroduced formations that do not correspond to the patterns just described. The suffix can be either shorter (e.g., It. *-ore* and Sp. *-or* vs. *-tore* and *-dor*) or longer (e.g., Fr. *-ateur* vs. *-eur*). Occasionally, we also find formal doublets, with a different use or meaning: Fr. *liseur* vs. *lecteur* 'reader', It. *leggitore* vs. *lettore*, Sp. *leedor* vs. *lector*. The borrowed forms can be related to other derivatives, for example Fr. *lecture* 'reading', It. *lettura*, Sp. *lectura*. The importance of these relationships is revealed by the diffusion of agent nouns parallel to action nouns without a corresponding verb: Fr. *aviateur/aviation*, It. *aviatore/aviazione*, Sp. *aviador/aviación*.

In Latin, the feminine gender of the agent was expressed by the suffix *-trīx*, *-trīcis*, where *-tr-* is the reduced degree of the masculine form. Some of these formations survived, but the pattern itself only very rarely remained productive, for example in Old Occitan (cf. Adams 1913: 51–54), where *-airitz* is the feminine equivalent of *-ador* (e.g., *balairitz* 'female dancer') and *-eiritz* the feminine of *-edor* and *-idor* (e.g., *defendeiritz* 'female defender', *menteiritz* 'female liar'). In Old French and Friulan the suffix *-trix* was blended with the synonymous suffix *-issa* (e.g., OFr. *ameresse*, Friul. *madrese* 'female lover'). But most of the new patterns were derived from the masculine form, the descendant of */-'tor-e/, by adding a mark designating the feminine: the result can be seen in dialectal Italian *-tora* or in Sp. *-dora*. In Romanian, the feminine form originates from *-toria*, which resulted in *-toare*. Still another solution was to borrow the form of another suffix, as in Modern French, where the feminine corresponding to *-eur*, that is *-euse*, was originally the feminine form of the adjectival suffix *-eux*. Finally, the return to the Latin form *-trīx*, in parallel to the masculine *-tor*, is closing the cycle: It. *editrice* 'female editor', Fr. *éditrice* vs. Rom. *editoare*, Sp. *editora*.

The Latin suffix *-ō*, *-ōnis* ~ */-'o/, */-'on-e/ was used in the formation of numerous agent nouns, such as *caupō* 'innkeeper', *laniō* 'butcher', *lēnō* 'pander', which were typical of the popular language: some of them have survived, like Lat. *latrō*, *-ōnis* ~ */'latr-o/, */la'tr-on-e/ 'bandit' > It. *ladro*, Fr. *larron*, Cat. *ladró*, Sp. *ladrón*, Port. *ladrão*. Where the suffix has survived as a means for forming personal nouns, it takes on a pejorative or augmentative connotation.

I n s t r u m e n t and p l a c e n o u n s: There are different types of deverbal nouns to designate instruments in Latin. The ones that remained productive during the whole Latin era contained the following suffixes: *-culum* (e.g., *gubernāre* → *gubernāculum*, *vehere* → *vehiculum*), *-bulum/-bula* (e.g., *stāre* → *stabulum*, *mandere* → *mandibula*) and *-tōrium/-sōrium* (e.g., *dormīre* → *dormītōrium*). The least productive of these three suffixes was *-bulum/-bula*; it has become completely unproductive in Romance. The suffix *-culum* disappeared in Romanian and has only survived in the Western part of Romance by generalising *-āculum*, which contains the thematic vowel of the first conjugation. From the frequency of retention of certain lexical types it can be assumed that their formation can be traced back to Proto-Romance: It. *battaglio* 'tongue of a bell', OFr. *batail*, Sp. *badajo*, Port. *badalo* justify the assumption of an etymon */bat'(t)a-kul-u/. Formations specific to the Romance languages are either rare (e.g., It. *sputare* 'to spit' → *sputacchio* 'spittle', OSp. *legar* 'to link' → *legajo* 'wad of papers') or more numerous, but nevertheless form a closed stock, like in French (e.g., *éventer* 'to fan' → *éventail*, *fermer* 'to close' → *fermail*). It is the third type of formation, which was also the most productive in Latin, that imposed itself on all Romance languages. The Latin suffix *-tōrius/-sōrius, -a~* */-'tori-u/, */-'tori-a/ / */-'sori-u/, */-'sori-a/, whose original function was to form relational adjectives corresponding to agent nouns in *-tōr/ -sōr*, was used to form instrument nouns, mainly neuter, more rarely feminine. This type of formation has survived in Romance, both with masculine and feminine gender, with different productivity and uses: Rom. *-tor* and *-toare*, It. *-toio* and *-toia*, Fr. *-oir* and *-oire*, Sp. *-dero* and *-dera*.

As Latin neatly separated agent nouns and instrument nouns, the use of an agentive suffix in a few Romance languages to designate instruments has to be secondary. The suffixes It. *-tore*, Fr. *-eur/-euse*, Occit. *-dour*, Sp. *-dor* are used in numerous nouns referring to instruments, devices, machines, or workplaces and are identical to the results of *-tor, -tōris* ~ */-'tor-e/. However, this fact does not imply a tendency to use this suffix metaphorically: OFr. *ovreour* 'workshop', OOccit. Cat. Sp. *obrador* either must be representatives of */opera-'tori-u/, as in, for example, Occitan, Catalan and in some French dialects where */-'tori-u/ and */-'tor-e/ yield the same result, or must be borrowings, as in Spanish (cf. Rainer 2005b, 2011).

4.2 Adjectival derivation

In Latin, adjectival derivation can use as bases verbs (e.g., *amāre* 'to love' → *amābilis* 'kind') or adjectives (e.g., *surdus* 'deaf' → *surdaster* 'a bit deaf'); both patterns remain in Romance. But it is predominately the denominal derivation which was and remains the most productive one in Romance languages, particularly for relational adjectives (cf. Lüdtke 1995). The suffix *-ōsu, -ōsa* ~ */-'os-u/, */-'os-a/ is widespread and attested early on; it has remained productive since Proto-Romance. Examples of this derivation include It. *amoroso* 'in love', Fr. *amoureux*, Cat. *amorós*, Sp. Port. *amoroso*, as well as modern formations such as Rom. *gazos* 'gaseous', It. *gassoso*, Fr. *gazeux*, Cat. *gazós*, Port. *gasoso*. The use of the three possessive suffixes *-ātu*, *-ītu*, and *-ūtu* was governed by the thematic vowel of the noun used as a base, but this distributional regularity has not prevailed. The variant *-ūtu*, *-ūta* ~ */-'ut-u/, */-'ut-a/ (e.g., It. *barbuto* 'bearded', Fr. *barbu*, Sp. Port. *barbudo*), whose use was limited in the beginning, witnessed a great development, as can be inferred from the fact that it competed with or even superseded the formations corresponding to classical Latin *barbātus* ~ */bar'bat-u/ 'bearded' (Rom. *bărbat* 'male human being', It. *barbato* 'bearded', OFr. *barbé*, Sp. Port. *barbado*).

The Latin suffix *-ēnsis*~ */-'es-e/ was originally added to city or country names, but then also spread to topographic nouns. Hence, from Late Latin *burgus* 'fortified castle; small town' and in parallel to medieval Latin *burgensis*, Romance formations like OIt. *borgese*, Fr. *bourgeois*, OSp. *burgés*, *burzés* (probably remade on the noun are It. *borghese*, Sp. *burgués*, Port. *burguês*); It. *forese* 'peasant', OOccit. *fores* 'foreigner'; Fr. *villageois* 'villager'; Sp. *montañés* 'montaineer', Port. *montanhês*. As can be seen in these examples, the adjectival formations were easily turned into nouns by conversion designating the inhabitants of a place or a country, but also the names of the languages (It. *francese* 'the French language'; cf. Malkiel and Uitti 1968).

The suffix *-ānus*~ */-'an-u/, in addition to its ethnic role (e.g., *Rōma* → *Rōmānus* vs. *Ostia* → *Ostiēnsis*; Rom. *român*, It. *romano*, Fr. *romain*, Sp. *romano*, OPort. *romão*, Port. *romano*) has developed new functions. Very early, the derivational bases were extended to adjectives and adverbs: the Latin adjective *certus* 'decided, determined; certain' is the base for OIt. *certano*, Fr. *certain*, Occit. *certan*, Cat. *certà*, OSp. *certan*, Port. *certão* and the adverb *super* 'above' is the base for It. *soprano* 'situated above; sovereign', Fr. *souverain*, OOccit. *sobran*, or, based on the Latin comparative form *superior*, *superius*, OOccit. *sobeiran*, Cat. *sobirà*, Sp. *soberano*. The nominal conversion has in a few cases superseded the adjectival function. Medieval Latin *cappellanus presbyter* m. 'priest attached to a chapel', whose adjective is derived from *cappella* f. 'chapel', is continued by the masculine nouns It. *cappellano* 'chaplain', Fr. *chapelain*, Cat. *capellà*, Sp. *capellán*, Port. *capelão*. The adjective derived from Latin *fons*, *-tis* 'spring', viz. Lat. *(aqua) fontana* 'spring (water)', has survived as a noun: Rom. *fântână* f., It. *fontana*, Fr. *fontaine*, Cat. *fontana*.

The suffix *-ālis*~ */-'al-e/, which was very productive in Latin, has survived in Romance, except in Romanian. Either the Latin derivations have been continued (e.g., Lat. *aequalis* 'equal' > It. *uguale*, OFr. *ivel*, Sp. Port. *igual*), or the learnèd language has reintroduced them. From a synchronic point of view, these two strands are difficult to distinguish. Without knowledge of the history of the words it is difficult to establish that It. *mortale* 'mortal', Fr. *mortel*, Sp. Port. *mortal* or It. *finale*, Fr. Sp. Port. *final* are descendants of Lat. *mortālis* 'mortal' and Lat. *fīnālis* 'final'. This suffix has also been chosen as a substitute when Latin derivatives were not ideal for adaptation, as with Lat. *colossēus, colossiœus, colossicus* (← *colossus* 'gigantic statue'), turned into It. *colossale*, Fr. *colossal*, Sp. Port. *colosal* and even Rom. *colosal* by means of adaptation or borrowing. But there is no need for a Latin model in order to get parallel Romance coinages (e.g., It. *derivazionale* 'derivational', Fr. *dérivationnel*, Sp. Port. *derivacional*). Since Latin times, this type of adjective has been nominalized by ellipsis, as in Lat. *dies nātālis* that became *nātālis* m. 'day of birth', also the name of Christmas (e.g., It. *natale*, OFr. *nael*, Occit. Cat. *Nadal*). Most of the time nominalization yielded a neuter noun: Lat. *digitāle* n. 'thimble', for example, is continued by It. *ditale*, OFr. *deel*, Sp. Port. *dedal* and maybe Rom. *degetar* n., if this is not an internal derivation. This type of elliptic formation has given rise to numerous denominations of objects and places such as the derivatives from the descendants of Lat. *porta* 'door' (e.g., It. *portale* 'portal', OFr. OOccit. Cat. Sp. Port. *portal*) or the ones from the descendants of Lat. *mercātus* 'trade; market' (e.g., OIt. *mercatale* 'market place', OOccit. *mercadal*, Gasc. *mercadáu*, Cat. OSp. *mercadal*).

Latin had a dissimilated variant of the suffix just discussed, *-āris*~ */-'ar-e/, used when the base already contained a liquid consonant. Unlike for the previous suffix, its adjectival function has rarely been conserved (e.g., Lat. *albāris* 'white' > Sp. *albar* 'white', Port. *alvar* 'whitish'). Most of the time, this suffix appears in nouns formed by ellipsis (e.g., Lat. *collāre* 'neckband' > It. *collare*, OFr. *coler*, Sp. *collar*, Port. *collar*). From Gallo-Romance, we can adduce OFr. *auber* m. 'sapwood', Occit. *aubar* 'white willow'. Sp. *dedo pulgar* and Port. *dedo polegar*, literally 'finger of the thumb', maintain the adjectival use of Lat. *pollicāris*, which most of the time appears in nominalized form, though (e.g., ORom. *pălicar* 'thumb', OOccit. *polgar*, Gasc. *pougà*, Sp. *pulgar*, Port. *polegar*). The primary adjectival function of the suffix declined but, in exchange, in the south-western area of the Romance domain, it gained new vitality in its secondary function as a nominalizer, especially for nouns designating places related to plants: OOccit. *milh* 'millet' → *milhar* 'millet field', Gasc. *geneste* 'broom' → *genestà* 'broom field', Cat. *canem* 'hemp' → *canemar* 'hemp field', Sp. *cañamo* → *cañamar*, OCat. *poma* 'apple' → *pomar* 'apple orchard', Sp. *pomo* 'seed fruit' → *pomar* 'orchard', Sp. *paloma* 'pigeon' → *palomar* 'dovecote'.

There are only a few derivatives with the variant *-īlis* ~ */-'il-e/ that have survived in Romance, such as Lat. *gentīlis* 'hereditary' which has possibly been continued by It. *gentile* 'gentle', Fr. Occit. Sp. *gentil*, despite the difference in meaning. Also quite rare are Late Latin formations like the adjective **axīlis*, which in nominalized form has regionally replaced Lat. *axis* 'axle' (cf. Romansh *ischel*, It. *assile*, Fr. *essieu*), or the derivative *focīlis* from *focus* 'fire', whence It. *fucile* 'flintstone; gunflint', OFr. *fuisil*, Port. *fuzil*. Its preferential use in Latin with bases designating human beings and animals has influenced its Romance coinages. After the model of *cīvīlis* (← *cīvis* 'citizen'), *juvenīlis* (← *juvenis* 'young'), *servīlis* (← *servus* 'slave') have been created adjectives like It. *signorile* 'seigniorial', Occit. *senhoril*, Sp. *señoril*, which add to loanwords such as It. *infantile* 'infantile', Fr. *infantile*, Sp. Port. *infantil*; It. *senile* 'senile', Fr. *sénile*, Sp. Port. *senil*. Latin denominations of shelters for animals or storage places for agricultural products have survived particularly well. These neutral nominalizations, after an ellipsis from Lat. *stabulum* 'barn', have been preserved as masculines: Lat. *cubīle* 'den, shelter for animals' > It. *covile* 'den', Sp. *cubil*, Port. *covil*; Lat. *fēnīle* 'hay barn' > It. *fienile*, Fr. Occit. *fenil*, Sp. *henil*. They have produced Romance formations in the same semantic fields: Lat. *canis* 'dog' → **canīle* 'kennel', from which It. *canile*, Fr. *chenil*, from Lat. *bōs*, *bovis* 'ox' → **bovīle*, from which It. *bovile* 'cowshed', Sp. *boil*, or specific to one language, Sp. *toro* 'bull' → *toril* 'grounds where the bull is locked up before the corrida', Fr. *four* 'bread oven' → *fournil* 'room where the oven is found', OOccit. *borda* 'rustic house' → *bordil* 'farmhouse'. From there, the suffix has extended its area of use: Sp. *carril* 'rut', Fr. *chartil* 'place where carts are stored', OOccit. *mercadil* 'market place'.

Since the Latin period, the products of the suffix *-ārius*, *-a*, *-um*~ */-'ari-u/, */-'ari-a/ have been increasingly nominalized, to the point where the adjectival formations appear regularly only with specific uses, for example in the domain of law or agriculture. The adjective *jugārius* 'related to the yoke', for example, is continued only by Rom. (*bou*) *jugar* 'coupling (ox)', *sōricārius* 'related to mice' by Béarnese *sourigué*. **Leviarius* 'light' has survived only in Fr. *léger* 'light', Occit. *leugier* and Cat. *lleuger* (which have been borrowed subsequently by other Romance languages). Other survivers are the result of the simplification of oppositions such as the one between Lat. *prīmus* 'first' and *prīmārius* 'principal, linked to the first', in favour of the latter, whence Fr. *premier* 'first', Cat. *primer*, Sp. *primero*, Port. *primeiro*, or between *tertius* 'third' and *tertiārius* 'containing a third', continued by Cat. *tercer* 'third', Sp. *tercero*, Port. *terceiro*. Although the adjectival function has been maintained (cf. also Fr. *ratier* '(dog, cat) that hunts mice, rats', Cat. *rater*, Sp. *ratero*, Port. *rateiro*, as well as Cat. *ratoner*), it was essentially the nominalizations that remained productive in the Romance languages, designating professions, places, instruments or fruit trees. The vitality of this type of formation can be seen in the fact that it appears in both popular and learnèd form (cf. Rom. *-ar*, *-ariu*, It. *-aio*, *-ario*, Fr. *-ier*, *-aire*, Sp. *-ero*, *-ario*, Port. *-eiro*, *-ario*), and that borrowing has introduced variants that have become autonomous, like *-iere*/*-iero*, in Italian, from French *-ier*. Among nouns designating professions can be found formations maintained since the Latin era, like *argentārius* m. 'silversmith' > Rom. *argintar*, It. *argentaio*, Fr. *argentier*, Cat. *argenter*, Sp. *argentero*; *ferrārius* 'smith' > Rom. *fierar*, It. *ferraio*, OFr. *ferrier*, Sp. *herrero*, Port.

ferreiro. Most of these lexemes, however, are native formations: It. *cioccolataio* 'person who makes or sells chocolate', Fr. *chocolatier*, Sp. *chocolatero*, Port. *chocolateiro*. Neuter nominalizations in Latin designated places, out of which numerous examples have survived: Lat. *grānu* m. 'grain' → Lat. *grānārium* 'granary', continued by Rom. *grânar* n., It. *granaio*, Fr. *grenier*, Cat. *graner*, Sp. *granero*. Romance formations have reinforced this model: from descendants of Lat. *formīca* 'ant' were derived Rom. *furnicar* n. 'anthill', It. *formicaio*, Occit. *formiguier*, Cat. *formiguer*, Sp. *hormiguero*, Port. *formigueiro*, while it is a feminine form that gave way to OFr. *formiere*. This is because, in parallel to the neuter noun, Latin developed feminine nominalizations, whose model has also been continued in the Romance languages, especially in the West, in order to designate places: OOccit. *feuziera* f. 'area where fens grow', Galician *filgueira*, and, by metonymic change, the plant itself: Fr. *fougère* 'fen', Occit. *falguiero*, Cat. *falguera*, Astur. *folguera*. The suffix has also been used in several Western Romance languages to designate fruit trees. In this case, the feminine and the masculine forms also alternate: Romansh *pirer* m. 'pear tree', Fr. *poirier*, Occit. *perier*, Cat. *perer* vs. Occit. *perièro* f., Cat. *perera*, Port. *pereira*, competing, in this case, with the suffix *-ālis* ~ */-'al-e/ in Spanish, where the noun is *peral*.

Only a few adjectival derivations in *-āticus*~ */-'atik-u/ have survived in Romance, e.g., *silvāticus*~ */sal'β-atik-u/ 'wild' (← *silva* 'forest'), continued by Rom. *sălbatec*, It. *salvatico*, Romansh *selvadi*, Fr. Occit. *sauvage*, Cat. *salvatge*. Most examples are old and rare, e.g., OFr. *marage* 'from the sea; situated on the sea shore' (← *mer* f. 'sea' < Lat. *mare*), *marage* 'that grows in marsh' (← *mare* f. 'pond' < ONorse *marr*), *ramage* 'bushy; that lives in the forest; wild' (← Fr. *raim* 'branch' < Lat. *ramus*). The suffix has developed into a nominalizer on the model of neuter nouns in Latin. As can be seen in the Latin example *granaticum* 'tax on granaries', the suffix served to form nouns designating royalties and charges: Medieval Latin *terraticum* n. (← Lat. *terra* 'land') > It. *terraggio* m. 'tax on lands and its products', Fr. *terrage*, Occit. Cat. *terratge*, Sp. *terrazgo*, Port. *terradego*. This type of formation has come to a second life in Romance languages through the imitation of French: Fr. *péage*, It. *pedaggio* 'toll', Cat. *peatge*, Sp. *peaje*. With bases designating persons, the suffix denotes state, condition, belonging to a group, as in Fr. *hommage*, It. *omaggio* 'acknowledgement of allegiance from a vassal to his lord', Occit. *omatge*, or, under the influence of Medieval Latin *hominaticum*, Fr. *homenage*, Occit. *omenatge*, Sp. *homenaje*. It is from this group that the collective value of the suffix has evolved (cf. Baldinger 1950: 152–174), as well as its use to form action nouns (cf. section 4.1.3; Fleischman 1977).

4.3 Verbal derivation

4.3.1 Denominal verbs

Prefixation: The vigour of Romance denominal verbal derivation goes back to spoken Latin: "the greatest fertility is seen in the department of compound verbs, which form one of the marked characteristics of the *sermo plebeius*" (Cooper 1975 [1895]: 246; see as well Moussy 2005). Involved prefixes are for instance *ad-* ~ */ad-/ 'toward', *con-* ~ */kon-/ 'with', *dē-* ~ */de-/ 'from', *dis-* ~ */dɪs-/ 'un-', *ex-* ~ */(ek)s-/ 'out of', or *in-* ~ */ɪn-/ 'into' (Anderson and Rochet 1979: 337–342). With respect to *dē-* ~ */de-/ and *dis-* ~ */dɪs-/, we are in the favorable (and uncommon) situation of being able to trace back the corresponding Romance suffixes not only to written Latin, but also to (spoken) Proto-Romance (Buchi 2009). With only three known derivatives lacking correlates from written Latin (*/de-'kad-e-/ 'to fall into an inferior state' < */'kad-e-/ 'to fall', */de-'pan-a-/ 'to unwind' < */'pan-a/ 'thread', and */de-'ren-a-/ 'to exhaust' < */'ren-e-/ 'loins'), Proto-Rom. */de-/ can be said to have been feebly productive. Chiefly denominative, */de-/ conveyed the meanings 'change of state' and 'deprivation', contrasting with *dē-* in written Latin which had a wider scope, since it also presented several other meanings. With the exception of French, where only */dɪs-/ survived, Proto-Rom. */de-/ was inherited by almost all Romance languages (although it is very scarcely productive in Spanish and Portuguese), where its continuators mostly serve the purpose of creating denominal verbs presenting the sense of 'deprivation' (It. *bosco* 'forest' → *diboscare* 'to deforest'). This kind of denominal derivation, which may be described as prefixation with a simultaneous change in part of speech, like in Fr. *embouteiller* 'to bottle' ← *bouteille* f. 'bottle', is traditionally analyzed as parasynthesis (see Reinheimer-Rîpeanu 1974 and Brachet 2009), which does not seem appropriate, as *-er* is an inflectional (and not a derivational) suffix.

Suffixation: The most common mode of formation for verbs in Latin was conversion of nouns and adjectives, which also remained the most frequent pattern in the Romance languages. However, a few derivational models witnessed significant developments in Late Latin and during the formative stage of the Romance languages. Leaving aside conversions derived from bases in *-ic-* (cf. *medicus* → *medicāre*, *jūdex*, *-icis* → *jūdicāre*), Latin also had a weakly productive suffix *-icāre* combining with verbal bases and adding an intensive value (*fodere* 'to dig' → *fodicāre*, *vellere* 'to tear, pull' → *vellicāre*), or with adjectival bases and adding an attenuative value (*albus* 'white' → *albicāre*, *niger* 'black' → *nigricāre*, *claudus* 'lame' → *claudicāre*). In Late Latin, this derivation spread to nominal bases: *follis* 'bellows' → *follicāre* 'to breathe like a bellows, pant'. This suffix became more productive in the formative stage of the Romance languages, attaching to new verbal bases (Lat. *figere* 'to fix' → **figicāre* ~ */'fig-ik-a-/ > It. *ficcare*, Fr. *ficher*, Occit. *ficar*, Gasc. *hicà*, Cat. Port. *ficar*) and to adjectival bases (Lat. *rasus* 'scraped; shaved' → **rasicāre* ~ */'ras-ik-a-/ 'to shave' > Sardinian *rasigare*, OFr. *racher*, Occit. Cat. Sp. Port. *rascar*). Derivatives from nominal bases which existed already in Latin have been continued (Lat. *follicāre* 'to breathe like a bellows, pant' > Cat. *folgar* 'to rest', Sp. *holgar*, Port. *folgar*; for Rom. *înfuleca* 'to eat like a glutton', cf. Buchi 2008: 293–298), and a numerous progeny has been added: Lat. *caballus* 'horse' → *caballicāre* ~ */ka'βall-ik-a-/ 'to ride a horse' > It. *cavalcare*, Fr. *chevaucher*, Sp. *cabalgar*, Port. *cavalgar*; Lat. *carrus* 'cart' → *carricāre* ~ */'karr-ik-a-/ 'to carry' > It. *caricare*, Fr. *charger*, Sp. *cargar*, Port. *carregar*. The vitality of both formations is also confirmed by the following prefixations with *in-* ~ */ɪn-/ and *dis-* ~*/dɪs-/, which are attested even in oriental Romania (cf. REW s.v. *cabăllĭcāre, carrĭcāre*, and *dĭscarrĭcāre*; Jactel and Buchi 2014 in DÉRom s.v. */ɪn-ka'βall-ik-a-/ and Hütsch and Buchi 2014 in DÉRom s.v. */dɪs-ka'βall-ik-a-/). The early vitality of this derivation can be seen in several formations that are specific to certain geographic areas, such as Fr. *plonger* 'to dive' (< **plumbicāre* ~ */'plʊmb-ik-a-/ ← *plumbum* 'lead'), Sp. Port. *salgar* 'to salt' (< **salicāre* ~ */'sal-ik-a-/ ← *sāl* 'salt'), OSp. *saborgar* 'to make tasty' (< **sapōricāre* ~ */sa'por-ik-a-/ ← *sapor* 'flavour'). Nevertheless, this type of derivation did not remain productive in Romance languages.

Another suffix has been more successful. Latin borrowed the Greek suffix *-ίζειν*, and adapted it as *-issāre*, later on as *-izzāre*. But it is the adaptation to *-idiāre* that took roots in the Western Romance languages. The beginning of this process can be seen particularly well in Latin bases such as **auridiāre* ~ */au'r-idi-a-/ 'to wind up, air' (← Lat. *aura* 'wind') > It. *oreggiare*, Occit. *aurejar*, Cat. *orejar*, Sp. *orear*, Galician *ourejar, ourear* (cf. Zamboni 1981). Numerous neologisms bear witness to the productivity of this suffix: Germanic *werra* 'war' > It. *guerreggiare* 'to make war', Fr. *guerroyer*, Sp. Port. *guerrear*; Germanic **bord* 'board, side of a ship' > It. *bordeggiare* 'to sail against the wind', Fr. *bordeyer*, Sp. *bordear*, Port. *bordejar*; Lat. *flamma* 'flame' > It. *fiammeggiare* 'to blaze', Sp. *llamear*, Port. *chamejar*; Lat. *flammula* > Fr. *flamboyer*. This suffix was also added to adjectival bases: Lat. *viridis* 'green' > It. *verdeggiare* 'to turn green', Fr. *verdoyer*, Sp. *verdear*, Port. *verdejar*; Germanic **blank* 'white' > It. *biancheggiare* 'to whiten', Fr. *blanchoyer*, Sp. *blanquear*, Port. *branquejar*. But it is the learnèd borrowing *-izzāre* which eventually took over: ecclesiastical Latin *baptizāre* > OIt. *battizare*, Fr. *baptiser*, Span. OPort. *bautizar*, competing with the popular type */bap't-idi-a-/ > It. *batteggiare, battezzare*, OFr. *batoyer*, Sp. Galician *batear*, Rom. *boteza*. Many new formations have been built upon this learnèd model: Rom. *automatiza* 'to automatize', It. *automatizzare*, Fr. *automatiser*, Sp. Port. *automatizar*, etc.

4.3.2 Deadjectival verbs

The most common way of forming deadjectival verbs is conversion. Nevertheless, a suffixal model also spread during Late Latinity. Adjectives of the type *brevis* 'short' → *breviare* 'to shorten', isolated in Classical Latin, became more common in Late Latin, as we can see from *humilis* 'humble' → *humiliāre* 'to humiliate', *levis* 'light' → *alleviāre* 'to make light'. Derivatives on the basis of comparatives may have furthered this evolution (*prope* adv. 'near' → *propius* 'nearer' → *propiāre* 'to come closer', *appropiāre* > 'to come closer'; *amplus* 'large' → *amplius* 'more' → *ampliāre* 'to increase'), as well as the alignment on the nominal derivation (*angustus* 'narrow' → *angustāre*, competing during later periods with *angustiāre*, from *angustiae* 'narrow passage; discomfort; critical situation'). As a consequence, a deadjectival suffix *-i-* ~ */-i-/ developed which had great success in Romance (cf. Walsh 1984). A few Latin examples have been continued: *abbreviāre* 'to abbreviate' ~ */ab-'breβ-i-a-/ > Fr. *abréger*, Occit. Cat. *abreujar*; *alleviāre* 'to make lighter' ~ */al-'leβ-i-a-/ > OIt. *alleviare*, Fr. *alléger*, Cat. *alleujar*, Sp. Port. *aliviar*; *angustiāre* 'to anguish' ~ */an'gʊst-i-a-/ > It. *angosciare*, Fr. *angoisser*; *appropiāre* 'to approach' ~ */ap-'prop-i-a-/ > Rom. *apropia*, Sardinian *approbiare*, Fr. *approcher*, Cat. *apropiar-se*. The regular Latin derivation *mollis* 'soft' → *mollīre* 'to soften' suffered competition early on by *molliāre* ~ */'moll-i-a-/, which has been continued by Rom. *muia*, Venetian *mogiar*, Fr. *mouiller*, Sp. *mojar*, Port. *molhar*. This model has also been extended to first class adjectives on a relatively large scale. The regular Latin verb *altāre* 'to raise' (← *altus* 'high') has left no trace in Romance, unlike **altiāre* ~ */'alt-i-a-/, continued by It. *alzare*, Fr. *hausser*, Sp. *alzar*, Port. *alçar* and the Romanian prefixed verb *înălţa*. Antonymous Lat. *bassus* 'low' also adopted this derivation, as can be seen in **bassiāre*~ */'bass-i-a-/ > South Italian *basciare*, Fr. *baisser*, Sp. *bajar*, Port. *baixar*. There exist approximately a hundred examples of continued derivatives of this type in Romance languages. Nevertheless, due to the unstressed character of the suffix, the model itself has not survived.

Late Latinity saw the development of factitive compounds in *-ficus*, from *facere* 'to make': *laetus* 'glad' → *laetificus* 'making glad'. After a conversion, this adjectival compound gave rise to the verb *laetificāre* 'to make glad, rejoice'. There were also parallel denominal formations: *ludus* 'game' → *ludificāre* 'to make a fool of'. After reanalysis, a direct connection of the verb to the base adjective was established. Late Latin literature gives testimony of verbs such as *dulcificāre*, *humilificāre*, *nūllificāre*, in which the *-ficus* adjectives, from which they should be derived, are missing. Thanks to the Christian literature, this derivation spread in the learnèd language. For example, corresponding to a derivative from *vīvus*, **advivificare* ~ */ad-βi'β-iɸik-a-/ 'to give life', is reflected in OIt. *abbeficare*, OFr. *aviger*, OCat. *aviugar* and OSp. *aviviguar*, while Rom. *vivifica*, It. *vivificare*, Fr. *vivi-*

fier, Sp. Port. *vivificar* constitute modern borrowings from Lat. *vivificare* 'to vivify'. This derivational pattern became independent of Latin, to the point where medical Latin modified Lat. *lūbricāre* 'to make slippery', derived from *lūbricus* 'slippery', into *lubrificare*, which was then adapted as Rom. *lubrefia*, It. *lubrificare*, Fr. *lubrifier*, Sp. Port. *lubrificar*. Furthermore, modern languages have no need of a Latin model to create formations such as It. *plastificare* 'to plasticize', Fr. *plastifier*, Sp. Port. *plastificar*.

4.3.3 Deverbal verbs

Prefixation: A traditional view (see, for instance, Meyer-Lübke 1895, § 595) holds that the Romance languages lost the Latin prefixes *ob-* 'against' (Lat. *obesse* 'to hinder' < *esse* 'to be', Ernoult and Meillet 1959 [1932] s.v. *ob, obs*) and *retro-* 'back' (Lat. *retrocedere* 'to move back' < *cedere* 'to go', Ernoult and Meillet 1959 [1932] s.v. *re-*, *red-*). However this is inaccurate, as there is no evidence whatsoever that these prefixes existed in Proto-Romance. Indeed, there are no inherited verbs in Romance (REW, FEW) containing the prefix *retro-*, and those etyma with *ob-* classically quoted are impossible to sustain: the cognates given by REW s.v. *ŏbstāre* rather call for */'ost-a-/ and */'dost-a-/, those from REW s.v. *obtūrāre/*attūrāre* unanimously call for */at'tur-a-/, and the survival of Lat. *obviāre* intr. v. 'to go against' (cf. REW s.v. *ŏbviāre*) is probably due to Lat. *obviam* adv. 'situated so as to confront' (cf. REW s.v. *ŏbviam*). Thus, the loss of these prefixes is strictly a matter of internal Latin diachrony (Cooper 1975 [1895]: 281 typically characterizes *ob-* as archaic).

The Romance languages inherited a small number of deverbal verb-forming prefixes from Proto-Romance, amongst which *dis-* ~ */dɪs-/ and *re-* ~ */re-/ are the most productive. In comparison with */de-/, Proto-Rom. */dɪs-/ was quite productive, more so than written Latin testimony suggests; as Cooper (1975 [1895]: 275) puts it: "verbs compounded with *dis-* [...] belong almost exclusively to the *sermo plebeius*". In the proto-language, both verbs (*/'dɪgn-a-/ 'to consider worthy' > */dɪs-'dɪgn-a-/ 'to consider unworthy') and nouns (*/'ram-a/ 'branch' > */dɪs-'ram-a-/ 'to prune') were used as bases (Buchi 2009), whereas the heirs of the prefix in the Romance languages only utilized its deverbal function. The meanings conveyed by the prefix in Proto-Romance were 'separation', 'change of state' (the latter probably passed on from */de-/, to which */dɪs-/ was close phonologically and semantically), and 'reversion', this last sense being the only one transmitted to the Romance languages: Fr. *capsule* 'bottle cap' → *décapsuler* 'to uncap', Spanish *cabello* 'hair' → *descabellar* 'to ruffle'. As for the Proto-Romance prefix */re-/, it conveyed the meanings 'return', 'repetition', and 'intensity' (REW s.v. **rĕjĕctāre* 'to throw back [repeatedly]' ← Lat. *jactāre* 'to throw', REW s.v. **rĕnĕgāre* 'to renounce' ← Lat. *negāre* 'to deny'). It has been inherited by all Romance languages except Romanian: It. *ricominciare* 'to begin again' ← *ri-* + *cominciare*, Fr. *retirer* 'to remove' ← *re-* + *tirer* 'to pull', Sp. *recargar* 'to load again' ← *re-* + *cargar* 'to load'. These prefixes have a functional match with Romanian *re-* (*recădea* 'to fall again' < *re-* + *cădea* 'to fall'), which however is not inherited, but borrowed from Latin (Bulgăr in SMFC 2: 67–78). Other quite productive inherited prefixes are *ad-* ~ */ad-/ (Sp. *abarrancar* 'to make cracks [in]' < *a-* + *barranco* 'cliff'), *e(x)-* ~ */(ek)s-/ (It. *sferrare* 'to unshoe, launch' < *s-* + *ferro* 'iron; tool'), and *in-* ~ */ɪn-/ (Romanian *a încheia* 'to finish' < *în-* + *cheie* 'key'), whose meanings are, however, often distinct in Romance from their Latin counterparts (Lüdtke 2007: 148–156).

S u f f i x a t i o n: Latin had a suffix *-sc-* ~ */-sk-/ (see Meul 2013) which formed verbs presenting a lexically bound inchoative aspect. Most formations were deverbal (*flōrēre* 'to flower' → *flōrescere* 'to begin to flower'), even in Late Latin (*apparēre* 'to appear' → *apparescere* 'to appear suddenly', ca 400, TLL), but some were also denominal (*ignis* 'fire' → *ignescere* 'to ignite') or deadjectival (*gravis* 'heavy' → *gravescere* 'to become heavy'). Rudes (1980) delineates the destiny of this suffix in Romance: the heirs of */-sk-/ lost the aspectual meaning and mutated from a derivative suffix to an inflectional suffix, a stem-extension (e.g., It. *finire* 'to finish': *finisco* '[I] finish').

4.4 Adverbial derivation

In Latin, adverbial derivation was characterized by a great deal of polymorphy (Leumann 1963, § 212–215; Löfstedt 1967; Krefeld 1999: 113): adverbs could be coined by adding *-ē* or *-ō* to the stem of adjectives in *-us* (*rectus* 'right' → *rectē* 'rightly'; *certus* 'certain' → *certō* 'certainly'), *-ter* to the stem of adjectives mostly in *-is* (*brevis* 'brief' → *breviter* adv. 'briefly') and to prepositions (*circā* 'near' → *circiter* 'nearly'), *-um* to selected adjective stems (*multus* 'many' → *multum* 'much'), *-tim* to noun stems (*pars* 'part' → *partim* 'partly'), rarely also *-tus* (*dīvīnus* 'divine' > *dīvīnitus* 'divinely'). Etymologically, most of these derivative suffixes go back, by way of grammaticalization (or more precisely morphologization), to inflectional suffixes: *-ē* and *-ō* initially marked the ablative case, *-tim* and *-um* the accusative case (although the latter could be a nominative if it represents a neuter). None of these derivational patterns live on in Romance. Instead, most Romance languages (with Romanian and Ladin being the exception) present the adverbial suffix *-mente*, which was morphologized from Proto-Rom. */'mɛnt-e/ f. 'manner' (see Groß 2011–2014 in DÉRom s.v. */'mɛnt-e/ III.). Whereas forrunners of */-'mɛnt-e/ as a suffix appear already in classical Latin – Cicero has *sānā mente* 'with a healthy mind', which lead to the future interpretation 'in a healthy manner' –, the noun is grammaticalized in Proto-Romance, where even the Latin adverb *quōmodo* 'how' (< *quō modō* 'in what way') was reanalyzed in */ko'mɛnt-e/ (> Sardinian *comenti*, Northern It. *comente*, Fr. *comment*, REW s.v. *quōmŏdo*).

As Krefeld (1999) shows very convincingly, the preeminent feature of this kind of morphologization lies in its original relationship with a human agent: semantically, the sequence was '(human) mind' > 'manner' > '(adverb marking suffix)', so much so that the first *-mente* adverbs had to determine verbs – moreover verbs with a personal noun as external argument, like Fr. *il écoutait calmement* 'he listened calmly' – rather than adjectives, as they may do in modern Romance languages (e.g., Fr. *c'est vraiment bête* 'this is really stupid').

Formally, *-mente* combines in most cases with the feminine form of the adjective stem, showing thereby its nominal origin: It. *chiaramente* 'clearly' (← *chiaro* 'clear'), Sardinian *distintamente* 'distinctly' (← *distintu* 'distinct'), Fr. *particulièrement* 'particularly' (← *particulier* 'particular'), Cat. *meravellosament* 'marvellously' (← *meravellós* 'marvellous'), Sp. *solamente* 'only' (← *solo* 'alone'), Port. *cruamente* 'crudely' (← *cru* 'crude'). As Rainer (2002: 111) points out, the grammaticalization process is however more complete in some languages than others: whilst Spanish still maintains a secondary accent in these adverbs and allows elision of the first suffix in coordination (*lisa y llanamente* 'in plain language'), French forms some of the adverbs in this series from the masculine stem of the adjective (*violent* 'violent' → *violemment* 'violently'). Maximum grammaticalization is obtained when even a borrowing from Latin like the Italian adverb *quasi* 'almost' receives the adverbal suffix: documented from the 13th century, It. *quasimente* 'almost' is now of dialectal use, whereas Fr. *quasiment*, documented since the 16th century, seems to represent a borrowing from Italian (DEI's etymology; TLF opts for an internal creation).

Apart from that, Italian and French share a more peripheral adverbial suffix *-oni* which takes its origin in the denominal suffix *-ōne* ~ */'-one/ and conveys the meaning 'peculiar form of appearance': It. *(a) tastoni*, Fr. *à tâtons* 'gropingly' (← It. *tastare*/Fr. *tâter* 'to touch'; see Krefeld 1999: 119–122, 126–127, providing a list of 21 Italian coinages, as well as Corona 2012). Subsequently, these adverbs went through categorial reanalysis: they may (in Italian) or must (in French) be introduced by the preposition *a* and therefore function like nouns. Romanian *-iş* (e.g., *brăţiş* adv. 'embracing' ← *braţ* 'arm'), whose origin also seems to lie in a nominal suffix (introduced through borrowings from Slavic languages, see Pascu 1916: 358), presents some functional and semantic parallelisms to *-oni* (Krefeld 1999: 122–123, 127, providing a list of 22 Romanian coinages). Finally, Romanian adverbs from adjectives in *-esc* (< *-iscu* ~ */-'isk-u/) present the suffix *-e* (*frăţesc* 'brotherly' → *frăţeşte* 'in a brotherly way').

5 Conversion

Conversion is very popular, both in Latin and in Romance, with nominalization representing the most common type. The bases for nominal conversion are mostly adjectives (Rom. *bun* 'good' → 'estate; virtue', It. *caldo* 'hot' → 'heat', Fr. *ridicule* 'ridiculous' → 'ridiculous feature', Sp. *rojo* 'red' → 'colour red; communist') or verbs (It. *valicare* 'to cross' → *valico* 'passage', Fr. *marcher* 'to walk' > *marche* 'walk', Sp. *contar* 'to count' → *cuenta* 'account'), but virtually all parts of speech are represented: Rom. *eu* pers. pron. 'I' → *eu* noun 'self', It. *perché?* adv. 'why?' → *perché* noun 'reason', Port. *onze* numeral 'eleven' → *onze* noun 'football team'.

Adjectival conversion is particularly frequent with Romance colour terms, the adjective being in general invariable: It. *arancia* 'orange' → *arancio* 'of orange colour', Fr. *orange* noun → *orange* adj., Sp. *naranja* noun → *naranja* adj., Port. *laranja* noun → *laranja* adj.

Latin made extensive use of denominal and deadjectival verbal conversion (see section 4.3.1), whose results were integrated into the *-a-* ~ */-'a-/ or the *-i-* ~ */-'i-/ declension: *mātūrus* 'mature' → *mātūrāre* 'to mature', *vestis* 'dress' → *vestīre* 'to dress'. The Romance languages inherited this double feature, most of them giving a preference to the inflectional class descended from */-'a-/ for denominal creations (Rom. *telefon* 'phone' → *telefona* 'to phone', It. *telefono* → *telefonare*, Fr. *téléphone* → *téléphoner*, Port. *telefone* → *telefonar*) and to the inflectional class inherited from */-'i/ for deadjectival creations (Rom. *alb* 'white' → *a albi* 'to whiten', It. *bianco* → *bianchire*, Fr. *blanc* → *blanchir*).

Adverbial conversion was productive in Latin, particularly in the colloquial language (Löfstedt 1967: 101–109). Three types coexisted: type 1a (neuter singular in *-um* ~ */u/ from *i*-stem adjectives: *multus* 'many' → *multum* 'greatly', *primus* 'first' → *primum* 'in the first place'), 1b (neuter singular in *-e* ~ */-e/ from *i*-stem adjectives: *difficilis* 'difficult' → *difficile* 'with difficulty', *fidelis* 'faithful' → *fidele* 'faithfully'), and type 2 (ablative masculine singular in *-o* ~ */-o/: *multo* 'a great deal', *raro* 'rarely'). The Romance languages inherited this threefold structure in a slightly adapted form (Dardel 1995). Indeed, as Romance adjectives are devoid of neuter forms, converted forms correspond to the unmarked (masculine singular) form: Rom. *a cînta frumos* 'to sing beautifully', Fr. *chanter faux* 'to sing out of tune', Sp. *trabajar duro* 'to work hard'. Adverbial conversion, which is clearly inherited from Proto-Romance (Hummel 2013), is monopolistic in Romanian, whereas it pertains, apart from some lexicalized exceptions, to the informal variants of Western Romance.

6 Minor processes

6.1 Reduplication

In Latin, reduplication – inherited from Proto-Indo-European, originally with intensitive meaning – pertains mostly to inflection: *dō* '(I) give' → *dedī* '(I) gave', *currō* '(I) run' → *cucurrī* '(I) ran' (Leumann 1963, § 222, 240). Reduplication is only scarcely used in Latin word-formation (the index of André 1978 contains more than 400 items, but most of them are not Latin coinages). Its function is then either iterative or intensive, mostly based on onomatopoeias (e.g., *murmur* 'murmur', Leumann 1963, § 177) and nursery words (Groß and Schweickard 2009–2014 in DÉRom s.v. */'baβ-a/ f. 'drool'), sometimes also on lexical bases (*furfurāculum* 'gimlet' < **bher-* 'drill', André 1978: 41), and there is no lexical opposition between reduplicated and not reduplicated items.

Word-formation based on reduplication has almost no role to play in most of the Romance languages, with the exception of French, where it is quite widespread (Mayerthaler 1977: 81–92 lists 222 lexemes, some of which are however inherited or borrowed and therefore not of French coinage). In this language, (mostly partial) reduplication is used for creating not only onomatopoeias, but also hypocorisms, mainly from nouns ([*un*] *ours* '[a] bear' → *nounours* 'teddy bear') and adjectives (*bête* 'stupid' → *bêbête* 'silly'). The reduplicative base is either a monosyllable (*fille* 'girl' → *fifille* 'little girl') or one syllable of a polysyllable (*nourrice* 'childminder' → *nounou* 'nanny') and presents the phonological structure CV. This phenomenon originated in child language – probably in the 17th century –, from where it migrated first to childminder language, then to colloquial language (Rainer 1998).

In a similar way, Brazilian Portuguese uses reduplication for hypocoristic kin terms (*pai* 'father' → *papai* 'daddy', *avó* 'grandmother' → *vovó* 'granny'), with secondary stress falling on the first syllable (Comrie 1989), as well as for some other coinages (*bibichinho* 'animal [pet name]' ← *bicho* 'animal', Kröll 1991: 37). In the other Romance languages, the role of reduplication is minor (see for instance Cabré Monné 2008: 910–920 for Catalan coinages like *pica-pica* 'appetizer' ← *picar* 'to snack' or Lloyd 1966 and Pharies 1986 for Spanish creations like *bulle-bulle* 'busybody' ← *bullir* 'to bustle').

There are considerable theoretical implications which follow from these findings, such as the three identified by Hurch and Mattes (2005): (1) reduplication is not a form of affixation, (2) partial reduplication does not always originate in total reduplication, and (3) reduplication does not necessarily implicate grammaticalization.

6.2 Blending

Blending was already used occasionally in former centuries (e.g., Rabelais' *sorbonnagres* 'students/professors of the Sorbonne' ← *Sorbonne* x *onagre* 'donkey'), but has only become more popular in recent times (e.g., Fr. *information* 'information' x *automatique* 'automatic' → *informatique* 'computer science').

6.3 Clipping

Whereas clipping was scarcely productive as a word-formation pattern in Latin (Biville 1989), it has developed in a spectacular way in colloquial Romance during the 20th century, quite independently from Proto-Romance. Romance clippings present a strong preference for disyllabicity: French *manifestation* 'demonstration' → *manif*, Catalan *ginecologia* 'gynaecology' → *gine*, Spanish *profesor* 'professor' → *profe*. They often convey hypocoristic and/or colloquial connotations. Many clipped words are certainly due to borrowing; cf. the parallelism between Fr. *télévision* → *télé*, Cat. *televisió* → *tele*, Sp. *televisión* → *tele*.

7 References

Adams, Edwards L. (1913): *Word-Formation in Provençal*. New York: MacMillan.

Anderson, James M. and Bernard Rochet (1979): *Historical Romance Morphology*. Ann Arbor: University Microfilms International.

André, Jacques (1978): *Les mots à redoublement en latin*. Paris: Klincksieck.

Badia i Margarit, Antoni M. (ed.) (1991): *Dictionnaire historique des noms de famille romans. Actes del III Col·loqui (Barcelona, 19–21 juny 1989)*. Tübingen: Niemeyer.

Badia i Margarit, Antoni M. (1994): *Gramàtica històrica catalana*. 3rd ed. Valencia: Tres i Quatre.

Baldinger, Kurt (1950): *Kollektivsuffixe und Kollektivbegriff. Ein Beitrag zur Bedeutungslehre im Französischen mit Berücksichtigung der Mundarten*. Berlin: Akademie Verlag.

Bauer, Brigitte L. M. (2011): Word formation. In: Martin Maiden, John Charles Smith and Adam Ledgeway (eds.), *The Cambridge History of the Romance Languages*. Vol. 1, 532–563. Cambridge: Cambridge University Press.

Biville, Frédérique (1989): Un processus dérivationnel méconnu du latin: La dérivation par troncation. *L'information grammaticale* 42: 15–22.

Bork, Hans Dieter (1990): *Die lateinisch-romanischen Zusammensetzungen Nomen + Verb und der Ursprung der romanischen Verb-Ergänzung-Komposita*. Bonn: Romanistischer Verlag.

Bosque, Ignacio and Violeta Demonte (eds.) (1999): *Gramática descriptiva de la lengua española*. Vol. 3: *Entre la oración y el discurso. Morfología*. Madrid: Espasa Calpe.

Brachet, Jean-Paul (2009): "Parasynthèse" et "hypostase": À propos de quelques verbes "parasynthétiques" latins. *Ktêma* 34: 25–32.

Bruguera, Jordi (2006): *Diccionari de la formació de mots*. Barcelona: Enciclopèdia Catalana.

Buchi, Éva (2008): Joan Coromines et l'étymologie lexicale romane: L'exemple roumain. In: Antoni M. Badia i Margarit and Joan Solà (eds.), *Joan Coromines, vida y obra*, 282–332. Madrid: Gredos.

Buchi, Éva (2009): La dérivation en */de-/ et en */dɪs-/ en protoroman: Contribution à la morphologie constructionnelle de l'ancêtre commun des langues romanes. *Recherches linguistiques de Vincennes* 38: 139–159.

Buchi, Éva (2010): Where Caesar's Latin does not belong: A comparative grammar based approach to Romance etymology. In: Charlotte Brewer (ed.), *Selected Proceedings of the Fifth International Conference on Historical Lexicography and Lexicology held at St Anne's College, Oxford, 16–18 June 2010*. Oxford: Oxford University Research Archive. [Online available at: http://ora.ox.ac.uk/objects/uuid%3A237856e6-a327-448b-898c-cb1860766e59]

Buchi, Éva (2022): À la recherche de la romanité du français. In: Franck Neveu, Sophie Prévost, Agnès Steuckardt, Gabriel Bergounioux and Badreddine Hamma (eds.), *8e Congrès mondial de linguistique française (Université d'Orléans, France, 4–8 juillet 2022)*. SHS Web of Conferences 138: 00002 [Online available at: https://doi.org/10.1051/shsconf/202213800002]

Burdy, Philipp (2013): *Die mittels* -aison *und Varianten gebildeten Nomina des Französischen von den Anfängen bis zur Gegenwart. Eine Studie zur diachronen Wortbildung*. Frankfurt/M.: Klostermann.

Cabré Monné, Teresa (2008): Altres sistemes de formació de mots. In: Joan Solà, Maria-Rosa Lloret, Joan Mascaró and Manuel Pérez Saldanya (eds.), *Gramàtica del català contemporani*. Vol. 1: *Introducció, fonètica i fonologia, morfologia*, 889–932. 4th ed. Barcelona: Empúries.

Carbonnelle, Hugo (2025): La nominalisation par dérivation suffixale dans la morphologie protoromane. Concurrence entre les suffixes */-'ur-a/, */-'jon-e/ et */-'or-e/. PhD Sorbonne Université.

Chauveau, Jean-Paul (2018): Du rôle de l'étymologie et de l'histoire lexicale. In: Martin Glessgen, Johannes Kabatek and Harald Völker (eds.), *Repenser la variation linguistique. Actes du colloque DIA IV à Zurich (12–14 sept. 2016)*, 125–153. Strasbourg: ELiPhi.

Comrie, Bernard (1989): The phonology of Brazilian Portuguese hypocoristic kin terms. In: Ursula Klenk (ed.), *Variatio linguarum. Beiträge zu Sprachvergleich und Sprachentwicklung. Festschrift zum 60. Geburtstag von Gustav Ineichen*, 63–66. Stuttgart: Steiner.

Cooper, Frederic Taber (1975 [1895]): *Word Formation in the Roman Sermo Plebeius*. Reprint. Hildesheim/New York: Olms.

Corona, Luisa (2012): Il suffisso italiano *-oni*. *Archivio Glottologico Italiano* 97: 34–77.

Dardel, Robert de (1995): Le protoroman comme héritier de l'indo-européen (à propos de la construction *clamare altum*). In: Louis Callebat (ed.), *Latin vulgaire – latin tardif IV. Actes du 4e colloque international sur le latin vulgaire et tardif. Caen, 2–5 septembre 1994*, 21–28. Hildesheim: Olms.

Dardel, Robert de (1999): Composés rectionnels nominaux nom + nom en protoroman. *Probus* 11: 177–208.

Dębowiak, Przemysław (2014): *La formation diminutive dans les langues romanes*. Frankfurt/M.: Lang.

Dębowiak, Przemysław and Hugo Carbonnelle (forthc.): Morphocréations. In: Éva Buchi (ed.), *Manuel d'étymologie lexicale romane*. Berlin/Boston: De Gruyter.

DEI = Carlo Battisti and Giovanni Alessio (1950–57): *Dizionario etimologico italiano*. Firenze: Barbèra.

DELI = Manlio Cortelazzo and Paolo Zolli (1999 [1979–1988]): *Dizionario etimologico della lingua italiana*. 2nd ed. Bologna: Zanichelli.

Delorme, Jérémie (forthc.): Lexique héréditaire remontant à des créations internes du protoroman. In: Éva Buchi (ed.), *Manuel d'étymologie lexicale romane*. Berlin/Boston: De Gruyter.

DÉRom = Éva Buchi and Wolfgang Schweickard (eds.) (2008): *Dictionnaire Étymologique Roman (DÉRom)*. Nancy: ATILF. http://www.atilf.fr/DERom.

DRG = Robert von Planta (1938): – *Dicziunari Rumantsch Grischun*. Chur: Bischofberger.

Ernout, Alfred and Antoine Meillet (1959 [1932]): *Dictionnaire étymologique de la langue latine. Histoire des mots*. 4th ed. Paris: Klincksieck.

FEW = Walther von Wartburg et al. (1922–2002): *Französisches Etymologisches Wörterbuch. Eine darstellung des galloromanischen sprachschatzes*. Bonn/Heidelberg/Leipzig-Berlin/Basel: Klopp/Winter/Teubner/Zbinden.

Fleischman, Suzanne (1977): *Cultural and Linguistic Factors in Word Formation. An Integrated Approach to the Development of the Suffix* -age. Berkeley/Los Angeles: University of California Publications.

Giurescu, Anca (1975): *Les mots composés dans les langues romanes*. La Haye/Paris: Mouton.

Grossmann, Maria and Franz Rainer (2004): *La formazione delle parole in italiano*. Tübingen: Niemeyer.

Hakamies, Reino (1951): *Étude sur l'origine et l'évolution du diminutif latin et sa survie dans les langues romanes*. Helsinki: Suomalaisen Kirjallisuuden Seuran Kirjapainon.

Hall, Robert A., Jr. (1983): *Proto-Romance Morphology*. Amsterdam/Philadelphia: Benjamins.

Hasselrot, Bengt (1957): *Études sur la formation diminutive dans les langues romanes*. Uppsala: Lundequist.

Heidemeier, Ulrike (2014): Reconstruction dérivationnelle. In: Éva Buchi and Wolfgang Schweickard (eds.), *Dictionnaire Étymologique Roman (DÉRom). Genèse, méthodes et résultats*, 211–246. Berlin: de Gruyter.

Hummel, Martin (2013): Attribution in Romance: Reconstructing the oral and written tradition. *Folia Linguistica Historica* 34: 1–42.

Hurch, Bernhard and Veronika Mattes (2005): Über die Entstehung von partieller Reduplikation. In: Gertraud Fenk-Oczlonand and Christian Winkler (eds.), *Sprache und NatürlichkeIt. Gedenkband für Willi Mayerthaler*, 137–156. Tübingen: Narr Francke Attempto.

Jochems, Helmut (1959): Beiträge zu einer vergleichenden Wortbildungslehre des heutigen Bündnerromanischen. Ph.D. dissertation, University of Cologne.

Kircher-Durand, Chantal (ed.) (2002): *Grammaire fondamentale du latin. Tome IX: Création lexicale: La formation des noms par dérivation suffixale*. Louvain/Paris: Peeters.

Koch, Peter and Wulf Oesterreicher (2008): Comparaison historique de l'architecture des langues romanes. In: Gerhard Ernst, Martin-Dietrich Gleßgen, Christian Schmitt and Wolfgang Schweickard (eds.), *Romanische Sprachgeschichte. Ein internationales Handbuch zur Geschichte der romanischen Sprachen*. Vol. 3, 2575–2610. Berlin/New York: de Gruyter.

Krefeld, Thomas (1999): Agens mit Leib und Seele: Zur Grammatikalisierung romanischer Adverbbildungen. In: Jürgen Lang and Ingrid Neumann-Holzschuh (eds.), *Reanalyse und Grammatikalisierung in den romanischen Sprachen*, 111–127. Tübingen: Niemeyer.

Kröll, Heinz (1990–91): Beitrag zu den Reduplikationen im Portugiesischen. *Lusorama* 11: 31–39; 15: 25–44.

Lausberg, Heinrich (1976): *Linguistica romanza*. 2nd ed. Milano: Feltrinelli.

Leumann, Manu (1963): *Lateinische Laut- und Formenlehre*. München: Beck.

Lindner, Thomas (1996): *Lateinische Komposita. Ein Glossar vornehmlich zum Wortschatz der Dichtersprache*. Innsbruck: Institut für Sprachwissenschaft der Universität Innsbruck.

Lloyd, Paul M. (1966): Some reduplicative words in colloquial Spanish. *Hispanic Review* 34: 135–142.

Löfstedt, Bengt (1967): Bemerkungen zum Adverb im Lateinischen. *Indogermanische Forschungen* 72: 79–109.

López del Castillo, Lluís (2002): *Diccionari de formació de paraules*. Barcelona: Edicions 62.

Lüdtke, Jens (1995): Grundzüge der Entwicklung der Relationsadjektive vom Latein zum Romanischen. In: Wolfgang Dahmen, Günter Holtus, Johannes Kramer, Michael Metzeltin, Wolfgang Schweickard and Otto Winkelmann (eds.), *Konvergenz und Divergenz in den romanischen Sprachen. Romanistisches Kolloquium VIII*, 138–150. Tübingen: Narr.

Lüdtke, Jens (1996): Gemeinromanische Tendenzen IV. Wortbildungslehre. In: Günter Holtus, Michael Metzeltin and Christian Schmitt (eds.), *Lexikon der Romanistischen Linguistik (LRL)*. Vol. II,1: *Latein und Romanisch. Historisch-vergleichende Grammatik der romanischen Sprachen*, 235–272. Tübingen: Niemeyer.

Lüdtke, Jens (2007): *Romanische Wortbildung. Inhaltlich – diachronisch – synchronisch*. Tübingen: Stauffenburg.

Malkiel, Yakov and Karl D. Uitti (1968): L'ancien français *gab-ois*, *ir-ois*, *jargon-ois* et leurs contreparties dans l'anglais d'Amérique. *Revue de Linguistique romane* 32: 126–174.

Mayerthaler, Willi (1977): *Studien zur theoretischen und zur französischen Morphologie. Reduplikation, Echowörter, morphologische Natürlichkeit, Haplologie, Produktivität, Regeltelescoping, paradigmatischer Ausgleich*. Tübingen: Niemeyer.

Mertens, Bianca (2021): *Le suffixe */-'ur-a/. Recherches sur la morphologie dérivationnelle du protoroman*. Berlin/Boston: De Gruyter.

Meul, Claire (2013): *The Romance reflexes of the Latin infixes* -I/ESC- *and* -IDI̯-. *Restructuring and remodeling processes*. Hamburg: Buske.

Meyer-Lübke, Wilhelm (1895): *Grammaire des langues romanes*. Vol. 2: *Morphologie*. Paris: Welter.

Moussy, Claude (ed.) (2005): *La composition et la préverbation en latin*. Paris: Presses de l'Université Paris-Sorbonne.

Müller, Peter O., Ingeborg Ohnheiser, Susan Olsen and Franz Rainer (eds.) (2015–2016): *Word-Formation. An International Handbook of the Languages of Europe*. 5 Vol. Berlin/Boston: De Gruyter Mouton.

Nyrop, Krystoffer (1908): *Grammaire historique de la langue française*. Vol. 3: *Formation des mots*. Copenhagen: Gyldendalske Boghandel.

Olcott, George N. (1898): *Studies in the Word Formation in the Latin Inscriptions. Substantives and Adjectives with Special Reference to the Latin Sermo Vulgaris*. Rome: Sallustian Typography.

Pascu, Giorge (1916): *Sufixele româneşti*. Bucureşti/Leipzig/Wien: Socec/Harrassowitz/Gerold.

Pharies, David A. (1986): *Structure and Analogy in the Playful Lexicon of Spanish*. Tübingen: Niemeyer.

Pharies, David (2002): *Diccionario etimológico de los sufijos españoles y de otros elementos finales*. Madrid: Gredos.

Rainer, Franz (1993): *Spanische Wortbildungslehre*. Tübingen: Niemeyer.

Rainer, Franz (1998): La réduplication française du type *fifille* d'un point de vue diachronique. In: Giovanni Ruffino (ed.), *Atti del XXI Congresso Internazionale di Linguistica e Filologia Romanza. Centro di studi filologici et linguistici siciliani, Università di Palermo 18–24 settembre 1995*. Vol. 1, 279–289. Tübingen: Niemeyer.

Rainer, Franz (2002): Convergencia y divergencia en la formación de palabras de las lenguas románicas. In: Joaquín García-Medall (ed.), *Aspectos de morfología derivativa del español*, 103–133. Lugo: Tris Tram.

Rainer, Franz (2003): L'intégration des composés latins du type *aurifer* en français. In: Bernard Fradin, Georgette Dal, Nabil Hathout, Françoise Kerleroux, Marc Plénat and Michel Roché (eds.), *Les unités morphologiques. Forum de morphologie (3èmes rencontres). Actes du colloque de Villeneuve d'Ascq (19–21 septembre 2002)*, 151–168. Villeneuve d'Ascq: SILEX.

Rainer, Franz (2004): From Latin to French. In: Geert Booij, Christian Lehmann, Joachim Mugdan and Stavros Skopeteas (eds), *Morphology. An International Handbook on Inflection and Word-Formation*. Vol. 2, 1698–1712. Berlin/New York: de Gruyter.

Rainer, Franz (2005a): Semantic change in word formation. *Linguistics* 43(2): 415–441.

Rainer, Franz (2005b): Noms d'instruments/de lieux en *-tor* dans la Galloromania. *Vox romanica* 64: 121–140.

Rainer, Franz (2008): Konvergenz- und Divergenzphänomene in der Romania: Wortbildung. In: Gerhard Ernst, Martin-Dietrich Gleßgen, Christian Schmitt and Wolfgang Schweickard (eds.), *Romanische Sprachgeschichte. Ein internationales Handbuch zur Geschichte der romanischen Sprachen*. Vol. 3, 3293–3307. Berlin/New York: de Gruyter.

Rainer, Franz (2011): The agent-instrument-place "polysemy" of the suffix -TOR in Romance. *STUF – Language Typology and Universals* 64: 8–32.

Rainer, Franz (2016): Derivational morphology. In: Adam Ledgeway and Martin Maiden (eds.), *The Oxford guide to the Romance languages*, 513–523. Oxford: Oxford University Press.

Rainer, Franz (2018): Patterns and niches in diachronic word formation: The fate of the suffix *-men* from Latin to Romance. *Morphology* 28(4): 397–465.

Rainer, Franz (2020): Sex-denoting patterns in the Romance languages. In: Mark Aronoff (ed.), *Oxford Research Encyclopedia of Linguistics*. Oxford: Oxford University Press [Online available at: https://doi.org/10.1093/acrefore/9780199384655.013.734]

Rainer, Franz (2021a): Compounding: From Latin to Romance. In: Mark Aronoff (ed.), *Oxford Research Encyclopedia of Linguistics*. Oxford: Oxford University Press [Online available at: https://doi.org/10.1093/acrefore/9780199384655.013.691]

Rainer, Franz (2021b): Instrument and place nouns in the Romance languages. In: Mark Aronoff (ed.), *Oxford Research Encyclopedia of Linguistics*. Oxford: Oxford University Press [Online available at: https://doi.org/10.1093/acrefore/9780199384655.013.461]

Rainer, Franz (2021c): Adjectival suffixes: From Latin to Romance. In: Mark Aronoff (ed.), *Oxford Research Encyclopedia of Linguistics*. Oxford: Oxford University Press [Online available at: https://doi.org/10.1093/acrefore/9780199384655.013.690]

Rainer, Franz (forthc.): Le témoignage de la morphologie. In: Éva Buchi (ed.), *Manuel d'étymologie lexicale romane*. Berlin/Boston: De Gruyter.

Reinheimer-Rîpeanu, Sandra (1974): *Lés dérivés parasynthétiques dans les langues romanes. Roumain, italien, français, espagnol*. Den Haag: Mouton.

REW = Wilhelm Meyer-Lübke (1930–35 [1911–20]): *Romanisches Etymologisches Wörterbuch*. 3rd ed. Heidelberg: Winter.

Rio-Torto, Graça (2013): *Gramática derivacional do português*. Coimbra: Universidade de Coimbra.

Rohlfs, Gerhard (1931): Beiträge zur Kenntnis der Pyrenäenmundarten. *Revue de linguistique romane* 7: 119–169.

Rohlfs, Gerhard (1954): *Historische Grammatik der italienischen Sprache und ihrer Mundarten*. Vol. 3: *Syntax und Wortbildung*. Bern: Francke.

Ronjat, Jules (1980 [1937]): *Grammaire istorique des parlers provençaux modernes*. Vol. 3: *Morphologie et formation des mots, notes de syntaxe*. Reprint. Geneva: Slatkine.

Rudes, Blair A. (1980): The functional development of the verbal suffix *+esc+* in Romance. In: Jacek Fisiak (ed.), *Historical Morphology*, 327–348. The Hague/Paris: Mouton.

Sandmann, Antônio José (1986): *Wortbildung im heutigen brasilianischen Portugiesisch*. Bonn: Romanistischer Verlag.

Schmitt, Christian (2000): À propos de l'européisation des langues romanes. In: Annick Englebert, Michel Pierrard, Laurence Rosier and Dan Van Raemdonck (eds.), *Actes du XXIIe Congrès International de Linguistique et de Philologie Romanes (Bruxelles, 23–29 juillet 1998)*. Vol. 6, 457–465. Tübingen: Niemeyer.

Siller-Runggaldier, Heidi (1989): *Grödnerische Wortbildung*. Innsbruck: Institut für Romanistik.

SMFC = (1959–72): *Studii şi materiale privitoare la formarea cuvintelor în limba română*. Bucureşti: Editura Academiei Republicii Populare Romîne.

Tekavčić, Pavao (1974): *Grammatica storica dell'italiano*. Vol. 3: *Lessico*. 2nd ed. Bologna: Il Mulino.

TLF = Paul Imbs and Bernard Quemada (eds.) (1971–94): *Trésor de la langue française. Dictionnaire de la langue du XIXe et du XXe siècle (1789–1960)*. Paris: Éditions du CNRS/Gallimard.

TLL = (1900): *Thesaurus Linguae Latinae*, Leipzig/Stuttgart/Berlin/New York: Teubner/Saur/De Gruyter.

Viaro, Mário Eduardo (ed.) (2014): *Morfologia histórica*. São Paulo: Cortez.

Villoing, Florence (1999): La querelle, au XIXe siècle, autour des mots composés du type $[VN]_N$: Quels enjeux pour la grammaire? *Linx* 40: 159–185.

Walsh, Thomas James (1984): The verbal suffix *-iāre*. Latin origin and development. Ann Arbor: University Microfilms International.

Weiss, Michael (2011): *Outline of the Historical and Comparative Grammar of Latin*. 2nd ed. Ann Arbor/New York: Beech Stave Press.

Williams, Edwin Bucher (1962 [1938]): *From Latin to Portuguese. Historical Phonology and Morphology of the Portuguese Language*. 2nd ed. Philadelphia: University of Pennsylvania Press.

Zamboni, Alberto (1981): Un problema di morfologia romanza: L'ampliamento verbale in *-idio, -izo*. *Quaderni patavini di linguistica* 2: 171–181.

Marina Rădulescu Sala

18 From Latin to Romanian

Abstract: This article aims to describe the particular features of Romanian as a Romance language and the transformation of Danubian Latin into Proto-Romanian on the basis of the data from Old Romanian (the 16th–18th centuries) in word-formation, leaving aside the phenomena present in all the Romance languages, as well as all the developments of Modern Romanian (the period spanning from the end of the 18th c. to the middle of the 20th c.).

1 Introduction

Romanian occupies a special position among the Romance languages, first of all because of its eccentric geographic position (the oriental extremity of the Romance territory) and of the socio-historical conditions in which Romanian emerged and developed (being cut off from Western Romance until the 18th c.). Secondly, there are no texts from two very old stages of Romanian: Proto-Romanian, before the 12th c. when the four historical dialects split – Daco-Romanian (henceforth: DRom.), north of the Danube, Aromanian/Macedo-Romanian (henceforth: ARom.), Megleno-Romanian (henceforth: MRom.) and Istro-Romanian (henceforth: IRom.), south of the river –, and Archaic Romanian, up to the 16th c.

The pre-literary Romanian language (beginning with the 12th c.) is partially known through attested Romanian words (especially proper names) or Romanian phrases inserted in Slavonic texts (inscriptions or documents), written or copied by Romanians or by Romanian-speaking Slavs; some documents (from Transylvania) written in Latin also contain Romanian phrases/words.

Marina Rădulescu Sala, Bucharest, Romania

https://doi.org/10.1515/9783111420530-018

The first text written entirely in Romanian, unanimously recognized as such, is a letter, *Neacşu's Letter* (1521), followed in the same century by many religious works, manuscripts or printed texts, translated from Slavonic and written in the Cyrillic alphabet (until the beginning of the 19th c. writing with the Cyrillic alphabet prevailed – Sala 2010: 853). In the following two centuries, religious texts continue to be the most frequent ones (the first translation of the Bible is published in 1688, in Bucharest), but the first codices of laws also appear and the chronicle literature develops, alongside the first original literary works. The period conventionally known as Old Romanian spans until the end of the 18th c. (the reference point is the year 1780, when the work *Elementa linguae daco-romanae sive valachicae*, by S. Micu and Gh. Şincai, was published).

2 Particular features of Romanian

2.1 The historical context

Dacia, inhabited by the Geto-Dacians (who belonged to the large group of the Thracians), was conquered by Emperor Trajan, who defeated the Dacian king Decebal in 106 AD, and was a Roman province until 271 AD, when Emperor Aurelian withdrew the administration and the army to the south of the Danube, because of the Gothic invasions. This does not entail that the Romanization process lasted only for 165 years. Out of the nearly 60,000 Roman soldiers brought in by Trajan, many (called "veterans") married Dacian women and settled in Dacia, where they received land; their descendants continued to live in the old deserted Roman cities (some historical sources mention approximately 44 cities in the first half of the 2nd c.) or took to farming in settlements founded by colonists. All spoke Vulgar Latin. When confronted with the waves of migratory populations (Germanic and Turkish), among which the Slavs occupy a special position (they massively migrated to the south and to the north of the Danube, in the 6th–7th c.), the (linguistically and genetically) Romanized Dacians temporarily withdrew to the mountains where they continued farming, grazing and woodworking.

2.2 The Thraco-Dacian substratum and its contact with Latin

Thraco-Dacian, a *satem*-type Indo-European language spoken by the autochthonous population of Dacia, constitutes the substratum of Romanian. There are very few data on this language: in the writings of some authors of Antiquity, in Greek and Latin inscriptions or on coins, various proper names are recorded (personal names, place names, names of rivers, lakes, mountains); a few glosses of Dacian medicinal plants appear in two treatises of medical botany (Dioscorides – 1st c. AD, Pseudo-Apuleius – 5th c. AD); also, a few inscriptions, undeciphered yet, have been discovered (ELR 2001: 584–585). In order to establish the inventory of substratum words in Romanian, most researchers resort to the comparison between Romanian and Albanian (henceforth: Alb.), considered a descendant of the Thracian languages (Brâncuş 1983: 10–11). Some researchers have reconstructed Thraco-Dacian elements also through comparison with old Indo-European languages (Poghirc 1969: 313–319).

The unstressed suffix *-(e/ă)ză* is attributed to the Thraco-Dacian substratum; it is identifiable in three words: DRom. *cínteză* 'chaffinch' ← *cint-* (expressive root that mimics a bird's song); DRom., ARom. *coácăză* 'black currant' ← **coacă* < Lat. *coccum*, pl. *cocca* (cf. ARom., MRom. *cocă* corresponding to Alb. *koqë* 'berry, fruit'); DRom., ARom. *púpăză* and MRom. *púpează* 'hoopoe' ← DRom. *pup* (expressive creation, cf. Alb. *pupë* 'crest') cf. ARom. *pupă*, MRom. *pupcă*; one may also include here *bogză* 'owl' ← *boghe* 'id.' (Cioränescu 2001: 6973). The suffix *-ză* is part of the Romanian complex suffix *-eáză: sfârleáză* 'whirligig' ← *sfârlă* 'flick', *speteáză* 'back of a chair' ← *spată* '(obsolete) shoulder blade', etc. (Cioränescu 2001: 7735, 8051).

Certain researchers (Graur 1936: 71–84; Rosetti 1986: 209–210, 567) argue that the adjectival suffix *-esc* (*bărbătesc* 'masculine' ← *bărbat* 'man', *strămoşesc* 'ancestral' ← *strămoş* 'ancestor'), also used as a patronymic suffix (*Vasilescu* ← *Vasile*), comes from the substratum; other researchers trace it back to Lat. *-iscus* (Pascu 1916: 69).

The suffix *-uş(ă)* might also come from the substratum; it is recognizable in three old Romanian words that have a Latin root: DRom., ARom. *auş* '(obsolete) old man, grandfather' < Lat. *auus* + *-uş* (REW 1935: 839; Cioränescu 2001: 536); DRom., ARom., MRom. *cătuşă* '(obsolete) cat' < Lat. *cattus* +*-uşă* (Cioränescu 2001: 1564); DRom. *mătuşă* 'aunt, elderly woman' < Lat. *mĭta* (← *amĭta*) + *-uşă* (REW 1935: 424; Cioränescu 2001: 5167).

During the Romanization process the autochthonous population gradually jettisoned its native language and shifted to Latin, initially imposed through administrative methods. The conversion of the Latin spoken in Dacia (which incorporated many autochthonous terms, especially names of plants and animals specific to the area – i.e. substratum elements) into Proto-Romanian occurred over several centuries. According to the majority of the researchers, the rise of Proto-Romanian (as different from Vulgar Latin) dates back to the 8th c., similarly to the other Romance languages (Fischer 1985: 210–211); this date can be taken as also marking the appearance of the Romanian people. According to certain researchers, the small fragment *torna frat(r)e* 'come back, brother', also known as *torna, torna/retorna, frat(r)e*, a quote from the 6th c. notated (with the aforementioned variants) by two Byzantine chroniclers (Theophylactos Simokattes – the 7th c. – and Theophanes Confesor – the 8th–9th c.), would represent the first clue as to the appearance of the Romanian language (thus, also being the first Romance text! – Philippide 1923: 504–508; Coteanu 1961: 53; Rosetti 1986: 591–592). There are, however, several scholars (Densusianu 1901: 390; Fischer 1985: 21–22) who argue that this is a Latin (not a Romanian) text.

2.3 Danubian Latin

The phrase "Danubian Latin" (henceforth: DL) is used to designate the spoken variety of Latin used in Antiquity in Moesia and Dacia, the place of origin of the four historical Romanian dialects. DL differs from *Oriental Latin*, which encompasses the south of Italy and the Balkans, as well as from *Balkan Latin*, a heterogeneous area which covers, besides DL, the Dalmatian area on the coast of the Adriatic Sea (closer to Northern Italy), the area of Via Egnatia (the source of the Latin borrowings found in Albanian) and probably another area, which represents the source of vulgar borrowings in Greek.

The sources of DL are the inscriptions from the area (which document deviations from the standards of literary Latin – approximately the same ones in all the areas of the Empire) and especially the reconstruction of Vulgar Latin forms starting from Old Romanian data.

Like the other Romance languages, Romanian inherited from Latin its grammatical structure and the basis of its fundamental vocabulary (i.e. the most frequently used words, which have many different meanings and derivatives – VRLR 1988: 13–14). In word-formation, DL displays the same tendencies as the Latin varieties spoken in the other Romance areas (Fischer 1985: 155–156, 184): (1) the preference for suffixes with a larger phonological shape (or for complex suffixes), which belonged to precise inflectional classes (the 1st and 2nd declensions) and had a clear sense (describing precise relations between the noun and the verb); (2) the reduction of suffix synonymy; (3) the reduction of the number of prefixes (Romanian inherited only 12 of the 21 Latin prefixes inherited by Western Romance).

2.4 The Slavic influence

Of the migratory populations that passed through the area where the Romanian language and people were formed, the Slavs had a very important role. The contact between the Slavs and the Romanized population north and south of the Danube (during the bilingualism) was strong and long lasting. Researchers have different points of view on the beginning of the Slavic influence: the 6th–7th centuries (Densusianu 1901: 241; Rosetti 1986: 267) or the 8th–9th centuries (Capidan 1925: 45, 51–52; Puşcariu 1940: 284). Spoken Slavic ceased to influence Romanian in the 11th–12th c. In the north of the Danube, the Slavs learned the language of the Romanized population; however, there are noteworthy traces of their influence on Romanian, especially in the vocabulary and in word-formation (numerous Slavic suffixes and prefixes have entered Romanian – see section 5). The Slavic influence represents the *superstratum* of Romanian (similarly to the Germanic influence on Western Romance).

A recurring question was the following: why did the Romance population and language survive north of the Danube, in the areas abandoned by the Romans in the face of barbarians (besides linguistic evidence, there are convincing archaeological proofs in this direction), while south of the Danube, where Roman life continued for a while, the vernacular Romance language disappeared and the population was assimilated by the Slavs? This Latin island in a Slavic sea has long been considered an "enigma" and a "historical miracle" (Lot 1937: 278–300); a Romanian historian answered to Lot by providing archaeological and linguistic evidence (Brătianu 1942). One explanation might be the following: the withdrawal of the Roman administration and army from Dacia actually favoured the persistence of Latinity, because if the Romans had attempted to resist, the barbarians would have destroyed the Romanized population; given the lack of military resistance north of the Danube, the invaders did not strike as forcefully as they did in the south, and consequently spread in all directions (Puşcariu 1940: 329–330). The Slavic population that came into these territories had the same destiny as the Germanic migrants in Western Europe (Sala 2006: 20): in the regions where they did not annihilate the Romanized population, such as Dacia, the Slavs were assimilated by the Romance population (similarly, the Germanic tribes were assimilated in Italy, Gallia and Iberia), while in the areas where the Romanized population was exterminated (such as the Balkan Peninsula), the Slavs assimilated the Romanized population (similarly, the Germanic tribes assimilated the Romanized population east of the Rhine). South of the Danube, Slav states were formed and, beginning with the 9th c., the number of Slavs gradually diminishes in Dacia, as an effect of their migration to the south.

2.5 The role of the Slavonic language

It is important to mention the role which the Slavonic language played in the evolution of the Romanian culture and how it was instrumental in distinguishing Romanian from its sister Romance languages.

Slavonic is a late literary variety of the (written) Old Slavic language. It was used as an ecclesiastical and cultural language north of the Danube in the 10th–16th centuries, and after the 16th c. it was used together with Romanian. After the emergence in the 14th c. of the first Romanian feudal states, Ţara Românească or Wallachia (south of the Carpathian mountains) and Moldavia (in the north-east), the documents of royal chanceries were also written in Slavonic, the ecclesiastical language of the area. Consequently, numerous Slavonic religious, cultural and administrative terms entered the vocabulary of Archaic Romanian (the new Romance language, originating in DL, with a Thraco-Dacian substratum and an Old Slavic superstratum). The south-Danubian dialects were spoken in the southern part of the Balkan Peninsula, given the migration of population to this area. Thus, Greek was the ecclesiastical language which played a part in the evolution of these dialects.

In the Western Romance area, the cultural language was Medieval Latin; this is why in the vocabulary of Western Romance languages one finds Medieval Latin terms or different forms "rectified" on the model of Latin ones. Consequently, Western Romance languages appear to be closer to Latin, in contrast to Romanian.

2.6 Other borrowings

Besides the words inherited from Latin, the ones from the substratum (identified by the comparison with Albanian), the ones from the Slavic superstratum (similar to the Germanic superstratum in Western Romance) and the ones borrowed from Slavonic, Romanian has also borrowed, at different times in its evolution, words from the languages with which it had contact. This is why there are Hungarian, Greek and Turkish derivatives in Old Romanian.

In the Modern Romanian period, there occurred a process called the "Re-Romanization" of Romanian (Puşcariu 1940: 370–371), via massive borrowings from the Romance languages (especially French, but also Italian) as well as from Medieval Latin. The Latino-Romance neologisms have often replaced old bookish Slavonic terms, which have become archaisms: for instance, the word *ostrov* 'island' was replaced by *insulă*, *iscoadă* 'spy' by *spion*, etc.

Romanian is later enriched with loanwords from the Modern Slavic languages, from German (especially from the dialectal German spoken by the Saxons of Transylvania), and currently from English.

3 Methodological questions

3.1 Derivatives inherited from Latin or formed in Romanian?

This is a question to be asked with regard to some old Romanian derivatives with attested Latin counterparts, but in which one can identify a base-word inherited from Latin and a productive Latin suffix; such is the case of *cercel* 'ear ring', which may be inherited from Lat. *circellus* 'small ring' or formed in Romanian from *cerc* 'circle, ring' (< Lat. *circus*) + the suffix *-el* (< Lat. *-ellus*). The answer to this question is given for each case in turn; certain linguists prefer an explanation in terms of Latin inheritance, while others favour an account in terms of derivation in Romanian. Lately, some criteria have been put forward (Sala 1999: 125–138), according to which the words in question can be classified as (a) derivatives clearly inherited in Romanian from Latin, (b) derivatives probably inherited from Latin, and (c) derivatives which are most probably Romanian creations.

a) A first criterion is a comparison within Romance. Thus, *apos* 'watery' (cf. *apă* 'water') < Lat. *aquosus* (REW 1935: 588) and *arătură* 'plough-land' (cf. *(a) ara* '(to) plough') < Lat. *aratura* (REW 1935: 602a) are most certainly inherited derivatives, since they are found in several Romance languages (Lat. *aratura* is actually present in all the Romance languages). A supplementary criterion is the existence of the derivative in question in Albanian (a language strongly influenced by Latin); this criterion functions for derivatives such as *legătură* 'link' (cf. *(a) lega* '(to) link') < Lat. *ligatura* (REW 1935: 20), *temoare* 'fear' (cf. *(a se) teme* '(to) fear') < Lat. *timor* (REW 1935: 8738), words which are also inherited by several other Romance languages. Yet another criterion is the semantic relation between the derivative and its presumed Romanian base: if in Romanian the derivative is motivated only from a formal point of view, but not semantically, then it may be considered as being inherited from Latin. Such an example is *iepar* 'guardian of horses', which could have been the outcome of Rom. *iapă* 'mare' + *-ar*; however, the word *equarius* 'guardian of horses' exists in Latin and, according to the phonetic laws, could have (and *has*) evolved into Rom. *iepar* (one should keep in mind that this word was also inherited by Spanish: *yegüero* – REW 1935: 2884).
b) The class of derivatives probably inherited from Latin includes, in the first place, the Latin derivatives existing only in Romanian, such as *blândeţe* 'kind-

ness' < Lat. *blanditia* (REW 1935: 1150), *cepar* 'onion merchant' < Lat. *ceparius* (REW 1935: 1818), etc. However, one cannot exclude the hypothesis that these words were created in Romanian by suffixation with *-e(a)ţe* < Lat. *-itia* or *-ar* < Lat. *-arius*. In the case of *cepar*, the functional status of the Latin derivative may also be taken into account: *ceparius* was not frequently used in Latin (it occurs only in two texts); however, it might have been frequently used in DL.

c) In contrast, a derivative such as *apar* 'water merchant' (cf. Lat. *aquarius*) represents a different situation. This word may be considered a Romanian creation, according to a socio-cultural criterion: it is hard to assume that, at the beginning of its history, the Romanian population – which always settled down next to sources of water – needed a word which would correspond to this notion; they could have created this word later, from *apă* 'water' (< Lat. *aqua*) + *-ar*.

The question "borrowed derivative or formed in Romanian?" can also be asked with respect to borrowings: was *pândar* 'guard' borrowed from Sl. *pǫdarь* or is it a Romanian creation, stemming from *(a) pândi* '(to) guard' + the suffix *-ar*? Given that this derivative also occurs in the southern Danubian dialects (ARom. and MRom.) and that the verb *(a) pândi* does not exist in ARom., it is very likely that *pândar* is a borrowing (Sala 1999: 175).

3.2 The reconstruction of Late Latin derivatives

The class of derivatives on which a clear stand cannot be taken (inherited from Latin or created in the Romance languages) also includes some Romance derivatives unattested in Latin. However, if the derivative occurs in a sufficiently large number of Romance languages, it may be assumed that this word had also existed in spoken Late Latin (including DL, if the derivative is also present in Romanian) and one may reconstruct the Latin word on the basis of the Romance forms; this is the case of Lat. **affundare* > Rom. *(a) afunda* '(to) sink' (also present in Italian, Old French, Spanish, Portuguese – REW 1935: 269), Lat. **ingrassiare* > Rom. *(a) îngrăşa* '(to) fatten' (also present in French, Occitan, Catalan, Portuguese – REW 1935: 4427), etc.

The particular case of Late Latin forms from DL reconstructed only on the basis of Romanian derivatives should also be considered: *albeaţă* 'white(ness)' < Lat. **albitia* (but also *alb* 'white' + *-eaţă*), *pielcea* 'small skin' < Lat. **pellicella* (but also *piele* 'skin' + the diminutive suffix *-cea*), etc. It is very likely that this type of derivative is inherited from Latin if they are also present in the south Danubian dialects; this is the case of *fecior* 'son, boy' < Lat. **fetiolus*, *mioară* 'ewe lamb' <

Lat. **agnelliola*, *sărbătoare* 'feast' < Lat. **servatoria* (Sala 1999: 129–130). Is one entitled to ascribe to Latin a word that perhaps never existed in Latin? Fisher (1985: 157) answers this question as follows: "provided that Romanian is the uninterrupted successor of Latin, the derivatives with productive suffixes, similarly to the grammatical forms, have a virtually uninterrupted existence since Antiquity to the present day; this does not mean that a derivative of this type has been used at all times in the current speech of all individuals, but that in the course of history such a word could be formed and understood by any speaker".

4 The Latin heritage

Romanian was genealogically defined as "the Latin language spoken uninterruptedly in the Oriental area of the Roman Empire, consisting of the Romanized Danubian provinces (Dacia, Southern Pannonia, Dardania, Moesia Superior and Inferior), from the moment when Latin penetrated in these provinces until our times" (Rosetti 1986: 75).

Since Romanian inherited a large number of analysable derivatives, it also took over from Latin many word-formation patterns. The affixes which are productive in Latin literary texts as well as in Old Romanian may also be considered productive in DL. Among the main word-formation processes in DL, the most important one is derivation and, first of all, derivation with suffixes (Fischer 1985: 155–191).

4.1 The suffixes

4.1.1 Deverbal and denominal abstract nouns

Romanian inherited certain Latin d e v e r b a l suffixes by means of transparent derivatives.

Lat. *-(t)ion-/-(s)ion-* became Rom. *-(ă/i)ciune* in *rogatio, -one* > *rugăciune* 'prayer' (cf. *(a se) ruga* '(to) pray' < *rogare*); it gave rise in Romanian to many derivatives from verbs (*asupriciune* 'oppression' ← *(a) asupri* '(to) oppress') as well as from adjectives (*înţelepciune* 'sapience' ← *înţelept* 'sapient'), and even from a numeral (*unu* 'one' → *uniciune* 'uniqueness') and a noun (*sete* 'thirst' → *seteciune* 'great thirst').

Lat. *-tūra/-sūra* > Rom. *-(ăt/it)ură* in *arsura* > *arsură* 'burn' (cf. *ars* 'burned' ← *(a) arde* '(to) burn' < *ardere*); it was highly productive, creating nouns not only from the infinitive (*cugetătură* 'thinking' ← *(a) cugeta* '(to) think'), but also from the participle (*chindisitură* 'embroidery' ← *chindisit* 'embroidered' ← *(a) chindisi* '(to) embroider').

Lat. *-tus*/*-sus* (cf. *cantus*, *risus*, etc.), turned into *-ĭtus* and became Rom. *-et* (unstressed) in *gemitus* > *gemet* 'groan/moan' (cf. *(a) geme* '(to) groan/moan' < *gemere*); the derivatives of Old Romanian are created from verbs of Latin or Slavic origin (*îmblet* '(the) walking' ← *(a) îmbla* '(to) walk', *scrâşnet* '(the) gnashing' ← *(a) scrâşni* '(to) gnash') as well as from an interjection (*vaet* 'lamentation' ← *vai!* 'Oh!').

Lat. *-mentum* (used in Late Latin to derive nouns denoting not only the event itself, but also its result) > Rom. *-(ă)mânt* (and *-(ă)minte*, a singular recreated by analogy with the plural) in *juramentum* > *jurământ* 'oath/the act of swearing' (cf. *(a) jura* '(to) swear' < *jurare*); it was rather productive, deriving nouns from verbs of Latin origin (*ascultământ* 'listening/obedience' ← *(a) asculta*, *rugăminte* 'request/the act of requesting' ← *(a) ruga*, etc.).

The complex suffix Lat. *-entia*/*-antia* > Rom. *-inţă* in *credentia* (attested in the 10th c.) > *credinţă* 'faith/belief' (cf. *(a) crede* '(to) believe' < *credere*), *potentia* > *putinţă* 'ability' (cf. *(a) putea* 'can/be able to' < *potere*), etc.; it derived nouns from verbs of Latin, Hungarian or Modern Greek origin (*cunoştinţă* 'knowledge' ← *(a) cunoaşte* '(to) know', *făgăduinţă* 'promise' ← *(a) făgădui* '(to) promise', *sosinţă* 'arrival' ← *(a) sosi* '(to) arrive') and even from a numeral (*întâinţă* 'firstness' ← *întâi* 'first').

Lat. *-or* (originally masculine; feminine in many Romance languages) became Rom. *-oare* in *sudor, -ore* > *sudoare* 'sweat' (an opaque derivative) or in transparent ones like *albor, -ore* > *alboare* 'whiteness' (cf. *(a) albi* '(to) whiten', but also *alb* 'white'), *timor, -ore* > *temoare* 'fear' (cf. *(a se) teme* '(to) fear'); the existence of certain new derivatives inherited only in Romanian such as **laudor* > *lăudoare* 'praise' and **uoluor* > *vâlvoare* 'big fire' (Fischer 1985: 159), and also **lucor* > ARom. *lucoare* 'shining' (REW 1935: 5144), testify to its relative productivity in DL; however, it was not productive in Romanian (its sole derivative in the 16th c. is *răcoare* 'coolness', created from the adjective *rece* 'cool').

Romanian inherited also certain Latin deadjectival and denominal suffixes such as Lat. *-tas, -tatis* > Rom. *-(t)ate* in the transparent derivative *bonitas* > *bunătate* 'kindness' (cf. *bun* 'good/kind'); it was productive in the 16th–17th c., attaching to adjectives of Latin, Slavic or Greek origin (*strâmbătate* 'injustice' ← *strâmb* 'injust', *bogătate* 'richness' ← *bogat* 'rich', *ieftinătate* 'cheapness' ← *ieftin* 'cheap'). Some forms have acquired a collective meaning, through the conversion of the base-adjective into a noun (*păgânătate* 'all the pagans' ← *păgân* 'pagan').

Lat. *-(ē)tum* > Rom. *-ét* in *fraxinetum* > *frăsinet* 'ash forest' (cf. *frasin* 'ash') was used to create collective nouns from nouns of Latin or Slavic origin (*mueret* 'group of women' ← *muere* 'women', *mlăjet* 'bush' ← *mlajă* 'osier').

Lat. *-alia* (neuter pl. of *-alis*) > Rom. *-aie* in the inherited collective derivative *minutalia* > *măruntaie* 'guts' (cf. *mărunt* 'small'); it was incorporated in the complex suffix *-ăraie* (*apăraie* 'a lot of water' ← *apă* 'water', *fumăraie* 'dense smoke' ← *fum* 'smoke').

Lat. *-itia* (a complex suffix) > Rom. *-eaţă/-e(a)ţe* in transparent derivatives such as *blanditia* > *blândeţe* 'gentleness' (cf. *blând* 'gentle') or in opaque ones like **grevitia* > *greaţă* 'nausea'; it was quite productive, creating qualitative abstract nouns from adjectives of Latin and, rarely, Slavic or Greek origin (*lineaţe* 'smoothness' ← *lin* 'smooth', *mândreaţe* 'beauty' ← *mândru* 'beautiful', *ieftineaţă* 'cheapness' ← *ieftin* 'cheap').

Lat. *-men*, which typically created nouns from verbs (*acūmen* 'needle' ← *acuĕre* '(to) sharpen'), in Late Latin began to derive collective nouns from adjectives (*uitreāmen* 'glassware' ← *uitreus* '(made) of glass') or from nouns (*linteāmen* 'bedclothes' ← *linteum* 'linen'); its successor in Old Romanian is *-ame* which testifies to this value in a few derivatives from nouns (*lotrame* 'all thieves' ← *lotru* 'thief', *prostame* 'the peasantry' ← *prost* '(bookish) peasant', etc.). The Romanian suffix *-ime* < Lat. *-imen*, was more productive with qualitative abstract nouns derived from adjectives (*desime* 'density' ← *des* 'dense', *iuţime* 'fastness' ← *iute* 'fast'); it was also used to create abstract nouns from verbs (*lucime* 'brightness' ← *(a) luci* '(to) bright'), and, starting with the 17th c., it yields collective nouns (*boierime* 'nobility (= all the boyars)' ← *boier* 'noble').

For Lat. *-ia* (*audacia* 'daringness' ← *audax* 'daring') > Rom. *-íe*, as well as for Lat. *-amen/-imen* > Rom. *-ame/-ime*, there are no analysable derivatives inherited from Latin, which would justify the productivity of these suffixes in Romanian; it may be assumed that, in the period spanning from the latest Latin text to the first Romanian attestations, the analysable derivatives disappeared (Fischer 1985: 161). The suffix *-íe* was very productive in Old Romanian, attaching to adjectives of Latin, Slavic or Hungarian origin (*blânzie* 'gentleness' ← *blând* 'gentle', *ghizdăvie* 'beauty' ← *ghizdav* 'beautiful', *viclenie* 'slyness' ← *viclean* 'sly'), to nouns of Latin, Slavic, Greek or Turkish origin (*soţie* 'wife' ← *soţ* 'husband', *slujnicie* 'maidishness' ← *slujnic* 'buttle/maid', *mărturie* 'deposition' ← *martur* 'witness', *păşie* 'the dignity of being pasha' ← *paşă* 'pasha') or, more rarely, to verbs (*ameţie* 'dizziness' ← *(a) ameţi* '(to) get dizzy'). It is one of the most productive suffixes that derive abstract nouns.

4.1.2 Deverbal and denominal agent nouns

In Latin the suffix *-tor*, *-tōris* typically encoded the agentive value; it was also productive in DL. Its Romanian counterpart is *-tor* (*dēbitor* > *dator* 'debtor' –

REW 1935: 2492). But given that neither the nominative *-tor* nor the accusative *-torem* could have evolved into Rom. *-tor(iu)*, it must be assumed that this form was recreated in Proto-Romanian, on the basis of the inherited feminine form *-toare* < Lat. *-toria* (which replaced in Late Latin the form *-trix*); the instrumental and locative values of the Romanian suffix (*ambulatōria* > *umblătoare* 'water closet' – REW 1935: 413) originate in the Latin adjectival suffix *-torius*, whose neuter derivatives in *-torium* became nouns (Graur 1929: 109–111). The suffix was highly productive in Old Romanian, creating agent nouns but also adjectives from verbs of Latin, Slavic, Hungarian and Greek origin (*cusător* 'tailor' ← *(a) coase* '(to) sew', *izbânditor* 'winner' ← *(a) izbândi* '(to) win', *gânditoriu* 'thinker/who thinks' ← *(a) gândi* '(to) think', *pătimitor* '(the one) who suffers' ← *(a) pătimi* '(to) suffer'). For the instrumental (*spălătoare* and *spălător* 'washer' ← *(a) spăla* '(to) wash') and locative values (*ieşitoare* 'exit' ← *(a) ieşi* '(to) exit'), more representative is the feminine form *-toare*.

A very productive Old Romanian suffix is *-ar(iu)*, which occurs in noun-based nouns denoting professionals or instruments. The adjectival suffix Lat. *-arius* (whose derivatives became nouns as early as the beginning of Latin) was inherited in transparent derivatives such as *molarius* > *morar* 'miller' (cf. *moară* 'mill'); the neuter form *-arium* entered Romanian through words like *granarium* > *grânar* 'granary' (cf. *grâne* 'cereals'); the neuter form *-āle* was transmitted to Romanian by words like *digitale* > *degetar* 'thimble' (cf. *deget* 'finger'). It was reinforced by transparent borrowings from Slavic and Greek. The suffix *-ar(iu)* created numerous derivatives from nouns of Latin, Slavic, Hungarian and Greek origin (*bucătar* 'cook' ← *bucate* 'food', *bivolar* 'buffalo guard' ← *bivol* 'buffalo', *cizmar* 'shoemaker' ← *cizmă* 'shoe', *cărămidar* 'brick manufacturer' ← *cărămidă* 'brick'). Only rarely did it create nouns also from verbal bases (*ştergariu* 'towel' ← *(a se) şterge* '(to) wipe (oneself)').

4.1.3 Diminutives

Lat. *-ellus* (an augmented form of *-(o)lus*, the only diminutive suffix of Latin) > Rom. *-el* in *vitellus* > *viţel* 'calf' (cf. *vită* 'cattle'); it attached to nouns of different origins (*cârligel* 'little hook' ← *cârlig* 'hook', *copăcel* 'little tree' ← *copac* 'tree'), but also to a few adjectives introducing an attenuating overtone (*(i)uşurel* ← *uşure* 'light/easy', *puţinel* ← *puţin* 'few'). The feminine form Lat. *-ella* became Rom. *-ea* in the inherited word *catella* > *căţea* 'female dog' – REW 1935: 1763 (cf. *căţel* 'little dog'); it has a few derivatives in Old Romanian (*fântânea* 'little well' ← *fântână* 'well').

Lat. *-(u)lus* survived only in a few opaque words (in fact, it had lost its diminutive value ever since Latin; its derivatives became synonymous with and later replaced their bases): Lat. *uet(u)lus* (← *uetus*) > Rom. *vechi* 'old', Lat. *genuculum* (← *genu*) > Rom. *genu(n)chi* 'knee', Lat. *auricula* (← *auris*) → *oricla* > Rom. *ureche* 'ear', Lat. *picula* (← *pix*) > Rom. *păcură* 'oil/tar'.

The basis for the assumption that Lat. *-ic(c)a* became Rom. *-ică* is a comparison within Romance: this value also exists in Iberian Romance (Fischer 1985: 167); it occurs in a few words in Old Romanian: *nepoţică* '(little) granddaughter' ← *nepot* 'grandson', *subţirică* 'delicate' ← *subţire* 'thin'.

4.1.4 Augmentatives

A comparison within Romance indicates that, in the late phases of Latin, the suffix *-on-* (which had many values) also became augmentative, often having a pejorative overtone.

It is presumed that (similarly to *-tor*, see section 4.1.2) Rom. *-oi* (which could not have phonetically evolved from *-on-*) is a masculine form reconstructed from the feminine *-oaie* (< Lat. *-onea* or *-onia*), which became a gender-changing suffix: *dumnezeoaie* 'goddess' ← *Dumnezeu* 'god', *păşoaie* 'wife of pasha' ← *paşă* 'pasha', *ursoaie* 'female bear' ← *urs* 'bear', etc. In Old Romanian, there are *-oi* derivatives with a gender-changing value (*broscoi* 'male frog' ← *broască* 'frog', *gâscoi* 'gander' ← *gâscă* 'goose'), but also with augmentative or pejorative meaning (*cămeşoi* 'big shirt' ← *cămaşă* 'shirt', *slugoi* '(pejorative) servant' ← *slugă* 'servant'). The shift of the suffix *-oi*, *-oaie* from the augmentative value to the gender-changing one probably took place in DL (Fischer 1985: 168).

4.1.5 Gender-changing suffixes

Lat. *-a* (*equus* 'horse' vs. *equa* 'mare') became Rom. *-ă* in *palumba* > *porumbă* 'female pigeon' (cf. *porumb* 'pigeon'), *socia* > *soaţă* 'wife' (cf. *soţ* 'husband'), etc. Derivatives like *asină* 'female donkey' ← *asin* 'donkey', *roabă* 'bondwoman' ← *rob* 'bond', *sfântă* 'female saint' ← *sfânt* 'saint' were created in Old Romanian.

Lat. *-issa* (a Late Latin suffix of Greek origin) became Rom. *-easă* in derivatives such as *imperatrissa* > *împărătească* 'empress, wife of the emperor' (cf. *împărat* 'emperor') and was productive in Romanian: *căpităneasă* 'wife of the captain' ← *căpitan* 'captain', *mireasă* 'bride' ← *mire* 'bridegroom', *preuteasă* 'priestess, wife of the priest' ← *preut* 'priest', etc.

Lat. *-īna* survived in the opaque derivative *gallina* > *găină* 'chicken' and Lat. *-ia* was transmitted via the complex suffix *-toria* (see section 4.1.2).

4.1.6 Deverbal and denominal adjectives

Lat. *-bundus* (cf. *furibundus, uagabundus*) seems to have regained a certain productivity in DL, since it is identifiable in some Old Romanian opaque derivatives, being absent from other Romance languages: **cascabundus* > *căscăund* 'booby' (REW 1935: 1732), *flammabundus* > *flămând* 'hungry' (REW 1935: 3351) or *palpabundus* > *plăpând* 'puny' (REW 1935: 6174). As a consequence of the weakening of the occlusion of *-b-* and, finally, of its disappearance, one cannot establish the precise moment of the weakening of *-bundus*; it is known that this phonetic change happened only in one part of the Romance area and was dated in the 6th c. This entails that *-bundus* lost its productivity in the final phase of DL or at the beginning of the Romance period (Fischer 1985: 156–157).

There is also a slight increase of adjectives in *-idus*, some of which are only found in Romanian: *languidus* > *lânced* 'feeble' (REW 1935: 4890), *marcidus* > *mârced* 'worn out' (REW 1935: 5346), *putridus* > *putred* 'rotted' (REW 1935: 6887). Since their verbal bases were not transmitted to Romanian, they are opaque derivatives; later on, new verbs were coined in Romanian on the basis of these adjectives: *(a) lâncezi* '(to) languish', *(a) putrezi* '(to) rotten'.

The suffix *-icius* was transmitted through the derivative Lat. *mixtĭcius* (literary: *mixtīcius*) 'obtained from a mixture' > Rom. *mistreţ* 'id.', hard to interpret even when the verb Rom. *(a) meşte* (< Lat. *miscēre* '(to) mix') was still in use.

Lat. *-aticus* > Rom. *-atec* in *siluaticus* > *sălbatec* 'savage' (an opaque derivative), but also in a transparent one: *hibernaticus* > *iernatec* 'winterish' (cf. *iarnă* 'winter'); the Romanian derivatives are based either on nouns (*ţărănatec* 'gross' ← *ţăran* 'peasant') or on adjectives (*roşiatec* 'almost red' ← *roşiu* 'red').

Lat. *-ĭscus* (a newer suffix, to which a Thracian origin was assigned, epigraphically attested in DL: *daciscus* 'Dacian', *frigiscus* 'Phrygian', *thraciscus* 'Thracian') seems to not have been inherited in Romanian through attested Latin derivatives (see section 2.2). Rom. *-esc* was very productive in Old Romanian, creating adjectives from nouns of Latin, Slavic, Greek, Hungarian and Turkish origin (*câinesc* 'canine, doggish' ← *câine* 'dog', *idolesc* 'specific to idols' ← *idol* 'idol', *demonesc* 'demonic(al)' ← *demon* 'devil', *meşterşugesc* 'skilful' ← *meşte(r)şug* 'craftsmanship', *mahmetesc* '(typical) of Mahomet' ← *Mah(o)met*).

Lat. *-ōsus* (extremely productive because of its unambiguous semantic content) became Rom. *-os* in some transparent derivatives like *foliōsus* > *foios* 'with leaves' (cf. *foi* 'leaves') or *carnōsus* > *cărnos* 'with meat' (cf. *carne* 'meat') and created in Romanian a lot of derivatives from nouns of Latin, Slavic or Greek origin (*păcătos* 'sinful' ← *păcat* 'sin', *ţepos* 'spiky' ← *ţepi* 'spikes', *mânios* 'angry' ← *mânie* 'anger').

Lat. *-tus* (denominal) was inherited in some hardly analysable words (*barbātus* 'bearded' > *bărbat* '(bookish) brave; man') or in opaque ones (*canūtus* > *cărunt* 'grey-haired'), and also in a transparent one: *cornūtus* > *cornut* 'horned' (cf. *corn* 'horn').

Lat. *-ivus* became Rom. *-iu* in the transparent derivative *timpuriu* 'early' (cf. *timpuri* 'times') < Lat. *tĕmpŏrīvus* (REW 1935: 8632); it created in Romanian derivatives from nouns of Latin origin (*mijlociu* 'medium' ← *mijloc* 'middle').

There are two other Latin adjectival suffixes which entered Romanian via opaque or hardly analysable nouns and which were consequently not productive: *-inus, -ina* (*circĭnus* > *cearcăn* 'dark ring', *capitīna* > *căpăţână* 'head') and *-aceus* (*carnaceus* > *cârnaţ* 'sausage', *gallinaceus* > *găinaţ* 'bird dung').

4.1.7 Adverbial derivation

The productivity of *-iscus* in DL also accounts for the productivity of its adverbial counterpart, formed with the suffix *-ē: *romanisce* > *româneşte* 'in a Romanian manner' (Fischer 1985: 169). Even though it was not inherited, *-eşte* was created in Romanian out of the adjectival suffix *-esc* (< Lat. *-ĭscus*) + *-e* (< Lat. *-ē*), on a Latin pattern. It was a productive suffix, deriving adverbs from nouns (*bărbăteşte* 'manly' ← *bărbat* 'man') and, less frequently, from adjectives (*vredniceşte* 'diligently' ← *vrednic* 'diligent').

It seems that the adverbial phrase composed of adjective + *mente* was not used to a large extent in DL, given that in Romanian it has only one (opaque) successor: *alia mente* or *altera mente* > *al(t)minteri* 'otherwise'.

4.1.8 Verbal derivation

Romanian inherited from Latin analysable verbs derived from nouns plus the suffix of the first (*hibernare* > *(a) ierna* cf. *iarnă* 'winter' – REW 1935: 4124, 4126) and fourth conjugations (*tussire* > *(a) tuşi* cf. *tuse* 'cough' – REW 1935: 9015, 9016); the process of zero derivation (conversion) became very productive in Romanian, especially for verbs of the fourth conjugation (for the form of the Romanian infinitive, see section 4.4).

Romanian also inherited from Latin a few derivatives with complex suffixes used to derive verbs; however, they were not productive in Old Romanian.

Lat. *-iāre* (also used in Late Latin) > Rom. *-ia* in *appropiare > (a) apropia* '(to) draw near(er)' – REW 1935: 557 (cf. *aproape* 'close'); in **ingrassiare > (a) îngrăşa* '(to) fatten' – REW 1935: 4427 (cf. *gras* 'fat') or **altiare > (a) (în)ălţa* '(to) raise' – REW 1935: 385 (cf. *înalt* 'high/tall') the suffix is no longer transparent, but the preceding consonant from the stem was altered because of *-i-*.

Lat. *-icare* > Rom. *-(e)ca* in a few opaque (denominal) derivatives such as *manicare > (a) mâneca* '(to) wake up at dawn' (REW 1935: 5301) or hardly transparent like *caballicare > (a) (în)căleca* '(to) mount a horse' (REW 1935: 1439) cf. *cal* 'horse', *carricare > (a) (în)cărca* '(to) load' (REW 1935: 1719) cf. *car* 'cart', *follicare > (a) (în)fuleca* '(to) wolf' (REW 1935: 3417) cf. *foale* 'belly'.

Lat. *-igare* became Rom. *-ega* in *rumigare > (a) rumega* '(to) chew, ruminate', an opaque word; later on, it derived *(a) spumega* '(to) foam' ← *spumă* 'foam' (Vasiliu 1989: 55).

Lat. *-itare* > Rom. *-(ă/i)ta* in some transparent deverbal derivatives like *dormitare > (a) durmita* '(to) doze' (REW 1935: 2752), cf. *(a) durmi* '(to) sleep' or **excloppitare > (a) şchiopăta* '(to) limp', cf. *şchiop* 'lame' < **excloppus*.

Lat. *-ulare* > Rom. *-ura* penetrated Romanian through opaque words like *(con)tremulare > (a) (cu)tremura* '(to) shake, tremble' and **turbulare > (a) turbura* '(to) (make) muddy' or hardly analysable derivatives like *excutulare > (a) scutura* '(to) shake (out)' (cf. *(a) scoate* '(to) pull out, extract') and also *ventulare > (a) vântura* '(to) winnow' (cf. *vânt* 'wind'; this one might have as well been formed in Romanian).

The Latin denominative suffixes *-izo* (*alapizare* 'to slap sb. in the face' ← *alapa* 'palm') and *-esco* (*floresco* 'to blossom' vs. *floreo* 'to bloom, blossom, flower' ← *flos* 'flower'), which became meaningless allomorphs of inflectional morphology, were inherited in Romanian as *-ez* and *-esc* only in opaque derivatives, thus only as grammatical suffixes: *(a) boteza* '(to) baptize', *(a) cuteza* '(to) dare', *(a) necheza* or *(a) râncheza* '(to) neigh', *(a) reteza* '(to) cut off' and *(a) creşte* '(to) grow', *(a) cunoaşte* '(to) know/get acquainted with', *(a) naşte* 'give birth', *(a) paşte* '(to) graze' (Fischer 1985: 170–171).

4.2 The prefixes

It may be assumed that DL did not have a poorer prefixation system than the rest of the Romance area, since the various prefixes available maintained here their productivity (Fischer 1985: 176–190), as it is shown by the data of Old Romanian (FCLRV 2007: 12–58).

Lat. *ad-* > Rom. *a-* in transparent derivatives with a locative value (*adducere > (a) aduce* '(to) bring (at)', cf. *(a) duce* '(to) lead, take') or an inchoative meaning (*addormire* > *(a) adormi* '(to) cause/fall asleep', cf. *(a) dormi* '(to) sleep') and produced derivatives such as *(a) apipăi* '(to) feel, touch' ← *(a) pipăi* 'id.'. This process is called "vocalic prosthesis" when the derivatives and their bases are synonymous.

Lat. *con-/com-* (which no longer established an opposition with *dis-*, as in *coniungere* '(to) conjoin' vs. *disiungere* '(to) disjoin', but had several vague values) > Rom. *cu-*; it was not productive in Romanian, even though it was inherited in transparent derivatives: *comprehendere* > *(a) cuprinde* '(to) comprise' (cf. *(a) prinde* '(to) catch'), **contremulare* > *(a) cutremura* '(to) shake' (cf. *(a) tremura* '(to) shake, shiver').

Lat. *de-* lost its meaning 'from top to bottom' (in opposition to *sub-* 'from bottom to top'). Romanian *de-* was inherited in transparent formations such as *deponere* > *(a) depune* '(to) deposit, lodge' (cf. *(a) pune* '(to) put, place') and was used to derive verbs like *(a se) delepăda* '(to) renounce' ← *(a se) lepăda* 'id.'.

Lat. *dis-* > Rom. *des-* (*dez-*) in transparent verbs like *disligare* > *(a) dezlega* '(to) untie' (cf. *(a) lega* '(to) tie'); it was very productive in Romanian, expressing especially the event opposed to the one expressed by its verbal (and sometimes nominal) base: *(a) despopi* '(to) unfrock' ← *(a) popi* '(to) ordain', *desfrâu* 'debauchery' ← *frâu* 'rein/means of restraint'.

Lat. *in-* > Rom. *în-* was not inherited with its locative value, but in transparent verbs such as *infrangere* > *(a) înfrânge* '(to) defeat' (cf. *(a) frânge* '(to) break') or *incalciare* > *(a) încălţa* '(to) put on sb.'s shoes' (cf. *(a) descălţa* '(to) take off sb.'s shoes'). It was productive in Romanian, creating verbs (*(a) încâştiga* '(to) win' ← *(a) câştiga* 'id.') and, rarely, adjectives (*înfricos* 'coward' ← *fricos* 'id.') or nouns (*înmulţime* 'abundance' ← *mulţime* 'crowd'). Alongside the verbal suffixes of conjugation 1 and 4, *în-* was used to derive verbs: *(a) încenuşa* '(to) cover with ash' ← *în-* + *cenuşă* 'ash' + *-a*, *(a) încălzi* '(to) heat/warm (up)' ← *în-* + *cald* 'warm' + *-i*.

Lat. *intro-* > Rom. *întru(-)* functioned in Old Romanian as a preposition and as a prefix. As a prefix, it was not inherited, but it occurs in a few verbs such as *(a) întraripa* '(to) gain wings; (fig.) (to) adorn' ← *într-* + *aripă* 'wing' + *-a* or *(a) întrauri* '(to) cover with gold' ← *(a) auri* 'id.' ← *aur* 'gold' + *-i*.

Losing in DL its locative value, Lat. *per-* (from Lat. *perīre* '(to) go ahead until the end; (to) perish' ← *īre* '(to) go') became Rom. *pre-*; it also was influenced by two other Latin prefixes, *prae-* 'ahead, on top' and *super-* 'above', as well as by the Slavic prefix *prě-* (> Rom. *prea-*). Lat. *per-* was inherited in transparent verbs such as *perambulare* > *(a) preumbla* '(to) walk' (cf. *(a) umbla* '(to) wander, walk') or *peruigilare* > *(a) preveghea* '(to) watch over' (cf. *(a) veghea* 'id.'); it created verbs such as *(a) presăra* '(to) sprinkle' ← *(a) săra* '(to) (powder with) salt' or *(a) prevesti* '(to) anticipate' ← *(a) vesti* '(to) announce'.

Lat. *re-* marked the return to a previous point/to an anterior state or added an iterative/intensifying meaning to the base: *redire* '(to) go, move, turn or come back' ← *īre* '(to) go', *reficere* '(to) make over, make anew' ← *facere* '(to) make'. It was inherited in Rom. *ră-* with vague values: *reponere* > *(a) răpune* '(to) defeat' (cf. *(a) pune* '(to) place, put'), **resalīre* > *(a) răsări* '(to) arise, spring' (cf. *(a) sări* '(to) jump'), *remanēre* > *(a) rămânea* '(to) remain' (cf. *(a) mânea* '(to) remain overnight'). Taking into account the productivity of this prefix in the other Romance languages, it may be that its productivity initially increased in DL, and subsequently decreased. Only two words seem to have been created in Old Romanian: *(a) răntu(r)na* '(to) overthrow' ← *(a) înturna* '(to) return' and *(a) răgloti* '(to) fight' ← *ră-* + *gloată* 'crowd' + *-i*. It is however hard to delimit it from the prefix *răs-* borrowed from Slavic: for instance *(a) răsuna* '(to) ring out' may be inherited from Lat. *resonare* or formed in Romanian from Sl. *răs-* + *(a) suna* '(to) ring'.

Lat. *ex-* (with a locative value in *exīre* '(to) exit' ← *īre*) > Rom. *s-* in inherited derivatives whose etymological relation with their bases, old in Romanian, is very hard to trace semantically: **excadere* > *(a) scădea* '(to) subtract, diminish' (cf. *(a) cădea* '(to) fall'), *exmulgere* > *(a) smulge* '(to) pull/tear out' (cf. *(a) mulge* '(to) milk, drain'), *exponere* > *(a) spune* '(to) say' (cf. *(a) pune* '(to) put'). In some derivatives, it has an intensifying meaning: *(a) smăcina* ← *(a) măcina* '(to) grind'. It was later reinforced by opaque borrowings from Slavic, which contain the homophonous prefix: *(a) spovedi* '(to) confess'.

Lat. *super* (adverb, preposition, and pre-verb) became Rom. *spre(-)*. In Romanian, the preposition *spre* is currently used, while the prefix occurs only sporadically. The prefix was inherited in the opaque word *supercilium* > *sprânceană* 'eyebrow'. Certain derivatives seem to be created in Romanian: *sprelung* 'oblong' ← *lung* 'long', *sprevăzător* 'pellucid' ← *văzător* '(one) that sees'; the word *sprepus* (from the phrase *nume sprepus* 'adjective') is a loan translation of Lat. *adiectiuum*.

Lat. *extra* 'outside of, beyond', rarely used as a prefix (*extracludere* '(to) close out(side)'), became Rom. *stră-*. *Extra* resembled phonetically and semantically the preposition *trans* 'across, beyond'. The prefix corresponding to the latter (*trans-*/*tra-*), quite productive in Latin, was gradually lost in the Romance languages; its traces in Romanian are *tramittere* > *(a) trămite* '(to) send, transmit' (REW 1935: 8849), *traicēre* > *(a) trece* '(to) pass' (REW 1935: 8842). The two prefixes were mixed up: *extra-* was interpreted by the speakers as *ex-* (intensifying) + *tra-*. Romanian *stră-* inherited the values of both prefixes. The verb *(a) străpunge* 'to bore/pierce/dig/strike through' seems to have been inherited from **extrapungere* = *transpungere*; other words like *(a) străluci* '(to) shine', *(a) strămuta* '(to) move, displace', etc., are hard to classify as inherited from Latin or derivationally created in Romanian. There are, however, clear derivatives in Romanian with this prefix:

strămoş 'ancestor' ← *moş* 'old man', *strănepot* 'great-grandson' ← *nepot* 'grandson', etc.

Lat. *sub-* > Rom. *su(b)-* has preserved its productivity in DL. Romanian inherited the transparent derivative *supponere* > *(a) supune* '(to) subdue, defeat' (cf. *(a) pune* '(to) put') and a few opaque verbs: *subīre* > *(a) sui* '(to) climb (up)', *sufferre* > *(a) suferi* '(to) suffer', etc.

The preposition Lat. *post* became in Romanian the prefix *poi-*, inherited in one single derivative, namely *poimâine* 'the day after tomorrow' < *post mane* (cf. *mâine* 'tomorrow'); by analogy, the ironical derivative *poimarţi* 'never' ← *poi-* + *marţi* 'Tuesday' was created quite recently.

4.3 Compounding

Similarly to the other varieties of Vulgar Latin, in DL compounding is not very productive. Certain compounds are no longer understood by speakers and are, consequently, deformed: *axungia* (← *axis* + *ung(u)ere*) 'grease used to smear the axis' became in Late Latin *auxungia* →**oxungia* > Rom. *osânză* 'lard'. Romanian inherited from Latin only two compounds; one of which is transparent (*trifolium* > *trifoi* 'clover', cf. *tri-* 'three' + *foi* 'leafs'), while the other is opaque (*lucifer* > *luceafăr* 'Venus'); cf. also *primăvară* 'spring' < *prima uera* (a late form for *primum uer*); *Dumnezeu* 'God' < *domine Deus* 'Lord God', *miazăzi* 'south' < *media dies* (the latter may be a recent formation).

4.4 Conversion (zero derivation)

Romanian took from Latin the infinitive form of the inherited verbs, shown by 16th c. constructions where this form had a verbal value, although it was preceded by the prepositions *a* and/or *de* (*e toată lumea de* [*şerbire*] *ţie* 'all people is here [to serve] your', *să aibă a* [*dare(a)*] 'to have in order [to give]' – FCLRV 2007: 167). Gradually, this form acquired the meaning of an abstract noun (name of event or of state, result of the event, object of the event, quality) and the nominal morpho-syntactic features of a feminine noun: it may accommodate the enclitic definite article *-a* (*den împărăţiia ceriului* [*cădearea*] '[the fall(ing)] from the sky's empire'), it may pluralize (*credinţa iaste ... şi lucrurilor ce nu se văd* [*dovediri*] 'faith constitutes [proofs] also of things that can't be seen') and it appears in syntactic positions typical of the noun. Under these circumstances, the forms with the suffixes *-are*, *-ire* (as well as with *-eare*, *-ere* < Lat. *-ēre*, *-ĕre: aveare* '(to) have, having' < *avēre*, *naştere* '(to) give birth, giving birth' < *nascĕre*) become ambiguous.

In order to avoid the confusion between verbs and deverbal abstract nouns, a "short infinitive" was created by reducing *-are, -eare, -ere, -ire* to *-a, -ea, -e, -i*. After a period of co-existence of the two infinitival forms (cf. *de a* [*mâncarea*] *şi de a* [*berea*] *şi a ne* [*îmbrăca*] '[to eat] and [to drink] and [to dress] ourselves'), the verbal usage of the "long infinitive" has gradually disappeared, being replaced by the short infinitive, an Archaic Romanian innovation (in MRom. and in ARom. the short infinitive does not exist; in MRom. the long infinitive conserved its verbal value, but in ARom. as well as in DRom. the long infinitive forms acquired a nominal value, cf. Byck 1959: 11; Caragiu-Marioţeanu 1975: 119, 252). Thus, the suffixes *-are, -eare, -ere* and *-ire*, identifiable in abstract nouns, move from the status of verbal grammatical suffixes to that of nominal lexical suffixes. Further evidence is provided by the occurrence of derivatives suffixed by *-are* from short infinitives with *-e* or *-ea: petrecare* 'feats, jollification' ← *(a) petrece* (← *petrecere*) '(to) amuse/enjoy oneself', *zăcare* 'falling ill' ← *(a) zăcea* (← *zăceare*) '(to) lie ill'.

The long infinitive is preserved in Non-Standard Romanian (as an archaism) only in a few imprecations (in the conditional mood – a complex verbal form, made up of the infinitive + an auxiliary): [*dormire-ar*] *somnul de veci!* lit. '[to sleep-would] the eternal sleep' = 'sleep the sleep that knows no breaking'.

5 The Slavic superstratum

During the cohabitation with the Slavs, Romanians (i.e. the Romanized Dacians) borrowed numerous words from Slavic or Old Bulgarian (both derivatives and their bases). Romanian was thus enriched with a series of Slavic suffixes detached from transparent derivatives: *-ac* (Sl. *prostakъ* >*prostac* 'dolt', cf. *prost* 'stupid'), *-anie* (Sl. *pokajanie* > *poca(i)anie* 'penance', cf. *(a se) pocăi* '(to) do penance'), *-că* (Bg. *arapka* >*arapcă* 'Arab/black woman', cf. *arap* 'Arab/blackamoor'), *-(l)ean* (Sl. *rymljaninъ* >*râmlean* 'inhabitant of Rome', cf. *Râm* 'Rome'), *-enie* (Sl. *sъměrenie* > *smerenie* 'humbleness', cf. *(a se) smeri* '(to) humble (oneself)'), *-işte* (Sl. *sъborište* > *zborişte* 'gathering place', cf. *zbor* 'council, assembly'), *-iţă* (Sl. *ǫdica* > *undiţă* 'fishing rod', cf. *(a) undi* '(to) angle'), *-nic* (Sl. *klevetьnikъ* >*clevetnic* 'slanderous', cf. *(a) cleveti* '(to) slander'), *-niţă* (Bg. *košьnica* >*coşniţă* 'market basket', cf. *coş* 'basket'), as well as the Romanian verbal suffix *-ui* < Sl. *-uj-* (the present tense inflectional ending of verbs ending in *-ovati*): Sl. *darovati, -ujǫ*> *(a) dărui* '(to) bestow (as a gift) on' (cf. *dar* 'gift').

There are also prefixes of Slavic origin: *ne-* (Sl. *nevinovatъ* > *nevinovat* 'innocent' cf. *vinovat* 'guilty'), *po-* (Sl. *pokajati sę* >*(a se) pocăi* '(to) do penance', cf. *(a se) căi* '(to) repent'), *prea-* (Sl. *pregrěšiti* > *(a) preagreşi* '(to) commit a serious sin', cf. *(a) greşi* '(to) err'), *răs-* (Sl. *razbolěti* > *(a) războli* '(to) fall ill', cf. *(a) boli* '(to) ail'). The prefixes *prea-* and *răs-* might have also been influenced by some homonymous or paronymous Latin prefixes (see section 4.2), and *ne-* was influenced by the negative adverb *nu* < Lat. *non*.

As to compounding, the pattern in the formation of the numerals from 11 to 19 is also the result of Slavic influence: *doisprezece* 'twelve' ← *doi* 'two' + *spre* 'over' + *zece* 'ten'.

6 Other borrowings

Romanian has borrowed lexical affixes through borrowed transparent derivatives as a result of the contact with other languages as well.

The suffixes *-ău* from *buduşlău* 'fugitive, wanderer' (cf. *(a) buduşlui* '(to) roam about'), *-şug* from *meşterşug* 'skill' (cf. *meşter* 'artisan, qualified worker') and the verbal suffix *-lui* from *(a) lăcăşlui* '(to) live' (cf. *lăcaş* 'slot') are due to Hungarian influence.

From Greek, Romanian took the following affixes: at the end of the 16th c., the suffix *-ache*, through masculine proper names (*Anghelache, Enachi*, cf. *Anghel, Ene*) and the prefix *arh(i)-* by means of Old Slavic: Gr. *αρχάγγελος* > OSl. *arxangelъ* > Rom. *arhanghel* 'archangel' (cf. *anghel* 'angel').

Also, in Romanian there are suffixes of Turkish origin: *-giu* (*pomanagiu* 'cadger', cf. *pomană* 'charity'), *-lâc* (*crailâc* 'debauchee life', cf. *crai* 'debauchee').

7 References

Brătianu, George Ion (1942): *Une énigme et un miracle historique. Le peuple roumain*. 2nd ed. Bucarest: [s.n.].

Brâncuş, Grigore (1983): *Vocabularul autohton al limbii române*. Bucureşti: Editura Ştiinţifică şi Enciclopedică.

Byck, Jacques (1959): Origine de l'infinitif abrégé en roumain. In: Ion Coteanu, Iorgu Iordan, Alexandru Rosetti and Marius Sala (eds.), *Recueil d'études romanes publié à l'occasion du IXe Congrès international de linguistique romane à Lisbonne*, 9–12. Bucarest: Editions de l'Académie.

Capidan, Theodor (1925): *Elementul slav în dialectul aromân*. Bucureşti: [s.n.].

Caragiu-Marioţeanu, Matilda (1975): *Compendiu de dialectologie română (nord- şi sud-dunăreană)*. Bucureşti: Editura Ştiinţifică şi Enciclopedică.

Ciorănescu, Alexandru (2001): *Dicţionar etimologic al limbii române*. Bucureşti: Saeculum I.O.

Coteanu, Ion (1961): *Originile limbii române*. Bucureşti: Editura Ştiinţifică.

Croitor, Blanca (2020): *Sufixele în limba română actuală. Formații recente*. București: Editura Universității din București.

Croitor, Blanca (ed.) (2024): *Formarea cuvintelor în limba română*. Vol. 4: *Sufixele. Derivarea nominală și adverbială*. Partea a II-a (E). Bucureşti: Editura Academiei Române.

Densusianu, Ovide (1901): *Histoire de la langue roumaine*. Vol. 1: *Les origines*. Paris: Dupuy.

ELR = Marius Sala (ed.) (2001): *Enciclopedia limbii române*. Bucureşti: Univers Enciclopedic.

FCLRV = Magdalena Popescu-Marin (ed.) (2007): *Formarea cuvintelor în limba română din secolele al XVI-lea – al XVIII-lea*. Bucureşti: Editura Academiei Române.

Fischer, Iancu (1985): *Latina dunăreană. Introducere în istoria limbii române*. Bucureşti: Editura Ştiinţifică şi Enciclopedică.

Fischer, Iancu (1989): Formation des mots. In: Günter Holtus, Michael Metzeltin and Christian Schmitt (eds.), *Lexikon der Romanistischen Linguistik*. Vol. 3, 33–55. Tübingen: Niemeyer.

Graur, Alexandru (1929): *Noms d'agent et adjectif en roumain*. Paris: [s.n.].

Graur, Alexandru (1936): *Mélanges linguistiques*. Paris/Bucureşti: [s.n.].

Lot, Ferdinand (1937): *Les Invasions barbares et le peuplement de l'Europe*. Vol. 1. Paris: Payot.

Maiden, Martin, Adina Dragomirescu, Gabriela Pană Dindelegan, Oana Uță Bărbulescu and Rodica Zafiu (2021): *The Oxford History of Romanian Morphology*. Oxford: Oxford University Press.

Pană-Dindelegan, Gabriela (ed.) (2013): *The Grammar of Romanian*. Oxford: Oxford University Press.

Pascu, Giorge (1916): *Sufixele româneşti*. Bucureşti: Ediţiunea Academiei Române.

Philippide, Alexandru (1923): *Originea românilor*. Vol. 1. Iaşi: [s.n.].

Poghirc, Cicerone (1969): Influenţe. In: Ion Coteanu (ed.), *Istoria limbii române*. Vol. 2. Bucureşti: Editura Academiei.

Puşcariu, Sextil (1940): *Limba română*. Vol. 1: *Privire generală*. Bucureşti: Fundaţia pentru literatură şi artă „Regele Carol II".

Rădulescu Sala, Marina (ed.) (2015): *Formarea cuvintelor în limba română*. Vol. 4: *Sufixele. Derivarea nominală și adverbială*. Partea I (A–C). Bucureşti: Editura Academiei Române.

Rainer, Franz (2021a): Adjectival Suffixes: From Latin to Romance. In: Mark Aronoff (ed.), *Oxford Research Encyclopedia of Linguistics*. Oxford: Oxford University Press [Online available at: https://doi.org/10.1093/acrefore/9780199384655.013.690]

Rainer, Franz (2021b): Instrument and Place Nouns in the Romance Languages. In: Mark Aronoff (ed.), *Oxford Research Encyclopedia of Linguistics*. Oxford: Oxford University Press [Online available at: https://doi.org/10.1093/acrefore/9780199384655.013.461]

REW (1935): Wilhelm Meyer-Lübke, *Romanisches Etymologisches Wörterbuch*. Heidelberg: Winter.

Rosetti, Alexandru (1986): *Istoria limbii române I. De la origini până la începutul secolului al XVII-lea*. Bucureşti: Editura Ştiinţifică şi Enciclopedică.

Sala, Marius (1999): *Introducere în etimologia limbii române*. Bucureşti: Univers Enciclopedic.

Sala, Marius (2006): *De la latină la română*. 2nd ed. Bucureşti: Univers Enciclopedic.

Sala, Marius (2010): Romanian. *Revue belge de philologie et d'histoire/Langues et littératures modernes* 88(3): 841–872.

Vasiliu, Laura (1989): *Formarea cuvintelor în limba română*. Vol. 3: *Sufixele. Derivarea verbală*. Bucureşti: Editura Academiei Române.

Vasiliu, Laura (2009): Histoire interne du roumain: Formation des mots. In: Gerhard Ernst, Martin-Dietrich Gleßgen, Christian Schmitt and Wolfgang Schweickard (eds.), *Romanische Sprachgeschichte*. Vol. 3, 2710–2721. Berlin/New York: de Gruyter.

VRLR (1988): Marius Sala (ed.), *Vocabularul reprezentativ al limbilor romanice*. Bucureşti: Editura Ştiinţifică şi Enciclopedică.

Franz Rainer and Claude Buridant

19 From Old French to Modern French

Abstract: This article provides a succinct overview of the evolution of central aspects of word-formation from Old to Modern French. The selective bibliographical references are meant to cover preferably works that could not yet be taken into account in the bibliographies of Schpak-Dolt (2003) and Piel's 1966 up-date of Meyer-Lübke (1921).

1 Introduction

The history of the French language is traditionally subdivided into three main periods: Old French (842–ca 1300), Middle French *sensu lato* (ca 1300–ca 1600), and Modern French. This rough division also makes sense for the history of French word-formation. In the Old French period, the dialects that had evolved from Vulgar Latin in the Northern half of the territory of Gaul were first used in writing. It is important to bear in mind that what is sloppily called "Old French" was not a homogeneous standard language, but a collection of regionally differentiated writing traditions (*scriptae*). These regional differences, genre traditions as well as the necessities of the rhyme explain, among other factors, the high degree of derivational synonymy in Old French (cf. Stefenelli 1967; Merk 1970; Merrilees 2006). The Middle French period was characterized by a growing trend towards a unification of these regional traditions after the model of the dialect of the Île-de-France (Paris; cf. Lodge 1993), as well as by a spectacular growth of the number of Latin loan words (3/5 of Latin and Greek roots entered French in this period,

Franz Rainer, Vienna, Austria
Claude Buridant, Strasbourg, France

https://doi.org/10.1515/9783111420530-019

according to Guiraud 1972: 53). This influx of Latinisms also transformed the word-formation system of French (cf. Zwanenburg 1985). In the 17th century, the definitive codification of the French language took place following the usage of the court and the "healthier part" of the inhabitants of Paris. Regionalisms that still lingered on in the language were banned, the number of synonyms was reduced, neologisms were proscribed. However, despite this considerable normative effort, the French language, and especially word-formation, did not come to a standstill. Beginning with the scientific revolution of the 17th century, technical and scientific progress made the coining of numerous new words inevitable, and from the 19th century onwards, popular patterns of word-formation became more and more accepted again.

Studies of French word-formation can build on an incomparable lexicographical basis. First and foremost, there is the magnificent *summa* of Gallo-Romance vocabulary constituted by Walther von Wartburg's *Französisches Etymologisches Wörterbuch* (*FEW*). The dictionaries of Godefroy and Tobler, Lommatzsch and Christmann cover the Old French period, for which Walker has provided a useful inverse dictionary. To these dictionaries we must add the still incomplete *Dictionnaire Étymologique de l'Ancien Français* (*DEAF*). The volumes corresponding to the letters G to K, published in print between 1974 and 2008, can be consulted online in the form of the *DEAF plus*, while the letter L is available only online as *DEAFpré*. Middle French is covered by the *Dictionnaire du Moyen Français* (*DMF*), an online dictionary whose articles can be searched in various ways, including by the beginning and end of words. Huguet (1925–1967), which is now also consultable online, is a dedicated dictionary in seven volumes for the 16th century, whose coverage, however, is far from complete (cf. Korfanty 1999). Among the Modern French dictionaries, we can only mention here the *Trésor de la langue française informatisé*, which concentrates on the 19th and 20th centuries and was originally published in print in 16 volumes from 1971 to 1994. The etymologies of the *Trésor*, many of which are of a disappointing quality, were partly updated in the project *TLF-étym*, whose results are also consultable online and contain important information concerning word-formation. Last but not least, specialized dictionaries of French dialects, popular French, as well as argot in all its manifestations constitute important complementary sources.

To these lexicographical sources, we may add a series of electronic text collections such as the *Base du Français Médiéval*, which contains 74 texts from the 9th to the 16th century, the *Anglo-Norman Online Hub*, a collection of 76 texts searchable by the beginning and end of words, the *Nouveau Corpus d'Amsterdam*, containing more than 3 million words of Old French, as well as *Frantext*, *Gallica* and Google Books for Modern French in general. For contemporary newspaper French, the CD-ROMs of *Le Monde* and similar corpora provide a valuable corpus.

Last but not least, commercial search engines as well as programs specifically designed for the needs of morphologists now permit including into morphological research all the treasures and trash that can be found on the world wide web.

2 General overview

In sharp contrast with the lexicographic and textual landscape outlined in the last section, the panorama concerning historical French word-formation still leaves a lot to be desired. The only handbooks, Nyrop (1936 [1908]) and Meyer-Lübke (1966 [1921]), were both published before French historical and etymological lexicography started flourishing. Though remarkable achievements a hundred years ago, they no longer reflect the current state of the art in etymology and word-formation (cf. the substantial reviews by Höfler 1967, Bork 1968 and Jänicke 1969 of Piel's 1966 revision of Meyer-Lübke's manual). The great progress that can be made in the historical study of French word-formation by systematically taking into account the *FEW* and the other lexicographic and textual sources mentioned in the last section has been demonstrated by monographs such as Baldinger (1950), Lindemann (1977), Bierbach (1982) or Burdy (2013). Many more such monographs will be needed in order to gain a solid basis on which a future manual of historical French word-formation can be based. The present sketch, of course, cannot fulfill such a task. It must limit itself to the more frequent patterns and to a brief overview of the principal changes observable from Old French to Modern French. The material will be arranged according to the general scheme adopted in this handbook, rather than chronologically, in order to avoid unnecessary repetition. At the same time, the article is intended to serve as a guide to the scattered literature on the history of French word-formation, especially to work published after Piel's 1966 bibliographical additions to Meyer-Lübke's manual (for a complete, annotated bibliography of the literature that appeared between 1875 and 1950, cf. Schpak-Dolt 2003).

3 Composition

Composition played a marginal role in Old French, but has gained in importance in Modern French. We will concentrate here on composition proper, i.e. patterns whose structure differs from that of syntactic phrases. So-called "syntagmatic compounds" – the *juxtaposés* (and *locutions par juxtaposition*) of Darmesteter (1894: 21–88) – can be mentioned only in passing. Old French expressions of the type *ostel Dieu* 'pilgrim hostel; lit. hostel God.OBL' look like noun-noun compounds from a present perspective, but in reality were syntactic combinations of a noun followed by a noun in the oblique case. Some of them have survived as fossils in Modern French, e.g., *Hôtel-Dieu* itself or *bain-marie* 'water bath; lit. bath Mary.OBL', as well as in many place names. The productive way of forming syntagmatic noun compounds in Modern French consists in combining the head noun with either an adjective or a prepositional phrase. The latter is normally introduced by *de* (e.g., *champ de bataille* 'battlefield; lit. field PREP battle') or *à* (e.g., *moulin à vent* 'windmill; lit. mill PREP wind'), but other prepositions can also be found. Adjectives can be pre- or postposed, following the rules of ordinary syntax obtaining when the compound was coined. In Old French, for example, even relational adjectives could still be preposed (e.g., *champel bataille* 'pitched battle; lit. field-REL battle'), an option that is no longer available in Modern French. The exocentric use of syntagmatic noun compounds, as in *Casque bleu* 'Blue Helmet', has been in use since Old French (e.g., OFr. *corsaint* 'Eucharist; lit. body holy'). While syntagmatic compounding has always been amply used with nouns and, in the older language also with particle verbs (cf. section 4.1), in the other parts of speech we have to do mostly with isolated univerbations that did not give rise to really productive word-formation patterns (cf., for example, adverbs such as OFr. *altrier* 'the day before yesterday; lit. other-yesterday', OFr. *tosdis* 'every day; lit. all days', which survives in the Picard dialect, *beaucoup* 'much; lit. nice stroke', etc.).

3.1 Nominal compounds

The most productive pattern of compounding in present-day French is constituted by left-headed noun-noun compounds, which may have coordinative (e.g., *boulangerie-pâtisserie* 'bread and cake shop; lit. bakery-cake shop') or subordinative (e.g., *pause-café* 'coffee break') semantics. Coordinative compounds go back to appositions (cf. Moliere's *bourgeois gentilhomme* 'bourgeois gentleman'), while subordinative compounds, whose number and semantic versatility has sharply increased during the last decades, have a variety of sources and should not be attributed exclusively to Anglo-Saxon influence (cf. Arnaud 2003). Old French also had a marginal pattern of right-headed noun-noun compounds (e.g., *banlieue* 'area of one mile (*lieue*) around a town where exclusive rights (*droit de ban*) prevailed', surviving in the sense of 'suburb'), which however disappeared in the further evolution of the language.

Already in Old French, verb-noun compounds (cf. Bierbach 1982) could refer to persons (e.g., *torche-pot* 'apprentice cook; lit. wipe-pot'), objects (e.g., *couvre-chef* 'headgear; lit. cover-head') and actions (e.g., OFr. *torneboele* 'somersault, tumble; lit. turn-guts'), as well as to toponyms (e.g., *Chanteraine* 'place where frogs quack; lit. quack-frog'). Of these types, instrument nouns have witnessed a great increase in productivity since the 18th century, while action nouns have always remained a rather rare phenomenon. Some verb-adverb compounds can already be found in Old French (e.g., *faitart* 'dawdler; lit. make-late'), but this type has always remained marginal.

The same is true for nominal verb-verb compounds (e.g., OFr. *dorme-veille* 'light sleep; lit. sleep-be awake', OFr. *saquebote* 'a kind of lance; lit. throw-push', OFr. *wirewire* 'weather cock; lit. turn-turn').

Adverb/preposition-noun compounds also reach back to Old French times: *avant-bras* 'forearm', *arriere-garde* 'reargarde', *entremain* 'a piece of armour; lit. between-hand', *forborc* 'suburb' (← *fors* 'outside' + *borc* 'town'), *sorcot* 'overcoat', etc. While such combinations are best considered as compounds from an Old French perspective, some patterns have become prefixal over time (cf. Amiot 2015).

3.2 Adjectival compounds

Adjective-adjective compounds are well represented in Modern French. Two types have to be distinguished, following Hatcher (1951). The adjectival pattern *aigre-doux* 'bittersweet' was introduced in the 16th century by the poets of the Pléiade, in imitation of Greek or Latin models. The pattern *ethico-moral*, on the contrary, first appears in 1635 in the combination *physico-mathématique* 'physico-mathematical', a *calque* of Neo-Latin *physico-mathematicus*. In Neo-Latin, the first member was generally an adjective in *-us*, while in the case of adjectives in *-is* the corresponding noun stem was used as a substitute, as in *sterno-thyroideus* (← *stern(um)*, instead of *sternalis*). French has adopted this habit in languages for specific purposes (cf. *sterno-thyroïdien*), but adjectives corresponding to Latin adjectives in *-is* now also tolerate the linking vowel *-o-* in French (e.g., *intellectualo-professoral*), because the distinction between the two Latin adjective classes has disappeared (Italian, which has maintained the distinction, does not allow such combinations).

Adverb-adjective compounds such as *clairvoyant* 'clear-sighted' or *nouveau-né* 'newborn' were syntagmatic compounds in Old French, when the adverb could still be placed in front of the verb in syntax. Since this syntactic option has disappeared in the meantime, they should be classified as compounds proper from a Modern French perspective. But this pattern has never become really productive.

The adjectival use of verb-noun compounds (cf. Bierbach 1982) is already occasionally attested in Old French (e.g., (*couteau*) *taillepain* 'bread knife; lit. (knife) cut-bread'), witnessed a spectacular, but momentary rise in the 16th century thanks to the poets of the Pléiade, and then has gained favour again from the 19th century onwards.

3.3 Verbal compounds

Noun-verb compounds of the type *maintenir* 'to maintain; lit. hand-hold' (< Lat. *manutenere*) are a negligible phenomenon in Modern French, but were still somewhat more important in Old French (cf. Klingebiel 1989): *clofermer* 'to nail; lit. nail-fix', *fervestir* 'to arm; lit. iron-dress', *orbatre* 'to hammer gold into gold leafs; lit. gold-beat', etc. Some isolated combinations of noun + participle such as OFr. *arcgetant* 'Sagittarius; lit. bow-throwing' or OFr. *champcheu* 'defeated; lit. field-fallen' probably are also best classified here. Among adverb-verb compounds, only those with *mal* showed some productivity (e.g., OFr. *malparler* 'to speak ill of; lit. ill-speak'; cf. also section 4.1). Adjective-verb compounds are no longer in use and seem to have been extremely rare also in Old French (e.g., *quiteclamer* 'to abandon; lit. free-declare').

3.4 Numeral compounds

Concerning cardinal numbers, the most notable aspect is the greater extension of the vigesimal system in Old and Middle French with respect to Modern French (cf. Reichenkron 1952). Since the 17th century, the only remnants have been the words from 70 to 99 (e.g., *quatre-vingt-dix-neuf* '99; lit. 4 × 20 + 19'). In Old and Middle French, we still find numbers such as *six vingts* '120; lit. 6 × 20' or *quinze vingts* '300; lit. 15 × 20' (the latter has survived as the name of a hospital). It must be noted that originally such combinations were syntagmatic compounds, i.e. *vingts* had the status of a noun, as the plural *-s* of *vingts* maintained in the orthography still indicates. A similar change from syntagmatic compounding to compounding proper can also be observed in additive cardinal numbers, which were linked with *et* 'and' until the 17th century (e.g., *vingt et trois* '23'). Today, numbers are joined asyndetically, except for the number '1' (e.g., *vingt-trois* '23' vs. *vingt-et-un* '21').

3.5 The integration of (Neo-)Latin compounds

Very few Latin patterns of composition have been handed down to French via popular transmission. However, Latin compounds were already borrowed again into Old French, most of them not fully transparent from the perspective of speakers of Old French without knowledge of Latin. Speakers of Old French could, for example, establish a relationship of identity between OFr. *mont* 'mountain' and the loanword *monticole* 'living in the mountains' (< Lat. *monticola*), or *ome* 'man' and *omicide* 'murder; murderer' (< Lat. *homicidium*; *homicida*), but *-cole* and *-cide* had no counterpart in the language. As Zwanenburg (1992) has pointed out, the same situation essentially obtained during the Middle French period. He tentatively identified the 18th century as the moment when the number of such compounds increased considerably. Though the number of compounds, most of which were taken over from Neo-Latin, steadily increased already during the 16th and 17th century, the corresponding patterns indeed were not applied to French bases before the 18th century: *-(o)manie* (< Lat. *-(o)mania*) in 1753 (*bureaumanie*; cf. Höfler 1972), *-(i)fère* (< Lat. *-(i)fer*) in 1786 (*gazifère*; cf. Rainer 2013), *-(i)forme* (< Lat. *-(i)formis*) in 1811 (*gazéiforme*; cf. Rainer 2009a). French formations such as *bureaumanie*, *gazifère* or *gazéiforme*, however, are not prototypical compounds from a French perspective: *-(o)manie*, it is true, can easily be identified with the independently occurring noun *manie* 'mania', but the relationship between adjectival *-(i)forme* and the noun *forme* 'form' is already somewhat indirect, and *-(i)fère* has no counterpart whatsoever, since the Latin verb *ferre* 'to bear' has been replaced by *porter* in French. In such cases it seems more appropriate to speak of a suffix in synchronic terms. The chronology just outlined also roughly applies to the case of coordinative adjectival compounds of the type *ethico-moral* (cf. section 3.2). Latin verbal compounds in *-(i)ficare* '-ify' have been borrowed since Old French times (e.g., 1190 *nidifier* 'to make a nest' < Lat. *nidificare*, relatable to *nid* 'nest'), but *-(i)fier* could never be identified with *faire* 'to make' and therefore qualifies as a suffix.

The standard scenario for the integration of foreign patterns of word-formation is as follows (see chapters VIII and IX in Müller et al. 2015–2016). In a first stage, compounds or derivatives are borrowed, in many cases along with the corresponding base word(s), which allows the receiving language to analyze them. In a second stage, the word-formation pattern abstracted from a series of loanwords is applied productively to foreign, and eventually even to native bases. This, however, is not the only kind of word-formation on a foreign basis. It can be observed that speakers of French (or any other European language, for that matter) with a profound knowledge of the classical languages sometimes also form new complex words by first creating in their mind a virtual word according to a word-formation pattern and lexical material of Greek or Latin and then adapt it to their native language phonologically and orthographically. This is how, for example, the French noun *mammifère* 'mammal' was formed at the end of the 18th century on the basis of a virtual Latin word *mammifer* (cf. Rainer 2007). By the same procedure, Bréal coined *polysémie* in 1887 on the basis of the virtual Ancient Greek word *polysêmía* ← *polýsêmos* 'with many meanings' (cf. *TLF-étym*, s. v.). This kind of word-formation, which scrupulously respects the patterns of the Classical languages must be distinguished from an assembly of roots or stems taken from the classical languages which violates the word-formation principles of these languages, as in the case of *microbe*, coined in 1878 by Sédillot. As Benveniste (1966) has pointed out, *mikró-bios* could never have meant 'small animal' in Ancient Greek.

4 Derivation

4.1 Prefixation

Nominal and adjectival prefixes were relatively rare in Old French in comparison with Modern French. Negation and intensification were the dominant categories. Among the negative prefixes we can mention *des-* (e.g., *desraison* 'unreasonableness', *despareil* 'dissimilar'; cf. Rothwell 1966), *mal-* (e.g., *malsage* 'unreasonable'), *mes-* (e.g., *meseur* 'misfortune', *mesacointe* 'ignorant' ← *acointe* 'familiar') and *non-*, which can also be analyzed as an adverb (e.g., *nonsavoir* 'ignorance' ← *savoir* 'knowledge', *nonsage* 'unwise'; note that there has been no continuity between OFr. *non-*, which soon disappeared, and the prefix *non-* that became popular in the 19th century; cf. Taylor 1976). The Latin negative prefix *in-* had disappeared from Proto-Romance and was only reestablished as a productive prefix in the 14th century on the basis of loanwords that began entering the language already in Old French. In Old French, Latin adjectives of the type *in-* + V + *-bilis* still used to be translated with a periphrasis (cf. Buridant 2010). Later on, *in-* split into two separate prefixes (cf. *irréalisable* vs. *inréalisable* 'unrealisable'; cf. Buchi 2012). Intensifying prefixes were *entre-* (e.g., *entrechenu* 'slightly hoary'), *oltre-* (e.g., *oltrevin* 'excellent wine'), *par-* (e.g., *parsome* 'total sum', *parnu* 'completely naked'), *re-* (e.g., *redisme* 'seconde tithe', *refol* 'completely mad'), *sor-* (e.g., *sorsome* 'excess load') and *tres-* (e.g., *tresaive* 'great-great-grandfather', *tres belle* 'very beautiful', also analyzable as an adverb). This category of intensification has undergone a substantial renewal in Middle and especially Modern French (cf. Guilbert and Dubois 1961; Widdig 1980; Amiot 2004) with the reintroduction of the Latin prefixes *extra-*, *super-* and *ultra-*, as well as the Greek prefixes *archi-*, *hyper-*, *mega-*, *micro-* and *macro-* (mostly via Neo-Latin). A prefix from a different semantic domain is *co-*, which appears in the 16th century as an imitation of Middle Latin models (cf. Väänänen 1979; e.g., 1500 *codétenteur* 'coholder').

One type of prefixation must be mentioned separately, viz. relational adjectives of the Latin type *extraordinarius*, whose analysis is still controversial. Formally, we seem to have to do with prefixation (*extra-* + *ordinarius*), but semantically a decomposition into *extraordin-* + *-arius* seems more adequate, which is why some scholars prefer analyzing them as "parasynthetic" (cf. Serrano-Dolader 2025). These adjectives had disappeared in Proto-Romance as a productive pattern, but already in Old French they appeared again in the form of isolated loan translations (e.g., *oltremarin* 'beyond the sea' < Lat. *ultramarinus*, *sosterin* 'subterranean' < Lat. *subterraneus*), giving rise to first timid imitations with native material (e.g., *ainsjornal* 'that is done before dawn; lit. before day-REL', *sorané* 'that has more than one year; lit. over year-REL'). However, it is only in modern French times that this pattern will reach its full productivity, especially in languages for special purposes (cf. Lüdtke 1995).

The system of v e r b a l p r e f i x a t i o n, on the contrary, though it had lost much of the remarkable flexibility of Latin "preverbs", was still more elaborate in Old French than it is in Modern French. In Latin, a verb (of motion) could freely be modulated by spatial preverbs, e.g., *ire* 'to go' → *abire* 'to go away', *inire* 'to go into', *exire* 'to go out', *subire* 'to go up', etc. This system had been reduced to inconspicuous remains in Old French (cf. *emplovoir*, *esduire*, *oltrenoier* in Table 19.1). The loss was partially compensated by the great expansion of particle verbs of the type OFr. *metre fors* 'to put outside' (cf. Buridant 1987). Particle verbs, however, dropped out of the language again at the end of the Middle French period, with few of them surviving in Modern standard French (more of them survived in the dialects).

It is out of question to describe the Old French situation in all its intricacies here, but Table 19.1 at least provides a rough idea. Those cases where the prefix was flanked by a preposition or an adverb – *contre-*, *entre-*, *for-*, *oltre-*, *sor-* and *sos-* – should probably better be classified as compounds from an Old French perspective in their literal use, but in their figurative uses they came close to real prefixes.

Old and Middle French prefixes have enjoyed much attention these last years. Among the more substantial studies, let us mention Buridant (1995), as well as Dufresne, Dupuis and Longtin (2001) and Martin (2001) on *a-*, Hamacher (2002) on *con-*, Martin (2006) on *dé(s)-*, Galli (2006) on *en-*, Tremblay (2008) and Nkollo (2013) on *entre-*, Aurnague and Plénat (2008) on *é-*, Librova (2010) on *re-*, Lebel (2009) on *par-* and Amiot (2015) on *sor-* and *sos-* (Modern *sur-* and *sous-*). One

Tab. 19.1: Old French verbal prefixes.

prefix	literal use	figurative use
a-	*porter* 'to carry' → *aporter* 'to bring'	*batre* 'to beat' → *abatre* 'to knock down'
con-	*batre* 'to beat' → *combatre* 'to fight with'	*pisser* 'to piss' → *compisser* '~ upon'
contre-	*batre* 'to fight' → *contrebatre* '~ against'	*loer* 'to let' → *contreloer* 'to sublet'
de-	*boter* 'to push' → *debater* '~ aside'	*batre* 'to beat' → *debatre* '~ severely'
des-	*clore* 'to close' → *desclore* 'to open'	
en-	*plovoir* 'to rain' → *emplovoir* '~ inside'	*hair* 'to hate' → *enhair* 'to start hating'
entre-	*boter* 'to hit' → *entreboter* 'to collide'	*oblier* 'to forget' → *entreoblier* '~ for a moment'
es-	*duire* 'to take' → *esduire* '~ outside'	*boillir* 'to boil' → *esboillir* 'to make ~'
for-	*geter* 'to throw' → *forgeter* '~ out'	*conter* 'to count' → *forconter* '~ wrongly'
mes-	*jugier* 'to judge' → *mesjugier* '~ badly'	
oltre-	*noer* 'to swim' → *oltrenoer* '~ across'	
par-	*abatre* 'to knock down' → *parabatre* '~ completely'	
por-	*aler* 'to go' → *poraler* '~ everywhere'	
re-	*cener* 'to dine' → *recener* '~ again'	*boter* 'to push' → *reboter* '~ back'
sor-	*aler* 'to go' → *soraler* '~ over'	*boivre* 'to drink' → *sorboivre* '~ too much'
sos-	*metre* 'to put' → *sosmetre* '~ under'	*entrer* 'to enter' → *sosentrer* '~ surreptitiously'
tres-	*aler* 'to go' → *tresaler* 'to go beyond'	*batre* 'to beat' → *tresbatre* '~ excessively'

question that has been discussed controversially is to what extent single prefixes have to be considered as polysemous, or can be reduced to a unitary abstract meaning. There is a general consensus, on the other hand, that some Old French prefixes had aspectual meanings which they lost in the Middle French period (cf. Buridant 2010: 46–47). Another phenomenon typical of Old French that disappeared in Middle French is the separability of the prefixes *par-* and *re-* (e.g., *la dame r-est forsissue* 'the lady went out again; lit. the lady again-is out gone').

The examples in Table 19.1 are all deverbal. It must be mentioned, however, that some of these prefixes could also be attached to adjectival and nominal bases, giving rise to so-called "parasynthetic" verbs. A verb such as OFr. *aviner* 'to supply the wine', for example, is derived from *vin* 'wine', and neither **avin* nor **viner* were Old French words. This kind of process, which goes back to Latin, has never ceased to be productive, especially with the prefixes *a-*, *dé(s)-* (e.g., OFr. *decerveler* 'to kill; lit. to take out the brains (*cervele*)') and *en-* (e.g., OFr. *enboser* 'to cover with dung (*bose*)'). The privative prefix *es-*, on the contrary, lost its productivity in Modern French (e.g., OFr. *esbraier* 'to clean' ← *brai* 'dirt').

4.2 Suffixation

The nominal suffixes of Old French have been treated from a synchronic perspective on the basis of homogeneous textual corpora by Sammet (1968), Diekmann (1969), Schmitz and Schmitz (1995), Middle French derivation by Lewicka (1960).

4.2.1 Nominal suffixes

Personal nouns can be deverbal or denominal, occasionally also deadjectival (e.g., *richard* 'rich person' ← *riche* 'rich'). Since Old French times, the central suffix for deriving deverbal agent nouns has been *-eur* (OFr. *-eor*). As long as the Old French two-case system subsisted, the nominative was *-ere* (< Lat. *-ator*), but eventually only the oblique form survived except for some irregular forms such as *peintre* 'painter' or *traître* 'traitor'. Many Latin nouns in *-ator* had not been transmitted to Old French, which is why in Old French translations these are often rendered with periphrases (cf. Buridant 2000: 16–17). The massive influx of Latinisms in the Middle French period not only expanded the stock of agent nouns in *-eur*, but led to the additional establishment of the learnèd variants *-ateur* and *-iteur*, which are chosen in Modern French when the corresponding action nouns end in *-ation* and *-ition*, two suffixes also borrowed from Latin in Middle French (e.g., *versificateur* 'verse-maker' ~ *versification* 'verse-making' vs. OFr. *versifieor*). The second important suffix producing agent nouns since Old French times has been *-ant*, a nominalized form of the Latin present participle *-ans*, *-antis* (e.g., *mendiant* 'beggar' ← *mendier* 'to beg'). The suffix *-ard* (cf. Peter 1951) was extracted in Old French times from German proper names like *Richard*, relatable to *riche* 'rich'. It is also used with verbal bases and distinguishes itself by its pejorative overtones (e.g., OFr. *faussart* 'traitor' ← *fausser* 'to deceive'; Mod. Fr. *chauffard* 'reckless driver', created by suffix substitution on the basis of *chauffeur* 'driver'). The suffix *-on* (< Lat. *-o*, *-onis*) retained some modest productivity in the older stages of the language (e.g., OFr. *preon* 'plunderer' ← *preer* 'to plunder'). In the realm of denominal personal nouns, the suffix *-ier* (< Lat. *-arius*) has remained productive until the present day (cf. Diekmann 1979; Roché 2006). Its learnèd counterpart, *-aire*, which we find already in the Old French loanword *libraire* 'librarian', relatable to *livre* 'book', became moderately productive in Modern French (e.g., *disquaire* 'record dealer' ← *disque* 'record'). The Latin suffix *-anus* had been transmitted as *-ain* and *-ien*. While the first one remained confined to a few words (e.g., *châtelain* 'lord of the manor (*château*)'), *-ien* became productive already in Old French (e.g., *artien* 'scholar' ← *art* 'liberal art'). It was also often used to adapt Latin personal nouns with no dedicated ending or with an ending different from *-anus* (e.g., OFr. *fisicien* 'doctor' ← *fisique* 'medicine' vs. Lat. *physicus*). The suffix *-iste* '-ist', already marginally present in Old French, witnessed a spectacular rise in Modern French under Neo-Latin influence, much like in other European languages. Old French also had a variant *-istre*, which is explained by Schweickard (1992) as the result of a contamination with personal nouns in *-tre* such as *traître* 'traitor', *apostre* 'apostle', and *ministre* 'minister'. The suffix *-eur* is fundamentally deverbal, but since Old French times we find a certain number of denominal derivatives such as *barbeor* 'barber' (← *barbe* 'beard'; Mod. Fr. *barbier*). The standard explanation for the rise of the denominal use resorts to reanalysis: according to this view, a word like *chasseur* 'hunter', derived from *chasser* 'to hunt', was directly related to the action noun *chasse* 'hunting', giving rise to a denominal pair of the type *chasse* → *chasseur*. Among the remaining personal suffixes, *-ard* is worth mentioning. It has become a truly productive suffix in French, distinguished from the other personal suffixes by its pejorative overtones (e.g., *trouillard* 'coward' ← *trouille* 'fear').

Feminization was expressed in Latin by conversion (*amicus* 'friend' → *amica* 'girl friend'), by affix substitution in the case of *-tor* → *-trix*, and, especially in Late Latin, by the suffix *-issa* of Greek provenance. Of these, the first process remained productive in French with certain endings, though in that language it is more appropriate to speak of the adjunction of a feminine suffix *-e* (cf. Melka and Zwanenburg 1993; e.g., OFr. *golpil, renard* 'fox' → *golpille, renarde* 'vixen'). The suffix *-trix* disappeared on the way to Old French, with the exception of a couple of words from the learnèd layer of vocabulary (e.g., *pecheor* 'sinner' → *pecheris*, which reflects Church Lat. *peccator* → *peccatrix*). The suffix *-issa*, on the contrary, continued its rise in Old French as *-esse* (e.g., *lion* 'lion' → *lionesse, duc* 'duke' → *duchesse*). Since it was often attached to agent nouns in *-ere*/*-eor* (e.g., *baleor* 'danser' → *balerece*), the sequence *-eresse* eventually became a suffixal variant that could also be attached to other nouns (e.g., *clerge* 'clergyman, scholar' → *clergesse, clergeresse*). This system, however, underwent a fundamental change in Middle French. According to Lindemann (1977: 172), the demise of the nouns in *-ere* in the 15th century brought about the demise of *-eresse* in the 16th century. It was replaced with *-euse* (e.g., *chanteur* 'singer' → *chanteuse*), originally the feminine form of the suffix *-eux*, in the core vocabulary, while with learnèd nouns in *-teur* the loan-suffix *-trice* stepped in (e.g., *provocateur* → *provocatrice*). This division of labor between *-euse* and *-trice* still obtains in Modern French, while *-eresse* only survived in a few relics (e.g., *chasseur* 'hunter' → *chasseresse*, a poetic word). In recent politically correct French, *-e* is recommended for nouns in *-eur* denoting higher professions (cf. Moreau and Botinelli 1999; e.g., *professeur* → *professeure*).

Denominal instrument nouns and nouns of artifacts have always been relatively rare (e.g., OFr. *banchier* 'blanket for covering a bench (*banc*)', OFr. *baviere* 'bib' ← *bave* 'dribble', OFr. *nasel* 'piece of armour covering the nose (*nes*)', *paillis* 'straw (*paille*) mattress'). Most instrument nouns are derived from the verb expressing the action performed with the instrument. The central suffix in Latin had been *-aculum* (cf. Tuttle 1975), which became *-ail*. It retained some modest productivity in Old French (e.g., *achopail* 'obstacle' ← *achoper* 'to collide'), but is unproductive in Modern French. It also existed in the feminine variant *-aille* (< Lat. *-acula*; e.g., OFr. *alumaille* 'what is used for lightening' ← *alumer* 'to light (fire)'). The instrumental suffix which dominated until the Industrial Revolution was *-oir* (< Lat. *-orium*), with a feminine variant *-oire* (< Lat. *-oria*): OFr. *escovoir* 'broom' (← *escover* 'to sweep'), OFr. *foloire* 'press' (← *foler* 'to press'), etc. An instrumental pattern that has also witnessed continuous productivity in French is the one ending in *-e* (e.g., *pince* 'pliers' ← *pincer* 'to pinch'), which can be considered as a case of conversion from a Modern French perspective, where the final *-e* is no longer pronounced. Since the Industrial Revolution, *-(at)eur* and *-euse* have dominated the scene: *condensateur* 'condenser', *batteuse* 'threshing machine' (← *battre* 'to thresh'), etc. This instrumental use of *-(at)eur* was due to borrowing (cf. *ventilateur* (1744) < Engl. *ventilator*) or to the ellipsis of the head noun and the concomitant conversion of the adjective in *-(at)eur* into a noun; in the case of *-euse*, this head noun was *machine*. The traditional semantic explanation as personification of instruments as agents must be rejected (cf. Rainer 2011). Instrument and place nouns in *-eor* can also be found in Old French (e.g., *mireor* 'mirror' ← *mirer* 'to look at', *parleor* 'parlor' ← *parler* 'to talk'), but these were regionalisms from dialects where Latin *-ator* and *-atorium* had been conflated as *-eor* (cf. Rainer 2005). By the end of Middle French they had disappeared in the process of standardization, being substituted by Parisian *-oir*. A further process for deriving instrument nouns that is productive in Modern French is the suffix *-et* (feminine variant: *-ette*), originally a diminutive suffix. First cases are already attested in Old French (e.g., *alumete*, a synonym of the derivative *alumaille* mentioned above; also *alumele*). They certainly arose through reanalysis: a word like *pincette* 'tweezers', a diminutive of *pince* 'pliers', could also plausibly be referred to the verb *pincer* 'to pinch' and hence reinterpreted as 'a small instrument for pinching'. A last, specifically French process is what Roché (1994) called "derivation by gender inversion" (cf. Roché 2002a). This process is available provided the base ends in a sequence that happens to be formally identical to a suffix of which there is both a masculine variant and a corresponding feminine variant in *-e*. Following this process, at the end of the 18th century the beheading machine invented by Guillotin was dubbed *guillotine*, and Montgolfier's balloon, *mongolfière*. The process seems to reach back to Middle French times, as *cocarde* 'cockade'

(16th c.; ← *cocard* 'vanitous person') and *cordelière* 'cord belt' (15th c.; ← *Cordelier* 'Fransciscan friar') suggest. It could even go back to Old French, if *béguin*, the headgear of the Beguines, where the masculine form is derived from a feminine base, is a case in point.

"Place noun" is a cover term for a range of denominal and deverbal derivatives referring to different kinds of places. Denominal place nouns referring to groves or plantations (cf. Tomassone and Combettes 1970) were formed with the suffixes *-oi* (< Lat. *-etum*) or its feminine counterpart *-oie* (< Lat. *-eta*) in Old French (e.g., *alnoi*, *alnoie* ← *alne* 'alder'). The feminine variant has survived into Modern French as *-aie*, or *-eraie*, whose interfix *-er-* was originally the tree suffix *-ier* (cf. Roché 2011). The suffix *-ier* (< Lat. *-arium*) and its feminine counterpart *-ière* (< Lat. *-aria*) have been productive since Old French times referring to different kinds of natural locations (e.g., *bourbier* 'mire' ← *bourbe* 'mud', OFr. *escailliere* 'slate quarry' ← *escaille* 'slate') or fields (e.g., OFr. *chanevier* 'hemp field' ← *chaneve* 'hemp', OFr. *faviere* 'field planted with broad beans' ← *feve* 'broad bean'), but also to dens (e.g., OFr. *lovier* 'wolf den' ← *lou* 'wolf', OFr. *coniliere* 'hare's den' ← *conil* 'hare') or receptacles (e.g., OFr. *aguillier* 'needle case' ← *aguille* 'needle', OFr. *leçonier* 'book containing lectures' ← *leçon* 'lecture'). The suffix *-ie*/*-erie* specialized in (work-)shops (e.g., OFr. *helmerie* 'helmet factory'), a meaning still very productive in Modern French, and stables (OFr. *boerie* 'ox stable' ← *buef* 'ox'), but also territories (e.g., OFr. *femenie* 'women's kingdom' ← *feme* 'woman', OFr. *gaianderie* 'giants' country' ← *gaiant* 'giant'). As one can see, the different suffixes have always tended to specialize in certain semantic niches, with little overlap among them. Deverbal place nouns denote a place by naming the typical activity associated with that place. The most important deverbal locative suffixes of French, *-oir* and *-oire*, also derive instrument nouns, as we have seen above, and the same syncretism also obtained for the Old French suffixes *-eor* (e.g., *ovreor* 'workshop' ← *ovrer* 'to work') and *-ail*/*-aille* (e.g., *degotail*, *-aille* 'gutter' ← *degoter* 'to drip'). This syncretism is quite widespread in the languages of the world (cf. Luschützky and Rainer 2013), but does not seem to be attributable, at least in most cases, to a semantic extension, as Meyer-Lübke once surmised. In the case of *-oir(e)*, it was the consequence of the ellipsis of an instrumental/locative head noun in the prehistory of Latin, while the syncretism of OFr. *-eor* was due to the homonymization of Lat. *-ator* and *-atorium*.

The category of action nouns has witnessed important changes not only from Latin to Old French, but also from Old to Modern French. The central Latin suffix, viz. *-io*, *-ionis*, was transmitted through the popular channel to Old French as *-aison* (among other forms). It retained some limited productivity in Old French, which, however, has waned on the way to Modern French (cf. Merk 1978; Burdy 2013). The central suffix of Old French, viz. *-ement* (< Lat. *-amentum*), has remained highly productive, but within a somewhat narrower scope (cf. Štichauer 2010). In part, its domain has been curtailed by the loan suffix *-ation* (Uth 2011: 262–271), introduced massively in Middle French (occasional loans such as *admiracion* were already used in the 12th century). The suffix *-ance* (< Lat. *-antia*; cf. François 1950) also suffered a retreat in Standard French in the 17th century, but regained the favour of literati in the 19th century and quite recently of journalists as a consequence of the borrowing of Engl. *governance*, which gave rise to *fumance* (← *fumer* 'to smoke') and similar jocular formations. Action nouns in *-e* (e.g., OFr. *adevine* f. 'foretelling' ← *adeviner* 'to foretell'), which go back to Latin conversions of the type *pugna* 'fight' (← *pugnare* 'to fight'), saw their productivity increase in Middle French, but eventually lost clout in the modern standard language. The suffix *-ëiz* (< Lat. *-aticium*; Malkiel 1986), which was also quite productive in Old French, has been reduced to inconspicuous remains (e.g., *clapotis* 'lapping' ← *clopoter* 'to lap'). The suffix *-age*, which shares with *-ëiz* the adjectival origin (< Lat. *-aticum*; on the nature of the semantic change, cf. the diverging views of Meyer-Lübke 1921: 62, Baldinger 1950: 152, Fleischman 1980 and Uth 2011: 216), has never ceased to be productive. A further French innovation was *-erie* (e.g., OFr. *baiserie* 'repeated kissing' ← *baisier* 'to kiss'), which originated from the reanalysis of abstract nouns in *-ie* derived from agent nouns in *-eor*. The suffix *-(e)ure* (< Lat. *-(at)ura*) of *ouverture* 'opening' (← *ouvrir* 'to open', past part. *ouvert*) has remained moderately productive throughout the history of French. The same seems to be true for action nouns which take the form of the feminine past participle, such as OFr. *choisie* 'choice' (← *choisir* 'to choose'; cf. Alsdorf-Bollée 1970: 150–162). The cognate suffix *-ade* (e.g., OFr. *balade* 'danse' ← *baler* 'to dance') is a loan suffix taken from Occitan and other southern Romance languages (cf. Gebhardt 1975). The English loan suffix *-ing* of *kidnapping*, etc. cannot yet be considered as fully integrated (cf. Söll 1968), despite a sizeable number of loan words. For conversion, cf. section 5. As in other languages, French action nouns can also express metonymically related notions such as result, instrument, place, etc.

Old French inherited most of its suffixes forming quality nouns from Latin. The suffixes *-ie* (< Lat. *-ía*; e.g., *courtoisie* 'courtesy' ← *courtois* 'courteous'), *-eur* (< Lat. *-or*; e.g., *grosseur* 'size' ← *gros* 'big, large') and *-esse* (< Lat. *-itia*; e.g., OFr. *altece* 'hight' ← *alt* 'high') enjoyed considerable productivity in Old French, but had lost it by the end of Middle French. The suffix *-ise* (cf. Breslin 1968–69), on the contrary, which also derived from *-itia*, has remained productive with adjectives ending in *-ard* (e.g., *roublardise* 'craftiness' ← *roublard* 'crafty'). Unstressed Latin *-ia* had also maintained some productivity in Old French as *-e* (cf. Zwanenburg 1997; e.g., *oisose* 'idleness' ← *oisos* 'idle'). But the most important suffix in Old French was *-té* (< Lat. *-tas*; e.g., *amerté* 'bitterness' ← *amer* 'bitter').

It retained its productivity until the end of Middle French, while in Modern French the loan suffix *-ité* prevailed, especially with the many Latinate adjectives (*stabilité* 'stability', for example, ousted OFr. *estableté*). Another loan suffix that came into the language in Middle French was *-itude* (< Lat. *-itudo*; e.g., *amplitude* 'id.'), whose traditional form *-tume* had always been marginal. In recent times, *-itude* has gained new vitality after the model of *négritude* 'id.' (cf. Bourquin 1979). In 2007, the coining of *bravitude* 'braveness' by presidential candidate Ségolène Royal sparked off a major debate about this suffix and gave rise to a host of jocular formations. A French innovation dating back to Old French times is *-erie* (e.g., *sauvagerie* 'savagery').

The main suffixes forming status nouns in Old French were *-é* (< Lat. *-atus*; e.g., *vevé* 'widowhood' ← *veve* 'widow') and its feminine variant *-ee* (e.g., *vevee*), *-ie* (< Lat. *-ía*; e.g., *senechalie* 'rank of a seneschal') and *-age* (e.g., *barnage* 'rank of a baron'), which comes from Lat. *-aticum*, though the nature of the semantic change involved is still disputed. The dominating suffix in Modern French is the learnèd suffix *-at* (< Lat. *-atus*) of *marquisat* 'rank of a marquis', etc. This kind of suffix has always given rise to locative, temporal and collective extensions.

As Baldinger (1950) has shown, Old and Middle French expanded the number of collective suffixes and derivatives considerably in comparison to Latin. But only two of these have remained moderately productive in Modern French, viz. *-aille* (e.g., *valetaille* 'menials' ← *valet* 'servant'), with pejorative overtones (cf. Aliquot-Suengas 1996), and *-erie* (e.g., *argenterie* 'silverware' ← *argent* 'silver'). Among the suffixes that became unproductive were *-age*, *-ain*, *-asse*, *-emente*, *-is* and *-ure*. We can also mention here the denumeral suffix *-aine* (e.g., *cinquantaine* 'a set of 50'), which was still applicable to more bases in the ancient language (e.g., OFr. *cinquaine* 'a set of 5').

Old French was fond of diminutive suffixes (cf. Golde 1929): *bastonet*, *bastoncel* 'small stick' (← *baston* 'stick'), *agnelin* 'lamb' (← *agnel* 'sheep'), *enfançon* 'small child' (← *enfant* 'child'), *pucelote* 'little girl' (← *pucele* 'girl'), *buschille* 'small log' (← *busche* 'log'), etc. Diminutive suffixes could also be combined into suffix chains such as *-el-et*, *-el-ot*, *-ill-on*, *-ot-in*, etc. The suffix *-at* was specialized in the designation of animal young (e.g., *cervat* 'fawn' ← *cerf* 'stag'). Augmentatives also existed in Old French, but remained comparatively rare: *tinas* 'big vat' (← *tine* 'vat'), etc. During the Middle French period evaluative suffixation began to decline. Though artificially boosted again by the poets of the Pléiade in the 16th century, it has eventually been relegated to popular and dialectal usage by the writers of the 17th century (cf. Eckert 1986: 284–318). In present-day French, only *-et*/*-ette* continues to be moderately productive as a notional diminutive, while evaluative diminution is expressed by the adjective *petit* 'little'. This demise of evaluative suffixation sets Modern French apart from most other Romance languages.

Most nominal suffixes fit into one of the derivational categories treated above, though many more marginal and isolated cases could be mentioned. Old French, for example, had an astonishing number of terms referring to all kinds of taxes, most of them formed with the suffix *-age* (e.g., OFr. *banchage* 'bench tax' ← *banc* 'bench'). Most of these terms disappeared with feudalism, one of the few extant examples being *péage* 'toll'. Suffixes that have remained at least moderately productive are the tree suffix *-ier* (e.g., OFr. *pomier* 'apple tree' ← *pome* 'apple'), the language suffix *-ois* (e.g., OFr. *sotois* 'language of fools' ← *sot* 'fool'; the Modern French form of the suffix is *-ais*) and the highly polysemous suffix *-ée* (e.g., OFr. *barilee* 'content of a barrel', *cornee* 'thrust with a bull's horn'). The suffix *-isme* witnessed a spectacular rise in Modern French, originally triggered by Neo-Latin, very much like in other European languages (cf. Roché 2007).

4.2.2 Adjectival suffixes

On the evolution of adjectival suffixation, a synthesis is available by Gawełko (1977). We will treat denominal, deverbal, deadjectival, deadverbial and denumeral derivatives in turn.

Denominal adjectives represent five main categories: relational, possessive, material, similative, and dispositional. Relational adjectives were certainly of less importance in Old French than in Latin, but nevertheless well represented (e.g., *evage* ← *eve* 'water', *boscain* ← *bos* 'wood', *lunal* ← *lune* 'moon', *champel* ← *champ* 'field', *corporien* ← *cors* 'body', *maisselier* ← *maissele* 'jaw', *clergil* ← *clerc* 'priest', *asnin* ← *asne* 'donkey', *cimatique* ← *cisme* 'schism'). Some of these suffixes disappeared, notably *-age*, while most of them strongly increased their productivity in Middle and Modern French under Latin influence. As regards *-ien*, it must be noted that it served as a means of adapting Latin words in *-eus* (e.g., *corporien* < Lat. *corporeus*), a suffix that had not survived in French (cf. Rainer 2009b; for other adaptive strategies, Thibault 1989). The relational use of *-iste* arose in Modern French through the adjectivization of the corresponding nouns. Forms reflecting the Latin genitive plural (e.g., *diablor* 'of (the) devils', *porcor* 'of (the) pigs') could also serve the function of relational adjectives in Old French. A special group of relational suffixes are the ones forming ethnic adjectives and nouns (cf. Wolf 1964). These were not much used in Old French (e.g., *chartrain* ← *Chartres*, *vianeis* ← *Vienne*, *provenisien* ← *Provins*, *parisin*, *parisis* ← *Paris*), but their use has increased steadily, especially since the 19th century, reaching some 10,000 items in present-day French (cf. Eggert 2005). The suffix *-eis* of Germanic origin (< *-isc*; e.g., *angleis* 'English') eventually fused with the *-eis* that continued Lat. *-ensis*, which is why the feminine form *-esche* (< *-iska*) dropped out of the language. The Old French suffix *-enc*, of Germanic origin, was replaced early on by *-and* and *-ain* (e.g., *flamenc* 'Flemish' > *flamand*, *loherenc* 'from Lorraine' > *lorrain*). The Old French suffix *-erez* (< Lat. *-aricius*; *truanderez* 'of crooks' ← *truand* 'crook') was also doomed. The history of adjectives derived from names of persons was similar: very rare in Old French (e.g., *jacobin* ← *Jacop*, *mahometique* ← *Mahomet*), with Middle French adding a substantial number of Latin loanwords such as *cicéronien* (← *Cicéron*) or *homérique* (← *Homère*), these suffixes were first added to native proper names in the 18th century (e.g., *racinien* ← *Racine*) and are now omnipresent in written French (e.g., *Chirac* → *chiraquien*). The main possessive suffixes have remained the same since Old French (e.g., OFr. *bavos* = Mod. Fr. *baveux* 'dribbling' ← *bave* 'dribble', OFr. *coé* 'with a tail' ← *coe* 'tail', *barbu* 'bearded' ← *barbe* 'beard'). As far as adjectives of resemblance are concerned, the same can be said of *-os*/*-eux* (e.g., OFr. *cendros* 'ashen' ← *cendre* 'ash'), but many other suffixes have secondary similative uses. The suffix *-esque* (cf. Malkiel 1972) was borrowed from Italian in the Renaissance (*chevaleresque* 'knightly' < it. *cavalleresco*). Material adjectives (cf. Ozolina 2013) were well represented in Old French (e.g., *acerin* 'made of steel' ← *acier* 'steel'), but have been ousted by prepositional phrases since Middle French times. Disposition has been expressed since Old French times by *-ier*, an extremely versatile suffix (cf. Roché 2006), or *-eux* (e.g., OFr. *mençongier*, *mençongeus* 'deceitful' ← *mençonge* 'lie').

In the domain of deverbal adjectives, Old French differed quite substantially from the modern language. The importance of the central active suffix of Old French, viz. *-eus* (e.g., *degabeus* 'mocking') declined in Middle French. Adjectives in *-able* were also mainly used with an active meaning in Old French (e.g., *muable* 'changing' ← *muer* 'to change'), but in Middle French the meaning of passive potentiality ('that can be Ved') was restored under the influence of Latin, while the active use was marginalized (cf. Thorné Hammar 1942). The central active suffix of Modern French, viz. *-(at)eur*, on the contrary, was still rare in the older stages of the language. The second most important suffix, viz. *-ant* (cf. Graff 1918), the descendant of the Latin present participle, has been available since Old French (e.g., *atraiant* 'attractive') but has increased in importance over time. The suffix *-ard* (e.g., OFr. *cuidart* 'credulous' ← *cuider* 'to believe'), of Germanic origin, has always distinguished itself by its pejorative connotations. Two active suffixes which started an important career in Middle French were *-(at)if* and *-(at)oire*, which established themselves as a result of the massive borrowing of Latin adjectives in *-(at)ivus* and *-(at)orius*. Since these loanwords were normally flanked by the corresponding loanwords in *-(at)io*, many of them have been reanalyzed as denominal (e.g., *agressif*/*agression*). The non-learnèd suffix *-if* of Old French (e.g., *aidif* 'helping'), on the contrary, declined. As far as passive meaning is concerned, the rise of *-able*/*-ible* in Middle French corresponded to the decline of OFr. *-(e)is* (< Lat. *-(at)icius*; e.g., *bateis* 'that is to be beaten' ← *batre* 'to beat', *fentis* 'split' ← *fendre* 'to split').

Deadjectival adjectives either express evaluative nuances or intensification. Diminutive suffixes were readily attached also to adjectival bases in Old French, expressing some kind of attenuation (e.g., *bloet* 'bluish' ← *blo* 'blue', *camusot* 'a bit snub' ← *camus* 'snub', *fauvel* 'fawnish' ← *fauve* 'fawn', *grandin* 'a bit big' ← *grant* 'big', *lordas* 'stupid' ← *lort* 'oaf'). Deadjectival evaluative suffixation suffered the same dire fate in Modern French as in the nominal domain (cf. section 4.2.1). In Middle French, the suffix *-âtre* took over the task of designating approximation with colour adjectives (e.g., *rougeâtre* 'reddish'), while with other bases it has a more distinctly pejorative meaning (e.g., *bellâtre* 'dandy' ← *beau* 'handsome'). The comparative suffix *-(i)or* (< Lat. *-ior*) was still present in a dozen words in Old French (e.g., *forçor* 'stronger' ← *fort* 'strong'), while it has disappeared as a suffix in Modern French (in *meilleur* 'better' it is no longer recognizable, let alone in *pire* 'worse'). The same is true of the Latin superlative suffix *-issimus* which occurred as an elative suffix in a dozen adjectives of Old French (e.g., *altisme* 'very high', *fortisme* 'very strong'). Middle French saw occasional Latinisms in *-issime* (e.g., *vaillantissime*, 1308), and in the 16th century great efforts were made to adapt Italian *-issimo* as *-issime*, but in the end only a few words have been retained in Standard French (e.g., *richissime* 'very rich'). In the last decades, however, the suffix has gained wider popularity again.

Old French also had a sizeable number of deadverbial adjectives in *-ain* (e.g., *arierain* 'rear' ← *ariere* 'backwards') which have disappeared from the modern language.

Denumeral adjectives were already well developed in Old French. For the formation of ordinal numbers, the suffix *-ième* (e.g., OFr. *noviesme* 'ninth') has survived into Modern French, while *-ain* fell out of use in this function.

4.2.3 Verbal suffixes

Among the verbal suffixes OFr. *-oier* (< Lat. *-idiare*; e.g., *cortoier* 'to live at the court', *grossoier* 'to become big (*gros*)') lost its productivity, while the Latinate suffixes *-iser* '-ize' and *-ifier* '-ify', though not completely unknown to Old French, began a great career in Middle French. Beside these denominal and deadjectival suffixes, French has had since Old French times half a dozen of evaluative suffixes – *-eler, -eter, -iller, -iner, -oter* –, linked to the corresponding denominal/deadjectival diminutive suffixes. On the more intricate case of *-ouiller*, cf. Roché (2002b).

4.2.4 Adverbial suffixes

Since Latin adjectives of the type *fortis* 'strong' still had the same form in the masculine and feminine gender (*fort*) in Old French, one might be misled to think from a modern perspective that the corresponding adverb in *-ment* was derived from the masculine stem form (e.g., OFr. *forment* ← *fort*). In some of the cases where the adjective later developed an analogical feminine form in *-e*, the adverb has been derived again on the basis of this feminine form (e.g., Mod. Fr. *forte-ment*), but some of the older derivatives have survived into Modern French as fossils (e.g., *élégamment* 'elegantly' vs. fem. *élégante*).

5 Conversion

Conversion has been an important process in French since Old French times.

Verbs can be derived by conversion from nouns (e.g., OFr. *bateler* 'to ship' ← *batel* 'ship') and adjectives (e.g., OFr. *foler* 'to drive or become mad (*fol*)'). The conjugation in *-ir* was still more productive in Old French than it is nowadays. In some cases palatalization accompanies conversion (e.g., *estrecier* 'to tighten' ← *estreit* 'tight'; cf. Walsh 1983), but this kind of formation had lost its productivity already in Old French. When conversion is combined with prefixation, it is customary to speak of "parasynthesis" (e.g., OFr. *aculvertir* 'to turn into a serf (*cul-vert*)', OFr. *afoletir* 'to drive mad (*folet*)'); cf. Serrano-Dolader (2025).

Nouns have always been formed by conversion in various ways. The action-noun pattern represented by OFr. *abri* m. 'sheltering' (← *abrier* 'to shelter') gave way in Middle French to those with the feminine suffix *-e* and to the learnèd suffix *-ation*. Some such formations, however, still linger around in the modern language (e.g., *abri* itself). Old and Middle French furthermore had the possibility to freely nominalize the infinitive, a possibility that was sharply reduced in the 17th century, but witnessed a new upswing in the literary register in the 20th century (cf. Buridant 2008). Adjectives can be turned into abstract nouns (e.g., *sérieux* 'serious' → 'seriousness', *préparatifs* 'preparative-PL' → 'preparations'), but also into nouns designating persons or things (e.g., *rouge* 'red' → 'communist; rouge'). In cases such as *rouge* 'red wine' it is preferable to speak of ellipsis (in the case at hand, of *vin* 'wine'). The intricacies of these kinds of conversion during the history of French have been analyzed by Malkiel (1938).

Nouns characterizing persons have been converted into adjectives since Latin times (e.g., OFr. *mastin* 'big dog' > 'servile'), but it is unclear to what extent such shifts are individual lexical changes or the result of a pattern of word-formation. Relational nouns have also occasionally been formed by conversion if the base noun ends in a sequence that is homonymous with a relational adjective (e.g., *Mazarin* → (*Bibliothèque*) *Mazarine* 'founded by Mazarin').

Last but not least, adjectives can be used as adverbs without formal change: *parler haut et clair* 'to speak loud and clear', etc., a possibility that was used more widely in the older stages of the language (cf. Hummel 2010). Lower varieties of French have retained some of this flexibility (e.g., *il faut trois heures facile* 'it takes you at least three hours').

6 Minor processes

Apart from the classical processes of word-formation treated in sections 3 to 5, French, to a more limited extent, also has recourse to the processes of backformation, reduplication, blending, clipping, and word-creation.

The point of departure of backformation is constituted by a word that is interpretable as morphologically complex but lacks a base from a synchronic point of view. In the process of backformation, this missing base is reconstructed by the speaker. The cases where we can be most confident of having to do with backformation are those where the backformed word is formally different from its Latin equivalent, e.g., *agresser* 'to aggress' (vs. Lat. *aggredi*), derived from *agression* 'aggression' in the 14th century. Most backformations are based on deverbal derivatives, but cf. also *mahom* 'Muhammad' (12th c.) ← *Mahomet*, whose ending *-et* was misinterpreted as a diminutive suffix, or *melancole* 'melancholic' (1318) ← *melancolie* 'melancholia'. In contemporary French, an important source for backformation is constituted by complex words that have undergone reanalysis. Namer (2012), for example, has shown that complex verbs consisting of a combining form and a verb, such as *thermocoller* 'to fuse', *prima facie* consisting of *thermo-* and *coller* 'to glue, bond', are not derived by adjoining the combining form directly to the verb, but through backformation from nouns whose second member is a deverbal noun, such as *thermocollage* 'fusing', regularly derivable by adjoining the combining form to the noun *collage* 'gluing, bonding'.

French is the only Romance language with a productive pattern of partial reduplication: *guerre* 'war' → *guéguerre* 'squabble', *bête* 'silly' → *bébête* 'dull', *dormir* 'to sleep' → *dodo* 'id.' (baby talk), etc. This pattern arose when people started imitating reduplicated words typical of the language of small children, attaching to them hypocoristic connotations typical of child-directed speech, but absent from the children's own language. The first attestations of this kind of hypocoristic/diminutive reduplication reach back to the final stage of Middle French (cf. Rainer 1998).

Blending is a potentially universal technique, but its massive use in French is a quite recent phenomenon, essentially of the second half of the 20th century, probably boosted by Anglo-American influence. The oldest example we have been able to find is *Moriant* (13th c.; Godefroy 1888) 'land of the Moors', a blend of *Maure* 'Moor' and *orient* 'Orient'. The conscious use of blending in word games can be traced back at least to François Rabelais (ca. 1494–1553), who famously called the professors and students of the Sorbonne *sorbonnagres*, a blend of *Sorbonne* and *onagre* 'donkey'.

The history of clipping resembles that of blending. Isolated instances can be found at all times, but its massive use seems to be relatively recent. From Old French, we only know of some cases of apheresis: *fançon* 'infant' ← *enfançon*, *gin* 'engine of war' ← *engin*. According to Kjellman (1920: 6), clipping by apocope, which is so popular nowadays in colloquial French, originated in the first half of the 19th century, when words such as *mac* 'pimp' (← *maquereau*) or *à perpète* 'for life' (← *à perpétuité*) are first documented in argot. In the second half of the 19th century this kind of clipping rapidly spread to ever wider social groups, eventually becoming part of the colloquial language of educated speakers, who nowadays not only prefer *vélo* 'bicycle' to *vélocipède*, but also *sympa* 'nice' to *sympatique* or *clim* 'air condition' to *climatisation*. The rise of abbreviations of the type *SNCF* /ɛsɛnseɛf/, shorthand for *Société Nationale des Chemins de Fer*, or *ONU* /ony/, shorthand for *Organisation des Nations Unies*, which is also traceable to the second half of the 19th century, is attributed by Kjellman (1920: 78) to Anglo-Saxon influence.

As cases of word-creation we could classify techniques, typical of French argot, that change the shape of words, rendering them difficult to identify for outsiders (cf. Guiraud 1956: 66–70). The *largonji*, used throughout the 19th century, consisted in substituting the first consonant by /l/ and adding it at the end of the word: *jargon* → *largonji* (*-ji* /ʒi/ is the name of the letter <j> in French), etc. A more complex form of this code is the *loucherbem*, originally practiced by the butchers of La Villette, where additionally a suffix was added: *boucher* 'butcher' → *loucherbem*, etc. These two codes are believed to have been imported from East Asia. They are no longer in use, but some lexicalized words have remained part of argot in the 20th century. A code of the 20th century, as it seems, is the *javanais*, which consists in the insertion of *-av-*: *non* 'no' → *navon*, etc. There is also a variant with *-ag-*: *moustaches* 'id.' → *moustagaches*, etc. (Guiraud says that he never encountered this variant, but it is well represented, for example, in the novels of A. Boudard.) The most popular code nowadays is the *verlan*, a kind of backward speaking (details are quite intricate): *(à) l'envers* 'backwards' → *verlan*, etc. First examples of *verlan* from argot reach back to the beginning of the 19th century, but only in the second half of the 20th century did it gain wider popularity.

A closely related phenomenon of French slang is what Guiraud (1956: 70–74) calls "parasitic suffixation" (*suffixation parasitaire*), i.e. the use of all kinds of endings to change the form of words: *américain* 'American' → *amerlot*, *chinois* 'Chinese' → *chinetoque*, *crasseux* 'dirty' → *craspec*, *sourd* 'deaf' → *sourdingue*, *poulet* 'policeman' → *poulaga*, *fort* 'strong' → *fortiche*, *valise* 'suitcase' → *valoche*, *dollar* → *dolluche*, etc. This kind of playful deformation, which is very widespread nowadays, reaches back to the Middle Ages. The origin of these suffixes is different in each case. The *-o* of *métallo* (← *métallurgiste* 'steel worker') and similar formations, which has been highly productive since the 19th century, is eventually traced back by Heinimann (1953) and Prigniel (1966) to the diminutive suffix *-ot* of *Margot* (← *Marguerite*) and similar words. Wolf (1969) has argued convincingly that the suffixes *-iche*, *-oche* and *-uche* do not descend from Latin suffixes, as had been claimed a hundred years ago. Baldinger (1997), for example, has shown that the suffix *-uche* is of dialectal origin and has been recycled as a parasitic suffix from the 18th century onwards. The suffix *-zingue* of *pompezingue* 'firefighter' (← *pompier*), attested from the middle of the 18th century, is interpreted in Baldinger (1995) as a variant of the suffix *-ingue*.

7 References

Aliquot-Suengas, Sophie (1996): Référence collective / sens collectif. La notion de collectif à travers les noms suffixes du lexique français. Ph.D. dissertation, Université de Lille III.

Alsdorf-Bollée, Annegret (1970): *Die lateinischen Verbalabstrakta der* u-*Deklination und ihre Umbildungen im Romanischen*. Bonn: Romanisches Seminar der Universität Bonn.

Amiot, Dany (2004): Haut degré et préfixation. In: Florence Lefeuvre and Michèle Noailly (eds.), *Intensité, comparaison, degree*, 91–104. Rennes: Presses Universitaires de Rennes.

Amiot, Dany (2015): The grammaticalization of prepositions in French word-formation. In: Peter O. Müller, Ingeborg Ohnheiser, Susan Olsen and Franz Rainer (eds.), *Word-Formation. An International Handbook of the Languages of Europe*. Vol. 3, 1811–1824. Berlin/Boston: De Gruyter Mouton.

Amiot, Dany (2020a) : Chapitre 29. Morphologie dérivationnelle vs. flexionnelle. In: Christiane Marchello-Nizia, Bernard Combettes, Sophie Prévost and Tobias Scheer (eds.), *Grande grammaire historique du français*. Vol. 1, 622–631. Berlin/Boston: De Gruyter Mouton.

Amiot, Dany (2020b) : Chapitre 48. Procédés morphologiques de création lexicale. In: Christiane Marchello-Nizia, Bernard Combettes, Sophie Prévost and Tobias Scheer (eds.), *Grande grammaire historique du français*. Vol. 2, 1894–1927. Berlin/Boston: De Gruyter Mouton.

Arnaud, Pierre J. L. (2003): *Les composés* timbre-poste. Lyon: Presses Universitaires de Lyon.
Aurnague, Michel and Marc Plénat (2008): Sémantique de l'espace et morphologie: Le cas de la préfixation en *é-*. *Bulletin de la Société de Linguistique de Paris* 103: 201–236.
Baldinger, Kurt (1950): *Kollektivsuffix und Kollektivbegriff. Ein Beitrag zur Bedeutungslehre im Französischen mit Berücksichtigung der Mundarten*. Berlin: Akademie Verlag.
Baldinger, Kurt (1995): Das Argotsuffix *-zingue*. In: Ulrich Hoinkes (ed.), *Panorama der Lexikalischen Semantik. Thematische Festschrift aus Anlaß des 60. Geburtstags von Horst Geckeler*, 65–75. Tübingen: Narr.
Baldinger, Kurt (1997): Das Suffix *-uche* in der Volkssprache und im Argot. In: Günter Holtus, Johannes Kramer and Wolfgang Schweickard (eds.), *Italica et Romanica. Festschrift für Max Pfister zum 65. Geburtstag*, 115–147. Tübingen: Niemeyer.
Benveniste, Émile (1966): Formes nouvelles de la composition nominale. *Bulletin de la Société de Linguistique de Paris* 61: 90–95.
Bierbach, Mechtild (1982): *Die Verbindung von Verbal- und Nominalelement im Französischen*. Tübingen: Narr.
Bork, Hans Dieter (1968): Review of Meyer-Lübke (1966 [1921]). *Romanische Forschungen* 80: 421–439.
Bourquin, Jacques (1979): Remarques sur la formation néologique récente de substantifs en *-itude* dérivés ou non. In: Rosine Adda (ed.), *Néologie et lexicologie. Hommage à Louis Guilbert*, 47–66. Paris: Larousse.
Breslin, Margret Sinclair (1968–69): The Old French abstract suffix *-ise*: Studies in its rise, internal diffusion, external spread, and retrenchment. *Romance Philology* 22: 408–420.
Büchi, Eva (2012): *Réel, irréel, inréel*: Depuis quand le français connaît-il deux préfixes négatifs *in-*? In: Mario Barra-Jover, Guylaine Brun-Trigaud, Jean-Philippe Dalbera, Patrick Sauzet and Tobias Scheer (eds.), *Études de linguistique gallo-romane*, 325–340. Saint-Denis: Presses Universitaires de Vincennes.
Burdy, Philipp (2013): *Die mittels* -aison *und Varianten gebildeten Nomina des Französischen. Eine Studie zur diachronen Wortbildung*. Frankfurt/M.: Klostermann.
Buridant, Claude (1987): Les particules séparées en ancien français. In: Claude Buridant (ed.), *Romanistique – germanistique. Une confrontation. Actes du colloque de Strasbourg, 23–24 mars 1984*, 166–204. Strasbourg: Presses de l'Université de Strasbourg.
Buridant, Claude (1995): Les préverbes en ancien français. In: André Rousseau (ed.), *Les préverbes dans les langues d'Europe. Introduction à l'étude de la préverbation*, 287–323. Villeneuve d'Ascq: Presses Universitaires du Septentrion.
Buridant, Claude (2000): Prolégomènes à une étude synthétique de la morphologie dérivationnelle en ancien français. *L'information grammaticale* 86: 14–20.
Buridant, Claude (2008): *La substantivation de l'infinitif en français. Étude historique*. Paris: Champion.
Buridant, Claude (2010): La morphologie dérivationnelle dans l'ancienne langue française: Esquisse d'un panorama. In: Peter Blumenthal and Salah Mejri (eds.), *Les configurations du sens*, 27–57. Stuttgart: Steiner.
Darmesteter, Arsène (1894 [1874]): *Traité de la formation des mots composés dans la langue française comparée aux autres langues romanes et au latin*. 2nd ed. Paris: Bouillon.
Diekmann, Erwin (1969): *Die Substantivbildung mit Suffixen in den Fabliaux*. Tübingen: Niemeyer.
Diekmann, Erwin (1979): Zu frz. *-ier*. In: Manfred Höfler, Henri Vernay and Lothar Wolf (eds.), *Festschrift Kurt Baldinger zum 60. Geburtstag*, 375–391. Tübingen: Niemeyer.
Dufresne, Monique, Fernande Dupuis and Catherine Marie Longtin (2001): Un changement dans la diachronie du français: La perte de la préfixation aspectuelle en *a-*. *Revue québécoise de linguistique* 29: 33–54.

Dufresne, Monique, Fernande Dupuis and Mireille Tremblay (2003): Preverbs and particles in Old French. In: Geert Booij and Jaap van Marle (eds.), *Yearbook of Morphology 2003*, 33–60. Dordrecht: Kluwer.

Dugas, Edwige (2016) : Non- dans le paradigme des préfixes de négation en français: étude synchronique et diachronique. Thèse de doctorat, Lille, Université de Lille 3.

Eckert, Gabriele (1986): *Sprachtypus und Geschichte. Untersuchungen zum typologischen Wandel des Französischen.* Tübingen: Narr.

Eggert, Elmar (2005): *Bisontins ou Besançonnais? À la recherche des règles pour la formation des gentilés pour une application au traitement automatique*. Tübingen: Narr.

Fleischman, Suzanne (1980): The French suffix *-age*. Its genesis, internal growth, and diffusion. Ph.D. dissertation, Ann Arbor, MI: UMI.

François, Alexis (1950): *La désinence "ance" dans le vocabulaire français. Une "pédale" de la langue et du style.* Genève: Droz.

Galli, Hugues (2006): Échappée en morphologie dérivationnelle. Approche épistémologique de la discipline avec application au préfixe français *en-*. Ph.D. dissertation, Universities of Zürich and Strasbourg.

Gawełko, Marek (1977): *Évolution des suffixes adjectivaux en français*. Wrocław: Zakład Narodowy im. Ossolińskich – Wydawnictwo Polskiej Akademii Nauk.

Gebhard, Karl (1975): Trois suffixes d'emprunt en français: *-ade*, *-ou/-ouse*, *-ole*: Étude lexicale. *Travaux de linguistique et de littérature* 13: 67–98.

Godefroy, Frédéric (1888): *Dictionnaire de l'ancienne langue française*. Tome 5. Paris: Vieweg-Bouillon.

Golde, Max (1929): Die altfranzösischen Diminutiva. *Romanische Forschungen* 41: 1–98.

Graff, Elisabeth (1918): *Das Participium praesentis im Französischen*. Greifswald: Panzig.

Guilbert, Louis and Jean Dubois (1961): Formation du système préfixal intensif en français moderne et contemporain. *Le Français Moderne* 29: 87–111.

Guiraud, Pierre (1956): *L'argot*. Paris: Presses Universitaires de France.

Guiraud, Pierre (1972): *Le moyen français*. Paris: Presses Universitaires de France.

Hamacher, Elisabeth (2002): La préfixation en français médiéval: Une étude du préfixe *con-*. Thèse de maîtrise, Université du Québec à Montréal.

Hatcher, Anna Granville (1951): *Modern English Word-Formation and Neo-Latin. A study of the origins of English (French, Italian, German) copulative compounds*. Baltimore: The Johns Hopkins Press.

Heinimann, Siegfried (1953): Les mots déformés et abrégés en *-o* dans l'argot, dans le langage populaire et dans la langue commune. In: *Mélanges de linguistique et de littérature romanes offerts à Mario Roques*. Vol. 2, 151–163. Paris: Didier.

Höfler, Manfred (1967): Review of Meyer-Lübke (1966 [1921]). *Zeitschrift für romanische Philologie* 83: 104–114.

Höfler, Manfred (1972): *Zur Integration der neulateinischen Kompositionsweise im Französischen. Dargestellt an den Bildungen auf* -(o)manie, -(o)mane. Tübingen: Niemeyer.

Huguet, Edmond (1925–1967): *Dictionnaire de la langue française du seizième siècle*. 7 Vol. Paris: Champion/Didier.

Hummel, Martin (2010): La diachronie du système adverbial des langues romanes: Tradition orale et tradition écrite. In: Maria Iliescu, Heidi Siller-Runggaldier and Paul Danler (eds.), *Actes du XXVe Congrès International de Linguistique et Philologie Romanes (Innsbruck, 3–8 septembre 2007)*. Vol. 4, 445–461. Berlin/New York: de Gruyter.

Hummel, Martin and Anna Gazdik (2021): *Dictionnaire historique de l'adjectif-adverbe*. Berlin/Boston: De Gruyter.

Jänicke, Otto (1969): Review of Meyer-Lübke 1966 [1921] *Vox Romanica* 28: 329–339.

Kjellman, Hilding (1920): *Mots abrégés et tendances d'abréviation en français*. Uppsala: A.-B. Akademiska Bokhandeln.
Klingebiel, Kathryn (1989): *Noun + verb compounding in Western Romance*. Berkeley: University of California Press.
Korfanty, Sylvie (1999): La lexicographie et glossographie en français du XVIe siècle. Prolégomènes à un dictionnaire du français préclassique. Ph.D. dissertation, Université Marc Bloch, Strasbourg.
Lebel, Marie Eleine (2009): Traitement assisté par ordinateur: À l'assaut du morphème *par* dans un corpus d'ancien français. *Revue québécoise de linguistique* 3: 88–108.
Lewicka, Halina (1960): *La langue et le style du théâtre comique français des XVe et XVIe siècles. La dérivation*. Paris: Klincksieck.
Librova, Bogdana (2010): La particule séparable *re-*, facteur de cohésion textuelle en français médiéval. In: Maria Iliescu, Heidi Siller-Runggaldier and Paul Danler (eds.), *Actes du XXVe Congrès International de Linguistique et de Philologie Romanes (Innsbruck, 3–8 Septembre 2007)*. Vol. 7, 455–464. Berlin/New York: de Gruyter.
Lindemann, Margarete (1977): *Zum Suffixwechsel von* -eresse *zu* -euse *und* -trice *im Französischen*. Tübingen: Narr.
Lodge, Anthony (1993): *Le français. Histoire d'un dialecte devenu langue*. Paris: Fayard.
Lüdtke, Jens (1995): Grundzüge der Entwicklung der Relationsadjektive vom Latein zum Romanischen. In: Wolfgang Dahmen, Günter Holtus, Johannes Kramer, Michael Metzeltin, Wolfgang Schweickard and Otto Winkelmann (eds.), *Konvergenz und Divergenz in den romanischen Sprachen. Romanistisches Kolloquium VIII*, 138–150. Tübingen: Narr.
Luschützky, Hans Christian and Franz Rainer (2013): Instrument and place nouns: A typological and diachronic perspective. *Linguistics* 51(6): 1301–1359.
Malkiel, Yakov (1938): *Das substantivierte Adjektiv im Französischen*. Berlin: Speer & Schmidt.
Malkiel, Yakov (1972): The pan-European suffix *-esco*, *-esque* in stratigraphic projection. In: Albert Valdman (ed.), *Papers in Linguistics and Phonetics to the Memory of P. Delattre*, 357–387. Den Haag/Paris: Mouton.
Malkiel, Yakov (1986): The Old French verbal abstracts in *-eiz*. *Zeitschrift für romanische Philologie* 102: 1–39.
Martin, Robert (2001): Le préfixe *a-/ad-* en moyen français. *Romania* 119: 289–322.
Martin, Robert (2006): Sémantique préfixale du moyen français: Les préfixes *de-/des-*. *Lexique* 17: 29–53.
Matrisciano, Sara and Franz Rainer (2021): Origine et diffusion des expressions romanes du type *jaune paille*. *Romanische Forschungen* 133(1): 3–27.
Melka, Francine and Wiecher Zwanenburg (1993): Femme et féminin en ancien français. *Cahiers de lexicologie* 62: 67–92.
Merk, Georges (1970): La vitalité des suffixes nominaux du latin au français. *Revue de linguistique romane* 34: 194–223.
Merk, Georges (1978): Les héritiers et les substituts du suffixe lat. *-ione* en Gallo-Romania. Lille: Atelier national de reproduction de thèses.
Merrilees, Brian (2006): La morphologie dérivationnelle en français médiéval: L'apport des lexiques. *Lexique* 17: 97–115.
Mertens, Bianca (2021): *Le suffixe */-'ur-a/. Recherches sur la morphologie dérivationnelle du protoroman*. Berlin/Boston: De Gruyter.
Meyer-Lübke, Wilhelm (1966 [1921]): *Historische Grammatik der französischen Sprache*. Vol. 2: *Wortbildungslehre*. 2nd revised ed. by J. M. Piel. Heidelberg: Winter.

Moreau, Thérèse and Mariane Botinelli (1999): *Dictionnaire féminin-masculin des professions, titres et fonctions électives*. Genève: Bureau de l'égalité entre homme et femme.

Müller, Peter O., Ingeborg Ohnheiser, Susan Olsen and Franz Rainer (eds.) (2015–2016): *Word-Formation. An International Handbook of the Languages of Europe*. 5 Vol. Berlin/Boston: De Gruyter Mouton.

Namer, Fiammetta (2012): Nominalisation et composition en français: D'où viennent les verbes composés. In: Rafael Marín and Florence Villoing (eds.), *Les nominalisations. Nouveaux aspects*, 173–205. Villeneuve d'Ascq: Presses Universitaires du Septentrion.

Nkollo, Mikołaj (2013): L'expression de la réciprocité en ancien français. *Romanische Forschungen* 125: 14–31.

Noailly, Michèle (1990): *Le substantif épithète*. Paris: Presses Universitaires de France.

Nyrop, Kristoffer (1936 [1908]): *Grammaire historique de la langue française*. Vol. 3: *Formation des mots*. 2nd revised ed. Copenhague: Gyldendal.

Ozolina, Olga (2013): La formation des mots dans le français médiéval et contemporain. In: Emili Casanova Herrero and Cesáreo Calvo Rigual (eds.), *Actas del XXVI Congreso Internacional de Lingüística y de Filología Románicas (Valencia, 6–11 septiembre 2010)*, 2206–2214. Berlin/Boston: de Gruyter.

Patard, Adeline and Walter De Mulder (2015) : La préverbation en *en-* en ancien français: un cas de préfixation aspectuelle? *Lexique* 22: 85–110.

Peter, Herbert (1951): Die Entwicklung des Suffixes *-ard* im Französischen. Ph.D. dissertation, Universität Innsbruck.

Rainer, Franz (1998): La réduplication française du type *fifille* d'un point de vue diachronique. In: Giovanni Ruffino (ed.), *Atti del XXI Congresso Internazionale di Linguistica e Filologia Romanza (Centro di studi filologici e linguistic siciliani, Università di Palermo, 18–24 settembre 1995)*, 279–289. Tübingen: Niemeyer.

Rainer, Franz (2005): Noms d'instruments/de lieux en *-tor* dans la Galloromania. *Vox Romanica* 64: 121–140.

Rainer, Franz (2007): Frz. *mammifère* oder: habent sua fata et termini technici. *Zeitschrift für französische Sprache und Literatur* 117: 14–24.

Rainer, Franz (2009a): Die Integration des lateinischen Kompositionstyps *tauriformis* im Französischen und Italienischen. *Zeitschrift für romanische Philologie* 125: 45–84.

Rainer, Franz (2009b): Étude diachronique des adjectifs de relation anatomiques, tout spécialement de ceux en *-ien*. *Revue de linguistique romane* 73: 371–425.

Rainer, Franz (2011): The agent-instrument-place "polysemy" of the suffix -TOR in Romance. *STUF – Language Typology and Universals* 64(1): 8–32.

Rainer, Franz (2013): L'intégration des composés latins du type *aurifer* en français. In: Georgette Dal and Dany Amiot (eds.), *Repères en morphologie*. Lille. http://stl.recherche.univ-lille3.fr/textesenligne/Reperes-Morphologie/Rainer-Reperes_morphologie_p182-214.pdf [last access 17 Apr 2015].

Rainer, Franz (2017): Étude diachronique sur l'emploi adjectival des noms en *-iste*. *Zeitschrift für französische Sprache und Literatur* 127: 23–44.

Rainer, Franz (2019): The benefit of the pan-Romance perspective: A new attempt to solve the *tecedor/tecedeira* puzzle. *Word Structure* 12(1): 127–151.

Reichenkron, Günter (1952): Einige grundsätzliche Bemerkungen zum Vigesimalsystem. In: *Festgabe Ernst Gamillscheg, zu seinem fünfundsechzigsten Geburtstag am 28. Oktober 1952 von Freunden und Schülern überreicht*, 164–184. Tübingen: Niemeyer.

Roché, Michel (2002a): Gender inversion in Romance derivatives with *-arius*. In: Sabrina Bendjaballah, Wolfgang U. Dressler, Oskar E. Pfeiffer and Maria D. Voeikova (eds.), *Morphology*

2000. Selected papers from the 9th Morphology Meeting, Vienna, 24–28 February 2000, 283–291. Amsterdam/Philadelphia: Benjamins.
Roché, Michel (2002b): Aux origines du suffixe *-ouille(r)*. In: Michel Aurnague and Michel Roché (eds.), *Hommage à Jacques Allières*. Vol. 2: *Romania sans frontières*, 561–572. Biarritz: Atlantica.
Roché, Michel (2006): La dérivation en *-ier(e)* en ancien français. *Lexique* 17: 55–96.
Roché, Michel (2007): Logique lexicale et morphologie: La dérivation en *-isme*. In: Fabio Montermini, Gilles Boyé and Nabil Hathout (eds.), *Morphology in Toulouse. Selected proceedings of the 5th Décembrettes*, 45–58. Somerville, MA: Cascadilla.
Roché, Michel (2011): Pression lexicale et contraintes phonologiques dans la dérivation en *-aie* du français. *Linguistica* 51: 5–22.
Rothwell, William (1966): A study of the prefix *de/des* in Anglo-Norman and some considerations arising therefrom. *Transactions of the Philological Society* 65: 24–41.
Sammet, Doris (1968): *Die Substantivbildung mit Suffixen bei Chrestien de Troyes*. Tübingen: Niemeyer.
Schmitz, Astrid and Beatrice Schmitz (1995): *Französische Wortbildung im 13. Jahrhundert. Untersuchung der Substantivbildung bei Rutebeuf und Adenet le Roi*. Bonn: Romanistischer Verlag.
Schpak-Dolt, Nikolaus (2003): *Bibliographische Materialien zur französischen Morphologie*. Frankfurt/M.: Lang.
Schweickard, Wolfgang (1992): Altfranzösisch *-istre* (< -ISTA) und entsprechende Varianten in anderen Sprachen. *Zeitschrift für romanische Philologie* 108: 435–442.
Serrano-Dolader, David (2025): Parasynthesis in Romance. In: Peter O. Müller, Susan Olsen and Franz Rainer (eds.), *Word-Formation – Special Patterns and Restrictions*, 1–15. Berlin/Boston: De Gruyter Mouton.
Söll, Ludwig (1968): *Shampooing* und die Integration des Suffixes *-ing*. In: *Verba et vocabula. Festschrift E. Gamillscheg*, 565–578. München: Fink.
Stefenelli, Arnulf (1967): *Der Synonymenreichtum der altfranzösischen Dichtersprache*. Wien: Braumüller.
Štichauer, Jaroslav (2010): L'évolution de la dérivation suffixale en français préclassique: Exemple des déverbaux en *-ment*. In: Bernard Combettes, Céline Guillot, Évelyne Oppermann-Marsaux, Sophie Prévost and Amalia Rodríguez-Somolinos (eds.), *Le changement en français. Études de linguistique diachronique*, 381–402. Bern: Lang.
Taylor, Robert (1976): Les préfixes de négation *non-* et *nient-* en ancien français. In: Marcel Boudreault and Frankwalt Möhren (eds.), *Actes du XIIIe Congrès International de Linguistique et Philologie Romanes (Québec, 29 août – 5 septembre 1971)*. Vol. 1, 647–658. Québec: Presses de l'Université Laval.
Thibault, André (1989): La terminaison lat. *-uus* dans les emprunts savants en français: Un problème d'adaptation morpholexicale. *Revue de linguistique romane* 53: 85–110.
Thorné Hammar, Eva (1942): *Le développement de sens du suffixe latin* -bilis *en français*. Lund: Gleerup.
TLF-étym http://www.atilf.fr/tlf-etym/
TLFi = *Trésor de la langue française informatisé* http://www.atilf.fr/Les-ressources/Ressources-informatisees/TLFi-Tresor-de-la-Langue-Francaise/
Tobler, Adolf, Erhard Lommatzsch and Hans Helmut Christmann (1925–2008): *Altfranzösisches Wörterbuch*. Wiesbaden: Steiner.
Tomassone, Roberte and Bernard Combettes (1970): Remarques sur la formation des collectifs de noms d'arbres et de plantes. *Revue de linguistique romane* 34: 224–233.

Tremblay, Mireille (2008): La préfixation en *entre-* en ancien français: Pluralité, réciprocité et valeur aspectuelle. In: Benjamin Fagard, Olivier Bertrand, Bernard Combettes and Sophie Prévost (eds.), *Évolutions en français. Études de linguistique diachronique*, 363–383. Bern: Lang.

Troberg, Michelle and Heather Burnett (2017): From Latin to Modern French: A punctuated shift. In: Éric Mathieu and Robert Truswell (eds.), *Micro-change and macro-change in diachronic syntax*, 104–124. Oxford: Oxford University Press.

Tuttle, Edward Fowler (1975): *Studies in the Derivational Suffix* -āculum. *Its Latin origin and its Romance development.* Tübingen: Niemeyer.

Uth, Melanie (2011): *Französische Ereignis-Nominalisierungen. Abstrakte Bedeutung und regelhafte Wortbildung.* Berlin/New York: de Gruyter.

Uth, Melanie (2016): The diachronic development of French *-age* between usage-related shifts and grammatical change. *Language Dynamics and Change* 6(2): 284–312.

Väänänen, Veikko (1979): *Co-*: Genèse d'un préfixe. In: Manfred Höfler, Henri Vernay and Lothar Wolf (eds.), *Festschrift Kurt Baldinger zum 60. Geburtstag*, 317–329. Tübingen: Niemeyer.

Walker, Douglas C. (1982): *Dictionnaire inverse de l'ancien français*. Ottawa: Éditions de l'Université d'Ottawa.

Walsh, Thomas J. (1983): The verbal suffix *-iare*. Latin origin and Romance development. Ph.D. dissertation, University of Berkeley.

Wartburg, Walther von and Jean-Paul Chauveau (1928–2002): *Französisches etymologisches Wörterbuch. Eine Darstellung des galloromanischen Sprachschatzes*. Basel: Zbinden.

Widdig, Walter (1982): Archi-, ultra-, maxi- *und andere Steigerungspräfixe im heutigen Französisch*. Genève: Droz.

Wolf, Heinz Jürgen (1964): *Die Bildung der französischen Ethnica*. Genève: Droz.

Wolf, Heinz Jürgen (1969): Frz. *-ache*, *-iche*, *-oche*, *-uche*. In: Wolf-Dieter Lange and Heinz Jürgen Wolf (eds.), *Philologische Studien für Joseph M. Piel*, 224–234. Heidelberg: Winter.

Zwanenburg, Wiecher (1985): La naissance de la dérivation savante en français. In: *Actes du XVIIème Congrès International de Linguistique et Philologie Romanes (Aix-en-Provence, 29 août–3 septembre 1983)*. Vol. 3, 177–188. Marseille: Lafitte.

Zwanenburg, Wiecher (1992): Composition savante et moyen français. *Vox Romanica* 51: 169–177.

Zwanenburg, Wiecher (1997): Le développement du suffixe dérivationnel *-e* en moyen français: La polyfonctionnalité et le blocage. In: Bernard Combettes and Simone Monsonégo (eds.), *Le moyen français*, 181–191. Paris: Didier.

David Stifter

20 From Old Irish to Modern Irish

Abstract: This article outlines the main changes that the processes of word-formation have undergone from Early Irish (Old Irish 7th–9th centuries, Middle Irish 10th–12th centuries) and its precursors to the modern spoken language (Classical Modern Irish 13th–17th centuries, dialectal Modern Irish 17th century to present), and puts them into a typological perspective.

1 Introduction

1.1 The Irish language

The Irish language forms a branch within the Celtic (Clt.) branch of the Indo-European macro-family. It is descended from Proto-Indo-European (PIE; c. 4th mill. BC) via Proto-Celtic (phps. 2nd mill. BC) and a possible further intervening sub-node Insular-Celtic (1st mill. BC). The earliest, fragmentarily attested stage of Irish is Primitive Irish, transmitted on the formulaic Ogam inscriptions of the 4th–6th centuries. This is followed by Early Old Irish (7th century) and Old Irish proper (OIr.; c. 700–900). The Irish language is fully documented in the Latin (Lat.) alphabet from the 7th c. AD onwards. Although a fair number of texts from Early Old Irish survive, and abundantly from Old Irish, almost all of them are extant only in much later manuscripts, sometimes a thousand years younger than the texts themselves. The intervening stages of manuscript copying have quite often led to an inextricable amalgamation of original and younger linguistic features. It has therefore been the practice to base the linguistic description of Classical Old Irish almost exclusively on the few sources in contemporary manuscripts from the 8th and 9th centuries, essentially three large Latin manuscripts that contain very extensive Old

David Stifter, Maynooth, Ireland

https://doi.org/10.1515/9783111420530-020

Irish interlinear glosses. The "Old-Irishness" of texts in later manuscripts is commonly measured against this linguistic standard. Old Irish is a remarkably uniform language. Evidently, texts from centres of learning across the whole country have survived, yet it has not been possible so far to identify unambiguous dialectal traits. With few exceptions, Old Irish literature has been transmitted without reliable information about its chronological and geographical origin. What linguistic variation can be found, is therefore usually ascribed to chronological differences. Old Irish can be characterised as an overspecifying language which encodes grammatical information that has no communicative and semantic significance, while adding to the morphological complexity (see Tristram 2010 on measuring morphological complexity). It is almost prototypical for a language whose grammatical behaviour cannot be described adequately by synchronic rules alone. Its notoriously complex surface allomorphies, especially in the inflectional morphology of verbs, but also in derivation, often make sense only from a diachronic perspective and receive elucidation only on the level of the quite dissimilar underlying forms.

The authoritative description of Old Irish is Thurneysen (1946). Pedersen (1909–13), McCone (1994) and Stifter (2009) provide supplementary information. The main lexicographic work is the *Dictionary of the Irish Language* (DIL = Quin 1983) in its second, revised online version (eDIL = Toner 2013). This dictionary includes attestations also from Middle (MIr.) and classical Modern Irish (ModIr.). The inconsistent spellings of the headwords in DIL vacillate between Old and Middle Irish practices, thereby on occasion concealing morphological information and restricting its use for systematic investigation into word-formation. The main etymological resource, the *Lexique étymologique de l'irlandais ancien* (LEIA), unfinished as of yet, organises the lexicon under roots or base forms. This allows one to study the derivational relationships within word families, but not to trace the distribution of morphemes across the language.

Any linguistic trait that deviates from the Old Irish standard but does not yet conform to what comes afterwards in Classical Modern Irish, is regarded as Middle Irish (c. 900–1200), irrespective of whether it is a genuine innovation or a hypercorrect aberration. Because of its transitional character and the concomitant uncertainty about the linguistic reality of many forms, the grammatical description of Middle Irish lags behind that of its ancestor and successor stages. Breatnach (1993) is the most extensive description, McCone (2005: 173–217) gives a concise overview of the main developments, and McCone (1997: 163–241) is a detailed study of the changes in the verbal system from Old to Middle Irish. For the entirety of linguistic stages up to Middle Irish the cover term Early Irish is used.

At the end of the Middle Irish re-structurings, simplifications and experiments emerges Classical Modern Irish (c. 1200–1650), a learned standard language again, which, however, ultimately gave way to the dialectally differentiated Modern Irish (c. 1600–present) when the social fabric, which had held the Gaelic World together, was forcefully removed in conflicts with England in the 17th century. The modern spoken form of Irish has three distinct dialects (Munster, Connacht, Ulster) and one officially superimposed standard form (*An Caighdeán Oifigiúil*). While the dialects diverge sufficiently to be on occasion mutually unintelligible, for the abstract purposes of historical word-formation the differences are negligible. A succinct description of Classical Modern Irish is McManus (1994); for the dialects and the closely related Scots Gaelic and Manx language (not treated here despite being on a par with Modern Irish as descendants of Old Irish) see the relevant chapters in McCone et al. (1994). Although following similar principles, the spelling rules of Old and Modern Irish differ in the details. Modern Irish practices are more explicit and on average use more letters in the representation of phonological distinctions. An orthographic reform was imposed in the 1950s (*An Caighdeán Oifigiúil*, Ó hAnluain 1999) to bring the, by then, historical spelling closer to the pronunciation of the language, but many earlier distinctions were obliterated this way by removing "silent letters". Usually, therefore, the difference between a medieval and a contemporary form looks more substantial than it is underlyingly. For the purposes of charting the diachrony of suffixal formations, the pre-reform dictionary (Dinneen 1927) is better suited than the standard modern dictionary (Ó Dónaill 1977) and *A Reverse Dictionary of Modern Irish* (Doyle and Gussman 2004). This defect will be remedied by a historical dictionary of Modern Irish (*Foclóir na Nua-Ghaeilge*), currently under way under the auspices of the Royal Irish Academy.

During its recorded history, Irish had contact with and was subject to influence mainly from the British Celtic languages, Latin, Norse, Normanno-French and English, as well as submerged prehistoric languages of the British Isles. These adstratal and substratal languages make themselves felt most notably in lexical borrowings, but occasionally they left their imprint in the form of suffixes or types of word-formation.

1.2 Preliminaries

Irish has inherited the traditional Indo-European types of word-formation: 1. a rich set of suffixes for creating derivatives within and across classes of words, and 2. formally and semantically diverse types of compounding, including the use of bound morphemes as first members of compounds. Although the system has remained stable in the outlines, during the recorded language history shifts in the relative importance of some of those strategies have occurred that are linked with other aspects of grammar, especially with its typological structure, but also language contact had a role to play. The general trend of Irish is one moving from synthetic to analytic, and this makes itself felt also in word-formation. Modern word-formation, officially imposed for the standard language, is sometimes artificial and counter to the natural tendencies of the spoken variant.

The numerous diachronic and synchronic sound rules of Irish, especially syncope, palatalisation, phonological lenition and concomitant phonetic weakening of sounds, and various kinds of assimilations, cannot be commented upon in detail in this survey. They cause a considerable amount of allomorphy which in turn is a potential source for morphemic splits and reanalyses. As the transparent connection between bases and derivatives became obscured by phonetic weakening, and lexemes with rare suffixes were abandoned, derivational processes became marginalised and were abandoned as well. Another major driving force for morphological change was the loss of distinct vowel qualities in unstressed syllables between the Old and Middle Irish periods. The obliteration of grammatical distinctions which had been conveyed by vowels in Old Irish had to be made up for by other means. One response to this structural challenge was to re-characterise derivational morphemes.

2 History of research

Whereas the inflectional morphology of Irish has attracted a lot of attention, its word-formation has been left largely neglected. The usual approach to the study of Irish word-formation has been diachronic, aiming to derive Old Irish structures from their Proto-Indo-European and Celtic ancestors. There have been no notable attempts to trace specific types of word-formation, or the formal expression of specific semantic classes, through the entire attested history of the language. The number of studies is therefore small. Pedersen devotes a long chapter to listing the historical nominal suffixes (1909–13: II 15–63) and verbal roots and their prefixes (1909–13: II 450–658). The verbal collection has been largely superseded by Schumacher (2004). Thurneysen (1946: 163–175, 218–223, 337–338, 445–455) and McCone (1994: 126–132, 176–181) contain concise remarks about historic and synchronic processes of word-formation. Only the last two decades have seen an upsurge in interest in Old Irish word-formation, the approach being either formal or functional, but almost always from a diachronic point of view. Abstracts with various types of dental suffixes are treated by Irslinger (2002), nasal stems by

Stüber (1998). A chapter in Stüber (2015: 105–135) is devoted to the derivational morphology of verbal abstracts. De Bernardo Stempel (1999) stands apart in that she aims at a description of Old Irish nominal morphology in its entirety. Rossiter (2004) and McCone (2006: 177–214) describe the processes of prefixal verb formation, Le Mair (2011) the suffixal formation of secondary verbs. Some relevant information is also contained in general Indo-Europeanist handbooks such as NIL, and under the lexical headings of the simple bases in LEIA. Synchronic variation and the development into younger stages of the language has seen less research. Wodtko (1995) and Russell (1990) treat productive adjective formations. Russell (2001) is about hypocoristic formations, a niche topic with formal peculiarities. McCone (1997) describes the pathways that led to the morphological simplification of the verbal complex from Old to Middle Irish, but mostly in respect to inflection and stem-formation. With the notable exception of the last work, none of these studies goes beyond Old Irish.

Doyle (1992) is the only monograph devoted to the word-formation of selected Modern Irish categories; lists of synchronic suffixes are found, for example, in De Bhaldraithe (1953: 239–256) and Ó hAnluain (1999: 241–255), all with a minimum of remarks about the origins of the suffixes. For other synchronic accounts of Irish word-formation see Ó Curnáin (2016).

Given the piecemeal state of research, despite the morphological richness of Irish, this article can only sketch representative topics to indicate the future directions of research into the diachrony of Irish word-formation. The focus will be on the system in the early, i.e. Old Irish language and on the tendencies of development towards the modern standard language. For the synchronic details of Modern Irish the reader is referred to Ó Curnáin (2016).

3 Nominal word-formation

The three major productive strategies of nominal word-formation in Old Irish are compounding, suffixation, and prefixation. Diachronically, prefixation is a subtype of compounding, but by the historical period it had developed a sufficient amount of unique formal and semantic features to qualify as a synchronically independent strategy. Other formal strategies, such as truncation or gemination, are very rare and are restricted to special functions. To a very limited degree, prefixation and suffixation compete with each other, like in the formation of feminines, or entail each other, like in the formation of hypocoristics. The three basic strategies have survived into the modern language, albeit with shifts in their relative importance. Compounding remains as a learned process in the standard language, but is of a much more restricted use in the spoken variant; prefixation has stood its ground; suffixation is the most prominent strategy. Compounding is most affected by the trend towards syntactic, i.e. analytic constructions to express concepts that previously found synthetic expression.

3.1 Compounding

Because compounding is a manifest diachronic source for a subset of morphemes in suffixation and in prefixation, it will be dealt with first. Irish had inherited a propensity for compounding, both in the verbal domain, stacking prefixes, called preverbs before verbal roots (cf. section 4.1), and in the nominal domain where it manifests itself in great formal and semantic variation. Basically, two (rarely more) independently attested lexical items (X, Y) are conjoined under a single stress to form a new item whose semantics can be more than just that of the two base elements added together. Only the last element (Y) is inflected. According to metrical evidence, the main stress in Old Irish compounds is on the initial syllable. The typical order is that the head, the determinatum (Y), is in the second position (right-headed, "hysterocentric", Ahlqvist 1985: 2), preceded by the determinans, or modifier (X). Compounds are typically equivalent to full clauses in that they create predicative statements between the two elements (e.g., 'a Y that is (of) X' = endocentric, i.e. referring to a concept that is verbalised in the head), or they make a predicative statement with the two elements about an unexpressed third entity (e.g., 'a Z whose Y is (of) X' = exocentric, bahuvrīhis). An exception are copulative compounds (dvandvas), where both elements are on an equal level ('X and Y'). Dvandvas are not formally distinguished from the other types, and their internal structure is only elucidated by the semantics. There are only few examples of endocentric head-first compounds, e.g., OIr. *maccóem* 'dear boy', *macc(ḟ)ind* 'fair boy', ModIr. *londubh* 'blackbird', which by their isolation are betrayed to result from unique developments (e.g., univerbation of vocatival phrases or imitation of English models?). A systematic exception to the preponderant right-headed order are the so-called "reversed bahuvrīhis", i.e. exocentric compounds ('a Z that is Y in respect to X'), called the "armstrong"-type (cf. Uhlich 1997).

The first element can belong to a variety of word classes, especially nouns, adjectives, prepositions, and even stems derived from verbs; those cases where the first element is a bound morpheme are treated under prefixation. The second element of a compound is a nominal stem or nominalised verbal stem (synthetic or verbal governing compounds; Uhlich 2002), and also the resulting form is nominal, either a noun or an adjective. Morphophonologically, nominal compounding in Irish is accompanied by lenition of the initial of the second element, with very few exceptions displaying no mutation (e.g., *fordorus* 'lintel' ← preposition *for* 'on, upon' + *dorus* 'door'), or, very exceptionally, nasalisation (e.g., *dícenn* 'headless' ← privative *dī* + *n* + *cenn* 'head', cf. O'Rahilly 1942; *sechtndelbach* 'septiform' ← *secht*^{n} 'seven' + *delbach* 'shaped'). Lenition frequently finds no graphic expression in Old Irish spelling, but there is no doubt that the same rules, including the same systematic exceptions (especially homorganic delenition), that obtain in Modern Irish operated in the early period. Stress on the first element normally entails phonetic reduction in the second element. This is proved by isolated forms like *gaisced* 'weapons' ← *gaí* 'spear' + *scíath* 'shield' which is synchronically no longer transparent as a dvandva-compound, or from anthroponyms that have lost their connection with the common lexicon. However, the speakers' synchronic linguistic awareness commonly aids to counteract the expected phonetic weakening.

The types and formal characteristics of Old Irish compounds, with specific reference to personal names, are conveniently discussed by Pedersen (1909–13: II 1–15), Uhlich (1993: 78–120; 2002) and Ziegler (1994: 66–89). The major semantic types of Old Irish compounds are: 1. endocentric determinative compounds (tatpuruṣas and karmadhārayas), i.e. where the first element qualifies the second, e.g., *béstindrem* 'idiomatic usage' ← *bés* 'habit' + *tindrem* 'behaviour', *túaisrenna* 'North' ← *túas* 'above' + plural of *rinn* 'star, constellation', *etraide* 'central part of the chariot' ← *eter* 'between' + *suide* 'seat'; 2. exocentric possessive compounds (bahuvrīhis), i.e. compounds that attribute the quality that is expressed by the members of the compound to an external entity, e.g., *cambṡrón* 'crooked-nosed one' ← *camb* 'crooked' + *srón* 'nose', *foltchain* 'fair-haired one' ← *folt* 'hair' + *cain* 'fair'; 3. copulative compounds (dvandvas) in which two elements of the same word class are conjoined. The latter are quite frequent with adjectives, e.g., *casmongach* 'curly and long-haired' ← *cas* 'curly' + *mongach* 'long-haired', less so, but still not uncommon, with nouns, e.g., *corpanim* 'body and soul' ← *corp* 'body' + *ainim* 'soul' (Binchy 1972).

In the modern language, compounds are still numerous as lexicalised items (e.g., *muicfheoil* 'pork' ← *muc* 'pig' + *feoil* 'meat', *bodóinseach* 'lusty woman' ← *bod* 'penis' + *óinseach* 'foolish woman'), but the process of compounding is restricted as a productive feature of the spoken language (De Bhaldraithe 1953: 254; Ahlqvist 1985; but cf. McManus 1994: 389–392 for Classical Modern Irish). It is more at home in learned contexts, especially neologisms are created this way, imitating the pattern of neoclassical determinative compounds, such as *fochonradh* 'subcontract' ← *fo* 'under, sub-' + *conradh* 'contract', *leasríocht* 'regency' ← *leas* 'vice-' + *ríocht* 'kingdom'. Substantival dvandvas can no longer be formed. Compounds of two adjectives are quite common (De Bhaldraithe 1953: 256), but they are no longer coordinated; rather, the first element is subordinated as a determiner to the second, e.g., *corrghlic* 'cunning < clever in a crooked way' ← *corr* 'odd, crooked' + *glic* 'clever', *bándearg* 'pink < whitish red' ← *bán* 'white' + *dearg* 'red'. Elsewhere in the spoken language, compounds have been replaced by lexicalised head-first phrasal nouns followed by an attributive genitive or an adverb (e.g., *bean tí* 'housewife' ← *bean* 'woman' + *tí* 'of house', *bualadh bos* 'applause' ← *bualadh* 'the beating' + *bos* 'of palms', *bealach isteach* 'entrance' ← *bealach* 'way' + *isteach* 'inside', *béal in airde* 'upright, open, unguarded' ← *béal* 'mouth' + *in* 'in(to)' + *airde* 'height', *cur síos* 'description' ← *cur* 'the putting' + *síos* 'down', nominalised from the verbal collocation *cuir síos* 'to describe'; cf. Greene 1977; Ahlqvist 1985; Doyle 1996; Uhlich 1997: 26). In the standard language, compounding may be artificially continued where the native speakers' practice differs, e.g., *bandochtúir* vs. *dochtúir mná* 'woman doctor' ← *dochtúir* 'doctor' + *mná* 'of woman'.

Ahlqvist (1985) ascribes this to a typological shift related to the emergence and consolidation of the word-order VSO and a concomitant change from morphology to syntax. The existence of fixed noun phrases can already be observed in Old Irish (Ahlqvist 1985: 4), particularly in the formation of place names and personal names, cf. the Old Clt. place name *Karbantoriton* 'chariot (*karbanto-*) ford (*riton*)' vs. OIr. *Áth Carpat* 'ford (*áth*) of chariots (*carpat*)'. The current development is one of further morphological simplification. Since awareness of the underlying grammatical structure, i.e. that the second noun in a phrasal noun is in the genitive, is vanishing among speakers of Irish, which today overwhelmingly means L2-speakers, the trend is to add the modifier after the head in the default, unmarked form.

3.2 Obscured compound heads

When lexemes habitually occur in particular positions in composition with varying partners, the way is open for them to bleach semantically and to be understood as mere modifiers. Compositional heads that undergo this transformation can be visualised to be on a continuum from compounding to derivation. In Irish, the phonetic reduction of post-tonic syllables facilitates the weakening of the formal and semantic connection between compound constituents and independent lexemes. Such elements are called "verdunkelte Komposita" (obscured compounds) by Pedersen (1909–13: II 13–15) and Russell (1996), and "Suffixoide" (suffixoids) by De Bernardo Stempel (1999: 461), but the term obscured compound heads will be employed here for greater preciseness. Occasionally, certain heads of compounds that had developed into derivational suffixes already in Proto-

Celtic can still be related morphologically to their fully stressed counterparts in phrasal variants almost until the present day, e.g., Proto-Clt. **māros* 'big, great' → suffix **X-māros* 'having a lot of X < being great in X', e.g., Gaulish *Nertomarus*, Welsh *nerthfawr*, OIr. *nertmar*, ModIr. *neartmhar*, all 'strong, vigorous', beside, e.g., OIr. *nert* 'strength'. The relationship of ModIr. *-mhar* with the simplex *mór* 'big' is still reasonably transparent, but no longer so in *lúfar* 'agile' < pre-reform *lúthmhar* from *lúth* 'activity'. Russell (1996: 125) identifies around a dozen of such obscured compound heads for Old Irish, De Bernardo Stempel (1999: 461–477) a few more. Special mention should be made of X-*amail* which was still analysable in Old Irish as meaning 'having the likeness of X' (*máthramail* 'motherlike'; cf. the simplex *samail* 'likeness'), but which due to phonetic attrition has become the bound adjective-forming denominal suffix *-úil* in Modern Irish. *Lann*, which exists as a rare, literary term for 'land, ground, site; building' in Modern Irish, is on its way to becoming exclusively a toponymic suffix for public buildings (*leabharlann* 'library' ← *leabhar* 'book', *bialann* 'restaurant' ← *bia* 'food'). *Gal* is a simple noun both in Old and Modern Irish covering semantic shades from 'seething heat, steam' to 'fury, valour'. While in Old Irish it retains its character as a free member of compounds (e.g., *fingal* 'slaying a relative, fratricide' ← *fine* 'kin, family'), it also combines with other nouns to form expressions for excited activities of the human body, e.g., *bonngal* 'fury of the soles > trampling' ← *bonn* 'sole of the foot' (Russell 1996: 119, 125; Lloyd-Jones 1947). From there, via phonological attrition, it develops into a Modern Irish suffix with a special application for abnormal movements or sounds, e.g., *bacaíl* 'lameness' ← *bac* 'to restrain, hinder'. The reformed spelling *-aíl* prevents an easy association with the base noun *gal*, even in inherited terms like *fionaíl* 'fratricide'.

Adjectives normally follow their nouns in Irish. Only a few attributive adjectives can precede the noun. They lose their inflection and are compounded with the noun; for some adjectives this is the only possible construction, e.g., OIr. *óen-*, ModIr. *aon* 'one', *sen-/sean-* 'old', *droch-* 'bad', *dag-*, *deg-/dea-* 'good', etc. In these instances, word-formation is a function of syntax. Again, there is a tendency for first elements of compounds that have a high frequency in speech to become bleached semantically and to turn into stereotyped prefixes (cf. section 3.4).

3.3 Suffixation

Suffixation transfers lexical elements from one part of speech to another, or it transfers elements within a word class from one semantic sub-class to another. Suffixation is the most diverse and most vibrant type of word-formation in Irish: apart from some minor types, nouns can be created from nouns, adjectives and verbs, adjectives from nouns and, via participles, from verbs, and verbs from nouns and adjectives. From the semantic point of view, the major types of derived nouns are collectives, abstracts, agent nouns, and diminutives. There is a wealth of suffixal variation for the formal expression of these semantic categories; in the following only the productive ones will be discussed.

The derivational base can be the default stem, i.e. the nom. sg. (e.g., abstract *flaith* 'lordship, rule' → agent noun *flaithem* 'ruler'), or, rarer, the inflectional ("oblique") stem (e.g., agent noun *druí* 'druid', inflectional stem *druid-* → abstract *druídecht* 'druidry', or noun *menmae*, inflectional stem *menman-* 'mind' → adjective *menmnach* 'mindful', → verb *menmnaigidir* 'to think, judge, deem'); occasionally both alternatives occur side by side, e.g., *cú*, inflectional stem *con-* 'dog' → hypocoristic anthroponym *Cúán* and *Conán*. Conversion occurs only in the substantivisation of adjectives, e.g., OIr. *dorchae* 'dark' → *dorchae* (neut.) 'darkness'; *dub* 'black' → *dub* (neut.) 'ink'; all other changes of word class require suffixation. On the juncture between the base and the suffix various phonetic phenomena may occur: 1. suffixation may be accompanied by palatalisation, e.g., from derivative chains such as OIr. *nertmar* 'strong' → *nertmaire* 'strength' → *nertmairecht* 'strengthening' the rule was abstracted that the addition of the abstract suffix *-acht* causes palatalisation of adjectives in *-mar*, so *lúthmar* 'agile' + *-acht* → *lúthmairecht* 'agility', as if there were a missing link **lúthmaire*; 2. assimilation rules operating on the underlying forms create suffixal allomorphs in the surface representations which, albeit predictable, can lead to the obliteration of derivational relationships. One instructive example will suffice: the Old Irish denominal adjectival suffix *-dae* (variants *-de*, *-aide*, *-ide*) is phonetically [(ə)ð$^{(j)}$e]. In Old Irish, the monosyllabic variant has an allomorph [de] after dental consonants, devoiced [te] after voiceless dentals (Wodtko 1995: 235–237). This synchronically predictable allomorphy increases in Middle and Modern Irish. Apart from the final vowel, which becomes schwa, the underlying voiced dental fricative undergoes further transformations: after *n* > *-na* [nə], after voiceless dental sounds > *-ta* [tə], after voiced dental sounds > *-da* [də], after vowels > MIr. [əjə] > *-aidhe* > reformed ModIr. *-í* [iː], elsewhere > *-dha* [ɣə], which frequently becomes *-ga* [gə] in Modern Irish. What started out as a unitary suffix has split into five allomorphs that bear no resemblance to each other any more.

The principles governing suffixation do not change from Old to Modern Irish. As a general tendency it can be observed that phonologically weak suffixes become re-characterised by double suffixing, or they are entirely replaced by phonologically more distinct ones. The free occurrence and recurrence of such processes of re-characterisation leads to great formal variation for suffixes of the same function among and even within the modern dialects. In all stages of the language, chains of derivative suffixes could be stacked onto each other, thereby leading to the creation of ever more complex suffixes. In the modern language, with its demand for subtly differentiated vocabulary, this can be brought to special use: 1. *daoine* 'people' → 2. *daoineach* 'populous', *daoiniúil* 'populous', *daonra* 'population', *daonna* 'human' → 3. *daoiniúlacht* 'populousness', *daonnachas* 'humanism', *daonnacht* 'humanity', *daonnaí* 'human being', *daonnaigh* 'to make human' → 4. *daonnachtaí* 'humanist', *daonnachtúil* 'humane', *daonnú* 'act of making human' → 5. *daonnachtúlacht* 'humaneness'. The seed for this proliferation of terms is already sown in Old Irish where *doíni* 'people' furnishes the basis for the derivatives *dóendae* 'human', *dóenacht* and *dóendacht* 'humanity', *dóendatu* 'status of a layman (?)', and MIr. *doínech* 'populous'.

Language-contact in the historic period had limited impact on Irish word-formation; the scale of prehistoric contact cannot be assessed. The list of recognisable loan suffixes is comparatively short. With the influx of specialised Christian terms in the early middle ages, the morphological patterns observable in some of them helped to establish new suffixes in Irish. The Latin agentive suffix *-arius* was borrowed twice, in the earliest period of contacts, perhaps in the 5th century, as *-aire* and then again as *-óir*, reflecting sound changes that the intermediary language Welsh had undergone in the meantime. De Bernardo Stempel (1999: 381–382) ascribes the more complex agentive suffix *-t(e)óir/-th(e)óir* likewise to a borrowing from Latin, but a native origin is also conceivable. The feminising suffix *-es* < *-issa* is of an extremely marginal status, fundamentally confined to less than a handful foreign words (De Bernardo Stempel 1999: 338–340). Enlarged by native *-ach* it yielded the weakly productive feminine suffix *-sech*, ModIr. *-seach*. The suffixes *-uc*, *-óc* and *-ín* came in via the pathway of affective onomastic formations, the first two from Welsh (Russell 1990: 108–116), the third from Latin. They were originally at home in the formation of hypocoristic names, but they expanded their functional remit on the way to Modern Irish. Normanno-French and English have contributed a number of suffixes that have, however, remained restricted to loan words. Under influence from English pairs with active *-er* vs. passive *-ee*, pairs with the (near) homophonous native elements *-óir* and *-aí* [iː] have assumed comparable functions in Modern Irish, e.g., *employer, employee* → *fostóir, fostaí*. English influence has perhaps to do with the rise of the glottonymic suffix *-(a)is* [ɪʃ] in the modern language, even though its roots lie in the native abstract suffix *-as/-ais*.

3.3.1 Abstract nouns

Abstract nouns can be derived from nominal, adjectival, verbal and even prepositional bases (Thurneysen 1946: 164–170). One of the commonest suffixes is *-e*, added to adjectives of all stem-classes, e.g., *tromm* 'heavy' → *trummae* 'weight', or *faílid* 'joyful' → *faílte* 'joy'. Only adjectives ending in *-e* themselves are excluded from this process to avoid homonymity. When added to pre-existing adjectival suffixes, various complex suffixes result, such as *-aige* < *-ach*. Abstract nouns in *-e* can even be created from prepositions, e.g., *inne* 'inmost part, essence' < *i*^{n} 'in' (Breatnach 1983). In Modern Irish, abstract nouns in *-e* are still numerous. Having fallen together in many instances with comparatives, Ó hAnluain's grammar (1999: 252–253) actually analyses them as a substantival use of the comparative, i.e. as instances of conversion, but see section 4.1.2 on deadjectival nouns in Ó Curnáin (2016) for the more natural way of describing them. Other common deadjectival abstract suffixes of Old Irish are *-etu/-atu/-tu*, *-us/-ius*, and other, less common types. Of these, *-us/-ius* in its younger form *-as* begins to spread and combine with other suffixes, resulting in such complex Modern Irish abstract suffixes like *-adas* (< *-atu* + *-us*), *-achas* (< *-ach* + *-us*) (Ó hAnluain 1999: 252; Greene 1977). The usual denominal abstract suffix is *-acht/-echt*. From the numerous instances when it was attached to already derived nouns, a plethora of complex suffixes ending in *-cht* resulted in Modern Irish (De Bhaldraithe 1953: 251–253; Ó hAnluain 1999: 250–252). Other more restricted denominal suffixes are *-as*, which fell together and was replaced by *-us* in Middle Irish, and *-ne/-ine/-sine*.

An especially important process for the grammar and syntax of Irish is the derivation of abstract nouns from verbal roots or stems. Such abstract nouns can take on various semantic roles (action nouns, agent nouns etc.; cf. Stüber 2010: 380–385), but a particularly prominent role in the grammar of the language is their use as verbal nouns (v.n.). Irish does not have a paradigmatically derived infinitive of verbal stems. Nominal functions of verbs are instead fulfilled by verbal abstracts. The diversity of their formations in Old Irish reveals the great time-depth behind them and the disparate sources from which they draw. There are no rules to predict the forms of the verbal nouns, they have to be identified for each verb separately (Thurneysen 1946: 444–455; Stüber 2015). Root suppletion is very rare (e.g., *caraid* 'to love' → *serc* 'love, the loving'); occasionally, the etymological connection between verbal stem and verbal noun is no longer discernable and creates the appearance of suppletion (e.g., *ibid* 'to drink' → *óol* 'the drinking' < PIE **piph*$_3$*eti* and **poi̯h*$_3$*etlom* (or the like) respectively, from the PIE root **pe(i̯)h*$_3$*-*). Zero-suffixing is rare (*ásaid* 'to grow' → *ás* 'growth, the growing'); the norm is the addition of an overt suffix to the root of inherited primary verbs, or to the default present stem of secondary verbs. The underlying connection between verbal stem and verbal noun is not always apparent on the surface, e.g., *do·gní* 'to do, make' → *dénum* 'deed, the doing' < **degnīmu-*, or *in·fét* 'to tell' → *indisiu* 'the telling' < **ande-u̯ei̯d-* and **ande-u̯id-ti̯ū* respectively. Stems ending in *-n*, which are a common but closed, historical category, are treated by Stüber

(1998). Dental suffixes, i.e. mostly ones involving *-t* and *-th/d* (Irslinger 2002) are very common, but by no means the norm. In Old Irish, the productive verbal noun suffix that is added to almost all secondary verbs is *-ad/-ed/-ud/-iud* (ModIr. *-adh/-eadh*), the allomorphy being the result of prehistoric sound changes. Added to the productive verbal stems in *-aig-* (cf. section 4.2), the resulting suffix is *-ugud*, which enjoys great productivity in Modern Irish as *-ughudh*, reformed spelling *-ú*.

The inherited verbal nouns have largely remained in Modern Irish (e.g., Ó hAnluain 1999: 193–197), but a good deal of normalisation or alignment has affected the suffixes on the way. Suppletive relationships between verbs and verbal nouns were reduced, e.g., *caraid* 'to love' received a more transparent verbal noun *carthain* in Middle Irish, OIr. *ibid* 'to drink' was replaced by a new verb ModIr. *ól* based on the homophonous verbal noun, creating the appearance of conversion. New suffixes with restricted productivity came into existence, e.g., OIr. *benaid* 'to strike', v.n. *bíth* became *bain* 'to reap, extract', v.n. *baint*; likewise, *canaid* 'to sing', v.n. *cétail* first became MIr. *canaid*, v.n. *canamain* and *caint*, before *céadal* 'recital', *caint* 'speech' and *canúint* 'accent, dialect' < *canamain* (influenced by *caint*) were detached from the verbal paradigm, and an even more regularised ModIr. *can*, v.n. *canadh* resulted; *ceilid* 'to hide', v.n. *cleth* → ModIr. *ceil*, v.n. *ceilt*. The suffix *-t* which displays limited productivity in these formations was probably abstracted from *geilt*, the verbal noun of *geilid* 'to graze' and transferred to other verbs on a purely formal analogy, thereby creating in *baint* and *caint* a final cluster *-nt* which was originally excluded by Irish phonotactics.

In Old Irish, the suffix *-áil* is limited to a single verb and its compounds, *gaibid* 'to take' → v.n. *gabáil*. When the relationship of *gabáil* with compounds like ModIr. *tógáil* 'the raising, lifting' < OIr. *tócbáil* (to *do·fócaib* 'to raise') was no longer transparent, it started to spread as a verbal noun suffix on its own and is now used as the default suffix for integrating English loan verbs, e.g., Engl. *to waste* → *vástáil*, *to hoover* → *húvaráil*, *to meet* → *míteáil*, *to tee off* → *tiáil*. Its prominence is no doubt due to the fact that it has a phonological shape that is not liable to phonetic reduction in Irish. In productivity it competes with *-(i)ú*, the verbal noun of the old denominal suffix *-(a)igh* which is more frequent in learned neologisms, e.g., *vaccine* → *vacsaín* → verbal stem *vacsaínigh*, v.n. *vacsaíniú*.

3.3.2 Collectives

Collectives in Old Irish are derived on the one hand from count nouns (*mac* 'boy' → *macrad* 'boygroup'; *ech* 'horse' → *echrad* 'horses, stud'), but also from mass nouns, perhaps referring to material in an abstract sense (Russell 1996: 121–123), e.g., *dám* 'company' → *dámrad* 'company', *lúaith* 'ashes' → *lúaithred* 'ashes'. Three homophonous, but inflectionally different and etymologically distinct suffixes with fairly similar meanings hide behind the productive *-rad*/*-red*. The feminine suffix is used to derive denotations for living beings, the neuter suffix is attached to inanimate mass nouns, and the third one forms a rather small group of words referring to seasons, e.g., *sam* 'summer' → *samrad* 'summertime'. As can be expected, the subtle formal distinctions were lost in the course of time. Such formations are still quite alive in Modern Irish, e.g., *míol* 'animal, insect' → *míolra* 'vermin', *cúl* 'back' → *cúlra* 'background', *daoine* 'people' → *daonra* 'population', but further suffixes are also adopted to express the notion of collectiveness, e.g., OIr. *lúaithred* 'ashes' → ModIr. *luaithreach*, OIr. *cnáimred* 'bones' → ModIr. *cnáfairt*. The loss of the collective semantics is witnessed by ModIr. *madra* 'dog' beside unsuffixed MIr. *matad* 'common dog'.

3.3.3 Agent nouns

Of the inherited suffixes for agent nouns, the most productive one in Old Irish is *-(a)id* which is usually added to verbal nouns or participles, themselves derived from verbal stems. Obsolescent suffixes are *-aige* and *-e* (Breatnach 1983a). *-am*/*-em* is tolerably alive and lends itself to demonstrate the concept of morphological attraction: the two loanwords OIr. *claideb* 'sword' and *felsub* 'philosopher', which could both be conceived of as being agentives, adapted to this class because of the phonetic similarity of their final *-b* [v] with *-m* [ṽ], yielding ModIr. *claíomh* (pre-reform spelling *claidheamh*) and *fealsamh*. The loan suffixes *-aire* and *-óir*, both from Lat. *-ārius*, assumed productivity very early. Already in Early Irish, there is a trend to re-characterise undercharacterised formations, e.g., *senchae* (containing an avatar of *-e*) → *senchaid* (McCone 1995). The suffix *-thóir* owes its existence possibly to the addition of Latinate *-óir* to inherited *-aid* in order to re-characterise it, although a loan from Lat. *-tōrem* is also conceivable. Its allomorphs *-tóir*/*-teóir*/*-theóir* are due to the usual assimilation processes on morphemic boundaries.

The diversity of agentive suffixes has largely survived into Modern Irish, and was further added to: *-aid* appears now as *-aí*, *-aire* remains as such, *-óir* has developed several allomorphs (*-adóir*, *-tóir*, *-theoir*), and the prominence of suffixes with *r* among agentives was strengthened by the adoption of Engl. *-er* as *-éir*. The class of agent nouns also attracted suffixes from other categories: *-án* started out among diminutives, but took on nominalising and agentive functions (*bodhar* 'deaf' → *bodhrán* 'deafener/object that creates deafness > hand drum'). An example of the obsolescence of an agentive term and its recreation is OIr. *rímid* 'computer', consisting of the root *rím-* 'to count' + the native agentive suffix *-(a)id*. With the demise of Easter calculations, the medieval term disappeared. When new demand for the term 'computer' in the modern sense arose, the more distinct suffix *-aire* was added to the root to give ModIr. *ríomhaire*, instead of the perfectly acceptable **ríomhaí*.

3.3.4 Diminutives

The formation of diminutives overlaps with, but is by no means restricted to, the formation of hypocoristics of personal nouns (cf. section 3.5). The most common suffixes of Old Irish are inherited *-án*, *-én*, themselves reflexes of the obscured compound head PIE **-ĝn(h$_1$)ó-* 'born'. An outwardly similar, but unrelated suffix *-ín* entered the language from Latin via names such as *Augustinus*. It was easily adopted because of its structural similarity with the inherited suffixes and because it filled the hitherto empty phonological slot of a high front vowel; the iconicity of the perceptionally salient vowel [iː] facilitated its ensuing success in Modern Irish as the default diminutive suffix. Old Irish differentiates diminutives by gender. While the suffixes above are used for masculines and neuters, *-nat* is as a rule added to feminines, e.g., *brú* 'belly' → *bronnat*, *altóir* 'altar' → *altóirnat*. Finally, *-ne* and *-éne* are open to all genders.

In Modern Irish, the formal diversity of expression has been reduced despite the language's strong predilection for diminutives. The gender distinction has been largely abandoned, *-nat* has dropped out of use. While *-án*, for masculines, and *-óg* (OIr. *-óc*), for feminines, can still form diminutives to a certain degree, masc. (!) *-ín* has expanded its sphere from hypocoristic names to common nouns of all genders (e.g., *cáilín* 'girl') and has thereby become the diminutive suffix of Modern Irish par excellence. It can even be added to parts of speech other than nouns to turn them into something concrete, e.g., *agus* 'and' → *aguisín* 'addition, addendum', and it has entered English as a loan suffix from Irish (Dolan 2004: 84). *-óc* slowly appears outside of the onomastic sphere in the Middle Irish period (Russell 1990: 109 suspects subliterary productivity already in Early Irish), not always with precisely definable semantics. While occasionally it has a diminutive value, perhaps facilitated by the folk-etymological association with the native adjective *óc* 'young' (e.g., *elit* 'doe' → *elteóc* 'fawn, young doe'), very often it appears to have no emotional quality at all, but its function can be rather analysed as nominalising and individualising (e.g., *crann* 'tree' → *crannóc* 'wooden structure, wooden drinking-container, basket; wooden lake-dwelling'; *fés* 'coarse (pubic) hair' → *fésoc*, ModIr. *féasóg* 'beard'). In Modern Irish, *-óg* has become very productive as a feminine suffix. Together with several lesser suffixes (some of foreign, British Celtic origin) *-án* appears in complex diminutive suffixes, such as *-cán, -chán, -gán, -tán* (Ó hAnluain 1999: 251), but it has assumed other nominalising functions as well.

3.3.5 Adjectival suffixations

Aside from adjectives formed by compounding, new adjectives are formed from other word classes by suffixation or prefixation. Old Irish has two productive suffixes to derive adjectives from nouns, *-dae* and *-a/ech*, "the former denotes quality, kind, appurtenance, origin, material, time, etc., whereas *-ach* denotes possession or […] residence or situation in the place in question" (Thurneysen 1946: 220; Wodtko 1995: 258–263). In addition, there are the two suffixoids *-amail* and *-mar* (Wodtko 1995: 312–319). In some forms *-amail* still retains its original semantics 'like', but like the corresponding elements in Germanic, already in Old Irish it is on the verge of turning into a mere adjectival suffix. Participles are a means of deriving adjectives from verbal stems, but they should best be viewed as part of verbal inflection.

Especially in contact with learned Latin culture, a large number of new adjectives were required to express hitherto unknown concepts. While borrowed nouns usually do not require an overt adaptation to the Irish morphological system but are relatively easily integrated into one of the inflectional classes on the basis of their morphophonemic properties, foreign adjectives have to undergo morphological re-characterisation to be adopted into the grammatical system of the vernacular. *-dae* serves this function, e.g., Lat. *Aegyptiacus* → *Égeptacdae* 'Egyptian'. Its phonetical weakness, making it subject to numerous changes and assimilations, furnishes enough motivation for replacing it with a more distinct and stable suffix in the course of time. Beside *-ach*, which still retains its position, *-úil* < OIr. *-amail* now has taken the position of being the primary adjectival formant in Modern Irish.

3.4 Prefixation

What is called prefixation here, developed diachronically out of compounding. Prefixation typically entails some kind of adverbial qualification or quantification. Both nouns and adjectives (Wodtko 1995: 29–219) can receive prefixes. Apart from the distinction between bound and unbound morphemes in use as prefixes, the class of free elements falls into two, not clearly separable classes: those whose meaning in prefixal usage is identical or similar to their usage as independent words, and those where a semantic shift (usually bleaching) has occurred. For instance, ModIr. *sean-* 'old', which is always compounded in Irish, can, among other things, serve as an intensifier and as a pejorative qualifier (Caerwyn Williams 1968); ModIr. *leath-* 'half', when prefixed to adjectives, can be equivalent to 'quite, considerably' (Mac Cana 2003). Although a subgroup of the bound prefixes resemble prepositions (and are historically identical with them), they have taken on special meanings. *In-*, which from its prepositional meaning must have referred to being 'in' a position, expresses capability in constructions such as *reic* 'sale' → *indraic* 'trustworthy < *fit for sale' (Greene 1966). The list of prefixes and premodifiers has remained relatively stable from Old into Modern Irish (Ó hAnluain 1999: 242–249).

Language comparison reveals that some lexemes must already have served this purpose in Common Celtic. In some formations, especially those with *su/o-* 'good' and *du/o-* 'bad', prefixation is accompanied by stem variation, e.g., *cenél* 'kindred, race' (*o*-stem) → *sochenéoil* 'being of good family', *dochenéuil* 'low-born, degenerate' (both *i*-stem) (Marstrander 1945: 340–343). Because of the homophony of the palatalised ending with the gen. sg. of *o*-stems, this morphological rule was later re-interpreted as a syntactical one, yet again indicating the general trend in Irish from morphology to syntax.

An important subclass of bound prefixes are those that convey negative or privative meaning. The inherited negative Clt. **an-* had split into several allomorphs, depending on the following sound: *an-/ain-/in-/é-*; an even older **ne-* is only found in a small number of formations that are no longer analysable (*námae* 'enemy < *not loving', *noídiu* 'infant < *not knowing'). Negative *é-* is not always easy to distinguish from privative *e-* < **exs-*, which, however, is rare beside more common *dí-*. *neph-/neb-*, later *nem-*, ModIr. *neamh-* serves for the plain negation of the simplex. Most of these formations are still productive in Modern Irish, but at the same time the negative prefix *an-* was extended semantically to become an intensifier *an(a)-* 'very' (Dillon 1944, however, separates the two etymologically).

Prefixing with bound morphemes overlaps to a certain degree with inflectional morphology in that several additional degrees of comparison, over and above the usual tripartite system, are formed by prefixation in Old Irish: the excessive degree ('too X') with the prefix *ro-*, the elative or absolute superlative ('very X') with the suffixes *ér-*, *der-*, *rug-*, *ro-*, and the equative ('as X as') with *com-* which in Early Irish is in competition with suffixal morphology (Meid 1967). Of these, *ró-* and *chomh-* are still alive in Modern Irish.

Old Irish is a language with a threefold gender distinction. The masculine is the unmarked gender and can be used for common-gender reference. When the female sex of generic nouns needs to be specifically referenced, the prefix *ban-* (an allomorph of *ben* 'woman') is used. Although this usage is still endorsed for the modern standard language, e.g., *banúdar* 'female author', the spoken language pushes into the direction of phrasal nouns, e.g., *údar mná*, where *mná* is the genitive singular of *bean* 'woman'. Suffixation for *Femininmotion* (femininisation) is relatively rare. Aside from isolated, non-productive suffixes (e.g., *rí*, stem *ríg-* 'king' → *rígain* 'queen'), there are just a few suffixes like *-sech* or diminutive *-nat* whose productivity is limited.

3.5 Onomastics

The area of name creation deserves to be treated separately. While there is much formal overlap with nominal compounding, onomastic word-formation also makes use of special processes of its own, or rules that pre-empt developments that become prominent elsewhere in the language much later. Furthermore, more than other aspects of the language, name-formation is influenced by extralinguistic, social developments. From its ancestral stages, Old Irish had inherited an onomastic system in which compounding was a central process in creating personal names. Names of this structure are well attested in the Ogam inscriptions of the Primitive Irish period (Ziegler 1994: 66–89; Uhlich 1993: 78–139; Stüber 2009), and they continue to be used through the medieval and modern periods, even though the constitutive elements are often not synchronically recognisable even in Old Irish. Many names must have manifestly lost their semantic content, but they are usually amenable to comparative-linguistic analysis. Beside compound names, uncompounded adjectives (*Báeth* 'stupid', *Donn* 'brown') and common nouns (*Art* 'bear', *Bran* 'raven') also serve as personal names in Old Irish (O'Brien 1973: 219).

Beside these central methods of name-formation stand two other strategies. One is the formation of hypocoristics, usually taking compound names as their derivational basis. The typical suffixes are shared with common nouns: *-án*, *-én*, *-ín*, *-ne*, *-íne*, *-éne*, but also *-ón*, absent in the common lexicon; feminine names receive the suffix *-nat*. In addition, special derivational processes come into play that diverge more crucially from the central types of word-formation (Russell 2001): 1. truncation of compounded bases, often insensitive to morphological boundaries; 2. gemination, usually of the final consonant of truncated stems; 3. palatalisation of consonants, following a common pattern whereby front vowels are preferred in hypocoristics (Russell 2001: 245); 4. prefixation of the possessive pronouns *Mo* 'my' and *To*/*Do* 'thy', often accompanied by the British loan suffix *-óc* (Russell 2001: 242–245). The restriction of the latter type to the Christian sphere suggests that this process is an import from Britain. These processes can occur in various combinations, e.g., *Diarmait* → *Dímma*, *Crónán* (itself a diminutive) →

MoChúa, *Íarnán* → *Ternóc*, *Éndae* → *Éinne*, *Fintan* → *Munnu* (< *Mu Ḟin°*; *Ḟ* = a silent sound). The interplay of processes leads to forms that are only tenuously linked with their bases. Having no processual support in non-onomastic word-formation, these special types of word-formation became obscured very early, perhaps in the 7th century (Russell 2001: 249), and only the more common processes like suffixation remain.

In a second, syntactic strategy of name-formation, supplanting the others during the 7th century, the modifier follows the head noun in the genitive case or as an adjective. This pattern is identical to that of the phrasal nouns that replace compound nouns in the common lexicon. O'Brien (1973: 218, 226–230) famously called this type of formation "non-Indo-European" since it has been suspected of reflecting the syntactic structures of a non-Indo-European substrate language in Ireland. The list of possible heads in this construction is surprisingly small: *Cenn* 'head', *Cú* 'dog', *Der*, *Dar*, *Tar*, *Derb* 'daughter (?)', *Donn* 'brown', *Dub* 'black', *Fer* 'man', *Gillae* 'lad', *Mac* 'son, boy', *Máel* 'shorn, servant', *Mess* 'fosterling', *Nia* 'warrior, nephew'. To these should be added the element of mythical or divine names *Da* 'god (?)'. The list of possible second elements is much longer. Apparently, any semantically suitable word could make it into second position. In a sense, the first elements, the heads, are in a quasi-prefixal position in that they are synchronically unstressed and may undergo phonetic reduction. Although being syntactically in the dependent position, the second element bears the stress and thus assumes a perceptionally more salient role. In the course of the Middle and Modern Irish period, many of these names are consolidated as surnames, but occasionally they survived as first names and even entered English, e.g., OIr. *Máel Choluim* > ModIr. *Maolcholuim*, Engl. *Malcolm*, OIr. *Der Biled*, *Dar Filed* > ModIr. *Deirbhile*, *Dairile*, Engl. *Dervla*.

In the early medieval period, individuals were identified by their individual name followed by the name of their father. From the 10th century, individual patronymics gave way to a system in which individuals were identified by reference to an ancestor whose name did not change through the generations. Surnames were thus created. Names in *Úa* 'grandson' were petrified first, names in *Mac* 'son' established themselves as surnames only in the late 12th century, perhaps in the wake of the Anglo-Norman invasion. A change in a very small section of word-formation was thus caused by societal changes.

The vernacular formation of new names and of diminutives has virtually come to a halt and has been replaced by English strategies in recent times. Apart from the ubiquitous availability of *-ín* (which has been even taken over into English, Dolan 2004: 84), the formation of pet names follows English patterns, e.g., *Séamus* → *Séimí* like *James* → *Jimmy*, or *Mícheál* → *Micí*, *Meic* like *Michael* → *Mickey*, *Mike*; the suffix *-í* has been virtually adopted from English *-y*.

4 Verbal word-formation

The entirety of semantic and syntactic items that are drawn into the sphere of the Old Irish verb has not inappropriately been termed "the verbal complex" (Watkins 1963: 3). Among all the elements that make up this complex (McCone 1997: 1–19), the central, indispensable ones are the verbal root which carries the semantic information and the ending which specifies the subject. Between the two, suffixes for derivation or stem formation may occur, and semantically modifying preverbs may precede the root. In Old Irish, new verbs can be created either through suffixation to a non-verbal base, or through compounding a verbal base with preverbs. This results in a rough dichotomy between suffixed denominal, secondary verbs, and prefixed primary verbs.

4.1 Verbal compounds

Compounding, which in the verbal system is synonymous with prefixation, operates only within the same word class: both the base and the semantically modified derivative are verbs. Diachronically, verbal compounding in Celtic and Irish arose out of the collocation and univerbation of adverbial preverbs and verbal forms (see, e.g., Watkins 1963: 39–40; McCone 2006: 41–61), so that this phenomenon is ultimately accessory to syntax. Like nominal compounding, Old Irish has a pronounced predilection for verbal compounding whereby one or several of the closed set of lexical preverbs (Thurneysen 1946: 495–534) are added in front of a pre-existing verbal stem, which itself may already be compounded. Up to four lexical preverbs (not counting grammatical prefixes) can be stacked onto each other in this manner before the root. Preverbs show certain preferences for positions (e.g., *to-* almost always comes first, *uss-* and *ne-* always come last), partly reflecting the chronological stage when they were drawn into the construction, but this is by no means a straightjacket (McCone 2006: 177–190). The semantic link between the compounded derivative and its base stretches from identity or great proximity (e.g., uncompounded *soid* 'to turn' → *in·soí* 'to turn, return' (*inde-so(u̯)-*) → *do·intai* 'to turn, return' (*to-inde-so(u̯)-*)) to being almost undiscernable (e.g., uncompounded *benaid* 'to strike' → *fris·ben* 'to heal' (*fris-ben-*), *imm·díben* 'to circumcise' (*ambi-dī-ben-*), *do·forban* 'to arrive, reach' (*to-for-ben-*)).

The propensity for compounding has its roots at least in the Common Celtic period, and intensified in Early Irish, compensating for the reduction of the number of inherited verbal roots on the way from Proto-Indo-European to Irish (Wodtko 2007). At the same time, the importance of the inherited roots was enervated in a self-reinforcing process by the very shift of semantic information from the roots to the preverbs. Eventually, in many synchronic stems the roots are no longer recognisable or are heavily truncated. For instance, in *do·intai* above the inherited root **so(u̯)* has been reduced to a devoicing effect on *d* and to a schwa which itself is eclipsed by what can be described as the ending *-i*. Old Irish has thus a very high proportion of compound verbs compared to simple verbs, especially among inherited primary roots. The process of prefixation is still synchronically on-going in Old Irish. New compounds are created as calques on Latin verbs in bilingual contexts, often mirroring Latin preverbs with phonetically – and etymologically – cognate Irish ones (e.g., Lat. *uertere* 'to turn' → *conuertere* 'to change, convert' is mirrored by OIr. *do·soí* 'to turn' (*to-so(u̯)-*) → *con·toí* 'to change, convert' (*con-to-so(u̯)-*), cf. McCone 1997: 90).

Aside from compounding with the lexical preverbs, there is the much rarer type where a nominal form serves as an adverb in the first position (e.g., *cain* 'fine', *ceta-* 'first', *mad* 'well', *mó* 'early', etc.). Unlike the normal type, no stable verbal stems are created this way that could be freely inflected in person, tense or mood. Being confined predominantly to poetry and to stereotyped phrases like greetings or exclamations (e.g., *céin·mair* lit. 'long lives > happy!'), this is a stylistically marked construction, and it is a function of syntax rather than of semantics.

It cannot be easily said when the active creation of new compounds came to a halt, but probably by the Middle Irish period its productivity had largely ceased. Around this time, the intricacies of the Irish verbal system are altogether drastically overhauled, the gradual elimination of compound verbs being one of the steps in this process. While Old Irish marked the distinction between simple and compound verbs morphologically, this dichotomy is eroded through the simultaneous operation of morphological, phonological and syntactic processes. In consequence, previous compounds were re-interpreted as new primary verbs on the basis of either the so-called dependent stem or the verbal noun. Lexicalisation, caused by the lack of phonological and morphological transparency, thus fuels the demise of prefixation as a living process. Modern Irish has come the full circle: while semantic nuances of verbs could be differentiated by a change of prefixes in Early Irish, the semantic modification of basic verbs needs to be expressed by syntactic means again. As was probably the case at the very starting point of the circle, in Proto-Indo-European, Modern Irish relies on combining verbs with a variety of postverbal adverbs and prepositions to express semantic nuances. This analytic pattern has no doubt been boosted by the English superstrate. Furthermore, there is a predilection to use light-verb constructions, with the trend towards them starting already in Old Irish (Ronan 2012). Yet again, here is a gray area between word-formation and syntax.

4.2 Suffixation

The normal way of creating new, i.e. denominal verbs in Old Irish is by means of suffixation (Le Mair 2011). This typically turns a noun or adjective into a verbal stem. Synchronically by far the most important suffix for this is *-aig-*, which in Old Irish inflects as a weak deponent verb, e.g., *slán* 'whole, safe, sound' → *slánaigidir* 'to heal, make whole', and as a normal active verb *slánaigid* after the demise of deponents in Middle Irish. This suffix has its roots already in Insular or maybe even Common Celtic (Joseph 1987). It survives as ModIr. *-aí-* (verbal noun *-ú*) which is still a very productive way of integrating new concepts into the verbal system, and it is also added to the verbal nouns in *-áil*, the main verbaliser of loan words. Rarer and no longer productive in Old Irish, but productive probably in the immediately preceding period, is the suffixation of **-ā-* or **-ī-* to nominal stems (Thurneysen 1946: 338), e.g., *mór* 'big' → *móraid* 'to praise', *rím* 'number' → *rímid* 'to count'. Because of the phonological rules of Old Irish, these suffixes do not usually appear on the surface, but they leave numerous phonotactic traces.

While verbal derivation from primary verbs via suffixation is no longer a productive option in Irish, it was at a remote stage in the prehistory of the language. The lexicalised remnants of this process, which on the formal side involved root ablaut and the addition of the suffix *-ī-, and which created causatives semantically, are easily identifiable through comparative study: *reithid* 'to run' → *rothaid* 'to make run', *laigid* 'to lie (down)' → *(do)·lugai* 'to forgive < *to make lay (down)'. At the prehistoric stage when this rule was productive, the formation of causatives can be viewed as a paradigmatic rather than a derivational process. In the Irish of the historic period, however, such pairs are just lexicalised items.

5 References

Ahlqvist, Anders (1985): The ordering of nominal compounds in Irish. In: Jacek Fisiak (ed.), *Historical Semantics – Historical Word Formation*, 1–9. Berlin/New York: Mouton de Gruyter.

An Caighdeán Oifigiúil. Gramadach na Gaeilge. Caighdeán Athbhreithnithe. (2012): Baile Átha Cliath: Seirbhís Thithe an Oireachtais.

Binchy, Daniel A. (1972): Varia Hibernica. 2. Substantival dvandva-compounds in Irish. In: Herbert Pilch and Joachim Thurow (eds.), *Indo-Celtica. Gedächtnisschrift für Alf Sommerfelt*, 38–41. München: Hueber.

Breatnach, Liam (1983a): Varia IV. 1. On the agent suffix *-e* in Irish. *Ériu* 34: 194.

Breatnach, Liam (1983b): On abstract nouns from prepositions in Irish. *Celtica* 15: 18–19.

Breatnach, Liam (1994): An Mheán-Ghaeilge. In: Kim McCone, Damian McManus, Cathal Ó Háinle, Nicholas Williams and Liam Breatnach (eds.), *Stair na Gaeilge in ómós do P[h]ádraig Ó Fiannachta*, 221–333. Maigh Nuad: Roinn na Sean-Ghaeilge, Coláiste Phádraig. [Italian translation by Elisa Roma: *Il medioirlandese / Middle Irish. A translation into Italian of the Gaelic text An Mheán-Ghaeilge by Liam Breatnach*. New York: Mellen Press 2013].

Caerwyn Williams, John Ellis (1968): Defnydd arbennig ar eiriau: Cym. *hen*, Gwydd. *sean*. *Bulletin of the Board of Celtic Studies* 22: 42–45.

De Bernardo Stempel, Patrizia (1999): *Nominale Wortbildung des älteren Irischen. Stammbildung und Derivation*. Tübingen: Niemeyer.

De Bhaldraithe, Tomás (1953): *Gaeilge Chois Fhairrge. An Deilbhíocht*. Baile Átha Cliath: Institiúid Árd-Léinn Bhaile Átha Cliath.

Dillon, Myles (1944): The negative and intensive prefixes in Irish and the origin of Modern Irish *an* 'very; great'. *Transactions of the Philological Society* 1944 [1945]: 94–107.

Dinneen, Patrick S. (1927): *Foclóir Gaedhilge agus Béarla. An Irish-English Dictionary*. New edition, revised and greatly enlarged. Dublin: Irish Texts Society.

Dolan, Terence Patrick (2004): *A Dictionary of Hiberno-English. The Irish Use of English*. 2nd ed. Dublin: Gill & Macmillan.

Doyle, Aidan (1992): *Noun Derivation in Modern Irish. Selected Categories, Rules and Suffixes*. Lublin: Redakcja Wydawnictw Katolickiego Uniwersytetu Lubelskiego.

Doyle, Aidan (1996): Compounds and syntactic phrases in Modern Irish. *Studia Anglica Posnaniensia* 30: 83–95.

Doyle, Aidan and Edmund Gussman (2004): *A Reverse Dictionary of Modern Irish*. 2nd ed. Lublin: Folium.

Greene, David (1966): The prefix *in-*. *Ériu* 20: 82–86.

Greene, David (1977): Varia IV. 1. *feras*, *banas*, and some related abstracts. *Ériu* 28: 155–160.

Greene, David (1992): Celtic. In: Jadranka Gvozdanović (ed.), *Indo-European Numerals*, 497–554. Berlin/New York: De Gruyter Mouton.

Griffith, Aaron (2021): Goidelic. In: Götz Keydana, Wolfgang Hock and Paul Widmer (eds.), *Comparison and Gradation in Indo-European*, 233–254. Berlin/Boston: De Gruyter Mouton.

Hickey, Raymond (1985): Segmental phonology and word-formation: Agency and abstraction in the history of Irish. In: Jacek Fisiak (ed.), *Historical Semantics – Historical Word Formation*, 199–219. Berlin/New York: Mouton de Gruyter.

Höfler, Stefan and David Stifter (2025): Caland verbs in Celtic. In: Laura Grestenberger, Viktoria Reiter and Melanie Malzahn (eds.), *Deadjectival Verb Formation in Indo-European and Beyond*, 83–113. Berlin: Language Science Press.

Irslinger, Britta (2002): *Abstrakta mit Dentalsuffixen im Altirischen*. Heidelberg: Winter.

Joseph, Lionel S. (1987): The origin of the Celtic denominatives in **-sag-*. In: Calvert Watkins (ed.), *Studies in Memory of Warren Cowgill (1929–1985)*, 113–159. Berlin/New York: de Gruyter.

LEIA = Joseph Vendryes, Édouard Bachellery, Pierre-Yves Lambert *Lexique étymologique de l'irlandais ancien*. Volumes: A [1959], B [1980], C [1987], D [1996], MNOP [1960], RS [1974], TU [1978]. Dublin: Dublin Institute for Advanced Studies/Paris: Centre National de la Recherche Scientifique.

Le Mair, Esther (2011): Secondary verbs in Old Irish. A comparative-historical study of patterns of verbal derivation in the Old Irish glosses. Ph.D. dissertation, Department of Old and Middle Irish and Celtic Philology, National University of Ireland Galway.

Lloyd-Jones, John (1947): The compounds of *gal*. In: Séamus Prender (ed.), *Féilscríbhinn Torna. Tráchtaisí léanta in onóir don Ollamh Tadhg Ua Donnchadha, D. Litt., in am a dheichiú bliana agus trí fichid, an ceathru lá de mhí Mheán Fhómhair 1944*, 83–89. Cork: Cló Ollscoile Corcaí.

Mac Cana, Proinsias (2003): Varia V. 2. Irish *leth-*, Welsh *lled* 'quite, considerably'. *Ériu* 53: 180–181.

Marstrander, Carl J. S. (1945): Sygnatrausti. *Norsk Tidsskrift for Sprogvidenskap* 13: 319–343.

McCone, Kim (1994): An tSean-Ghaeilge agus a Réamhstair. In: Kim McCone, Damian McManus, Cathal Ó Háinle, Nicholas Williams and Liam Breatnach (eds.), *Stair na Gaeilge in ómós do P[h]ádraig Ó Fiannachta*, 61–219. Maigh Nuad: Roinn na Sean-Ghaeilge, Coláiste Phádraig.

McCone, Kim (1995): OIr. *senchae, senchaid* and preliminaries on agent noun formation in Celtic. *Ériu* 46: 1–10.

McCone, Kim (1997): *The Early Irish Verb*. Revised 2nd ed. with Index Verborum. Maynooth: An Sagart.

McCone, Kim (2005): *A First Old Irish Grammar and Reader. Including an Introduction to Middle Irish*. Maynooth: Department of Old and Middle Irish, NUI Maynooth.

McCone, Kim (2006): *The Origins and Development of the Insular Celtic Verbal Complex*. Maynooth: Department of Old and Middle Irish.

McCone, Kim, Damian McManus, Cathal Ó Háinle, Nicholas Williams and Liam Breatnach (eds.) (1994): *Stair na Gaeilge in ómós do P[h]ádraig Ó Fiannachta*. Maigh Nuad: Roinn na Sean-Ghaeilge, Coláiste Phádraig.

McManus, Damian (1994): An Nua-Ghaeilge Chlasaiceach. In: Kim McCone, Damian McManus, Cathal Ó Háinle, Nicholas Williams and Liam Breatnach (eds.), *Stair na Gaeilge in ómós do P[h]ádraig Ó Fiannachta*, 335–445. Maigh Nuad: Roinn na Sean-Ghaeilge, Coláiste Phádraig.

Meid, Wolfgang (1967): Zum Aequativ der keltischen Sprachen, besonders des Irischen. In: Wolfgang Meid (ed.), *Beiträge zur Indogermanistik und Keltologie. Julius Pokorny zum 80. Geburtstag gewidmet*, 223–242. Innsbruck: Institut für Sprachwissenschaft der Universität Innsbruck.

NIL = Dagmar Wodtko, Britta Irslinger, Caroline Schneider (eds.) (2008): *Nomina im indogermanischen Lexikon*. Heidelberg: Winter.

O'Brien, Michael (1973): Old Irish personal names. *Celtica* 10: 211–236.

Ó Curnáin, Brian (2016): Irish. In: Peter O. Müller, Ingeborg Ohnheiser, Susan Olsen and Franz Rainer (eds.), *Word-Formation. An International Handbook of the Languages of Europe*. Vol. 4, 2782–2810. Berlin/Boston: De Gruyter Mouton.

Ó Dónaill, Niall (1977): *Foclóir Gaeilge-Béarla*. Baile Átha Cliath: An Gúm.

Ó hAnluain, Liam A. (1999): *Graiméar Gaeilge na mBráithre Críostaí. Éagrán Nua*. Baile Átha Cliath: An Gúm.

Ó Muircheartaigh, Peadar (2018): The sociolinguistics of the superlative adjective in the Milan Glosses. *Ériu* 68: 129–144.

O'Rahilly, Thomas F. (1942): *-genn* for *-chenn*. *Ériu* 13: 140–143.

Pedersen, Holger (1909–13): *Vergleichende Grammatik der keltischen Sprachen*. 2 Vol. Göttingen: Vandenhoeck & Ruprecht.

Quin, Ernest G. (ed.) (1983): *Dictionary of the Irish Language Based Mainly on Old and Middle Irish Materials*. Compact Edition. Dublin: Royal Irish Academy.

Ronan, Patricia (2012): *Make Peace and Take Victory. Support Verb Constructions in Old English in Comparison with Old Irish*. Odense: University of Southern Denmark.

Rossiter, Trudy (2004): Verbal composition in Old Irish with special reference to multi-preverb compounds. Ph.D. dissertation, Department of Old and Middle Irish, National University of Ireland Maynooth.

Russell, Paul (1990): *Celtic Word-Formation. The Velar Suffixes*. Dublin: Dublin Institute for Advanced Studies.

Russell, Paul (1996): 'Verdunkelte Komposita' in Celtic. *Studia Celtica* 30: 113–125.

Russell, Paul (2001): Patterns of Hypocorism in Early Irish Hagiography. In: John Carey, Máire Herbert and Pádraig Ó Riain (eds.), *Studies in Irish Hagiography. Saints and Scholars*, 237–249. Dublin: Four Courts Press.

Schumacher, Stefan (2004): *Die keltischen Primärverben. Ein vergleichendes, etymologisches und morphologisches Lexikon*. Unter Mitarbeit von Britta Schulze-Thulin und Caroline aan de Wiel. Innsbruck: Institut für Sprachwissenschaft der Universität Innsbruck.

Stifter, David (2009): Early Irish. In: Martin J. Ball and Nicole Müller (eds.), *The Celtic Languages*, 55–116. 2nd ed. Abingdon/New York: Routledge.

Stifter, David (2011): Lack of Syncope and other nichtlautgesetzlich vowel developments in OIr. consonant-stem nouns. Animacy rearing its head in morphology? In: Thomas Krisch and Thomas Lindner (eds.), *Indogermanistik und Linguistik im Dialog. Akten der XIII. Fachtagung der Indogermanischen Gesellschaft*, 556–565. Wiesbaden: Reichert.

Stüber, Karin (1998): *The Historical Morphology of* n-*Stems in Celtic*. Maynooth: Dept. of Old Irish, National University of Ireland Maynooth.

Stüber, Karin (2009): 6. Keltisch. In: Karin Stüber, Thomas Zehnder and Ulla Remmer (eds.), *Indogermanische Frauennamen*, 243–278. Heidelberg: Winter.

Stüber, Karin (2010): Verbalabstrakta im Altirischen: Verbalnomina und verwandte Kategorien. In: Karin Stüber, Thomas Zehnder and Dieter Bachmann (eds.), *Akten des 5. Deutschsprachigen Keltologensymposiums. Zürich, 7.–10. September 2009*, 377–393. Wien: Praesens.

Stüber, Karin (2015): *Die Verbalabstrakta des Altirischen*. Bremen: Hempen.

Stüber, Karin (2017): The morphology of Celtic. In: Jared Klein, Brian Joseph and Matthias Fritz (eds.), *Handbook of Comparative and Historical Indo-European Linguistics. An International Handbook*, 1203–1218. Berlin/Boston: De Gruyter Mouton.

Stüber, Karin (2022): Zwischen Wortbildung und Flexion. Verbalnomina auf *-mu- im Altirischen. In: Florian Sommer, Karin Stüber, Paul Widmer and Yoko Yamazaki (eds.), *Indogermanische Morphologie in erweiterter Sicht. Grenzfälle und Übergänge. Beiträge zu einer 2020 in Zürich geplanten, aber nicht stattgefundenen Fachtagung der Indogermanischen Gesellschaft*, 175–184. Innsbruck: Universität Innsbruck.

Thurneysen, Rudolf (1946): *A Grammar of Old Irish*. Dublin: Dublin Institute for Advanced Studies.

Toner, Gregory (2013): *Electronic Dictionary of the Irish Language 2013*. Belfast: Queens University. http://edil.qub.ac.uk/dictionary/search.php [last access 21 Jan 2015].

Tristram, Hildegard L. C. (2010): Probleme bei der Quantifizierung morphologischer Komplexität im Altirischen. In: Karin Stüber, Thomas Zehnder and Dieter Bachmann (eds.), *Akten des 5. Deutschsprachigen Keltologensymposiums. Zürich, 7.–10. September 2009*, 407–426. Wien: Praesens.

Uhlich, Jürgen (1993): *Die Morphologie der komponierten Personennamen des Altirischen*. Bonn/Witterschlick: Wehle.

Uhlich, Jürgen (1997): Der Kompositionstyp 'Armstrong' in den indogermanischen Sprachen. *Historische Sprachforschung* 110(1): 21–46.

Uhlich, Jürgen (2002): Verbal governing compounds (synthetics) in early Irish and other Celtic languages. *Transactions of the Philological Society* 100(3): 403–433.

Veselinović, Elvira (2003): *Suppletion im irischen Verb*. Hamburg: Kovač.

Watkins, Calvert (1963): Preliminaries to a historical and comparative analysis of the syntax of the Old Irish verb. *Celtica* 6: 1–49.

Wodtko, Dagmar S. (1995): *Sekundäradjektive in den altirischen Glossen. Untersuchungen zur präfixalen und suffixalen Wortbildung*. Innsbruck: Institut für Sprachwissenschaft der Universität Innsbruck.

Wodtko, Dagmar S. (2007): Das Verb im Lexikon: Indogermanisch und Irisch. *International Journal of Diachronic Linguistics and Linguistic Reconstruction* 4(2): 91–133.

Wodtko, Dagmar S. (forthc.): The morphology of Old Irish. In: Joseph F. Eska, Silva Nurmio, Peadar Ó Muircheartaigh and Paul Russell (eds.), *The Palgrave Handbook of Celtic Languages and Linguistics*. Basingstoke: Palgrave Macmillan.

Ziegler, Sabine (1994): *Die Sprache der altirischen Ogam-Inschriften*. Göttingen: Vandenhoeck & Ruprecht.

Swetlana Mengel

21 Historical word-formation in Slavic

Abstract: The most important peculiarity of Slavic word-formation as compared to other Indo-European languages is the enormous productivity of affixation. Derivation surpasses compounding in importance and offers a wide range of affixes, particularly suffixes in noun formation. This is a result of diachronic changes in the structure of Proto-Slavonic due to the influence of specific sound changes which led to a gradual shift of morpheme boundaries in the word, thus increasing the number and the formal complexity of the suffixes, and subsequently consolidating the semantic categories of word-formation. A further influence was exerted by the peculiarities of word-formation in Old Church Slavonic on the development of the word-formation systems of the written standard languages in the Slavia Orthodoxa.

1 Introduction

The diachronic study of word-formation aims at the reconstruction of the historically "real" processes employed in the formation of new words, i.e. it seeks to analyze word-formation in its dynamics, in the relationship of the derivational stem and the derived word as well as the means of word-formation in their origin and subsequent development on the morphological and semantic level.

Linguistic reconstruction includes an historical-comparative approach and the use of etymological methods. This has had the consequence that the historical word-formation of the Slavic languages has traditionally been confined to the etymological scrutiny of Proto-Slavonic (Varbot 1984), and its morpheme inventory was the centre of interest (Efimova 2006).

Swetlana Mengel, Halle/S., Germany

https://doi.org/10.1515/9783111420530-021

The most significant feature of Slavic word-formation as compared to that of other Indo-European languages is the enormous productivity of affixation. Derivation plays a leading role and exceeds compounding in importance. It makes use of a wide range of affixes, especially of suffixes in noun formation. In view of this fact, the two above mentioned approaches (etymology and morphemics) to a diachronic study of word-formation become plausible. They form the basis and backbone of this kind of linguistic investigation (Meillet 1961 [1902–05]; Vaillant 1964 [1948]).

The present description of the historical word-formation of Slavic is meant to complement the above-mentioned traditional etymological approaches with concepts and findings of contemporary word-formation theory. For this reason we operate with complex concepts (types and categories of word-formation) and include in the analysis both morphological and semantic aspects (cf. Mengel 1997, 2002, 2007). Our presentation is not meant to list each and every affix or word-formation procedure for all word classes, but rather aims at the description of the central phenomenon of the derivation of nouns by means of numerous suffixes with different forms and meanings, which constitutes a unique feature of Slavic compared to other Indo-European languages. The great diversity of suffixes arose as a consequence of specific phonetic laws in Classical Proto-Slavonic (5th–8th centuries AC). The historic dynamics of this development is presented in this article in its application to the word class of nouns.

Another specific feature of historical word-formation in Slavic goes back to characteristics of the first written language of the Slavs which arose as the language of translations of religious texts from Greek into Slavic in the course of the Christianization of the Slavs in the second half of the 9th century and which evolved in the 10th–11th centuries. This written language, which is known as classical Old Church Slavonic, Old Bulgarian or Old Slavonic is considered the first written fixation of Proto-Slavonic ever and was based on the living South-Slavonic, Macedonian-Bulgarian dialects in the vicinity of Thessalonica. It was later enriched by West-Slavic (Moravian) and East-Slavic influences. However, Old Church Slavonic was from its very beginning heavily reliant on the creativity of the translators for the transmission of complex religious and abstract concepts that were missing from the everyday Slavic language of that time. The means, structures and processes of word-formation developed as a result of these translation activities and had repercussions for the word-formation procedures in the later Slavic languages.

On the other hand, Old Church Slavonic (9th–11th centuries) reflects, as mentioned above, the late state of Proto-Slavonic (7th–9th centuries). In this particular period of time, the phonetic laws which determined the specific Slavic means of word-formation and are generally responsible for the development of the particularities of a given word-formation system (cf. section 2), lost their former vigour. As a consequence, the Slavic word-formation system develops and stabilizes in this very period. Later on, the individual Slavic languages do not develop word-formation systems of their own that would considerably differ from these original word-formation routines in Common Slavonic. Slight differences may be observed with respect to the productivity of particular affixes and the influence of morphemes borrowed from other languages in the course of history (cf. section 4). This is why it is necessary to pay special attention to the word-formation of Old Church Slavonic when describing historical Slavic word-formation (cf. section 3).

In the following the abbreviations Psl. and OCsl. will stand respectively for the reconstructed Proto-Slavonic, the Proto-Slavonic elements in Old Church Slavonic and the Old Church Slavonic elements resulting from the activity of the first translators. All examples provided in this article are taken from historical dictionaries, language testimonies examined by myself (cf. Mengel 1997, 1998, 2007) and from further works cited individually.

For the above-mentioned reasons, the present article concentrates on derivation, particularly on suffixation in nominal structures. The derivation of adjectives and verbal word-formation, predominantly by prefixes descended from adverbs and prepositions (as in other Indo-European languages), will be referred to in smaller overviews only.

The formal and semantic mechanisms of the development of the suffixal word-formation of adjectives run parallel to those of nouns. Due to the fact that nouns and adjectives in Slavic originally constituted a single class of words, the derivation of both adjectives and nouns relies on the same primary suffixes. A description of the individual suffixes for adjectives in Old Church Slavonic (which remains valid for the individual Slavic languages, too) may be obtained from investigations dedicated to this particular topic (Brodowska-Honowska 1960; Grammatika 1993; Birnbaum and Schaeken 1997). For the sake of exemplification, we will only mention here the most important word-formation categories of the adjectives. To the latter belong qualitative adjectives (cf. OCsl. *kras-ьn-ъ* 'beautiful, red', *dob-r-ъ* 'good, benign', *slad-ok-ъ* 'sweet'), relational adjectives (OCsl. *osobь* [*osob-j-ь*] 'isolated, special'), and possessive adjectives (OCsl. *adam-ov-ъ* 'of Adam', *božь* [*bog-j-ь*] 'God's').

Prefixation as a word-formation procedure is not typical of Slavic nouns or adjectives, whereas it is highly productive in verbal word-formation. From the earliest stages of development right on to the present day, prefixes serve in the Slavic languages as a means of forming different *aktionsarten*. Worth mentioning here are the following: ingressive (cf. OCsl. *za-žešti* 'to set alight'), finitive (OCsl. *sъ-plesti* 'to finish with binding'), completive (Russ. *do-pisat'* 'to complete a writing'), delimitative (Russ. *po-stojat'* 'to stand a while'), perdurative (Russ. *pro-rabot-*

at' (*ves' den'*) 'to work (all day long)'), distributive (Russ. *po-zapirat'* (*vse dveri*) 'to close (all the doors [one after the other])'), cumulative (OCsl. *sъ-zvati* 'to call [all] together'), total (Russ. *is-pisat'* 'to fill with letters') and attenuative (Russ. *pri-otkryt'* (*okno*) 'to open (the window) a bit'); cf. Grammatika (1993); Birnbaum and Schaeken (1997).

Compounding will be dealt with in connection with Old Church Slavonic translations (cf. section 3.2).

2 Development of the word-formation system in Proto-Slavonic

2.1 Word-formation in early Proto-Slavonic

The difficulty of determining from an etymological point of view the motivational direction of designations with the same roots in words such as Psl. **chvala* 'praise' and **chvaliti* 'to praise' (cf. Russ. *chvala* : *chvalit'*, Pol. *chwała* : *chwalić*, Serb. *chvala* : *chvaliti*, OCsl. *chvala* : *chvaliti*) (see Meillet 1961: 27), reflects the original interdependence in the designation of objects (nouns) and variable characteristics of these objects (verbs, adjectives). The example **chvala* – **chvaliti* also shows the early occurrence of the naming function of word-formation: new words were built up from already existing ones by means of formal non-lexical elements.

The formation of new words and of word forms was based on the same mechanisms. Originally the main role was played by v o w e l c h a n g e s in the root morpheme and the final sound of the stem, e.g., Psl. **mer-* : **mor-* in **merěti* 'to die' : **moriti* 'to kill', **morъ* 'plague' (cf. OCsl. *merěti* : *moriti*, *morъ*, Russ. *umeret'* : *umorit'*, *mor*); Psl. **chvatati* (durative action) 'to seize' : **chvatiti* (sudden action) 'to grab' (OCsl. *chvatati* : *chvatiti*, Russ. *chvatat'* : *schvatit'*); Psl. **orbŏs* 'worker' : **orbās* 'female worker' (OCsl. *rabъ* : *raba*, Russ. *rab* : *raba*).

Regarding the regular vocalic stem endings in the noun-declension as well as the theme-vowels of the verbs in the four verb classes, one can assume genuine form-building and word-building morphemes or suffixes. Already in its earliest period, Proto-Slavonic had other word-formation morphemes similar to the ones mentioned above, all of which were inherited from Proto-Indo-European. The suffix **-j-* proved very productive both in verbal inflection, for instance, as a supplement to the thematic suffixes of the verbs of the third class **-jo/je-* as in Psl. **plakati* 'to weep' – **plak-jo-on* 1st pers. sg. (OCsl. *plakati* – *plačǫ*, Russ. *plakat'* – *plaču*) and in the formation of nouns such as Psl. **zem-j-ā-s* > **zemlja* 'earth' (OCsl. *zemlja*), Psl. **kon-j-ŏ-s* > **kon'* 'horse' (OCsl. *konь*); Psl. **suchъ* 'dry'

→ *such-j-ь > *suš'ъ 'drought', Psl. *such-j-a > suš'a 'dry land' (OCsl. suchъ → sušь, suša), Psl. *čędo 'child' → *čęd-j-ь > *čęďь 'people' (OCsl. čędo → čędь). The suffix is still used today, for instance, in the formation of Slavic generic adjectives (cf. Russ. *lisьjanora* 'fox hole' from *lisa* 'fox').

The above-mentioned Proto-Slavonic morphemes are primary suffixes that, as the examples show, were not yet clearly differentiated semantically and functionally.

The effect of the phonetic laws in Proto-Slavonic (5th–8th centuries), i.e. the tendency towards increasing the sonority of the syllables ("law of the open syllable") and a further tendency towards palatalization of consonants, led to a remodeling of the word structure and to the development of new morphemes both in word-formation and inflection. Above all, the law of the open syllable, a tendency in Common Slavonic which resulted in the (re)arrangement of phonemes in a syllable from lower to higher sonority, caused a profound shift of morpheme boundaries, a phenomenon called metanalysis.

The most important consequence was a striking peculiarity of Slavonic word-formation in comparison with other Indo-European languages: the enormous productivity of word-formation by suffixation with a vast array of suffixes, especially in noun formation. Therefore, the most important word-formation procedure in Slavic, viz. derivation, will be dealt with in more detail and particular attention will be paid in the following to the diachronic developments in noun formation.

2.2 Effects of phonetic laws on derivation

The regular co-occurrence of a specific affix with the derivational stems of a specific word class and the parallel semantic increase in the derivative, i.e. the word-formation meaning, proves the existence of specific morphological word-formation structures (patterns) as well as of semantic word-formation types in the systems of the Slavic languages.

Word-formation types – according to Dokulil (1962) and Lopatin and Uluchanov (1970) – fulfill the following criteria: 1) identical word class of the base, 2) identical meaning/function of the formant, 3) identical semantic relation between the base and the derivative. Types with different formants, but identical word-formation meanings, and identical semantic relations between the base and the derivative can be united in word-formation categories (cf. section 2.2.3).

The diachronic development of the Slavic system of word-formation initially produced new word-formation suffixes on the basis of the inherited primary morphemes of Indo-European and resulted finally in the growth of the morphological variety and the consolidation of the respective semantic structures.

2.2.1 Increase in the number of suffixes and their formal extension

Relevant investigations (Meillet 1961 [1902–05]; Vaillant 1964 [1948]; Seliščev 1952; Grammatika 1993; Birnbaum and Schaeken 1997) confirmed that early Proto-Slavonic, apart from the above-mentioned stem endings **-ŏ*, **-ā*, **-ĭ*, **-ŭ*, **-ū* had the following Indo-European primary suffixes for the formation of nouns: **-b-*, **-v-*, **-g-*, **-j-*, **-k-*, **-l-*, **-n-*, **-r-*, **-t-*.

The remodeling of the word structure, due to the law of the open syllable, resulted in a shift of the morpheme boundaries in the words (metanalysis). The above-mentioned primary suffixes were eventually fused with the word root, a phenomenon comparable to the process of fusion of vocalic stem endings with the new word endings. The primary suffixes eventually lost their original functions, cf. Psl. **zvon-ŏ-s* (> *zvonъ*) 'sound, ringing' → **zvon*-k-*ŏ-s* > **zvǫkъ* 'sound' (OCsl. *zvonъ*, *zvǫkъ*), Psl. **byti* 'to be, exist' → **by*-l-ь > **bylь* 'true story' (OCsl. *byti*, *bylь*), Psl. **dati* 'to give' → **da*-r-ъ > **darъ* 'gift, present' (OCsl. *dati*, *darъ*), Psl. **sъpati* 'to sleep' → **sъp*-n-ъ > **sъnъ* 'sleep' (OCsl. *sъpati*, *sъnъ*), Psl. **vōldti* (> **vlasti*) 'to rule' → **vōld*-t-ь > **vōlttь* > **vōlstь* > **vlastь* 'power' (OCsl. *vlasti*, *vlastь*).

On the other hand, metanalysis led to a formally larger suffix by:

a) fusion of the primary consonantal suffixes with the stem endings,
b) combination of two (or more) primary (or newly formed) suffixes,
c) extension of the new suffixes by means of new endings.

As a result of this development, several new word-formation morphemes evolved, which were formally more complex and at the same time served to distinguish their function/meaning more clearly. The number of derivational morphemes increased sharply, since one primary suffix gave rise to several new ones.

This will be demonstrated by the suffix **-k-*, which proved to be especially productive in early Proto-Slavonic. As in Indo-European, it was used for extending several word stems, originally without any significant semantic change (Meillet 1961: 333). The process of morpheme boundary shift resulted in the combination of the vocalic stem endings **-ŏ* (> *-o*) **-ā* (> *a*), **-ī* (> *-i*), **-ĭ* (> ь), **-ŭ* (> -ъ), **-ū* (> *-y*) with the suffix **-k-* and thus in the formation of the new suffixes *-ok-*, *-ak-*, *-ik-*, *-ьk-*, *-ъk-*, *-yk-* (cf. OCsl. *vid-ok-ъ* 'witness', *bliz-ok-ъ* 'relative'; ORuss. *ryb-ak-ъ* 'fisherman', *prost-ak-ъ* 'simpleton'; *zlat-ik-ъ* 'gold coin', Russ.-OCsl. *nož-ik-ъ* 'small knife'; OCsl. *dobyt-ъk-ъ* 'gain', *pęt-ъk-ъ* 'five pieces', *cvět-ъk-ъ* 'small flower'). The tendency towards palatalization affected a still larger number of new suffixes: in the third palatalization, the velar consonant **k* became *c* after the vowels *i* und ь; this led to the development of the suffixes *-ic-* < *-ik-* (cf. OCsl. *čarodě-ic-ь* 'magician'), and *-ьc-* < *-ьk-* (OCsl. *vid-ьc-ь* 'witness', *star-ьc-ь* 'the elderly', *čгьn-ьc-ь* 'monk', *cvět-ьc-ь* 'small flower', *studen-ьc-ь* 'well'), whereas the suffixes *-ik-* und *-ьk-* remained in use due to the inconsistencies in the remodeling process.

By the fusion of (two) suffixes more new suffixes were formed in early Proto-Slavonic. This was frequently caused by the regressive effect of the suffix *-j-* on preceding consonants with a tendency towards palatalization, e.g., Psl. **kj > č*: *-ak-jo > -ačь* (Seliščev 1952: 59; cf. OCsl. *kov-ačь* 'blacksmith', Russ. *borodačь* 'bearded', Cz. *bradáč* 'id.'), and *-ik-jo > -ičь* (OCsl. *gospod-ičь* 'son of the lord', ORuss. *sestr-ičь* 'nephew, son of the sister', *pьsov-ičь* 'dog-keeper'). The combination of the suffixes *-ak-* and **-ĭ-j-* resulted in the new suffix *-ъčii/-ьčii* (Seliščev 1952: 63; cf. OCsl. *kъnig-ъčii* 'book expert', *krъm-ьčii* 'helmsman').

The number of new suffixes was further increased by adding new endings: *-ika < -ik-a* (cf. OCsl. *bliž-ika* 'relative', *ǫž-ika* 'relative'); *-ьka < ьk-a* (OCsl. *rǫč-ьka* 'handle'); *-ъka < -ъk-a* (OCsl. *kot-ъka* 'cat', *tet-ъka* 'aunt'); *-ica < -ic-a* (OCsl. *proroč-ica* 'fortune teller f.', *čarodě-ica* 'magician', *tьmьn-ica* 'dungeon', *grъl-ica* 'turtle-dove', *ryb-ica* 'small fish'); *-ьce < -ic-e* (OCsl. *slъn-ьce* < Psl. **sъlnьce* < Indo-European **sāul-/sul-* 'sun', *čęd-ьce* 'small child', *bljud-ьce* 'small bowl'); *-ьca < -ьc-a* (OCsl. *dvьr-ьca* 'small door', *sěč-ьca* 'hangman'); *-yka < -yk-a* (OCsl. *vlad-yka* 'ruler, sovereign').

The growth of the complexity of suffixes by the shift of morpheme boundaries (metanalysis) continued after the phonetic law of the open syllable had expired in late Proto-Slavonic. Mostly from the combination of two (or more) new suffixes, complex new suffixes of the second generation evolved.

The suffix *-ik-*, for example, was extended by the adjectival suffix *-ьn-*, and the suffix of the passive past participle *-en-* was extended to the new complex suffix *-ьnik-/-enik-*; cf. a) OCsl. *grěšьnikъ* 'sinner' (Psl. **grěchъ* 'sin' → **grěch-ĭ-n-ъ* > **grěš-ьn-ъ* 'sinful'; OCsl. *grěšьnъ* 'sinful' → *grěšьn-ik-ъ* 'sinner'; at the same time, OCsl. *grěšnikъ* can now be perceived as a denominal derivative (N → N): *grěchъ* 'sin' → *grěš-ьnik-ъ* 'sinner') and b) OCsl. *ljublenikъ* 'lover, beloved' (OCsl. *ljubiti* 'to love' → *ljubl-en-ъ* 'beloved' → *ljublen-ik-ъ* 'lover'; with *-enikъ* as a new complex suffix the noun has to be regarded as a deverbal derivative (V → N): OCsl. *ljubiti* 'to love' → *ljubl-enikъ* 'lover, beloved').

The following derivatives can thus be analyzed (without referring to an intermediate stage of derivation) as

- deverbal: OCsl. *zaštitьnikъ* 'guardian' (← *zaštititi* 'to protect'), *mǫčenikъ* 'martyr' (← *mǫčiti* 'to torment'), *istočьnikъ* 'spring' (← *istočati* 'to flow out'),
- denominal: OCsl. *kъnižьnikъ* 'book expert' (← *kъniga* 'book'), *žrьtvьnikь* 'sacrificial altar' (← *žrьtva* 'sacrifice'), and
- deadjectival: OCsl. *prazdьnikъ* 'holiday' (← *prazdьnъ* 'empty, free').

Thus in late Proto-Slavonic (as well as in Old Church Slavonic as its first written fixation), the following secondary suffixes occur: *-*k*- > OCsl. *-ok-ъ*, *-ak-ъ*, *-ik-ъ*, *-ika*, *-ьk-ъ*, *-ьka*, *-ъkъ*, *-ъka*, *-yka*, *-ьcь*, *-ьce*, *-ьca*, *-ica*, *-ačь*, *-ičь*, *-ъčii*/*-ьčii*, *-ьnikъ*/*-enikъ*.

The increase of the formal complexity of suffixes was furthermore enhanced by the doubling of a new suffix in certain derivations without creating a new meaning (affix pleonasm), as, for example, ORuss. *sestr-ičь*, *sestr-ič-ičь* (from *sestra* 'sister'), Russ. dial. *sestr-ičъ*, *sestr-ič-ičъ* (Dal' 1956 [1880–82]: IV, 179) 'nephew, son of the sister'; ORuss. *brat-ičь*, *brat-ič-ičь* (from *bratъ* 'brother') 'nephew, son of the brother', or it was due to the use of two different new suffixes in derivatives such as Russ.-OCsl. *bratъ* 'brother' → *brat-an-ьcь* 'brother' and ORuss. *brat-anъ* 'nephew'; OCsl. *vlasti* 'to reign' → *vlas-telь*, but also *vlas-telь-nikъ*, *vlas-tel-inъ*, *vlas-tel-janinъ* 'sovereign'. These approaches were largely practised by the translators of texts into Old Church Slavonic (and later into Church Slavonic) (see section 3.1.2).

2.2.2 Consolidation of word-formation semantics

In comparison to primary suffixes (including final stem vowels) with their primarily stem-extending function (Psl. **orb*- [cf. Russ. dial. *robi-ti* 'to work'] → **orb-ŏ-s* 'worker', **orb-ā-s* 'female worker'; **moriti* 'to kill' → **mor-ŏ-s* 'plague', **chvaliti* 'to praise' : **chval-ā-s* 'praise', see section 2.1), the new suffixes, thanks to their strength of formal expression are in a position to consolidate their share of meaning in the newly created word structures and to transmit these shares of meaning to derivatives of identical word structure, cf. Psl. **pēns-ŭ-k-ŏ-s* (originally without any diminutive meaning) > **pěs-ъk-ъ* (Grammatika 1993: 182) 'sand' (OCsl. *pěsъkъ*) vs. **domъ* (< **dom-ŏ-s*) 'house' → **dom-ъk-ъ* 'small house' (OCsl. *domъ* → *domъkъ*).

It is in this manner that regular word-formation structures (word-formation types) evolved which, by the combination of a certain suffix with the derivational stem of a certain morphological category (but independent of the individual lexical meaning), regularly produce an identical semantic increase compared to the meaning of the stem (in the examples cited above, e.g., diminutiveness), in contemporary word-formation theory referred to as word-formation meaning (Lopatin and Uluchanov 1980: 136; cf. Mengel 2009: 776 ff.).

According to the nature of the semantic increase, transmitted and consolidated by the new suffixes, one can distinguish three major semantic types (cf. Dokulil 1968: 203 ff.):

a) Transposition: The results are derivatives in which the affix merely has a syntactic function, changing the base's part of speech. Here belongs, for instance, the formation of abstract nouns (reification of features, qualities and processes), cf. OCsl. *bogat-ьstvo* 'wealth' (← *bogatъ* 'rich'), *prišьl-ьstvo* 'arrival' (← *prišьlъ* 'arrived'), *rožd-ьstvo* 'birth' (← *roždьnъ* 'born'); *grъd-ostь* 'pride' (← *grъdъ* 'proud'), *prav-ostь* 'justice' (← *pravъ* 'just'), *krotъk-ostь* 'gentleness' (← *krot-ъkъ* 'gentle'); *prav-ota* 'justice' (← *pravъ* 'just'), *kras-ota* 'beauty' (← *kras-ьnъ* 'beautiful', *krasa* 'beauty'); *grъd-yni* 'pride' (← *grъdъ* 'proud'), *prav-yni* 'justice' (← *pravъ* 'just'); *spasen-ie* 'rescue' (← *spas-enъ* 'rescued'), *trьpě-nie* 'patience' (← *trьpěti* 'to endure') and others more.

b) Modification: The derivatives and their bases refer to the same kind of objects, i.e. they always represent the same part of speech. The affix modifies the meaning of the base as, for example, in diminutives, cf. OCsl. *grad-ьcь* 'small town' (← *gradъ* 'town'), *cvět-ьcь* 'small flower' (← *cvětъ* 'flower'); *cvět-ъkъ* 'small flower' (← *cvětъ* 'flower'); *ryb-ica* 'small fish' (← *ryba* 'fish'), *crьkъv-ica* 'small church' (← *crьky* 'church'); collective nouns, cf. OCsl. *kamen-ie* 'rock' (← *kamy/kamenь* 'stone') or female personal nouns, cf. OCsl. *proroč-ica* 'female fortune teller' (← *prorokъ* 'fortune teller'), *vratar-ica* 'female guardian of the gate' (← *vrat-arь* 'guardian of the gate'); *gospod-yni* 'mistress' (← *gospodь* 'master') and others.

c) Mutation: The meaning of the derivative is distinct from that of its base; the semantic change may (but need not) coincide with a change in the part of speech. Mutation is primarily characteristic of the formation of names for concrete objects or personal nouns, cf. the above mentioned examples with the suffix *-ьnikъ* and OCsl. *tvor-ьcь* 'creator' (← *tvoriti* 'to create'), *vid-ьcь* 'witness' (← *viděti* 'to see'), *star-ьcь* 'elder' (← *starъ* 'old'), *črьn-ьcь* 'monk' (← *črьnъ* 'black'), *studen-ьcь* 'well' (← *studenъ* 'cold'); *čarodě-ica* 'magician' (← *čaroděti* 'to conjure'), *tьmьn-ica* 'dungeon, prison' (← *tьmьnъ* 'dark'), *grъl-ica* 'turtledove' (← *grъlo* 'throat'); *dobyt-ъkъ* 'gain' (← *dobyti* 'to acquire'), *pęt-ъkъ* 'five pieces' (← *pętъ* 'fifth'); *kъnig-ъčii* 'book expert' (← *kъniga* 'book'), *krъm-ьčii* 'helmsman' (← *kъrma* 'stern'); *sir-ota* 'orphan' (← *sirъ* 'orphaned') and others.

The old stem extension by primary, polyfunctional, semantically undifferentiated suffixes, is thus replaced by new, semantically specified, word-formation structures with a distinct categorial meaning. The latter is based on new, semantically specialized suffixes. In this manner, instead of formations such as **chval-ā-s* (OCsl. *chvala*) 'praise', **orb-ŏ-s* (OCsl. *rabъ*) 'worker', **orb-ā-s* (OCsl. *raba*) 'female worker' (see section 2.1), new formally and semantically distinct types evolved such as OCsl. *chvalenъ* 'praised' (from *chvaliti* 'to praise') → *chvalen-ie* 'praise', *rabotati* 'to work' → *rabot-ьnikъ* 'worker', *rabъ* 'worker, slave' → *rab-yni* 'female worker, female slave'. The old (suffixless) word-formation procedure remains only in derivatives from verbal stems (Vaillant 1952: 228), cf. OCsl. *vъzrasti* 'to grow up' →

vъzrastъ 'age'; *pojasati* 'to gird' → *pojasъ* 'girdle'; *voda* + *nositi* 'to carry water' → *vodonosъ* 'water carrier'; *izměniti* 'to betray' → *izměna* 'betrayal'; *ograditi* 'to enclose' → *ograda* 'fence'.

Owing to their genesis, the new suffixes combine with derivational stems of several word classes and – within a word class – with stems of different morphological categories (deverbal formations, e.g., can be derived from the infinitive stem or the present tense stem, or from participles) and convey different word-formation meanings, depending on the particular stems, e.g.:

a) *-yni*: ABSTR ← A; FEM.PERS ← N
   The suffix *-yni*, combined with an adjectival stem, denotes an abstract concept (*grъdyni* 'pride'), whereas combined with a noun stem of a masculine personal noun it conveys the meaning of the female counterpart (*gospodyni* 'mistress').
b) *-ie*: ABSTR ← V; COLLECT ← N
   The suffix *-ie* denotes an abstract verbal quality when combined with a passive past participle (*spasenie* 'rescue'), and when combined with a noun stem it expresses the meaning of a collective noun (*kamenie* 'rock' ← *kamy/kamen*' 'stone').
c) *-ica*: FEM.PERS ← N; AGENT FEM ← V; VARIA
   The suffix *-ica* expresses the meaning 'female person' when combined with the stem of a masculine personal noun (*proročica* 'female fortune teller' ← *prorokъ*, *vratarica* 'female guardian of the gate' ← *vratarъ*). It also denotes a diminutive when combined with feminine noun stems, which can stand for living beings as well as concrete objects (*rybica* 'small fish', *crъkъvica* 'small church'). When combined with a verbal stem (infinitive stem) the suffix transmits the meaning of a personal noun (*čaroděica* 'magician'). In combination with adjectival and nominal stems it forms expressions for concrete objects and animals (*tьmьnica* 'dungeon, prison', *grъlica* 'turtledove').
d) *-ьcь*: DIM ← N; PERS ← V, A; VARIA ← A
   The suffix -ьcь, combined with a noun stem conveys the meaning of a diminutive (*gradьcь* 'small town', *cvětьcь* 'small flower'), combined with verbal and adjectival stems it denotes personal nouns (*tvorьcь* 'creator', *vidьcь* 'witness'; *starьcь* 'elder', *črьnьcь* 'monk') as well as denominations of concrete objects when combined with adjectival stems (*studenьcь* 'well').
e) *-ъkъ*: DIM ← N; N ← NUM
   The meaning of a diminutive is transmitted by the suffix *-ъkъ* combined with a noun stem (*stanъkъ* 'small camp', *cvětъkъ* 'small flower', *domъkъ* 'small house'). It is used for the formation of concrete terms when combined with verbal stems or cardinal numbers (*dobytъkъ* 'gain', *pętъkъ* 'five pieces').

f) *-ьnikъ*: PERS ← A, V, N
The new suffix of the second generation *-ьnikъ*, in combination with adjectival, verbal and nominal stems forms personal nouns (*grěšьnikъ* 'sinner', *ljublenikъ* 'lover', *mǫčenikъ* 'martyr', *kъnižьnikъ* 'book expert') or denominations of objects (*prazdьnikъ* 'holiday', *istočьnikъ* 'source', *žrьtvьnikь* 'sacrificial altar').

g) *-ota*: ABSTR ← A; PERS ← A
The suffix *-ota*, when combined with adjectives, can form both abstract quality nouns (*pravota* 'justice', *krasota* 'beauty') and personal nouns (*sirota* 'orphan').

The above-mentioned examples show that suffixes can establish different word-formation types fulfilling the criteria 1) identical word class of the base, 2) identical meaning/function of the formant, 3) identical semantic relation between the base and the derivative (cf. Dokulil 1962; Lopatin and Uluchanov 1970), and that types with different formants, but identical word-formation meanings and identical semantic relations between the base and the derivative can be united in word-formation categories:

a) Quality nouns
The meaning of an abstract quality is conveyed by combining the suffixes *-ьstvo*, *-ostь*, *-ota*, *-yni* (and others) with an adjectival stem (cf. *bogatьstvo* 'wealth', *grъdostь* 'pride', *pravostь* 'justice', *krotъkostь* 'gentleness', *pravota* 'justice', *krasota* 'beauty', *grъdyni* 'pride', *pravyni* 'justice') and others.

b) Action nouns
The meaning of action nouns is transmitted by combining the suffixes *-ьstvo*, *-ie*, *-nie* (and others) with verbal stems (cf. *prišьlьstvo* 'arrival', *roždьstvo* 'birth', *spasenie* 'rescue', *trьpěnie* 'patience').

c) Agent nouns/personal nouns
Personal nouns are formed by combining
   - the suffixes *-ьсь*, *-icь*, *-ьca*, *-ica*, *-ьnikъ*, *-ačь*, *-yka*, *-okъ* (and others) with verbal stems (cf. *tvorьсь* 'creator', *čaroděicь* 'magician', *sěčьca* 'hangman; warrier', *čaroděica* 'magician', *zaštitьnikъ* 'guardian', *kovačь* 'blacksmith', *vladyka* 'sovereign, ruler', *vidokъ* 'witness'),
   - the suffixes *-ьсь*, *-okъ*, *-ika*, *-akъ*, *-ičь*, *-ota* (and others) with adjectival stems (cf. *starьсь* 'elder', *blizokъ* 'relative', *bližika* 'relative', *prostakъ* 'simpleton', *pьsovičь* 'dog-keeper', *sirota* 'orphan'), and
   - the suffixes *-ьnikъ*, *-akъ*, *-ačь*, *-arь*, *-ičь*, *-ъčii/ьčii* (and others) with noun stems (cf. *kъnižьnikъ* 'book expert', *rybakъ* 'fisherman', *rybarь* 'id.', *gospodičь* 'son of the lord', *kъnigъčii* 'book expert', *krъmьčii* 'helmsman').

d) Feminine personal nouns
   The feminine counterparts are generated by combining masculine personal nouns with the suffixes *-ica*, *-yni* (and others) (cf. *proročica* 'female fortune teller', *vratarica* 'female guardian of the gate', *gospodyni* 'mistress').
e) Non-personal nouns
   Most of the suffixes that generate personal nouns (and partly also those that produce diminutives) are similarly used to form designations of non-personal nouns (cf. *žrьtvьnikъ* 'sacrificial altar', *istočьnikъ* 'spring', *prazdьnikъ* 'holiday', *studenьcь* 'well', *tьmьnica* 'dungeon, prison', *dobytъkъ* 'gain', *zlatikъ* 'gold coin', *ręčьka* 'vessel').
f) Diminutives
   Diminutive meaning is expressed by the suffixes *-ьcь*, *-ъkъ*, *-ikъ*, *-ica*, *-ьca*, *-ьce* (and others) when combined with noun stems (cf. *cvětьcь* 'small flower', *cvětъkъ* 'id.', *nožikъ* 'small knife', *rybica* 'small fish', *dvьrьca* 'small door', *čjadьce* 'small child', *bljudьce* 'small bowl').

Derivatives belonging to the same category of word-formation, can also have identical roots/stems combined with different suffixes and sometimes even identical lexical meaning, referred to as word-formation synonymy (Ohnheiser 1979; Mengel 1997: 49 ff.), as the following examples show:

a) Abstract nouns: *grъd-ostь* : *grъd-yni* 'pride' (← *grъdъ* 'proud'), *prav-ostь* : *prav-ota* : *prav-yni* 'justice' (← *pravъ* 'just').
b) Agent nouns and denominal personal nouns: *vid-ьcь* : *vid-okъ* 'witness' (← *viděti* 'to see'), *kov-ьcь* : *kov-ačь* 'blacksmith' (← *kovati* 'to forge'), *čarodě-icь* : *čarodě-ica* 'magician' (← *čaroděti* 'to conjure'); *bliz-okъ* : *bliž-ika* 'relative' (← *blizъ* 'near'); *kъniž-ьnikъ* : *kъnig-ъčii* 'book expert' (← *kniga* 'book'), *ryb-akъ* : *ryb-ьnikъ* 'fisherman' (← *ryba* 'fish'), *pьs-arь* (← *pьsъ* 'dog') : *pьsovičь* (← *pьsovъ* 'dog- (adj.)') 'dog-keeper' and many others.
c) Diminutives: *cvět-ьcь* : *cvět-ъkъ* 'small flower' (← *cvětъ* 'flower').

2.2.3 Consolidation of specialized word-formation structures

The extensive synonymy of word-formation types and the corresponding derivatives described in the previous section has been gradually suppressed/diminished by language use. This is reflected in the varying productivity of synonymous (and sometimes also homonymous) word-formation types.

For example, the suffix *-ota*, combined with adjectival stems for the derivation of personal nouns (cf. *sirota*), is already unproductive in Proto-Slavonic (Grammatika 1993: 189). However, it remains productive in the contemporary

Slavic languages for the formation of deadjectival abstract nouns (OCsl. *pravota* 'justice'; Russ. *širota* 'breadth', Bul. *dobrota* 'benevolence').

The suffix *-yni*, combined with adjectival stems, by contrast, loses its productivity for the formation of deadjectival abstract nouns (cf. OCsl. *grъdyni*). In combination with stems of personal nouns, *-yni* in the meaning 'female person' (cf. OCsl. *gospodyni*) soon follows the productive word-formation type with the suffix *-ica*, which develops a high productivity for forming feminine personal nouns (cf. OCsl. *proročica, vratarica*) (Cejtlin 1977: 133).

The formation of personal nouns with the following suffixes becomes less and less productive:

a) *-icь, -ьca, -ica, -ačь, -yka, -okъ* (and some others) combined with verbal stems (cf. OCsl. *čaroděicь, sěčьca, čaroděica, kovačь, vladyka, vidokъ*),
b) *-okъ, -ika, -ičь* (and some others) combined with adjectival stems (cf. OCsl. *blizokъ, bližika, prostakъ, pьsovičь*) and also
c) *-akъ, -ačь, -ъčii/ьčii* (and others) in combination with noun stems (cf. OCsl. *rybakъ, kъnigъčii*).

The highest productivity is shown by the new suffix *-ьnikъ* (Cejtlin 1977: 90) combined with verbal, nominal and adjectival stems, followed by the suffix *-ьcь*, when joined to verbal and adjectival stems.

As has been mentioned above, all word-formation types which share a common general word-formation meaning belong to one and the same word-formation category.

The word-formation structures of transposition and modification show from the very beginning of their existence a relatively narrow specialization of their word-formation categories, cf.

Transposition: The category of abstract nouns (transposition) is based on two word classes, on verbs (→ action nouns) and adjectives (→ quality nouns).

Modification: The meaning of feminine personal nouns is transmitted by word-formation types in only one word-formation category, exclusively in combination with stems of masculine agent/personal nouns. The formation of diminutives is also a matter of word-formation types in only one word-formation category, which comprises derivatives from noun stems of the group "objects" (in a broader sense persons are included).

Mutation: The word-formation structures of mutation, in the course of their development, are involved in far more complex semantic structures. If one presupposes, according to the above-cited examples, two word-formation categories (personal nouns; non-personal object nouns) the respective word-formation structures form derivatives from at least three parts of speech (N, A, V), cf. Mengel (1997: 187 ff., 2002); see also section 3.2.2.

3 Further development of the Proto-Slavonic word-formation system in Old Church Slavonic

The first written language of the Slavs, Old Church Slavonic, at its origin in 863 was based upon late Proto-Slavonic Macedonian-Bulgarian dialects in the Thessalonica region. During the 10th–11th centuries it was enriched by further West, South and East Slavic elements. In a sense, Old Church Slavonic adopted the word-formation system of Proto-Slavonic.

On the other hand, Old Church Slavonic evolves as the language of Bible translations and translations of religious, edifying literature from the highly developed Greek written standard language into one of the dialects of a language that had so far been unaffected by any rigid written norm. The receiving language was not in a position to adequately and fully render the subtle concepts of the books to be translated. On the lexical level, certain concepts and corresponding terms and denominations were missing. Apart from the numerous direct borrowings from Greek, the first translators had to rely on the denominative function of word-formation in order to solve the problem, i.e. they had to create the necessary abstract terms and designations of persons with their differing characteristic features.

The first translators, in their creative activity, used the available word-formation procedures and conventions of late Proto-Slavonic. Sometimes, though, they changed the very system.

3.1 Derivation

In the field of derivation, the increase in the length of suffixes and the consolidation of means of expression were deliberately continued.

3.1.1 Peculiarities in the formation of abstract nouns

Expressions of abstract features appear in Proto-Slavonic mostly in the form of deadjectival abstract nouns. As the above-mentioned examples show (see sections 2.1.2 and 2.1.3), they are formed by the combination of certain suffixes with adjective stems and are morphologically of the feminine gender. The formation of deverbal abstract nouns is less productive. They were originally formed by stems of participles (which represent the verbal features) in combination with the suffixes *-ie* (*spasen-ie* 'rescue', *chvalen-ie* 'praise') and *-ьstvo* (*prišьl-ьstvo* 'arrival', *rožd-ьstvo* 'birth'), which in combination with adjectival stems form deadjectival abstract nouns (*bogat-ьstvo* 'wealth'). As for their morphological gender, deverbal abstract nouns are neuter. By morpheme boundary shifting (metanalysis) the suffix *-ie* combined with the suffix of the passive past participle. This lead to the emergence of the new suffix of the second generation *-nie* which combined with infinitive stems (*trьpě-nie* 'patience').

For new abstract concepts the first translators preferably made use of the available Proto-Slavonic word-formation structures with the three above-mentioned suffixes *-ie*, *-nie*, *-stvo* (cf. OCsl. *ugožden-ie* 'favour', *blagoslavlen-ie* 'benediction'; *lichoima-nie* 'corruptibility', *oblada-nie* 'possession'; *blažen-stvo* 'blissfulness'). The suffix *-ie* enjoys the highest productivity amongst them. Based upon the word-formation type for collective nouns (*kamen-ie* 'rock', cf. section 2.1.2), it is also used in combination with nouns to form abstract terms (cf. OCsl. *bezzakon-ie* 'lawlessness; lit. without-law-ABSTR' ← *bezъ zakona* 'without law', *bezum-ie* 'madness; lit. without-reason-ABSTR' ← *bezъ uma* 'without reason', *velič-ie* 'greatness' ← *velikъ* 'great'), and develops in Old Church Slavonic into a specific mark for abstract terms (Chaburgaev 1986: 122). The use of the suffix *-ьstvo* in combination with noun stems, is also extended for forming abstract nouns (cf. OCsl. *bož-ьstvo* 'deity' ← *bogъ* 'God', *brat-ьstvo* 'brotherhood' ← *bratъ* 'brother', *episkop-ьstvo* 'bishopric' ← *episkopъ* 'bishop').

On the formal side of expression, the applicability of these suffixes is further extended. Analogous to the Proto-Slavonic process of suffix extension by morpheme boundary shifts (metanalysis), the two most productive suffixes *-ьstvo* and *-ie*, which transmit the same word-formation meaning in parallel word-formation structures, are arbitrarily combined into a new, complex suffix *-ьstvie*. Formations with this suffix (without word-formation synonyms) exist already in the most ancient documents of Old Church Slavonic (cf. *bratoljub-ьstvie* 'brotherly love' ← *bratъ* 'brother' + *ljubiti* 'to love', *podob-ьstvie* 'resemblance' ← *podobiti* 'to resemble', *synobož-ьstvie* 'God's sonship' ← *synъ Božii* 'God's son; lit. son God-POSS.ADJ') (Chaburgaev 1986: 123). Their productivity in the course of the history of Church Slavonic, especially in its Eastern Slavonic variant, is constantly increasing. This is reflected to a striking degree in the word-formation system of the contemporary Russian standard language, cf. Russ. *sledstvie* 'consequence' (← *sledovat'* 'to follow'), *spokojstvie* 'silence' (← *spokojnyj* 'silent').

When forming new abstract nouns, the first translators' approach in Old Church Slavonic was concentrated on having the suffix, e.g., *-stvo* or *-ie*, transmit initially the simple and transparent word-formation meaning of the Proto-Slavonic derivatives of the transposition type (deadjectival and deverbal abstract nouns). Later, the suffix was capable of combining with derivational stems of the main word classes and various morphological categories in the formation of derivatives with an abstract meaning.

3.1.2 Peculiarities in the formation of personal nouns

For coining new personal nouns in late Proto-Slavonic, several word-formation structures with a whole series of productive suffixes were available. They combined with derivational stems of various word classes, thus belonging to various word-formation types and producing different word-formation meanings of mutation (cf. sections 2.1.2–2.1.3). The first translators preferred the morphologically and semantically unequivocal word-formation structures.

In the translations into Old Church Slavonic the suffix *-telь* acquires very high productivity. Its origin is not fully traceable, but most probably goes back to Proto-Slavonic dialects. In combination with infinitive stems (most frequently of verbs ending in *-iti*), it formed new agent nouns (Grammatika 1993: 191), cf. OCsl. *krъsti-telь* 'baptist' (← *krъstiti* 'to baptize'), *iskusi-telь* 'seducer' (← *iskusiti* 'to seduce'), *iscěli-telь* 'healer' (← *iscěliti* 'to heal'), *obliči-telь* 'accuser' (← *obličiti* 'to accuse'), *světi-telь* 'light bearer' (← *světiti* 'to shine'), *mǫči-telь* 'torturer' (← *mǫčiti* 'to torture'), *uči-telь* 'teacher' (← *učiti* 'to teach') and others. Derivatives from other verbs are in a minority, cf. *vlas-telь* 'ruler, sovereign' (← *vlasti* 'to rule, reign'), *ži-telь* 'inhabitant' (← *žiti* 'to live'), *žę-telь* 'harvester' (← *žęti* 'to harvest'), *prěda-telь* 'traitor' (← *prědati* 'to betray') and others. Under the influence of Old Church Slavonic this productive word-formation type occurred in later Slavic written standard languages, cf. Russ. *izobretatelь* 'inventor' (← *izobretat'* 'to invent'), *potrebitelь* 'consumer' (← *potrebit'* 'to consume'), Bul. *potrebitel* 'consumer' (← *potrjabva* 'to be in need'), *poluča-tel* 'recipient' (← *polučava* 'to receive'), etc.

The suffix *-arь*, borrowed from Germanic and not productive in Proto-Slavonic (cf. Gothic *motareis*, OCsl. *mytarь* 'tax collector', see Meillet 1961 [1902–05]: 211, cf. also Lat. *-ārius*), is used in the most ancient documents of Old Church Slavonic exclusively to form personal nouns in combination with noun stems. These personal nouns mostly represent denominations of trades and professions according to the object of the respective activity mentioned in the derivational stem, cf. *vrat-arь* 'guardian of the door' (← *vrata* 'door'), *ryb-arь* 'fisherman' (← *ryba* 'fish'), *vrьtograd-arь* 'gardener' (← *vrьtogradъ* 'garden'), *klevet-arь* 'accuser' (← *kleveta* 'accusation') and others more. This word-formation type develops a high productivity in Old Church Slavonic and competes with the very productive Proto-Slavonic suffix *-ьnikъ* among others (cf. Meillet 1961 [1902/1905]: 212, see also sections 2.2.1 and 2.2.2). Thus it was possible for derivatives of these two word-formation types to be used in Old Church Slavonic translations with the same roots to specify the lexical meaning, cf. *klevet-arь* (Gr. *katégoros*) 'accuser' : *klevet-ьnikъ* (Gr. *sukophántes*) 'slanderer'. This word-formation type also played an essential role in the subsequent history of certain written standard languages; in Bulgarian, for instance, it is used to form names of inhabitants (Duridanov 1970: 863 ff.).

In Old Church Slavonic translations, the translators created a new complex suffix to render the Greek terms for inhabitants. Based upon the Proto-Slavonic word-formation type with the suffix *-jan/ěn-* (< **-jē-n-*), which was used to form collective nouns according to the place of residence, tribal association, etc. (e.g., OCsl. *slav-jane* 'Slavs', *gražd-ane* 'citizens', cf. in Nestor's Chronicle (beginning of the 12th century) ORuss. *pol-jane* 'the Polyans', *drěvl-jane* 'the Drevlyans' and other Old Russian tribes, see Iljinskij 1902: 31 ff.), and also upon the morpheme *-in/ьn-ъ* (< **-jŏ-n/ĭ-n-*) with the meaning 'singulative' (cf. OCsl. *židov-inъ* 'jew' ← *židovy* 'jews'), the suffix *-janinъ/-ěninъ* has evolved. (The morpheme *-in-* was also used to render the Greek root *mon-* mainly in compounds, cf. OCsl. *in-ok-ъ* (Gr. *moniós*) 'hermit', *in-o-rogъ* (Gr. *monókeros*) 'unicorn', *in-o-čędъ* (Gr. *monogenénes*) 'single child'.) The newly developed word-formation type is restricted to noun stems of the lexical-semantic group of (geographic) places of residence, cf. OCsl. *galilě-janinъ* 'Galilean', *riml-janinъ* 'Roman', *samar-janinъ* 'Samarian', *egypt-ěninъ* 'Egyptian', *solun-janinъ* 'inhabitant of Thessalonica', etc. In later Slavonic written standard languages, especially in Russian, this word-formation type enjoys a high productivity in forming names of city dwellers, cf. Russ. *kirovčanin* 'inhabitant of Kirov' and others (cf. section 4).

The above-mentioned approach of the first translators in creating new denominations for persons in Old Church Slavonic is intended to achieve the most unequivocal meaning of mutation in the resulting derivatives. This is done by employing highly specialized word-formation structures with a certain suffix which combines with the derivational stem of only one particular class of words. The word-formation semantics of the personal nouns (in analogy to the formation of new abstract nouns) is thus consolidated and concentrated in the suffix.

By combining several morphemes into one new suffix (cf. *-janinъ/-ěninъ*) and by forming the derivatives by means of both the new and the already existing productive suffixes (e.g., *-tel'*, *-ьnikъ* and *-ьcь*), the number of suffixes and their length are further increased to underline their semantic weight, cf. *vlas-telь* 'sovereign, ruler' (← *vlas-t-i* 'to reign') → *vlas-tel-inъ*, *vlas-tel-janinъ*, *vlas-tel-ьnikъ* 'id.', *čelęd-inъ* 'servant' (← *čelędь* collective noun 'servants') → *čelęd-in-ьcь* 'id.', and others. Especially this latter approach becomes a characteristic trait of Old Church Slavonic as the written and cultural language of the Slavs in comparison with their living colloquial languages and dialects (Uspenskij 1984). – In the field of adjectival word-formation, the doubling of the suffix *-n-* is a characteristic operation, e.g., *blaženьnъ* 'blessed, blissful', *vъždelenьnъ* 'desired, longed for', *neizglagolanьnъ* 'ineffable' (cf. Dobrev 2004: 22).

One of the most important principles of the first translators was the principle of variability, according to which a Greek word could be translated by several equivalent Slavonic lexical units in order to reach an improved understanding (Vereščagin 1972; Mengel 1998), cf. Gr. *katégoros* – *klevet-arь* (← *kleveta* 'claim'), *obliči-telь* (← *obliči-t-i* 'to accuse') both meaning 'accuser'; Gr. *telōnēs* – *myt-arь* (← *myt-o* 'tax'), *mьzdo-im-ьcь* (lit. 'tax-have/get/take-AGENT') both in the meaning 'tax collector'; Gr. *phoneús, miaphónos* – *ubi-ica* (← *ubi-t-i* 'to murder, kill'), *ubi-telьnikъ* 'murderer'; Gr. *agathós, philágathos* – *blagodě-telь* lit. 'good-doer' (← *blago* + *dět'* lit. 'good (n.) do'), *blagoda-telь* lit. 'good-giver' (← *blago* + *dat'* lit. 'good (n.) to give'), *blagodat-ьnikъ, blagodav-ьcь* 'benefactor'. Thus, several synonymous denominations developed (rich synonymy was equally characteristic of the highly developed Greek written language), word-formation synonyms amongst others. As the above-mentioned examples show, new word-formations with new, specialized word-formation structures and suffixes (cf. *ubitelьnikъ*) were introduced in addition to the denominations already existent in Proto-Slavonic (e.g., *ubiica*).

In the course of the history of Church Slavonic, the procedure used by the first translators for coining new denominations of persons lead to a specialization of the other inherited word-formation types belonging to the word-formation category "personal nouns". By combining a certain suffix with the derivational stem of a word class within a definite lexical-semantic group, a very precise word-formation meaning was obtained (e.g., trades and professions, inhabitants, etc.). Our own studies of Russian Church Slavonic in the 11th–14th and 15th–17th centuries, in comparison to the East Slavic of the 11th–14th centuries and the East Slavic languages Old Russian, Old Ukrainian, Old Belarusian during the 15th–17th centuries, confirm such a specialization (Mengel 1997, 2002).

For translating designations of concrete objects and every-day events, the first translators into Old Church Slavonic made use of the colloquial vocabulary of the late Proto-Slavonic period or, if terms were missing in the local dialects, they usually took loan words from Greek (Chaburgaev 1986: 118), cf. *alavastrъ* 'vessel made of alabaster' (Gr. *alábastros*), *talantъ* 'monetary unit' (Gr. *tálantos*) and others. As a consequence, Church Slavonic is lacking in specialized word-formation structures of mutation in this semantic field.

The Modern Russian standard language, which consolidated itself in the second half of the 18th century by fusing Russian and Church Slavonic (i.e. the cult language of Russia from the 11th to the 17th centuries and beyond), included Church Slavonic in the new norm. Its word-formation system shows clear traces of this development in the field of expressions for persons and concrete objects, as explained in this section.

3.2 Composition

An important peculiarity of the translations into the Old Church Slavonic of the 10th–11th centuries consists in the large number of compounds in its lexis: 611 out of 9,616 words are compounds (Cejtlin 1977: 186, 273). The impression that the first translators deliberately promoted compounding in imitation of the Greek originals does not, however, correspond to reality.

Compounding of two existing words is already a typical trait of word-formation in the oldest known Indo-European languages (Jagić 1898: 528; Meillet 1961 [1902–05]: 300). Compounds represent a considerable part of the vocabulary in the individual languages including Slavonic. A large part of the compounds in the Old Church Slavonic translations is undoubtedly of Proto-Slavonic origin (Jagić 1898: 535; Taseva 2000: 205). Proof of the productivity of this word-formation procedure in Proto-Slavonic is the large number of compounds in the most ancient Slavonic toponymy and anthroponymy (Miklosich 1927 [1860–74]; Taseva 2008: 231 f.), and in the folk tales of the pre-Christian period (Grammatika 1993: 192).

A comparison of the corpus of Old Church Slavonic translations with their Greek originals reveals that the first translators employed a wide range of possibilities to render Greek compounds in Slavonic. They could be translated by a word group, cf. Gr. *lithoktoneĩn* – OCsl. *kameniemь pobiti* 'to stone; lit. stone-INSTR to beat' (Rečnik 2003: 289), by an available Slavonic equivalent that was not a compound, cf. Gr. *laxeutérion* – OCsl. *oskrъdъ* 'pickaxe' (Rečnik 2003: 286) or by borrowing from Greek, cf. Gr. *koinobiárkhes* – OCsl. *kinovi-archъ* 'abbot' (Rečnik 2003: 272).

Moreover, the translators used other word-formation procedures to render Greek compounds (cf. section 3.1.2), especially the prefixation of verbs. Prefixes (< adverbs and prepositions) formed the first component of the compound to be translated, cf. Gr. *makrothumeĩn* – OCsl. *po-trъpěti, prě-trъpěti, u-trъpěti* 'to endure, suffer much' (Rečnik 2003: 295).

Loan translations from Greek (cf. Gr. *makrothumeĩn*, corresponding to OCsl. *dlъgotrъpěti* lit. 'long-ADV-suffer', *mnogotrъpěti* lit. 'to much-suffer', both in the meaning 'to suffer long, much; to endure'; Rečnik 2003: 295) and the new creations on their pattern, represent a considerable part of the compounds in Old Church Slavonic. For the most part, they are denominations of abstract concepts and philosophical or religious terms which had not previously existed in the target language.

The specific nature of their word-formation structure in comparison with Proto-Slavonic suffixless compounds (cf. *vodonosъ* 'water carrier', cf. section 2.2.2) lies in the fact that the Old Church Slavonic compounds, as borrowings or new creations, contain the above-mentioned productive suffixes for the formation of abstract nouns *-ie*, *-nie*, *-ьstvo*, *-stvie* (cf. section 3.1.1): OCsl. *blago-slavlen-ie* 'benediction, blessing' (← *blagoslaviti*, a calque of Gr. *eu-logeĩn* 'to benedict'), *licho-imanie* 'corruptibility', *brato-ljub-ьstvie* 'brotherly love; lit. brother-love-ABSTR', *syno-bož-ьstvie* 'being God's son; lit. son-God-POSS.ADJ-ABSTR', *sьrebro-ljub-ьstvo* 'avarice; lit. silver-love-ABSTR', cf. Gr. *philarguría*, and for denominations of persons *-telь*, *-ьсь*, *-ьnikъ* (cf. section 3.1.2): OCsl. *blago-dě-telь*, *blago-da-telь*, *blago-dat-ьnikъ*, *blago-dav-ьсь* 'benefactor', *mьzdo-im-ьсь* 'tax collector' (cf. Grammatika 1993: 194).

On the other hand, the majority of these borrowings and new creations consists of a denominal first and a deverbal second component, which is due to the model of the original language, and, in addition, to their specific lexical meaning. That is, they belong to a certain semantic group: abstract concepts (deverbal abstract nouns), and philosophical and religious terms (deverbal abstract and agent nouns). The high productivity of the first components *blago-* 'well' and *bog(o)-* 'God' is a common feature. As second components, *-ljubьсь* 'lover', *-tvorьсь* 'creator', *-davьсь* 'donator'; *-ljubie* 'love', *-tvorenie* 'creation' prove to be especially productive (Grammatika 1993: 192 ff.).

The combination of compounding and suffixation, developed in Old Church Slavonic, had a strong influence on the word-formation systems of subsequent Slavic languages, in which it enjoys a high productivity, cf. Russ. *nov-o-sel-ie* 'moving into a new home' (← *novyj* 'new' + *selit'sja* 'to settle down'), *perv-o-klass-nik* 'school beginner' (← *pervyj* 'first' + *klass* 'class') and others.

4 Outlook

The Proto-Slavonic word-formation system with its specific features with regard to the productivity of nominal derivation for the formation of new terms for objects, persons and their characteristics was inherited by the individual Slavic languages and the contemporary Slavic standard languages.

The word-formation system of Common Slavonic, as it is retraceable in late Proto-Slavonic (7th–9th centuries) and in Old Church Slavonic (written testimonies from the 9th/10th century onwards), experiences hardly any fundamental changes in later times. Slight changes do occur, but are limited to variability in the actual phonetic realization of some affixes as a result of particular phonetic laws valid in the individual Slavic languages. The reduction or full vocalization of the so-called reduced vowels or half-vowels (ь, ъ) may serve as an example which occurred at different points of time in the Western, Southern and Eastern group of Slavic languages respectively (in the Southern group in the 10th/11th centuries, in the Eastern in the 12th/14th centuries), triggering partly different results. As a consequence, ь and ъ occurring in Proto-Slavonic suffixes are realized in the individual Slavic languages as *a*, *e*, *o* or *ø* (zero) respectively, cf. *-ькъ* (Psl.), *-ькъ/-окъ/-къ* (OCsl.), *-ok/-k* (Russ.), *-ak/-k* (Belarus.). Due to specific phonetic laws in the individual Slavic languages, the suffix *-ost'* (Psl./OCsl.) is realized as *-ość* (Pol.), *-ist'*/genitive *-osti* (Ukr.), *-asc'* (Belarus.), *-ost'* (Russ.), and the suffix *-tel'* (OCsl.) as, for instance, *-ciel* (Pol.), *-tel* (Czech), *-tel'* (Russ.). One and the same suffix can occur with a different frequency and can have a different productivity in different Slavic languages, such as the agent noun suffixes *-tel* and *-lac*, which nowadays are often exploited in language policy to underline the difference between Croatian and Serbian (cf. Tošović 2015). Some suffixes are well codified in one standard language, whereas they occur in other languages merely in dialects or other non-standard varieties. New suffixes only arise by affix merger or due to direct language contact, for example, with Turkish in Bulgarian (cf. Avramova and Baltova 2016), Macedonian (cf. Arizankovska 2016), Bosnian (cf. Tošović 2016) and Serbian (cf. Ćorić 2016). More recently, international affixes have been integrated. The conservation of patterns of composition, which proved less active in the Slavic languages, often also depends on direct language contact (cf. calques of German compounds, for instance, in Upper Sorbian – see Pohontsch 2016). Those languages whose literary tradition suffered historic interruptions (as, for instance, Czech or several Southern Slavic languages) experienced a revival of their original literary tradition during the "national resurrection" in the 19th century (as in Czech) or have stuck to the popular vernacular as the point of reference for the development of the standard language (as in Southern Slavic languages). Bulgarian, in its elevated style, has "reimported" numerous deverbal abstract nouns from Russian which had once been borrowed by the Russian language from Old Church Slavonic (i.e. Old Bulgarian).

The characteristic influences of (Old) Church Slavonic word-formation, which are attributable to the activities of the early translators, are evident and fertile in the development of the word-formation systems in the written standard languages of the *Slavia Orthodoxa*.

Church Slavonic played a decisive role especially in the development of the modern Russian literary language (i.e. the Russian standard language) during the 18th century. In the field of word-formation, the productive affixes of Old Church Slavonic and the complex suffixes derived from them prove to be enormously productive in modern Standard Russian. They serve the formal and semantic specialization of certain word-formation types within the framework of the word-formation categories. Thus, when it comes to form new names for certain city dwellers, the word-formation type "noun stem (name of the location) + (Old Church Slavonic) suffix *-anin*" is almost exclusively used, cf. Russ. *kirovčanin* 'inhabitant of Kirov', *narymčanin* 'inhabitant of Narym' (see above section 3.1.2). Its main rival is the word-formation type using the Proto-Slavonic (Common Slavonic) suffix *-ec*, cf., e.g., *leningradec* 'inhabitant of Leningrad'. Nevertheless, the suffix *-anin* is largely preferred when forming new names of inhabitants for two major reasons: firstly, its semantics was already narrowly specialized in Old Church Slavonic. The semantics of the suffix *-ec* is much broader, cf. Russ. *sverdlovec* 'student (staff) of the Sverdlov-Academy' as opposed to *sverdlovčanin* 'inhabitant of Sverdlovsk' (1924–1991; afterwards renamed Ekaterinburg), cf. also *kirovec* 'worker in the Kirov car factories' and *kirovčanin* 'inhabitant of Kirov'. Secondly, Russian names of inhabitants inherit by means of the suffix *-anin* the prestige which Old Church Slavonic traditionally enjoyed as the language of cult and culture until the 17th century and beyond. Thus, *-anin* preferably serves to form names of city dwellers, whereas when used to designate inhabitants of a village, it obtains a connotation of politeness, cf. *berezovčanin* 'inhabitant of the village of Berezovo' (Mengel 1997). The old suffixes stemming from Common Slavonic gradually lose their productivity within the word-formation category "name of inhabitants", as, for example, the suffix *-ič* (cf. *moskvič* 'inhabitant of Moscow').

5 References

Arizankovska, Lidija (2016): Macedonian. In: Peter O. Müller, Ingeborg Ohnheiser, Susan Olsen and Franz Rainer (eds.), *Word-Formation. An International Handbook of the Languages of Europe*. Vol. 4, 3070–3086. Berlin/Boston: De Gruyter Mouton.

Avramova, Cvetanka and Julia Baltova (2016): Bulgarian. In: Peter O. Müller, Ingeborg Ohnheiser, Susan Olsen and Franz Rainer (eds.), *Word-Formation. An International Handbook of the Languages of Europe*. Vol. 4, 3049–3069. Berlin/Boston: De Gruyter Mouton.

Birnbaum, Henrik and Jos Schaeken (1997): *Das altkirchenslawische Wort. Bildung – Bedeutung – Herleitung*. München: Sagner.

Brodowska-Honowska, Maria (1960): *Słowotwórstwo przymiotnika w języku staro-cerkiewno-słowiańskim*. Kraków: Zakład Narodowy imienia Ossolińskich.

Cejtlin, Ralja Michajlovna (1977): *Leksika staroslavjanskogo jazyka*. Moskva: Nauka.

Chaburgaev, Georgij Aleksandrovič (1986): *Staroslavjanskij jazyk*. Moskva: Prosveščenie.

Ćorić, Božo (2016): Serbian. In: Peter O. Müller, Ingeborg Ohnheiser, Susan Olsen and Franz Rainer (eds.), *Word-Formation. An International Handbook of the Languages of Europe*. Vol. 4, 3017–3037. Berlin/Boston: De Gruyter Mouton.

Dal', Vladimir Ivanovič (1956 [1880–82]): *Tolkovoj slovar' živogo velikorusskogo jazyka*. Vol. 4. Moskva: Gosudarstvennoe izdateľstvo inostrannych i nacional'nych slovarej.

Dobrev, Ivan (2004): XIV vek – klasicizăm ili prakriti. In: Lora Taseva (ed.), *Prevodi prez XIV stoletie na Balkanite. Dokladi ot meždunarodnata konferencija (Sofija, 26–28 juni 2003)*, 17–26. Sofija: Goreks Press.

Dokulil, Miloš (1962): *Tvoření slov v češtine*. Vol. 1: *Teorie odvozování slov*. Praha: Nakladatelství Československé akademie věd.

Dokulil, Miloš (1968): Zur Theorie der Wortbildung. *Wissenschaftliche Zeitschrift der Karl-Marx-Universität Leipzig. Gesellschafts- und sprachwissenschaftliche Reihe* 17: 203–211.

Duridanov, Ivan Vasilev (1970): Edin nepoznat slovoobrazuvatelen tip v bălgarski: Žitelski imena na *-ar* (s usporedici ot drugite slavjanski ezici). *Isvestija ot Institut na bălgarski ezik* 19: 863–869.

Efimova, Valerija Sergeevna (2006): *Staroslavjanskaja slovoobrazovatel'naja morfemika*. Moskva: Institut slavjanovedenija RAN.

Grammatika = Duridanov, Ivan Vasilev (ed.) (1993): *Grammatika na starobălgarski ezik*. Sofija: Izdatelstvo na Bălgarskata Akademija na naukite.

Il'inskij, Grigorij Andreevič (1902): *O nekotorych archaizmach i novoobrazovanijach praslavjanskogo jazyka*. Praha: Grégr.

Jagić, Vatroslav (1898): Die slavischen Composita in ihrem zeitgeschichtlichen Auftreten. *Archiv für slavische Philologie* 20: 519–556.

Lopatin, Vladimir Vladimirovič and Igor' Stepanovič Uluchanov (1980): Slovoobrazovanie. In: Natal'ja Jur'evna Švedova (ed.), *Russkaja grammatika*. Vol. 1, 133–452. Moskva: Nauka.

Meillet, Antoine (1961 [1902–05]): *Études sur l'étymologie et le vocabulaire du vieux slave*. 2 Vol. Paris: Champion.

Mengel, Swetlana (1997): *Wege der Herausbildung der Wortbildungsnorm im Ostslawischen des 11.–17. Jahrhunderts*. Frankfurt/M.: Lang.

Mengel, Swetlana (1998): Variabilität als Übersetzungsprinzip. In: Elena Bogdanova and Margot Sobieroj (eds.), *Florilegium Slavicum. Liber ad honorandum Herbert Jelitte*, 165–175. Frankfurt/M.: Lang.

Mengel, Swetlana (2002): Semantičeskie i formal'nye korreljacii vnutri slovoobrazovatel'noj kategorii i slovoobrazovatel'noj paradigmy. In: Swetlana Mengel (ed.), *Slavische Wortbildung. Semantik und Kombinatorik*, 329–342. Münster: LIT.

Mengel, Swetlana (2007): Slovoobrazovatel'nye sinonimy: Jazykovoj fenomen meždu leksikoj, grammatikoj i slovoobrazovaniem. In: Hanna Burkhardt and Alicja Nagórko (eds.), *Sprachliche Kategorien und die slawische Wortbildung*, 131–142. Hildesheim: Olms.

Mengel, Swetlana (2009): Wortbildungsbedeutung. In: Sebastian Kempgen, Peter Kosta, Tilman Berger and Karl Gutschmidt (eds.), *The Slavic Languages. An International Handbook of their Structure, their History and their Investigation*. Vol. 1, 775–781. Berlin/New York: de Gruyter.

Mengel, Swetlana (2022): O gendernoj problematike v russkom jazyke: novoobrazovanija poslednich let i diachronnyj aspekt. In: Martin Ološtiak, Ľudmila Liptáková and Klaudia Bednárová-Gibová (eds.), *Slovanská slovotvorba. Synchrónia, inovácie, neologizácia*, 35–56. Prešov: Vydavatelstvo Prešovskej Univerzity.

Mengel, Swetlana (2024): K voprosu o naimenovanii ženščin i mužčin v slavjanskich jazykach. Diachronnyj aspekt. In: *Slovoobrazovanie. Stilistika. Lingvističeskaja poėtika*, 156–171. Moskva: AN Rossii.

Miklosich [Miklošič], Franz (1927 [1860–74]): *Die Bildung der slawischen Personen- und Ortsnamen*. Heidelberg: Winter.

Ohnheiser, Ingeborg (1979): *Wortbildung und Synonymie. Untersuchungen zur nominalen Wortbildungssynonymie in der russischen Gegenwartssprache*. Leipzig: Enzyklopädie.

Pohontsch, Anja (2016): Upper Sorbian. In: Peter O. Müller, Ingeborg Ohnheiser, Susan Olsen and Franz Rainer (eds.), *Word-Formation. An International Handbook of the Languages of Europe*. Vol. 4, 2811–2831. Berlin/Boston: De Gruyter Mouton.

Rečnik = Argirovski, Mito, Natalija Andrijevska and Aleksandra Gurkova (eds.) (2003): *Rečnik na grčko-crkovnoslovenski leksički paraleli*. Skopje: Institut za makedonski jazik „Krste Misirkov".

Seliščev, Afanasij Matveevič (1952): *Staroslavjanskij jazyk*. Vol. 2. Moskva: Prosveščenie.

Taseva, Lora (2000): Ezikăt na prevodača Zakchej: Meždu knižovnoto nasledstvo i formalističnite tendencii na epochata. *Slavia* 69: 189–210.

Taseva, Lora (2008): Imenuvaneto v srednevekovna Makedonija. In: *XXXIV naučna konferencija na XL međunaroden seminar za makedonski jazyk, literatura i kultura (Ochrid, 13.–30. VIII 2007)*, 223–235. Skopje: Lingvistika.

Tošović, Branko (2015): Word-formation and purism in Croatian. In: Peter O. Müller, Ingeborg Ohnheiser, Susan Olsen and Franz Rainer (eds.), *Word-Formation. An International Handbook of the Languages of Europe*. Vol. 3, 1720–1730. Berlin/Boston: De Gruyter Mouton.

Tošović, Branko (2016): Bosnian. In: Peter O. Müller, Ingeborg Ohnheiser, Susan Olsen and Franz Rainer (eds.), *Word-Formation. An International Handbook of the Languages of Europe*. Vol. 4, 3038–3049. Berlin/Boston: De Gruyter Mouton.

Uspenskij, Boris Andreevič (1984): Staroslavjanskij i Cerkovnoslavjanskij. In: Klavdija Vasil'evna Gorškova (ed.), *Aktual'nyje problemy izučenija i prepodovanija staroslavjanskogo jazyka*, 43–69. Moskva: Izdatel'stvo Moskovskogo univerziteta.

Vaillant, André (1964 [1948]): *Manuel du vieux slave*. Vol. 1: *Grammaire*. 2nd ed. Paris: Institut d'Études Slaves.

Vaillant, André (1952): *Rukovodstvo po staroslavjanskomu jazyku*. Moskva: Izdatel'stvo inostrannoj literatury.

Varbot, Žanna Žanovna (1984): *Pravoslavjanskaja morfologija, slovoobrazovanie i ėtimologija*. Moskva: Nauka.

Vereščagin, Evgenij Michajlovič (1972): *Iz istorii vozniknovenija pervogo literaturnogo jazyka slavjan*. Vol. 1: *Perevodčeskaja dejatel'nost' Kirila i Mefodija*. Moskva: Izdatel'stvo Moskovskogo universiteta.

Zemskaja, Elena Andreevna (1992): *Slovoobrazovanie kak dejatel'nost'*. Moskva: Nauka.

Io Manolessou and Angela Ralli

22 From Ancient Greek to Modern Greek

Abstract: This article deals with word-formation in the diachrony of the Greek language. It provides a basic description of the structure, the properties and the evolution of affixal derivation (prefixation and suffixation) as well as compounding, while there are hints about the evolution of formations created by processes such as ablaut, backformation and reduplication. All issues are illustrated with examples, which, for reasons of clarity, are given in a phonological transcription.

1 Bibliographic sources

Unexpectedly for such a well-researched language as Greek, word-formation has received little attention from a diachronic point of view, and, in the case of Ancient Greek (hereafter AG), from a theoretical point of view as well. No diachronic accounts exist of the phenomenon, apart from the brief comparative overview (AG derivational suffixes and their survival or loss in Modern Greek (hereafter MG)) in the outdated Jannaris (1897: 287–311) and from Dieterich's (1928) list of MG derivational prefixes and suffixes with their previous history and origins. The only full-length description of AG word-formation remains Debrunner (1917), which can be complemented by Chantraine (1933) and Lühr (2008) for the nominal domain only. Fortunately, the historical description of Homeric word-formation by Risch (1973) can be applied to AG in general. The data (lists of suffixes by part of speech) is set out in the traditional grammars of Buck (1933: 441–530), Schwyzer (1939: 415–544) and Bornemann and Risch (1978: 306–319), while a survey of suffix productivity is possible through the reverse dictionaries of Buck and

Io Manolessou, Athens, Greece
Angela Ralli, Patras, Greece

https://doi.org/10.1515/9783111420530-022

Petersen (1945) (for nominal suffixes only, but with an historical introduction and a bibliography for each suffix) and Kretschmer and Locker (1977). There is, on the other hand, a considerable bibliography on specific suffixes or word-formation types, cf. Meier-Brügger (1992: 33–39), Meissner and Tribulato (2002) and Lühr (2008).

Word-formation in Koine Greek (ca 3rd c. BC to 3rd c. AD) is much less researched; the data can be viewed in the grammars of Mayser (1923: 415–510), Moulton (1963: 267–410) and Palmer (1964), while much information is provided by Filos (2008). For Medieval Greek (hereafter MedG), no grammatical description is available apart from Minas (1994: 139–159), and data can be collected only through historical overviews of MG derivation, such as Dieterich (1904, 1909, 1928), Anastasiadi-Symeonidi (1983), Andriotis (1939, 1956). Considerable evidence concerning suffixation in late Medieval and Early MG can be found in Karantzola and Giannoulopoulou (2000, 2001) and Karantzola (2004).

Studies dealing with specific suffixes in MG usually include a diachronic component, where the origin of the suffix and its use in the medieval, early modern and modern period is discussed, but data are rare. A comparison of the amount of research on word-formation for each period, as listed in Heidermanns (2005), easily shows how far behind research in Koine and MedG is lagging.

2 Word-formation overview

Greek word-formation can be subdivided in two main domains, derivation and composition. Both domains are in general comparatively stable diachronically, as Greek is a remarkably conservative language from a morphological point of view, mainly due to the fact that there is no phonological erosion at the end of the word, which would have destroyed inflectional and derivational suffixes as has happened in most Indo-European (hereafter IE) languages. An additional factor is the long diglossic history of the language, which has led to the retention of archaic derivational and compounding patterns. In a similar vein, the diachronic prestige of AG and its influence on European civilization (and thence, European languages) has caused the re-importation of much AG word-formation material into MG through borrowing: the so-called "neoclassical" suffixes and neoclassical compounds fit easily into MG and contribute to its overall conservative morphological outlook.

The morphological make-up of Greek words is diachronically stable. They consist of roots (bearers of the main lexical meaning of the word) + derivational suffixes and/or prefixes + inflectional suffixes. The combination of root + affix gives the stem, which is available for further derivational processes, i.e. affixation of additional derivational suffixes. One may therefore distinguish between simple and complex stems.

IE and to a large extent AG made a fundamental distinction between athematic and thematic formations which affected their inflectional behaviour: athematic nouns and verbs are formed by the direct affixation of inflectional suffixes onto the stem, while in thematic nouns and verbs a so-called "thematic vowel" intervenes between the root (or the stem) and the inflectional suffix. In the nominal domain, analyses of AG word-formation thus make a basic division between root nouns (*Wurzelnomina*, from a traditional point of view belonging to the 3rd "athematic" declension) (cf. (1) below) and nouns derived through suffixation of the base with a thematic vowel (2). In the verbal domain, one may distinguish between the athematic conjugation (the so called *-mi* verbs) (3), in which the inflectional suffix is attached directly onto the stem, and the thematic conjugation (the *-o* verbs), in which a thematic vowel intervenes (4).

(1)	a.	*thɛːr-*	+	∅			→	*thɛ́ːr*
		root		infl. suffix				
		'animal'		nom. sg.				
	b.	*phylak-*	+			*-s*	→	*phýlaks*
		root				infl. suffix		
		'guard'				nom. sg.		
(2)		*log-*	+	*-o-*	+	*-s*	→	*lógos*
		root		them. vowel		infl. suffix		
		'reason'				nom. sg.		
(3)		*deik-ny*	+			*-te*	→	*deíknyte*
		stem				infl. suffix		
		'to show'				2nd pl.		
(4)		*leg-*	+	*-e-*	+	*-te*	→	*légete*
		root		them. vowel		infl. suffix		
		'to say'				2nd pl.		

NB: Following the IPA model, the AG pitch accent is noted as a tone on the vowel that bears it, whereas the MedG and MG dynamic accent is noted as a stress mark preceding the accent-bearing syllable.

The status of the thematic vowel in a synchronic theoretical analysis of AG inflectional and derivational morphology is debatable, in view of the fact that it also has inflectional properties (see, e.g., Luraghi 2004, Kakarikos 2010 for nominal inflection; Duhoux 2000 for verbal inflection).

The distinction between athematic and thematic inflected items disappeared from Greek when the overall inflectional system changed, and led to the incorporation of the thematic vowel onto the stem (or onto the suffix, depending on the approach adopted, see Ralli 2005). In the nominal domain, this happened in conjunction with important changes in the inflectional system, which brought about the demise of the athematic 3rd declension and its merger with the 1st (*a*-stem) declension. In the verbal domain, the athematic declension disappeared entirely during the Koine period, and all its members were reformed according to the thematic pattern (see Holton and Manolessou 2010 and references therein for these changes).

From the viewpoint of the overall evolution of Greek morphology, therefore, the most important diachronic changes in Greek word-formation do not consist in the creation of new suffixes or loss of old ones (although both processes do take place) but in the reanalysis of the same words in different ways.

As already mentioned, another major difference between AG and MG word-formation is caused by the influence of the diglossic history of the language. All historical phases of Greek, from the Koine onwards, display a distinction between learned/high and vernacular/low which widens with the passage of time, involving more and more phonetic and morphological differentiation. As a result, the vocabulary contains lexical items of different chronological periods and different morphological properties. Thus, there are many items belonging to non-productive derivational and compositional patterns, which makes their synchronic morphological analysis difficult. Moreover, several suffixes have two allomorphs, one learned and one popular, both of which might be productive (e.g., AG suffix *-té:rion* > MG *-ˈtirio* and *-ˈtiri* (5a, b); AG denominal agent suffix *-eús* > MG *-ˈeas* and *-ˈjas* (6a, b)), and some suffixes combine exclusively with either learned or popular lexical bases. To take an example from adjective-forming suffixes: *-iˈðis* (< AG *-eidɛ́:s*) and *-ˈoðis* (< AG *-o:dɛ:s-* see Anastasiadi-Symeonidi 2001) are learned suffixes (7a, b), whereas *-ˈenjos* and *-ˈutsikos* are exclusively popular (8a, b). For the notion of "learned" in the MG vocabulary, see Symeonidi and Fliatouras (2004).

(5)	a.	*poˈlo* 'to sell'	→	*poli-ˈtirio* 'sales point'
		proskaˈlo 'to invite'	→	*proskli-ˈtirio* 'invitation'
	b.	*poˈtizo* 'to water'	→	*potis-ˈtiri* 'watering can'
		ksiˈpno 'to wake up'	→	*ksipni-ˈtiri* 'alarm clock'

(6) a. *ˈɣrama* ‘letter’ → *ɣramaˈt-eas* ‘secretary’
ˈfero ‘bear’ → *foˈr-eas* ‘bearer, vector’
b. *ˈfonos* ‘murder’ → *foˈn-jas* ‘murderer’

(7) a. *oˈsto* ‘bone’ (learned) → *oste-ˈoðis* ‘bony’ vs.
ˈkokalo ‘bone’ (pop.) → **kokalˈ-oðis*
b. *ˈialos* ‘glass’ (learned) → *ialˈ-oðis* ‘glassy’ vs.
jaˈli ‘glass’ (cognate pop.) → **jalˈ-oðis*

(8) a. *moˈlivi* ‘lead’ (pop.) → *moliˈv-enjos* ‘made of lead’ vs.
molivðos ‘lead’ (cognate learned) → **molivˈð-enjos*
b. *ˈsinefo* ‘cloud’ (pop.) → *sineˈf-enjos* ‘cloudy’ vs.
ˈnefos ‘cloud, smog’ (cognate learned) → **neˈf-enjos*

3 Derivation

3.1 Suffixation and prefixation

3.1.1 Suffixation

The basic properties of AG suffixes are the following:

- Most suffixes are of IE descent, and their previous history is discussed in works on IE word-formation, such as Lindner (2011). AG suffixes are therefore almost exclusively native, and there is no borrowing of suffixes in AG, if one exempts a number of pre-Greek loans (for details see Beekes 2010: xxxiii–xl), which are opaque and non-productive and, thus, no longer felt as suffixes. On the contrary, in later periods there is considerable suffix borrowing, initially from Latin (cf. Filos 2008), e.g., *-arius*, and later from Italian/Venetian (*-are*, *-ada*) and Turkish (*-lı*, *-lık* > MG *-lis*, *-ˈliki*); examples will be given under (d) below.
- Suffixes may have several allomorphs with an initial vowel added through reanalysis (shift of morpheme boundary) and analogical extension. For example, -V*rós* has the allomorphs *-erós*, *-arós*, *-yrós*, *-ɛːrós* (9):

(9) a. *kŷ:d-os* ‘glory’, *kýd-istos* ‘very glorious’ → *kyd-rós* ‘glorious’
anth-éo: ‘to bloom’, *ánthɛː-sa* ‘bloomed’ → *anthɛː-rós* ‘blooming’
b. *trém-o:* ‘to fear, tremble’, *tróm-os* ‘terror’ → *trom-erós* ‘terrible’
steíb-o: ‘to tread’, *stíb-os* ‘trodden track’ → *stib-arós* ‘compact, sturdy’
haîma ‘blood’, *haímat-os* ‘blood GEN.SG.’ → *haimat-ɛːrós* ‘bloody’

– Nominal suffixes may be used for more than one part of speech, i.e. both for nouns and adjectives. For example, the AG suffix *-mós* creates adjectives from nominal stems and nouns from verbal stems (10). This suffixal property of polyfunctionality is also shared by the later phases of the language.

(10) *thér-os* 'warmth, summer' → *ther-mós* 'hot' (cognate with Engl. *warm*)
dió:k-o: 'to pursue, chase' → *dio:k-mós* > *dio:g-mós* 'chase, persecution'

One may distinguish the following types of evolution in Greek suffixal derivation:

a) Preservation of morphologically-intact suffixes: Of course, one cannot speak of complete identity of form, since AG and MG phonology are quite different; identity can be understood as a phoneme-per-phoneme correspondence, where correspondence has its usual historical linguistic meaning of "direct inheritance through regular phonological evolution". For example, the masculine deverbal suffix *-tɛ:s* (Leukart 1994) was in AG and still is in MG one of the main suffixes creating agent nouns, e.g., *po:lô:* 'to sell' → AG *po:lɛ:tɛ́:s*, MG *poliˈtis* 'seller' (for reasons of clarity, the derivational suffix is taken together with the inflectional ending). Phonologically, the suffix appears in AG as /tɛ:s/ and in MedG and MG as /tis/, while in the Pontic dialect of MG it preserves its ancient form /tes/ when unaccented (e.g., Pontic *ˈrafto* 'to sew' → *ˈraftes* 'tailor'). In other cases, the phonological difference is minimal, e.g., the adjective-creating suffix *-imos* (AG and MG /imos/): AG and MG *nóm-os* 'law' → *nóm-imos* 'legal', AG *nóst-os* 'return' → *nóst-imos* 'belonging to the day of the return' → MG 'tasty'.

b) Preservation of suffixes with major phonological and morphological changes: Evolution in the inflectional morphology of the language has led to changes in the "citation form" (the nom. sg.) and the inflectional pattern of many nominal suffixes, as in the AG fem. denominal suffix *-tɛ:s*, gen. *-tɛ:t-os* > MG *-tita*, gen. *-titas* (11) or AG masc. deverbal suffix *-tɛ:r*, gen. *-tɛ:r-os* > MG *-tiras*, gen. *-tira* (12):

(11) AG *ánthro:pos* 'man' → AG *anthro:pó-tɛ:s*, MG *anθroˈpo-tita* 'humanity'
AG *takʰýs* 'quick' → AG *takhý-tɛ:s*, MG *taˈxi-tita* 'quickness'

(12) AG *só:-idzo:* 'to save' → AG *so:-tɛ́:r*, MG *so-ˈtiras* 'saviour'
AG *antidrô:* 'to react' → MG *andiðras-ˈtiras* 'reactor'

The major vowel change of "synizesis" (glide formation), which took place around the 13th c. AD, has greatly altered the form of several suffixes, e.g., the deverbal neuter suffix [ion] > [ˈjo] forming nouns where an activity takes place: MedG *maɣir-évo* 'to cook' → *maɣiˈrio* /*maɣiˈrjo* 'kitchen, cook-shop'.

As already mentioned, due to the double (learned and vernacular) linguistic tradition, a suffix may have two allomorphs in MG, one forming high register words and one for "lower" vocabulary. See the "high" *metaksur'γ-io* 'silk factory', *zaxaroplas't-io* 'pastry shop', *kosmimatopo'l-io* 'jewellery store', *stratoði'k-io* 'court martial' vs. the "low" *krasopu'l-jo* 'wine shop, tavern', *ljotri'v-jo* 'olive press', *kambana'r-jo* 'belfry'. Occasionally, the same stem may be combined with the two allomorphs of the same suffix, creating words with different meanings (etymological doublets), e.g., *sti'x-io* 'element' but *sti'x-jo* 'ghost'. Synizesis has also caused merging of initially distinct suffixes, as in the case of AG *-éa*, *-ía*, *-eia* and *-iá*, now all *-'ja*, e.g., *ma'xeri* 'knife' → *maxe'r-ja* 'knife-wound', *'milo* 'apple' → *mil-'ja* 'apple tree', *tar'zan* 'Tarzan' → *tarza'n-ja* 'foolhardy action'. It is doubtful whether the contemporary native speaker makes any distinction between the homophonous suffixes, and the distinctions made by the Ancient and the Medieval speaker must have also been different from each other. The picture is further complicated by the existence of "learned" variants of the suffix, preserving the form ['ia] without synizesis, and creating etymological doublets, sometimes without a change of meaning (e.g., *elefθe'r-ia*/*lefte'r-ja* 'freedom', *sxo'l-io*/*sxo'l-jo* 'school') and sometimes with difference of meaning (e.g., *ðu'l-ia* 'slavery'/*ðu'l-ja* 'work'). Additionally, a number of MG dialects, such as those of Megara, Mani and Pontus, also preserve the Medieval form ['ea] without synizesis, e.g., *mi'l-ea* 'apple tree', *maxe'rea* 'knife-wound'. For the complex history of these suffixes see Petrounias (1987).

Another characteristic example is the nominal suffix *-eús* (Leukart 1994), which, due to alternative phonological or analogical evolutions as well as to the learned tradition, has acquired the allomorphs *-'eas*, *-'jas* and *-'jos*, applying to the same stem (13a), depending on the register or dialect, or to different stems (13b): nouns formed with this suffix constitute a problem for MG morphology, because they form a small inflectional class with a mixed paradigm. In MG, this suffix has acquired an additional colloquial meaning (apart from the formation of agent nouns), yielding pejorative augmentative nouns (13c).

(13)	a.	AG *basil-eús* 'king'	>	MG *vasi'l-eas*, *vasi'l-jas*, *vasi'l-jos*
		AG *graph-eús* 'scribe'	>	MG *γra'f-eas* / *γra'f-jas* 'clerk'
	b.	AG *grammat-eús* 'secretary'	>	MG *γrama't-eas*
		AG *drom-eús* 'runner'	>	MG *ðro'm-eas*
		AG *phon-eús* 'killer'	>	MG *fo'n-jas*
		AG *gon-eús* 'parent'	>	MG *γo'n-jos*
	c.	MG *psi'l-os* 'tall'	→	*psi'l-eas* 'tall guy'
		MG *'mavr-os* 'black'	→	*ma'vr-eas* 'Blackie (surname)'

c) L o s s o f s u f f i x e s: A number of AG suffixes were lost during the Koine or the Medieval period. "Loss" means cessation of productivity and of ability to create new lexical items, although, due to the conservative character of the language a suffix may survive. For example, AG possessed a neuter suffix creating instrument nouns, with four allomorphs: *-tron, -tʰron, -tlon, -tʰlon,* e.g., *aró-o:* 'to plough' → *áro-tron* 'plough', *kleí-o:* 'to close' → *kleí-tʰron* 'latch', *gén-os* 'race, kin' → *géne-tʰlon* 'offspring, descent'. The suffix ceased to be productive in MedG, but survives lexically, as a number of AG words bearing the allomorph *-tro* are still used, having recognizable verbal stems: *'θea-tro* 'theatre', *'kini-tro* 'motive', *'γoi-tro* 'charm', *'plik-tro* 'key (of keyboard)', *'komis-tro* 'fare', etc. In the case of the much rarer survivals of the allomorph *-tʰron,* the derivational process is probably no longer felt: *'elki-θro* 'sledge'. The allomorphs *-tlon* and *-tʰlon* have completely disappeared.

d) Borrowing of new suffixes: As already mentioned, a number of derivational suffixes were borrowed into Greek during different periods. These are mostly nominal suffixes. Examples include Latin *-arius* > *-'arios/-'aris* (forming nouns, e.g., *peri'voli* 'garden' → *perivo'l-aris* 'gardener' and adjectives, e.g., *'zil-ja* 'jealousy' → *zi'lj-aris* 'jealous'), Latin *-atus* (forming adjectives, e.g., *'trexo* 'to run' → *tre'x-atos* 'running'), Turkish *-ci* (forming professional nouns, e.g., *ta'ksi* 'taxi' → *taksi-'dzis* 'taxi-driver', *'suvla* 'roasting spit' → *suvla-'dzis* 'souvlaki seller'), Venetian *-ada* (forming nouns, e.g., *'eksipnos* 'clever' → *eksi'pn-aða* 'cleverness', *porto'kali* 'orange' → *portoka'l-aða* 'orange juice'). The borrowing of verbal suffixes, such as the Italian *-are,* is much rarer, and limited to stems of foreign origin, e.g., Italian *sollazzo* 'amusement' → *sollazz-are* 'to entertain' > MG *su'latso* 'stroll' → *sula'ts-aro* 'to stroll' or English *google* → *gu'gl-aro* 'to google' '(Ralli 2012a). As this distribution shows, the borrowing of suffixes may have started from the transfer of the entire lexical items bearing the suffix in question, which initially combined with stems from the language of origin, and had the same function. A suffix may later extend its meaning range and its usage to native stems. For example, the Turkish suffix *-cı* first appears with stems of Turkish origin: the Medieval dictionary of Kriaras (1967–) contains items like *balta-'dzis* 'wood-cutter' < Turk. *balta-cı* < *balta* 'axe'; *aba-'dzis* 'robe-maker' < Turk. *aba-cı* < *aba* 'cloth, cloak'; *bostan-'dzis* 'gardener' < Turk. *bostancı* < *bostan* 'vegetable garden'. Later the suffix spreads to Greek stems, e.g., *'suvla* 'roasting spit' → *suvla-'dzis* 'souvlaki seller', *forti'γo* 'truck' → *fortiγa-'dzis* 'truck driver', *'aspros* 'white' → *aspri-'dzis* 'whitewasher'. Finally, it also acquires a more general sense not necessarily connected with professions, e.g., *AEK* 'a Greek football team' → *aek-'dzis* 'supporter of the team AEK', *xora'to* 'joke' → *xorata-'dzis* 'joker', *fasa'ria* 'trouble, noise' → *fasar-'dzis* 'troublemaker' (Ralli 2005).

In some cases, a native suffix merges with a borrowed suffix, creating a new range of functions. For example, the AG masc. nominal suffix *-to:r* creates agent nouns (*r^{h}ε̂:-ma* 'word, speech' → *r^{h}έ:to:r* 'orator', *prak-jo: > prátto:* 'to act, do' → *prák-to:r* 'doer', *gennáo:* 'to give birth' → *gennε:´-tor* 'parent'). In Hellenistic and MedG this suffix (its inflectional form changed to *-toras*) merged with the cognate Latin suffix *-tor*, allowing the importation of many Latin loanwords, e.g., *vi'ɣlatoras* 'watcher', *ro'ɣatoras* 'mercenary', *ði'ktatoras* 'dictator', *'pretoras* 'praetor'. This type of words, most of them from the Italian verbs in *-are* (e.g., *vigilare, rogare*), together with the frequent derivatives of the AG verb *kratéo:* 'to rule, prevail' (MedG *afto-'krator* 'emperor', *panto-'krator* '(of God) ruler of all', *kliðo-'krator* 'key-master', *kosmo-'krator* 'ruler of the world', *θalaso-'krator* 'ruler of the seas') led to an extended form of the suffix in *-'atoras*, which attaches to both verbal and nominal stems: MedG *simvu'l-evo* 'to advise' → *simvu'l-atoras* 'advisor', *kini'ɣ-o* 'to hunt' → *kini'ɣ-atoras* 'hunter', *ðo'ksari* 'bow' → *ðoksa'r-atoras* 'archer', MG *maɣa'zi* 'store' → *maɣa'z-atoras* 'store-keeper'.

e) Creation of new suffixes through reanalysis: A considerable number of new suffixes were created during the history of Greek through the mechanism of reanalysis and shift of morpheme boundaries. A characteristic case is the AG masculine suffix *-mos*, which combines with aorist (perfective) verbal stems to create action nouns (cf. Bader 1974; Rico 2002) (14a). When attached to the extremely frequent verbs bearing the derivational suffixes *-ídz-o:* and *-ádz-o:*, reanalysis took place, in the context of the sigmatic forms of the aorist (+perfective, +past), which led to the creation of the new suffix *-ismos* or *-asmos* (14b).

(14) a. *odýr-omai* 'to wail' → *odyr-mós* 'wailing'
kat^{h}ár-jo: > kat^{h}aíro: 'to purify' → *kat^{h}ar-mós* 'purification'
b. *k^{h}o:r-ídz-o:* 'to separate' → *kho:r-is-mós* 'separation'
syllabέ: 'syllable' → *syllab-ídzo:* 'to spell' → *syllab-is-mós* 'spelling'
kalp-ádzo: 'to gallop' → *kalp-as-mós* 'gallop n.'
en-thu:si-ádzo: 'to be inspired by a god' → *enthu:si-as-mós* 'enthusiasm'

This suffix, apart from a new (extended) form, acquired a new function, namely attachment to nominal bases in order to form abstract nouns, e.g., *xristia'nos* 'Christian' → *xristiani'smos* 'Christianity', *'ðoɣma* → *ðoɣmati'smos* 'dogmatism' (both first attested in the Hellenistic period). The new suffix was subsequently borrowed into Latin (as *-ismus*), with a greatly increased productivity in the Neolatin of the Renaissance, from whence it passed into the major European languages (a characteristic case of neoclassical word-formation). In this new guise, it came back into Greek during the Enlightenment period, following three paths: a) via words formed in a foreign language on the basis of Greek elements, subsequently borrowed into Greek. E.g., *mixa'ni* 'machine' → *mixani'smos* 'mechanism', attested since 1761, from French *mécanisme* attested since 1701; b) via calques, e.g., *γi'mnos* 'nude' → *γimn-i'smos* 'nudism' on the basis of English *nudism*; c) via phonetically adapted foreign terms, e.g., *femini'smos, sinðikali'smos* from French *féminisme, syndicalisme*. A similar evolution applies to the reanalyzed morpheme *-is'tis* (English *-ist*) from the AG *-tɛ:s*, through verbs in *-idzo* (cf. Haspelmath 1995: 5).

Another characteristic case of affix creation through reanalysis is the extremely productive diminutive suffix *-'aki* (Jannaris 1897: 292–293). Its origin lies in the AG diminutive *-ion*, e.g., AG *bíbl-os* 'book' → *bibl-íon* 'small book', *sphŷ:r-a* 'hammer' → *sphy:r-íon* 'small hammer', whose diminutive meaning was subsequently bleached (in MG *vi'vlio* and *sfi'ri* mean simply 'book' and 'hammer', respectively, without any diminutive meaning, while the original words have disappeared). When the suffix *-ion* was attached to nominal bases in /k/, the diminutive item ended in *-akion*, which through phonological erosion became *-'aki*, e.g., AG *rýak-s* 'brook' → *ryák-ion* 'small brook' > MG *ri'aki* 'brook'. The final phonemes of the stem were reanalyzed as part of the suffix (*ry'ak-ion* > *ry-'akion*) and the new suffix spread to new nominal bases, e.g., *sfi'ri* 'hammer' → *sfi'r-aki* 'small hammer', *mo'ro* 'baby' → *mo'r-aki* 'small baby'.

3.1.2 Prefixation

Prefixation in AG involves a very small number of prefixes which attach to nominal bases (e.g., AG *sop^{h}ós* 'wise' → *á-sop^{h}os* 'unwise'), and the very productive mechanism of prefixing verbs by preverbs, which originate from prepositions with adverbial locative meaning (e.g., *katá* 'towards, with downward motion' + *grápho:* 'I write' → *kata-grápho:* 'I write down, list', *antí* 'opposite' + *grápho:* → *antigrápho:* 'I write back, copy', *hypó* 'under' + *grápho:* → *hypográpho:* 'I sign, subscribe'). Traditional accounts (e.g., Debrunner 1917) treat the attachment of preverbs under composition, where compound verbs are considered to consist of a preposition and a full verb. However, recent accounts demand a distinction between prepositions and preverbs, i.e. prepositions prefixed to verbs (see Bortone 2010: 119–121), mainly because the meanings of preverbs are not always the same as the meanings of the prepositions from which they derive. Even if in AG a grouping together of prepositions and preverbs is possible, since for every preverb there exists a homonymous preposition with a similar meaning, it ceases to be so in later Greek, since many AG prepositions are lost and survive only as preverbs. Moreover, preverbs have different morphological and semantic properties from the surviving free-form prepositions (see Ralli 2004). For example, the AG preposition and preverb *diá* 'through, for' survives in MG as a preverb *ði'a* (e.g., *ði'a +'γrafo* 'I write' → *ðia'γrafo* 'I delete', *ði'a +'krino* 'I judge' → *ðia'krino* 'I distinguish') but the corresponding preposition has changed through phonological evolution to *ja* 'for' and its relation to the preverb is no longer obvious.

Apart from this major change in the domain of prefixation, the following changes can be observed in the diachrony of Greek:

a) Preservation of morphologically-intact prefixes: The most characteristic case is the very productive privative prefix *a-* (before consonant) and *an-* before vowel, etymologically a cognate of the Latin *in-* (English *un-*). This prefix attaches to nouns, adjectives and adverbs, and has remained stable throughout the history of Greek. E.g., AG *sop^hós* 'wise' → *á-sop^hos* 'unwise', *st^hénos* 'strength' → *a-sthenέ:s* 'weak' (> MG *asθe'nis* 'ill'), *ónoma* 'name' → *anó:nymos* 'anonymous', MG *xa'ra* 'joy' → *'a-xar-os* 'joyless', *ar'moðios* 'responsible, in charge' → *an-ar'moðios* 'not in charge'. Another case of prefix preservation can be seen in the also productive qualitative adverbial prefixes *dys-* 'un-, mis-, bad' and its opposite *eu-* 'well, good', continued in MG as *ðis-* and *ef-* with the same meaning and function. E.g., AG *eu-tyk^hέ:s* ~ *dys-tyk^hέ:s*, MG *ef-tixi'smenos* ~ *ðis-tixi'smenos* 'happy, lucky'~ 'unhappy, unlucky', AG *eu-k^háristos* ~ *dys-árestos*, MG *ef-'xaristos* ~ *ði's-arestos* 'pleasant/unpleasant'. Most words formed from these suffixes are directly inherited from AG, but new words are also formed in a higher register, e.g., *ðis-litur'γia* 'malfunction', *ðis-le'ksia* 'dyslexia' (neoclassical loan), *ðis-'profer-tos* 'hard to pronounce'.

b) Preservation of prefixes with major phonological and morphological changes: The IE root **sem-* 'one' gives, in the lengthened grade, the prefix *hε:mi-* (cf. Latin *semi-*) 'half-', e.g., *hέ:mi-sys* 'half' (adj.), *hε:mi-t^hanέ:s* 'half-dead', *hε:mí-t^heos* 'demi-god', *hε:mí-p^ho:non* 'semi-vowel'. The prefix continues in the high register vocabulary of MG as *i'mi-* (e.g., *imi-θa'nis, i'mi-θeos, i'mi-fono*), while popular language elements contain instead the cognate nominal *mis(o)-* as first member of compounds (*-o-* is the linking vowel whose presence is compulsory in compounds, see Ralli 2008). *miso-* derives from the adjective *mi'sos* < AG *hέ:mi-sys* 'half', first appearing in the Medieval period, e.g., *mi's-o-trelos* 'half-mad', *mis-o-fayo'menos* 'half-eaten', *mi's-o-loγa* 'minced words'. "Learned" and "popular" variants may co-exist with the same meaning, e.g., *imiθa'nis* and *miso-peθa-'menos* 'half-dead', *imi-te'lis* and *miso-telio-'menos* 'half-finished', *i'mi-γimnos* and *mi'so-γimnos* 'half-naked', while in MG many new high register *imi*-derivatives, non-existent in AG, are created, e.g., *imi-a'ftonomos* 'semi-autonomous', *imi-ðiatro'fi* 'half-board', *imi-po'litimos* 'semi-precious'.

c) Loss of prefixes: A number of AG nominal prefixes disappeared, mostly during the Koine period. The lost prefixes were mainly those whose meaning and etymology were no longer transparent, and thus were not very productive even in AG. An example is the negative prefix *nɛ:-* of the same IE etymology as *a-* (both < *n̥), attached to stems beginning with a vowel, e.g., *épos* 'word' → *nɛ́:pios* 'not speaking > stupid', *ánemos* 'wind' → *nɛ:nemía* 'calm'. The prefix *nɛ:-* did not survive after AG, but still exists as a fossil in a number of MG words such as *'nipio* 'infant' (from AG *nɛ́:pios* 'stupid').

d) Borrowing of prefixes: The borrowing of prefixes is not attested in any phase of the history of Greek. A possible exception might be the MG colloquial intensive prefix *kara-* 'very', from the Turkish adjective *kara* 'black': *i'liθios* 'silly' → *kara-i'liθios* 'very silly', *tsek-'aro* 'I check' → *kara-tse'karo* 'I check very thoroughly'. The use as an intensive prefix probably started from the borrowing of Turkish words where *kara* was a component with an intensifying function, e.g., Turkish *sevda* 'love, passion' → *kara-sevda-lı* 'deeply in love (adjective) > MG *karasevda'lis* 'id.'

e) Creation of new prefixes or prefixoids through reanalysis: One may distinguish two cases: i) creation of prefixes from grammatical/functional elements and ii) creation of prefixoids from lexical elements. The first case involves the prefix *kse-*, which derives from the combination of the AG preverb *ek* 'of, from' and the augment *e-* which marked the past tense of AG verbs and was prefixed on the left side (15a) of the verbal stem. In later Greek, the augment lost its status as an inflectional element when unaccented, through a general phonetic process deleting unaccented initial vowels from the Medieval period onwards (15b). In certain cases where a verb is prefixed by a preverb, the augment is attached internally (15c):

(15) a. *gráph-o:* 'I write' → *é-graph-on* 'I wrote (imperfective, past)', *é-grap-s-a* 'I wrote (perfective, past)'
b. *'e-ɣrap-s-a* 1st sg. vs. *e-'ɣrap-s-amen* → *'ɣrapsame* 1st plur.
c. *anti-grápho:* → *ant-é-grap-s-a*, *kata-grápho:* → *kat-é-grap-s-a*

Crucially, in the case of verbs formed with the preverb *ek-* 'out, off' (*eks-* before vowel), the past tenses show the surface form *ekse-*, as in *ek* + *kathar-ízo:* 'to clean' → *ekkatharízo:* 'to clean out, clean completely' → *eks-e-kathár-iz-on* and *eks-e-kathár-is-a*. Phonetic erosion of the unaccented initial /e/ of *eks-*, together with the destabilization of the augment through the same phenomenon, led to past forms like *ksekatharisa* which were reanalyzed not as *ks-e-katharisa* but as *kse-katharisa*. Thence, a new prefix *kse-* appeared in the medieval period, which was able to attach to verbs (*kse-'ɣrafo* 'to write off', *kse-'pleno* 'to wash off') and adjectives (*kse-'katharos* 'utterly clear'), with the limitation that the stems which accept it belong to the vernacular and not to the learned register.

It is important to note that a similar evolution occurred in the case of the MG adverb *ksana* 'again', which derives from the sequence of two AG preverbs, *ek* (its allomorph *eks*) and *ana-*, with phonetic erosion of the initial unstressed vowel, e.g., *eks-ana-ˈɣrafo* > *ksana-ˈɣrafo*. However, contrary to *kse-* which is a clear-cut bound morpheme (prefix), *ksana* has become a free word, i.e. an adverb meaning 'again' (see Ralli 2004 for the compound nature of combination involving *ksana* and a verb). Thus, the further development of *ksana* from a prefix to the status of a free word suggests the occurrence of a degrammaticalization process (cf. Méndez Dosuna 1997).

The second process of prefixoid creation involves the prefixation of full lexical items which were originally first members of compounds, and subsequently underwent generalization and bleaching of their meaning. A case in point is *θeo-* (Anastasiadi-Symeonidi 2008), from the noun *θeˈos* 'God', which initially participated in compounds such as *θeˈo-ðotos* 'God-given', *θeo-ˈfilak-tos* 'guarded by God', but now behaves like a prefix with an intensifying function, attached to adjectives: *xonˈdros* 'fat' → *θeˈo-xondros* 'very very fat', *ɣimˈnos* 'naked' → *θεˈo-ɣimnos* 'utterly naked'.

3.2 Ablaut

Nominal derivation in AG is also connected with the phenomenon of ablaut, i.e. the change of the root vowel. Ablaut is a residual effect of IE word-formation, where it was connected with the accent (accented roots remained stable, unaccented roots underwent change). In other words, it was originally a phonologically-driven alternation. However, from a synchronic point of view within AG, it should be considered as a purely morphological phenomenon (16):

(16) *phér-o:* 'to bear, bring' → *phór-os* 'tribute', *phor-á:* 'carrying, tendency', *phor-eús* 'carrier'
trép-o: 'to turn' → *tróp-os* 'direction, manner', *trop-έ:* 'turn, turning', *trop-eús* 'door-hinge'
ném-o: 'to dispense, distribute' → *nóm-os* 'dispensation, law', *nom-έ:* 'distribution', *nom-eús* 'distributor'

It is doubtful whether ablaut was a productive mechanism in AG, i.e. whether new nouns could be formed using it or whether all the word families participating in the pattern were of IE inheritance. Of course, there can be no question of ablaut as a productive mechanism after AG. However, most of the relevant word families survived diachronically until MG in unchanged form (disregarding changes in pronunciation), and, therefore, the pattern is almost as obvious as it was in AG.

3.3 Backformation

Sometimes, simplex words (inflection disregarded) can be created from derived words through the analogical process of backformation, which may produce the following categories:

a) nouns from verbs, e.g., *hɛ:ttô:mai* 'to be defeated' → *hɛ̂:tta* 'defeat', *gennô:* 'to give birth' → *génna* 'birth', *ereunô:* 'to investigate' → *éreuna* 'investigation' (on the analogy of regular denominal formations like *dípsa* 'thirst' → *dipsô:* 'to be thirsty', *peína* 'hunger' → *peinô:* 'to be hungry', *lýssa* 'rage, rabies' → *lyssô:* 'to be enraged, rabid'). The process continues in MedG and MG, creating nouns like *ɣnoˈrizo* 'to know' → *ˈɣnora* 'sign of recognition', *anaˈseno* 'to breathe' → *aˈnasa* 'breath', *kaˈvlono* 'to be turned on' → *ˈkavla* 'erection'.
b) Simple adjectives from prefixed words, e.g., *pseûdos* 'lie, falsehood' → *a-pseudɛ́:s* 'not false, true' → *pseudɛ́:s* 'false' (for the process see Meissner 2005).
c) Derived nouns from compounds, e.g., *polítɛ:s* 'citizen' → *politeía* 'citizenship, constitution' → *iso-politeía* 'equality of civic rights' → *iso-polítɛ:s* 'citizen with equal rights'; *eleútheros* 'free' → *ap-eleutheróo:* 'set free' → *apeleútheros* 'freed slave, freeman'. Similar backformations can also be found in MedG and MG, e.g., AG and MG *ˈorkos* 'oath' → *eks-orˈk-izo* 'to exorcise' → MedG *eˈksorkin*, MG *ˈksorki* 'magic spell'.

3.4 Reduplication

Reduplication was originally a non-systematic mechanism to denote emphasis through repetition, a cross-linguistically common phenomenon. In AG (< IE) it had become grammaticalized in verbal inflection where it regularly formed the Perfect stem, e.g., *lýo:* → *lé-ly-ka*, *grápho:* → *gé-graph-a* (for the mechanism of reduplication in AG see Steriade 1982; Niepokuj 1997), and in a subset of verbs also the present stem ("present reduplication", e.g., *bi-bá-dzo:* 'to cause to go', *di-dá-sko:* 'to cause to know > to teach', *pí-pt-o:* 'to fall', *gí-gn-omai* 'to become'). Furthermore, emphatic reduplication of the whole word existed as a marginal phenomenon, e.g., *pan* 'all, whole' (neuter adjective) *pámpan* 'completely, wholly', *pró* 'before, in front' (preposition) → *propró* 'on and on, thoroughly', and it also participated, albeit non-systematically, in nominal derivation, often involving onomatopoeia. E.g., *bárbaros* 'barbarian', *bórboros* 'mire, filth', *mórmuros* 'murmur', *kókkuks* 'cuckoo'. Most of these words survive into MG, which still possesses emphatic lexical reduplication as a productive mechanism (e.g., *murmu'rizo* 'to murmur', *xaxa'nizo* 'to giggle', *tsitsi'rizo* 'to sizzle', *'kokoras* 'rooster', *psi'psina* 'kitty', *'dzidzikas* 'cicada'). However, grammatical reduplication is no longer a living process in MG, having become obsolete since Koine times.

A difficult problem from a synchronic morphological point of view is the considerable number of perfect participles still in use in MG, which continue to show reduplication (17):

(17)	*sin-'krino* 'to compare'	→	*sin-ke-kri-'men-os* 'definite'
	per'no 'to pass, pass through'	→	*pe-pera's-men-os* 'finite'
	'piθo 'to convince'	→	*pe-pi's-men-os* 'convinced'
	pros-ka'lo 'to invite'	→	*pros-ke-kli-'men-os* 'invited, guest'
	vi'azome 'to be in a hurry'	→	*ve-via's-menos* 'hasty, forced'
	si'meno 'to signal, denote'	→	*se-sima's-men-os* 'marked criminal'

In most cases, it can be argued that the link to the relevant verb has been lost through semantic change, and that it is no longer felt by the speaker, which entails that the stem of such items is a fossil, no longer part of the verbal paradigm. However, the high number of such items in the lexicon, the presence of the synchronically-common adjectival/participial suffix *-'men* and their productive inflectional paradigms in the three gender values, masculine, feminine and neuter, make them subject to an analysis procedure.

4 Composition

4.1 Form of compounds

In AG, composition was very rich, and this continues throughout the history of the language. With few differences, most compound patterns continue the IE types, and, thus, overviews of IE and Sanskrit composition are also applicable to AG (see Lindner 2011; Lühr 2010). The basic sequence of the constituents of AG compounds is member1 + linking vowel + member2 (+ derivational suffix) + inflectional suffix.

Regularly, the first member of a compound is a bare stem, deprived of the inflectional suffix, but the appearance of an inflected first member is also possible. The first member may appear in any case-form, depending on its syntactic relationship with the second member (the head). Compounds with full-word first members often serve as relic testimonies of the lost (syncretized) cases, i.e. the locative and the instrumental, but these are rather rare, whereas the genitive case is comparatively common (18):

(18) *Neá-polis* 'new town, Naples' < *néa* 'new, fem.' + *pólis* 'city, fem.'
Pelopón-nɛ:sos 'the island of Pelops, Peloponnese' < *Pélop-os* 'Pelops, gen.' + *nɛ̂:sos* 'island'
Diós-ku:roi 'sons of Zeus, Dioscuri' < *Di-ós* 'Zeus, gen.' + *kû:roi* 'sons'
pasí-philos 'beloved by all' < *pa-sí* 'all, dat. plur.' + *phílos* 'beloved'
nu:n-ekh-é:s 'sensible, wise' < *nû:n* 'mind, acc. sg.' + *ék*^{h}*o:* 'to have'
earí-drep-tos 'harvested in spring' < *éar-i* 'spring, locative' + *drépo:* 'to pluck'
pyrí-kaus-tos 'burnt by fire' < *pyr-í* 'fire, instrumental' + *kaío:* 'to burn'

With the demise of the locative and instrumental cases, most of these compounds were already fossilized in AG, and appear mostly in poetic texts. In later Greek such formations disappear, and in MG a number of words survive in the learned vocabulary and in place names, but they can no longer be considered as the result of a morphological process (Ralli 2013a).

Of course, when the first member of a compound is an uninflected word (numeral, preposition, adverb) its entire form appears in composition. E.g., *déka* 'ten' + *heptá* 'seven' → *deka-eptá* 'seventeen', *déka* + *étos* 'year' → *deka-etɛ́:s* 'ten years old', *áno:* 'up' + *gaîa* 'earth' → *anó:-gaion* 'upper floor'. Also, due to right-headedness, when the adverb is the second member of a compound, the whole compound is uninflected, e.g., *pró* 'before' + *pálai* 'ago' → *pró-palai* 'long ago'.

The second member of the compound may be a whole word (e.g., *mégas* 'great' + *t*^{h}*ymós* 'soul' → *megá-t*^{h}*ymos* 'great-souled, generous') or a stem with a derivational suffix (e.g., *t*^{h}*rasýs* 'brave' + *kardía* 'heart' → *t*^{h}*rasy-kárd-ios* 'brave-heart'). The same two patterns are available throughout the history of Greek.

AG compounds have recessive accentuation, i.e. the accent shifts as far as possible from the final syllable, restricted only by the law of limitation, i.e. the restriction whereby the accent cannot fall further than three morae from the end of the word (see Allen 1973: 236–240 and references therein), unless the derivational suffix is inherently accented. Again, recessive accentuation remains a diachronic property of Greek composition, but in MG, accent has been replaced by stress which can climb up to the antepenultimate syllable (with few exceptions in certain MG dialects). As noted by Ralli (2013a, 2016), MG compounds bear antepenultimate stress if their second member is a stem (compounds of a [stem stem] structural pattern). However, they follow the stress of their second member if it is a fully inflected word (compounds of a [stem word] pattern).

In AG, the order of the compound constituents (see Andriotis 1939) is generally considered to reflect the syntactic word order: thus, adjective-noun compounds display the order modifier + head (e.g., *t^hrasýs* 'brave' + *kardía* 'heart' → *t^hrasy-kárd-ios* 'braveheart', *ákros* 'topmost, edgemost' + *pólis* 'city' → *akrópolis* 'fortified city on a hill'), while noun-verb subordinating compounds display the order argument + head (e.g., *pŷ:r* 'fire' + *phéro:* 'to bear' → *pyrphóros* 'fire-bearing'). The AG compositional system was generally right-headed (Tribulato 2006; Raftopoulou 2005), due to the fact that the unmarked word order in AG syntax, at least initially, was adjective + noun and object + verb. Of course, there existed a number of exceptions to the general pattern. For example, a non-productive and archaic subclass, subsequently lost, had a verb with a thematic vowel /e/ as its first member, followed by a nominal second member (e.g., *p^hér-o:* 'to bear' + *oîkos* 'house' → *p^heréoikos* 'snail; lit. house-bearer', *ék^ho:* 'to have' + *pô:los* 'foal' → *ek^hépo:los* 'having many foals'). In later Greek, compounds continue to be right-headed, but occasionally, especially in slang or dialectal vocabulary, items with the reverse order appear (19) (Ralli 2013a):

(19) *'asximo* 'ugly' + *pa'pi* 'duck' → *asxi'mopapo* 'ugly duckling'
'xar(os) 'death' + *pa'levo* 'to fight' → *'xaropa'levo* 'to fight (with) death'
vs.
aya'po 'to love' + *'adras* 'man' → *ayapsa'dru* 'woman who loves men' (Lesbian dialect)

4.2 Juncture between compound members

4.2.1 Linking vowel

IE composition did not have a linking element; instead, the first member stood as a bare stem, deprived of the inflectional suffix. However, a large number of AG first compound constituents were nouns and adjectives belonging to the *-o-* thematic inflection (2nd declension), i.e. having an *-o-* thematic vowel. This led to the reanalysis of [o] as a linking element and its analogical spread to compound first members which etymologically did not belong to the *-o-* inflection, i.e. they either had an [a:] > [ɛ:] thematic vowel (1st declension), e.g., *hýlɛ:* 'forest' + *tém-no* 'to cut' → *hylɛ:-tóm-os* 'wood-cutter', later *hylotómos*, or were athematic (3rd declension), e.g., *pŷ:r* 'fire' + *phéro:* 'to bear' → *pyrphóros* 'fire-bearing', but later *pŷ:r* 'fire' + *ballo:* 'to throw' → *pyrobólos* 'fire-throwing, firearm', *pŷ:r* 'fire' + *manteía* 'divination' → *pyromanteía* 'divination by fire' (see Anastasiadi-Symeonidi 1983 and Raftopoulou and Ralli 1999). Recent views date the evolution of [o] as far back as the Mycenaean period (see Meissner and Tribulato 2002: 320–323; Lindner 2011: 46–47 and references therein). In fact, [o] has been a regular characteristic of composition throughout the history of Greek, and nowadays, it has assumed the role of a compound marker (Ralli 2008).

Instead of the regular linking vowel [o], a long vowel [ɛ:] appears in a number of AG compounds, whose first members probably originate from stems ending in [ɛ:]: (*níkɛ:* 'victory' + *p^héro:* 'to bear, bring' → *nikɛ:p^hóros* 'victorious' and analogically *t^hánatos* 'death' + *p^héro:* 'to bear, bring' → *thanatɛ:p^hóros* 'deadly', *lampás* 'torch' + **drémo:* 'run' → *lampadɛ:drómos* 'runner at a torch-race'). This pattern does not go beyond AG, since during the Koine and Medieval period no new compounds with [ɛ:] > [i] as a linking vowel are formed. A number of these words appear in the high registers of MG as archaisms, e.g., *θanat-iˈ-foros* 'deadly', *θalam-i-polos* 'butler'.

4.2.2 Wackernagel's law

According to Wackernagel's law II (not the well known syntactic "law" concerning clitic positioning, but a lesser, morphological, generalization by the same scholar), in AG, when the second member of a compound begins with a vowel, it becomes lengthened in contact with the final vowel of the first member or with the linking vowel (20a). The phenomenon (see Collinge 1986: 238–239; Lindner 2011: 53–57) has many exceptions and analogical extensions, even in cases where the first member of the compound does not end in a vowel (20b).

(20)	a.	*stratós* 'army' + *ágo:* 'to lead'	→	*stratoagos* > *stratɛ:gós* 'general'
		dýo 'two' + *órop^hos* 'floor'	→	*dioorop^{h}os* > *dió:rop^{h}os* 'two-storey'
	b.	*kýo:n* 'hound' + *ágo:* 'to lead'	→	*kynɛ:gós* 'hunter'
		dys- 'bad, ill' + *ónoma* 'name'	→	*dysó:nymos* 'bearing a name of ill-omen'

Wackernagel's law was phonological in origin (contraction as a hiatus resolving strategy), but already in AG, it had become morphologized as a marker of composition. With the loss of quantity distinctions in the Koine period, the law became meaningless; nevertheless, its results are still obvious in items which have survived as fossils in the MG vocabulary, such as *stratiˈγos* 'general', *kiniˈγos* 'hunter'.

4.3 Types of compounds

AG compounds can be classified in two ways: a) formally, according to the grammatical category of each member and of the formation as a whole (noun, adjective, verb, pronoun, etc.) and b) semantically, according to the dependency relationship between the two members (possession, addition, determination, etc.). In addition, one may further distinguish between endocentric and exocentric compounds, depending on whether the designatum is contained or not within the compound. For a list of AG compound types, see Meissner and Tribulato (2002) and Lindner (2011).

As in the case of derivation, one may observe the following evolutions:

a) Retention of a compound type: In general, the same compound types are maintained throughout the history of Greek, and Greek remains a language where compounding is an extremely productive process (see Ralli 2009b, 2013a, 2016).
b) Loss of a compound type: No compound formation was lost during the history of Greek, with the exception of a specific sub-type which was already non-productive and opaque in AG, namely, the nominal verb-noun pattern (e.g., *pʰeré-oikos*). The loss of this compound type was in all probability due both to the obscurity of the pattern that created it and to its uncommon left-headed structure.
c) Borrowing of a compound type: Greek is a language with a much richer compounding system than the languages it has come into contact with (e.g., Turkish and Italian). Thus, borrowing of "proper" compound types did not take place. However, a recent (20th c.) innovation in MG are the so-called "phrasal (or syntagmatic) compounds" introduced as calques through the influence of French and English (see Ralli 2013b). Phrasal compounds may have the form Adj+N (e.g., Engl. *cold war* > *psi'xros 'polemos, atom bomb* > *atomi'ki 'vomva*), N+N in the genitive case (e.g., Fr. *agence de voyages* > *prakto'rio taksi'ðion, safety belt* > *'zoni asfa'lias*) or N+N in the nominative (e.g., Fr. *voyage-éclair* > *ta'ksiði astra'pi, enfant-prodige* > *pe'ði-'θavma*).
d) Creation of a new compound type: Two major innovations can be mentioned in the domain of composition, one concerning subordinative and one concerning coordinative compounds.

In the first case, the innovation consists of the creation of verbal compounds. IE and the ancient IE languages had no compound verbs, if one excepts composition with preverbs, as already discussed (Lindner 2011: 36); the same can be said for AG as well (Meissner and Tribulato 2002: 301) and for most, if not all, modern European languages. AG does possess a type of apparently compound verbs which are secondary formations (backformations) from corresponding compound nouns and adjectives (21):

(21) *pétra* 'stone' + *bállo:* 'to throw' → *petrobólos* 'stone-thrower' → *petrobol-ô:* 'to throw stones'
t^hálassa 'sea' + *kratô:* 'to rule' → *thalassokráto:r* 'sea-ruler' → *thalassokrat-ô:* 'to rule the seas'
orp^hanós 'orphan' + *tréph^o* 'to feed, raise' → *orp^hanotróp^hos* 'orphan-raiser' → *orp^hanotroph-ô:* 'to raise orphans'

Their derivative character is obvious from the fact that the second (verbal) member is in most cases not identical to the original verb (e.g., *-troph-ô:* not *tréph-o:*, *-bol-ô:* not *báll-o:*).

Secondary verbal formations are also those which originate from the exocentric V+N nominal compounds, such as the examples given in (22):

(22) *mémp^homai* 'to blame, complain' + *moîra* 'fate' → *mempsímoir-os* 'fault-finding' → *mempsimoirô:* 'to rail against fate'
p^heúgo: 'to leave, run away' + *mákhɛ:* 'combat' → *p^hygómakhos* 'shunning battle, coward' → *p^hygomakhô:* 'to run from combat'

Verbal compounds continue to exist in the learned registers of Greek, but true verbal subordinative compounds, whose second member does not show the ancient verbal ending *-éo* > *-ô:* are a Medieval evolution. E.g., *ˈema* 'blood' + *poˈtizo* 'to water' → *ematopoˈtizo* 'to drench with blood', *karˈðia* 'heart' + *floˈγizo* 'to burn' → *karðiofloˈγizo* 'to burn the heart', *ˈalisos* 'chain' + *ˈðeno* 'to tie' → *alisoˈðeno* 'to tie with chains' (all from the dictionary of Kriaras 1967–).

A medieval innovation is the creation of exocentric compound adjectives with an *-is* derivational suffix, e.g., *ˈkokinos* 'red' + *leˈmos* 'neck' → *kokinoˈlem-is* 'redneck (the bird robin)', *aniˈxtos* 'open' + *ˈxeri* 'hand' → *anixtoˈxer-is* 'open-handed, generous', *maˈkris* 'long' + *maˈli* 'hair' → *makriˈmalis* 'long-haired'. AG and Koine Greek did not possess this compound formation, and, more generally, did not possess *a*-stem ("first declension") adjectives at all (NB *-a:s* > Attic *-ɛ:s* > MG *-is*).

In the domain of coordinative compounds, Greek shows a particularly important innovation: the creation of V+V compounds, which were non-existent in Ancient and Koine Greek, and first appeared during the Medieval period, after the 13th c. AD (Manolessou and Tsolakidis 2009; Ralli 2009b). E.g., *aneˈveno* 'to go up' + *kateˈveno* 'to go down' → *anevokateˈveno* 'to go up and down', *ˈpezo* 'to play' + *γeˈlo* 'to laugh' → *pezoγeˈlo* 'to play and laugh'.

Nominal coordinative compounds were a regular feature of AG, which had appositive N+N compounds, such as *klausí-gelo:s* 'laughter mingled with tears' and *iatró-mantis* 'healer and diviner', and appositive A+A compounds, such as *glyký-pikros* 'bittersweet' and *leuk-érythros* 'white-and-red'. N+N compounds were very productive and to this category belongs the longest attested word in AG, the name of a dish/food in Aristophanes' *Ecclesiazusae* (1169–1174) taking up four lines and consisting of 26 compound members. A+A compounds, on the contrary, were comparatively rare in AG and Koine Greek, but became much more productive in Medieval and Modern Greek.

Finally, during the Medieval period, a new type of N+N compound appeared (Manolessou and Tsolakidis 2009): the plural number coordinative compound which denotes groups of entities, e.g., *γi'neka* 'woman' + *pe'ði* 'child' → *γine'kopeða* 'women and children', *ma'xeri* 'knife' + *pi'runi* 'fork' → *maxero'piruna* 'knives and forks, cutlery'.

5 Conclusion

In this article, we have tried to describe the evolution of Greek word-formation focusing on the period from Koine to Modern Greek, in spite of the fact that studies dealing with specific phenomena and data are rare. We hope to have shown that there is a range of innovations that are worth studying, although Greek is a remarkably conservative language from the morphological point of view as compared to other European languages. More particularly, we tackled issues referring to prefixation, suffixation and composition, where Greek seems to be affected by both language-internal factors and by borrowing from languages it has been in contact with through its long attested history.

6 References

Allen, W. Sidney (1973): *Accent and Rhythm. Prosodic Features of Latin and Greek. A Study in Theory and Reconstruction.* Cambridge: Cambridge University Press.

Anastasiadi-Symeonidi, Anna (1983): La composition en grec moderne d'un point de vue diachronique. *Lalies* 2: 77–90.

Anastasiadi-Symeonidi, Anna (2001): To stixio *-od(is)* stin elliniki: Mia periptosi grammatikopiisis. In: Yorgia Agouraki, Amalia Arvaniti, Jim Davy, Dionysis Goutsos, Marilena Karyolemou, Anna Panayiotou-Triandafillidou, Andreas Papapavlou, Pavlos Pavlou and Anna Roussou (eds.), *Greek Linguistics '99: Proceedings of the 4th International Conference on Greek Language, University of Cyprus, Nicosia 1999*, 71–86. Thessaloniki: University Studio Press.

Anastasiadi-Symeonidi, Anna (2008): To morphima *theo-* stin elliniki. In: Amalia Mozer, Aikaterini Bakakou-Orfanou, Christophoros Charalambakis and Despina Cheila-Markopoulou (eds.), *Glossis Charin. A Festschrift for George Babiniotis*, 99–113. Athens: Ellinika Grammata.
Anastasiadi-Symeonidi, Anna and Asimakis Fliatouras (2004): I diakrisi [logio] ke [laiko] stin elliniki glossa: Orismos ke taksinomisi. In: *Proceedings of the 6th International Conference of Greek Linguistics, Rethymnon, 18–21 September 2003* [e-book]. http://www.philology.uoc.gr/conferences/6thICGL/
Andriotis, Nikolaos (1939): Die wechselnde Stellung von Kompositionsgliedern im Spät-, Mittel- und Neugriechischen. *Glotta* 27: 92–134.
Andriotis, Nikolaos (1956): Die Amredita-Zusammensetzung im Alt- und Neugriechischen. In: Heinz Kronasser (ed.), *Μνήμης χάριν. Gedenkschrift Paul Kretschmer*, 24–30. Wien: Wiener Sprachgesellschaft.
Bader, Françoise (1974): *Suffixes grecs en* -m-. *Recherches comparatives sur l'heteroclisie nominale*. Genève: Droz.
Beekes, Robert (2010): *Etymological Dictionary of Greek*. Leiden: Brill.
Bornemann, Eduard and Ernst Risch (1978): *Griechische Grammatik*. Frankfurt/M.: Diesterweg.
Bortone, Pietro (2010): *Greek Prepositions. From Antiquity to the Present*. Oxford: Oxford University Press.
Buck, Carl D. (1933): *A Comparative Grammar of Greek and Latin*. Chicago: University of Chicago Press.
Buck, Carl D. and Walter Petersen (1945): *A Reverse Index of Greek Nouns and Adjectives*. Chicago: University of Chicago Press.
Chantraine, Pierre (1933): *La formation des noms en grec ancien*. Paris: Klincksieck.
Collinge, Neville Edgar (1986): *The Laws of Indo-European*. Amsterdam/Philadelphia: Benjamins.
Debrunner, Albert (1917): *Griechische Wortbildungslehre*. Heidelberg: Winter.
Dieterich, Karl (1904): Akzent- und Bedeutungsverschiebung im Mittel- und Neugriechischen. *Indogermanische Forschungen* 16: 1–26.
Dieterich, Karl (1909): Die präpositionalen Präfixe in der griechischen Sprachentwicklung mit besonderer Berücksichtigung des Mittel- und Neugriechischen. *Indogermanische Forschungen* 24: 87–158.
Dieterich, Karl (1928): Die Suffixbildung im Neugriechischen. *Balkan-Archiv* 4: 104–167.
Duhoux, Yves (2000): *Le verbe grec ancien. Élements de morphologie et de syntaxe historiques*. 2nd ed. Louvain-la-Neuve: Peeters.
Filos, Panagiotis (2008): Studies in the morphology of Latin loanwords into Greek. Evidence from the papyri. Ph.D. dissertation, Oxford University.
Haspelmath, Martin (1995): The growth of affixes in morphological reanalysis. In: Geert Booij and Jaap van Marle (eds.), *Yearbook of Morphology 1994*, 1–29. Dordrecht: Kluwer.
Heidermanns, Frank (2005): *Bibliographie zur Indogermanischen Wortforschung*. Vol. 3: *Wortbildung, Etymologie, Onomasiologie und Lehnwortschichten der alten und modernen Indogermanischen Sprachen in systematischen Publikationen ab 1800*. Berlin/New York: de Gruyter.
Holton, David, Panagiotis Toufexis, Io Manolessou, Geoffrey Horrocks, Stamatina Lentari and Marjolijne Janssen (2019): *The Cambridge Grammar of Medieval and Early Modern Greek*. Cambridge: Cambridge University Press.
Jannaris, Antonius (1897): *An Historical Greek Grammar, chiefly of the Attic Dialect*. London: McMillan.
Joseph, Brian D. and Angela Ralli (2024): Something out of nothing: Degrammaticalizing Grammaticalization. In: Bethwyn Evans, Maria Kristina Gallego and Luisa Miceli (eds.), *Historical Linguistics 2019. Selected papers from the 24th International Conference on Historical Linguistics, Canberra, 1–5 July 2019*, 240–259. Amsterdam/Philadelphia: Benjamins.

Kakarikos, Kostas (2010): Feature hierarchy and nominal inflection: Evidence from Ancient Greek. In: Geert Booij, Marianna Katsoyannou, Angela Ralli and Sergio Scalise (eds.), *Proceedings of the 7th Mediterranean Morphology Meeting, Nicosia, Cyprus, 10–13 September 2009*, 18–37. Patras: University of Patras.

Karantzola, Eleni (2004): Morphologikes ke simasiologikes opsis tis epithimatopiisis stin proimi neoelliniki. *Studies in Greek Linguistics* 24: 218–229.

Karantzola, Eleni and Giannoula Giannoulopoulou (2000): Simasiologika stixia ja ti sinthesi ke paragogi stin proimi neoelliniki. *Studies in Greek Linguistics* 20: 193–202.

Karantzola, Eleni and Giannoula Giannoulopoulou (2001): Simasiologika stixia ja ti sinthesi ke paragogi stin proimi neoelliniki b: Epithimatopiisi. *Studies in Greek Linguistics* 21: 245–256.

Kretschmer, Paul and Ernst Locker (1977): *Rückläufiges Wörterbuch der griechischen Sprache.* Göttingen: Vandenhoeck & Rupprecht.

Kriaras, Emmanouil (ed.) (1967–): *Leksiko tis meseonikis ellinikis dimodous grammatias 1100–1669.* Thessaloniki: Kentro Ellinikis Glossas.

Leukart, Alex (1994): *Die frühgriechischen Nomina auf* -tas *und* -as. *Untersuchungen zu ihrer Herkunft und Ausbreitung unter Vergleich mit den Nomina auf* -eus. Wien: Österreichische Akademie der Wissenschaften.

Lindner, Thomas (2011): *Indogermanische Grammatik.* Vol. 4/1: *Komposition.* Heidelberg: Winter.

Lühr, Rosemarie (2004): Nominalkomposition im Altindischen und Altgriechischen. In: Elke Nowak (ed.), *Komplexe Wortstrukturen. Komposition, Inkorporation, Polysynthese*, 107–214. Berlin: Technische Universität Berlin, Institut für Sprache und Kommunikation.

Lühr, Rosemarie (ed.) (2008): *Nominale Wortbildung des Indogermanischen in Grundzügen. Die Wortbildungsmuster ausgewählter indogermanischer Einzelsprachen. Band 1: Latein, Altgriechisch.* Hamburg: Kovač.

Luraghi, Silvia (2004): The evolution of the Greek nominal paradigms from Mycenaean to Modern Greek. *Classica e Medievalia* 55: 361–380.

Manolessou, Io and Symeon Tsolakidis (2009): Greek coordinated compounds: Synchrony and diachrony. *Patras Working Papers in Linguistics* 1: 23–39.

Mayser, Edwin (1923): *Grammatik der griechischen Papyri aus der Ptolemäerzeit.* Vol. I: *Laut- und Wortlehre.* Berlin: de Gruyter.

Meier-Brügger, Michael (1992): *Griechische Sprachwissenschaft.* Berlin: de Gruyter.

Meissner, Torsten (2005): *S-stem Nouns and Adjectives in Greek and Proto-Indo-European. A Diachronic Study in Word-Formation.* Oxford: Oxford University Press.

Meissner, Torsten and Olga Tribulato (2002): Nominal composition in Mycenaean Greek. *Transactions of the Philological Society* 100: 289–330.

Méndez Dosuna, Julian (1997): Fusion, fission and relevance in language change: De-univerbation in Greek verb morphology. *Studies in Language* 21: 577–612.

Minas, Konstantinos (1994): *I glossa ton dimosievmenon meseonikon ellinikon engrafon tis Kato Italias ke tis Sikelias.* Athens: Academy of Athens.

Moulton, James H. (1963): *A Grammar of New Testament Greek.* Vol. 2: *Accidence and Word-formation.* London: Clark.

Niepokuj, Mary (1997): *The Development of Verbal Reduplication in Indo-European.* Washington: Institute for the study of Man.

Palmer, Leonard R. (1945): *A Grammar of the Post-Ptolemaic Papyri.* Vol. 1: *Accidence and Word-formation.* Part 1: *The Suffixes.* Oxford: Oxford University Press.

Petrounias, Evangelos (1987): Ellinika epithimata koinis katagogis kai syggenikis ekseliksis: I omada '-ia'. *Studies in Greek Linguistics* 8: 193–214.

Raftopoulou, Maria (2005): Sinthesi stin Archaia Elliniki. Ta rimatika sintheta stin Iliada ke stin Odysseia. Ph.D. dissertation, University of Athens.

Ralli, Angela (2004): Stem-based versus word-based morphological configurations: The case of Modern Greek preverbs. *Lingue e Linguaggio* 2: 241–275.

Ralli, Angela (2005): *Morphology*. Athens: Patakis.

Ralli, Angela (2008): Compound markers and parametric variation. *STUF – Linguistic Typology and Universals* 61: 19–38.

Ralli, Angela (2009a): Modern Greek dvandva V+V compounds: A linguistic innovation in the history of the Indo-European languages. *Word Structure* 2: 48–68.

Ralli, Angela (2009b): IE, Hellenic. In: Rochelle Lieber and Pavol Štekauer (eds.), *The Oxford Handbook of Compounding*, 453–464. Oxford: Oxford University Press.

Ralli, Angela (2012a): Verbal loanblends in Griko and Heptanesian: A case study of contact morphology. *L'Italia Dialettale* 73: 111–132.

Ralli, Angela (2012b): Greek. *Revue belge de philologie et d'histoire* 90(3): 939–966.

Ralli, Angela (2013a): *Compounding in Modern Greek*. Dordrecht: Springer.

Ralli, Angela (2013b): Compounding and its locus of realization: Evidence from Greek and Turkish. *Word Structure* 6(2): 181–200.

Ralli, Angela (2016): Greek. In: Peter O. Müller, Ingeborg Ohnheiser, Susan Olsen and Franz Rainer (eds.), *Word-Formation. An International Handbook of the Languages of Europe*. Vol. 5, 3138–3156. Berlin/Boston: De Gruyter Mouton.

Ralli, Angela (2019): Greek in contact with Romance. In: Mark Aronoff (ed.), *The Oxford Research Encyclopedia of Linguistics*. Oxford: Oxford University Press [Online available at: DOI: 10.1093/acrefore/9780199384655.013.422]

Ralli, Angela (2021): Contrasting Romance and Turkish as source languages. Evidence from Borrowing verbs in Modern Greek dialects. *Journal of Language Contact* 14: 220–252.

Ralli, Angela (2024) Compounding in Medieval and Modern Greek. In: Georgios K. Giannakis (ed.), *Encyclopedia of Greek Language and Linguistics*. Leiden: Brill [Online available at: https://referenceworks.brill.com/display/db/eglo]

Ralli, Angela (forthc.): Morphology: From Hellenistic to Modern Greek. In: Georgios K. Giannakis (ed.), *Encyclopedia of Greek Language and Linguistics*. Leiden: Brill [Online available at: https://referenceworks.brill.com/display/db/eglo]

Ralli, Angela and Maria Raftopoulou (1999): Compounding as a diachronic word-formation process in Greek. *Studies in Greek Linguistics* 1998: 389–403.

Rico, Christophe (2002): Le suffixe *-μος/-μός* dans la recherche linguistique, de Ferdinand de Saussure à nos jours. *Emerita* 70: 304–320.

Risch, Ernst (1973): *Wortbildung der homerischen Sprache*. Berlin: de Gruyter.

Schwyzer, Eduard (1939): *Griechische Grammatik*. Vol. 1. München: Beck.

Steriade, Donca (1982): Greek prosodies and the nature of syllabification. Ph.D. dissertation, MIT.

Tribulato, Olga (2006): Homeric θυμολέων and the question of Greek "reversed bahuvrīhis". *Oxford Working Papers in Linguistics, Philology and Phonetics* 11: 162–178.

Tribulato, Olga (2015): *Ancient Greek Verb-Initial Compounds. Their Diachronic Development within the Greek Compound System*. Berlin/Boston: De Gruyter.

Johanna Laakso

23 The history of word-formation in Uralic

Abstract: Since the Uralic language family represents a time depth and internal diversity comparable to Indo-European and for most of its languages there is very little historical documentation, this article only presents a survey of the most important common characteristics of word-formation in Uralic. As a rule, Uralic languages are fairly agglutinative and display a rich suffixal word-formation morphology, forming both verbs and nouns (as well as adjectives and adverbs) from both verbs and nouns. Some suffixes are transparent grammaticalisations, but many of the derivational suffixes are ancient, although their original functions and especially their original position between word-formation and inflection may be unclear. Compounding is found across Uralic, and at least the western-most Uralic languages display (mostly marginal or nascent) prefixation.

1 Introduction

1.1 The Uralic languages

Describing any phenomenon from the viewpoint of "Uralic" as a whole is an almost insurmountable challenge. First of all, the Uralic/Finno-Ugric language family represents an internal diversity and a time depth comparable to those of Indo-European. Secondly, the Uralic languages are very unevenly researched, and their history is often only sparsely documented. The first complete texts in Uralic languages stem from the Middle Ages, but for the most Uralic languages, literary documentation only begins with the Reformation (Finnish, Estonian, some Sámi varieties) or even later (for many minor Uralic languages, in the 19th or 20th cen-

Johanna Laakso, Vienna, Austria

https://doi.org/10.1515/9783111420530-023

tury!). Thus, this article, instead of presenting a comprehensive description of the history of derivation in Uralic, will merely describe the common points of departure and some general features of Uralic word-formation.

The Uralic languages are spoken in a large area stretching from Eastern and Northern Europe (Russia, Estonia and Latvia, Scandinavia) to Western Siberia; Hungarian, due to the semi-nomadic prehistory of the Hungarians, forms a geographic outlier. The internal taxonomy of the Uralic language family is subject to some controversy (especially as to whether the nodes should represent binary or multiple splits, in particular as concerns the basic division of Uralic into Samoyedic and Finno-Ugric = non-Samoyedic), but there is a consensus that the family consists of six main branches:

1. Finnic (Finnish, Estonian and some minority languages: Livonian in Latvia, Vote, Ingrian, Veps and Karelian in Northwest Russia, plus some Finnish and Estonian varieties now recognised or seeking recognition as independent languages) and Sámi (a chain of sister varieties stretching from Northern Scandinavia to the Kola Peninsula);
2. Mordvin (two varieties, Erzya and Moksha, in European Russia);
3. Mari (two standard varieties in European Russia);
4. Permic: Komi (with two standard varieties) and Udmurt in European Russia;
5. Ugric (Hungarian in Hungary and adjacent areas; the Ob-Ugric languages Mansi and Khanty in Western Siberia);
6. Samoyedic (Nenets, Enets, Nganasan, Selkup and some corpus languages in Siberia, Nenets also in the Far North of European Russia).

1.2 On the research tradition

The existing studies on Uralic word-formation can be roughly divided into the following types:

a) The two standard works dealing with (the history of) derivation in Uralic as a whole: Györke (1934) and Lehtisalo (1936), followed by some general reflections by Kangasmaa-Minn (1987, 1992). Pan-Uralic comparisons concentrating on a certain derivational suffix or function have only been undertaken in a few cases (e.g., Lazar 1975 on the derivation of abstract nouns; Laakso 1997 on "verbaliser" suffixes). Compounding in Uralic from a comparative point of view has been investigated by Fejes (2005).
b) Chapters on word-formation (usually fairly scanty, sometimes not very far beyond listing examples of the "famous opulence of derivatives" in the major Uralic languages) can be found in general introductions into Uralic compara-

tive grammar: e.g., Majtinskaja (1974); Collinder (1960: 220–232); Hajdú (1987: 257–260).

c) Language-specific studies on word- (often: verb- or noun-) formation in a "minor" Uralic language. Most of these have been written from a historical-comparative point of view, and/or on the basis of classical dialect material collected before World War I; see, e.g., Sauer (1967) for Khanty, Kneisl (1978) for Komi, Riese (2001a) for Mansi. However, there are also some descriptive studies based on more recent fieldwork, such as Wagner-Nagy (2001) for Nganasan, or even written by native speakers, such as Ruong (1943) on Pite Sámi, Zajceva (1978) on Veps, or Markianova (1985) on Karelian.
d) Language-specific studies on word-formation, describing a modern standard language and often with a strong emphasis on language correctness, or chapters of this type as part of a standard "academic grammar".
e) Studies on a suffix, a suffix group or a type of suffixes in a certain language or a subgroup of the Uralic languages.

The historical-comparative tradition of Uralic word-formation research, resting heavily on historical phonology and etymology, has often largely concentrated on listing and classifying derivatives and reconstructing the original forms of suffixes. Word-formation systems, the interaction between different derivational suffixes, or the diachronic developments of the meanings (functions) of individual suffixes have received far less attention.

There is also a more general problem which concerns the research of Uralic historical morphosyntax in general: Even until the 1950s and -60s, Uralicists could speculate with the "primitive" character of the reconstructed Proto-Uralic, confusing the reconstructed proto-language with the evolution of human language in general. For word-formation, this could mean an excuse for not dealing with semantics in greater detail: it was assumed that derivational suffixes in the proto-language only had a very vague, "primitive" meaning, even that they could denote "any kind of connection between two concepts" (Majtinskaja 1974: 331). This original, "primitive" meaning is sometimes dubbed "diminutive". Lehtisalo (1936: 3) claims that diminutive meanings can be expected to appear in "the most primitive language", while in the languages of "culturally more highly developed peoples" the meanings of derivational suffixes are specified, so that from the multiplicity of meanings only one is chosen and generalised for each suffix. Needless to say, a reconstruction with a multitude of derivational suffixes, all without a clearly defined meaning (other than "diminutive") is unrealistic.

Seeing the reconstructed Proto-Uralic as an essentially "primitive" language also gave an all too obvious explanation for the cross-categorial use of many suffixes: it was believed that the proto-language originally had no noun/verb distinction at all. However, the hypothesis of Proto-Uralic lacking word classes altogether does not hold up to a closer scrutiny (for criticism, see Laakso 1990b; Ritter 1991), especially as there are ancient derivational suffixes in Uralic which only serve to form verbs from nouns (cf. Laakso 1997).

2 General characteristics of word-formation in Uralic

2.1 Phonotactics and word architectonics in Proto-Uralic

Despite differences of opinion as concerns the vowel system or the possibility of vowel quantity correlation, most features of the Proto-Uralic sound system and word architecture can be reconstructed beyond major debates (see, e.g., Janhunen 1981; Sammallahti 1988). The mainstream reconstruction relies heavily on the conservative peripheries in the Northwest and the Northeast, viz. Finnic-Sámi and Samoyedic; the main challenge consists of fitting the sometimes problematic and controversial reconstructions of the central branches of Uralic, Ugric in particular, into the framework based on Finnic-Sámi and Samoyedic (see especially Sammallahti 1988).

Proto-Uralic word stems obviously fell into two major classes: grammatical stems (such as pronouns or the negative auxiliary **e-*) were monosyllabic, while underived content word stems had two syllables and ended in a vowel. This would imply that all word stems with three or more syllables were derivatives; for some ancient trisyllabic words no underived bases or derivation can be reconstructed, but quite obviously there were lexicalised, opaque derivatives already in the earliest reconstructible proto-language stages (Janhunen 1992; Hahmo 1994). The canonic disyllabicity also means that in the historical morphophonology of Uralic there is a clear division in *radical* (pertaining to the stem, i.e. up to the vowel nucleus of the second syllable) and *suffixal* (by definition, all elements starting with the coda of the second syllable) elements.

2.2 Suffix types in Proto-Uralic

The most reliably reconstructable suffix types in Proto-Uralic (see Janhunen 1981: 28–29) were the following:

(i) one consonant (in particular, stop or nasal) or glide (*j*, *w*);
(ii) one consonant (stop, nasal, sibilant, liquid) or two consonants (geminate stop or a consonant sequence ending with a stop) followed by an illabial vowel. (Sequences of three or more consonants, or two syllable-final consonants were not allowed.)

There were also suffixes or suffix combinations with two or more syllables, such as the caritive **ktAmA* or **ptAmA* (cf. Finnish *silmä-tön* [stem *silmä-ttömä-*] 'eye-less, without eyes' ~ Komi *śin-töm* 'blind' < **śilmä-ktämä*). These were probably originally complex suffixes; **ktAmA*, for instance, obviously consists of the caritive **ktA* also present in the Finnic abessive case suffix (Finnish *raha-tta* 'without money') and the nominaliser suffix **mA*.

Complex suffixes may also be monosyllabic, as the factitive verb suffix **mtA* (from translative *m(V)* and causative *tA*) in, e.g., Finnish *piene-ntä-* 'to make small(er)'. This has given rise to a tradition of calling all single-consonant suffixes "primary" and all suffixes with consonant sequences "secondary". However, it is not clear whether, for instance, the ancient comparative suffix *mpA* (translative **m(V)* + participle/agent noun **pA*?) or the wide-spread causative verb suffix **ptA* ~ **ktA* really reflect a fusion of two original suffixes (cf. Janhunen 1981: 33). As both the concatenation of suffixes and reanalyses of complex suffixes (or suffixes and stem-final elements) into new ones are usual throughout the Uralic language family, it is also possible that reanalyses in the opposite direction take place and parts of suffixes are separated to new functions. (This is what Lehtinen 1984 has suggested in the case of Finnic verbs in TA: from the causative suffix TTA, as in Finnish *hajotta-* 'to disperse, break up' [transitive], the TA perceived as the carrier of the causative meaning was "reduced", which gave rise to a new intransitive verb type in **tA*, as in Finnish *hajoa-* < **hajo-ta-* 'to be dispersed, fall apart'.)

Thus, it cannot be straightforwardly stated that the simplest suffixes are the most original and ancient ones. Most probably, already Proto-Uralic, similarly to today's Uralic languages, had a host of both simple ("primary") and complex derivational suffixes of different ages.

As pointed out by, e.g., Hajdú (1987: 260), there was probably a separate subgroup of suffixes which was only used in pronouns and had no function other than to extend the monosyllabic pronoun stem to fit in with the canonic disyllabicity. Traces of such suffixes may be reflected in Finnic-Sámi-Mordvin *n(V)* (e.g., Finnish *mi-nä* 'I' ~ Mordvin, Sámi *mo-n*) or Hungarian *g* in the accusative forms *en-g-em* 'me', *té-g-ed* 'thee'.

3 Strategies of word-formation in Uralic

3.1 Suffixal vs. prefixal morphology

In all Uralic languages, both inflectional and derivational morphology is solely or predominantly suffixal. Prefixes, if any, are clearly innovations and only used in a few exceptional cases, mainly in derivational morphology. The most productive and also the most debated case are the verb prefixes or preverbs (pre-adverbs) in Hungarian. Kiefer (2010) argues that although the Hungarian verb prefixes are old, inherited elements with cognates in other Ugric languages, the complex process by which the verbal prefix system came into being was also affected by contacts, so that Hungarian can be claimed to belong to a "verbal prefix alliance" together with German, Slavic, Baltic, Romani and Yiddish. Borrowed verbal prefixes for aspectual meanings can be found in Livonian (from Latvian) and in some Karelian dialects (from Russian); for a critical overview of verbal prefixes in Uralic see Kiefer and Honti (2003).

Negative prefixes for various types of adnominal negation or for forming antonyms also appear in some Uralic languages. Finnish *epä-*, Estonian *eba-* and Northern Sámi *eahpe-* (as in *epä-selvä* / *eba-selge* / *eahpe-čielggas* 'unclear'; at least the Estonian prefix, perhaps the Sámi one as well, could be a borrowing from Finnish; cf. Sammallahti 1998: 94) are etymologically present participles of the negative auxiliary *e-*. Negation words proper may also be used as prefixes, as in Estonian *mitte-suitsetaja*, Hungarian *nem-dohányzó* 'non-smoker' (Estonian *mitte* is a particle used for non-finite or intensified negation, Hungarian *nem* is the regular negation particle).

Furthermore, at least the three major Uralic languages know bound morphs which can already be regarded as derivational prefixes or prefixoids. Examples include Finnish *ali-*/*ala-*, Estonian *all-*/*alem-*, Hungarian *al-* 'under-, sub-' (as in Hungarian *almenedzser* 'sub-, lower-ranking manager', Finnish *aliupseeri* 'non-commanding officer'), or Estonian *liba-* (originally abstracted from *libahunt* 'werewolf') and Hungarian *ál-* 'pseudo-' (e.g., Estonian *libateadlane*, Hungarian *áltudós* 'pseudo-scientist'; cf. Fejes 2005: 109–110). These are sometimes equivalents and possibly calques of Germanic or Greek/Latinate prefixes such as *under-*, *pre-*, *sub-* or *pseudo-*. Thus, it seems possible that the literarisation process, involving massive translation and creation of terminology, and the model of Standard Average European languages have contributed to the development of these "prefixoids", but the issue still awaits further research, especially into the minor Uralic languages.

3.2 Conversion (zero derivation)

Conversion or zero derivation typically only plays a marginal role in Uralic languages, and it is restricted to some specific cases, none of which can unambiguously be regarded as true conversion or traced back to original Proto-Uralic zero derivation:

(i) Ambiguous noun/verb stems, such as Hungarian *fagy* 'to freeze; frost' appear in all Uralic languages. However, they typically only form a very small, closed subclass in each language, and although some of them are old, no etymologically coherent group of original "Nomen-Verba" can be reconstructed (cf. Laakso 1990b).

(ii) Ambiguity within the "nomen" macroclass: adjectives can be "nouny" (Moravcsik 2001), or nouns with appropriate semantics can take comparative or superlative endings, as in Finnish *ranne-mpa-na* (shore-COMP-ESS) 'closer to the shore'.

(iii) Conjugation of predicate nouns: in Mordvin (cf. Turunen 2010) and at least some Samoyed languages, person and tense-aspect-modality suffixes can be attached to the predicate noun, as in Nenets *ńe-dmʔ* (woman-1SG) 'I am a woman'. This, however, should be seen as a syntactic phenomenon, rather than as true noun-to-verb conversion.

(iv) Secondary "conversion" caused by the coincidental homonymy of verb and noun types, as in Estonian *luba(-)* 'to allow; permission' or *arst(i-)* 'to heal; physician'. In the former case, the erosion of suffixal syllables has caused the complete loss of the derivational suffix (cf. Finnish *lupa* 'permission' – *lupaa-* [< **lupa-ta-*] 'to promise'). In the latter case, the verb suffix *i* (cf. *sõda* 'war' – *sõdi-* 'to wage war') happens to be homonymous with the stem vowel *i* usually added to the inflection stem of loanwords (*arst* < German *Arzt* 'doctor').

3.3 Fusion and stem alternation in derivation

Although the Uralic languages are often called "agglutinative", all of them are far from the ideal agglutinative type (for calculated indices of agglutination and synthesis, see Korhonen 1969: 219–226) and display morphophonological alternations in their inflectional and derivational morphology.

Steinitz (see, e.g., Steinitz 1944), who based his reconstructions of Proto-Finno-Ugric on Ob-Ugric, especially Eastern Khanty, thought that stem-internal vowel alternations could be an ancient phenomenon, as some obviously ancient vowel alternations in a handful of etyma seem to indicate (cf. Finnish *kuole-* 'to die', *kuolema* 'death' ~ *kalma* 'death, grave, corpse'; Hungarian *(meg)hal* 'to die' ~ *holt* 'dead'). However, contrary to Steinitz' expectations, no additional etymological material has turned up that would lend further support to this hypothesis.

3.4 Correlation, "suffix alternation", truncation, holistic "word patterns"

Throughout Uralic, correlations within the derivation system appear: obviously cognate derivatives with different suffixes have no existing independent base. For instance, Finnish has patterns of continuative (*hypp-i-* 'to jump (many times, for a longer time)') and momentaneous (*hyppä-ä-* 'to jump (once)') verbs without an underived base (there is no **hyppä(-)*).

Correlational patterns of "suffix alternation" are clearly visible in the Finnic languages, the subgroup with the most conservative word structure. This pattern, described in the seminal article of Nikkilä (1998), implies reanalysis and truncation: a disyllabic word is interpreted as a derivative, cut down to a monosyllabic "root" and supplied with another suffix, as in the case of Finnish *hieta* 'sand', a Germanic loanword, and its secondary synonyms *hiekka* and *hiesu*. This technique obviously also explains the Finnic phenomenon known as "stem extension" or the addition of consonants to the stem: cf. Finnish *ylä-* 'upper, above' – *ylp-eä* 'proud', *valo* 'light n.' – *valk-ea* 'white; fire'. Nikkilä's examples are mainly Finnic but also include some more ancient, Pre-Finnic cases such as Finnish *salmi* 'strait, narrow waterway' (< Proto-Finnic-Sámi **śolma* < **śol-ma*) – *suoli* 'gut, intestine' (< Proto-Finnic-Sámi **śola* < Indo-European?).

On the other hand, seemingly underived disyllabic stems may represent ancient derivatives now turned opaque. Janhunen (1992) has interpreted some well-established Uralic reconstructs as "petrified" deverbal nouns carrying the nominaliser suffix **mA*: **ńälmä* 'tongue' or 'mouth' (e.g., Hungarian *nyelv* 'tongue, language'; from **ńäxli-* 'to swallow'), Finnish *kalma* 'death' (from **kaxli-* 'to die') and **ńoma(la)* 'hare' (e.g., Hungarian *nyúl*; from **ńoxi-* 'to hunt, to pursue').

The idea of truncated monosyllabic "abstract roots" has especially been applied in the analysis of expressive and ideophonic words in Finnish (for a critical review of the debate, see Koivulehto 2001 – but cf. Jarva 2001), together with the insight that seemingly irregular vowel alternations are characteristic of expressive vocabulary in general. For instance, in Finnish the verbs *sihistä* ~ *sähistä* ~ *suhista* ~ *sahista* ~ *sohista* can be used to denote different kinds of hissing or rustling sounds. Considering the tendency of expressive words to "bleach" and lose their expressive character, irregular vowel correspondences might reflect original expressive word-formation, e.g., Finnish *tora* 'quarrel', *terä* 'sharp edge', *tör-mä* 'steep bank' and *tar-kka* 'precise; attentive' could be original expressive words based on the "root" $^{\surd}$*tVr-* (Koponen 1998: 51–58). Forsberg (2010) has developed this idea further by introducing the idea of phonesthemic "patterns" functioning as holistic models for new expressive words which are created by way of analogy. Thus, for instance, although the words for 'butterfly' such as Finnish *liippo*, Estonian *liblikas* and Hungarian *lepke* are not regular cognates, they (together with other words for something flapping or fluttering, such as Finnish *lippu* 'flag') represent an expressive word-formation schema **lVpV* or **LIPI* which in itself might be ancient.

3.5 Compounding

Compound words – in particular, compound nouns – appear throughout the Uralic language family. Both endocentric and exocentric compound nouns are attested. Typically, there are also productive models for deriving compound adjectives of the type "blue-eyed".

Compound verbs are far less frequently attested, and at least in the Western Uralic languages, are often interpreted either as backformations from nouns (e.g., Hungarian *kép-visel* picture-wear 'to represent' from the participle or agent noun *képviselő* picture-wearing 'representative'; cf. Fejes 2005: 177) or as calques from the neighbouring Indo-European languages (e.g., Finnish *alle-kirjoittaa*, Hungarian *alá-ír* under-write 'to (under)sign', cf. German *unter-schreiben*; Northern Sámi *bajás-geassit* up-pull 'to educate' < Norwegian *opp-dra*, Sammallahti 1998: 94). Verbs of the latter type sometimes belong to the grey zone between compounds and prefixed derivatives, as the first part can also be analysed as a prefix(oid).

The comparative analysis of Uralic compounds reveals numerous problems. Above all, there seem to be no clear nor compatible criteria for distinguishing compound words from phrases or compound words from derivatives. Grammar traditions differ and borderline cases abound. For instance, certain types of noun-noun compounds (e.g., Hungarian *ló-fej* 'horse's head', *vas-ágy* 'iron bed') can be interpreted as two-word constructions with "modifier nouns"; this is the normal practice, for instance, in the grammars of Standard Komi (e.g., *vöv jur* horse head 'horse's head', *kört tuj* iron road 'railway'), possibly due to the influence of Russian where the equivalents of these expressions are formed using derived adjective modifiers (cf. Fejes 2005: 16–17).

Many Uralic languages also have elements which resemble derivational suffixes (or prefixes) but share features with independent words, i.e. seem to be in the process of being grammaticalised. For example, the collective suffixoid *-kond* in Estonian (as in *mees-kond* 'team' from *mees* 'man' – cf. German *Mannschaft* – and *inim-kond* 'mankind' from *inimene* 'human being') has phonologically word-like features, e.g., the vowel *o* which otherwise never appears in non-first syllables in native words. Etymologically, *-kond* stems from an independent word (cf. cognates such as Finnish *kunta* 'municipality', Hungarian *had* 'army') but in Modern Standard Estonian it does not appear as a free morph. Or the words for 'man' and 'woman' in Ob-Ugric come close functionally to agent noun suffixes, as in Mansi *χańśtėn nē* teaching woman '(female) teacher' – *χańśtėn χum* teaching man '(male) teacher' (Munkácsi and Kálmán 1986: 78); Sauer (1967: 215–216) calls the corresponding elements in Khanty "nachgestellte Nomina mit wortbildendem Charakter" [postposed nouns with word-formational character].

Kont (1973: 165) claims that there is a systematic difference between "Western" (Finnic-Sámi, Hungarian) and "Eastern" Finno-Ugric languages: in the "Western" languages, noun modifiers denoting type, substance or class fuse with their head to form a compound, while in the "Eastern" type, the corresponding constructions only form compounds if they are lexicalised, otherwise they remain phrases of distinct words (cf. the examples *lófej* – *vöv jur* above). However, Fejes (2005), in his comparative analysis of compounding in Finnish, Estonian, Hungarian and Permic (Komi and Udmurt), has not found any support for this view. The only unambiguous difference, as noted by Kont and many others, is the use of genitive modifier parts in Finnic and Sámi, as in Estonian *hamba-hari* tooth.GEN-brush 'toothbrush' – in this respect, however, there already are differences within Finnic and Sámi (cf. Finnish *hammas-harja* tooth.(NOM)-brush).

Fejes (2005: 191) concludes that the compounding systems in Finnic, Permic and Hungarian show more similarities than could be expected on the basis of merely convergent developments. This seems to indicate that compounding strategies can be ancient and inherited, contrary to the traditional assumption that (noun-modifier) compounds – which often are calques or connected with foreign influences – are a recent or "even a regional phenomenon" (Kont 1973: 166).

4 Types and functions of suffixal derivation in Uralic

In most handbooks, derivational suffixes are divided into four (2 × 2) types on the basis of the word class of the base and the derivative: denominal and deverbal verb-forming and noun-forming suffixes. However, there are typically major overlaps between these types, in particular between denominal and deverbal suffixes. Many derivational suffixes can be attached to both noun and verb stems (cf. the nominaliser **mA* in Finnish *rinta-ma* 'front' from *rinta* 'breast' – *kuole-ma* 'death' from *kuole-* 'to die'), and it can even be claimed that some similar-looking suffixes which appear in all four functions are, ultimately, etymologically related (Kangasmaa-Minn 1987, 1992).

4.1 Noun derivation

Among the types of deverbal nouns, action, agent and instrument nouns as well as nouns denoting the result, object, place or conditions of the action are types which occur across the language family. The boundary between nominaliser suffixes and suffixes for non-finite verb forms, infinitives or participles (which sometimes may develop into tense or mood markers) is often fuzzy (cf. Ylikoski 2003). For instance, the agent noun suffix *-jA* has in some Finnic varieties partly or completely replaced the present participle marker **-pA*, and in Livonian, the same suffix *-jA* is developing further into the marker of the quotative ("hearsay") mood. Referring to the Finnic 3rd-person forms, which are etymologically present participles, Kangasmaa-Minn (1987: 12) goes as far as to claim that "[I]n order to function as a finite verb form, a verb stem must first be converted to a noun, and for this purpose several non-specific noun suffixes can be employed".

The most widespread Uralic nominaliser suffix **mA* probably originally denoted accomplished action; in some Uralic languages, it has developed further into a (past) participle or even (narrative) past tense marker (e.g., the narrative perfect in Komi: *Ivan mun-öma* 'Ivan has gone (, they say)'). The agent noun suffix **jV* (e.g., Finnish *opetta-ja* 'teacher', Northern Sámi *muital-eaddji* 'story-teller') also seems to be ancient.

Probably already in Proto-Uralic there were derivational suffixes for instruments, objects, results, conditions or places of action; typically, these functions often overlap and the most original function is difficult to reconstruct. Sammallahti (1998: 90) traces, e.g., **ntA* (in Northern Sámi part of a complex suffix for condition, e.g., *oainn-ádat* 'seeing, clear weather' from *oaidnit* 'to see'; in Finnic a suffix for action nouns, e.g., *lue-nta* 'reading' from *luke-* 'to read') back to Proto-Uralic.

As for the original or basic functions of denominal noun derivation, Hajdú (1987: 260) only mentions the diminutive, augmentative and "determining" suffixes, but many other functions, such as collective suffixes ('group of X', 'X and his/her associates') or suffixes expressing home or origin ('coming from X') appear across Uralic and can also be ancient. On the other hand, diminutive suffixes in modern Uralic languages may often be the result of relatively recent borrowing or adaptation (for *-ke(ne)* in Estonian and its possibly Low German origins, see Laakso 2004), and true augmentative suffixes are rare. Thus, it is questionable whether diminutive or augmentative suffixes can be reconstructed for Proto-Uralic.

Lazar (1975), in a vulgar-Whorfian way, claims that the occurrence of abstract nouns correlates with "the level of development" of the speakers, which also implies that the "western" Uralic languages have more abstract nouns while the Ob-Ugric and Samoyedic languages "have no formation of abstract nouns at all in the true sense of the word" (Lazar 1975: 309; for counter-examples see, e.g., Wagner-Nagy 2001: 167). Lazar's argumentation is also based on the fact that many Uralic suffixes which form abstract nouns are transparent grammaticalisations from independent nouns (often nouns designating periods of time), e.g., Mordvin *-či* (*paro-či* 'goodness' from *paro* 'good'), Komi *-lun* (*bur-lun* 'goodness' from *bur* 'good'), Livonian *-pǟva* (*rujā-pǟva* 'illness' from *rujā* 'ill(ness)'), all still identical with the noun 'day' (*či* ~ *lun* ~ *pǟva*). However, possibly cognate suffixes containing the consonant *t* occur across Uralic in this function, forming not only nouns (or adjectives) which indicate measure or comparison (e.g., Mansi *χosit* '(of the) length of' ← *χosa* 'long'; Lazar 1975: 238) but also true abstract nouns (e.g., Nganasan *-TU"* in *d'ürađi"* 'depth' (Wagner-Nagy l.c.), Finnish *-UUTE-* in *syvyys* [: *syvyyte-*] 'depth' ← *syvä* 'deep').

The Uralic languages lack grammatical gender, but – obviously due to foreign influences and the needs of language planning – Hungarian, Finnish and Estonian have developed (or, partly, borrowed) suffixes for deriving feminine versions of occupational terms and the like (Laakso 2005: 110–118).

4.2 Adjective derivation

Typically, the border between adjectives and nouns in Uralic is not clear-cut, and at least the ordinal numbers are an example of a derivative type on the border of these two categories. The ordinal suffix **mti* can be traced back to Proto-Uralic (cf. Finnish (*neljäs* :) *neljä-nte-*, Northern Sámi *njealjá-t*, Komi *ńol'-öd*, Hungarian *negye-d-ik* 'fourth').

Caritive adjectives ('lacking X', 'X-less') as well as other relative adjectives which denote quality ('like X', 'resembling X'), origin ('coming from X'), possession or abundance ('having (plenty of) X') are characteristic of most, if not all, Uralic languages.

Of the suffixes deriving adjectives, in addition to the caritive suffix **ktAmA* ~ **ptAmA* mentioned above (section 2.1.2), at least **ŋ* for possession or abundance ('having (plenty of) X') seems to be ancient, if both Northern Sámi *-i* (e.g., *geađgá-i* 'stony' from *geađgi* 'stone') and Finnic *-vA* (e.g., Finnish *liha-va* 'fat, obese' from *liha* 'meat, flesh') can be traced back to it (Sammallahti 1998: 91). The suffix **tA*, typically present in adjectives (such as Finnish *pimeä* 'dark' < **pimetä* ~ Komi *pemyd*), but unproductive, also seems to be ancient.

Of moderative adjective suffixes (pertaining to the grade of the quality or the attitude of the speaker), the suffix **mpA* has been subject to some debate; it has the clear comparative function in Finnic-Sámi and in Hungarian (Finnish *suure-mpi*, Hungarian *nagyo-bb* 'bigger'), but as adjective comparison is expressed in most other Uralic languages with other suffixes or by other syntactic means, it is not clear whether the original function of this suffix was to express adjective comparison. Beside comparison proper, many Uralic languages know adjective suffixes which modify the grade of the quality ('fairly X', 'very X').

4.3 Verb derivation

The functions of verb derivation can be divided into three types; Kangasmaa-Minn (1987) speaks of "intercategory transformers" (forming verbs from nouns), "inner transformers" (changing transitive verbs into intransitive ones, or vice versa) and "modifiers" (changing the meaning of the verb without affecting its (in)transitivity). Alternatively, instead of changes in transitivity we might speak of suffixes which modify the argument structure of the verb; this group includes not only passive or reflexive derivatives (intransitive from transitive) but also the curative-causative ones ('to make somebody X (something), have something X-ed (by somebody), cause X-ing to take place') which can be formed from both transitive and intransitive verbs.

As already mentioned, verb suffixes are seldom exclusively denominal or deverbal; the same suffixes can occur across all the derivation types described in what follows.

4.3.1 Denominal verb derivation

Kytömäki (1992) divides the denominal verb suffixes in Finnish into three types: (i) suffixes with a clear semantic function that can be translated or reformulated with a paraphrase (e.g., *ne* in Finnish forms verbs which denote a change into the state indicated by the base, as in *piene-ne-* 'to become small(er)'), (ii) suffixes with no function other than forming verbs from nouns, viz. the so-called "verbers", and (iii) an intermediate group between these two.

The meaning of the verbs derived with "verber" suffixes is determined by the semantics of the base and by encyclopedic knowledge. So, for instance, the Finnish verbs formed with the suffix TA can be 'causative' (*kaunis-ta-* 'to make beautiful' from *kaunis* 'beautiful'), 'instrumental' (*pyydys-tä-* 'to catch with a trap' from *pyydys* 'trap'), 'essive' (*sairas-ta-* 'to be ill' from *sairas* 'sick'), 'instructive' (*kulta-a-* 'to gild' from *kulta* 'gold'), etc. Verbers are also often used for the adaptation of loan verbs.

Throughout Uralic, the same three suffixes, viz. TA (**ta/*tä*), L (**li?*) and J, occur in verber functions: forming verbs with very diverse semantics and also in borrowed verbs (Laakso 1997). This indicates that the semantic diversity of these suffixes is neither a result of diversification (from an originally clear-cut semantic function) nor a remnant of a "primitive" stage in which the functions of derivational suffixes had not yet differentiated – the semantic diversity is simply due to their verber character, which may well have been present already in Proto-Uralic.

Of the suffixes with a more clear-cut semantic function, at least **m(i)* (> Finnic *ne*, cf. Laakso 1990), forming translative verbs ('to become (more) X') occurs throughout Uralic in this function and is obviously ancient. Translative verbs can also be formed with the same suffixes as deverbal intransitive (passive or reflexive) verbs, most notably **w*, or combinations of such suffixes. The suffix **mtA*, combination of **m(i)* with the causative **tA*, forming causative verbs ('to make something (more) X'), is attested throughout Uralic as well.

Today's Uralic languages often display a broad spectrum of semantic functions for denominal verb derivation. In addition to the examples given above, handbooks typically distinguish functions such as 'captative' ('to catch X'), 'privative' ('to take X away, deprive of X') or 'sensive' ('to consider as X'), sometimes formed with verber suffixes, sometimes with a specific (often etymologically complex) suffix. Even within these functions, shades and grades can be distinguished, as in Ruong's (1943: 170) example from Pite Sámi, which has two sensive suffixes. Ruong's informant illustrated the difference between the verbs *guhkâluššât* and *guhkâhit* ('to consider something long', from *guh'ke* 'long') with the following sentence: *Jus šuohpânâw guhkâlušâw, dœ ânaw liik nǫwtǫg, mœn jus guhkâhâw, jâlâstâw vânj dœ dâlanâg* 'if I think that the lasso is long, I'll use it as it is, but if I think it's (too) long, I'll shorten it at once'.

4.3.2 Deverbal verb derivation

Of the deverbal verb suffixes which change the argument structure of the base, the two main types, viz. intransitive (reflexive, anticausative or passive) and transitive (curative-causative: 'to make somebody X') are attested throughout Uralic, and their suffixes, the reflexive-anticausative **w* and the causative **ktA* or **ptA*, can be traced back to Proto-Uralic. In today's Uralic languages, these suffixes may form complex formatives with other suffixes, such as the Finnish *UTU* (**w* + **tA* + **w*) for true reflexive verbs (*peseyty-* 'to wash oneself' from *pese-* 'to wash'), or the passive suffixes which both in Finnic and in Hungarian stem from a combination of the causative **ktA*/**ptA* and a reflexive suffix. In Sámi and Mansi, the markers of the passive voice are descendants of the ancient reflexive suffix **w* (Sammallahti 1998: 84–85; Kulonen 1989).

The deverbal verb suffixes which do not affect the argument structure cover a broad range of aspect, aktionsart and other semantic functions. Many Uralic languages have a host of these suffixes (including combined and reanalysed complex suffixes). In the literature they are often classified into seemingly clear-cut categories such as 'momentaneous' or 'subitive' ('X once, quickly, sharply'), 'continuative' or 'durative' ('X for a longer time'), 'frequentative' ('X many times', 'X often'), 'inchoative-ingressive' ('to start X-ing'), etc. In reality, however, the categories are fuzzy, overlapping and interconnected – or sometimes too crude to account for finer semantic shades which may represent combinations of different features. This is one of the central issues tackled by Ruong (1943) and illustrated, e.g., in his Pite Sámi examples of 'frequentative' and 'momentaneous' 'diminutivity': *čuoigâstit* means 'to ski a little bit (and then stop)', while *čuoigâdit* can be translated with something like 'to ski slowly, softly' (Ruong 1943: 28).

The semantics of deverbal verb suffixes are connected to aspect: Kangasmaa-Minn (1987: 23–24) points out that "verbs designating inchoative or momentaneous or terminative action are inherently perfective while durative or iterative verbs seem to contain the idea of imperfectiveness". In the Uralic languages of Russia, the influence of Russian may render the aktionsart suffixes more and more "aspect"-like, as can be seen, for instance, in the increasing use of frequentative and momentative derivatives in Veps (Lehtinen 1990; Puura 2010). Aktionsart suffixes may also express something that resembles number agreement; for instance in Sámi, the use of frequentative suffixes may be connected to subject or object plurality (Northern Sámi *láhp-ad-it* 'to lose (many objects)' from *láhppit* 'to lose', *čohkán-adda-t* 'to sit down (of many)' from *čohkánit* 'to sit down'; Sammallahti 1998: 92).

Of the aktionsart suffixes, at least the frequentative SK (**śk*) and L seem to occur throughout the language family.

4.4 Adverb derivation

Adverb suffixes, occurring in various forms throughout the Uralic language family, are typically a category difficult to define, as the border between them and the adverbial (local, causal and other) case suffixes is fuzzy. The most famous example is probably Hungarian, in which the number of cases according to different grammars varies between 16 and almost 30, depending on whether certain suffixes such as the sociative *-stUl(fia-stul* 'with his/her son') or the distributive-temporal *-nta* (*napo-nta* 'daily') are regarded as case endings or adverb suffixes (cf. Kiefer 1987).

As concerns the reconstruction of adverb suffixes, the basic problem is the same as with the suffixes for verb derivation and tense-aspect-modality inflection: a host of elements can be traced back to Proto-Uralic, in today's Uralic languages they appear in different combinations (often forming complex suffixes), but their original role remains somewhat unclear. Because of the above-mentioned demarcation problems and the fact that adverb suffixes often are complex and transparently secondary, traditional handbooks often do not even mention the possibility of adverb derivation in Proto-Uralic. However, the lack of reconstructible clearly adverbial suffixes does not mean that adverb derivation as a category could not have existed already at the earliest reconstructible stages.

5 Remarks on development tendencies in Uralic derivation

5.1 Grammaticalisation

Across the Uralic language family, there are derivational (as well as inflectional) suffixes which seem to have developed from independent words. Examples include the feminine suffixes in Finnish (*-tAr* as in *laulaja-tar* '(female) singer', from *tytär* 'daughter') and Hungarian (*-nő*, *-né* from *nő* 'woman'; cf. Laakso 2005: 110–118) and the previously mentioned abstract noun suffixes from the noun 'day' (cf. section 4.1). However, the major part of derivational suffixes seem to be ancient suffixes, possibly recombined and reanalysed; whether their original function belonged to derivation or inflection may stand to debate.

As already mentioned, the border between derivation and inflection – nominalisations and nominal verb forms, tense-aspect-modality and aktionsart suffixes, or derived adverbs and adverbial case forms – is often fuzzy in Uralic, and the direction of possible category shifts cannot always be defined. There are some examples of category shifts from derivation to inflection. The Finnish (Finnic) translative case suffix *-ksi* (e.g., *prinssi muuttui sammako-ksi* 'the prince turned into a frog') may originate from a derivational suffix **-ks(V)* forming nouns for 'raw material' (e.g., *aida-kse-t* [pl.] 'material for building a fence', from *aita* 'fence'), and in Mansi, the diminutive noun suffixes *-k*^{w}*e* and *-riś* are also used as markers of the so-called diminutive conjugation (e.g., *amkkem ōli-riś-əm* 'poor little me lives alone' [live-DIM-1SG]; Riese 2001b: 59).

5.2 Typological and areal factors

In accordance with the fairly agglutinative and synthetic character of the Uralic languages, the derivation systems in Uralic are not only rich – usually having dozens of different derivational suffixes – but also characterised by an abundance of suffix chains and combinations. Concatenation of suffixes, often with a corresponding composition of meaning, is not unusual. For instance, Finnish often allows the combination of momentaneous and frequentative suffixes: *hyp-ähtä-ä* 'to make one little jump' > *hyp-ähd-el-lä* 'to make little jumps repeatedly'. In this respect, it is interesting to observe the changes in Estonian and Livonian, the two Finnic languages which are generally developing into a more fusional direction (see, e.g., Grünthal 2000; Kasik 1997; Metslang 2009; Ojutkangas 1997). In Estonian, there is an obvious tendency towards minimising the number of suffixes (inflectional and derivational!) per word, and suffix chains which are typical of Finnish are, in Estonian, often perceived as either ungrammatical or stylistically deviant. Whether this phenomenon is a natural consequence of the typological shift (which today's Estonian researchers often in a fairly straightforward way explain with intensive language contacts, particularly with (Low and High) German), or whether it was directly caused by language contacts remains to be investigated.

Effects of language contacts on derivation can be observed in all branches of Uralic. Intensive contacts have led to a borrowing of whole suffixes at least in the Volga region (Mari and Udmurt have borrowed derivational suffixes from the neighbouring Turkic languages, such as the abstract noun suffix *-lyk*, as in Udmurt *eš-lyk* 'friendship' from *eš* 'friend') or from Germanic to Finnic (Hahmo 1997). In some cases, there are competing explanations (as with the Estonian diminutive suffix *-ke(ne)*, which might reflect the intertwining of an inherited suffix and a borrowed Low German one, cf. Laakso 2004). More generally, areal developments and language contacts may have affected the functions of derivation: a good example is the formation of diminutive nouns, which is productive in the Eastern Finnic languages (as in Russian) and in Estonian (as in German), while Finnish patterns with Swedish in not having a regular suffixal diminutive derivation at all (Laakso 2004).

Contacts between related Uralic varieties may also lead to the borrowing of derivational suffixes. Sámi varieties and their Northern Finnic neighbours (Finnish and Karelian), despite lack of mutual intelligibility, have numerous structural similarities which bilingual speakers will easily detect and which greatly facilitate morphological borrowing. Some productive derivational suffixes in Northern Sámi are borrowed from Finnic (e.g., the deverbal adjective suffix *-meahttun* 'not X-ing', as in *duhtameahttun* 'dissatisfied' from *duhtat* 'to be satisfied', cf. Finnish *tyytymätön*; Sammallahti 1998: 89). An example of borrowing in the opposite direction is the superlative suffix *-mUs* in the Finnish dialects of the Far North; in fact, the same cognate suffix appears throughout Finnic, but at least its superlative function must be ascribed to the influence of Sámi.

5.3 Effects of language planning and literarisation

In connection with the national emancipation and the development of modern standard literary languages from the 19th century on, the three major Uralic languages (Hungarian, Finnish and Estonian; on the latter, cf. Raag 2015) have undergone intensive language planning in which the enhancement of the vocabulary played an important role. New words were formed by means of morphological derivation and compounding (and also in less regular ways such as truncation, backformation or coinage of completely new word stems). In this process, some derivational suffixes were revitalised or even created, and, typically, there were general tendencies towards the standardisation of derivational suffixes, their meaning, use, and distribution. In the history of language planning in the three Uralic-speaking nation states, discussions on the correctness and regularity of derivatives were not unusual. (For instance, language planners could argue for or against the introduction of a certain neologism on the basis of whether it was regularly or "correctly" derived.)

Sometimes, research into the history of a derivational suffix reveals major differences between the semantically and morphologically regular modern standard language and the much more heterogeneous derivational types in pre-20th-century sources (for an Estonian example, see Laakso 2007). This suggests that there might be fundamental differences between the "planned" and standardised derivation systems of the major Uralic standard languages and the "unplanned" ones of the Uralic minority languages; however, this issue has not been systematically investigated.

6 References

Bakró-Nagy, Marianne, Johanna Laakso and Elena Skribnik (eds.) (2022): *The Oxford Guide to the Uralic Languages*. Oxford: Oxford University Press.

Collinder, Björn (1960): *Comparative Grammar of the Uralic Languages.* Stockholm: Almqvist & Wiksell.
Fejes, László (2005): Összetett szavak finnugor nyelvekben. Ph.D. dissertation, ELTE University Budapest. http://nytud.hu/~fejes/phd/PHD.pdf [last access 23 Aug 2011].
Forsberg [= Kulonen], Ulla-Maija (2010): Expressive vocabulary in the early phases of Finno-Ugrian. In: Sándor Csúcs, Nóra Falk, Viktória Püspök, Viktória Tóth and Gábor Zaicz (eds.), *Congressus XI Internationalis Fenno-Ugristarum: Pars I. Orationes Plenariae*, 5–19. Piliscsaba: Reguly Társaság.
Grünthal, Riho (2000): Typological characteristics of the Finnic languages: A reappraisal. In: Johanna Laakso (ed.), *Facing Finnic. Some Challenges to Historical and Contact Linguistics*, 31–63. Helsinki: Helsingin yliopisto, suomalais-ugrilainen laitos.
Györke, J[ózsef] (1934): *Die Wortbildungslehre des Uralischen. (Primäre Bildungssuffixe.)* Tartu: Krüger.
Hahmo, Sirkka-Liisa (1994): *Grundlexem oder Ableitung? Die finnischen Nomina der Typen* kämmen *und* pähkinä *und ihre Geschichte.* Helsinki: Finnish Literature Society.
Hahmo, Sirkka-Liisa (1997): Finnische nominale Ableitungssuffixe fremder Herkunft. In: Sirkka-Liisa Hahmo, Tette Hofstra, László Honti, Paul van Linde and Osmo Nikkilä (eds.), *Finnisch-ugrische Sprachen in Kontakt*, 95–102. Maastricht: Shaker.
Hajdú, Péter (1987): Die uralischen Sprachen. In: Péter Hajdú and Péter Domokos, *Die uralischen Sprachen und Literaturen*, 21–450. Budapest: Akadémiai Kiadó.
Janhunen, Juha (1981): On the structure of Proto-Uralic. *Finnisch-Ugrische Forschungen* 44: 23–42.
Janhunen, Juha (1992): Petrified verbal nouns in Early Uralic. In: Pál Deréky, Timothy Riese, Marianne Sz. Bakró-Nagy and Hajdú Péter (eds.), *Festschrift für Károly Rédei zum 60. Geburtstag*, 239–244. Wien/Budapest: Institut für Finno-Ugristik der Universität Wien/ELTE BTK Finnugor Tanszék, MTA Nyelvtudományi Intézet.
Jarva, Vesa (2001): Some expressive and borrowed elements in the lexicon of Finnish dialects. In: F. K. Erhard Voeltz and Christa Kilian-Hatz (eds.), *Ideophones*, 111–119. Amsterdam/ Philadelphia: Benjamins.
Kangasmaa-Minn, Eeva (1987): Functional derivation in Finno-Ugric. In: *Papers on Derivation in Uralic. Szegeder und Turkuer Beiträge zur uralischen Derivation*, 5–27. Szeged: University of Szeged.
Kangasmaa-Minn, Eeva (1992): Pienimuotoinen kieliperimämme. *Sananjalka* 34: 21–31.
Kasik, Reet (1997): Typology of Estonian and Finnish word-formation: The verb. In: Mati Erelt (ed.), *Estonian. Typological Studies II*, 43–72. Tartu: Tartu University Press.
Kiefer, Ferenc (1987): The cases of Hungarian nouns. *Acta Linguistica Hungarica* 37(1–4): 93–101.
Kiefer, Ferenc (2010): Areal-typological aspects of word-formation: The case of aktionsart-formation in German, Hungarian, Slavic, Baltic, Romani and Yiddish. In: Franz Rainer, Wolfgang U. Dressler, Dieter Kastovsky and Hans Christian Luschützky (eds.), *Variation and Change in Morphology. Selected papers from the International Morphology Meeting, Vienna, February 2008*, 129–147. Amsterdam/Philadelphia: Benjamins.
Kiefer, Ferenc and László Honti (2003): Verbal 'prefixation' in Uralic languages. *Acta Linguistica Hungarica* 50: 137–153.
Kiefer, Ferenc and Johanna Laakso (2015): Uralic. In: Rochelle Lieber and Pavol Štekauer (eds.), *The Oxford Handbook of Derivational Morphology*, 473–492. Oxford: Oxford University Press.
Kneisl, Marianne (1978): *Die Verbalbildung im Syrjänischen.* München: Traut.
Koivulehto, Jorma (2001): Etymologie und Lehnwortforschung: Ein Überblick um 2000. *Finnisch-Ugrische Forschungen* 56: 42–78.
Kont, Karl (1973): Substantiivsest atribuudist soome-ugri keeltes. In: *Commentationes Fenno-Ugricae in honorem Erkki Itkonen sexagenarii*, 165–173. Helsinki: Finno-Ugrian Society.

Koponen, Eino (1998): *Eteläviron murteen sanaston alkuperä. Itämerensuomalaista etymologiaa.* Helsinki: Finno-Ugrian Society.
Korhonen, Mikko (1969): Die Entwicklung der morphologischen Methode im Lappischen. *Finnisch-Ugrische Forschungen* 37: 203–362. [Reprinted in: Tapani Salminen (ed.), *Typological and historical studies in language by Mikko Korhonen*, 17–142. Helsinki: Finno-Ugrian Society 1996.]
Kulonen [= Forsberg], Ulla-Maija (1989): *The Passive in Ob-Ugrian.* Helsinki: Finno-Ugrian Society.
Kytömäki, Leena (1992): Suomen verbinjohto ja sen kuvausongelmat. *Sananjalka* 34: 69–75.
Laakso, Johanna (1990a): *Translatiivinen verbinjohdin NE itämerensuomalaisissa kielissä.* Helsinki: Finno-Ugrian Society.
Laakso, Johanna (1990b): Reflections on the problem of Uralic N/V word stems. In: László Jakab, László Keresztes, Antal Kiss and Sándor Maticsák (eds.), *Congressus septimus internationalis fenno-ugristarum* 3A, 153–157. Debrecen: s.n.
Laakso, Johanna (1997): On verbalising nouns in Uralic. *Finnisch-Ugrische Forschungen* 54(3): 267–304.
Laakso, Johanna (2004): Derivation, morphopragmatics, and language contact – on the role of German influence in Estonian word-formation. In: Irma Hyvärinen, Petri Kallio and Jarmo Korhonen (eds.), *Etymologie, Entlehnungen und Entwicklungen. Festschrift für Jorma Koivulehto zum 70. Geburtstag*, 171–180. Helsinki: Société Néophilologique/Uusfilologinen yhdistys.
Laakso, Johanna (2005): *Our Otherness. Finno-Ugrian approaches to Women's Studies, or vice versa.* Wien: LIT-Verlag.
Laakso, Johanna (2007): Transitivität und Intransitivität in der Wortbildung: Estnisch und Deutsch. In: Hans Fix (ed.), *Beiträge zur Morphologie. Germanisch, Baltisch, Ostseefinnisch*, 433–447. Odense: University Press of Southern Denmark.
Lazar, Oscar (1975): *The Formation of Abstract Nouns in the Uralic Languages.* Uppsala/Stockholm: Almqvist & Wiksell.
Lehtinen, Tapani (1984): *Itämerensuomen passiivin alkuperästä.* Helsinki: Finnish Literature Society.
Lehtinen, Tapani (1990): Venäjän aspektien heijastumia vepsän verbijärjestelmässä. In: Sari Vaula (ed.), *Itämerensuomalaiset kielikontaktit = Läänemeresoome keelekontaktid*, 59–68. Helsinki: Kotimaisten kielten tutkimuskeskus.
Lehtisalo, Toivo V. (1936): *Über die primären ururalischen Ableitungssuffixe.* Helsinki: Finno-Ugrian Society.
Majtinskaja, Klara E. (1974): Sravnitel'naja morfologija finno-ugorskix jazykov. In: *Osnovy finno-ugorskogo jazykoznanija. Voprosy proisxoždenija i razvitija finno-ugorskix jazykov*, 214–382. Moskva: Nauka.
Markianova, Ljudmila F. (1985): *Glagol'noe slovoobrazovanie v karel'skom jazyke.* Petrozavodsk: s.n.
Metslang, Helle (2009): Estonian grammar between Finnic and SAE: Some comparisons. *STUF – Language Typology and Universals* 62: 49–71.
Moravcsik, Edith (2001): On the nouniness of Hungarian adjectives. In: Chris Schaner-Wolles, John Rennison and Friedrich Neubarth (eds.), *Naturally! Linguistic studies in honor of Wolfgang Ulrich Dressler presented on the occasion of his 60th birthday*, 337–346. Torino: Rosenberg and Sellier.
Munkácsi, Bernát and Béla Kálmán (1986): *Wogulisches Wörterbuch.* Budapest: Akadémiai Kiadó.
Nikkilä, Osmo (1998): *nop-ea* → *nop- sa*, *sel-keä* → *sel-vä*: Suffiksinvaihto ja suomen sanojen etymologiointi. In: Urho Määttä and Klaus Laalo (eds.), *Kirjoituksia muoto- ja merkitysopista*, 77–101. Tampere: Tampere University Press.
Ojutkangas, Krista (1997): Suomen ja viron *U-* ja *ne*-verbijohdosten käytön vertailua. *Virittäjä* 101: 358–379.
Puura, Ulriikka (2010): Frequentative and momentative verbal derivation in Veps. *Linguistica Uralica* 46(4): 261–280.

Raag, Virve (2015): Word-formation and language planning in Estonian. In: Peter O. Müller, Ingeborg Ohnheiser, Susan Olsen and Franz Rainer (eds.), *Word-Formation. An International Handbook of the Languages of Europe*. Vol. 3, 1730–1744. Berlin/Boston: De Gruyter Mouton.

Riese, Timothy (2001a): *Historische Nominalderivation des Wogulischen.* Wiesbaden: Harrassowitz.

Riese, Timothy (2001b): *Vogul.* München: LINCOM Europa.

Ritter, Ralf-Peter (1991): Über einige vermeintliche Besonderheiten der Wortarten in den finnisch-ugrischen Sprachen. *Linguistica Uralica* 27(1): 3–11.

Ruong, Israel (1943): *Lappische Verbalableitung dargestellt auf Grundlage des Pitelappischen.* Uppsala/Leipzig: Lundequist/Harrassowitz.

Sammallahti, Pekka (1988): Historical phonology of the Uralic languages with special reference to Samoyed, Ugric, and Permic. In: Denis Sinor (ed.), *The Uralic Languages*, 478–554. Leiden/New York: Brill.

Sammallahti, Pekka (1998): *The Saami Languages. An introduction.* Kárášjohka: Girji.

Sauer, Gert (1967): *Die Nominalbildung im Ostjakischen.* Berlin: Akademie Verlag.

Sőrés, Anna and Krisztina Hevér-Joly (2019): Morphology in Uralic Languages. In: Mark Aronoff (ed.), *Oxford Research Encyclopedia of Linguistics*. Oxford: Oxford University Press [Online available at: https://doi.org/10.1093/acrefore/9780199384655.013.536]

Steinitz, Wolfgang (1944): *Geschichte des finnisch-ugrischen Vokalismus.* Stockholm: Universität, Ungarisches Institut.

Turunen, Rigina (2010): Nonverbal predication in Erzya: Studies on morphosyntactic variation and part of speech distinctions. Ph.D. dissertation, University of Helsinki. http://urn.fi/URN:ISBN:978-952-10-6277-3 [last access 21 Jan 2015].

Wagner-Nagy, Beáta Boglárka (2001): *Die Wortbildung im Nganasanischen.* Szeged: Universitas Szegediensis and Amsterdam/Philadelphia: Benjamins.

Ylikoski, Jussi (2003): Defining non-finites: Action nominals, converbs and infinitives. *SKY Journal of Linguistics* 16: 185–237. http://cc.oulu.fi/~jylikosk/defining.pdf [last access 25 Nov 2008].

Zajceva, Marija I. (1978): *Suffiksal'noe glagol'noe slovoobrazovanie v vepsskom jazyke.* Leningrad: Nauka.

Tamás Forgács

24 From Old Hungarian to Modern Hungarian

Abstract: The aim of the present article is to provide an overview of the history of Hungarian word-formation. After a brief outline of the history of research on this topic, the paper discusses in a chronological order the main methods of word-formation characteristic for the various periods in the history of the Hungarian language with a special focus on derivation and compounding and their relative prominence. The paper also touches on the origins of derivational suffixes and the historical process of the formation of compounds. It also examines the less common methods of word-formation, documented only since the Middle Hungarian period, such as backformation, blending, clipping, and acronym formation as well as the conscious word-formation endeavors of the language reform movement of early 19th-century Hungary, an important era of its cultural history.

1 Introduction

Just like in most languages of the world, in Hungarian the words resulting from word-formation processes form the largest lexical category as far as the origin of words is concerned (Gerstner 2006: 465). The independent history of Hungarian (i.e. the time since it split from the other Finno-Ugric languages) goes back roughly 3000 years. During this time, Hungarian has used many methods of word-formation, with the two most important being derivation and compounding. The present article discusses these in most detail, while overviewing some of the other processes as well.

Tamás Forgács, Szeged, Hungary

https://doi.org/10.1515/9783111420530-024

The proportion of words formed by derivation vs. compounding has changed somewhat during the history of Hungarian: as attested in early linguistic sources, derived words initially constituted a larger group than that of compounds. In time, however, the situation changed: starting from the Middle Hungarian period, and especially in the Modern Hungarian period, compounds have become more numerous and the proportion of derived words has decreased.

2 History of research

In the late 19th century and even in the inter-war period, the dominant trend in Hungarian linguistics was historical linguistics, with historical phonology (especially of the Old Hungarian period) being the most researched topic. The first major work providing a theoretical summary was the first volume of József Simonyi and Zsigmond Balassa's *A Thorough Hungarian Grammar*, providing an overview of the historical phonological and morphological research up until then. No other monograph followed this summary for a long time. By the mid-20th century, however, the need for a more substantial historical linguistic synthesis was apparent. What filled this need was a multi-volume series of slim textbooks published under the title *University Booklets on Hungarian Linguistics*. Two of these booklets were written on morphology: Bárczi's *Word roots* (1958) and D. Bartha's *The History of Hungarian Word-Formation* (1958). The latter provides an excellent insight into morphological issues of derivational morphemes, their origin, and functions.

In the 1950s several monographs on linguistic sources of the Old Hungarian period were written, which, naturally, discussed in detail the word-formation characteristics of these texts as well (Bárczi 1951, B. Lőrinczy 1953 and Imre 1958). An abbreviated and integrated version of the university booklets was published in 1967 by Bárczi, Benkő and Berrár in which word-formation was given a separate chapter, albeit a short one (pp. 316–350).

The challenge of writing a really thorough monographic account of the historical morphological knowledge of Hungarian linguistics (including word-formation) was taken up by the group of authors in what became the monumental work *An Historical Grammar of the Hungarian Language*. This work (Benkő 1991–92) is extremely detailed but extends only up to the late Old Hungarian period: the other periods of Hungarian language history were not processed for it due to the lack of resources. This makes the university textbook *Hungarian Linguistic History* (Kiss and Pusztai 2003) all the more important: even though it is only "textbook deep", it extends over the entire history of the Hungarian language, providing important chapters on more recent periods which are relevant to our focus.

3 Word-formation in Proto-Hungarian

3.1 Derivation

Derivation was, most likely, one of the most productive means of word-formation in the Uralic (Finno-Ugric) proto-language. On the basis of comparative historical investigations we can conclude that the Hungarian language had a relatively rich system of derivational affixes at the beginning of its independent life.

At the beginning of the Proto-Hungarian period (1000 BC–900 AD) Hungarian had inherited a series of one-element derivational affixes both for the derivation of nominals (e.g., *-g*, *-j*, *-k*, *-l~ly*, *-r*, *-s*) and for the derivation of verbs (e.g., *-d*, *-g*, *-r*, *-s*, *-sz*, *-z*). These formed numerous derivatives (whose derived nature has been obscured by now), both nominals and verbs (e.g., *boldog* 'happy', *világ* 'world', *tolvaj* 'thief', *torok* 'throat', and *fárad* 'to get tired', *forog* 'to turn, gyrate', *kapar* 'to scratch', *olvas* 'to read'; cf. D. Bartha 1991: 60, and Szegfű 1991: 188–193).

Several new derivational affixes (e.g., *-nt*, *-rog*/*-reg*/*-rög*, *-tat*/*-tet*, *-hat*/*-het*, etc.) were formed in the Proto-Hungarian period, mostly through the fusion of simple derivational affixes with each other, a phenomenon made possible by the fact that derived words may become the input to further derivation. Such further derivation was motivated by functional needs, either to modify the meaning of the existing derivational affix (in such cases the new derivation is done with an affix of a different function, e.g., *rette-n* 'to be scared' → *rette-nt* 'to scare'), or because the original derivational affix deriving the relative stem becomes obsolete and, thus, its function needs to be reinforced (in such cases the new derivation is carried out with a more current affix of the same function, e.g., *hábo-r* → *hábo-rog* 'to seethe', or sometimes even with the new variant of the same derivational affix made more up-to-date by adding a stem-final vowel, e.g., *gyón-t* → *gyón-tat* 'take confession'). In the Proto-Hungarian period the fusion of derivational affixes of different functions was typical, since the meanings of the ancient derivational affixes were still transparent, and re-derivation due to opaqueness became more common starting in the Old Hungarian period (D. Bartha 1991: 60–61).

Another way in which derivational affixes were formed is through independent words being agglutinated. This is how the *-hat*/*-het* suffix (e.g., *alhat* 'can/may sleep', *élhet* 'can/may live'), deriving verbs from verbs, or the *-ság*/*-ség* suffix (e.g., *imádság* 'prayer', *szépség* 'beauty'), deriving nouns from nominals (nouns, adjectives, or numerals) were formed in Proto-Hungarian. The suffix *-hat*/*-het* most likely originated in the verb *hat* 'to know, be able', while *-ság*/*-ség* can be traced back to the noun *ság* ~ *szág* 'mound, hill'. Earlier, they had formed phrases and later compounds with the preceding verb or noun (in some Old Hungarian sources *-ság/-ség* appears written separately, e.g., ca. 1405: *nemzet seg* 'genus; blood line', cf. Szegfű 1991: 211). Finally, the second part of the compound grammaticalized and became a derivational suffix (which, at the same time, also changed the nature of the morphological structure, cf. Károly 1980: 153), and started obeying Hungarian phonotactic rules of vowel harmony.

Some derivational suffixes formed as the result of morphophonological change through the fusion of the typically Finno-Ugric and Hungarian stem-final vowel with a suffix that had previously been one element. Stem-final vowels – detached from their stems and phonetically lengthened – reattached to derivational suffixes which were no longer productive forming new derivational suffixes such as *-sz* becoming the profession-name denoting suffix *-ász/-ész* (*hal-ász* 'fisherman', *vad-ász* 'hunter', *lov-ász* 'groom', etc.) or the suffix *-ék* (*köny-ék* 'elbow', *körny-ék* 'vicinity', etc.); cf. Szegfű (1991: 212).

A relatively rare way of forming new derivational suffixes is when another type of affix turns into a derivational suffix, as happened in the case of the *-i* and *-nyi* nominal derivational suffixes. The suffix *-i*, expressing possession, was formed in the Proto-Hungarian period through a formal and functional split from the *-é* possessive inflection. The most likely path of its development was from a predicative structure (*a birtok a királyé* 'the estate is the king's') which enabled a free word order variant (*a királyé (a) birtok* 'the king's [is] (the) estate') to develop, producing the attributive adjectival form in the structure *királyi birtok* 'royal estate' (Szegfű 1991: 210). The long process of the lative adverbial inflection *-n(y)é* ~ *-n(y)í* turning into a derivational suffix most likely started in the second half of the Proto-Hungarian period but was completed only in the late Old Hungarian period (and will, thus, be discussed in section 4.1, under the latter period).

3.2 Compounding

There were few compound nouns in the Hungarian lexicon of Finno-Ugric origin, and most of them have become completely opaque by now. Some of them represent coordinate compounding and mostly have compositional meaning, e.g., *arc* ~ *orca* 'face; lit. nose mouth' (nose + mouth), *ember* 'person, human' (< *em* 'woman' + *bër* 'man'), while in a few of them the parts of the compound are synonyms, e.g., *férj* 'husband' (< *fi* 'man' + **er(j)* 'man'). Other early compounds had a subordinate structure: most have a qualitative or quantitative adjective plus noun structure, e.g., *leány* 'girl' (< **laj* 'young' + *any(a)* 'mother'), or *ötven* 'fifty' (< *öt* 'five' + *tíz* 'ten'), *harminc* 'thirty' (< *három* 'three' + *tíz* 'ten'), cf. Zelliger (1991: 524), and Kiss and Pusztai (2003: 198).

Several of the earliest Hungarian compounds are of a form similar to what can be found in other Finno-Ugric languages: e.g., Hungarian *hat-van* ~ Mansi *χōt-pan* 'sixty; lit. six-ten'; Hungarian *or-ca* ~ Mansi *ńol* + *tus* 'face; lit. nose-mouth'. This fact makes it likely that certain compound types may have had a shared origin on the level of collocations, with their development into compounds happening later as an independent parallel development (Zelliger 1991: 524). Since compounds can be found in numerous Old Hungarian sources, a more detailed overview of the compound types will be given in section 4.2 on that period.

4 Word-formation in Old Hungarian

4.1 Derivation

By the early Old Hungarian period the simple and complex derivational suffixes inherited from the Uralic proto-language and originating in the Proto-Hungarian period formed a relatively rich system, with further complex derivational suffixes added in the Old Hungarian period (900–1526), motivated not so much by functional need but by the intention to increase variability and shades of meanings (cf. Szegfű 1991: 213 and 1992: 268). The new complex derivational suffixes were formed by the fusion of two primary derivational suffixes in this period as well, although there are also examples of complex suffixes growing more complex. Usually, the derivational suffix attached to a stem fused with another suffix (e.g., *mara-d* 'to remain, stay' → *mara-doz* 'to stay frequently'), forming what is called "right complex derivational suffixes" in the Hungarian historical linguistics literature. In later periods "left complex derivational suffixes" were occasionally formed: *butá-skodik* 'to behave silly; lit. silly + derivational suffix', *kutyá-lkodik* 'josh; lit. dog + derivational suffix', cf. D. Bartha (1991: 64). In the Old Hungarian period complex derivational suffixes with an iterative function were mostly formed from verbs, e.g., *-gat*/*-get* (*csörget* 'to rattle'), *-dos*/*-des*/*-dös* (*szálldos* 'to fly about'), some of them of three forms *-dogál*/*-dëgél*/*-dögél* (*mendegél* 'to wander'), cf. D. Bartha (1991: 66). New complex nominal derivational suffixes were mostly diminutive-forming suffixes, e.g., *-ócs*/*-őcs* (archaic *Petőcs* 'Pete'), *-kó*/*-kő* (*Jankó* 'Johnny', *csikó* 'foal'); cf. Szegfű (1991: 213).

In the Old Hungarian period the first borrowed derivational suffix entered the Hungarian language, thereby adding a new source of word-formation. The suffix in question is *-nok*/*-nëk*/*-nök*, originating in Slavic *-nik*, which entered Hungarian as part of loanwords, e.g., *bajnok* 'champion', *udvarnok* 'free medieval peasant' (cf. Serbian and Croatian *bojnik*, *dvôrnīk*). Since the roots of these words (*baj* 'trouble', *udvar* 'yard') were also borrowed into Hungarian, speakers may have identified them in derived forms as well, using the derivational suffix on other stems later. According to sources, the suffix, which had only one variant form in Slavic, had different forms, following vowel harmony, in the derivatives in Hungarian (cf. *Boynuc* [family name], from ca. 1208–1235, or *Aztalnak* [family name] from 1382), serving as the basis for the three harmonic variants, *-nok*/ *-nëk*/*-nök*. The late Old Hungarian and the Middle Hungarian periods saw the borrowing of further derivational suffixes in Hungarian – more on this in section 5.

As was mentioned before, the *-nyi* derivational suffix forming quantifiers had its origin in another suffix, in the lative inflection *-n(y)é* ~ *-n(y)í*, from which it developed through a change of function in the Old Hungarian period. The process may have been aided by the relatively limited geographical area in which this inflection was used, contributing to its function becoming opaque and the inflection being used in conjunction with the newer *-ra*/*-re* suffix of similar function: e.g., *kőhagyejtás-né-ra* 'at a stone's throw'. Since only one case inflection can occur on one stem, the suffix closer to the stem was later reinterpreted as a derivational affix (Szegfű 1991: 210–211).

4.2 Compounding

Sources from the Old Hungarian period contain several Hungarian language compounds (most of them being proper names and consisting of two parts, some of them of more) in the Latin language texts which share the same characteristic features of compounds dated from later as far as their structural and semantic features are concerned. (Coordinate compounds are, for instance, the place names *Kozmadamján* (from the names of saints Kosmas and Damian) from 1199 and *Hontpázmány* (from the names Hont and Pázmány) from 1262; while subordinate compounds include the place name *Kerekegyház* lit. 'round church' from 1241 and the family name *Farkasverő* lit. 'wolf beater' from 1272). From this it can be concluded that, even though in the Old Hungarian period compounding could not compete with derivation in productivity, it played an ever increasing role in word-formation (Kiss and Pusztai 2003: 378). Beginning with the second half of this period, sources written fully in Hungarian became common, and these contained more and more compounded common nouns as well. Most compounds are subordinate or coordinate compounds (rather than exocentric compounds).

4.2.1 Subordinate compounds

Pais (1951: 141) illustrates very plausibly the origin of subordinate compounds with historical examples such as the compound *drágakő* 'jewel; lit. expensive stone', which had precursors in synonymous phrases such as *drágalátus kő* 'costly stone', *nemes kő* 'noble stone', *drága avagy nemes kő* 'expensive or noble stone', and *drága kő* 'expensive stone'. Of these, the use of the structure *drága kő* became predominant starting from the 16th century and, due to habitual use, its spelling as one word became usual. It became a compound when, in addition to its change in form, it underwent semantic change as well: the meaning expressing a functional relation ('an expensive stone') changed into a single, unified notion ('jewel') (Pais 1951: 144).

Among endocentric compounds expressing a subordinate structural relationship there must have been some already in the Proto-Hungarian period which were subject compounds originating in noun + past or present adjectival participles (or deverbal nominals) such as *istenadta* 'God-given', *napsütötte* 'sun-baked', and *szélfútta* 'wind-blown'. Similar examples can also be found among personal and place names in legal documents, e.g., *Istenwetthe* 'God-forsaken' from 1333, or *Menittemezev* 'lightning struck field' from 1363, and common noun forms from later times such as *eszeveszett* 'frantic; lit. mind-lost' or *agyafúrt* 'shrewd; lit. brain-drilled' (cf. Zelliger 1991: 529 and Lőrinczi 1992: 861). Compounds of the subjective genitive type also belong here, most of them formed with the second part of the compound derived in *-ás/-és* (a deverbal noun-forming suffix), such as *vízfolyás* 'watercourse, river; lit. water flow', *hideglelés* 'shivers; lit. cold find', *földindulás* 'earthquake; lit. land start-out', but in Old Hungarian they also occurred with other derivational suffixes as well (sometimes even the exact same stems, cf. with *-at/-et: hideglelet, földindulat*, etc.).

Object compounds also occurred already in the Proto-Hungarian period. The modifier of the compound is a noun, while the head is usually a present adjectival participle or deverbal adjective with privative meaning (*szófogadatlan* 'disobedient; lit. word-to take-PRIVATIVE', *írástudatlan* 'illiterate; lit. writing-to know-PRIVATIVE'). The earliest examples among these are, stemming from the nature of the sources, also place and family names (*Cuhurdovhut* 'stone carrying road' from 1300, *Kenersytou* 'bread baker' from 1357, *Wyzmereu* 'water measurer' from 1340, etc.), whereas common nouns appear later, e.g., *pénzváltó* 'money changer', *írástudó* 'scribe; lit. writing knower', and *favágó* 'logger; lit. tree cutter'. The base word of the object compound can contain various deverbal noun-forming suffixes, most frequent among them is *-ás/-és: pártütés* 'forming an opposing party; lit. group creation', *hitszegés* 'heresy; lit. faith breaking', but other suffixes are also used, e.g., *igazságtétel* 'doing justice [to somebody]; lit. justice doing', *bajviadal* 'tournament; lit. fight combat'. Semantically, most of them are words denoting professions or objects: *nyereggyártó* 'saddle maker', and *gyertyatartó* 'candle holder', etc. (cf. Lőrinczi 1992: 863–865).

Most of the adverbial compounds of the early Old Hungarian period contain inflection on the determining element. On the basis of this, those few lexemes where the adverbial relationship is unmarked by inflection are considered to be very early compounds from Proto-Hungarian, *Vizkuzureu* 'whetstone working with water; lit. water whetstone' from 1327, or *vakmere* 'foolhardy; lit. blind brave' from 1456. Another unmarked compound is the word *kesztyű* 'glove' (cf. *vas kezthew* 'iron glove', from ca. 1395), which is a by now opaque compound originally meaning literally 'onto-the-hand putter', with the head of the compound being an archaic, by now non-existent participial form of the verb *tesz* 'to put' (cf. Zelliger 1991: 530). The superessive adverbial relationship is marked in the numerals *tizenegy* 'eleven', *huszonegy* 'twenty-one', etc. involving the modifiers *tizen-* 'teen; lit. on ten' and *huszon-* 'twenty-; lit. on twenty', originating from the Proto-Hungarian period, which are similarly constructed in several other Finno-Ugric languages, e.g., in Mansi: *lu-tọmọr-uki* 'eleven' (with *tọmọr* meaning 'onto'), cf. Zelliger (1991: 530).

Hungarian language sources contain primarily marked determining members whose head is usually a participle, or, rarely, a noun derived in *-ás*/*-és* or *-at*/*-et*, e.g., *alabualo* 'inferior; lit. lower being' from 1470, *Nyakbawetew* 'necklace; lit. onto-neck casting' from 1415, *Napra nezo (fy)* 'sunflower; lit. onto-sun looking [grass]', *ketſegben* (sic!) *eſſes* 'dispair; lit. in-doubt falling', today *kétségbeesés*, and *menÿbenmenet* 'Ascension; lit. in-heaven going', today *mennybemenetel*. Compounds with a head verb (e.g., *bejön* 'to come in; lit. in-come', *kimegy* 'to go out; lit. out-go', *lefekszik* 'to lie down; lit. down-lie') constitute a special group among adverbial compounds: they have grammaticalized adverb complements as modifiers, which have developed into preverbs. The earliest Hungarian preverbs (*meg-* 'back', *el-* 'away', *be-* 'in', *ki-* 'out', *le-* 'down', *fel-* 'up') are of Finno-Ugric origin, of them, *meg-* carries a perfective meaning already in the early Hungarian sources, with its directional meaning no longer present. The other preverbs also lost some of their directional meaning, acquiring an additional aspectual meaning. From the late Old Hungarian period on, preverbs were formed from polysyllabic adverbials (e.g., *hátra|fordul* 'to turn around; lit. back-onto turn', and *vissza|tér* 'to return; lit. back-come') and from parts of idioms (e.g., *agyon-* 'to death; lit. brain-on', as in *agyon|ver* 'to beat to death'). For more on their origin and development, see Forgács (2004) and Ladányi (2015).

While in the above compound types the head of the compound is a participle or deverbal noun, adjectival compounds have nominals as their heads and fall into three types: they can have quantitative, qualitative, or possessive adjectives as modifiers.

A great number of qualitative adjectival compounds occur among the place names mentioned in historical charters. The head of such a compound is a noun, while its modifier is an adjective. Place names can contain the name of the nationality of the inhabitants (e.g., *Magyarfalu* lit. 'Hungarian village', *Németfalu* 'German village'), it can signal that the village has a church or a castle (*Egyházasharaszti* lit. 'church Haraszti', and *Váraskécs* lit. 'castle Kécs') or indicate the shape or color of its church (*Kerekegyház* lit. 'round church', *Veresegyház* 'red church'), etc. The place names *Hatház* lit. 'six houses' and *Mindszent* lit. 'all saints', originate in quantitative adjectival compounds, while *Mihályfalva* lit. 'Michael's village', and *Ispánlaka* lit. 'governor's home' contain possessive modifiers; see Kiss and Pusztai (2003: 378).

Rarely, adjectival participles also occur as adjectival modifiers in compounds, cf. *Verofyn* 'sunshine; lit. casting light' from 1312, *vefel* 'best man; lit. buying person', from ca. 1405. There are numerous similar examples from later periods: in most of them the head indicates the place where the action expressed in the modifier occurs, cf. *mosóház* 'washing house', *sütőház* 'baking house', etc.

The structures with a head adjective derived in *-ú/-ű* constitute collocations rather than compounds (*szőke hajú* 'blond haired', etc.). But when the meaning is different than the sum of the meanings of the parts, they become compounds: *jókedvű* 'joyful; lit. good mooded', etc.

Nouns often served as qualitative adjectival premodifiers in early Old Hungarian, especially in names of trees and bushes: *tölgyfa* 'oak tree', *fenyőfa* 'fir tree', *körtefa* 'pear tree', *mogyoróbokor* 'hazelnut bush', *csipkebokor* 'hawthorn; lit. hawthorn bush', etc. Such adjectival premodifiers can also express the aim, material, or use of the entity expressed by the head: *füstpénz* 'household tax; lit. smoke money', *hegyvám* 'hillside use fee; lit. mountain toll', *vámsó* 'salt paid as toll; lit. toll salt', *vaspénz* 'iron coin', *földvár* 'hill fort; lit. earth fort', etc. Some of the compounds formed like this have by now become opaque: for example, the word *némber*, which originally meant 'female person' (< *né* 'woman' + *ember* 'person') has acquired the pejorative meaning 'dishonorable woman' (cf. Zelliger 1991: 533).

Collocations involving quantitative adjectival premodifiers relatively rarely developed into compounds since the quantity of the entity expressed through the head could change, thus impeding their structural stabilization (Zelliger 1991: 534). The only existing examples are compounded numerals such as *háromszáz* 'three hundred', *négyszáz* 'four hundred', and compounds where the numeral has an indirect meaning, e.g., *ezerjó (fű)* 'centaurium', a plant name; lit. 'thousand good (grass)'. Relatively frequent are the compounds with *fél-* 'half' as the modifier, primarily because this quantifier is also used to express the incompleteness or lower rank of a quality or state, *féldrágakő* 'semi-precious stone', *félpap* 'Levite; lit. semi-priest', etc. (Lőrinczi 1992: 871).

In compounds involving possessive adjectival premodifiers both the head and the modifier are nouns. The earliest examples of this type have by now become opaque, e.g., *hónalj* 'armpit; lit. the cavity under the base of the arm + lower part', *hónap* 'month; lit. moon day', *hétfő* 'Monday; lit. week head', *vasárnap* 'Sunday; lit. market day'. Early compounds of this type usually are unmarked for the possessive relationship (see the previous examples, also *birſagnop* 'Judgment Day; lit. toll day' from 1200, or *buthuruth* 'dagger of sorrow' (cf. Latin *gladium doloris*) from ca. 1300. This type of compound was very productive in Old Hungarian, partly due to the semantic complexity of the possessive relationship, since, in addition to possession, it also referred to more abstract relationships as well, e.g., *házfedél* 'roof; lit. house top', *tanácsház* 'town hall', *ebédidő* 'lunchtime', *ítéletnap* 'Judgment Day', *udvarbíró* 'a type of judge; lit. court judge' (Lőrinczi 1992: 872).

Compounds with the head marked for possessive are rare (e.g., *Ispanpeze* 'governor's money' from ca. 1510, *Spanbora* 'governor's wine' from 1422), and sometimes the marking of the possessive is missing from the head noun, with orthography being variable (cf. *eb nÿelw* from ca. 1525 ~ *Eb nyelue* '[plant name]; lit. dog's tongue' from 1533; *haʒhenak*, with *házhéj* 'roof; lit. house surface', from 1493~1519: *haz heiara* '[onto the] house's roof'). This is probably connected to the fact that, due to being marked, these constructions preserve their syntagmatic nature, while unmarked variants are more compound-like.

In a small group of compounds the relationship of the parts is not subordinate but predicative. These compounds are very similar to subject compounds, except their heads are not participles or deverbal nouns but finite verbs, since they combine the subject and the predicate, *Mendoͤroͤk* 'thunder; lit. heaven rumbles' from 1493, cf. Lőrinczi (1992: 879).

Exocentric compounds also occur already at this time, for instance, when the neighboring words of an often repeated phrase which are not in any relationship with each other are fused. Such compounds must have existed already in the Proto-Hungarian period (e.g., parts of oaths or beginning words of prayers), but when these texts were no longer repeated, the compounds were also lost (Zelliger 1991: 536). Thus, the earliest such compound is *idueʒleg* 'Hail Mary; lit. be hailed', from the Königsberg Fragment (14th c.), and later examples are *hiszekegy* 'Creed; lit. I believe' and *miatyánk* 'Lord's prayer; lit. our father'.

Further such compounds can be formed by words with no syntactic function (such as negative particles or interjections) connecting to lexemes that constitute sentence elements (Lőrinczi 1992: 879). Examples are old personal names (e.g., *Bornemisza* lit. 'wine no drinker' from 1442, or *Nemdeák* lit. 'no student') and common nouns, e.g., *Jay vezic* lit. 'alas I'm dying' from 1512, which was not preserved in Hungarian in this form, only in its derived verbal form *jajveszékel* 'to lament'. Exocentric compounds also include conjunctions, pronouns, and adverbs (e.g., *minthogy* 'since; lit. as that', *valaki* 'somebody', and *néhány* 'some').

A transitional category between endocentric and exocentric compounds is composed of adverbs formed from nouns plus postpositions, e.g., *délelőtt* 'morning; lit. noon before', *délután* 'afternoon; lit. noon after', *holnapután* 'day after tomorrow; lit. tomorrow after', *ezenkívül* 'besides; lit. this-superessive outside'. Some kind of endocentric relationship can be traced between the parts of the compound, but the reason for their being is not founded in a syntagmatic relationship but in the linear ordering of a sentence (cf. Gerstner 2006: 471).

The history of compounds shows that they typically originate in sentences through univerbation. They proliferate, however, mostly due to analogical creation, since by analogy language users can create new compounds by following certain patterns of structuring without these compounds being fused in sentences (Gerstner 2006: 471).

The following patterns also play an important role in copying compounds from other languages. As we could see in connection with derivational suffixes, the Hungarian language was greatly affected by language contact already in the Old Hungarian period, and the same is true of compounds as well, as calques and partial translations originating in this period indicate. (Their numbers are only to increase later.) They are mostly nouns. As Lőrinczi (1992: 880) expounds, the difference between the two types is that in the case of partial translations the modifying element is a word borrowed from the source language, while in calquing it is only the pattern of the compound that is borrowed, and both parts of the compound are lexical items from the borrowing language, in this case Hungarian (cf., e.g., *Galycz kew* 'vitriol; lit. sulphate stone' < Bavarian and Austrian *galitzn-staə* 'sulphate stone', from ca. 1520, *hofmeiſter* 'courtier; lit. court master' < German *Hofmeister*, from 1529, and *nag penthek*en (today *nagypénteken*) 'on Good Friday; lit. on great Friday', modeled on the Slavic pattern; cf. Old Bulgarian *velikaja nedělja* 'passion week; lit. great week' from 1456).

Interestingly, some examples of compounds formed via folk etymology also date back to the late Old Hungarian period (cf. Lőrinczi 1992: 881). On the basis of their origin, they can be categorized into two types. One of the types is simple folk etymology, in examples of which speakers replaced a part of a compound which they considered foreign (or unknown) with a Hungarian word of a similar form, e.g., *Ostoradó* 'tax' from 1434, where the modifier goes back to German *Steuer* 'tax' but its form is identical with the Hungarian word *ostor* 'whip', or *mely feldet* 'mile (earth)' from after 1372, where the modifier is the German word *Meile*, Middle High German *mīle* 'mile' but its form is the same as the Hungarian word *mély* 'deep'. The other type, found in a greater range of examples, can be called compositional folk etymology. Examples of this type are created because speakers (correctly or incorrectly) consider some foreign words to be morphologically composed. In some cases it is only the head that is considered a separate lexeme, and the modifier a fictitious loanword, e.g., *Cymteremeben* '(in the) graveyard; lit. (in the) tin room', from Latin *coemeterium* 'graveyard' from after 1372, whereas in other examples both "parts of the compound" are existing Hungarian lexemes. An example of the latter is the word *számszeríj* 'weapon similar to bow', which is a Slavic borrowing (cf. Slovak *samostrel* 'self shooter') but looks like a three part compound consisting of the Hungarian words *szám* 'number', *szer* 'matter' and *íj* 'bow'.

Opaque compounds, which occurred in small numbers in the Proto-Hungarian period, are more numerous in Old Hungarian times (cf. Lőrinczi 1992: 882). Sometimes opacity originates solely in one factor, which is usually phonological (e.g., *folu nagy* 'village leader; lit. village big', > *folnagy* > *fónagy*; or *hálaadatos* 'thankful; lit. gratitude giving' > *háládatos*). Sometimes, however, opacity results from a combination of two or more factors, most likely in the case of *keszkenő* 'small kerchief': the word was originally of the form *kéz* 'hand' + *kenő* 'wiper' (cf. *kezkene* from around 1405). Later its modifier changed as *kéz* > *kesz*, and the head lost its 'wiper' meaning, these two factors together contributing to the opacity of the compound. Another example is the development of the form **idnap* into *idnep* and into today's *ünnep*, with the meaning changing from 'holy day' to 'holiday', resulting in the compounded nature of the word becoming opaque, and the *id-* ~ *üd-* part also being lost as a lexeme.

4.2.2 Coordinate compounds

Coordinate compounds have two basic types as far as the phonological and semantic affinity between the parts is concerned. The simpler and less frequent type involves coordinating reduplication, which is a simple manifestation of the archaic figure of repetition. The more complex and more frequent type is coordinating cumulation, which is a manifestation of another archaic figure, that of parallelism (Lőrinczi 1992: 853).

Reduplication may involve a real syntagmatic relationship or be simple reduplication without it. The former also has two types: simple coordination (exact reduplication) (e.g., *már-már* 'almost; lit. already-already'), and stem reduplication, which is morphologically not complete, repeating only the stem for a rhetorical purpose (figura etymologica), and producing collocations rather than compounds (e.g., *nőttön-nő* 'to grow continuously; lit. to grown-much grow', and *körös-körül* 'all around; lit. round and round').

Simple reduplication involves a repetition of the form and constitutes a rather rare form of word-formation characteristic only of adjectives, numerals and pronouns in Hungarian (e.g., *fő-fő* 'most important; lit. important-important', *ki-ki* 'everyone; lit. who-who').

Simple reduplication not expressing a syntagmatic relationship – and a special case of it, called proliferating reduplication in Hungarian linguistics – is morphologically very similar to reduplication expressing syntagmatic relationship. This way of word-formation produces playful and expressive forms which, for normative and semantic reasons, did not make their way into early sources (Zelliger 1991: 527) but appear in abundance towards the late Old Hungarian period. As far as their form is concerned, two types can be identified. In one type, an existing lexeme is appended to its phonologically modified variant, whereas in the other type neither part is used in itself (Lőrinczi 1992: 855, cf. in addition Szikszainé 1993). The sources of the phonological similarity of the parts of the compound are various, including vowel harmony (*mendemonda* 'hearsay', cf. *monda* 'legend'; *diribdarab* 'odds and ends', cf. *darab* 'piece'; *tarkabarka* 'motley', cf. *tarka* 'multicolored'; and *dibdáb* 'paltry', with neither part existing in itself, etc.), labial/non-labial opposition (*csigabiga* 'snail [children's form]', cf. *csiga* 'snail', etc.), or vocalic/labial word-initial opposition (*izeg-mozog* 'to fidget', cf. *mozog* 'to move'; *ireg-forog* 'to keep turning', cf. *forog* 'to revolve'). Proliferating reduplication is used in the formation of verbs, nouns and adjectives. Similarly to other coordinate compounds, such forms are also inflected on both their parts, cf., e.g., *ihagtok-vihagtok* 'they giggled' from 1541.

The other large group of coordinate compounds is cumulative compounds, with three main types as far as their form and meaning are concerned: (a) amalgamating reduplications, (b) true (amalgamated) coordinating compounds, and (c) collocations.

While in the case of proliferating reduplication a word is appended to its own playfully formed variant, in amalgamating reduplication two separate but similar words are fused – thus, making it very similar in form to proliferating reduplication. The similarity of the two parts may be due to the palatal/labial opposition (*hébe-hóba* 'rarely; lit. in heat and in snow') or to the labial-nonlabial opposition of vowels (*csúszó|mászó* 'cringing, sneaking; lit. sliding-crawling'). Amalgamating reduplication produces verbs, nouns, and adjectives, which are usually inflected on both parts (especially the verbs) – this guaranteeing that the coordinating nature of their relationship is preserved. Semantically, the two parts of the compound can be synonyms (e.g., *per|patvar* 'altercation; lit. legal proceedings squabble', *locs|pocs* 'squashy mud; lit. wetness puddle' (< archaic *locsé-pocsé*)', but they can also be cohyponyms or members of the same semantic field (*ágas-bogas* 'branchy, complicated; lit. branchy-knotty', *dúl-fúl* 'fume [with rage]; lit. destroy choke', etc.), cf. Lőrinczi (1992: 857).

The parts of true coordinating compounds have a different form and constitute cumulation only semantically. Their first part is usually a one or two-syllable word, while the second part is longer by one syllable (e.g., *kőszikla* 'rock, cliff; lit. rock cliff', *vízözön* 'flood; lit. water torrent'). Rarely, words of the same number of syllables attach together: *szélvész* 'wind storm; lit. wind disaster', or *hírnév* 'fame; lit. news name'.

5 Word-formation in Middle Hungarian

Few new derivational affixes were formed in the Middle Hungarian period (1526–1772), but derivation as a form of word-formation continued to be a major source of new words. Among verbs, the number of derived iterative and punctual verbs increased (e.g., *irkál* 'to scribble', from *ír* 'to write', and the iterative suffix *-kál*, 1585; *rugdal* 'to keep kicking', from *rúg* 'to kick' and the iterative suffix *-dal*, 1768; *futamodik* 'to flee', from *fut* 'to run' and *-amodik* 'inchoative', from around 1550; and *köhint* 'to cough [once]', with the punctual suffix *-int*, 1604; cf. Kiss and Pusztai 2003: 620). Because several suffixes had the same function, synonyms were also often formed (e.g., iterative derivations of *fut* → *futkos* from 1590 and *futkároz* from 1621). In this period noun and adjective derivation began to develop separately, and derivational suffixes started to develop individual functions. For instance, the deverbal nominal suffix *-at*/*-et* was used in the 15th and 16th centuries to form action nouns (e.g., *arat* 'to harvest' → *aratat* 'harvest, the process of harvesting', or *művelkedik* 'to act' → *művelkedet* 'action, i.e. the process of acting'). This kind of meaning is expressed now by the suffix *-ás*/*-és* (*aratás* 'harvest', *futás* 'running'), and the suffix *-at*/*-et* expresses the result of the action (*épület* 'building [structure]', *irat* 'document'), cf. Gerstner (2006: 469).

In addition, new borrowed derivational suffixes (*-izál*, *-ista*, *-izmus*, *-órium*/*-tórium* from Latin, and *-éroz*/*-íroz* from German) also appear in Hungarian at this time. The derivational suffixes of Latin verbs borrowed directly or indirectly (via German) (*kanonizál* 'to canonize', *katolizál* 'to convert to Catholicism', *politizál* 'to engage in politics') were now used with some native stems (e.g., *úr* 'lord' → *urizál* 'to live idly', from 1708, or *hiú* 'vain' → *hévizál* 'to behave idly'). Borrowed noun derivational suffixes include *-ista*, which previously occurred in *pápista* 'papist' and *kálvinista* 'Calvinist', deriving new words using native stems such as *ördög* 'devil' → *ördögista* 'devil's follower' in the 17th century, or later *egyetem* 'university' → *egyetemista* 'university student', *forgalom* 'traffic' → *forgalmista* 'traffic manager (of railway)', *iroda* 'office' → *irodista* 'office worker', etc.

A new tendency among the formation of compounds at the time was that several compounds formed using the same first or second part (e.g., *farkas-* 'wolf': *farkasfű* 'wolf's bane; lit. wolf grass', from 1578, *farkasgyökér* 'northern wolfsbane; lit. wolf root', from 1767, *farkasseb* 'skin cancer; lit. wolf wound', from 1508, *farkashályog* 'night blindness; lit. wolf cataract', from 1577, or *-ház* 'house': *borház* 'tavern; lit. wine house', from 1604, *fegyverház* 'armory; lit. weapon house', from 1621, *áruház* 'store house; lit. merchandise house', from 1685. This signals the quickening of the pace with which compounds were formed at this time, and also the growing importance of their role in developing special registers (e.g., medical and botanical) (cf. Kiss and Pusztai 2003: 622).

The written sources of the Middle Hungarian period contain numerous examples of a less frequent method of word-formation, namely, backformation (which were very scarce earlier, in the Old Hungarian period). Backformation produces a new word by taking away a part of it which is interpreted as a derivational affix by analogy to existing derived words. For instance, the Slavic verb *kopati* 'to hoe' was borrowed in Hungarian with the Hungarian derivational suffix *-l* as *kapál*. Since *-l* is one of the most productive verb derivational suffixes in Hungarian (e.g., *fűrész* 'saw' → *fűrész-el* 'to saw', *gomb* 'button' → *gomb-ol* 'to button'), in time, the new noun *kapa* 'hoe' was formed by backformation from *kapál*. Similarly, other nouns were formed by taking away a 'presumed' *-l* suffix: from verbs of Slavic origin such as *hahotál* 'to laugh' → *hahota* 'laughter', *parancsol* 'to order' → *parancs* 'order', or from onomatopoetic words such as *fütyül* 'to whistle' → *fütty* 'whistle', *löttyen* 'to spill' → *lötty* 'thin soup/wine, etc.' (cf. Gerstner 2006: 473).

Sometimes the ending of borrowed words was reinterpreted as a Hungarian derivational suffix. The Hungarian adjective-forming *-s* suffix is very common, and thus the element *-us* is often left off of Latin loanwords, creating a new stem: *Paulus* → *Pál* 'Paul', *angelus* → *angyal* 'angel', and *apostolus* → *apostol* 'apostle'. Loanwords ending in *-k* often get reinterpreted as containing the Hungarian plural marker *-k*, producing, by backformation, for instance, *csárda* 'tavern' (< Slavic *csárdák* orig. 'military guard tower').

Gerstner (2006: 473) considers the method of word-formation called "meaning adhesion" in Hungarian linguistic terminology to be a special subtype of backformation during which members of compounds or collocations can become independent, taking the meaning of the compound or collocation with them: *fekete|kávé* 'black coffee' → *fekete* 'coffee; lit. black', *nap|kelet* 'east; lit. sun's rise' → *kelet* 'east', and *tokaji bor* 'Tokaji wine' → *tokaji* 'Tokaji wine'. Since in most cases such examples involve change of part of speech (usually in the adjective → noun direction) in addition to being instances of backformation, they constitute a combination of backformation and zero derivation (bordering on ellipsis, and, therefore, syntax), in my opinion.

Blending is a method somewhat similar to backformation. It can be spontaneous or the result of conscious word-formation. Spontaneous examples include *csokor* 'bunch' + *bokréta* 'bouquet' → *csokréta* 'nosegay', *csupa* 'all' + *kopasz* 'bald' → *csupasz* 'naked', *rémít* 'to frighten' + *ijeszt* 'to scare' → *rémiszt* 'to frighten', etc. Conscious word-formation produced a few decades ago the lexemes *levlap* 'postcard' from *levelezőlap* 'postcard; lit. corresponding card' or *csalagút* 'Chunnel' (*csatorna* 'channel' + *alagút* 'tunnel').

Less frequent methods of word-formation also include clipping and further derivation of clipped forms. Both were documented already in the Old Hungarian period, but only in proper names (e.g., *Petrus* → *Pet*, *Benedictus* → *Ben*), although this can be connected to the fact that most linguistic sources from this time are charters and inventories of estates. The names created by means of this method, however, lived on derived further with a diminutive suffix rather than in their clipped form, e.g., *Pet* → *Pete*, *Pető*, and *Ben* → *Bene*, *Benkő* (today they are used mostly as family names) or *Peti*, *Petya*, and *Benő* (given names). Further derivation of clipped forms is a very productive process in the formation of diminutive name forms in modern Hungarian as well (e.g., *Katalin* → *Kati*, *Ágnes* → *Ági*, *Andrea* → *Andi*, etc.; cf. Gerstner 2006: 472). The clipping of common nouns was a rare phenomenon for a long time; examples of it from the Middle Hungarian period include *bácsi* 'uncle' → *bá*, *kegyelmed* 'your worship (address form)' → *kend* and *hiszen* 'but, since' → *hisz*.

The Hungarian linguistic literature (cf. Grétsy 1962; Gerstner 2006) considers what has been called "word splitting" to be a method of word-formation, although an infrequent one. It can be regarded as a special case of zero derivation occurring when a polysemous word develops phonological or morphological variants (N.B.: form variants without a difference in meanings do not cause word splitting – cf. *veder* ~ *vödör* both meaning 'bucket', *csoda* ~ *csuda* both meaning 'miracle'). When the meaning of a polysemous word starts to be attached to one of the variants, the connection may become fixed, producing a pair of words with related forms and meanings: *szaru* 'keratin' ~ *szarv* 'horn', *nevel* 'nurture' ~ *növel* 'increase', *bozótos* 'bushy' ~ *bozontos* 'hairy', etc.

6 Word-formation in Early Modern Hungarian and Modern Hungarian

The beginning of the Early Modern Hungarian period (1772–1920) coincides with the beginning of the Hungarian enlightenment and, from an historical linguistic point of view, with the beginning of the Hungarian language reform movement. The latter did not confine itself purely to language cultivation but was important socially and politically as well, since at this time Latin was the official language of the country. The leading figures of the movement clearly understood that the spiritual rise of the nation and the spreading of learning in wider social circles can only be hoped for if sciences and literature are written in the mother tongue of the users of the language (cf. Bárczi, Benkő and Berrár 1967: 542). The language reform aimed to renew and reform the then fairly provincial Hungarian language and, especially, its lexicon – both as far as the literary and the scientific language are concerned. The language reform, thus, meant conscious word-formation.

Attempts to consciously form words existed in earlier times as well. As was discussed above, the expressions *bírságnap* 'Judgment Day' and *bútőr* 'dagger of sorrow', dating back to the Old Hungarian period, can be regarded as such, or creations from the Hussite Bible (15th c.) such as *sósolat* 'alkali wilderness', *hangoslat* 'singing', or *címerlet* 'inscription', derived from *só* 'salt', *hangos* 'loud', and *címer* 'coat of arms', respectively, which did not get preserved in the language. The Middle Hungarian period saw the conscious creation of lexemes for the terminology of some sciences. János Sylvester's creations of grammar terminology, for instance, include terms such as *köznév* 'common noun' and *tulajdonnév* 'proper noun', and János Apáczai Csere's mathematical terms such as *számláló* 'numerator', *nevező* 'denominator' and *osztó* 'divisor' are still in use today (Kiss and Pusztai 2003: 624).

Compared to these earlier attempts, the era of the language reform produced and attempted to popularize a multitude of new words. It was not only writers but almost all representatives of social and natural sciences who felt it to be their responsibility to create the lexical items missing from the Hungarian language. Their methods included the incorporation of regional vocabulary into the literary language (e.g., *betyár* 'outlaw', *hullám* 'wave', *kandalló* 'fireplace'), the revival of old, archaic words (e.g., *szobor* 'statue', *vihar* 'storm', *aggastyán* 'very old man'). Most words dating back to this era were, however, created with traditional methods of word-formation, i.e. via derivation, compounding, and backformation.

The most productive method used at the time was derivation. The language reformers used almost all the derivational suffixes existing at the time, as well as many, by this time, obsolete ones. They also created new derivational suffixes, with varying degrees of success (Bárczi, Benkő and Berrár 1967: 552–553). The newly created lexemes were often criticized by the users of the language, so not all of them remained in the language – but, all in all, it is safe to say that hundreds of impeccably derived words came out of the workshops of the language reformers. Existing suffixes were used to derive these words: *fagy* 'to freeze, itr.' → *fagy-aszt* 'to freeze, tr.', *fog* 'to understand' → *fog-alom* 'notion', *igazol* 'to certify'

→ *igazol-vány* 'certificate', *gyúl* 'to ignite' → *gyúl-ékony* 'flammable', etc. Obsolete derivational suffixes were revived to form the words *enged-ély* 'permission' (← *enged* 'to allow'), *szeg-ecs* 'rivet' (← *szeg* 'nail') and *alak-zat* 'pattern' (← *alak* 'figure'). Completely new derivational suffixes were formed by taking away, via artificial adaptation, commonly occurring word endings such as *-c*, *-nc*, *-da*/*-de*, and *-ma*/*me*, then used in creating *bohó-c* 'clown' (← *bohó* 'playful'), *kegy-enc* 'favorite; minion' (← *kegy* 'benevolence'), *új-onc* 'recruit' (← *új* 'new'); *jár-da* 'sidewalk' (← *jár* 'to walk (regularly)'), *gyur-ma* 'dough' (← *gyúr* 'to knead'), etc.

Compounding was also used extensively in the language reform. One of the reasons for this is that many German words were adopted at the time, and the original shades of the meanings of compounded German nouns could be preserved this way (Bárczi, Benkő and Berrár 1967: 555). Many new compounds followed the traditions of Hungarian compounding (e.g., *bús*|*komor* 'sullen; lit. sad sullen', *föld*|*rengés* 'earthquake; lit. earth trembling', *alva*|*járó* 'sleep walker; lit. sleeping walker', etc.), but numerous foreign sounding compounds, formed on German patterns, were also created, e.g., using uninflected adverbs such as *szellem*|*dús* 'witty; lit. spirit rich', *szolgálat*|*kész* 'obliging; lit. service ready', *jog*|*erős* 'legally binding; lit. law strong', etc. Such compounds are not completely foreign to Hungarian, since there are examples such as these from both Proto-Hungarian and Old Hungarian (see the discussion of *kesztyű* in section 4.2.1), but by the time of the language reform movement they were obsolete and slightly foreign-sounding. Compounds that used as their first part a pure verb stem (or "presumed" verb stem), such as *fek*|*hely* 'resting place; lit. lie place', *forr*|*pont* 'boiling point; lit. boil point', are even more foreign. The compounds that involve the blending of clipped nouns and adjectives are also unusual (e.g., *könnyelmű* 'light headed; reckless' ← *könnyű elméjű* 'light minded', *lég* 'air' ← *levegő ég* 'air sky', *csőr* 'beak' ← *cső* 'tube' + *orr* 'nose'). In spite of this, many such lexemes "seamlessly" adapted to the Hungarian vocabulary and are no longer felt to be foreign (with the compounded nature of some of them also completely forgotten).

The Hungarian language reformers also used backformation, forming new words from derived or seemingly derived words as well as from compounds. This is the way the words *vizsga* 'examination' (← *vizsgál* 'to examine'), *roncs* 'wreckage' (← *roncsol* 'to break'), *taps* 'applause' (← *tapsol* 'to applaud') were formed from non-compounds, and *kelet* 'east' (← *napkelet* 'sunrise'), and *nyugat* 'west' (← *napnyugat* 'sunset') were formed from compounds. Incorrect assumptions led to the creation of *gyár* 'factory' (← *gyárt* 'to manufacture': the word ending is part of the borrowed Turkish stem), *cég* 'company' (← *cégér* 'sign-board': the word ending is part of the borrowed German stem).

In the past two hundred years compounding has clearly taken over in word-formation at the expense of derivation, for a variety of reasons (cf. Kiss and

Pusztai 2003: 727). New words are created mostly through compounding now, and among compounds the proportion of preverb-verb compounds is also increasing. While in earlier periods derivation played an important role in expressing aspect and quality of action, in the Early Modern Hungarian period, and especially in the Modern Hungarian period (since 1920) preverbs have taken over this function. This leads to the decrease of derived forms and a continuous increase of preverb-verb compounds.

Both at the time of the language reform movement and later the influence of the German language has been considerable in the formation of new compounds and preverb-verb combinations through "mirror translation" (cf. German *Stand|punkt* > *állás|pont* 'standpoint', German *Tier|garten* > *állat|kert* 'zoo; lit. animal garden', and German *ein|sehen* > *be|lát* 'to comprehend; lit. in-see', German *aus|werten* > *ki|értékel* 'to evaluate; lit. out-evaluate'; German *Ein|sicht* > *be|látás* 'comprehension; lit. in-seeing', etc.). Derived German forms are translated into Hungarian rarely, although some examples exist: German *Kellner* > *pincér* 'waiter', German *Stimmung* > *hangulat* 'mood, atmosphere', etc.

A decrease in the productivity of derivation was also affected by the great number of loanwords borrowed in Hungarian in the Early Modern Hungarian period especially in the fields of politics, economy and science. When, driven by purist considerations, the language reformers sought to replace these with words from the native stock, they replaced them with compounds (*állampolgár* 'citizen; lit. state burgher', *köztársaság* 'republic; lit. common company') and not derived forms.

Among the various methods of word-formation, derivation has been losing ground ever since the time of the language reform. This is manifested especially in the considerable decrease of the productivity of some of the derivational suffixes. Despite this, there are still very productive derivational suffixes in Hungarian today, for instance, the verb deriving suffixes *-l* and *-z*, which can form verbs of native or nativized stems (e.g., *korongoz* 'to work the potter's wheel', from *korong* 'potter's wheel', *kukázik* 'to salvage things from garbage', from *kuka* 'garbage can'), as well as from recently borrowed words (e.g., *lízingel* 'to lease', from *lízing* 'leasing', *chatel* 'to chat (electronically)', *internetez* 'to use the internet').

In the Early Modern Hungarian period, especially in the last century, the use of the diminutive affix *-i* has increased considerably in the formation of nominals. It is very productive especially in the derivation of clipped forms: partly in the derivation of names (see section 5), and partly in youth slang, where it lends a familiar, endearing touch to the newly produced word: *husi* (← *hús*) 'meat', *süti* (← *sütemény*) 'pastry', etc. Such forms occurred only in spoken language before, but many of them have made their way into written language use as well by now (Gerstner 2006: 472). Forms such as *bugyi* (← *bugyogó* 'panties', now archaic), *csoki* (← *csokoládé* 'chocolate'), and *pulcsi* (← *pulóver* 'pullover') are earlier creations, whereas *nari* (←*narancs* 'orange'), *ubi sali* (← *uborkasaláta* 'cucumber salad') and *tali* (← *találka* 'date (appointment)'), etc. are more recent ones.

The function of the adjective-forming suffix *-s* has increased to include reference to affiliation with a group, e.g., *töris* 'history major', *magyaros* 'Hungarian major', *BTK-s* 'arts faculty', *TTK-s* 'science faculty' as adjectives referring to students; *fideszes* and *MSZP-s* 'voters or backers of Hungarian political parties FIDESZ and MSZP', respectively.

As far as the compounds of the most recent decades are concerned, many of them have greatly condensed meanings (e.g., *benzinturizmus* 'gasoline tourism', i.e. travel abroad to buy cheaper gasoline there, *béranya* 'surrogate mother; lit. lease mother', *kopogtatócédula* 'pre-election note of support collected by Hungarian political parties; lit. knocking slip'). Even the syntactically analyzable formations are semantically rather than grammatically motivated (cf. Kiss and Pusztai 2003: 806), e.g., *kerékbilincs* 'wheel clamp', *zsebszerződés* 'illegal land contract; lit. pocket contract', and *pénzmosás* 'money laundering; lit. money washing'. Newly borrowed words are quickly used in compounding nowadays (sometimes through mirror translation), e.g., *drogbáró* 'drug lord; lit. drug baron', *drogbarlang* 'den of drug crime; lit. drug cave', *drogstratégia* 'drug policy; lit. drug strategy'.

In the Early Modern Hungarian period backformation is employed less in the verb → nominal direction than before. Instead, a related method has gained more prominence which takes away the derivational suffix from the second part of compounds formed by mirror translation and creates a new verb, e.g., *gyorsúszás* 'freestyle swimming; lit. fast swimming' → *gyorsúsz-ik* 'to swim freestyle', *hőszigetelés* 'insulation; lit. heat isolation' → *hőszigetel* 'to insulate', *nagytakarítás* 'seasonal cleaning; lit. big cleaning' → *nagytakarít* 'to do seasonal cleaning'. These forms are especially interesting since their internal structure changes: syntactically analyzable complex nouns (*nagy* + *takarítás* adjectival subordination, *hő* + *szigetelés* meaning condensing compound) turn into mostly unanalyzable verbs, since the first part of the compound becomes an unmarked adverb, which is a non-typical way of verb formation (cf. Gerstner 2006: 473). The most recent examples are often used ironically: *közvéleménykutatás* 'public opinion poll; lit. common opinion research' → *közvéleménykutat* 'to carry out public opinion poll', *tényfeltárás* 'uncovering of facts' → *tényfeltár* 'to do fact uncovering', etc.

Towards the end of the Early Modern Hungarian period a new method of word-formation developed in Hungarian: the formation of acronyms. While clipping is very similar to acronym formation, it is mostly spontaneous, whereas acronym formation is a mostly conscious, and thus, separate process. This method first occurred in Hungarian in the late 19th century but became widespread only in the mid-20th. A very productive process, it has two main types, one of which is initialism or alphabetism, using the first letters of names (e.g., *MÁV* for *Magyar Államvasutak* 'Hungarian State Railways', *MTA* for *Magyar Tudományos Akadémia* 'Hungarian Academy of Sciences', *OTP* for *Országos Takarékpénztár* 'National Savings Bank', etc.). Some of these are equivalents of international names (e.g., *ENSZ* 'UN'), others are borrowed into Hungarian unchanged (e.g., *NATO, WHO*). The other type of acronyms is abbreviation, using parts of the words which compose it, e.g., *MOL* = *Magyar Olaj- és Gázipari Rt.* 'Hungarian Oil and Gas Company'. In addition to proper-noun acronyms, there are also some common-noun examples as well: *tbc* or *tébécé* 'tuberculosis'; *tv* or *tévé* (← *televízió*) 'TV', etc.

For an overview of word-formation in Modern Hungarian, cf. also Kiefer (2016).

7 References

Bárczi, Géza (1951): *A Tihanyi Apátság Alapítólevele mint nyelvi emlék*. Budapest: Akadémiai Kiadó.

Bárczi, Géza (1958): *A szótövek*. Egyetemi Magyar Nyelvészeti Füzetek. Budapest: Tankönyvkiadó.

Bárczi, Géza, Loránd Benkő and Jolán Berrár (1967): *A magyar nyelv története*. Budapest: Tankönyvkiadó.

Benkő, Loránd (1984): *A magyar fiktív (passzív) tövű igék*. Budapest: Akadémiai Kiadó.

Benkő, Loránd (ed.) (1991–92): *A magyar nyelv történeti nyelvtana I. és II/1*. Budapest: Akadémiai Kiadó.

B. Lőrinczy, Éva (1953): *A Königsbergi Töredék és Szalagjai mint nyelvi emlék*. Budapest: Akadémiai Kiadó.

D. Bartha, Katalin (1958): *A magyar szóképzés története*. Egyetemi Magyar Nyelvészeti Füzetek. Budapest: Tankönyvkiadó.

D. Bartha, Katalin (1991): Az igeképzés. In: Loránd Benkő (ed.), *A magyar nyelv történeti nyelvtana I*, 60–103. Budapest: Akadémiai Kiadó.

D. Bartha, Katalin (1992): Az igeképzés. In: Loránd Benkő (ed.), *A magyar nyelv történeti nyelvtana II/1*, 55–119. Budapest: Akadémiai Kiadó.

Forgács, Tamás (2004): Grammaticalisation and preverbs. *Acta Linguistica Hungarica* 51: 45–84.

Gerstner, Károly (2006): A magyar nyelv szókészlete. In: Ferenc Kiefer (ed.), *Magyar nyelv*, 437–480. Budapest: Akadémiai Kiadó.

Grétsy, László (1962): *A szóhasadás*. Budapest: Akadémiai Kiadó.

Imre, Samu (1958): *A Szabács Viadala*. Budapest: Akadémiai Kiadó.

Károly, Sándor (1980): Szavak, szerkezetek morfológiai tagoltságának változásai és a jelentés. In: Endre Rácz and István Szathmári (eds.), *Tanulmányok a mai magyar nyelv szókészlettana és jelentéstana köréből*, 121–155. Budapest: Tankönyvkiadó.

Kiefer, Ferenc (2000): A szóösszetétel. In: Ferenc Kiefer (ed.), *Strukturális magyar nyelvtan. 3. Morfológia*, 519–567. Budapest: Akadémiai Kiadó.

Kiefer, Ferenc (2006): Alaktan. In: Ferenc Kiefer (ed.), *A magyar nyelv*, 54–79. Budapest: Akadémiai Kiadó.

Kiefer, Ferenc (2016): Hungarian. In: Peter O. Müller, Ingeborg Ohnheiser, Susan Olsen and Franz Rainer (eds.), *Word-Formation. An International Handbook of the Languages of Europe*. Vol. 5, 3308–3326. Berlin/Boston: De Gruyter Mouton.

Kiefer, Ferenc and Mária Ladányi (2000): A szóképzés. In: Ferenc Kiefer (ed.), *Strukturális magyar nyelvtan. 3. Morfológia*, 137–164. Budapest: Akadémiai Kiadó.

Kiss, Jenő and Ferenc Pusztai (ed.) (2003): *Magyar nyelvtörténet*. Budapest: Osiris Kiadó.

Ladányi, Mária (2015): Particle verbs in Hungarian. In: Peter O. Müller, Ingeborg Ohnheiser, Susan Olsen and Franz Rainer (eds.), *Word-Formation. An International Handbook of the Languages of Europe*. Vol. 1, 660–672. Berlin/Boston: De Gruyter Mouton.

Lőrinczi, Réka (1992): Összetett szavak és szoros szókapcsolatok. In: Loránd Benkő (ed.), *A magyar nyelv történeti nyelvtana II/1*, 853–910. Budapest: Akadémiai Kiadó.

Pais, Dezső (1951): Kérdések és szempontok a szóösszetételek vizsgálatához. *Magyar Nyelv* 47: 135–154.

Sárosi, Zsófia (2003): Morfématörténet. In: Jenő Kiss and Ferenc Pusztai (eds.), *Magyar nyelvtörténet*, 129–172, 352–371, 610–617, 719–724, 800–803. Budapest: Osiris Kiadó.

Simonyi, Zsigmond and József Balassa (1895): *Tüzetes magyar nyelvtan történeti alapon*. Budapest: Magyar Tudományos Akadémia.

Szegfű, Mária (1991): A névszóképzés. In: Loránd Benkő (ed.), *A magyar nyelv történeti nyelvtana I*, 188–258. Budapest: Akadémiai Kiadó.

Szegfű, Mária (1992): A névszóképzés. In: Loránd Benkő (ed.), *A magyar nyelv történeti nyelvtana II/1*, 268–320. Budapest: Akadémiai Kiadó.

Szikszainé, Nagy Irma (1993): *Az ikerítés helye, szerepe, szabályszerűségei a magyar nyelvben*. Budapest: Magyar Nyelvtudományi Társaság.

Zelliger, Erzsébet (1991): A szóösszetétel. In: Loránd Benkő (ed.), *A magyar nyelv történeti nyelvtana I*, 523–552. Budapest: Akadémiai Kiadó.

T. Szabó, Csilla (2003): *A deverbális igeképzés a XVI–XVIII. században az Erdélyi magyar szótörténeti tár adatanyaga alapján*. Kolozsvár: Erdélyi Múzeum-Egyesület kiadása.

Claus Schönig

25 Historical word-formation in Turkish

Abstract: The aim of the present article is to provide an overview of the history of Turkish word-formation. After a brief outline of the development and structure of the Turkic language family and a short history of research on this topic, the article presents the different kinds of word-formation strategies in Turkish and their historical development. The main focus is on the history of Turkish and its forerunners in western Asia Minor. The article concentrates on the continuity of many derivational suffixes throughout the historical development of Turkish, but at the same time tries to demonstrate individual features of this member of the Western Wing of Western Oghuz Turkic. Ottoman was the language of a multilingual empire and Turkish still is the most influential Turkic language. In addition this article tries to underscore the role of the influence of contact-languages, especially of the languages of the various "minorities" as well as the manipulations by language reformers, especially the "Türk Dil Kurumu" (Turkish Language Foundation)

1 Introduction

Turkish, the standard language of the Turkish Republic (*Türkiye Cumhuriyeti*) (see also Wilkens 2016), is a member of the Western Wing of Western Oghuz; it is based on the sociolect of the intellectuals of Istanbul and gained much (most?) of its modern shape during the last two hundred years. Together with Azeri, the dialects of the Eastern Wing of Western Oghuz, Khorasan Turkic, and Eastern Oghuz Turkmen, Turkish and associated dialects form the Oghuz branch of Turkic; Gagauz (cf. Menz 2016) is a member of the European part of the Western Wing of Western Oghuz under strong Indo-European (mainly Slavic) influence. The

Claus Schönig, Berlin, Germany

https://doi.org/10.1515/9783111420530-025

Oghuz branch of Turkic is part of Central Turkic (like most of the modern Turkic languages). The history of the Oghuz language can be traced back by texts to the Old Ottoman (sometimes called Old Anatolian Turkish) from the late thirteenth century, i.e. to the beginning of the Middle Turkic period. The sources of the Ancient Turkic period are attested in the Old Turkic sources of the early eighth to the thirteenth century in Runiform, Soghdian, Manichaean, Syrian, Uighur, Tibetan, Brahmi, etc. scripts; Arabic script has probably been used since the late Ancient Turkic period. It is still not possible to connect the Oghuz of the Middle and Ancient Turkic periods with specific sources of the Old Turkic corpus. None of the Old Turkic sources shows specific traces of Oghuz, but most exhibit some features which have only survived in Oghuz (besides features common to many modern Turkic languages). In this article I try to present the various techniques of word-formation of Turkish and connect them to their place within the diachronic and areal landscape of Turkic.

The morphemes are written according to Turkological tradition, i.e. the sounds which change depending on vowel harmony and position are noted with capital letters. Thus, we have *A* = *a*, *e*; *I* = *ı*, *i*, *u*, *ü*; *C* = *c*, *ç*; *D* = *d*, *t*; *K* = *k*, *g*, *ğ*. For Old Turkic: *G* = *g*, *gh* [ɣ], *k*, *q*; *O* = *o*, *ö*; *U* = *u*, *ü*; *V* = any vowel.

2 History of research

The Near Eastern (Arabic) tradition has produced the enormous dictionary of Kashgari (*Dīwān Luġāt at-Turk*) in the eleventh century (see Dankoff and Kelly 1982; Schönig 2007) and some Mamluk Kipchak works from the thirteenth to the fifteenth centuries. Even if these surveys are far away from modern linguistic standards, they give precious information about the development of Turkic, but unfortunately not of the forerunner of Ottoman-Turkish.

The history of the systematic research on Ottoman-Turkish and thus on Turkish word-formation begins with manuals, collections of sentences and idioms, etc., often composed by European merchants, travelers, soldiers or diplomats in the Ottoman Empire and other Turkic regions mainly since the fifteenth century. There follows the literature dedicated, for instance, to the "Scythian languages" (from the eighteenth century on), the "Ural-Altaic languages" (from the nineteenth century on) and the "Altaic languages" (mainly from the nineteenth century on). The interest in Turkic word-formation increased with the discovery of the oldest Turkic inscriptions, the so-called Orkhon inscription in Mongolia and their decipherment by the Danish scholar Vilhelm Thomsen in the 1890es. The interest especially in Turkish word-formation was nourished by the development of Turkish “nationalism” which became politically important at the beginning of the twentieth century during the last years of the decline of the Ottoman Empire. With the breakdown of the Ottoman Empire after World War I and the political dominance of Mustafa Kemal Atatürk since 1924, word-formation was one of the main instruments of language “purification” in the cultural struggle against Islamic influence as well as against other foreign (European and American) lexical influence (as a part of the nation-building process within the Turkish Republic). This political background has constituted a heavy burden for serious scholars in Turkey until today.

The scientific investigation of Turkish word-formation is still not sufficiently developed. At present there is no reliable monographic investigation on this topic. The chapters on word-formation in grammars of modern Turkish are highly incomplete and mostly depend on outdated investigations and descriptions; a reliable grammar of at least one phase of the 600 year history of the Ottoman language is not even in sight. An important contribution to the investigation of Turkic word-formation was Erdal (1991) which still must be considered a milestone in this field of Turkology. In the field of modern Turkish the grammar by Kononov (1956) deserves mention, which covers a wide range of linguistic information of various types. Furthermore, there is the grammar of Lewis (1967), a short but very concise work with many important notes and interesting details; many examples in this article are taken from this remarkable work. Of the Turkish works dealing with word-formation, the enormous grammar of Korkmaz (2009) tries to incorporate the knowledge collected in previous works; it contains a good bibliography which can be used for further investigations in the field of Turkish studies on word-formation.

If we compare the materials from the different stages of Turkic and Turkish language development, we find numerous derivational elements which are still present in modern Turkish. Some of them show certain changes in function. But because the Ottoman written language is very conservative, thus concealing changes that have taken place in the spoken language, it is often impossible to say when these changes took place. Some of the old suffixes seem to have vanished and then have been subsequently revived during the Kemalist language reform (sometimes with a different meaning). Therefore, we are far away from being able to write a detailed history of Turkish word-formation: it is still impossible to treat the techniques and tools of word-derivation in chronological order.

3 Word-formation from Proto-Turkic to the modern Turkic languages

Turkish as a member of the Turkic language family mainly uses derivation by suffixes as the central instrument of word-formation. Furthermore, we find compounding, (complete and incomplete) reduplication and echoing. These means of word-formation are already attested in the Old Turkic sources and can sometimes be reconstructed for Proto-Turkic period(s) much older than the Ancient Turkic period.

Some derivatives exhibit phonetic (and prosodic) peculiarities in addition to suffixation and compounding, most of which can be explained as secondary effects of derivational processes. The double *n* in the originally affectionate form *anne* 'dear mother' (in Modern Turkish just 'mother') can be explained by expressive (emotional) pronunciation, the palatalization goes back to a diminutive suffix *-y* (added to older *ana* 'mother') and thus can be explained on the phonetic level. They are not due to "inflectional" elements in Turkic derivation like the kind of *ablaut* which appears in connection with plural of personal pronouns and demonstratives and cannot be explained by phonetic processes; comparable phenomena can be found in neighboring language families like Mongolic and Tungusic.

Prefixation appears under the influence of Indo-European languages (mainly Persian); for the use of prefix-like elements in neologistic derivations see section 3.3.

3.1 Derivation by suffixes

3.1.1 Formation of nouns and adjectives

a) Denominal derivatives

Derivation by use of suffixes is the most common means of word-formation in all Turkic languages and thus most probably also in Proto-Turkic. By means of internal reconstruction based on comparative historical investigations we can reconstruct a comprehensive system of derivational suffixes.

There seems to be an old suffix *-(I)z* which appears in designations of paired parts of the body, e.g., *ağız* 'mouth' (perhaps originally 'lips'?), *diz* 'knee', *göğüz* 'breast', *göz* 'eye', *omuz* 'shoulder blade'. Furthermore, we find derivations from numerals like *ikiz* 'twin' from *iki* 'two' (see below in this section). Perhaps *yıldız* < *yulduz* 'star' belongs here, too. This leads to the conclusion that *-(I)z* is a kind of collective or plural suffix which designates things which normally do not appear as single units. It may be compared with the *-(I)z* of the plural forms of the personal pronouns and the corresponding possessive suffixes of the first and second person which may be called a personal plural sign, see *ben(-[I]m)* 'I/my' : *biz(-[I]mIz)* 'we/our' and *sen(-[I]n)* 'you/your-SG': *siz(-[I]nIz)* 'you/your-PL'.

The non-harmonic suffix *-gil* (sometimes *-giller* with a nominal plural suffix) may be treated as a special plural suffix (sometimes reinforced by the current plural suffix) which creates designations for the family community of a person from a personal name, a kinship term, a title, etc., see *Mehmet-gil(ler)* 'Mehmet and his family', *Komutan-gil(ler)* 'the commander and his family'. The nominal plural suffix *-lAr* used with nouns bearing a numeral attribute works as a determiner and creates individual names, e.g., *on iki ada* 'twelve islands', *on iki adalar* 'The Twelve Islands, i.e. The Dodekanes', *kırk haramiler* 'The Forty Thieves', etc.

We still find the expressions *oğlan* 'boy' and *eren* 'man' which are said to contain an old collective suffix *-An*; in Turkish these words are used as singular forms.

The suffix *-lIK* is used to create abstract nouns, cf. *ağır* 'heavy' → *ağırlık* 'weight', *bir* 'one' → *birlik* 'unity'. The suffix *-lIK* also produces purposive adjectives, e.g., *kira* 'hire' → *kiralık* 'for hire', *göz* 'eye' → *gözlük* 'glasses', *şehit* 'martyr' → *şehitlik* 'military cemetery, martyrdom'. The suffix can also be added to locative case forms, see *yüzde* 'in a hundred' → *yüzdelik* 'percentage', *günde* 'in the day' → *gündelik* 'daily wage', *şimdi* 'now' → *şimdilik* 'for the present', etc.

The non-harmonic suffix *-Daş* is used to form personal nouns which have something in common with each other, e.g., *meslek* 'profession' → *meslektaş* 'colleague', *vatan* 'motherland' → *vatandaş* 'compatriot', *yol* 'way' → *yoldaş* 'companion'. Cf. also *arkadaş* 'comrade' going back to Old Turkic *arka* 'backing, support'.

The essentially denominal agent noun-suffix *-CI* is one of the most successful common suffixes of Turkic and Mongolic; from these groups the suffix reached many other languages of different language families, e.g., Balkan Slavic and the Tungus languages. It is attested very early, e.g., in Tabghach (a kind of Proto-Mongolic) for the fifth and sixth century as *-Cin*, e.g., *bitig* 'writing' (← *bitigçin* 'scribe'); see also Middle Mongolic *Temüçin* 'blacksmith' (← *temür* 'iron' + *-Cin*), the personal name of Chenggis Khan. As we can see from *bitigçin*, the suffix has been combined since earliest times with a verbal noun (in *-G*) to derive a complex suffix to designate agent nouns of the structure *X(-G)* + *-CI* 'who/what does X' of a verbal stem with the meaning 'X' in Turkic and the Mongolic languages. The old agent noun in *-(I)GcI* appears as *-(y)IcI*, e.g., *yaz-ıcı* 'writer', *temizle-yici* 'cleaner'. The suffix *-CI* appears very frequently for actors of different types, e.g., *iş* 'work' → *işçi* 'worksman', *balık* 'fish' → *balıkçı* 'fisherman', *yol* 'way' → *yolcu* 'traveller', *milliyet* 'nationality' → *milliyetçi* 'nationalist', *toptan* 'wholesale' → *toptancı* 'wholesaler', cf. also *ne* 'what?' → *neci* 'of what profession?', etc.

Of the diminutive suffixes mainly *-CIK* and to a certain extent-*CAGIz* are used, e.g., *kuşçuk* 'little bird' (← *kuş* 'bird'), *evcik* 'little house' (← *ev* 'house'), *kızcağız* 'dear little girl' (← *kız* 'girl'), *hayvancağız* 'poor little creature' (← *hayvan* 'animal'). With personal names and kinship terms it is used to express an affectionate meaning, often combined with the possessive suffix of the first person singular, see *kızcığım* 'my dear girl', *Aliciğim* 'my dear Ali', etc. The diminutive form *Mehmetçik* became a synonym for the common soldier. Other diminutive forms of personal names are of the type *Mehmet* → *Memiş*, *Fatma* → *Fatoş*, *Hasan* → *Haso*, *Ibrahim* → *Ibo*. It also combines with adjectives in *-CA* (see below in this section) to express approximative meaning, e.g., *genişçecik* 'pretty wide' (← *geniş* 'wide') and *yakıncacık* 'pretty near' (← *yakın* 'near') (cf. Lewis 1967: 58). Other suffixes like *-CAK* and *-AK* are no longer used actively, e.g., (older) *küçücek* (besides *küçücük*) 'very small' (← *küçük* 'small') and the old petrified forms *başak* 'ear of corn; lit. little head' (← *baş* 'head') and *taşak* 'testicle; lit. little stone' (← *taş* 'stone'); for *-AK* see Erdal (1991: 40).

Furthermore, Turkish exhibits the suffixes *-lA* and *-lAK* to derive place nouns, e.g., *yayla* 'summer pasture' (← *yay* (old) 'summer'), *kışlak* 'winter settlement' (← *kış* 'winter').

The sociative suffix *-lI* expresses the presence and the privative suffix *-sIz* the absence of the referent of the base noun, e.g., *atlı* 'with horse, having a horse', *evli* 'married; lit. having a house(-hold)', *hız* 'speed' → *hızlı* 'rapid', *sevgi* 'affection' → *sevgili* 'beloved'; *atsız* 'without horse, being without horse', *sensiz* 'without you' (from *at* 'horse', *ev* 'house', *sen* 'you-SG'). The suffix *-lI* is also used to derive ethnic adjectives and inhabitant names, e.g., *Polonyalı* 'Pole, from Poland', *İsviçreli* 'Swiss (noun), from Switzerland', *Berlinli* 'Berliner', *köylü* 'villager, peasant'. The expression *Türkiyeli* 'from, of the Turkish Republic' was used to designate political groups of different beliefs; in the East of Turkey it is used to designate persons connected with the Turkish state.

The suffix *-ki* has a pronominal *-n*, which appears in oblique cases, as in the demonstrative pronouns *bu(n-)*, *şu(n-)* and *o(n-)* (in older Ottoman language *ol*, oblique stem *an-*), the third person possessive suffix *-(s)I(n)-*, and *kendi* 'self', alternatively as *-y* with the impersonal interrogative pronoun *ne* 'what?'; it normally is non-harmonic and keeps its *k* in intervocalic position. The suffix *-ki* can be added to adverbial expressions of time to derive relational adjectives, see *bugün* 'today' → *bugünkü* 'of today', *dün* 'yesterday' → *dünkü* 'of yesterday', etc. It can also be added to genitives, e.g., *anneminki* 'my mother's' and is used to derive possessive pronouns, see *benimki* 'mine', *bizimki* 'ours', *onlarınkı* 'theirs'. The suffix *-ki* can also be added to locatives, e.g., *köprüdeki* '(located) on the bridge' (← *köprü-de* 'on the bridge'), *İstanbul'daki* '(located) in Istanbul', (*senin*) *yanındaki* '(being) on your-SG side' (← *yan-ın-da* 'on your side; lit. side-yours-on'). The postposition *aşağı* 'lower (part)' is an old derivation and contains the suffix *-ki* in a harmonic form.

The suffix *-CA*, a kind of similative suffix (in Turkologic terminology: equative suffix) is sometimes treated as a "secondary case suffix"; in contradistinction to case, plural and possessive suffixes it never takes the stress, e.g., *erkekçe* 'masculine, like a man' (← *erkek* 'male'), *kadınca* 'feminine, like a woman' (← *kadın* 'woman'), *onca* 'according to him/her/it' (← *o* 'he, she, it'). The suffix *-CA* is also used to derive adjectives from designations for nationalities, cultures, religions, etc.; as nouns the *-CA*-derivatives are used to designate languages, e.g., *Türkçe* 'Turkish', *Almanca* 'German', *İngilizce* 'English'. With adjectives the suffix expresses approximative meaning, see *güzel* 'nice, good' → *güzelce* 'quite nice, quite good', *uzun* 'long' → *uzunca* 'rather long'. (For derivatives in *-CA* + diminutive *-CIK* see above.) It is also attached to verbal nouns in *-mA* to derive some nouns like *bilmece* 'riddle' (← *bilme* 'knowing'), *bulmaca* 'puzzle' (← *bulma* 'finding'), *çekmece* 'drawer' (← *çekme* 'drawing').

The old comparative suffix *-(I)rAK* was given up in late Ottoman, but has survived in Turkish word-formation. Here we find forms like *küçürek* 'rather small' (← *küçük* 'small'), *bozrak* 'light grey' (← *boz* 'grey'), *ufurak* 'rather tiny' (← *ufuk* 'tiny'), cf. Lewis (1967: 57). It appears in the suffix *-(I)mtrAK* which mainly combines with adjectives which denote colours, tastes, etc., to form approximative derivatives, see *yeşilimtrak* 'greenish' (← *yeşil* 'green'), *ekşimtrak* 'sourish' (← *ekşi* 'sour'). Other suffixes (expressing similarity) are *-sI* and *-(I)msI* as in *erkeksi* 'mannish' (← *erkek* 'male'), *çocuksu* 'childish' (← *çocuk* 'child'), *duvarımsı* 'wall-like' (← *duvar* 'wall'), etc.

The suffix *-CIl* is added to nouns and derives adjectives which express some kind of orientation or connection to the referent of the base noun, e.g., *ölüm* 'death' → *ölümcül* 'moribund', *ben* 'I' → *bencil* 'selfish', *ev* 'house' → *evcil* 'domesticated'.

Adjectives designating colours take some special suffixes to derive personal nouns like, e.g., *sarışın* 'a blonde' (← *sarı* 'yellow'). An old denominal suffix *-(I)s* has survived in *maviş* 'a blonde and blue-eyed girl' (← *mavi* 'blue'), see Erdal (1991: 105).

The old suffix *-mAn* signalizes intensification, see the adjective *kocaman* 'huge' (← *koca* 'big'). In the Kemalist language reform, it was used to derive nouns like *okutman* 'lecturer' (← *okut-* 'to make read' (deverbal!)), *eroinmen* 'addicted to heroin' (← *eroin* 'heroin'). Another suffix revived by the reformers is *-kAn* used to create "names of divine beings, honorifics and the like" (Erdal 1991: 76), see *başkan* 'president' (← *baş* 'head'). The old suffix *-sIG* has been revived under regular loss of the final *G* in forms like the proper name *Tansu* 'resembling the dawn' from *tan* 'dawn'.

Finally, worth mentioning is the derivation of spatial, temporal and abstract adverbial expressions. Some spatial nouns took a suffix *-rA*, e.g., *içre* 'in' (← *iç* 'inner part') which is found today only in archaizing language, as in *cihan içre* 'in the world' – cf. Lewis (1967: 85) and *taşra* 'province (as an invective); everywhere outside Istanbul'. The form *üz(e)re* mainly appears with verbal nouns in *-mAK* (infinitives) to express 'to be about', but see also *yol üzere* 'on the road'. The form *sonra* 'after' is frequently used. The postpositions *beri* 'since; this side of' and (rare) *ötürü* 'because of' exhibit the old directive suffix *-rU* which seems to be contained in the old directive suffix *-GArU*. This suffix has survived in derivatives like *içeri* 'inside', *dışarı* 'outside' and *yukarı* 'upper side'.

b) Deverbal derivatives

As to deverbal derivations, some participles are petrified and used as nouns, e.g., *tanı-dık* 'acquaintance' (← *tanı-* 'to be acquainted with'), *gel-ir* 'income' (← *gel-* 'to come'). We also find adjectival use of the so-called aorist participles which go back to their old use as predicates of relative clauses, see *akar su* 'running water' (← *ak-* 'to flow') (petrified and/or dialectal). Today we find many negative passive forms like *bilinmez* 'unknown' (← *bilin-* 'to be known'), *beklenmez* 'unexpected' (← *beklen-* 'to be awaited'), *inanılmaz* 'unbelievable' (← *inanıl-* 'to be believed'), etc. The form *olur* (← *ol-* 'to become; to be') is also used to express 'all right! O.K.!'. The active participle in *-(y)An* appears in collocations like *geçen yıl* 'last year' and *geçen hafta* 'last week' (← *geç-* 'to pass') but also in lexicalized forms like *bakan* 'minister' (← *bak-* 'to look'). The future participle in *-(y)AcAK* is used in *içecek* 'something to drink' and *yiyecek* 'something to eat' (from *iç-* 'to drink', *ye-* 'to eat'). Petrified forms of the perfect participle are, e.g., *okumuş* 'educated' (from *oku-* 'to read'), etc.

In Turkish we find *yemiş* for 'fruit' and *yazmış* 'fate, destiny' (in older and regional sources sometimes *durmuş* 'life') from *ye-* 'to eat', *yaz-* 'to write', *dur-* 'to stand'. These words were probably derived in an early (Ancient Turkic) period, when the participle in *-mIş* was used in a way different from its modern usage in Turkish. For *yemiş* we may assume an underlying meaning 'what one eats', for *yazmış* 'what one (God) has written (e.g., on one's forehead)', for *durmuş* 'what (the time) one stays (alive)'.

The deverbal form in *-mA* functions like the *-mIş*-forms mentioned above in the meaning of result nouns, e.g., *dövme* 'tattoo; lit. what one has beaten'. Such derivations often occur in kitchen vocabulary, e.g., *sarma* 'wrap; lit. what one has wrapped', *kıyma* 'minced meat; lit. what one has minced', *dondurma* 'ice cream; lit. what one has caused to freeze', *asmaköprü* 'hanging bridge; lit. bridge which one has hung'. If the verb contained in the *-mA*-forms is transitive, the derivation designates the state which an internal argument (the object in an active clause with the transitive verb in the predicate) takes on if the action expressed by the verb is applied to it. If the verb is intransitive, the derivation designates the external argument (the subject in an active clause with the intransitive verb in the predicate), e.g., *dönme* 'one who converted [to Islam]' and *dolma* 'stuffed (wine leaves, egg-plants, etc.); lit. what has become full'.

The old adjective suffix *-(I)K*, *-AK* < *-(O)k* produces derivatives with a meaning comparable to that of the passive/resultative meaning of *-mA*-forms, see *bozuk* 'spoiled' (← *boz-* 'to spoil' ← *buz-*), *kırık* 'broken' (← *kır-* 'to break (into pieces)'), *ürkek* 'timid' (← *ürk-* 'to shy'), etc. The old suffix *-(I)G* has become *-I*, e.g., *dolu* 'full' (← *dol-* 'to be filled'), *ölü* 'dead' (← *öl-* 'to die'); a good part of these derivatives are used as nouns, see *koşu* 'race' (← *koş-* 'to run'), *yapı* 'construction' (← *yap-* 'to make, build'), *korku* 'fear' (← *kork-* 'to fear'). In the case of base verbs ending in vowels the derivative looks like the verbal stem, see *kuru* 'dry' (← *kuru-* 'to become dry').

Semantically the same type of derivatives are produced by the old noun suffixes *-tI* (*belirti* 'symptom' ← *belir-* 'to appear'), *-(I)ntI* (*akıntı* 'stream' ← *ak-* 'to flow'), *-(I)t* (*geçit* 'passage' ← *geç-* 'to pass') and the quite frequent *-(I)m* (*ölüm* 'death' ← *öl-* 'to die', *yudum* 'a swallow, mouthful' ← *yut-* 'to swallow'). The suffix *-GI* may also be mentioned here, see: *çalgı* 'musical instrument' (← *çal-* 'to play an instrument'), *içki* 'alcoholic drink' (← *iç-* 'to drink'), *sevgi* 'affection' (← *sev-* 'to love'). The suffix *-(I)n* appears in very old derivatives like *san* 'number' (← Old Turkic *sa-* 'to think, count'). Of course, the language reformers made use of these suffixes to create, e.g., *yazıt* 'inscription' (← *yaz-* 'to write'), *basım* 'printing', *basın* 'the Press' (← *bas-* 'to press').

Deverbal instrument and place nouns can be derived by means of the suffix *-AK*, see *durak* 'stopping place' (← *dur-* 'to stand'), *batak* 'swamp' (← *bat-* 'to sink'), *elek* 'sifter' (← *ele-* 'to sieve'). Another type of instrument noun became very popular among the Kemalist reformers, the nouns in *-GIc* (< Old Turkic *-GUc*) and *-GAç*, see the (most probably) neologistic expressions *dalgıç* 'diver' (← *dal-* 'to plunge') and *süzgeç* 'filter' (← *süz-* 'to filter'); for denominal *dumangaç* see below in this section. Of Kipchak (Tatar) origin are neologistic verbal nouns in *-(A)v* like *söylev* 'speech' (← *söyle-* 'to speak') and *görev* 'obligation' (← *gör-* 'to see'). The suffix *-(A)y* was another favorite of the language reformers who created words like *yatay* 'horizontal' (← *yat-* 'to lie') and *yüzey* 'surface' (← *yüz* 'face'; denominal!).

The adjectives in *-(I)nç* denote a characteristic feature expressed or caused by a verbal action, e.g., *gülünç* 'ridiculous' (← *gül-* 'to laugh'), *korkunç* 'terrible' (← *kork-* 'to fear'); *kıskanç* 'jealous' (← *kıskan-* 'to envy'). The suffix *-GIn* expresses the resultant state of an action, see *kızgın* 'glowing; upset' (← *kız-* 'to become heated'), *bitkin* 'exhausted' (← *bit-* 'to come to an end').

The deverbal suffix *-GAn* is used to derive adjectives with active meaning, partially combined with the meaning of inclination: *çalışkan* 'busy' (← *çalış-* 'to work'), *ısırgan* 'itchy' (← *ısır-* 'to bite'). Probably, this suffix originally designated a kind of present participle and became re-categorized as a derivational suffix during the formative phase of Western Oghuz at the beginning of the Middle Turkic period since the Chinggisid Mongol expansion in the thirteenth century. Western Oghuz materials of these times exhibit a present participle in *-AGAn*; the language reformers used this suffix to produce *Öztürkçe* ("pure Turkish") forms like *olağan* 'regular' (from *ol-* 'to become; to be').

3.1.2 Formation of numerals and pronouns

In Turkish (as in most of the remaining modern Turkic languages) the cardinal numerals exhibit the same shape and structure as in the Old Turkic sources. The numbers from one to five (*bir, iki, üç, dört, beş*) and the tens from ten to fifty (*on, yirmi* [< *yigirmi*], *otuz, kırk, elli*), *yüz* 'hundred' and *bin* 'thousand' are individual designations which are structurally independent from each other, i.e. they do not exhibit any formal connection. The numerals *altı* 'six' and *yedi* 'seven' end in **...tI*. The designations for the tens, *altmış* 'sixty' and *yetmiş* 'seventy', have replaced the final *I* by *-mIş*; they may go back to *...I* + *mIş*-forms in which the final *I* was later dropped. The forms *sekiz* 'eight' and *dokuz* 'nine' are combined with *on* 'ten' to designate the corresponding tens 'eighty' and 'ninety': *seksen* (Old Turkic *sekiz on*) and *doksan* (Old Turkic *tokuz on*). The designations for higher potencies of ten like *milyon* 'million', *milyar* 'billion' are borrowed from French.

The numerals and the corresponding interrogative pronoun *kaç* 'how much?, how many?' take a special set of suffixes like the ordinal suffix *-ncI* and the distributive suffix *-(ş)Ar*, see *iki* 'two', *ikinci* 'second', *ikişer* 'two (of each)', *on* 'ten', *onuncu* 'tenth', *onar* 'ten (of each)'; see also *kaçıncı* 'how many' and *kaçar* 'how many of each'. The expression *son* 'end; last' can take the ordinal suffix (*sonuncu* 'the last'); *ilk* 'first' may be used instead of *birinci* (← *bir* 'one'). The suffix *-(I)z* (see section 3.1.1) is used to derive designations like *ikiz* 'twin', mostly used with the plural suffix as *ikizler*; see also *üçüzler* 'triplets' (← *üc* 'three'), *dördüzler* 'quadruplets' (← *dört* 'four'), etc. To derive names of polygons we find the neologistic suffix *-gen* (always with *g*, even after voiceless consonants; probably inspired by *-gon* in designations like Fr. *octogone*, G. *Oktogon*), see *üçgen* 'triangle', *dörtgen* 'quadrangle'.

The demonstrative pronouns *bu*, *şu* and *o* show derivatives of the type *böyle*, *şöyle* and *öyle* 'so, such'. Furthermore, the demonstrative pronouns and the impersonal interrogative pronoun *ne* 'what' exhibit derivatives in *-ra*/*-re* to designate corresponding pronouns with local meaning, i.e. *bura-*, *şura-*, *ora-*, and *nere-*; in combination with the dative, locative and ablative suffix they are used to ask for directions, places and starting points. These local pronouns are a typically (modern) Oghuz feature. It is absent in the sources of the Ancient Turkic period. Both the *böyle*, etc. and the *bura*, etc. pronouns can take the possessive suffix of the third person *-I* (*-s-I* after a vowel) and thus become nouns, e.g., *böylesi* 'such a person, this sort of person', *burası Türkiye* 'this here is Turkey'. In the same way *kimi* 'some' is derived from *kim* 'who?'.

The numeral *bir* is used as the base of the indefinite pronouns *biri* and *birisi* 'one, some (of ...)' which are derived by a single and a double possessive suffix of the third person; see also *kimisi* 'some people'. The form *hepsi* 'all (of ...)' is also derived by means of a double possessive suffix, but has lost the *i* of the middle syllable; for other indefinite pronouns see section 3.3. Of the same origin perhaps we find the *-si* in *evvelsi gün* 'the day before yesterday'.

Turkish (like the other Turkic languages) has a set of s p a t i a l n o u n s like *iç* 'inner part' (older *dahil*), *dış* (Old Turkic *taş*; older *hariç*) 'outer part', *üst* 'top', *alt* 'underside', *ara* 'space between', *arka*, *art* 'back', etc.; many of these nouns (especially in older stages of the Turkish-Ottoman language development) are of foreign origin (mainly borrowings from Arabic-Persian), e.g., *etraf* 'surroundings' (modern: *çevre*). This type of noun has played an important role in the orientational system of Turkic since the earliest periods. The form *son* 'end' has a spatial as well as a temporal meaning. For a t e m p o r a l relation like 'before' we find the neologistic derivation *önce* which has replaced *evvel* (a borrowing from Arabic via Persian, originally 'first'). Beside spatial and temporal nouns there is a third category of nouns to designate abstract relations like *hak* 'concern' (Arabic via Persian *haqq* 'right') and *taraf* 'by' (originally 'side'), e.g., *benim hakkımda* 'concerning me; lit. 1PERS-GEN concern1POSS+LOC', *devlet tarafından* 'by the state; lit. state side3POSS+ABL'. Formally, they represent a combination of compounding and suffixation.

3.1.3 Verb formation

In the field of verbal word-formation we do not have the same number of functional suffixes. Thus we find the denominal suffix *-lA-* (and its diathetical derivations in *-lAş-*, *-lAn-*, *-lAt-*, etc.) already known from Old Turkic and the other Turkic languages. Furthermore, denominal verb suffixes like *-(A)r-* (from designations of colours, see *ağar-* 'to become white' ← *ak-* 'white'), *-A-* (*kana-* 'to bleed' ← *kan* 'blood') and *-(I)k-* (*gecik-* 'to be late' ← *geç* 'late') have survived. A suffix *-Al-* appears, for instance, in *azal-* 'to decrease' (← *az* 'few') and *yüksel-* 'to increase' (← *yüksek* 'high' (with loss of the final *k*)).

As in other Turkic languages onomatopoetic verbs can be derived by a suffix *-gIr-*, see *bağır-* 'to shout', *çağır-* 'to call'. Of the verbs called simulative by Erdal ('to be A' or 'to pretend to be A') we find *-(I)msA-*, see *iyimse-* 'to be optimistic' (← *iyi* 'good'). The old desiderative *-sA-* is also still detectable, e.g., *susa-* 'to be thirsty' (← *su* 'water').

We also find suffixes indicating aktionsarten like *-(I)klA-*, *-ala-* and *-(I)ştIr-*. They specify phases of an action, the execution of an action in small consecutive steps (which may be accompanied by an intensification), or the repetition of an action. In modern Turkish the examples for *-AlA-* which appears as *-gAlA-* in other Turkic languages and older stages of development are very limited, e.g., *şaş-* 'to be astonished' → *şaşala-* 'to be bewildered'. For *-(I)klA-* cf. *it-* 'to push' → *itikle-* 'to manhandle', *sür-* 'to drive' → *sürükle-* 'to drag', *uyu-* 'to sleep' → *uyukla-* 'to keep dozing off', etc. The form *-(I)ştIr-* is by far more common, e.g., *ara-* 'to search' → *araştır-* 'to investigate' (i.e. 'to perform a series of searchings'), *sür-* 'to smear' → *sürüştür-* 'to put on make-up' (i.e. 'to perform a series of smearings') (see Lewis 1967: 148).

The diathetical, i.e. valency-changing suffixes are *-(I)l-* (passive), *-(I)n-* (reflexive, passive), *-(I)t-*, *-(I)r-*, *-Ar-*, *-DIr-*, etc. (causative) and *-(I)ş-* (reciprocal-cooperative). The reciprocal-cooperative suffix *-(I)ş-* does not show any special features. The suffix *-n-* is used as a passive suffix on verbs in *-l-* (because a sequence *-l-l-* is forbidden by the rules of euphony), e.g., *al-ın-* 'to be taken', *böl-ün-* 'to be divided'; see also the deverbal forms in *-lAn-*. Verbs ending in a vowel take *-(I)n-*, too, see *oku-n-* 'to be read', *kapa-n-* 'to be shut'. Together with very short verbs like *de-* and *ye-* we find a complex suffix *-nIl-* which produces forms with meanings different from the passive forms in *-(I)n*.

Like the other Turkic languages, Turkish exhibits a whole variety of causative suffixes, *-(I)t-* (on polysyllabic stems in vowel, *l* and *r*), *-(I)r-* (on monosyllabic stems), *-Ar-* (only in a few verbs), *-DIr-* (remaining cases), etc. *-GUr-*, one of the Old Turkic causative suffixes has vanished because of the loss of *g* after the first syllable border during the development in the Oghuz branch of Turkic; it became more or less identical with *-(I)r-*. Many of the Old Turkic *-(I)t-*causatives are replaced by *-DIr-*. The form *göster-* 'to show' has survived from ancient times; due to phonetic developments we find *getir-* 'to bring' < *keltür-* 'to make come' (and under the influence of *götür-* 'to carry away') and *kaldır-* 'to raise, remove' (from *kalk-* 'to rise'). The old *-(I)z-*causatives have also vanished. For Old Turkic *emiz-* 'to suckle' we find *emzir-* (already in the Middle Turkic period), i.e. the causative meaning of the form is strengthened by adding a further and still comprehensible causative suffix. There are also some double causative forms with simple causative meaning, e.g., *de-dir-*, *de-dir-t-* 'to make say' and *kon-dur-*, *kon-dur-t-* 'to make settle'.

In the case of the modal gerund in *-(y)ArAk* we find the old comparative suffix *-(I)rAk* because the Western Oghuz cognate *-(y)A* of the Old Turkic vocalic gerund in *-(y)V* was too short to survive outside its use in biverbal forms like the possibilative in *-Abil*, i.e. a gerundial form of a verb and *bil-* 'to know'. The new gerund in *-(y)ArAk* carries the same function as the previous form in *-(y)V.* In contemporary Turkish, the old suffix *-(I)rAk* (still preserved in Old Ottoman and Modern Azeri) only functions to provide the short element *-(y)V* with more phonological substance. It has become a formal means to express an action which accompanies the main action, e.g., *şarkı söyleyerek eve döndü* 'singing a song he/she returned home'. Another denominal suffix, the equative suffix *-CA*, is part of the gerund in *-(y)IncA*. The Old Turkic gerund in *-(I)bAn* (still in Old Ottoman) seems to be composed of the gerund in *-(I)p* and an instrumental suffix. During the development from the languages of the Ancient Turkic to the languages of the New Turkic period and thus to Turkish, the instrumental is more or less petrified in adverbial forms like *yazın* 'in summer' from *yaz* 'summer' and the gerund in *-mAksIzIn* (Ottoman, rarely used in modern Turkic) consisting of the verbal noun (lexical infinitive) in *-mAk*, the privative suffix in *-sIz* and the instrumental in *-In*. It may have been helpful for the recategorization of the former instrumental case suffix as an adverbial derivational suffix that forms like *sabahleyin* 'in the morning' (consisting of *sabah* 'morning', the deverbal suffix for verb derivation *-lA-*, and the archaic gerund in *-yIn* which has only survived in petrified forms) sound the same and thus helped to establish a secondary category of "adverbs in *-In*".

The gerund in *-(y)A* is used to derive postpositions like *göre* 'according to' (from *gör-* 'to see') and *bile* 'even' (from *bil-* 'to know').

3.1.4 Word-formation and borrowing

Persian suffixes like *-baz*, *-ban*, *-perest*, *-perver*, *-istan* appear in borrowings such as *sekban* 'dog-keeper (a kind of Ottoman military police)' (from Persian *sag* 'dog' + *bān* 'keeper'), *botperest* 'idolator' (from Persian *but* 'idol' + *parast* 'adorator, admirer'); some forms were replaced during the Kemalist language reform by *Öztürkçe*-forms, e.g., *vatanperver* by *yurtsever* (Arabic *vatan* 'patria; fatherland', Persian *perver* 'one who likes', *yurt* (neologistic) for *vatan*, *sever* 'one who loves' from *sev-* 'to love'). The suffix *-istan* to derive designations for countries like *Hırvatistan* 'Croatia', *Yunanistan* 'Greece' can still be used for ad hoc-derivations.

Because many (relational) adjectives for new ideas, inventions, discoveries, etc. borrowed from French into Ottoman-Turkish ended in *-Ik*, it is regarded as something like a suffix for deriving adjectives, see *demokratik, minik, pratik, turistik*; the same holds true for *-ist* denoting an adherent of a religious, political, etc. program, e.g., *sosyalist, faşist, Zionist, Kemalist, İslamist* and the abstract nouns in *-izm*, e.g., *sosyalizm, faşizm, Zionizm, Kemalizm, İslamizm.*

Already at the end of the nineteenth century, there were attempts to create expressions for newly developed or discovered things and concepts which were previously not so important, differentiated, relevant or even existent. Some reformers proposed to use not only the derivational elements of Turkic, but also of French and Arabic. In Ottoman the word *tayyare* 'airplane' was derived from Classical Arabic (from the root *ṭ-y-r* 'to fly', arranged according to the pattern *faʿʿāl* deriving a noun of the habitual (professional) actor, and a feminine suffix *-a* to form a sort of instrument noun) and then passed over to the living Arabic vernaculars and the modern standard language as a borrowing. A word like *uydurmasyon* 'fake' contains a Turkish verbal noun *uydurma* 'inventing' combined with a French suffix (*-ation*). Towards the end of the twentieth century, we find many examples for combinations of Turkish and Western language material in advertisements, e.g., *Halıdrom* for a large carpet (*halı*) store (in analogy to Western word coinings like *Motodrom* which itself is analogous to *Hippodrom*) and *Raksotek* (← *Raks*, a company name) for a place where they sell tapes, CDs, etc. (in analogy to *Discothek*). Especially in the language of educated young people we find spontaneous creations of Turkish and foreign elements as, for instance, *-et* (cf. Fr. *-ette*) in *Çapulet*, a pseudonym of a young woman as a reaction of Prime Minister Erdogan's use of *çapulcu* 'marauder' for the Gezi Park activists in 2013.

The Kemalist language reform which began in the late 1920es produced new material. Some of the new words were taken from Turkish dialects, from other Turkic languages and from Ottoman (sometimes erroneously). To compile a material base for the purification of modern Turkish great efforts were made to collect lexical material from the dialects spoken in the Turkish Republic which finally led to the composition of, e.g., the *Derleme Sözlüğü*, a dictionary of Turkish dialects. The search for Turkic words which had been replaced by Arabic-Persian borrowings from the sixteenth century on (e.g., *barış* 'peace', later *sulh*) resulted in the *Tarama Sözlüğü*, a dictionary of Ottoman words of Turkic origin. Unfortunately, some non-Turkic words, e.g., borrowings from Middle Mongolian passed over into *Öztürkçe* ("pure Turkish"), see *ülke* 'land, territory', *şölen* '(official) dinner' and the famous *kurultay* 'assembly'. From Old Ottoman *kurultay* 'assembly (of tribal nobility)' the suffix *-tay* has been deduced. (The form has been traced back to *kurul-* 'to be founded' from *kur-* 'to found', but *kurultay* is a borrowing from Middle Mongolic; it is derived from the verb *guru-* 'to assemble' by means of the suffix *-(I)lta* with a secondary form *-(I)ltay*.) The suffix was used to create designations of assemblies of people which are concerned with the same thing (from nouns and from verbs!), e.g., *sayıştay* 'Exchequer and Audit' (← *sayış-* 'to settle accounts'), *danıştay* 'Council of State' (← *danış-* 'consultation'), *yargıtay* 'Supreme court of appeal' (← *yargı* '(juridical) decision'), *çalıştay* 'workshop' (← *çalış-* 'to work, be busy').

Other lexical material is synthetic and sometimes formed according to rules which contradict the natural rules of sound development, areal distribution, morphological correctness, etymology, etc. Some expressions were accepted by the population, others were not (like *tütünsel dumangaç* 'cigarette' ← *tütün* 'tobacco' + *-sAl* 'belonging to, made of', *duman* 'smoke' + *-gAç* 'instrument'). The suffix *-sAl* (after *-z*, *-s* only *-Al*) was officially created on the basis of old words like *kumsal* 'sandy' from *kum* 'sand'; in fact, it seems to have been inspired by the French suffix *-al*. Derivations in *-sAl* were launched to replace older Arabic-Persian derivations like *siyasi* (in older spelling *siyasî*) 'political' from *siyaset* 'politic(s)', *dini* (*dinî*) 'religious' from *din* 'religion', *tarihi* (*tarihî*) from *tarih* 'history', some of which are still in use (as, e.g., in *tarihî otel* 'historical hotel'). The suffix caused some political (!) trouble in the 1970es and 1980es; but today forms like *siyasal* 'political', *tarihsel* 'historical', *fiziksel* 'physical' (from *fizik* 'physics'), *bilimsel* 'scientific' (from *bilim* 'science'), *özel* 'private' (from *öz* 'self') are commonly accepted.

The neologism *ortaç* 'participle' is probably influenced by German *Mittelwort* ('middle word', i.e. a word mediating between nominals and verbs) for 'participle'; for other traces of Indo-European inspiration in *Öztürkçe* see section 3.3.

The language reform then was slowed down by the *Güneş Dil Teorisi* ("Sun Language theory"), one of the absurdities which appeared in the context of language planning in the twentieth century. But until today the language reform goes on and has produced many new terms in the fields of technique, science, social and cultural developments, etc. Even if the roots of many *Öztürkçe* ("pure Turkish") forms have no solid etymological and morphological grounding, they have to be treated together with the natural, inherited material in a survey on modern Turkish derivation, because they are part of the linguistic reality of Turkish. For more details see Laut (2000) and Röhrborn (2003).

3.2 Derivation by prefixes and the Persian *ezafet*

Word-formation by prefixes is limited to borrowings. The most prominent elements are the Arabic prefix *bi-* 'with' (*bizzat* 'self, personally') and the Persian prefix *bi-* with privative meaning (*biaman* = *amansız* 'merciless' ← *aman* 'mercy'). For preposed nouns in *Öztürkçe* see section 3.3.

There exist some derivations in Turkish which are Persian *ezafet*-constructions; the lexical elements are often borrowings from Arabic as in *katl-i am* 'massacre, mass murder; lit. general murder/slaughter'. The pronominal form *bazı* from *ba'z-i* 'some of' belong here, too. Today it is treated like a regular pronoun, see *bazı insanlar* 'some people', *bazıları* 'some of them'.

The form *gayri* 'un-, non-' has fallen out of function but is still understood and used in special contexts, e.g., in *gayri Müslim* 'Non-Muslim' during a period of nostalgia for the Pre-World War I Istanbul and its minorities at the beginning of the twenty first century.

3.3 Compounding

Because Turkic has no suffixes to mark gender, the categories "masculine" and "feminine" in biological, social, metaphysical, etc. contexts have to be expressed by words like *dişi* 'female' (in later Ottoman and modern Turkish only for non-humans) and *erkek* 'male'. The sexual state of humans and domesticated animals is expressed by a set of nouns which designate species, gender (including castration, sterilization, etc.), and in most cases age of an entity. If female sex has to be attributed explicitly to an expression for humans, the nouns *kız* 'girl' and *kadın* 'woman' are used (see below in this section). The dichotomy of the designations for human females into a designation for an un-married and a married female, i.e. for a virgin and a "legal" ex-virgin, is typical for the treatment of sexuality in the (majority of the) Turkish (and related) society. Another reflex of this attitude is the use of *dul* for 'widow' as well as for 'divorced woman'.

Titles and specifications of kinship relations appear as preposed appositions, e.g., *Sultan Selim*, *Başbakan Erdoğan* 'Prime Minister Erdoğan', *Özlem'in eşi Özgür* 'Özlem's spouse Özgür'. In older layers of Turkic we find functional titles postponed (except *Sultan* for the ruling member of the dynasty), e.g., *Bilge Kagan* in Old Tukic and *Kemal Paşa*. The old way to address persons was *Mehmet Bey* (after the replacement of *efendi* by *bey*) and *Zühal Hanım*. This way of addressing a person is still alive and could not be replaced by the modernist *Bay Öztürk* 'Mr Öztürk' and *Bayan Öztürk* 'Ms Öztürk' (with "Western" placement of the term before the name). Whereas *bay* is attested very early in the meaning 'rich', *bayan* is a neologism without any etymological base. It seems that during the last years of the twentieth century the word *bayan* has replaced the word *kadın* in the language of the uneducated traditionalist parts of the population as a reference term for 'matured female', because it contains no statement to the marital status (with all its consequences) of the person concerned.

If the referent of the second noun consists of the referent of the first noun, the second noun does not take a possessive suffix, e.g., *taş köprü* 'stone bridge', *asfalt yol* 'asphalt road', *demir perde* 'iron curtain', *kadın doktor* 'female doctor', *kız talebe* 'girl student'.

The expressions *ana* and *baş* are also attached to other nouns without a possessive suffix, in the meaning 'basic, main, arch-, etc.', see *başkomutan* 'High Commander', *başbakan* 'Prime Minister', *anavatan* 'motherland'.

Already in the Old Turkic sources we find combinations of the so-called e z a f e t-type (a very unsatisfactory designation) *XY* + *-(s)I*, where two nouns *X* and *Y* are bound together by a possessive suffix of the third person on the second noun, e.g., *ev kapısı* 'house door', *kadın doktoru* 'gynaecologist', *posta kutusu* 'mail box'. A chain of three nouns has a possessive suffix only on the third noun, see *Alman Erkek Lisesi* 'German Boys' Lycée; lit. German male lycée-3POSS', *Türk Dil Kurumu* 'Turkish Language Society; lit. Turkish language society-3POSS'. Only a limited number of possessive-marked compounds can be used as the first element of another possessive-marked compound, e.g., *Diyanet İşleri Bakanlığı* 'Religion-affairs Ministry; lit. what belongs to religion affair-PL-3POSS ministry-3POSS', see Lewis (1967: 46). A part of these combinations consists of a specific name or designation followed by a noun which designates the category to which the specimen belongs, e.g., *elma ağacı* 'apple tree; apple tree-3POSS', *Salı günü* 'Tuesday; lit. Tuesday day-3POSS', etc. In the same way persons may be categorized, e.g., *Nuri çapkını* 'that rascal of a Nuri!; lit. Nuri rascal-3POSS'.

These compounds always express that the referent of the second noun is determined to serve in a more or less concrete sense for the referent of the first noun ('a door for a house', 'a doctor for medical treatment of women', 'a box in which letters can be placed'). Such compounds can even consist of a noun and the postposition *gibi* 'like' (with respect to quality), e.g., *İstanbul gibisi* 'something (a town) like Istanbul'; see also the substantivation in *bundan sonrası* 'that which is after this'.

Different from Old Turkic sources (and, e.g., modern Sayan Turkic, see Schönig 1999) designations for nations, regions and the like (*Türk*, *Alman*, *Rus*, etc.) in combination with a noun require a possessive suffix, e.g., *Türk halkı* 'the Turkish people; lit. Turkish people-3POSS', analogously *Alman ekmeği* 'German bread', *Rus kadınları* 'Russian women; lit. Russian woman-PL-3POSS', *İstanbul meyhaneleri* 'the wine houses of Istanbul; lit. Istanbul winehouse-PL-3POSS', etc.; for Old Turkic cf. *Türük bodun* 'the *Türk* people', Tuvan *Dıva tıl* 'Tuvan language' (without possessive suffix), but *Tavgaç eli* (with possessive suffix) 'Tavghach land, i.e. China' (Tonyukuk inscription, 8th century).

In some segments of the Turkish lexicon, e.g., in kitchen vocabulary, names of streets, quarters, etc. we can find combinations like *Adana kebap*, *Sultan kebap*, *Susam Sokak* 'Sesame Street', *Arnavutköy* 'quarter of Istanbul; lit. Albanian village' which should carry the possessive suffix, but do not. This may be due to the high percentage of Greek, Armenian, Ladino, etc., speaking population in those towns of the late Ottoman Empire in which modern gastronomy, street-naming, etc., developed under European (mainly French) influence in the nineteenth century. In the case of the names of the type X + *köy* 'village' we may assume a previous form X + *köyü* which lost its final vowel due to a phonetic process. For a funny, but nevertheless probable, interpretation for *Türk iş* 'Turkish muddle' as German *türkisch!* ("accompanied by a heavenward rolling of the eyes") from the time of the German military instructors before 1918, see Lewis (1967: 44).

The postposition *gibi* 'like' (with respect to quality) has been derived from **kep* 'form, shape' + possessive suffix of the third person 'his/her/its shape'.

A product of language reform is the adjective *uluslar arası* 'international; lit. nations-in between', older *milletler arası*; see also *olağanüstü* 'extraordinary; lit. what is above regular'.

In a phase of the Kemalist language reform the reformers were inspired by Indo-European languages. Thus, we find lexical creations with a spatial noun placed before the noun to be specified, e.g., *ön yargı* 'prejudice; lit. (the) before decision', *sonsöz* 'afterword; lit. endword'. The formation *yan cümle* 'subordinated clause; lit. side clause' makes it probable that especially German (cf. G. *Nebensatz*) was a source of inspiration for this type of word-formation; see also *ortaç* in section 3.1.

An adjectival attribute and its head noun can also be combined to form a compound, e.g., *büyükanne* 'grandmother' (← *büyük* 'big, great' + *anne* 'mother'), *kırkayak* 'centipede' (← *kırk* 'forty' + *ayak* 'foot'). A noun may also appear as the first element of such compounds, see *sütbeyaz* 'milk-white' (← *süt* 'milk' + *beyaz* 'white').

Combinations of numerals have an additive meaning, if the preceding form designates a higher power of ten than the following one, see *yüz elli iki* 'hundred fifty-two', etc. If the second component expresses a higher power than the first one, the interpretation is multiplicative, e.g., *seksen* 'eighty' (← *sekiz on* lit. 'eight ten'), *iki yüz* 'two hundred', *yedi bin* 'seven thousand'. For fractions we find the denominator in the locative case preceding the numerator, see *beşte üç* 'three fifth; lit. five-in three', etc.

For counting, the numerals appear with classifiers like *baş* 'head' for animals and *tane* 'grain' (from Persian) for most of the remaining things. Of these old classifiers mainly *tane* and *parça* 'piece' are in frequent use until today. Modern

Turkish makes, of course, also use of "international" classifiers like *kişi* 'person', *bardak* and *kadeh* 'glass', *kutu* 'box'.

Indefinite pronouns are formed by the combination of *her* (a borrowing of Persian *har* 'each, every, any') and pronouns (*her hangi* 'any; lit. everyone who', *her kim* 'whoever', *her ne* 'whatever') and quasi-pronominal words (*her bir* 'everyone', *her kes* 'everybody'); see also forms like *her ikisi* 'both of them', *her üçünüz* 'all the three of you', *her birimiz* 'each one of us'. Other expressions like *her halde* 'in any case', *her yerde* 'everywhere', *her zaman* 'everytime' designate indefinite adverbials. With the help of *bir* 'one' and *takım* 'set' the form *birtakım* 'several' is formed, e.g., *birtakımı* 'some of them'. Furthermore we find *biraz* 'a little' and *birkaç* 'a few, several'. There are also combinations of demonstrative pronouns *bu, şu, o* and the personal and impersonal interrogative pronouns *kim* and *ne* with the conditional copula *ise* < **ärsä* 'if-is'. The forms *buysa, şuysa, oysa, neyse*, and *kimise* 'some' are relatively young and formed by means of the recent form *ise*. The form *kimse* 'somebody' is an older form directly from **kim ärsä* 'who if-is'.

Indefinite negative pronouns are formed by combinations with *hiç* (also a borrowing from Persian), e.g., *hiç kimse* 'nobody' and *hiç bir* 'no one'; combinations with other expressions require *bir* (indicating non-definiteness), e.g., *hiç bir şey* 'nothing at all', *hiç bir zaman* 'never'.

Some interrogative pronouns are also formed by compounding the impersonal interrogative pronoun *ne* 'what?' with expressions designating time, quantity, purpose, etc., e.g., *ne zaman* 'when; lit. what time?', *ne kadar* 'how much?'; fused forms appear in *niçin̩* 'why?' (← *ne için* 'what for?') and *nasıl* 'how?, what sort of ...?' < **ne asıl* 'what basis?'.

The borrowings of Arabic origin *falan* and *filân* are used to express 'so and so'; they can be used as attributes, e.g., *falan tarih* 'such and such a date'. To express 'X and so on' *falan* and *filân* are postponed, e.g., *Mayıs filân* '[in] May or so', *yüz lira falan* 'hundred lira or so'.

To form verbs from nouns (often of foreign origin) Turkish uses a combination of the foreign noun and a light verb (also called auxiliary or phraseological verb). In Old Turkic sources we find *kıl-* 'to do, act' which also functioned as a full verb; in modern Turkish its use is restricted to verbs related to belief and religion, see *namaz* 'Muslim prayer' and *namaz kıl-* 'to pray (Muslim style)'. The verb *et-* 'to do, make, build' is the most frequent in denominal formations, e.g., *yardım* 'help' → *yardım et-* 'to help', *kabul* 'acceptance' → *kabul et-* 'to accept', *ispat* 'proof' → *ispat et-* 'to proof', *izole* (from French) 'isolated' → *izole et-* 'to isolate', *organize* (from French) 'organized' → *organize et-* 'to organize'; sometimes the words are written together, see *af* 'forgiveness' → *affet-* 'to forgive', *fikir* 'thought' → *fikret-* 'to think'. The verb *et-* is no longer used for word-formation.

The verb *eyle-* has fallen totally out of use; in rare cases it can be found in formulas like *Allah rahmet eylesin* 'God have mercy'. There are other verbs like *gör-* 'to see', *ye-* 'to eat', *bul-* 'to find', also used to form new verbs from nouns, e.g., *ceza gör-* 'to be punished' (← *ceza* 'penalty'), *dayak ye-* 'to be beaten up' (← *dayak* 'beating (n.)'), *şifa bul-* 'to find release' (← *şifa* 'release'). Most of these forms are translations of Persian verbal formations, the nominal part of which often consists of the same loan from Arabic, e.g., Persian *şifa yaftan* 'to find release'. The modern light verb in denominal verb formation is *yap-* 'to build, glue', e.g., *hesap yap-* 'to calculate; lit. calculation build'.

The combinations with *ol-* 'to become; to be' are used to form inchoative verbs, among others, e.g., *hasta olmak* 'to fall sick'. In some cases the combinations with *ol-* seem to mean 'to undergo, be subjected to', e.g., *ameliyat* 'operation' → *ameliyat ol-* 'to undergo an operation' (see Lewis 1967: 156). Only in some cases does *ol-* function like a passive of the corresponding *et*-form, see *mahvet-* 'to destroy' and *mahvol-* 'to be destroyed'. A part of the *ol*-forms serve as bases for inflectional suffixes, if there does not exist a corresponding inflectional form of the defective verb *i-* 'to be', e.g., *olma* 'being' instead of **ime*. These forms do not belong to word-formation in the strict sense of the word.

A gerundial form of a verb which bears the semantic load may be combined with another verb which modifies the action expressed by the first verb with respect to phase structure, intensity, extension in time, etc. (i.e. types of *aktionsarten*), to beginning and failing to perform an action, and to (im-)possibility (the latter does not belong to word-formation). Some of the combinations of the first type have developed into aspecto-temporal forms, e.g., the Turkish present tense in *-(I)yor* which has developed from a kind of durative form **-A yorı-r* (a combination of the vocalic gerund and the old present tense form of the verb *yorı-* 'to go, move'). Different from most of the New and Middle Turkic languages, Western Oghuz and thus Turkish does not apply this type of deverbal verb formation very frequently. According to Lewis (1967: 191) we find, e.g., *dur-* with the gerund in *-(y)Ip* and *-(y)A*, e.g., *söylenedur-* and *söylenip dur-* 'to keep grumbling; lit. grumbling keep'; the same modification can be made by (partially) reduplicated finite forms, see *söylenir durur* 'keeps grumbling', *söylendi durdu* 'kept grumbling'. With *gel-* 'to come' we find forms like *yapıla gel-* 'to be constantly made' and *ola gel-* 'to happen always', but also *çık-a-gel-* 'to come up suddenly'. With *kal-* we find *bak-a-kal-* 'to remain staring'. The combination *-Iver-* (vocalic gerund + *ver-* 'to give') expresses quickness, cf. *köprü çök-ü-verdi* 'the bridge suddenly collapsed'.

3.4 Phrasal and synthetic compounds

Some suffixes may be added to a word which itself serves as the head of attributes or as a verbal core with complements. Suffixes like *-lI*, *-lIK*, *-CI* encompass also the attributes of their basic nouns, e.g., *üç günlük yemek* 'food for three days; lit. three day-SUFF food', *sarı saçlı* 'blond-haired; lit. blond hair-SUFF', *hazır elbiseci* 'dealer in ready-made clothes; lit. ready clothes-SUFF' (the latter according to Lewis 1967: 60). If compounds with a possessive suffix take such a suffix, the possessive suffix drops, cf. *koyunbaşlı* 'mutton-headed' (← *koyunbaşı* 'mutton head').

There are several types of lexicalized phrases: One type of complex adjective consists of participles with unmarked (accusative) objects or other complements, e.g., *kafa yemiş bir derviş* 'a crazy dervish; lit. head eaten a dervish, i.e. a dervish who has eaten his head', *sonradan görmüş* 'nouveau riche' (*sonra* 'later, after' + *görmüş* 'has seen'). Such forms (as headless relative clauses) may be used as nouns, e.g., *köpek öldüren* 'what kills a dog (designation for a very cheap wine)' and the neologism *bilgisayar* 'computer; lit. data counter'. There are also lexicalized imperative clauses with object like *albeni* 'sexy; lit. take me!'. Note that the neologistic formation *soykırım* 'genocide; lit. people/tribe massacre' is based on a deverbal form in *-(I)m* which normally does not carry complements.

Another type of complex nouns consists of a noun and a deverbal adjective (which does not function as a participle). The noun is marked by a possessive suffix pointing to the bearer of the quality which is expressed by the following deverbal adjective, e.g., *başı bozuk* lit. 'head-POSS spoiled – a type of crazy fighter in Ottoman times', *karnı yarık* lit. 'his body cut – a type of egg plant dish'.

Examples for lexicalized phrases with finite predicates in final position are *gecekondu* lit. 'settled at night' (the designation for an illegal settlement on somebody else's ground not in use by its owner) and *imambayıldı* 'the Imam fell unconscious' (name of an egg-plant dish); see also personal names, etc. in section 4. An adjective of this type is *vurdumduymaz* 'thick-skinned' (← *vurdum* 'I hit' + *duymaz* 'he/she does not feel it').

3.5 Reduplicative patterns and combination of synonyms and antonyms

Adjectives designating colours and some other adjectives like *yeni* 'new' and *boş* 'empty' exhibit forms with intensifying meaning which consist of mostly incomplete and phonetically slightly deviant cognates of the adjective in question which follows, e.g., *kara* 'black' → *kapkara* 'pitch black', *ak* 'white' → *apak* 'snow-white', *yeşil* 'green' → *yemyeşil* 'intensive green', *mor* 'violet' → *mosmor* 'deep violet'; see also *apaçık* 'totally open' (← *açık* 'open'), *bomboş* 'totally empty' (← *boş* 'empty'), *dosdoğru* 'totally straight' (← *doğru* 'straight'), *tertemiz* 'totally clean' (← *temiz* 'clean'). Enlarged forms of the same basic type are, e.g., *yapayalnız* 'totally alone' (beside *yapyalnız* 'id.'), *güpegündüz* 'in broad daylight' (from *gündüz* 'daylight'); see Lewis (1967: 55 f.).

Reduplication of adjectives often appears in adverbial use to signal higher intensity or duration of the quality expressed by the single adjective, e.g., *yavaşyavaş* 'very slowly', *güzel güzel* 'very beautifully'.

The gerund in *-(y)A* only appears in reduplicated forms in syntactically free use. Thus we find *güle güle* lit. 'laughing laughing'; also used as a farewell formula by the remaining person. These forms signal intensity (duration). It is also possible to combine two antonymic verbs, e.g., *düşe kalka* '(permanently) falling down getting up' signalizing duration. Instead of one specific action, the following combination expresses two extremes of actions, e.g., *düşe kalka eve döndü* 'falling down getting up he went home'.

The reciprocal pronoun *birbir* or *biribir* 'one another' is a reduplication of the numeral *bir* 'one', sometimes with the possessive suffix of the third person on the first *bir*. This pronoun takes possessive suffixes and the adverbial cases accusative (*birbirini*), dative (*birbirine*), locative (*birbirinde*), and ablative (*birbirinden*).

Combinations of antonymic adjectives designate antagonistic extremes of qualities and thus may express 'all', e.g., in attributively and adverbially used double adjectives of the type *X-lI Y-lI* with *X* being an antonym of *Y*, see *geceli gündüzlü* 'day and night' (← *gece* 'night' + *gün* 'day'). Combinations of spatial expressions appear in *aşağı yukarı* 'about, approximately' (← *aşağı* 'down, downwards' + *yukarı* 'up, upwards') to express that the following information has to be interpreted as an average value oscillating between an upper and a lower border. The combination *alt üst* behaves different. It consists of *alt* 'lower part; downside' and *üst* 'upper part; upside' and means 'upside down'.

Two nouns of related meaning may be combined to express a complex idea by using two characteristic components, e.g., *iş güç* 'employment' (← *iş* 'work' + *güç* 'toil'), *kanlı canlı* 'robust' (← *kanlı* 'having blood' + *canlı* 'having life'), cf. also the term co-compound, see Wälchli (2025). There are combinations of one meaningful component and an element without any meaning, e.g., *çoluk çocuk* 'wife and children', composed of *çoluk* (which does not exist as an independent word) and *çocuk* 'child'; sometimes both components do not exist as single words, see *abuk sabuk* 'nonsensical'.

We find a special set of initial "echo consonants", see *sıkı fıkı* 'intimate' (← *sıkı* 'close'). Sometimes the vowels (of the first syllable) of the echo word are labialized (*çarpık çurpuk* 'crooked and twisted' ← *carpık* 'crooked'); sometimes the initial consonant of the second word is changed and the vowel of its first syllable is labial, e.g., *alaca bulaca* 'garish and discordant of colour' (← *alaca* 'motley'). Since the late Ancient Turkic period we find the pattern *(C)-X m-X*, e.g., *fabrika mabrika* 'factories and the like', *kokteyl mokteyl* 'cocktails and the like'.

3.6 Word-formation by ablaut

There seems to have been a kind of ablaut with the personal pronouns and the demonstratives which cannot be explained by phonetical processes. The demonstrative pronouns in modern Turkish do not exhibit any trace of former ablaut, but see Ottoman *ol* 'that', oblique stem *an-* (modern *o*, oblique stem *on-*).

We meet a kind of secondary ablaut in connection with the impersonal interrogative pronoun. The dative form of this pronoun can appear as *neye* and *niye*. Today *neye* is used as the regular dative 'for what?' (*neye yarar?* 'for what is it suitable?'), whereas *niye* is used for 'what for, why?'. The same holds true for the equative forms *nece* 'in what language' (see section 3.3) and *nice* (older) 'how many?', in modern Turkish mostly 'many'.

4 Turkish names

In Turkish (but also in other Turkic languages) we are confronted with many different layers from foreign languages which mainly came in by way of the different religions the Turkic speaking peoples have espoused in the course of time. In Turkish we find a mixture of personal names, which is, of course, influenced by (Sunni) Islam (with subsets acceptable for non-Sunni groups and used by them to hide their identity) besides Christian and Jewish elements. The language reform brought a wave of "national" prenames, sometimes wrong interpretations of names in ancient Chinese sources. But the laicist state gave way to Turkish (neologistic) names instead of older Arabic-Persian forms (*Dilek* 'wish, desire' for *Arzu*), new creations like *Mavisu* 'Blue Water' (if the honeymoon had taken place in the Aegean region), and programmatic names like *Özgür* 'free'. Names like *Kaptan* and *Volkan* for men are possible as are *Venüs* and *İştar* for women. For girls the name *İlknur* 'First Light' may be used for the first (female) child of a family project line, the name for the last female of such a line may be called *Songül* 'Last Rose'; if the series does not stop, the next girl may be named *Yeter* 'It's enough', probably followed by an *İmdat* 'Help!'. This is only one example for folkloristic motivated name-giving in Turkish. Sentence names like *Tanrı-*

verdi and *Allahverdi* ('God-gave', like Slavic *Bogdan*) are rarely used for persons in modern language, but still appear as place names, etc. Non-Muslims carry names related to their religion, neutral Turkish names or foreign names.

The toponymy of the former Ottoman Empire and Turkey has undergone considerable transformations during the last few hundred years. In some regions a Turkification of formerly non-Turkic place names (Greek *Sebasteia*, Turkish *Sivas*) followed a period of replacing some of these names in non-Turkish speaking successor states of the Ottoman Empire and also in the Turkish Republic. After religious upheavals in the East of Turkey among Kurds in the 1920es and 1930es the town of *Dersim* has been renamed *Tunceli*. To hide the enormous ethnic heterogenity of Asia Minor, the designation *Anadolu* (the name of a Byzantine district which is now *İç Anadolu*) was enlarged to cover more or less the whole Asian part of Turkey. In the case of the toponym *Diyarbekir*, Mustafa Kemal Atatürk himself made the name harmonic: *Diyarbakır*.

In the field of family names, the legal reform during the formation phase of the Republic has produced a lot of interesting material. People could create their own family names like *Öztürk* 'Original Turk', *Akyüz* 'White Face', *Orkun* 'Orkhon (a river in Mongolia close to which the oldest Turkic inscriptions were found)', *Sümer* 'Sumerian (because the Sumerians were considered as Turks)', etc. Names, going back to the old way of connecting a person to his/her family, like *Mehmedoğlu* 'Mehmed's son' (and *Mehmed kızı* 'Mehmed's daughter') often became family names (in the case of noble families the personal name refers to the founder of the family, e.g., *Osmanoğlu* 'of the Ottoman family', *Osmanoğulları* 'the Ottoman family'). Thus it is possible in modern Turkic that women carry names like *Özlem Yiğitoğlu* 'Özlem Brave-Young-Man-His-Son'.

5 References

Dankoff, Robert and James Kelly (1982–85): *Mamūd al-Kāšġārī. Compendium of the Turkic dialects (Dīwān Luγat at-Turk)*. Harvard: Harvard University Printing Office.

Derleme Sözlüğü I–XII (1963–82): Ankara: Türk Dil Kurumu Yayınları.

Erdal, Marcel (1991): *Old Turkic Word-Formation*. Wiesbaden: Harrassowitz.

Kononov, Andrej N. (1956): *Grammatika sovremennogo tureckogo literaturnogo jazyka*. Moskva/Leningrad: Izdatel'stvo AN SSSR.

Korkmaz, Zeynep (2009): *Türkiye Türkçesi Grameri. Şekil bilgisi*. Ankara: Türk Dil Kurumu.

Kupayeva, Aisulu (2015): Suffixation in Old Turkic Inscriptions. *GSTF Journal of Education* 2(2): 61–67.

Laut, Jens Peter (2000): *Das Türkische als Ursprache? Sprachwissenschaftliche Theorien in der Zeit des erwachenden türkischen Nationalismus*. Wiesbaden: Harrassowitz.

Lewis, Geoffrey L. (1967): *Turkish Grammar*. Oxford: Oxford University Press.

Menz, Astrid (2016): Gagauz. In: Peter O. Müller, Ingeborg Ohnheiser, Susan Olsen and Franz Rainer (eds.), *Word-Formation. An International Handbook of the Languages of Europe*. Vol. 5, 3433–3442. Berlin/Boston: De Gruyter Mouton.
Röhrborn, Klaus (2003): *Interlinguale Angleichung der Lexik*. Göttingen: Vandenhoek & Ruprecht.
Schönig, Claus (1999): The internal division of Modern Turkic and its historical implications. *Acta Orientalia Academiae Scientiarum Hungaricae* 52(1): 63–95.
Schönig, Claus (2007): On some unclear, doubtful and contradictory passages in Mahmūd al-Kāšġarī's "Dīwān Luġāt at-Turk". *Türk Dilleri Araştırmaları* 14: 35–56.
Tarama Sözlüğü I–VIII (1963–77): Ankara: Türk Dil Kurumu Yayınları.
Wälchli, Bernhard (2025): Co-compounds. In: Peter O. Müller, Susan Olsen and Franz Rainer (eds.), *Word-Formation – Special Patterns and Restrictions*, 145–169. Berlin/Boston: De Gruyter Mouton.
Wilkens, Jens (2016): Turkish. In: Peter O. Müller, Ingeborg Ohnheiser, Susan Olsen and Franz Rainer (eds.), *Word-Formation. An International Handbook of the Languages of Europe*. Vol. 5, 3367–3385. Berlin/Boston: De Gruyter Mouton.

Index

https://doi.org/10.1515/9783111420530-026